Notebooks, 1922–86

Michael Oakeshott, *Selected Writings*

Volume I (2004):
What is History? and other essays
edited by Luke O'Sullivan, 978-0907845836

Volume II (2006):
Lectures in the History of Political Thought
edited by Terry Nardin & Luke O'Sullivan, 978-1845400934

Volume III (2007):
The Concept of a Philosophical Jurisprudence:
Essays and Reviews 1926–51
edited by Luke O'Sullivan, 978-1845400309

Volume IV (2008):
The Vocabulary of a Modern European State:
Essays and Reviews 1952–88
edited by Luke O'Sullivan, 978-1845400316

Volume V (2010):
Early Political Writings 1925–30
edited by Luke O'Sullivan, 978-1845400538

Michael Oakeshott

Notebooks, 1922–86

Edited by
Luke O'Sullivan

imprint-academic.com

Published in the UK by
Imprint Academic, PO Box 200, Exeter EX5 5YX, UK

Distributed in the USA by
Ingram Book Company,
One Ingram Blvd., La Vergne, TN 37086, USA

ISBN 978-1845400545 hardback
ISBN 978-1845409562 paperback

A CIP catalogue record for this book is available from the
British Library and US Library of Congress

Contents

Preface

In the decade during which this series has been in preparation, Oakeshott's reputation has continued to grow. The recent appearance of a volume devoted to him in the series of *Cambridge Companions* effectively acknowledges that he has achieved a canonical status accorded to relatively few writers. Only the most important modern philosophers merit inclusion in such a series, and when a writer is recognized to have achieved this kind of status, the presumption is that everything he had to say is of potential interest.

Many of the other authors of the same rank have had their unpublished as well as their published works exhaustively dissected. In particular, where they left collections of notebooks, these have eventually seen publication. This has certainly been the case for Nietzsche and Wittgenstein, for example, and few would argue that bringing their private reflections to light has been a wasted endeavour. Readers will hopefully come to think the same of the present volume, which includes selections from over forty of Oakeshott's notebooks, spanning his entire career.

The notebooks open a window onto Oakeshott's intellectual development that simply cannot be found elsewhere amongst his writings. They are a unique source of aphorisms and miniature essays that have no parallel in his books, articles, and reviews, although they certainly form a valuable complement to the published works. As the editorial introduction will show, they indicate connections between his private and scholarly life that have only recently begun to come to light, and make clear continuities in his thought, such as a persistent interest in Christianity, which are much less visible elsewhere.

The original intention was for this sixth volume in the *Selected Writings* series to be the final one. It was to have consisted in selections from both Oakeshott's letters and his notebooks. But as work proceeded, it became clear that combining the notebooks with the letters in this fashion would have meant sacrificing too much interesting material. This conviction was only reinforced by the emergence of eleven new notebooks from the years 1928–34, which delayed completion of this volume by over a year while this new material was assimilated.

Imprint Academic thus graciously consented to a change of plan, and a separate seventh volume of correspondence will now hopefully follow in due course. Even this does not quite exhaust the material that deserves to be made more widely available, and so an eighth (and hopefully final) volume collecting up the more miscellaneous items amongst Oakeshott's papers is also planned.

This is the second volume in the series to have been completed mainly at the Political Science Department of the National University of Singapore, and once again I am pleased to be able to acknowledge the financial help I received when making a trip to the London School of Economics in June and July 2012 to carry out archival work.

The generosity of Mr. Simon Oakeshott in making available his father's private notebooks, and in granting his permission for early publication of excerpts from the writings they contain, deserves particular thanks. Professor Robert Grant was kind enough to share his digital photographs of both the new and existing notebooks which made preparing this edition at a distance feasible. I am also grateful to Mr. Chris Thomas of the Powys Society for his assistance with a query regarding the *Cornhill Magazine*. The continuing support of the Archive at the British Library of Political and Economic Science was essential for the volume to appear at all. As for the burden of transcribing the notebooks, it fell entirely on the editor, who as usual must be held solely accountable for all the mistakes that were made. Finally, profuse editorial thanks are owed to Mr. Graham Horswell for his patience in dealing with a particularly troublesome set of proofs.

Singapore, 2013

Oakeshott attached considerable importance to his notebooks. He kept them all his life, and specifically mentioned them in his will as amongst the literary remains that his executor was to take charge of.[1] He also revealed their existence to those who knew him personally, and from time to time passing references to them would appear in print.[2] After his death they became part of the collection of his papers at the British Library of Political and Economic Science, but until now there has been no way to consult them without visiting the archive. Even those prepared to make the trip will not find them easily digestible in the form in which Oakeshott left them. In their unedited state they consist of several hundred thousand words and include material of all sorts, including quotations, transcriptions, reflections, and miniature essays.[3]

This volume contains selections from over forty of the notebooks. They begin in the early 1920s and break off around the mid-1980s. They fall into four more or less distinct groups. The first, largest, group is a series which Oakeshott kept throughout his career. The notebooks in this group are numbered one to twenty-one, indicating unmistakably that he regarded them as a single series. The second is a group of eleven notebooks containing reflections on love and women composed over a relatively short period, 1928 to 1934. Though unnumbered, their dating and subject matter means that they too must be regarded as a single set. The third group is devoted to a close analysis of some of the major works of Plato, Aristotle, and Spinoza, and dates mostly from an even shorter period, 1923-4. It derives its unity from the period and purpose of its composition. Finally, there are a couple of individual notebooks compiled around the end of the war in 1945.[4]

Oakeshott remarked in one of his very last notebooks that 'This is a sort of *Zibaldone*: a written chaos.'[5] Whether he meant the individual notebook or the whole series is unclear, but the comparison with Giacomo Leopardi, whose own

---

[1]   Oakeshott left 'all manuscripts notebooks letters and copyrights' to his literary executor.

[2]   See T. Fuller (ed.), 'Preface' to M. Oakeshott, *Religion, Politics, and the Moral Life* (New Haven, CT, and London: Yale University Press, 1993), p. vii n. 2, and R. Grant, 'Inside the Hedge: Oakeshott's Early Life and Work', Special Issue: Remembering Michael Oakeshott, *Cambridge Review*, 112, 106–9, at p. 109.

[3]   All of these notebooks are now in the Oakeshott archive at the British Library for Political and Economic Science. They are referred to in the footnotes by their catalogue reference number or by the page numberings used throughout this volume, as appropriate; see the final section of the editorial introduction for more details.

[4]   Other notebooks do survive amongst Oakeshott's papers but are not represented in this volume because of the nature of the material they contain; there is one devoted to poems he had composed himself, for example.

[5]   See p. 520.

notebooks were published as the *Zibaldone di pensieri*, is significant. In drawing it, Oakeshott was connecting himself to a European aphoristic tradition. That this was a well-meditated observation rather than a passing comment is suggested by the fact that his notebooks feature remarks by a whole host of contributors to the genre. The list includes Pascal, La Rochefoucauld, Vauvenargues, Charles Duclos, Georg Lichtenberg, Antoine de Rivarol, Richard Garnett, Charles Colton, Nietzsche, and F.H. Bradley, amongst others.

A successful aphorism, according to one of its modern students, should be brief, definitive, personal, and philosophical; and it should have a twist, a sting in the tail.[6] There are plenty of examples in these notebooks of aphorisms that Oakeshott seems to have coined himself which meet these criteria. For example, 'Prejudice is knowing the answer to a question without knowing that it is an answer to a question'[7] gives a pithy definition which invokes the philosophical proposition that all ideas involve assumptions, while also providing a sharp reminder of the limits of common sense. There are plenty of others — 'Loneliness is not living alone; it is loving alone', and 'A book is a mirror; we see only ourselves', are two more examples — which readers will discover for themselves.[8]

The notebooks are much more than a collection of aphorisms, however. A number of major twentieth-century philosophers routinely drew inspiration from poetry and the novel; George Santayana, Iris Murdoch, and Jean-Paul Sartre are notable examples. Though he would not have enjoyed the comparison with Sartre, Oakeshott, too, belongs to this group. A lifelong interest in literature informed his entire intellectual outlook. In general, the novelists Oakeshott favoured were themselves philosophically inclined, and in his notebooks he treated literary depictions of characters, ideas, and situations as either incipiently philosophical in themselves or as material for further philosophical reflection. Amongst his favourites were Spanish and Russian authors such as Cervantes, Turgenev, and Tolstoy, although he also had considerable affection for writers in English such as Henry James and Joseph Conrad. An idea encountered in a novel could assume lasting importance for him, as was the case with Conrad's notion of the 'shadow line' that separates the illusions of youth from the realities of adulthood.

Oakeshott treated poetry in the same way, and was especially drawn to the Romantics. His early admiration for Wordsworth and Coleridge is familiar; they both appear, albeit briefly, in a consideration of the nature of 'the State' which concluded, in keeping with Idealist philosophy, that State, Self, and Society were ultimately all aspects of a single whole. So, indeed, does Shelley; Oakeshott wrote approvingly that he had grasped 'the true notion that literature, art, and

---

6   See James Geary, *The World in a Phrase* (New York: Bloomsbury USA, 2005).
7   See p. 427.
8   See pp. 405, 416.

institutions are the valid expressions of…a single social will'.[9] But the notebooks indicate that there were other authors from the Romantic era, such as Keats and Goethe, who were also important to him. Moreover, as we shall see, the notebooks suggest very strongly that his interest in Romanticism was not purely academic; in his youth in particular he treated it as a living tradition which had a major impact on his approach to life.

While the present volume hopefully gives the reader a good sense of the nature and range of Oakeshott's literary interests, it aims to present his own thoughts rather than simply reproduce the passages he selected for transcription. The early notebooks in particular are notebooks in the most literal sense; they were used simply to record passages, sometimes at considerable length, from his reading. As a result, very little of the material in the early notebooks has been included here. For those readers who nevertheless wish to know exactly what he read and when, the first footnote to every notebook contains some information on what has been omitted.

Once Oakeshott ceased to treat the notebooks exclusively as repositories for transcription, he did not use them instead to make detailed drafts of whatever paper he was currently working on, but to record particular thoughts. References to any of his own books and essays are actually extremely rare.[10] Mostly he used the notebooks to record his reactions to whatever he was currently reading, but this was as likely to be a novel or newspaper as a work of philosophy. Often he appears simply to have seized on a passing notion to scrutinize it further without necessarily seeking to develop it into anything intended for more general consumption.

Anyone familiar with Oakeshott's published works will soon discover that their main themes can all also be found in the notebooks. Philosophy, politics, history, morals, education, aesthetics, religion — all are present. Yet the treatment they received in the notebooks does not simply mirror their handling in print. History, for example, receives much less attention in the notebooks than in Oakeshott's published writings. There is relatively little discussion of the narrative of post-Renaissance European history that figured so prominently in his published works from the 1950s onwards. Nor, indeed, are there more than occasional remarks on the philosophy of historical knowledge, to which he devoted so much thought in *Experience and its Modes* and *On History*.

There is more on politics — Oakeshott exaggerated when he told a friend that they contained 'almost nothing' on the subject — but much of what there is takes a withering tone.[11] Still, some overlap with the published writings is unmis-

9   M. Oakeshott, 'A Discussion of Some Matters Preliminary to the Study of Political Philosophy' in *Early Political Writings 1925–30. Selected Writings vol. 5 (SW)*, ed. L. O'Sullivan (Exeter: Imprint Academic, 2007), pp. 74, 75 n.

10   For the only mention of *Experience and its Modes* see p. 246. M. Oakeshott, *Experience and its Modes* (Cambridge: Cambridge University Press, 1991 [1933]).

11   Grant, 'Inside the Hedge', p. 109.

takable; the theory of civil association, for example, is mentioned a couple of times in the later notebooks, and its precursor, the 'politics of scepticism', can be seen in the modified form of 'the politics of conversation'. Philosophy in the strict sense is also rather under-represented. Oakeshott did not use the note-books to work out ideas for his own theories of modality and categoriality in any detail, nor in many cases did he have much to say about the thinkers whom we know from other sources to have been very important to him.

There is almost nothing in the notebooks on Hobbes, for instance, even though Oakeshott published more on him than on any other writer. This is per-haps partly a reflection of how Oakeshott worked. Once he had decided to read a philosophical work closely, rather than make notes in one of the notebooks, he worked on loose paper or annotated a personal copy of a book or a pamphlet directly, as he did, for example, with Hegel's *Phenomenology of Spirit*. Neverthe-less, there are exceptions to this rule, and the main numbered series of notebooks does provide some valuable evidence about his philosophical reading.

They contain conclusive evidence, for example, that Oakeshott sustained an interest in Nietzsche throughout the 1920s and 1930s that was much more exten-sive than his published writings, which mention Nietzsche only a handful of times, would indicate. The published writings also show little trace of the fact that he read many of Santayana's major works, including the multi-volume treatise on the *Life of Reason*, with some care. There is proof, too, that he succumbed to the fashion for Bergson that was so prevalent in the first decades of the twentieth century.

Remarks in the later notebooks suggest that Oakeshott's attitude to philo-sophy was far more equivocal than it had been in his youth. His statement that 'I too have tried to be a philosopher, but happiness keeps breaking in' may be taken as at least partly in jest, but he seems to have been entirely in earnest when he wrote in old age that 'Strangely enough, I have always preferred practice to theory', and wondered to himself whether he had simply 'not enough intellect to be a philosopher'.[12] As a young man, he showed no such qualms about his competence in or attraction to philosophy, which, as readers of *Experience and its Modes* will remember, he was inclined to think of as absolute experience.

The view of philosophy as absolute experience was derived from Oakeshott's early studies of Idealist and Rationalist thought, and those with a particular interest in his relationship to these schools of thought will want to pay especially close attention to the early notebooks on Plato, Aristotle, and Spinoza. They are an exception to the general lack of close engagement with particular thinkers which characterizes the main numbered series. At first glance, they appear to be direct commentaries on the relevant texts, albeit in English translation. This impression, however, is misleading. What we are dealing with in every case is in

---

[12] See pp. 481, 519.

fact a digest of the commentaries of several of the leading scholars of the day rather than Oakeshott's spontaneous responses to the text in question.

In studying Aristotle's *Politics*, for example, Oakeshott quite clearly had Jowett, Congreve, and Newman all open before him at once as he went through their various translations of the Greek text and their voluminous accompanying notes. But his manner of working is less important than the fact that he was using commentaries produced by Victorian scholars most if not all of whom had felt the attraction of Idealism in both its ancient and modern varieties. This situation is a perfect example of why the problem of 'influence' in intellectual history is so notoriously tricky; to say simply that Oakeshott was influenced by the ancient Idealism of Plato ignores the fact that this 'Plato' was mostly the creation of nineteenth-century Anglo-German Idealist scholarship.

Oakeshott's reception of ancient and modern Idealist thought was thus fused in a manner which it is impossible to separate, as an example will show. Take, for example, the first notebook on Plato, dated 1923. On the first page a quotation appears from 'Nettleship', which is traceable easily enough to R.L. Nettleship's *Lectures on the Republic of Plato*. It is very obviously a quotation, as it appears in quotation marks. But much of the rest of the material on the first pages of this notebook does not announce itself as quotation, although one only has to read a little of Nettleship to realise that Oakeshott was summarizing his commentary. Then, however, eleven pages into the notebook, numerical references begin to appear which are clearly not to the canonical Stephanus numbers used to refer to Plato's works, but which do not correlate with Nettleship's work either.

It is not immediately obvious what these Roman numerals (which are accompanied by headings and followed by Arabic numerals separated by full stops) refer to. In fact, they were taken from Bosanquet's *Companion to the Republic of Plato*, which was in turn keyed to a translation by Davies and Vaughan. Much of the subsequent text of the notebook, when it is not paraphrasing Nettleship, turns out to be condensing Bosanquet instead. Before one could consider any of the remarks on Plato in this notebook to be exclusively attributable to 'Oakeshott', then, one must look carefully at several different texts. The other notebooks in this sequence pose similar puzzles. The notes on Spinoza's *Tractatus De Intellectus Emendatione*, for example, turn out to be particularly indebted to H.H. Joachim's *Study of the Ethics of Spinoza*. Some readers will care deeply about the precise sources of Oakeshott's notes, and others will be indifferent, but in general it is wise to be aware that he began from a context in which the thought of the nineteenth century was still very much alive.

It is safe on the whole to assume that when Oakeshott made these notes, his intention was not simply to collect information but to form some opinions which could serve as his own. That the young Oakeshott lacked the keen historical sense he would later develop is clear from descriptions like that of Socrates from his notebook on 'Early Greek Philosophy' as both a 'Conservative' and a

'Radical'. One of his later precepts for understanding the history of thought was to avoid using the contemporary vocabulary of practical politics and moral judgment as far as possible, but in these early notebooks past thinkers are effectively treated as if they were contemporaries. The same lack of historical awareness is clearly visible in the way Oakeshott singled out the Aristotelian ideal of the good man as a forerunner of the character type of the English gentleman.

Aristotle remained important for Oakeshott long after he had learned to see him in his proper historical context, as the only serious study of his notebooks on Aristotle to date has made clear.[13] In light of the longer-term importance of Aristotle for Oakeshott, it is worth pointing out that in his early notebooks he devoted far more space to the study of Aristotle's *Ethics* than to the *Politics*. It seems likely that in addition to the emphasis on the importance of character for understanding action, topics such as play and conversation as essential elements of civilized life entered Oakeshott's thought at least partly via the study of that particular text.

With the exception of the notebooks on Plato, Aristotle, and Spinoza just described, however, Oakeshott seems mostly to have used his notebooks to record his thoughts on the great problems of life: love and mortality, religion and morality. While the subject of 'Oakeshott on life' has occasionally engaged his readers, he never produced a systematic treatise on the topic.[14] But if we are tempted to speculate about what he might have written had he done so, the notebooks are far and away our best source. In particular, the material they contain on religion (which most of the time was a synonym for Christianity) transforms the conventional view of his thought on the subject.

The conventional view is that Oakeshott had an early interest in religion which waned significantly as he got older, although it flickered briefly once again in old age. In the 1920s and early 1930s, he published two essays on religion, wrote many more, and regularly reviewed works on the subject.[15] In the early 1930s, *Experience and its Modes* developed the idea of religion as the most

---

[13] See C. Abel, 'Appropriating Aristotle', in C. Abel and T. Fuller (eds.), *The Intellectual Legacy of Michael Oakeshott* (Exeter: Imprint Academic, 2005), pp. 37–60.

[14] See G. Worthington, 'Michael Oakeshott on Life: Waiting With Godot', *History of Political Thought*, 16 (1995), 105–19.

[15] See 'Religion and the Moral Life', 'The Importance of the Historical Element in Christianity' (first published in 1927 and 1928 respectively), and 'Religion and the World' (composed in 1929), in *Religion, Politics, and the Moral Life*, and the numerous reviews republished in *The Concept of a Philosophical Jurisprudence: Essays and Reviews 1926–51. Selected Writings vol. 3*, ed. L. O'Sullivan (Exeter: Imprint Academic, 2007). In 1982 Oakeshott mentioned in a letter (to Noël O'Sullivan, 12 March 1982) that when he moved out of his office at LSE he had found that 'I have kept almost everything from the last 50 years & it has been fascinating to discover in it my past life – my undergraduate notebooks, an almost endless collection of papers I had written for historical & theological societies', but that he threw most of this material away. The current archive of his papers thus contains only what survived this cull.

complete form of practical experience, but after that, he fell virtually silent on the issue. Many years later, in *On Human Conduct*, written in the 1970s, he treated it as one means of reconciliation to the inevitable finitude of human life.[16] Both books, however, devoted only a handful of pages to the theme.

From Oakeshott's correspondence, as well as from the notebooks, it is clear that the conventional view needs serious correction. More than once, he contemplated writing an entire book on Christianity.[17] This, admittedly, was only one of several major projects he never accomplished. The notebooks contain material for at least three other books he did not write, including an auto-biographical treatise on love, a biography of Nelson, and a dramatic dialogue (to have been entitled 'A Conversation') on the problems of modernity. But religion, the notebooks make very clear, was not one of the subjects he toyed with and then dropped, only to come back to it much later, as the published writings tend to suggest. Rather, it was a persistent focus of attention, one that occupied a much more central role in his thinking than has been evident hitherto.

It was still possible for a discerning reader to suspect that religion had more ongoing importance than Oakeshott's published works seemed to suggest.[18] But even a careful reader lacked the benefit of being able to consult the notebooks, which make clear that even if Oakeshott was 'probably not [a Christian] in any ordinary sense', he certainly considered himself to be one throughout his life, even into his old age. So, while it is true that 'he was not much drawn to theology' in the sense of being keenly interested in dogmatics, he continuously reflected on the meaning of Christianity for contemporary life, and believed strongly that the modern abandonment of it was a great loss.[19]

Reading through the notebooks allows us to follow the development of Oakeshott's ideas on religion in a way that is not possible using any other

---

[16] *Experience and its Modes*, pp. 292–5; *On Human Conduct* (Oxford: Clarendon Press, 1975), pp. 81–6.

[17] There are two references of this sort from the 1920s. At p. 3 there are headings for a work, probably an essay, on 'The Psychology of the Saints', and at p. 106 'A work on the nature of Religion & the philosophy of the Christian Religion' is listed amongst a number of 'Projected Labours'. Oakeshott wrote in a letter (to Dorothea Krook, 10 April 1970), in the context of a discussion of Christian belief, that 'I once thought I might write a history of modern European moral sentiments, but the thought came too late.'

[18] E. Corey, *Michael Oakeshott on Religion, Aesthetics, and Politics* (Missouri: University of Missouri Press, 2006).

[19] See E. Corey, 'The Religious Sensibility of Michael Oakeshott', in *A Companion to Michael Oakeshott*, pp. 134–50, at pp. 140, 148. 'What rot. We're not apes but good Christians' was Oakeshott's derisive response to a comparison between humans and apes in 1970: see p. 516. In his final notebooks he remarked that 'The twentieth century is distinguished by the large number of people who do not think it worthwhile to remake Christianity for themselves': see p. 510. Nevertheless, he considered that 'we could not do without [the scriptures], but they have been fatally misrepresented': see p. 545.

source. The first phase of his intellectual trajectory is, admittedly, already well known. He was committed to a modernistic Anglicanism which minimized the importance of liturgy and opposed literalism in the interpretation of the Bible. Studying *Types of Christian Saintliness* (1915) by William Inge, Dean of St Paul's, he noted the view that 'The religion of authority is Catholicism' and 'the religion of the Spirit is Liberal Protestantism'; Oakeshott was firmly on the side of the Spirit.[20] Such views lead him to argue for an explicit recognition that religion was perpetually changing in tandem with the needs of the society it served. This meant he was unruffled by the implications of research in history, geology, biology, and anthropology for Christianity, since he was not concerned with its truth but with its ability to give spiritual sustenance.[21]

Typically, the first notebook begins with an extract from a novel, *The Man of the World* (1907) by the Italian writer Antonio Fogazzaro, a Catholic with mystical and reforming tendencies. In the passage Oakeshott seized upon, a young man has been debating whether or not to enter a monastery. The excerpt begins with the words of an old priest to him: 'My son, you must remain in the world, and still you must withdraw from it.'[22] This tension between worldly and spiritual values would remain an enduring opposition in Oakeshott's thought; it would be just about a pardonable exaggeration to say that it summarizes the main theme of the notebooks in their entirety.

Oakeshott came to think of life, or, in technical terms, 'practical experience', as necessarily defined by the attempt to realize the 'ought' latent in the 'is'. As such, practice is at once the realm of instrumental action and consequentialist thinking, and the scene of the realization of the non-instrumental values of love and friendship. Religion is this non-instrumental side of practical experience taken to its logical conclusion. But the tension between worldly and spiritual values also marked the distinction between practice in general and the pursuit of theoretical knowledge and aesthetic experience for their own sake.

Early in his career, Oakeshott was inclined to assimilate religion to philosophy in a way that he would not do later on. 'Philosophy is really the clear thinking of what is felt in religion – the oneness. If we have no religion we have but a poor starting place for philosophy.'[23] This assimilation was characteristic of the Idealist and Rationalist thought which largely determined his philosophical horizons in the 1920s and into the 1930s. The influence of Idealist logic is clearly visible, for example, in his description of the doctrine of the Trinity as the solution to the problem of 'the relation of the universal to the particular'.[24]

---

[20] LSE 2/1/1.
[21] For a lengthier discussion see the introduction to Oakeshott, *The Concept of a Philosophical Jurisprudence, SW* iii.2–5.
[22] LSE 2/1/1.
[23] See p. 13.
[24] See p. 94.

By the later 1920s, however, there is already a discernible shift away from the vocabulary of Idealism. A note for another essay on 'Modern Religion' which was either never completed or has not survived was supposed 'to call attention to…the Epicurean element in Christianity'.[25] This was a radical move to make, because for centuries Epicureanism had been conventionally regarded as unchristian, sensual, hedonistic, and selfish; J.S. Mill still felt obliged to distance himself from this view of it when identifying Bentham and Epicurus as both utilitarians in 1861.[26] But Oakeshott did not see Epicureanism in this negative light; nor did he see Epicurus as Mill did, as a proto-utilitarian. The pagan figure of Epicurus became an example for him of a possible form of reconciliation to life based on a refusal of instrumentalist and consequentialist values: a rejection of 'the world'. He took from Epicureanism the belief that one should concentrate on those relationships and activities and ideas that are intrinsically rewarding, and strive to live in the present.

One of the greatest problems with conventional Christianity, Oakeshott increasingly came to think, was its literal attachment to the notion of an afterlife which left it open to contamination by the worldly, consequentialist way of thinking. Salvation was not something to be endlessly postponed into the future, like a retirement fund which relies on the willingness of savers to defer gratification, but an attitude to life that was possible here and now. What Christianity really offered was a rich set of metaphors for understanding the human condition, and in particular for acceptance of the inevitability of death. This is perhaps what Oakeshott meant when he described sin and God as being solutions rather than problems.[27]

By the early 1930s Oakeshott was convinced that it was important to 'Attempt to restate the doctrines of Christianity for the contemporary mind' by emphasizing the fact that Christianity is something which we have *made*.[28] He seems to have thought that accepting that Christianity was what might now be called a social construct was not to devalue it but to bring it into harmony with modernity. The view put forward by the Victorian author Samuel Butler that 'Either Jesus was the son of God, or He was not' struck him as 'entirely out of date'.[29] Abandoning the commitment to literalism would be a radical transformation, but it would not be the first time Christianity had radically changed its character. In any case, such a transformation was necessary to its survival. 'To *defend* Christianity is always to transform it. Each defence has been a readjustment.'[30]

---

[25] See p. 140.

[26] J.S. Mill, *Utilitarianism*, in *Collected Works of John Stuart Mill*, ed. J.M. Robson, 33 vols. (Toronto: University of Toronto Press, 1963–91), x.209.

[27] See p. 144.

[28] See p. 216.

[29] See p. 217.

[30] See p. 225.

If all of this sounds rather abstract, it is clear that it was intended to be compatible with a conception of Christianity as a way of life. 'Christian festivals, worship, prayer' were definitely to have a place in Oakeshott's reformed religion.[31] 'Are not the gods, from earliest times, associated with dancing, feasting, laughter, poetry, holiday, joy, gifts?' he asked himself rhetorically. Religious observances provided an important focus for 'human need and aspiration', though he never really addressed the problem of how spontaneous products of popular belief could be consciously remade without suffering from the kinds of problems he exposed in a political context in his critique of Rationalism.[32]

Oakeshott continued developing his critique of traditional Christianity during the 1940s, sometimes comparing it unfavourably with paganism. The belief in the Incarnation now struck him as a device for bridging the gap between man and God, something which had not been a problem for Greek religion in which men and gods inhabited the same world.[33] He also became increasingly convinced that the idea of an afterlife had actually become a means of avoiding the problem of mortality. The traditional Christian doctrine was not entirely valueless insofar as it really had helped people to accept their mortality, but this had never been its explicit purpose.[34] The disappointment of the imminent expectation of Christ's return which characterized the earliest years of Christian faith had been met by a promise of an ultimate redemption that did not necessarily address the need for redemption in the present.[35]

Late in life, pondering Foucault's views on Christian attitudes to sexuality, Oakeshott still remained convinced that Christianity had 'never succeeded in divesting itself of a notion of "salvation" as a future condition to be awaited or promoted'.[36] By that point he had long been convinced that the transformation Christianity had to undergo was into a religion not of immortality but mortality. In the mid-1950s, for example, he suggested that Confucianism and humanism, as well as 'the religions of Greece', could serve as guides as to how to achieve this.[37]

While human beings could not escape the fact of their own mortality, they also had to contend constantly with the fatality of action. What is done can never be undone, and given the liability of human beings to error, this brought with it the possibility of crushing feelings of guilt and remorse. It was because 'everything is irreparable' in this sense that the notion of sin could serve as a solution. A wrong done to another could be conceived in ultimate terms as an injury to

---

[31] See p. 216.
[32] See p. 343.
[33] See p. 342.
[34] See p. 335.
[35] See p. 352.
[36] See p. 548.
[37] See p. 375.

God which could be forgiven, thus creating the possibility of absolution and a fresh beginning.[38]

One might, of course, dismiss this as simply a psychological device, and a possible criticism of Oakeshott's position is that this God is a very insubstantial one. He was happy nevertheless to accept that the idea of God as 'not a being or a person', but as 'a way of thinking about human life' was a consequence of his view that Christianity was a human invention.[39] He seems to have conceived of the idea of God as offering a kind of ultimate or unconditional perspective on life which reached beyond the limits of ordinary morality. 'What is staggering is God's imagination: no human inventor could possibly have imagined relationships such as love. There is nothing humane about this imagination, it is pure fantasy.'[40]

The imaginative and metaphorical approach Oakeshott took to understanding God is equally visible in an analysis of 'The History of Creation' which was written in the early 1960s. The creation of both man and the angels 'so that he should not be alone' gave the impression of a 'restless, discontented' God. Oakeshott's interpretation of the Fall which resulted in our expulsion from the Garden of Eden deserves particularly close attention. The outcome of eating the fruit of the tree of knowledge was that Adam and Eve became aware of their own nakedness, and indeed their own mortality. Thus, in Oakeshott's understanding of it, 'The burden of original sin is "self-consciousness."'[41]

Oakeshott actually gave two somewhat different accounts of what occasioned the Fall in the first place. At one point in the notebooks he ascribes it to human pride stemming from a desire to be God's equal. Elsewhere, he describes it as 'an unavoidable consequence of the character with which God had endowed mankind: imagination'. But although he was inconsistent in the grounds he gave for the cause of the Fall, one could argue that either of these reasons would still allow his interpretation to make sense. Moreover, his two reasons are not mutually exclusive: imagination is presumably a precondition of pride.

The profound implication of the story, which Oakeshott thought St Augustine had appreciated, was that (whether pride or imagination was the cause) the Fall was not an accident. The birth of self-consciousness represented the awakening of a quality that was already latent in humanity. 'There was no point in creating the possibility of "sin" if in fact there were to be no sinners.' Here we are quite clearly dealing with the view that Oakeshott put forth in *On Human Conduct*, of a God 'who, when he might have devised an untroublesome universe, had the nerve to create one composed of self-employed adventurers of

---

[38] See p. 395.

[39] See p. 399.

[40] See p. 416.

[41] See p. 433.

unpredictable fancy', with the aim of acquiring 'convives capable of "answering back"'.[42]

Oakeshott's God rather resembles the gods of the pagans in having very human qualities. Commenting on the decline of the Roman Empire, he remarked that '*Change* is what people long for, not better or worse. In this they are like God.'[43] Given the human inability to escape more than temporarily from the ceaseless flow of activity, what mattered in the end was the reality of the inevitability of change. From this point of view the process rather than the result was the important thing. The problem with modernity, so Oakeshott believed, was a characteristic failure to recognize this. An obsession with achievements and outcomes had distracted Western civilization from what was truly worthwhile. The 'only *human* value lies in the adventure & the excitement of discovery ...It is our non-recognition of this, our rejection of it, which makes our civilization...non-Christian.'[44] This conception of it as a 'religion of "non-achievement"' casts important light on the kind of salvation his modernized Christianity was able to provide.

It offers eternal life, not in the form of a life after death, but in the metaphorical sense of 'a note of timelessness, of the unconditioned, of the absolute which may be heard in the hubbub of the transitory & the conditional'.[45] This form of salvation is potentially open to all, for 'Every man is an attempt on the part of God to make a human being', but it also presents a major challenge, as it requires people to be capable of 'self-enactment'. The self for Oakeshott was not a natural endowment; like Christianity, it was something that had to be made, and the education necessary for this self-fashioning was a process that could fail, or even never take place. There was thus a sense for him in which 'Some never become human' in the full meaning of the term, though he also recognized that even people falling into this category deserved consideration; 'they must all be treated as if they were human.'[46]

The outline of the book Oakeshott never wrote on Christianity is clear, then. It would have proposed, in deliberate imitation of William Blake (an ideal example for anyone wishing to argue that we must create our religion for ourselves), that 'all deities reside in the human breast', and that what were once called the 'evidences' of Christianity, its historical proofs, were in fact '"events" in the history of human imagination, in human self-understanding'.[47] But far from treating this historicization of Christianity as a way of undermining it, it would have gone on to argue that Christianity should be celebrated as 'a stupen-

---

[42] See p. 549. Cp. *On Human Conduct*, p. 324 (reading 'adventurers' for 'adventures' in the original).

[43] See p. 446.

[44] See p. 468.

[45] See p. 500.

[46] See p. 514.

[47] See p. 545.

dous imaginative engagement, a poem whose first languages were Hebrew & Greek & Latin but which has since been written in all the languages of the world'.[48]

It cannot be pretended that this conception of Christianity 'in which the Cross [is] understood as a *symbol* of the character of God' was one that Oakeshott ever completely worked out. Some of his remarks seem plainly contradictory. For example, his characterization of God as 'remote, untouched, caring nothing for suffering, for the desires & the longings of men, for their life or death' and as one who 'cares only about good & evil' seems plainly at odds with his idea of God's 'love' as 'a delight in difference which must be capable of including the acceptance of errancy'.[49] If God indeed cares nothing for suffering, why would He ever bother to grant forgiveness? Yet we can be certain that Oakeshott went on pondering over such matters virtually until the end of his days. The last entry in the notebooks returns once more to the advent of self-consciousness after the Fall, and asks, in respect of this new self-knowledge, 'Was God repairing a mistake or did he intend it all along?'

In *On Human Conduct*, the discussion of religion immediately follows that of morality, and it should already be clear that these two subjects were very closely linked, if not indeed inseparable, so far as Oakeshott was concerned. After all, they addressed the same problem, of how best to live a mortal life. However, the sources for Oakeshott's moral thought were somewhat different. He drew, for example, on Aristotle's *Ethics*, as well as on a variety of medieval and early modern authors, for what might be called an aristocratic ideal of conduct which clearly parallels his portrait of the religious personality without quite being identical with it. His work on this subject led him to argue, following Burckhardt, that there was a distinctive European post-Renaissance practice of moral individualism which is familiar from a number of his published essays, including 'The Masses in Representative Democracy'. But although the notebooks are not quite so important for understanding his ideas on morality as they are for his view of religion, they once again allow us to see these ideas in formation, and add significant extra detail with respect to their sources.

Perhaps the single moral virtue to receive the most attention in the notebooks is courage, for which, once more, Aristotle seems to have been a major source.[50] Courage was a necessity in the face of mortality; it was a condition of being able to realize the Aristotelian injunction to live as an immortal, a saying which is quoted several times throughout the notebooks.[51] It was a characteristic which Oakeshott thought distinguished Nelson, one of his great heroes, on whom some of the fragmentary notes which survive from the material he collected in the

---

[48] See p. 533.
[49] Cp. p. 501 and p. 549.
[50] See p. 45.
[51] See for example pp. 107 n. 1, 118, 376, 504.

later 1940s for his unwritten biography are included here. Nelson, he believed, was driven not by 'exterior success' or 'tangible ends' ('wealth, power, position') but by *'interior* success' – 'honour, reputation, fame'.[52]

There was, however, a period during which this Aristotelian outlook, with its emphasis on courage and integrity, was pushed into the background. In his later twenties and early thirties, after an unrequited passion lead to an extended period of introspection, Oakeshott broke off for a time from his numbered series of notebooks to concentrate on writing what we shall call the 'Belle Dame' notebooks. The first bears the heading 'La Belle Dame Sans Merci', after the title of a poem by Keats. In Keats' poem, a 'knight-at-arms' is found 'palely loitering' following a meeting with a mysterious lady who took him back to her grotto where he was lulled to sleep, only to awaken alone 'on the cold hill's side'.[53] For Oakeshott, 'La Belle Dame' came to represent something akin to a Platonic form of womanhood, different fragments of which he found instantiated both in women he knew and in complete strangers, but which never fully revealed itself.

We have already noted that Oakeshott treated Romanticism as a living literary tradition, but this statement deserves considerable emphasis. He actually tried to live out his interpretation of Keats' poem in his pursuit of the figure of the 'Belle Dame' in a manner that was entirely self-conscious and also inevitably doomed, something which he gradually seems to have realised himself.[54] The unhappiness of his love life seems, for a time, to have pitched him into depression and even lead him to contemplate suicide, or at least to long for death. These too were sentiments quite in keeping with the darker side of the Romantic tradition, but they can hardly be described as classical.[55]

These notebooks were not simply private diaries; it is incontrovertibly clear that they were conceived as material for yet another book Oakeshott did not write, namely the semi-autobiographical reflection on love mentioned above.[56] The book he did write during these years was *Experience and its Modes*, and when it is placed beside the 'Belle Dame' notebooks there is no better illustration of the contrast or even contradiction between the two sides of Oakeshott's personality.

---

[52] See p. 364.

[53] As Grant points out, 'La Belle Dame Sans Merci' was a sufficiently important figure in Romanticism – being the subject, for example, of several paintings – for Praz to use the phrase as the title of an entire section of *The Romantic Agony*, but this cannot have been Oakeshott's source for the term. He certainly knew Praz's book, but it was published in 1933, five years after the first of the 'Belle Dame' notebooks was written. See R. Grant, 'The Pursuit of Intimacy, or Rationalism in Love', in P. Franco and L. Marsh (eds.), *A Companion to Michael Oakeshott* (Pennsylvania: Pennsylvania State University Press, 2012), pp. 15–44, at p. 44 n. 59.

[54] See p. 197. For a full discussion of the Belle Dame notebooks and Oakeshott's love life in general, as well as its relationship to his intellectual life, see Grant, 'The Pursuit of Intimacy'.

[55] See pp. 259, 260.

[56] See pp. 206, 210, 266.

There was what Grant calls the Apollonian side, for which a supremely rational approach to philosophy was the only form of experience which could escape modality, and the 'radical Dionysiac' side which could declare that love, not philosophy, was 'the absolute category of experience'.[57] Yet these two sides were not totally separate; they flowed into one another. In his most intensely Romantic phase, Oakeshott still thought of himself as pursuing the Aristotelian goal of immortality. Only the means had changed; the realization of a perfect love was now what was required.

Thus, depending on his mood, the young Oakeshott could regard any one of religion, love, and philosophy as the way to transcend mortality and repudiate worldly values. But a man of thirty, though far from old, is no longer in the first flush of youth, and he could not escape the fear that worldliness eventually overtakes us all, however we try to evade it. The remark that 'The story [of *Don Quixote*] is played out in the lives of each of us' so that 'At the expense of Don Quixote, Sancho Panza grows in each of us & comes to dominate us' is revealing.[58] What worried Oakeshott was not suffering from delusions, like Don Quixote who believed himself to be a medieval knight in an age of chivalry which was not only long past but had never really existed in the manner in which he imagined it in the first place. Rather, his worry was about *not* being able to suffer from delusions of this sort. Sancho Panza, the elderly Don's faithful squire who is forever shattering his illusions, was precisely the kind of person Oakeshott did not want to become, or to have any more to do with than was necessary.

For Oakeshott, it seems, Cervantes had hit upon a fundamental feature of human life, namely, that it is grounded in imagination. This, we have already noted, was crucial to his understanding of religion, but it was also a central feature of his moral thought. Just as in religion, he considered it important to guard against allowing the future to dominate our imagination. Even when the intense Romanticism of his late twenties and early thirties had passed, the great problem remained of how to deal with the fears to which knowledge of their own finitude left human beings exposed. It seems to have been this problem which prompted him to declare that Epicureanism was of permanent interest.[59]

Once more, there is an overlap with Oakeshott's approach to Christianity, but the emphasis changes somewhat. The problem of mortality raises the question of how best to spend the time one has as well as of how to confront one's final demise, and here Epicurus was important because of his connection to the thought of the Renaissance and the early modern era, and in particular to Montaigne. There is no doubt about the reality of this connection; Montaigne expressed an affinity for Epicurus in his *Essays* and was widely regarded by later

---

[57]   See p. 259.
[58]   See p. 172.
[59]   See p. 245.

generations as an Epicurean.[60] Oakeshott thus had good grounds for grouping Montaigne with Epicurus. What matters, though, is what he made of Montaigne. What the Frenchman had to offer, he believed, was not a consistent set of arguments with which to answer problems of the human condition,[61] but (like Aristotle) a feeling for balance and an ability to live without the need for certainty. Moreover, he had a sense of his own integrity; late in life, Oakeshott made a note of Montaigne's remark that 'The greatest thing in the world is to know how to belong to oneself.'[62]

Oakeshott was as attracted to the French thought of this period as a source of moral and ethical example as he was repelled by the French authors of his own day. It seemed to him to provide a range of moral personae — the *homme habile*, the *honnête homme*, the *prudhomme* — illustrating his conviction of the importance of holding fast to one's own identity (though it is fair to say that he found it in some of his contemporaries, too — in D.H. Lawrence, for example). In the mid-1960s he inserted a quotation from Pierre Charron's work *De la sagesse* into a character sketch of the idea of *Prud'homie* which is a distilled summary of this ideal: 'True *Prud'homie*…is free, candid, manly, generous, cheerful, pleasant, *self-possessed*, constant, it walks with a firm tread, is bold and confident, pursuing its own path…not changing its gait & pace for wind or weather or any other circumstance.'[63] It insists, above all else, on a self-chosen life; the kind of life that he believed Nelson had lived in a later era, for example.

In one of the late notebooks Oakeshott made the intriguing remark that his ideal ethical theory would be a kind of fusion of the ideas of Montaigne and Pascal. He mused that 'Pascal misunderstood Montaigne…and Montaigne would never have understood Pascal. But there is a land, an island, where they meet & understand one another. I have not found it; but this is what I have looked for, without knowing what I looked for.'[64] It is well established that Pascal knew Montaigne's *Essais* in detail and admired him as a stylist, while disliking his lack of piety and relative indifference to religious questions. Perhaps the misunderstanding Oakeshott had in mind refers, as some have suggested, to Pascal's failure to appreciate sufficiently that Montaigne shared his own deep scepticism about the ability of reason alone to provide answers for the fundamental problems of life, and that Montaigne was just as convinced as Pascal himself was of the importance of self-knowledge for living well.[65]

---

[60] See F. Hugo, *Montaigne* (Berkeley, CA: University of California Press, 1991 [1949]), p. 67.

[61] See pp. 284–5, 371.

[62] See p. 483.

[63] See p. 461.

[64] See p. 521.

[65] On the relationship between Pascal and Montaigne see F.M. Chambers, 'Pascal's Montaigne', *PMLA*, 65:5 (1950), 790–804; R.C. La Charité, 'Pascal's Ambivalence toward Montaigne', *Studies in Philology*, 70:2 (1973), 187–98; and P. Force, 'Innovation

The ethical ideal that Montaigne and Pascal represented to Oakeshott was not one that he thought of as exclusively European. As with religion, he found it in Chinese culture too, particularly in Confucius, but also in the Daoists. The notebooks help us to date his interest in Chinese thought, which notably informed his conception of practical activity in the essays in *Rationalism in Politics*, to the early 1930s. In a notebook begun in 1931, he drew an explicit comparison between 'The "superior man" of Confucius' and 'the "*homme habile*" of La Rochefoucauld'; later, he compared Chuang Tzu and Epicurus, making an analogy between the Daoist's stress on the 'importance of seeming unimportant' and the Greek's injunction to 'live unknown'.[66] All of this had nothing to do with philosophy, in any technical sense of the term. Oakeshott explicitly rejected the *vita contemplativa* as an answer to the kinds of problems raised by a concern with mortality and integrity — if the aim was to be 'free' in the sense of being 'superior to fortune', good or bad, and to that extent 'unconquerable', then what was necessary was not 'Platonic wisdom' but 'Platonic courage' and 'Hobbesian "pride"'.[67]

The question of how widely this ethic, which is plainly radical and demanding, could be shared was certainly one that occurred to Oakeshott. In his published writings, he made plain that the practice of individualism was by no means the only moral tendency visible in modern Europe. Some never acquired it, and others were actively hostile to it. In the notebooks, the alternatives tend perhaps to be presented less starkly, but they are certainly there. The bourgeois, concerned with security, actually makes the world habitable for the 'extremist' who refuses to compromise; he 'keeps the world going' and ensures it is 'a world in which to be extremist is not absolute disaster'.[68] Radical individualists determined to live out the life of a Don Quixote, it turns out, have a genuine need of their Sancho Panzas. Sancho was, after all, the one who was always there to dust the Don down and patch him up after his frequent (largely self-inflicted) mishaps, only to watch him sally forth once again in search of more adventures.

Oakeshott certainly seems to have done his best to live a life of radical moral individualism himself, though not, it must be said, without imposing considerable costs on some of those around him, particularly the women in his life. There was, he wrote as a young man, 'something wild in me', and in old age he thought of himself as having been 'born under a wandering star'.[69] Following this star certainly ensured, as he put it, that he 'wasted a lot of time living',[70] and the wistful remark in the 'Preface' to *On Human Conduct* that 'when I look back

---

as Spiritual Exercise: Montaigne and Pascal', *Journal of the History of Ideas*, 66:1 (2005), 17–35.

[66] See pp. 248, 424.
[67] See p. 426.
[68] See p. 502.
[69] See p. 208.
[70] See p. 507.

upon the path my footprints make in the snow I wish it might have been less rambling' may perhaps be read as a tacit confession of regret at the cost to his intellectual life of his often chaotic private circumstances. Perhaps, too, we ought not to overlook the way in which his ethical values lead him to regard intellectual work in a manner which may partially explain the equivocal attitude to philosophy we noted earlier. When he was young, at least, he was inclined to regard it as an 'escape' in a negative sense, a means of avoiding life, and one that also imposed a worldly standard of productivity.[71] There is, after all, an enormous difference between talking philosophy with friends when the mood strikes, and writing, much less publishing, a book of philosophy.

There is also the question of how Quixotic Oakeshott became as a result of his insistence on a self-chosen life. In one sense, he was very successful in avoiding the fate he had feared in his youth, of becoming Sancho. As an old man he declared to himself that 'those marvelous ambiguous centuries of the early Christian era, which carried with them reminiscences of ancient Athens & Sparta, & the realities of Rome' constituted '*my world*'.[72] Admittedly, he believed, also, that the twelfth century had survived into the present, and remained a shared fate: it was 'the century in which we are all born'. But this view, if taken literally, can only be described as eccentric. Certainly, there are parts of the modern world that really have survived from the medieval past. But by the mid-twentieth century the differences between modernity and the medieval world were surely greater, when viewed in a genuinely historical fashion, than the similarities.

When Oakeshott made these remarks, however, he was not aiming at historical truth. Rather, he was composing a practical present for himself, one that was rooted in imagination—as indeed he thought that such a present must be. No doubt his claim that 'I & Charlemagne & Roland & Oliver are contemporaries' was true, for him. But it is significant that at the head of the passage in question he placed a quote from the nineteenth-century French Romantic poet Alfred de Vigny. One of Vigny's early poems was a reworking of the medieval epic of *The Song of Roland*, a heroic narrative set during Charlemagne's wars in Spain in the late eighth century. This kind of faux medievalism was typical of Romanticism, which was always trying to leap from the present into either the past or the future; Keats, as it happens, had also taken the title of 'La Belle Dame' from a late medieval poem. So it is significant that the period seems to have acquired its emotional resonance for Oakeshott via Vigny, rather than from the original epic. Even as an old man, his values were still mediated by nineteenth-century Romanticism in a way that he himself was not always fully conscious of.

What Oakeshott did know was that he disliked more or less everything that he judged distinctively modern. The hostility to modernity which comes

---

[71] See pp. 152–3.

[72] See p. 520.

through strongly in the notebooks is important, because some of his interpreters have tried to argue that he was a defender of it. In fact, all of the things which really mattered to Oakeshott were products of earlier periods that now seemed to him to be in danger of disappearing altogether. We have seen that this was true of Christianity, but it is equally true of other things that he also considered hallmarks of English civilization (as he tended to think of it), including the rule of law, education, and standards of civility in general. The rule of law, he liked to observe, was best understood by the Romans and the Normans in Sicily, and Englishmen of the seventeenth century such as Halifax showed a far greater attachment to and grasp of it than contemporary politicians. As for contemporary popular culture, it disgusted him on the rare occasions that he took any notice of it. 'The indescribable vulgarity of *Sergeant Pepper*' shows what he thought of the Beatles.[73]

In defending ethical individualism and moral and intellectual pluralism, as he undoubtedly did, Oakeshott saw himself not as defending modernity (which was characterized by Rationalism and the spirit of enterprise) but as fighting a rearguard action against it. Although he never became a true reactionary, he had a certain sympathy for spirits of this type (Joseph de Maistre is a case in point), and there can be no doubt of where he thought modernity was going. His second telling of the story of the Tower of Babel, the version which appeared in *On History*, may well have had its germ in the narrative of the Creation noticed above.[74] It has perhaps not been emphasized enough that although he thought all cultures had myths warning of the dangers of pride and over-ambition, it was a Christian myth that he chose to re-tell to make his point. But whatever the reason he decided to write the essay, its message was clear: the materialistic and acquisitive nature of modern civilization, and its neglect of everything incompatible with its goal of ever greater productivity, meant that it was heading for disaster.

Some of this hostility may be an expression of the disappointed hopes of Oakeshott's youth. As a young man, he had taken the view (which, typically, he derived from Spinoza) that 'Citizenship is a spiritual experience—not a legal relationship.'[75] At least, he believed, having imbibed deeply in his youth of Rationalisms and Idealisms both ancient and modern, that this was what citizenship ought to be, and seems to have hoped that society was on the brink of an imminent transformation for the better. But his experience of the rise of totalitarian ideology in the thirties set him on a long road towards just the oppo-

---

[73] See p. 519.
[74] See pp. 434–6. Cp. 'The Tower of Babel' in M. Oakeshott, *On History and Other Essays* (Blackwell: Oxford, 1983), pp. 165–94.
[75] See p. 13.

site conclusion.[76] By the time he wrote *On Human Conduct*, a legal relationship was precisely what he now thought citizenship was; spiritual matters belonged to another part of life entirely. His early religious yearnings for unity slowly became detached from politics as well as philosophy.

The first steps on the road to the theory of civil association seem to have consisted of an attempt to restate the principles of democracy in the face of the totalitarian threat. The remarks on this subject, particularly those contained in the long notebook 'A Conversation', are entirely consistent with the moral and religious concerns we have encountered thus far. This notebook lies outside the main numbered series, but it is an important one, for it seems to have been the seedbed for many of the essays written in the 1940s and 1950s which eventually appeared in *Rationalism in Politics*. The roots of the essay on 'The Voice of Poetry in the Conversation of Mankind' also seem ultimately to lie in this notebook. This essay is important for having introduced the idea that there was a distinctively aesthetic form of experience which had not been included in *Experience and its Modes*. But what Oakeshott originally appears to have contemplated was a dialogue between a number of characters who represented different tendencies in contemporary society.

The opening pages of 'A Conversation' conceive of politics as the interchange between the different voices of the poet, the scientist, the soldier, the religious man, and so on. The aim was apparently to show a style of 'politics become conversable', in which the aim was to avoid dogmatism at all costs. It was also to be a style to which modern democratic politics might ideally conform. Oakeshott's conception of what democracy ought to be shared in the Romantic vision that shaped his moral and religious ideas. He noted, apparently with approval, Walt Whitman's belief that democracy should be 'based upon *individualism*, & equality',[77] but even more important, once again, was the figure of Montaigne: 'The principle in democracy. *Que sais-je*? Montaigne. Humility & not presumption; enquiry & not scepticism.'[78]

The scepticism being ruled out here is presumably the absolute or Pyrrhonian variety, for it is evident that the approach to politics Oakeshott favoured was most definitely sceptical in the sense of being critical and questioning. He wanted a kind of democracy which would be 'the expression of *mortality*'.[79] At least part of what was meant by this, presumably, was that democratic politics should avoid the pursuit of Quixotic projects of the sort that the Tower of Babel came to symbolize. Utopianism of any kind became a particular species of dogmatism, or a fatal insistence on being right at all costs. 'Utopian ideals have

---

[76] See p. 302. For Oakeshott's early views on politics and the relationship of his lectures on 'The Philosophical Approach to Politics' to *Experience and its Modes* see the editorial introduction to Oakeshott, *Early Political Writings, SW* v.

[77] See p. 301.

[78] See p. 318.

[79] See p. 299.

always turned to blood when they have touched the earth — & they *must* always do so. "Truths" always kill; errors are better, they are sometimes merciful.'[80]

How to ensure that this undogmatic style prevailed in politics was not a question Oakeshott believed that the modern world had discovered how to answer. 'How to be the enemy of superstition without being the friend of "truth" — a problem never solved by J.S. Mill or any "liberal"', he noted in the early 1960s.[81] His own answer was to concentrate on processes rather than outcomes; for the 'politics of scepticism', 'what you do is much less important than how you do it.'[82] This presumes, of course, that there were some kinds of things that the politics of scepticism would not even attempt in the first place, but the general thrust of the remark is clear; the true political priority was, as he put it in his essay on 'Political Education', not to get anywhere but simply 'to keep afloat on an even keel'.[83]

When the phrase 'civil association' first appears in the notebooks in the late 1950s, the emphasis is clearly on the art of living well amongst strangers. Civil association is 'concerned with people whom we do not particularly like, with whom we do not agree, whom we may even despise or even hate, but with whom we must have a relationship because we live near them'.[84] One of its chief characteristics might be described as what has latterly been called 'disattendability';[85] it emphasizes the importance for freedom of leaving well enough alone. This aspect of civil association also comes out strongly in another brief statement of the aims of politics a few years later, in the early 1960s. 'Politics is the art of living together & of being "just" to one another — *not* of imposing a way of life, but of organizing a common life. The art of peace; the art of accommodating moralities to one another.'[86]

Correctly understood, politics was an important means of preserving the individual capacity for choice which gives life the possibility of religious and moral significance in the face of contingency. 'Where there is no choice we are for ever at the mercy of chance.'[87] The framework of rules which results from political deliberation in the form of legislation provides the structure within which people are free to pursue their own devices. From this point of view, individuals should be made the targets of policy as little as possible; not executive decision, but the civil and criminal law, should set the limits to their actions.

---

[80] See p. 408.

[81] See p. 444.

[82] See p. 429.

[83] M. Oakeshott, *Rationalism in Politics*, 2nd edn., ed. T. Fuller (Liberty Press: Indianapolis, 1991), p. 60.

[84] See p. 421.

[85] Raymond Geuss, *Private Goods, Public Goods* (Princeton, NJ: Princeton University Press, 2001), p. 32.

[86] See p. 444.

[87] See p. 403.

Only thus could one hope fully to realize the possibility of the sole kind of life which Oakeshott considered truly meaningful, namely a self-chosen life. Such a life might as well consist in a decision to succeed in business as to live on a kibbutz; the point was that it should belong to the person choosing it, in the sense of being intelligibly related to their own choices.

Yet Oakeshott believed the reality of political practice fell far short of providing the protection necessary to ensure the liberty of individual choice. Privately, he condemned it in the harshest terms. 'Rape', he wrote, 'is the typical crime of modern politics; politicians rape their victims, rulers rape their subjects; technology is the rape of the earth.'[88] This statement reinforces the observation already made in relation to his moral thought, that far from being any kind of defender of modernity, he was revolted by its exploitative excesses. Worse, this exploitation was now no longer simply a European problem, but thanks to Imperialism, a global one. 'The liquidation of colonial government is an incident overshadowed by a revolution with which it is not very closely connected – a revolution in which Africans have learned to *want*.'[89] The future he foresaw was a bleak one in which the rest of the world would imitate the materialistic and acquisitive habits which were making Western civilization so miserable.

When considering the contemporary fortunes of education it is no surprise, then, that Oakeshott was similarly pessimistic. 'For centuries..."Education" has meant a release from the current vulgarities of the world...Now, education is merely instruction in the current vulgarities.'[90] His own defence of the values of liberal learning appears in this light as also something of a rearguard action, one from which, moreover, his own view of the limitations of philosophy meant that he could not expect much in the way of success. He had already posed the problem to himself in the 1930s. 'Will a synthesis, a system, a corpus, teach, when we have failed to learn from those who given us insight into our civilization already?' He answered his own question: 'No.'[91]

Yet the effort itself was 'worth trying'. Even if its value was 'small', it was 'not pretentious' to make the attempt. Though we have seen that Oakeshott condemned the idea of philosophy insofar as it was an 'escape' from the pressing religious and ethical problems life raised, in another sense he thought of the ability of philosophy and other forms of theoretical and artistic experience to offer temporary relief from the banality of daily life as extremely important. It was difficult if not impossible to avoid 'work', his synonym for instrumental activity, altogether in life, but if it could be balanced with 'play', which included the diversions of conversation and leisure (whether a trip to the races or a camp-

---

[88] See p. 444.
[89] See p. 441.
[90] See p. 442.
[91] See p. 302.

ing expedition) as well as intellectual and aesthetic pursuits, life became less burdensome.

Education was crucial to making this possible. Although Oakeshott only began publishing his thoughts on the subject in the later 1940s, the notebooks demonstrate that he had been thinking about it since the early 1920s. In his youth, he seems to have been particularly interested in progressive education movements such as that lead by Maria Montessori. He took a very broad view of the things that were relevant to education, including, for example, music and dance. Somewhat later, in the 1930s, he seems to have been so concerned about the threat to liberal and humanistic learning that he went through a period of being actively hostile to science, fulminating that 'this science-ridden civilization is a menace to civilized life.'[92] But it was unusual for him to rant in this fashion, and further reflection convinced him that not scientific education, but scientism, or Rationalism, was the real problem. To the end of his life he remained grateful for his own education, telling himself in his eighties that 'I was lucky: my schooldays were filled with wonder', although he clearly felt in old age that education was not providing the same experience for modern children. 'How can we stop education from killing the sense of wonder?' he asked himself; but this time the question went unanswered.[93]

The literary sensibility which did so much to colour Oakeshott's views on religion, morality, and politics seems to have been at work in his ideas on education and philosophy also. There is a list of 'escapes' in one of the early notebooks from the 1920s based on his notes on Symons's *The Symbolist Movement in Literature*, and a possible source for the term 'mode of experience' is Murry's *The Problem of Style* which he encountered in the same period.[94] While his use of the concept of a mode of experience was mostly indebted to Spinoza and to Idealist thought, the term itself may well have had a literary source. One might wonder, too, whether there is not something fundamentally aesthetic in Oakeshott's notion of a mode or a category of understanding: at least, any kind of perspectivalism which emphasizes that the world must always be seen from a particular point of view is potentially liable to develop in this direction.

After all, Oakeshott reflected to himself when he was still young that he had chosen to live life as if it were a novel; it would be no surprise if the aestheticism which informed his moral and religious values turned out to have informed his philosophy also.[95] Perhaps the lesson of the notebooks as a whole is that Oakeshott was really the last great representative, not only of British Idealism, but also of English Romanticism; and that, indeed, he continued to cleave to the latter long after he had abandoned the former. Whether this was the case is

---

[92] See p. 305.
[93] See p. 551.
[94] See p. 11.
[95] See p. 183.

something that readers can now reflect on for themselves. Hopefully, they will find, too, that there is far more in them to discover than has been covered here.

A Note on the Texts

The notebooks required considerably more editorial intervention than the other material from amongst Oakeshott's papers published in this series so far. The problem of how to present the material on the page in an orderly fashion was the first problem that needed solving. The solution adopted for the recent Cambridge editions of Nietzsche's notebooks, of prefacing each passage with the number of the notebook and its accompanying page number (where available), seemed to be the most elegant answer.[96] It both provided an absolute reference point for citation and allowed any reader wishing to find the relevant text in the original notebook to do so easily.

A more minor problem was the presence in the notebooks of various notes on loose sheets which could not always be reliably tied to a particular point in the text and which in any case could not be ascertained to have remained in the place where Oakeshott originally inserted them (assuming that he did in fact do so himself). In some cases they did appear closely connected to passages in the notebooks, but in other instances their placement seemed arbitrary. In the interests of consistency, notes on loose sheets have been placed at the end of the notebook in question and given a letter rather than a page number, with a note indicating their original location where appropriate. Some of them have been numbered, apparently by an archivist, and these numberings have also been noted.

It was also in the nature of the material that it contained copious abbreviations, such as 'Xt' and 'Xtianity' for 'Christ' and 'Christianity', for example. Most of these abbreviations have been expanded in the interests of readability. Spelling, punctuation, and capitalization have also been standardized and corrected where it seemed desirable. But where Oakeshott wrote in note form rather than in complete sentences, his phrasing has been allowed to stand. At the same time, to preserve as much of the flavour of reading the originals as possible, Oakeshott's underlinings have been preserved, and certain abbreviations (such as 'Cp.' for 'Compare') have been retained, as have his ampersands. An effort has been made in the first footnote to each chapter to describe the notebook physically and to record the quotations Oakeshott sometimes used to embellish the title page, where appropriate.

On the whole, passages of continuous prose have been favoured over the more fragmentary entries in the notebooks. Instances of these, such as lists, have only been included when they seemed to be of exceptional interest; for example, Oakeshott's list of projected works at 07[A]. As already noted, most of the

---

[96] F. Nietzsche, *Writings from the Early Notebooks*, ed. R. Geuss and A. Nehemas (Cambridge: Cambridge University Press, 2009).

material in the notebooks which consisted exclusively of quotations from other writers has been omitted; even though they are often of interest to read through, their inclusion was not appropriate in a volume of this kind.

Since, however, some readers will inevitably wish for more detail about Oakeshott's reading than an edition of this kind can provide, the editor has also tried to list in the first footnote those works from which at least roughly a page or so of notes were copied out. It must be remarked, however, that the notebooks also contain very many individual quotations which were simply too numerous to be included, and any mention of these has been silently omitted. Very occasionally, an unaccompanied quotation has been included in the main text if it seemed to have particular significance for Oakeshott's thought; for example, Santayana's reflections on the use of the term *theoria*.[97]

Then there was the question of what to do with Oakeshott's own references. It can probably be assumed that readers of Oakeshott will not need guidance regarding the works of Hobbes and Hegel, but many of the other authors mentioned are now generally forgotten, so some annotation seemed called for. Oakeshott's references are typically cursory; in general, an author, short title, and perhaps a page number or other indication of a book or chapter is the most one can hope for. His notes, such as they are, are given in the footnotes, and where possible they have been put into a standard short form. If it were possible to be sure of the edition that Oakeshott was using, his note has been expanded into a full bibliographic reference. Where there is some doubt, a full citation has been placed after his note. In cases where no information was supplied at all, an editorial note has been inserted. These inserted notes are based on a first edition, another contemporary edition, or a modern edition if available, in that order of preference.

A final word of warning is required — many times during the preparation of this volume a phrase which gave no indication of being a quotation turned out to be such. While the editor would like to believe that everything represented in this volume as being Oakeshott's own words really falls into that category, the possibility of error can never be entirely excluded. And on that note, it must also be said that (owing chiefly to a lack of time and wherewithal), the annotation has been almost exclusively reliant on electronic sources. Although a gratifyingly large number of the nineteenth and early twentieth century works that figure in the notebooks can now be found online as scanned digital copies, which for the purpose of bibliographic reference is as often as good as being able to consult the original, this is not uniformly the case.

Hundreds of the books Oakeshott refers to were available in this form, but sometimes a reference had to be based on the electronic catalogue of a national or university library, or even in some cases of an antiquarian bookseller. The perils of this approach are too obvious to be worth emphasizing, but the benefit

---

[97] See pp. 124–5.

to the reader was felt overall to outweigh the inevitable mistakes which it entails. Similarly, while some of the persons mentioned in the notebooks will need no introduction, many of those named are now also forgotten, and they, too, have been identified where possible in the hope of saving the reader some trouble.

Lastly, as for the problem of selection, it can only be acknowledged that another editor would have chosen differently. Much had to be omitted in order to fit this volume within a single pair of covers. At least until the notebooks can be made available in their entirety in electronic form, the present volume, whatever its inadequacies, will have to serve as the public record of Oakeshott's private thoughts.

"The terrible aboriginal calamity". But Newman, who is usually right, was here unexpectedly astray. It must be understood not as a weakness in the design of the Creation but as a subtlety which distinguishes the Creation from a piece of commonplace engineering.

For Augustine (who unfortunately got caught up with the notion of 'Salvation' & who erred in some of the eccentric parts of his doctrine of 'Salvation') the 'Fall', 'Original sin' was not a simple 'calamity', the outcome of a flaw in the design, but an unavoidable consequence of the character with which God had endowed mankind: imagination, the capability of choosing & doing: self-creation. And when Augustine was asked why God did not endow mankind with unalterable 'perfection', he replied that God created Man because he was lonely, & that a companion who was himself a god, or a faultless automaton, would be insufferably boring. There was no point in creating the possibility of 'sin' if in fact there were to be no sinners. What (among much else) Augustine meant when he understood the relationship of God to Mankind was one of 'love' was that God was interested in comedy other than perfection. 'Love' is a delight in difference which must be capable of including the acceptance of error. Zeus had to suffer the errancy of men & responded with displeasure & anger. Jehovah had to suffer the errancy of his Chosen & responded with punishment (since recognized responsibility) and forgiveness. The Christian (Augustinian) God purposely created the unalterable and responded to (at least the more endearing antics of his creation) with 'love.' But this is not quite the whole story.

01[05]

In arguing for a national church we must not forget to distinguish between what is national in a nation and what is merely incidental — such as education etc: The difference between <u>personality</u> & <u>faddy habits</u>.[2]

01[05]

Be of good cheer, I have overcome the world![3]

01[14]

To make allegories was the aim of medieval Christianity.[4]

01[19–20]

<u>The Trinity</u>[5]

(Power) God. The Absolute creator.

(Wisdom) The Son. God turned towards the world. The word (will) made flesh. Means by which all was created. Immanent in man's soul.

(Goodness) The spirit. Witness of the will. The interpreter.

Argument from (i) Our own personality.
                (ii) The meaning of 'persons' — utterly reasonable.

01[29]

Love and knowledge go on acting and reacting upon one another till love finally is made perfect and reigns supreme.

---

[1]   LSE 2/1/1. Soft cover, green, 20 cm x 15 cm, ruled. Recto folios numbered 1–62. Autograph, pencil and ink. Cover: 'Notes / Michael Oakeshott / I.' Undated.
      Other works from which Oakeshott made excerpts in this notebook but which are not mentioned in the text include: Fos. 2–4, A. Fogazzaro, *The Man of the World*, tr. M. Prichard Agnetti, 3rd edn (London: Hodder and Stoughton, 1907); 57–8, John Keats, *Life, Letters, and Literary Remains*, ed. R.M. Milnes, 2 vols. (London: Edward Moxon, 1848); 59–60, Plato, *Symposium* and *Phaedrus*, probably from *The Dialogues of Plato*, tr. B. Jowett, 4 vols. (Oxford: Clarendon Press, 1871).

[2]   Fos. 5–6 contain notes on Thomas à Kempis, *De imitatione Christi* (c.1418–27).

[3]   John 16:33.

[4]   Fos. 6–16 contain notes on W.R. Inge, *Types of Christian Saintliness* (London: Longmans, Green & Co., 1915).

[5]   Fos. 17–38 contain notes on W.R. Inge, *Studies of English Mystics* (London: John Murray, 1906).

01[35]

Jesus Christ is the sure proof of the sacramentality of our life. A life with an inner meaning—a material body with the spirit within. In Him it was God wholly possessing the body.

01[35]

The first act of a democratic state would be to form an aristocracy.

01[36]

We must not condemn the world as evil because it seems to be evil at the moment, any more than it would be just to condemn a policy which was stopped half way.

01[36]

Father & Son

Those fragile loves to which men look back with tenderness & passion, emotions only to be explained as Montaigne explained them, '*parceque c'était lui, parceque c'était moi.*'[6]

01[37]

Flowers are spring's whisperings.

01[39]

If you admit no possibility of fall you can admit none of rise.[7]

01[39]

Allegory is what prose writers use where the poet uses symbols.[8]

01[41]

There are more molecules in one tear than there are people on the Earth.[9]

01[41]

The perfect Christian character.

---

[6] See Montaigne, *Essais*, 'Of Friendship.'

[7] Fos. 38–40 contain notes on Emile Gebhart, *L'Italie mystique: histoire de la renaissance religieuse au moyen age* (Paris: Librairie Hachette, 1890).

[8] Oakeshott's note: 'Symons.' Probably Arthur William Symons (1865–1945), Welsh poet.

[9] Fos. 40–1 contain notes on W.R. Inge, *Truth and Falsehood in Religion Six Lectures Delivered in Cambridge to Undergraduates in the Lent Term 1906* (London: John Murray, Albermarle Street, 1906).

The balanced mind.

The man who has all good qualities at his command and the necessary judgment to know when to use them.

01[48]

In Indian art we see the realization that the infinite is the goal of India's ideal by the accumulation of images.[10]

Infinite accumulation is India's expression of her ideal.

01[50]

Birds & flowers and all beauty are rainbows — they are promises, assurances that all is well, from God.

01[50]

In love is our existence made intelligible. For in love are all contraries reconciled.

01[60]

Plan[11]

The Psychology of the Saints

Monasticism — the externalizing properties of the church.
From freedom to authority — the philosophy of Papalism. From Doubt to belief.
Religion — bearing or borne.
The sense of sin.
The meaning of poverty. Celibacy, etc:
Children — their message & significance to the saints.
The Balanced mind. Liberal Theologians. Liberal-Conservative.

---

[10] Fos. 46–50 contain notes on R. Tagore, *Sādhanā: The Realisation of Life* (Leipzig: Bernhard Tauchnitz, 1921).

[11] This page crossed out in pencil.

02[07]

The complexity of our eye enables us to see things simply — see things as a whole.[2]

02[12]

'But through the words, lives & verses, runs the simple inspiration which is the whole poem. So, among the dislocated individuals one life goes on moving.'[3]

Individuals joining together in a society; but the society soon becomes an individual in itself able in its turn to be part and parcel of a new association.

[1]   LSE 2/1/2. Soft cover, green, 20 cm x 15 cm, blank. Recto folios numbered 1–97. Autograph, pencil and ink. Cover: 'II.' Undated.
      Other works from which Oakeshott made excerpts in this notebook but which are not mentioned in the text include: Fos. 1–4, H. Bergson, *Dreams*, tr. E.E. Slosson (New York: B.W. Huebsch, 1914); 17–20, H. Bergson, *Le rire. Essai sur la signification du comique* (Paris: F. Alcan, 1900); 36–40, *One Hundred Poems of Kabir*, tr. R. Tagore and E. Underhill (London: Macmillan and Co., Limited, 1915); 55–7, R.L. Stevenson, *Lay Morals, and Other Papers* (London: Chatto and Windus, 1911); 58–9, John Fiske, *The Unseen World, and Other Essays*, 5th edn (Boston, MA: Houghton, Mifflin & Co., 1876); 60, 'Kingsley, Life, 18th ed.', probably *Charles Kingsley His Letters And Memories of his Life*, ed. F.E. Kingsley, 2 vols. (London: H.S. King, 1876); 61, W.R. Inge, *Faith and Knowledge* (Edinburgh: T. & T. Clark, 1904); 64–5, R. Tagore, *The Gardener* (London: Macmillan and Co., Limited, 1913); 68, H. Black, *Edinburgh Sermons Listening to God* (London, Edinburgh, New York, Chicago and Toronto: Fleming H. Revell Company, 1906); 73–5, J.B. Bury, *The Idea of Progress An Inquiry Into Its Origin and Growth* (London: Macmillan and Co., Limited, 1920); 76–7, F. Nietzsche, *Beyond Good and Evil*, tr. H. Zimmern (Edinburgh and London: T. Foulis, 1907); 79–82, J. Combarieu, *Music Its Laws and Evolution* (London: Kegan Paul, Trench, Trübner & Co. Ltd, 1910); 83–4, T.H. Huxley, *Method and Results Essays* (London: Macmillan and Co., Limited, 1893); George William Russell, aka 'A.E.,' *Imaginations and Reveries* (Dublin and London: Mansel & Company, Ltd., 1915); 86, C.K.D. Patmore, *The Rod, The Root, and the Flower* (London: George Bell and Sons, 1895); 87–8, A.V. Dicey, *Introduction to the Study of the Law of the Constitution*, 8th edn (London: Macmillan and Co., Limited, 1915); 88–90, J. Bryce, *Modern Democracies*, 2 vols. (London: Macmillan and Co., Limited, 1921); 92–4, B. de Selincourt, 'Rhyme in English Poetry' and A.H. Fox Strangways, 'Words and Music in Song', in *Essays and Studies by Members of the English Association*, vol. vii, ed. J. Bailey (Oxford: Clarendon Press, 1921), 7–29, 30–56.
[2]   Fos. 5–16 contain notes on H. Bergson, *Evolution créatrice* (Paris: F. Alcan, 1907).
[3]   Bergson, *Evolution créatrice*, p. 272.

02[27]

'Joy is a soul-force…joy illuminates thought.'[4]

02[31]

'The complete citizen should leave school capable not only of living normally, but of feeling life. He should be in a position both to create and to respond to the creation of others.'[5]

That response to the creations of others which is itself creation.

02[43]

The child must be armed against the present, must be protected from falling prey to a view of life which knows only the present, by that knowledge and feeling of eternity, which is behind, which upholds time, without which no time could exist, which comes to us in religion. The slaves of petty desires, of materialism, of 'rationalism' are the slaves of a restricted view, and can only be freed by the impulse of natural religion springing up within him and showing him the spiritual world which is above all time and place, which includes all times & places & people.[6]

02[43]

Religion is the poetry of morality. A code of morality only rules bad, unloving souls in order that they first may become better & then good. As an eagle flies high above the highest mountains so the transport of religion transcends the persuasion of our moral law.

02[44]

A child is to you, that which is in your heart. Children will be loving, gentle, beautiful, thoughtful, unselfish if in your heart they can, all unawares, find these virtues. Cf. Jeremy Taylor.

02[44]

Church = fellowship = Friendship with God

02[47]

Joy is spiritual pleasure. Cheerfulness is the result of spiritual enjoyment.

---

[4] Fos. 21–35 contain notes on Emile-Jacques Dalcroze, *Rhythm, Music and Education* (New York and London: G.P. Putnam's Sons, 1921). The quotation is attributed by Dalcroze to Henri Bois at p. 175 n.

[5] Dalcroze, *Rhythm, Music and Education*, p. 137.

[6] Fos. 40–54 contain notes on Jean Paul Richter, *Levana; Or, The Doctrine Of Education*, tr. S. Wood (London: Swan Sonnenschein, Lowrey & Co., 1887).

02[67]

Practice & improvement

Improvement takes place actually during the interruption of practice.

It has been found that the memory is more retentive if after it has 'memorized' the facts it is given a period of rest before use for any other purpose. In this period of 'rest' the facts are engraved in the memory more indelibly.

02[67]

Thought is always spasmodic. There is no such thing as an unbroken chain of thought. The revelation comes suddenly & categorically.

Our actions do not come as the fruit of an unbroken train of thought, they are the materialization of a sudden, unexpected desire, passionate longing, of the whole soul.

02[69]

1. Logic.[7]
2. The Philosophy of the practical.
3. Aesthetic.
4. History.

02[A][8]

Jesus' saying—'Mother behold thy son.'

Astounding when viewed according to Jewish ideas—women & children in Jewish society.

---

7   Fos. 69–72 contain notes on B. Croce, *Theory and History of Historiography*, tr. D. Ainslie (London: George G. Harrap & Co., 1921).
8   On a loose sheet inserted at 02[51], crossed out.

03[62]

Repentance. 'Repent ye for the Kingdom of Heaven is at hand.'[2] To the Hebrew & the Greek, Repentance means turning round – one of life, other of mind. No emphasis on the backward look. 'Open your hearts & minds or you will not see a Good thing when it comes, or understand it when you see it.' Jesus' 'repentance' is a casting off of preconceptions, a becoming as a little child, & it is

---

[1] LSE 2/1/3. Soft cover, green, 20 cm x 16 cm, ruled, 20 cm x 16 cm, ruled. Recto folios numbered 1–62. Autograph, pencil and ink. Title page: 'Michael Oakeshott / Notes. / Volume III. / August. 1922.'

Other works from which Oakeshott made excerpts in this notebook but which are not mentioned in the text include: Fos. 1–8, W. Pater, *Marius the Epicurean: His Sensations and Ideas*, 2 vols. (London: Macmillan and Co., 1895); 8–10, Ella Fuller Maitland, *Pages from the Day-Book of Bethia Hardacre* (London: Chapman & Hall, 1895), and *More Pages from the Day-Book of Bethia Hardacre* (London: Archibald Constable & Co., 1907); 10–11, W.F. de Morgan, *It Never Can Happen Again* (New York: Grosset and Dunlap, 1909); 14–18, P.T. Forsyth, *Christ on Parnassus Lectures on Art, Ethic, and Theology* (London: Independent Press, 1911); 19–22, Leslie Stephen, *History of English Thought in the Eighteenth Century*, 2 vols. (London: Smith, Elder, & Co., 1876); 23–30, Henry Jones, *A Faith That Enquires: The Gifford Lectures delivered in the University of Glasgow in the years 1920 and 1921*, (London: Macmillan, 1922); 30–3, E.G.A. Holmes, *What Is Philosophy?* (London and New York: John Lane: The Bodley Head, 1905); 32, J.S. Mill, *Dissertations and Discussions Political, Philosophical, and Historical*, 3 vols. (London: Longmans, Green, Reader, and Dyer, 1867); 34–5, T.H. Green, *Works*, ed. R.L. Nettleship, 3 vols. (London and New York: Longmans, Green, And Co., 1888); 35, W.E. Soothill, *The Three Religions of China. Lectures delivered at Oxford* (London: Hodder & Stoughton, 1913); 36–9, L.P. Jacks, *The Legends of Smokeover* (Toronto, London, and New York: Hodder and Stoughton, 1921); 40–2, A.J. Balfour, *Essays Speculative and Political* (London: Hodder and Stoughton, 1920); 43–6, G. Santayana, *The Life of Reason or the Phases of Human Progress Reason in Art* (London: Archibald Constable & Co., 1905); 47–51, H. Bergson, *Introduction to Metaphysics*, tr. T.E. Hulme (New York and London: G.P. Putnam's Sons, 1912); 51–2, L.P. Jacks, *Religious Perplexities* (New York: George H. Doran Company, 1923); 54–6, J.W. von Goethe, *Maxims and Reflections*, tr. B. Saunders (New York: The Macmillan Company; London, Macmillan & Co., Ltd., 1906); 58–9, B. Bosanquet, *What Religion Is* (London: Macmillan and Co., 1920); 60–1, K. Stephen, *The Misuse of Mind: A Study of Bergson's Attack on Intellectualism* (London: Kegan Paul Trench Trübner and Co. Ltd., 1922); 70–72, J.P. Richter, *Hesperus or Forty-Five Dog-Post-Days*, tr. C.T. Brooks, 2 vols. (Boston: Ticknor and Fields, 1865); 84–6, P.T. Forsyth, *Marriage: Its Ethic and Religion* (London: Hodder & Stoughton, 1912); 87–90, M. Rutherford, *Pages From A Journal With Other Papers* (London: T.F. Unwin, 1900), *More Pages From A Journal With Other Papers* (London, Edinburgh, New York, Toronto, and Melbourne: Henry Frowde Oxford University Press, 1910), and *Last Pages From A Journal With Other Papers*, ed. D.V. White (London: Humphrey Milford, 1915); 91–3, G. Santayana, *Poems* (London, Bombay, and Sydney: Constable and Company Ltd, 1922).

[2] Matthew 3:2.

followed by the Kingdom of Heaven. It is a freeing of the mind, it is joyful &
forward looking.[3]

03[62–3]

The Vision of the Spirit. Jesus lived in a world where the hand of God was
visible everywhere. In every happening he was drawn close to His Father. Thus
in the Storm on the Sea of Gallilee, he is awakened suddenly among men who
do not see the world thus—and who are consequently afraid & perplexed. The
fear of the disciples is so evident, that for a moment Jesus himself is dazed—then
he comes to himself & says 'You cowards.'

Also, after the mystic Transfiguration, he is met on his return by the blind
man & his father & the disciples who have failed to effect a cure. He is so full of
the reality of God everywhere that he cannot at first understand the difficulty
felt by others. He then crys out to the men before him—'Believe.' You have no
faith—no vision of the Spirit.

03[65]

Men & women are often more fairly judged by the way in which they bear the
burden of what they have done, than by the prime act which laid the burden on
their lives.

03[82]

General Argument[4]

General assumption throughout—Christianity is Roman Catholicism.

Modernism = position adopted by many who wish to remain Catholic but
who have pursued   (i) Rationalistic study of Bible & Church History.
                                (ii) Modern Philosophy.
Christianity thinks, *a priori*, that a miracle is probable. It must stand apart from
the intellectual world of any particular day. It is always anti the world. (In what
sense does Santayana use the word 'world'?)

Modernism is an allegiance to God & the World. It tries to reconcile the ever
irreconcilable—Christianity & 'Modern' thought. Church & the World. Tries to
take all dogmas in a 'purely symbolic or moral sense.' Christianity came to
announce salvation from the world. Catholicism etc. 'gives out the full & exact
note of the New Testament.' The wish 'to preserve a continuity of moral
traditions,' to take good out of all human activities, is a Pagan, Renaissance wish
& contrary to Christiantity. Modernists think that the weakness of the Church is

---

3   Oakeshott's note: 'See Burkitt, *Christian Beginnings.*' F.C. Burkitt, *Christian Beginnings
     Three Lectures* (London: University of London Press, 1924).
4   Fos. 79–84 contain notes on G. Santayana, *Winds of Doctrine Studies In Contemporary
     Opinion* (London: J.M. Dent & Sons; New York: Charles Scribner's Sons, 1913).

that it does not follow the impulse of the age—but this may well prove its strength. The real power in all Churches lies with those who believe in the sacraments & miracles literally, who preach 'foolishness.'[5]

03[83]

Modernism is suicide—it gives up all the essential dignity of Christianity.[6]

Whatever the 'world' is, Christianity by definition is different?

03[A][7]

Philosophy & temperament. We cannot exclude this factor—Everyman an Aristotelian or a Platonist by nature. What is this factor?

03[A]

Can it be conceived that such books as W. James, *Varieties*, will give anyone real belief, faith.[8] It is a scientific examination of facts which adds to our knowledge about (correct language here) these things, but does not help us to know them.

03[B][9]

To produce great literature we must have within us that spirit of quiet, that 'central peace Subsisting at the heart of endless agitation.' The world is agitated but behind it is peace; and he who has cleft the veil and can see, has eternal life. See Carroll, 'Preface' to *Silvie & Bruno* etc.—full of life, but in harmony with 'those deeper cadences of life.'[10]

03[C][11]

I. Is there such a sensation as one of pure admiration? Is it not usually—always—mixed with an active desire to emulate?

If the sovereignty of personality is a fact then it is not possible. If we admire a picture then we cannot wish to emulate the picture.

---

5 See Santayana, *Winds of Doctrine*, pp. 36–7, 50–1, 59.

6 See Santayana, *Winds of Doctrine*, pp. 35, 56.

7 On a loose sheet inserted at 03[24], headed 'The Ultimate Belief.' Apparently a note on A. Clutton-Brock, *The Ultimate Belief* (London: Archibald Constable & Co., 1916).

8 W. James, *Varieties of Religious Experience: A Study in Human Nature. Being the Gifford Lectures on Natural Religion delivered at Edinburgh in 1901–2* (London and Bombay: Longman's, Green, and Co., 1902).

9 On a loose sheet inserted at 03[26].

10 L. Carroll, *Sylvie and Bruno* (London: Macmillan and Co., 1889).

11 On pencil on the reverse of a mutilated letter to J.F. Oakeshott from the *Encyclopedia Britannica*, inserted at 03[78]. Apparently notes on J.S. Blackie, *On Beauty: Three Discourses Delivered in the University of Edinburgh. With an Exposition of the Doctrine of the Beautiful According to Plato* (Edinburgh: Sunderland and Knox; London: Simpkin, Marshall, and Co., 1858), including pp. 118, 148, 150.

Which is to say that we can never <u>merely contemplate</u> human character.

II. Beauty of a process? Scientific mans point of view was aesthetic?

IV, & V. Then a simple, unrestricted mass of colour cannot be called, 'Beautiful.'

VI. Sometimes, when the shape can be perceived as a whole in one glance, <u>memory</u> is not a factor in sense perception — only <u>extent</u>.[12]

VII. Then greater ability of mind will find fewer things ugly.

XIII. Aesthetic <u>appreciation</u> came before <u>production</u>.

XVIII. Cf. Keat's attempt at incompleteness. It can at times be right to leave a work of art incomplete.

XX. The lyric.

---

[12] Oakeshott's note: 'Bergson.'

Notebook 4 (1923)

04[45]

Escapes. Fantasy — (Bennett — *Hugo*.)[2] Romance, Dreams.[3]

Sleep, insensibility, poetry of escape, wine, the past, childhood (Vaughan).[4]

---

[1] LSE 2/1/4. Hard cover, black and red marbling, 20 cm x 14 cm, blank. Recto folios numbered 1–85. Autograph, ink. Title page: 'NOTES. IV. / July 2nd 1923.'

Other works from which Oakeshott made excerpts in this notebook but which are not mentioned in the text include: Fos. 1–2, W.S. Landor, *Pericles & Aspasia*, ed. C.G. Crump, 2 vols. (London: J.M. Dent and Co., 1890); 3, W.S. Landor, *The Hellenics of Walter Savage Landor. Enlarged and Completed* (Edward Moxon: London, 1847); 5–13, W.B. Yeats, *Ideas of Good and Evil* (London: A.H. Bullen, 1903); 18–20, J.M. Murry, *The Problem of Style* (London, Edinburgh, Glasgow, Copehagen, New York, Toronto, Melbourne, Cape Town, Bombay, Calcutta, Madras, Shanghai: Humphrey Milford Oxford University Press, 1922); 21–26, B. Bosanquet, *Essays and Addresses* (London: Swan Sonnenschein & Co., 1891); 30–3, J.M.E. McTaggart, 'The Necessity of Dogma', *International Journal of Ethics*, 5 (1895), 147–62; 34–7, G. Santayana, *Soliloquies in England and Later Soliloquies* (London, Bombay, and Sydney: Constable and Company Ltd., 1922); 37–8, T.E. Brown, *Letters of Thomas Edward Brown Author of 'Fo'c'sle Yarns'*, ed. S.T. Irwin, 2 vols. (London: Archibald Constable and Co., Ltd., 1900); 38–40, D. Merejkowski, *Christ and Anti-Christ The Romance of Leonardo da Vinci The Forerunner*, tr. H. Trench (New York and London: G.P. Putnam's Sons, 1908); 41–2, J.M.E. McTaggart, 'Mysticism', *New Quarterly*, 2 (1909), 315–39; 45–6, W.H. White, *The Autobiography of Mark Rutherford, Dissenting Minister. Edited by his Friend Reuben Shapcott* (London: Trübner and Co., 1881); 49–50, R.L. Stevenson, *Weir of Hermiston: An Unfinished Romance* (London: Chatto and Windus, 1896); 51–4, G. Macdonald, *Phantastes A Faërie Romance for Men and Women* (London: Smith, Elder & Co., 1858); 55–6, T. Carlyle, *The Life of John Sterling* (London: Chapman and Hall, 1871); 60–1, R. Browning, *Prince Hohenstiel-Schwangau, Saviour of Society* (London: Smith, Elder and Co., 1871); 62–3, G. Moore, *The Brook Kerith A Syrian Story* (Edinburgh: Dunedin Press, 1921); 63, B. Pascal, *Discours sur les passions de l'amour avec un commentaire de Emile Faguet* (Paris: Bernard Grasset, 1911); 64–5, M. Pattison, *Essays by the Late Mark Pattison Sometime Rector of Lincoln College*, ed. H. Nettleship, 2 vols. (Oxford: Clarendon Press, 1889); 68–9, possibly G.T.W. Patrick, *The Fragments of the Work of Heraclitus of Ephesus on Nature Translated from the Greek Text of Bywater with an Introduction Historical and Critical* (Baltimore: N. Murray, 1889); 69–71, J.M.E. McTaggart, *Some Dogmas of Religion* (London: Edward Arnold, 1906); 72–77, G. Santayana, *The Life of Reason or the Phases of Human Progress Reason in Society* (New York: Charles Scribner's Sons, 1905); 78–80, W.M. Thackeray, *Vanity Fair: A Novel Without A Hero* (London: Bradbury and Evans, 1849); 81–3, W.E.H. Lecky, *The Map of Life Conduct and Character* (London: Longman's, Green, and Co., 1901); 84–5, B. Russell, *Prospects of Industrial Civilization* (London: Allen and Unwin, 1923).

[2] Arnold Bennett, *Hugo. A Fantasia on Modern Themes* (London: Chatto and Windus, 1906).

[3] Fos. 42–5 contain notes on A. Symons, *The Symbolist Movement in Literature*, 2nd edn (1908).

[4] Possibly a reference to 'Childhood' by Henry Vaughan (1621–95), which begins 'I cannot reach it; and my striving eye / Dazzles at it, as at eternity.'

04[48]

Milton was not the proverbial puritan without any sensitiveness to beauty — he was a man who knew only too well the force of temptation & his life was a long struggle against it.[5] All his poems treat of temptation either succumbed to or thwarted.

Paradise Regained is not a continuation of *Paradise Lost* but a new theme, a new temptation & a final victory.

We are all Miltons in at least a part of our lives.

04[67]

'Pascal is naturally & rightly taken by those who found their Apologetic upon Immanence as their leader.'[6]

Cf. Schleiermacher. Pascal was his precusor in his attempt to build up an 'Immanent' apologetic.

04[84]

Habit

Socrates defined excellence in terms of knowledge — which is the opposite of Habit. Fichte said that to form a habit was to fail; & Shelley describes it as 'The queen of slaves, the hoodwinked angel of the blind & dead.' But cf. Bosanquet, *Philosophical Theory of the State*, for the value of habit.[7]

04[A][8]

The poet's business to reveal the real under the symbol.
See Shelley's 'Defence.'[9]

04[A]

We must get back to the idea that all philosophy is built on experience & that some experience is more profound, truer than other. And that the true poet's experience is the profoundest — because we mean by poet, 'he who experiences best what is true' — feels unity when others only feel diversity; knows spirit, mind, when others see only material & physical expression.

---

[5] Fos. 47–9 contain notes on Sir W. Raleigh, *Milton* (London: Edward Arnold, 1913).

[6] Oakeshott's note: 'H.F. Stewart, *The Holiness of Pascal* (Cambridge: Cambridge University Press, 1915), p. 89.'

[7] B. Bosanquet, *The Philosophical Theory of the State* (London: Macmillan and Co., 1899).

[8] On a loose sheet inserted into Notebook 4.

[9] i.e. Percy Bysshe Shelley, 'A Defence of Poetry.'

04[A]

Philosophy is really the clear thinking of what is felt in religion — the <u>oneness</u>. If we have no religion we have but a poor starting place for philosophy.

04[B][10]

<u>The Poetry of A.E.</u>

Poetry & politics.

Politics of time; politics of eternity. How to join.
    Few have dared not believe that here we are in exile — Paul, Augustine; —
    But what sort of exile?
    A vale of soul-making? Prometheus, Psyche.

04[B]

It were too much, perhaps, to ask that every worker should envisage the whole — that were to demand the quarryman should build the temple in his mind — but we may ask that those who profess to see it whole should not leave out half — & that the invisible, eternal half.

04[C][11]

See Bosanquet, *Aspects*, essay I — the true citizen sees life whole.[12]

04[C]

Citizenship is a spiritual experience — not a legal relationship.
    See Spinoza — *De intellectus emendatione* & *Ethics* & *Tractatus theologico-politicus*.

04[D][13]

<u>Read Plato</u>

The great question is, what exactly is the social experience?
    The poet takes us behind forms which are dissimilar to show us the unity.

---

[10] On a loose sheet inserted into Notebook 4.
[11] On a loose sheet inserted into Notebook 4.
[12] B. Bosanquet, 'The Duties of Citizenship,' in B. Bosanquet (ed.), *Aspects of the Social Problem* (London and New York: Macmillan and Co., 1895), pp. 1–13.
[13] On a loose sheet inserted into Notebook 4.

PL1[01]

Plato's conception—The best life can only be lived in some form of organized community, ∴ he calls it 'The Republic.' So the question 'What is the best life?' is the same as 'What is the best order or organization of society?'

PL1[01]

Greeks did not distinguish between ethical & political aspects of life—but they did not therefore confuse them. Nowadays we have come to distinguish—for good or for evil.

PL1[01]

The Republic is also a book of a <u>reformer</u>. (Unlike Aristotle in this way.)

PL1[04]

Plato's aim was to awaken Athens to her desperate need of discipline. Sparta, he saw, took life seriously, was scientifically organized—for a purpose—war. 'The children of this world are wiser than the children of light' (Luke 16:8). Athens must be disciplined, scientifically organized for the purpose of—'the good life.' It is the old, old trouble which Jesus saw in the religious life of men.

PL1[21]

35.41[2]

Is this the question which Political Philosophy sets itself to answer?—'the manner in which a man ought to live.'

PL1[26]

The idea that God blesses the just, that virtue should have its reward is instinctive in man. In purest form found in Old Testament. Later is corrupted by making material prosperity a criterion of justice. In early times it was but a

---

[1] LSE 2/2/1. Hard cover, black and red marbling, 20 cm x 12.5 cm, blank. Recto folios numbered 1–86. Autograph, ink. Title page: 'I. / <u>Plato</u>. <u>Republic</u>. / July. 1923.'
    The notebooks on Plato make extensive use of B. Bosanquet, *A Companion to Plato's Republic For English Readers Being a Commentary Adapted to Davies and Vaughan's Translation* (London: Rivington and Co., 1895); R.L. Nettleship, *Lectures on the Republic of Plato*, ed. G.R. Benson (London: Macmillan and Co, 1898); and *The Republic of Plato Translated into English with an Analysis and Notes*, tr. J.L. Davies and D.J. Vaughan (Cambridge: Macmillan and Co., 1866).
[2] Oakeshott's numberings refer to the page and line number in Davies and Vaughan.

convenient way of expressing the fact that righteousness rules the world. But ordinary facts contradict it as a theory of life.[3]

PL1[29]

'While every man is insufficient for himself, every man has it in him to give to others what they have not got. This is what we may call the principle of reciprocity.'[4]

Cp. Hegel's principle that unity requires differentiation, & that the greater the differentiation, the greater the unity.

PL1[34]

66. 2-5

The Quest for God is the whole business of human life. This idea puts meaning into the living history of man's mental & physical struggles.

PL1[35]

Whole argument from 70.35-71.14 lies against the Christian conception of God.

But does this idea necessitate the idea of <u>change</u> in God? (Note Plato merely says that it is 'very unlikely.')[5]

PL1[36]

Bradley leaves open the question as to why there should be <u>appearance</u> as well as reality. Appearance seems like a lie of God in Plato's sense. That is, if we can speak of appearances as created by Him.

PL1[38]

Cf. Spinoza, *Ethics*. Ideal of <u>Freedom</u>. It is really the same thing as Plato's Temperance. Cf. 292.34.

PL1[44]

The problem of Christian theology — Man is sinful, God is good — there is no common ground in either, no analogy. A gulf to be bridged — the Divine Initiative. 'While we were yet in sin.'

---

3 Oakeshott's note: 'Cf. J.E. Acton, *Historical Essays & Studies*, ed. J.N. Figgis and R.V. Laurence (London: Macmillan and Co., 1907), p. 286, and Plato, *Laws*, 662.'

4 Oakeshott's note: 'Nettleship, *Lectures*, p. 71.'

5 Oakeshott's note: 'Cf. Plato, *Phaedrus*, 381e.'

PL1[51]

Plato's idea that the thing to do is to get the State to a certain level of life & then keep it there at all costs. No idea of continuing progress.[6]

PL1[54–55]

The basis of all political theory must be sought in the individual consciousness.

This is fundamental in Plato & Aristotle. The justification & nature of the State is in the mind of man.

PL1[59]

(a) <u>Communism</u> & (b) the <u>Sovereignty of Philosophy</u> are the subjects of book V.

(a) As advocated by Plato only applies to the Guardians. It is supplementary machinery to give effect to & reinforce the spirit which education is to create.

Plato sees the enormous dangers, socially, which come from property & family. They are the great strongholds of selfishness.

(b) Two elements — (i) 'speculative.' This is possessed by all, but in very varying degrees. To do good it must, like art, be enlisted in the service of the State. (ii) 'Spiritual' cf. Roman Catholic Church & England in the 17th century.[7]

PL1[61–62]

Plato is so taken up with the different elements & abilities of woman's nature, that he does not question whether her real nature can or cannot be said to be the sum of these abilities. Or whether, having these abilities, to a degree, the same as men, she has not, perhaps, others, higher & more suited to her nature. There is a logical fallacy. A is similar to B ∴ B has nothing other than A.

The more co-operation in a community the better — this is Plato's <u>principle</u>. But how? Plato takes what we should call a restricted view of woman & her capabilities. Partly owing to his time and place. Greece was almost Oriental in its treatment of women. Plato makes a great advance.[8]

Cf. Rousseau & his protest against woman's neglect of her family. And Rousseau was, in many ways, a true Platonist.[9]

PL1[63]

Such phenomena as 'crowd suggestion,' & such observations as 'corporations have no conscience,' point out the fact that human nature is limited in the degree

---

[6]   Compare Nettleship, *Lectures*, p. 142.
[7]   Compare Nettleship, *Lectures*, pp. 166–9.
[8]   Compare Bosanquet, *Companion*, p. 182; Nettleship, *Lectures*, p. 173.
[9]   Compare Bosanquet, *Companion*, p. 187.

to which it can really lead a common life. To force it further means the loss of all the greatness of a higher individuality.

Family may often be the greatest source of selfishness — dynastic wars, nepotism, etc: — but it is also the occasion of the highest unselfishness.

Are we to enforce unity, to say that the Family is on occasion evil & so must be done away & the whole ruled by 'wise men,' or are we to seek to limit the evil & give fullest scope for the good, i.e. to eliminate evil by slow education of the whole & not by authority in these matters?[10]

PL1[64]

It is nothing against the Ideal that it cannot be made actual. The actual is never more than an approximation to the ideal pattern.

Justice is a pattern for human action; true human life would be lived in an ideal community. Actual life is, to a degree, a falsification of the Truth.[11]

'Theory' a misleading word. The antithesis between 'theory & practice' is vulgar. Read, 'Is it possible for things to be done as they are said?'[12]

PL1[66]

What are called 'forms' then, are the elements of unity in the manifold objects or things which we apprehend by the senses.[13]

PL1[66]

The object of knowledge is what is; or, in other words, the operation of knowledge is to produce consciousness of what is. Opinion must have an object; but it cannot be the same as that of knowledge.[14]

PL1[77]

Simile of the Cave. Everything is seen from a fixed standpoint — prejudice. Man sees what he <u>can</u>, not what <u>is</u>, as a rule. No open minded observation.
Education is painful.[15]

---

[10] Compare Nettleship, *Lectures*, pp. 178–9.

[11] Compare Nettleship, *Lectures*, pp. 184–5.

[12] Compare Bosanquet, *Companion*, p. 201.

[13] A direct quotation from Nettleship, *Lectures*, p. 191. See also Nettleship, *Lectures*, p. 195: 'The world as it is for science, the world of what Plato calls forms, is not a second, shadowy, unreal world, it is the same world better understood.'

[14] The first sentence is direct quotation, the second a digest of Nettleship, *Lectures*, p. 193.

[15] Compare Nettleship, *Lectures*, p. 261.

PL1[78]

When a 'philosopher' returns to ordinary life he is, at first, unable to grasp the awful reality of ordinary life. (Cf. Christ after the Transfiguration. Matthew 17:17.)

But cf. 'You will see a thousand times better' — This is the final justification for the sovereignty of philosophy.[16]

PL1[79]

The relation between society & great men should be one of mutual recognition & service.

The great man must remember that he owes a tremendous amount of his greatness & character to society; & he will willingly serve society in return.

PL1[81]

The truths of science 'always' <u>are</u>, granted the assumptions on which they are based.[17]

PL1[83]

258.17

Dialectic is Rational. It does not even use diagrams to the extent which geometry does.[18]

PL1[83]

260.17

Dialectic is <u>critical</u>; & its result, <u>categorical</u>.[19]

PL1[84–5]

Plato's principles of Education: —

1. Education must be complete, meeting all the demands that human nature brings with it.

2. Education should be co-extensive with life, for education simply means keeping the soul alive.

---

16 Oakeshott's note: '242.22; 239.11–26.' The context is a discussion of Plato's myth of the cave.
17 Compare Bosanquet, *Companion*, p. 287.
18 Compare Bosanquet, *Companion*, p. 297.
19 Compare Bosanquet, *Companion*, p. 301.

3. The organs of education are simply the great things of life — Religion, art, science, philosophy, etc: —

4. Its aim is to realize the harmonious & complete man — whose completeness is found in service of the community.

These principles, & not any method suggested, are Plato's gift to the world.[20]

PL1[85]

Note: The idea of <u>Government</u> in Greece. We have narrowed it tremendously. There it meant the total <u>leadership</u> afforded to the people. Now, it means simply politics. But there are other leaders than political.

---

[20] Compare Nettleship, *Lectures*, p. 292.

PL2[01]

Books II–VII of the *Republic* may be regarded as a philosophy of history. But it is in no sense an 'historical' account. And for this reason all account of the reaction from without, which plays so great a part in actual societies, is omitted.

Did Plato think that reactions from without were only the results, the occasions of fall, & that the whole health of society was ruled internally?

PL2[06]

299.10

The tyrant grows from the public champion. The despotism of the Thirty did not arise in this manner, but that of Dionysius the elder did.[2]

PL2[12]

334.13

'Perhaps in heaven there is laid up a pattern [of the city] for him who wishes to behold it, and, beholding, to organize himself accordingly.'

'Heaven' is here a mere passing figure of speech. Each must try to organize his life according to the scheme of a community in which man's being would find perfect expression.

Present society is pretty well calculated to demoralize a great character. But such a man will always carry his ideal with him & live the life of it. The philosopher neither does the best for himself, nor for society, until he finds a state & a part into which he fits — προσήκουσα πολιτειά.[3]

PL2[15–16]

339.34

There is no question of the artist seeking reality. It is fundamentally impossible for him ever to have a glimpse of what is — qua artist. As an artist he places himself in a state of unreality & cultivates ignorance of what is.

---

1   LSE 2/2/2. Hard cover, black and red marbling, 20 cm x 12.5 cm, blank. Recto folios numbered 1–79. Autograph, ink. Title page: 'II. / Plato. *Republic* / *Phaedo*. p. 40. / *Politicus*. p. 42. / July. 1923.'

2   Compare Bosanquet, *Companion*, p. 338.

3   Oakeshott's note 'Cf. 208.8.' Compare also Nettleship, *Lectures*, p. 338.

The artist's knowledge is mere 'conjecture' (εἰκασία). (The craftsman has a certain right opinion (ὀρθή δόξα). The artist is not in earnest, but <u>plays</u>.[4]

PL2[16]

344.20

So far as a man grasps the purpose or function of an object, <u>so far</u> he has knowledge about it. The 'user' alone has real knowledge.[5]

PL2[19]

The proper place of poetry in life — for it has a proper place & is only harmful when used for improper purposes.[6]

---

[4] Compare Nettleship, *Lectures*, pp. 347–8.
[5] Compare Bosanquet, *Companion*, p. 390.
[6] Compare Nettleship, *Lectures*, pp. 348–9.

Early Greek Philosophy (October 1923)

GK[12]

Socrates was a Conservative in that he equated the just & the legal. A real loyalty & love of law. There is no such thing as natural justice. What the law commands, that is just.

But he was also a Radical. He taught men to think & to question everything. He refused to cease his teaching in spite of prohibition. All except conscience must be under the control of the State. But even life must be given up readily if it is the will of the State to take it. Even Plato never resolved this antithesis.

GK[14]

Doctrine of Ideas. Whatever the Platonic 'ideas' really are, it is certain that they are something connected with all kinds of thought, & not merely with mere scientific thinking. Their connection with the more elementary kinds of thinking may not be the same as that with 'philosophy', but none the less it is there.

They are, in essence, a property of thought qua thought.

Whenever we think we make use of 'ideas' — for the most part unconsciously, but the philosopher examines these 'ideas' & knows that he is using them.

(And since a man of mere 'sensation' is an abstraction, whenever we 'feel' we make use of them also.)

'Ideas' are the models or archetypes according to which God fabricates all things. They are not separate things. All men have 'ideas' (or know things according to their idea), but only the instructed mind is conscious of this.

---

1   LSE 2/4/1. Soft cover, white, 23.5 cm x 18.5 cm, blank. Recto folios numbered 1–21. Autograph, ink. Title page: '[EARLY] GREEK PHILOSOPHY. / Order in development, tho' not necessarily in chronology. 1. Ionic School. / Thales, Anaximander, Anaximenes. / 2. Italic School. / Pythagoras. / 3. Eleatics. / Xenophanes, Parmenides, Zeno. / 4. Heraclitus / 5. Empedocles / 6. Atomic School. / Leucippus & Democritus. / 7. Anaxagoras. / 8. Sophists. / Protagoras, Gorgias, Prodicus. / 9. Socrates. / 10. Cyrenaics. / 11. Cynics. / 12. Megaric School. / 13. Plato. 14. Aristotle. 15. Stoics. 16. Epicureans. / [October 1923] / Oct. 1925.'
   The notebook on Early Greek Philosophy makes extensive use of J.E. Erdmann, *A History of Philosophy*, ed. W.S. Hough, 3 vols. (London: George Allen and Unwin, 1889); J. Burnet, *Early Greek Philosophy* (London: Adam and Charles Black, 1892); *Lectures on Greek Philosophy and Other Philosophical Remains of James Frederick Ferrier*, ed. Sir A. Grant and E.L. Lushington, 2 vols. (Edinburgh and London: William Blackwood and Sons, 1866); and E. Zeller, *A History of Greek Philosophy from the Earliest Period to the Time of Socrates*, tr. S.F. Alleyne, 2 vols. (London: Longmans, Green, and Co., 1881).

The doctrine of ideas is Plato's effort to turn men from the abstract sensation-alism of the Sophists to the contemplation of the concrete whole of the things of experience.

<u>Thinking</u>, of any sort, (but in varying degrees) necessitates passing from the particular (the abstract object of sensation) to the universal or concrete whole of experience. The idea cannot be pictured or represented, for that would reduce it to a particular.

GK[18]

Stoicism & Epicureanism <u>agree</u> that 'happiness' is the end of man, that man must live 'according to his nature' to achieve happiness, & that this life is 'virtuous.' They <u>differ</u> upon <u>what</u> is happiness, 'nature,' & virtue. Socrates was a life according to <u>reason</u>; Epicurus, a life according to sensation.

Spinoza (October 1923)

SP[08]

Spinoza's conception that all 'reasonable' men agree.

SP[10]

'It is part of my happiness to lend a helping hand, that many others may understand even as I do, so that their understanding and desire may entirely agree with my own.'[2]

The 'good life' is essentially social. The principle of Fraternity — bound together by an unseen chain of common desire & enlightenment.

SP[10]

'It is necessary…to form a social order such as is most conducive to the attainment of this character by the greatest number with the least difficulty and danger.'[3]

The object of the State. The State is a society formed for the purpose of enabling the greatest number to acquire this new nature, which is Wisdom.

SP[10]

'But before all things, a means must be devised for improving the understanding and purifying it, as far as may be at the outset, so that it may apprehend things without error, and in the best possible way.'[4]

Spinoza is 'methodical.' And yet it is no lifeless method. It is a true 'taking by storm' of the citadel of Truth. We can see in this, the same desire which

---

1   LSE 2/4/2. Hard cover, black and red marbling, 20 cm x 12.5 cm, blank. Recto folios numbered 1–39. Autograph, ink. Title page: 'Spinoza. / I. / *Tractatus de Intellectus Emendatione*. pp. 1–39. / Oct. 1923.'

      Oakeshott appears to have been using both the Hale Wight and Elwes translations of the *Tractatus*: see *Tractatus de intellectus emandatione et de via, qua optime in veram rerum cognitionem dirigitur. Translated From The Latin Of Benedict Spinoza By W. Hale Wight. Translation Revised By Amelia Hutchinson Stirling* (New York: Macmillan & Co., 1895), and *The Chief Works of Benedict de Spinoza, Translated from the Latin, with an Introduction by R.H.M Elwes*, 2 vols. (London: George Bell and Sons, 1891). The notebook on Spinoza also includes quotations and summaries from F. Pollock, *Spinoza His Life And Philosophy* (London: C. Kegan Paul & Co., 1880), and H.H. Joachim, *A Study of the Ethics of Spinoza* (Oxford: Clarendon Press, 1901).

2   Spinoza, *Works*, i.6.

3   Spinoza, *Works*, i.6–7.

4   Spinoza, *Works*, i.7.

consumed Plato — to leave no stone unturned if by any chance we can come to know the truth.

SP[11]

Experientia vaga.[5]

Un-examined 'experience' can be turned to <u>any</u> use.

SP[11]

'Reflection shows that all modes of perception or knowledge may be reduced to four.'[6]

Presuppositions must be made, but we must understand what they are & their import.

SP[13]

Essentiam rei, cf. the 'thing itself' in Plato,[7] not to be confused with the Kantian 'thing-in-itself.'

'To understand a thing is to know why it is what it is — to see the necessity of its being.'[8]

This is what Spinoza calls seeing it *sub specie aeternitatis*. Cf. the Platonic conception of 'eternal' & 'infinite.'[9]

SP[14]

'The method of knowledge is that knowledge reflected on itself — the thinking of our thinking, "*cognitio reflexiva*" or "*idea ideae*."'[10]

SP[16]

As soon as an 'idea' becomes an object of thought it is an '*ideatum.*' Thus to Spinoza the difference between 'objective' & 'subjective' is not fundamental, i.e., is merely psychological. An 'idea' can be the <u>object</u> of thought, though its existence is nowhere but in thought, i.e. subjective.[11]

---

5   Oakeshott's note: 'See Bacon, *Novum organum*, Aphorism 100: "For vague and arbitrary experience is (as we have observed), mere groping in the dark, and rather astonishes than instructs." Qv. Cf. F.H. Bradley, *The Presuppositions of Critical History* (Oxford: J. Parker and Co., 1874), p. 6.'

6   Spinoza, *Works*, ii.8.

7   Oakeshott's note: 'Plato, *Republic*, pp. 190, 196 etc.'

8   Joachim, *Ethics*, p. 5.

9   Oakeshott's note: 'Cf. §1 (*Republic*, pp. 362, 370).'

10   Joachim, *Ethics*, p. 5.

11   Compare Joachim, *Ethics*, pp. 6–7.

'Essence' — essential. That which makes a thing what it is. We are said to know *per essentiam* when we see that if two lines are parallel to a third they are parallel to one another. The essence of a thing is what it actually is in its whole nature & relations.

SP[18–19]

The nature of method

It is 'nothing else than reflective knowledge, or the idea of an idea.'

And the best method will be that which reflects on the truest idea — the most perfect knowledge.

The relation between ideas & ideas = relation between formal essences. Thus body & mind are parallel. Mind & matter are co-existing differentiations of an activity connected yet separate & (equally) real.

The most perfect thing — 'formal essence' — has a corresponding perfect 'idea,' or 'objective essence.'

SP[20–21]

True knowledge is knowledge of the totality of a thing's relations. We must know its 'place in Nature' before we can understand it. And as we gradually come to understand our place in Nature we come to know how we can best live to fulfill the 'duties of our station' — to keep ourselves from useless things. The mind that understands is undistracted.

SP[21–22]

If we have an idea of God — 'the origin & fountain of the whole of Nature' — then we have an idea which can help us in seeking all other knowledge. For this is the one common factor & life of all that is.

Cf. 'Seek ye first the Kingdom of Heaven, & all these things shall be added unto you.'[12]

SP[23]

The difference between knowledge of the Truth & the ability to explain it to others. The double task of the teacher (i) To possess & foster his knowledge & love of the ideal. And (ii) to seek the basis & principle of human nature & study how it may be touched, moved & at last transported to the ideal. (i) Ideal. (ii) Method.

---

12 Matthew 6:33.

SP[25]

Spinoza makes a distinction between the imagination & the understanding. But both are included in 'Reason' — which is the sum total of man's epistemological faculties.

The need for distinction emphasized. Hegel was driven to stress the need for unity. Both conceptions are found in Spinoza & Hegel.

SP[26]

The nature of the imagination. It rests upon experience. It is an act of memory, — in most cases unconscious.[13]

SP[27]

The positive attitude. It matters little what statement we take as our starting place, we can get at truth from it. For everything is in a measure true; & there are degrees of truth. All expression is in its degree adequate or inadequate. No expression is without its background of truth.

This is the problem of education. We must start at what our pupils are thinking of. Get from them its truth & advance from that. All knowledge is progress from inadequacy to greater adequacy.[14]

SP[28]

The secret of adequacy of thought is clear distinction.

SP[30]

Ultimately there is no external test of truth. An idea may be true apart from any formal existence.

This cuts both ways. We can claim truth for an idea not formally realized. But we can claim truth for no idea which, though it be formally realized, we are ignorant of. It is a 'high standard' of truth. To tell the truth unwittingly is not telling the truth — it is a lucky shot. Often we ourselves are the only possible judges of the truth of our statements — we must be imperious in our judgments.

SP[30]

Ideas possess reality. That reality is true; & by investigating it we shall arrive at some standard by which we can judge whether an idea is true or false.

SP[31]

Not the bare possession of fact, but ordered knowledge constitutes truth.

---

[13] Oakeshott's note: 'Cf. Montessori on the imagination.' Maria Montessori (1870–1952), Italian educationalist.

[14] Oakeshott's note: 'Cp. Richter, *Levana.*'

SP[32]

A knowledge of the whole will clarify our ideas of the particular.

The idea which is fundamental to Spinoza's thought is that of the uniformity of nature. The universe is 'all of a piece.'[15] We can understand the parts only in the whole, & the whole only through the parts.

SP[33]

Spinoza never for a moment supposes that doubt is a healthy state of mind. It is a symptom of disease.

SP[33]

It is possible to have as clear an idea of God as of a triangle & when we have it we cannot think of him as a deceiver. No man can doubt that the three angles of a Δ make two right angles, whatever theory he has about a deceiving God.

SP[34–35]

The imagination — which is something different from the intellect — is the seat of error. It matters little what it is so long as we are freed from it.

SP[35–36]

Words have, nor can have, no definite meaning. It depends wholly upon the hearer what he understands by them & the meaning he reads into them. We must use language accurately and reduce to a minimum the danger of misunderstanding from this quarter.

SP[36]

Language does not necessarily correspond to fact — & distinctions we can make in words are not necessarily real distinctions. We shall only save ourselves from being deluded by words if we constantly refer them to actuality.

SP[37]

It is to know God — the unity — that all our effort must be finally expended.

SP[37]

Thought must have a starting place — it can have none better than a good definition. As a particular thing coordinates the mind & leads it to the truth; so a good definition centres the mind upon the essential nature of a particular thing & keeps it from 'useless' speculation.

---

15 Oakeshott's note: 'Pollock, *Spinoza*, pp. 84, 136, 143.'

SP[37–38]

'Res creata' = 'modus' of the *Ethics* & Spinoza speaks of 'infinite modes.' But still, it = more or less a <u>finite thing</u>.

SP[38]

Spinoza requires far more of a definition than an ordinary logician would. It is, rather, a scientific explanation.

SP[39]

'Things fixed and eternal.' What are these? They are themselves particular (*singularia*). Are they the constant relations between phenomena which we call Laws of Nature? No. Spinoza would not confuse abstract relations with things. 'Eternal things' have laws of their own. Sigwart identifies the 'eternal things' of Spinoza with the 'forms' of Bacon. But Baconian 'Forms' are not <u>things</u>.

Pollock — the 'eternal things' = the 'infinite modes' of the *Ethics*. Motion, the material universe, etc.

Aristotle 1 (November 1923)

AR1[13]

I.iii.4–9[2]

The Individual & the State[3]

'The political faculty' or 'the social purpose' (πολιτική) is the greatest end a man can set himself, for if he follows it he will realize his nature most fully. The good of society & the good of the individual are the same.[4]

With the discovery of the true social purpose will come the knowledge of our individual stations within that purpose.

Cf. Hobbes, *Leviathan*, Ch. XVII: The State is 'that <u>mortal God</u> to which we owe, under the immortal God, our peace & defence.'

Social purpose is the lesser Absolute — the Absolute within our relative experience — which we must hold ever before our eyes.

AR1[23]

I.vi.5

Stewart remarks that Platonic 'ideas' hold a very similar position as our 'laws of Nature.'[5] They are <u>fixed</u> & so can be known scientifically. The absolute is a <u>law</u> & not a separate <u>thing</u>.[6]

---

1   LSE 2/3/1. Hard cover, black and red marbling, 20 cm x 12.5 cm, blank. Recto folios numbered 2–83. Autograph, ink. Title page: 'Aristotle. / I / *Nicomachean Ethics* I.1.1 to III.2.17. / November 1923.'
    The notebooks on Aristotle's *Nicomachean Ethics* make extensive use of Sir W.D. Ross, *Aristotle* (London: Methuen and Co., 1923); J.A. Stewart, *Notes on the Nichomachean Ethics of Aristotle*, 2 vols. (Oxford: Clarendon Press, 1892); Sir A. Grant, *The Ethics of Aristotle Illustrated with Essays and Notes*, 2 vols. (London: J.W. Parker and Son, 1857); and *The Nicomachean Ethics of Aristotle*, tr. F.H. Peters (London: Kegan Paul, 1881).
2   Oakeshott's numberings refer to the divisions of the *Ethics*.
3   Compare Stewart, *Notes*, i.24–5.
4   Oakeshott's note: 'Cf. M. Aurelius, *Meditations*, Bk V §xv.' Marcus Aurelius, *Meditations* (London: J.M. Dent & Sons Ltd, 1906), p. 50: 'Society therefore is the proper good of a rational creature.'
5   See Stewart, *Notes*, i.71.
6   Oakeshott's note: 'Cf. W.R. Inge, "*Confessio Fidei*", in *Outspoken Essays (Second Series)* (London: Longman's, Green and Co.), 1922, 1–59.'

AR1[26]

I.vi.15–16

Ethics 1097a is not a fair criticism of <u>Plato</u>. For he reserves the study of διαλεκτική for those only who have undergone a very rigorous preparatory training.[7] It is not for the artisan — but for those who are to rule & lead — the Guardians.[8]

What it comes to is that this knowledge of the Idea is necessary to all the finer & higher development of the spirit — which is apt to be called an unpractical life. While it can be dispensed with in the crafts & occupations of every-day life. But as life has no 'pass' standard to those who take it seriously, Plato's remains the truer theory.

AR1[27]

I.vii.3

Aristotle suggests a compromise. He will call that the chief good which, if there is no obvious <u>single</u> end to all action, is the most predominant. It is a matter of degree. The final good is the same <u>in kind</u> as any other good.[9]

AR1[29]

I.vii

We must live in the present. And our study of the past must be used for this purpose & not for the purpose of prolonging the rule of the past into the present.[10]

So too with regard to the future. We may take a quietistic view — the world is young, many changes must come, the span of individual life is too short for an estimate in terms of the universal, what we do matters but little. But we <u>must</u> act & live by the light we possess & not 'jack' the race because we are not hares or horses but only men.[11]

AR1[33–34]

I.vii.16

βιος implies form and duration of life.[12] Happiness comes to be inseparable from something which we might call a <u>career</u>. It must be active throughout.[13]

---

[7] Oakeshott's note: 'Plato, *Republic*, Bk VII.'

[8] Compare Stewart, *Notes*, i.89.

[9] Compare Grant, *Ethics*, i.447, and Stewart, *Notes*, i.92.

[10] Oakeshott's note: 'Cf. A. Schweitzer, *The Decay & Restoration of Civilization The Philosophy of Civilization Part I*, tr. C.T. Campion, 2 vols. (London: Adam & Charles Black, Ltd., 1923), p. 47.'

[11] Oakeshott's note: 'Cf. *Ethics*, Bk I ch. iii §4.'

[12] Compare Grant, *Ethics*, i.451.

[13] Oakeshott's note: 'Cf. *Ethics*, Bk I ch. v §6.'

Cf. also St Paul's continual comparison of his life to a 'race.'[14]

Happiness without a kind of 'habit of happiness' does not truly exist.[15] It is a condemnation of 'quick salvation.'[16]

AR1[35]

Mathematical exactness is not suited to Ethics — too much subtlety must not be expected — too much detail is to be avoided. A knowledge of <u>tendencies</u> — not a complete knowledge.[17]

AR1[38]

I.viii.9

Aristotle is always optimistic; he never doubts that the Good is attainable in life. He is heedless of many difficulties because so intent upon the end. Cf. Spinoza & Plato.

AR1[38]

It is fairly easy to forget scientific truth, but very difficult to lose the basis of virtuous action — 'knowledge' is less stable & so less reliable than character.[18]

AR1[38]

I.x.10

Aristotle tries to discover the true aspect of this popular difficulty, i.e. of not being able to predicate happiness except retrospectively.[19] It shows that men do consider happiness as something more abiding that the fluctuations of fortune — which supports Aristotle's own theory. Cf. Spinoza's attitude of search. In a monistic universe nothing can be entirely without relevance; it matters not from what point we start, if we examine it acutely truth can be reached.

---

14 Oakeshott's note: 'Pater, *Marius the Epicurean*, ii.220.'
15 Oakeshott's note: 'Cf. *Ethics*, Bk II ch. iv.'
16 Oakeshott's note: 'Cf. Plato, *Republic*, 362.39.'
17 Compare Grant, *Ethics*, i.452.
18 Oakeshott's note: 'Cf. *Ethics*, Bk I ch. x §14.'
19 Compare Grant, *Ethics*, i.465.

AR1[50]

I.xiii.8

The extent of this 'higher' knowledge [of the ψυχή] must be measured by practical value — the Politician must not be led to spend his whole time on questions of pure metaphysics.[20]

AR1[51]

I.xiii.18–20

Aristotle comes to a conclusion different from that reached by Plato & Spinoza, both of whom place morality in the intellectual sphere. Aristotle was wrong in taking popular opinion on a psychological point; but right when he refers moral judgments to current practice & opinion.

 The 'soul' to Aristotle is much the same as 'Reason' to Plato, Spinoza, Hegel, Green etc.

'Aristotle is founding the distinction between the moral & the intellectual which has lasted ever since.'[21]

AR1[53]

'I do not know any inborn propensity which may not be moralized into good or turned into bad.'[22]

Custom possesses the power of transmutation or sublimation — not of creation. It can mould power, but not generate it.

AR1[54]

II.i.5

But Aristotle had not grasped the truth that 'constitutions are not made but grow.'[23]

AR1[54]

II.i.7

'This is Aristotle's famous doctrine of habits.'[24]

Circumstances will unfailingly mould character, but whether it makes it stronger or weaker, better or worse depends on other factors.

---

[20] Oakeshott's note: 'Cf. *Ethics*, Bk I ch. xiii §10.' See also Grant, *Ethics*, i.474.

[21] Oakeshott's note: 'Grant, *Ethics*, i.479.'

[22] Oakeshott's note: 'F.H. Bradley, *Ethical Studies* (London: Henry S. King, 1876), p. 249.'

[23] Compare Stewart, *Notes*, i.171.

[24] Oakeshott's note: 'Grant, *Ethics*, i.485.'

AR1[56–57]

II.ii.6–7

The principle of the Mean.

'The doctrine that medical treatment ought to aim at the mean had been laid down by Hippocrates.'[25]

This illustrates the truth that there is very little absolute originality, but new discoveries are made by the application of facts of other branches of studies — or methods or principles — to your own study. A rigid system of specialization will therefore tend to deaden originality, whether it is self-imposed or imposed by university regulations.

Ideas are necessarily fluid, they act & interact, & we cannot really grasp them separately. The great mind is that which sees a truth & all its relations in one vision.

AR1[56–57]

I.vi.14 (note).

The principle of the Mean connects itself with the ideas of self-control, Freedom, Harmony, etc. Plato, Spinoza. Kant. Hegel.

It is the very spirit of Greece. And the ideal of Plato. Ideals are usually extensions of the present. They grow out of the actual soil, & carry with them some of its properties to the end. Virtue reproduces the actions out of which it is formed.[26]

AR1[56–57]

II.ii.9

Theory of Education — Aristotle really asserts a theory of 'technical' education. That is to say, practice of bravery only will make us brave. We must learn the actual thing we wish to know. This is the reverse of the theory of liberal education, which tries to educate so that a man shall be able to do that which he has not specially practised.

AR1[60]

Virtue is the highest — & so hardest — we know — & by experience it is the most difficult thing to contend against pleasure & pain — the contest therefore is worthy of Politics — the Art of Life.[27]

---

25 Oakeshott's note: 'Stewart, *Notes*, i.175.'
26 Oakeshott's note: 'Cf. *Ethics*, Bk II ch. ii §8.'
27 Oakeshott's note: 'Spinoza, *Ethics*, Bk V §42 schol. cf. Aristotle, *Politics*, Bk V ch. ii §31.'

AR1[61]

II.iv.3

'The real object of the moral judgment is not the isolated action, but the system of conduct to which it belongs.'[28]

This includes <u>motive</u>. It ought to represent a permanent outlook, & so can be counted on for repetition. We can never judge an act from the outside alone.
Knowledge and purity of purpose are the internal requisites of a good action. But knowledge without anything else is of little avail for virtue. A reaction against the Platonic idea of virtue as knowledge. Knowledge & will must be combined.

But Aristotle uses 'knowledge' in two senses here. (i) Man must <u>know</u> he is doing an act for it to have moral significance. But (ii) man may act well without <u>a theory of action</u>, if his moral habits are good. But a <u>theory</u> will vastly help to make a system of life — a character. Plato & Aristotle really hold similar opinions about the place of knowledge in moral life.[29]

A good act must be chosen for its own sake.

AR1[64–65]

II.vi.5

Aristotle unwittingly lays his theory open to a grave distortion — i.e., the recognition of only a quantitative difference between Virtue & Vice. But he does not himself make this mistake. To him, 'the mean,' though it is explained & described as something equidistant from either extreme, does not in itself depend upon these extremes — that is, is a positive value, with a real meaning apart from that derived from its mere descriptive position. <u>Quantity</u> changes into <u>quality</u>. A quantity which is 'just right' for the purpose in hand, by being so transcends all thought of mere quantity & degree. It is either right or wrong. A very little less would have been useless. The fact that the quantity is <u>exactly</u> suitable excludes ideas of degree and changes the whole thing on to a qualitative basis.[30]

AR1[66]

II.vi.10,11

'Moral excellence,' 'Virtue,' 'the mean of conduct or harmony of character' is the principle which should govern & organize our instincts & emotions, which in themselves are natural, i.e., non-moral.

---

[28] Oakeshott's note: 'Stewart i.183.'
[29] Oakeshott's note: 'See Stewart, *Notes,* i.185.'
[30] Compare Stewart, *Notes,* i.194–5.

AR1[76]

III.i.2

This is not a disquisition on Free Will. Aristotle assumes that man is an ἀρχή of his own actions. In what sense, & how, the individual is an ἀρχή is the point where Aristotle stops short in the enquiry.

The enquiry is about <u>responsibility</u>; & Aristotle shows that it is meaningless except as a resting on the immediate cause of an act, i.e. with the concrete individual whose function the act is. The individual is 'responsible' for acts which can be assigned to his <u>character</u> as immediate cause. 'Free' means 'caused immediately by a character.' It is only the individual, as affected by particular circumstances, who can put forth acts, & be responsible for them, i.e., come in for their consequences.

Antecedents are not 'responsible.' Individual character alone is. Character is the product of the universe, so is environment. The individual performs acts & must bear consequences — the Universe is irresponsible.

All living beings are 'responsible' i.e. come in for the consequences of their acts. This is what it means to be alive.[31]

AR1[77]

III.i.3

Aristotle is content with the ordinary meaning of words — at any rate to start with. It is not a metaphysical enquiry.[32]

AR1[79]

III.i.16

The particulars — (i) The active person. (ii) The thing done. (iii) The thing or person acted upon. (iv) The instrument used. (v) The purpose. (vi) The manner. Ignorance can exist about all except about (i).[33]

AR1[82]

III.ii.11

Moral choice is a matter of character; opinion changes with the changing content of the mind. Our moral character does not depend on our opinions on good & evil, but in the deliberate acts of our will.

---

[31] Compare Stewart, *Notes*, i.225–7.
[32] Compare Grant, *Ethics*, ii.6.
[33] Compare Grant, *Ethics*, ii.12.

05[05]

'An Englishman never thinks he is really impartial til he has voted against his better judgment.'

Cf. J.F. Bethune-Baker's remark[2] — it was suggested that the idea of an Earthly Paradise was peculiar to the Anglo-Saxon race; he replied, 'But don't you believe that we really are the highest point in human evolution?' He rose above the English fear of prejudice.

05[05]

Patriotism — love of family, school — love of God usward, etc.

Why do we love? Because the object <u>merits</u> it? Because it is the best of all schools? This is the popular theory; and it rests in the uncertain basis of a kindly sentiment often blind to fact. We love because the object <u>needs</u> our love. Love answers <u>need</u>, not rewards merit.

---

[1] LSE 2/1/5. Hard cover, black and red marbling, 20 cm x 12.5 cm, blank. Recto folios numbered 1–85. Autograph, ink. Title page: '<u>Notes V.</u> / <u>November</u> 1923.'

Other works from which Oakeshott made excerpts in this notebook but which are not mentioned in the text include: Fos. 15–24, M. Arnold, *Culture and Anarchy: An Essay in Social and Political Criticism* (London: Smith, Elder, and Co., 1889) ; 29–30, B. Bosanquet, *Social and International Ideals* (London: Macmillan and Co., 1917); 32–6, E.W. Hobson, *The Domain of Natural Science The Gifford Lecures Delivered in the University of Aberdeen in 1921 and 1922* (Aberdeen: University of Aberdeen, 1923); 40–2, Sir Sidney Colvin, *Keats* (London: Macmillan and Co., 1887); 44–7, Bolton King, *Life of Mazzini* (London: J.M. Dent and Sons, 1912); 48–50, A.J. Balfour, *Theism and Humanism Being the Gifford Lectures Delivered at the University of Glasgow, 1914* (London: Hodder and Stoughton, 1915); 51–3, E. Faure, *History of Art*, tr. W. Pack, 5 vols. (London: John Lane; New York: Harper and Bros., 1921–30); 54–5, J.W. von Goethe, *Torquato Tasso*, in *Dramatic Works of Goethe: Comprising Faust, Iphigenia in Taurus, Torquato Tasso, Egmont, and Goetz von Berlichingen*, tr. A. Swan, Sir Walter Scott, and H.G. Bohn (London: Henry G. Bohn, 1860); 59–61, I. Disraeli, *Sybil, or The Two Nations*, 3 vols. (London: Henry Colburn, 1845) ; 65–7, C.S. Loch (ed.), *Methods of Social Advance Short Studies in Social Practice by various Authors* (London: Macmillan and Co., 1904); 69–71, A. Clutton-Brock, *Studies in Christianity* (London: Constable and Company Limited, 1918); 73–4, W.E. Hocking, *The Meaning of God in Human Experience A Philosophic Study of Religion* (New Haven and London: Yale University Press, 1912); 75–6, G. Lowes Dickinson, *Justice and Liberty* (London: J.M. Dent and Co., 1908); 78–80, W.F. de Morgan, *Joseph Vance An Ill-written Autobiography* (London: William Heinemann, 1906).

[2] James Franklin Bethune Baker (1861–1951), modernist Anglican theologian, founder of the Cambridge D Society for the discussion of philosophical and systematic theology, and editor of the *Journal of Theological Studies*, 1903–35.

05[07–08]

'It is well nigh impossible to devise a League which does not demand from the nations concerned in it, & especially from the great nations, something which they are unwilling to give up. It demands a considerable surrender of their power, or, as we call it, their sovereign rights, for the common good.'[3]

(But rights come from moral law, & if there existed a moral law governing the nations these rights would no longer be demanded in vain.)

05[09]

'I recollect his (his father's) indignation at my using the common expression that something was true in theory but required correction in practice.'[4]

But there is something of a true meaning in this form of speech — notice how Aristotle is persistent that ethical theory can give an account of ethical practice — only 'in outline.'

05[26]

Natural self & moral self — clearly this cannot <u>exist</u> apart from the group, & yet we are told that it is just this <u>moral</u> self that demands complete independence.[5]

05[30]

The Meaning & Necessity of Becoming as little Children.[6]

05[31]

Nietzsche — the state is simply 'nature's roundabout way of making a few great individuals.'

(Yes: but it is the *raison d'être* of the State to struggle to make the million what the one attains to be.)

---

3   Fos. 6–8 contain notes on L.P. Jacks, *A Living Universe Three Lectures* (London: Hodder and Stoughton, 1923). See Jacks, *Living Universe*, p. 74.

4   Fos. 9–13 contain notes on J.S. Mill, *Autobiography* (London: Longmans, Green, Reader, & Dyer, 1873). See Mill, *Autobiography*, p. 32.

5   Fos. 25–7 contain notes on a review of M.P. Follett, *The New State Group Organization The Solution of Popular Government* (London: Longmans, Green and Co., 1923), in *Times Literary Supplement*, 3 July 1919.

6   Oakeshott's note: 'See Baron Friedrich von Hügel, "Preliminaries to Religious Belief" in *Essays & Addresses on the Philosophy of Religion* (London and Toronto: J.M Dent & Sons Limited; New York: E.P. Dutton & Co., 1921), pp. 98–116.'

05[37]

International Relations

'The promises & bargains for truck, etc., between the two men in Soldania, in or between a Swiss and an Indian, in the woods of America, are binding on them, though they are perfectly in a state of nature in reference to one another, for truth & keeping of faith belongs to man as man, and not as members of society.'[7]

But Locke forgets that without the idea of society there could not be an idea of bargaining, of faith, of truth etc.

05[37]

'No man wants happiness; only the Englishman desires that.' Nietzsche. — The result of the hedonist philosophy of early utilitarianism.

05[37]

'Had you seen these roads before they were made,
You'd throw up your hands & bless General Wade.'

On a wayside obelisk between Inverness & Inverary.

05[38]

'A is like B' = 'A has some qualities in common with B.'

So, A must also be <u>un</u>like B — i.e., have some qualities peculiar to itself.

Thus, 'A is like B' implies 'A is unlike B.'

All judgments, except those which affirm totality of identity — $A \equiv B$ — are subject to the law of thesis & antithesis.

05[38–39]

Education

'*Educere*': first meaning is the fact of birth. Then it comes to mean the rearing of the child by the mother — cf. Virgil, where it means 'bring forth'; and 'reared.'[8]

Further extension of meaning. Tacitus, *Annals* — '*Eductum in domo regnatrice*' — 'reared' again, rather than 'educated.'[9]

'*Educare*' begins where '*educere*' leaves off; & is used primarily of the nurse who rears the child. So, Varro: '*Educit obstetrix, educat nutrix.*'[10]

---

[7] Oakeshott's note: 'Cf. J. Locke, *Second Treatise on Government*, Bk II §ii.'
[8] Oakeshott's note: 'Virgil, *Aeneid*, Bk VI, 764–5, 769; Bk VII, 762–3; Bk VIII, 413; Bk IX, 584.'
[9] Oakeshott's note: 'Tacitus, *Annals*, Bk I ch. 4.'
[10] Oakeshott's note: 'Varro, *Apud nonium*, 447.'

('Educs' would go 'Eduction' not 'Educ<u>a</u>tion,' like 'Induco' — Induction (not 'Induc<u>a</u>tion') or 'deduco' — Deduction. It is *reductio ad absurdum*, <u>not</u> *reduc<u>a</u>tio*.)

Cf. Cicero, *De finibus*, uses *'educatio'* as nurture; in *De oratore*, *'sit modo is, qui dicet aut scribet, institutus liberaliter educatione doctrinaque puerile*,' it means what we call 'education.'[11] Cf. Tacitus, *Annals*, *'Sosibius Britannici educator';* *'Optimum quemque educatorem filii exilis aut morte afficit.'*[12]

05[58–59]

The Ordeal of Richard Feverel shows the reaction caused in a truly sensitive & artistic mind by the early advances of science as a panacea in the 19th century.[13]

Meredith is continually referring to the fact that Science has a limited scope & if used indiscriminately (e.g. in education) will lead us astray.

He contrasts science & nature; mans inventions & orderings & Gods.
But this is a false contrast. Science, if it is anything, is a systematic attempt at <u>discovery</u>, not manufacture. In its imperfect stages it may well lead us astray, yet its imperfections are not a necessary part of science, & true science will but reveal to us what is the will of nature.

What is to be feared & guarded against are the inaccuracies of science. A Comte will try & systematize human life, but if the laws he pretends to have discovered are not laws at all, but fictions, then the harm he will do will be just the harm of Sir Austin Feverel.[14]

Another point of interest is Meredith's insight into the fact that a science attempting to surplant nature is the outcome of a Manichee philosophy. To fear nature, to treat it as evil, to think to better it is Manichaeism.[15] But true science leads us not away from, but to nature. So in education, Montessori returns to nature. The Rousseauian pose & the idea of a return to nature by a path other than that of science is pure barbarism, but excusable in the 18th Century, when the reaction was not against science but social convention.

Cf. T.E. Brown — 'Pain' — 'timorous manichee' & Bradley, *Ethical Studies*.[16] Things are not good & evil, but there is nothing that may not be moralized into good or turned to evil.

---

11 Oakeshott's note: 'Cicero, *De finibus*, Bk III ch. 19; *De oratore*, Bk III ch. 31.'

12 Oakeshott's note: 'Tacitus, *Annals*, Bk XI ch. 1; Bk XII ch. 41.'

13 Fos. 58–9 contain notes on George Meredith, *The Ordeal of Richard Feverel: A History of Father and Son* (London: Chapman and Hall, 1859).

14 Oakeshott's note: 'Science & Nature — pp. 205–6, Ch. XXVI, & Ch. XLIII.' The character of Sir Austin Feverel appears in *The Ordeal of Richard Feverel*.

15 Oakeshott's note: 'see p. 299 (Ch. XXXIV), p. 308.'

16 See 'Pain,' ll. 20–8 by T.E. Brown (1830–97): 'Nay, the great passions are His veriest thought, / Which whoso can absorb, / Nor, querulous halting, violate their orb, / In him the mind of God is fullest wrought. / Thrice happy such an one ! Far other he Who dallies on the edge / Of the great vortex, clinging to a sedge / Of patent good, a timorous Manichee.'

05[61]

There is no such thing as a final & unexplainable anachronism.[17]

05[63]

'As wise historians are now beginning to recognize, the part of a nations life which attains notoriety, or gets itself visibly & audibly published, is a small affair compared with other parts which never come into public at all, these latter being transacted, like the best deeds & major operations of the universe, under conditions which do not invite the presence of reporters.'[18]

But, a fact which L.P. Jacks does not realize, in all the best usage 'the State' is the name given to the sum of all possible communities of this nature—i.e., conducive to the 'good life.'

05[67]

George IV the only King who has aesthetic taste & showed it by building Brighton pavilion.

05[67–68]

History. It is a feature of these days that an immense amount of scholarship is expended on the reversal of the hitherto accepted verdict of history. For instance—P.B. Bronte is made out to be the genius of his family; Tolstoy's ruling motive was vanity; Henry VIII's fault an ill judged indulgence of the whims of his wives; Judas Iscariot a far-sighted financial genius. And the rest. While M. Aurelius was a bad man, Pitt an incompetent scoundrel, Palmerstone an unprincipled grabber of power & land & Jesus the first Anglican Clergyman or a modern slum worker.

What does this mean?

1. It is a good sign. 'The first lesson of history is the good of evil.' (Creighton). We are beginning to depart from our judgments (childish) of simply good & wicked. (Cf. Mazzini. 'Individuals were to him too much wholly good or wholly bad.'[19] And the Hebrew element of our civilization.) A more refined judgment of character is called for.

2. It is a bad sign. Cf. Acton's strictures of condoning evil in history. It is a sign of merely the changing point of view of our age. We are writing history from our point of view; yesterday wrote from its point of view; & not until we

---

[17] This remark occurs on the verso facing a quotation from Theodore Golobensky from A.P. Stanley, *Lectures on the History of the Eastern Church*, p. 378, which Oakeshott employed in 'A Discussion of Some Matters Preliminary to the Study of Political Philosophy' (1925): see *SW*, v.60, n. 7.

[18] Fos. 62–4 contain notes on L.P. Jacks, *Realities & Shams* (London: Williams and Norgate, 1923). Oakeshott's note: 'p. 17.'

[19] Oakeshott's note 'Bolton King, *Mazzini*, p. 336.'

know the <u>truth</u> finally (which we never shall) shall we be able to write true history.

The evolution of this factor in the writing of history is most clearly seen in the researches of New Testament scholars.

It may, of course, be simply bad history in some case — but the motive for these attempted explanations is what is significant.

05[A][20]

<u>Divorce</u>

Moral & other laws | Is it a friendly Universe.

It is often ignorance that leads men to fight against economic laws for the sake of a supposed moral principle, but on this account let us not persuade ourselves that there is an eternal agreement between moral & economic laws. The Christian must defy economic laws. But unlike others he is not restricted. Immortality. He can <u>die</u> with a sure hope. There is <u>always</u> the opening of death. — Not suicide though — Schiller's line. — 'Life is not the highest thing.'[21]

05[B][22]

<u>Sea</u>

The experience of the Red Sea in the history of the Jews evidently influenced them greatly — it was their experience of the sea — its mightiness & the greater strength of God.

So largely did it bulk in their minds that the 'west' & the 'sea' are synonymous. The Mediterranean — after they settled in Canaan — was the 'great sea.'[23]

05[B]

Jews not seafaring. For most of their history debarred from the coast. Their view of sea entirely contemplative. No utilitarian motive could enter. They were oppressed with fear & its mystery & the 'sorrow of the sea' — so we are not surprised that in heaven there is 'no more sea.'[24]

---

[20] On a loose sheet in ink inserted at the front of Notebook 5.

[21] Probably an allusion to the concluding lines of Friedrich Schiller, *The Bride of Messina*. See *The Works of Charles Follen, With A Memoir Of His Life*, 5 vols (Boston, MA: Hilliard, Gray, and Company, 1841), vol. iv, *On Schiller's Life and Dramas*, p. 324: 'One thing, indeed, I feel and know it clearly / That life is not the highest of all goods; / But guilt, guilt is the greatest of all evils.'

[22] On a loose sheet in ink, inserted at the rear of Notebook 5 on notepaper headed 'GONVILLE & CAIUS COLLEGE, / CAMBRIDGE.'

[23] Oakeshott's note: 'Exodus 36:22; Joshua 5:1; 1 Kings 8:25 etc.'

[24] Oakeshott's note: 'Revelation 21:1.'

05[B]

The stars have lost much of their mystery. They are in human thought a symbol for the silent forces of destiny. Astrology purports to have discovered the secret of their influence on human life—but who would dare to say that he had discovered the secret of the sea?

05[C][25]

1. The English Constitution. Theory; law; practice & history
2. Philosophical Theorists. Plato to to-day.
3. Social etc: psychology. Modern writers.
4. Religion. The individuals relation to God—history & validity.
5. Religion—Institutional.
6. General History of Philosophy & political theory.
7. The Philosophy of History.
8. Outlines of Jurisprudence & legal practice.

Greek.
German.

05[D][26]

The Charm of the Past.

05[D]

Sleep & the Sea. Cf. Hopkins' poems. They express the two poles—views of life, one of retirement, the other of danger—*Odyssey*.

05[E][27]

Dante's idea that the will of God—which is our peace—is the sea to which all things which it created moves.[28]

05[E]

The sea breeds energy of soul—which Aristotle called happiness.

---

[25] On a loose sheet inserted at the front of Notebook 5 on notepaper embossed: 'VALE COTTAGE, / DOWNLEY, / HIGH WYCOMBE.'

[26] On a loose sheet in pencil inserted at the front of Notebook 5.

[27] On a loose sheet inserted at the rear of Notebook 5 on notepaper headed 'GONVILLE & CAIUS COLLEGE, / CAMBRIDGE.'

[28] Oakeshott's note: 'Dante, *Paradiso*, Canto III, l. 87.' See D. Johnston, *A Translation of Dante's Paradiso* (Bath: The Chronicle, 1868), Canto III, ll. 85–7, at p. 16: 'And in His will it is our peace resides; / It is the oceans whither all things move / By Him created or by nature made.'

05[F][29]

The first sight of the sea is a great experience in the life of a nation – but also of the individual. 'I doubt whether I shall ever receive a stronger impression than when, from the rising ground above Cromer, we caught sight of the sparkling expanse.'[30]

05[G][31]

Shipwreck

The Sea used to express the idea of total loss of personality etc: – mergence.
Death – a flask of water broken in the Sea.

The sea, it appears, will always be somewhat of a mystery, expressing inexpressible thoughts & feelings to humanity. For familiarity has not bred contempt, & we are hardly less in awe of it, we hardly less wonder at it now than did those nations long ago when its vast expanses & restless waves first met their gaze after long wanderings.
    Perplexed.

05[G]

Whenever man has attempted to express the immensity that surrounds him he has thought not, primarily of the stars, of the distant desert horizon, the heavens with their worlds on worlds, but of the sea. The sea in all human experience is the symbol of immensity.

Start with this:

Restlessness – the lady who went to stay in cottage on the shore – got on her nerves.

05[H][32]

Divorce

Life is serious. Or as Plato puts it – 'we have work to do.'[33]

---

[29] On a scrap of paper inserted at the rear of Notebook 5.
[30] Oakeshott's note: '*Harriet Martineau's Autobiography*, ed. M.W. Chapman, 3 vols. (Boston, MA: James R. Osgood and Company), i.45.'
[31] On a scrap of paper inserted at the rear of Notebook 5.
[32] On a scrap of paper inserted at the front of Notebook 5.
[33] Oakeshott's note: 'Plato, *Republic*, 406.'

Aristotle 2 (December 1923)

AR2[09]

At the bottom of the whole doctrine of the Mean lies the idea that it is man's function to maintain his own nature—to rise above or fall below is failure.

Cf. Spinoza. Man's first business 'to preserve his own being.'

AR2[09]

III.vii.1

Aristotle never treats of the 'perfect' man & never ventures on a counsel of perfection. It is 'man' whom he is studying, not a 'god or a beast.'

AR2[14]

III.ix

Courage is no mere matter of discipline, but is an energy of the individual soul— a quality of character.

AR2[15]

III.ix.4

The whole essence of the 'safety first' cry as a guide to life (it is all very well in getting off a bus!) is immoral.[2]

AR2[18]

III.x.7

For a pleasure to be beyond the realm of Temperance it must be enjoyed for its own sake—i.e. <u>aesthetically</u>.

AR2[20]

III.xi.7

Monasticism tends to deaden natural pleasure, producing that disinterestedness in life which is a parody of the true principle of equanimity—the mean.[3]

---

[1]   LSE 2/3/2. Hard cover, black and red marbling, 20 cm x 12.5 cm, blank. Recto folios numbered 1–82. Autograph, ink. Title page: 'ARISTOTLE. / II / NICOMACHEAN ETHICS. III.3 to VI.7 / December 1923.'

[2]   See Grant, *Ethics*, ii.45.

[3]   See Grant, *Ethics*, ii.51.

AR2[25]

IV.i.15

Wealth in itself is not valued by the Liberal man, for it can only be of use when used, & its greatest value is to be rightly used. Miserliness contains a fallacious conception of the nature of 'wealth.'

AR2[27]

IV.i.17

The duty of care in charitable acts. To give indiscriminately may do great harm. The Liberal man takes all precautions necessary to enable him to make the best use of his wealth.[4] Not moved by monetary sentiment.

AR2[28]

IV.i.26, 27

The liberal man, when all is said & done, has a leaning to carelessness in matters of money — he would rather sin on one side than the other. A minute precision of conduct is inhuman — the principle of the mean is but 'an outline.'

AR2[32]

IV.ii.9

This is the great principle of both Platonic & Aristotelian Ethics — a thing should be well done, and it should be the sole aim of the doer to do it well. Excellence is the *porro unum necessarium*, expense, time, trouble & the rest are not to be measured or considered at all.

The Modern World has deserted this, the whole principle of Trade Unions, Rings, Combines etc. is against it.

AR2[32]

IV.ii.18

The 'poor' man who lives beyond his means so as to appear richer than he is, is one of the perennial objects of laughter (& pity) in the world. He has forgotten his 'station.'

The other type, well known to *Punch* in our day, is the 'Profiteer' — 'Nouveau Riche.' He is the man with wealth enough to be truly magnificent, but so utterly devoid of taste or knowledge that he fails in his objects and becomes a laughing stock to many.[5]

---

4   Compare Grant, *Ethics*, ii.60.

5   Oakeshott's note: 'Cf. Aristotle, *Ethics*, Bk IV ch. iii §21; Bk IV ch. vii.'

Cf. The 'Catechism,' & compare with Bradley's 'My Station and its Duties.'[6]

AR2[34]

IV.iii

'Highmindedness is nothing else than a certain loftiness of spirit possessed by great men.'[7]

This is a picture of what Aristotle finds in great men; it is in no sense an 'ought to be.' It is one of the criteria of greatness.

In this we see the means of moral development. Moral behavior, convention, etc., cannot stipulate for certain ways of living before these have been discovered. The great man discovers new ways, higher ways & reveals them in his life & perhaps, teaching – e.g. Jesus – society gradually conforms to these, man's moral nature develops, then the moral philosopher finally makes men conscious of the advance by placing moral behavior in a system – by viewing it not, as in daily life, in parts as circumstances demand, but as a whole, and a consistent whole.

AR2[35]

IV.iii.3

The great-souled one knows himself. And is not afraid of knowing himself to be great – cf. Keats.

But great men often see defects in themselves & their work which others fail to see, simply because they know more about themselves & it than anyone else.

Cf. Dedication of Bradley's *Appearance & Reality*.[8]

AR2[37]

IV.iii.23

'Excellence' is the name which the great-souled man would give to his aim in life, and death is a little thing, not to be counted, in comparison with a fall from excellence already attained.

---

6   See F.H. Bradley, *Ethical Studies*, Essay V.

7   Oakeshott's note: 'Grant, *Ethics*, ii.72.'

8   The 'Dedication' to F.H. Bradley, *Appearance and Reality: A Metaphysical Essay* (London: Swan Sonnenschein and Co., 1902) reads: 'To my friend E.R. this unworthy volume is respectfully dedicated.'

AR2[39]

IV.v.3

The near relation of Gentleness or Mildness to Perfect Self mastery is shown. The Mild man is imperturbable. He is a <u>free man</u> 'not carried away by passion.'[9]

AR2[42]

IV.vii.4

The Truthful man is he whose judgments & acts are his own. He does not, while seeing clearly what he ought to do & be, confuse this with what he is, & no-one can persuade him that he is other than he is. It is a matter of Reality. He is a Real Individual who knows himself, & harbours no delusions. He is unaffected, what we call a 'simple-minded man.' It will be seen how this quality combines with & flows into that of 'friendliness' in the last chapter.

AR2[42]

IV.vii.8,9

It is easier to delude oneself than to do anything else in the world. The Truthful man is brave enough to refuse to be deluded — he is a <u>free man</u>, & a wise man, & a good man because of his love of Truth & freedom.

AR2[44]

IV.viii

'The εὐτράπελοσ, or ἐπιδέξιοσ, is the man whose conversation in society is easy, bright & playful, contributing to the pleasure & amusement of the company, without offending against good taste or hurting susceptibilities.'[10]

The Gentleman. This is the standard of Hellenic Life & Culture.

AR2[44–45]

IV.viii.1

It is, then, not jocularity or wit in any narrow sense of which Aristotle speaks. The Gentleman is one who can <u>play</u> well. It is easy, comparatively speaking, to keep the mean in serious moments of concentrated attention, but far more difficult to do so in the 'pauses of life' — moments when we may easily be 'taken off our guard.'

---

9   Compare Grant, *Ethics*, ii.81.
10   Stewart, *Notes*, i.365.

AR2[45]

IV.viii.5

'Tact':[11] it might almost be said that this English word, when used in its best sense, is the most adequate epitome of Aristotle's philosophy of the Mean in the conduct of life.

AR2[46]

IV.ix.3

Shame is a means of forming the moral character of a man and so is right in the young; but in the old it shows a deficiency of character & is a symptom of lack of development. It is not wrong, in itself, in the old, but a symptom of wrong.

Aristotle protests against the substitution of the subject's feeling in place of an objective moral standard.

AR2[46]

IV.ix.6

'Shame is felt at voluntary actions only.'

Shame, we constantly see, is felt at many involuntary matters. To-day a sensitive man feels shame at being unemployed, & it is often this feeling, when not too acute, which saves him from moral degeneration.

AR2[47]

V.i.3

Justice is a state of mind which implies: —   (i) Capacity of doing what is just.
(ii) Doing what is just.
(iii) Wishing what is just.

Aristotle's principle of virtue as an <u>energy</u>, ethics as a theory of <u>action</u>. But at the same time the morality of an action is judged by its motive as well as its effect.

AR2[49]

V.i.9

Aristotle bids us not pray for <u>things</u>, but for a better state of ourselves (or the selves of our friends). This but follows the psychology of desire — We always desire a state (better) of ourselves — Green, *Prolegomena to Ethics*.[12]

---

[11] Peters, *Nicomachean Ethics*, uses 'tact.'

[12] T.H. Green, *Prolegomena to Ethics*, ed. A.C. Bradley (Oxford: Clarendon Press, 1883).

AR2[50]

V.i.13

The end of the <u>State</u> — the common good of all — is expressed in its laws only when the 'determining power' in the State aims at 'real goodness.'

AR2[51]

V.i.13

'Plato and Aristotle both make the mistake of wishing for entire state-control over individual life.'[13]

This statement must be modified (i) By the whole meaning of νόμος. (ii) By the meaning of 'state.' (iii) By Plato's desire for the reform of present abuses in Athens which led him to exaggeration.[14] (iv) By Plato following the Spartan ideal of discipline too far in order to counteract the opposite tendencies of Athens.

AR2[51]

V.i.15

Justice is perfect <u>social</u> virtue. Aristotle implies that there are virtues which are not to be designated primarily 'social.' 'Ethics' (i.e. 'individual ethics') are a part of Politics. A true conception of the State will lead to a right individual life.

    Cf. Spinoza, *Tractatus theologico-politicus*, Bk IV — politics is a part of ethics. A true individual life will issue in the welfare of the whole.

AR2[52]

V.i

Aristotle tends to think that there are such things as self-regarding acts, but he does not quite commit himself — i.e., no further than saying that some acts have a predominating self-regarding aspect. It is almost a matter of degree — all acts are social, but some more than others.[15]

AR2[52]

V.i.17

Justice is a good to all for it is a state of mind which bestows good.[16]

---

13   Oakeshott's note: 'Grant, *Ethics*, ii.102.'
14   Oakeshott's note: 'Cf. M. Arnold, *Culture & Anarchy*, Ch. 2.'
15   Compare Grant, *Ethics*, ii.102.
16   Oakeshott's note: 'Cp. Plato, *Republic*, 343c.'

AR2[56–57]

V.iv–v

Ethics, for the most part, has created no vocabulary of its own, for, being a late development in human history, finds language in a more or less rigid state.

Hence (i). The main difficulties of Ethics — i.e., verbal disputes; & (ii) Perennial misunderstandings arising from the use of words which derive their meanings from other, non-ethical associations.

And again, the true expression of the whole of morality can only be in <u>action</u> — 'The Highest cannot be spoken' (Goethe) — & so 'Ethics' — Moral Theory — can at most present morality 'in outline' — a point on which Aristotle is never tired of insisting.

AR2[59]

V.v.6

Mutual need as the basis for civil society — Plato, *Republic*.[17] Dawn of political economy. But it was a false scent to place the basis of civil society on this need. The basis is deeper, is ethical.[18]

AR2[61]

V.vi.5

Justice does not depend upon law, but law is evidence that the idea of justice exists. Nor can there be justice without law — e.g., as between a father & son there is no law, & so no justice.[19]

AR2[61–62]

V.vi.8, 9

Aristotle seems to admit the existence of an individual apart & separate from all social relations. Justice exists in social relations because men are not <u>one</u> in aim & life, for were they one indivisible & complete whole there could be no justice — 'for no man chooses to hurt himself.'

Later idealist theorists seem to hold that, <u>in fact</u>, the individual is an abstraction, that society — or the State — is a single whole & that 'Each individual is not only himself but also the State,'[20] but that man has an evil, individual, selfish inclination or 'will' which must be converted into a good, social, real, general will. From the conflict of these wills — one is really only an uncoordinated inclination — arises the necessity of law, justice, punishment, etc.

---

[17] Oakeshott's note: 'Plato, *Republic*, 369b.'
[18] Compare Grant, *Ethics*, ii.117.
[19] Compare Grant, *Ethics*, ii.124.
[20] Oakeshott's note: 'Bosanquet, *Philosophical Theory of the State*, 3rd edn, p. lvii.'

AR2[62–63]

V.vii.1

Distinction between Nature & Convention.[21] Here & in Plato we see the first signs of that idea of a Law of Nature developed by the Stoics, Cicero, & Roman law.

AR2[62–63]

V.vii.2

This was a favourite Sophist argument, & one which occurred inevitably to one who had travelled at all.[22]

Locke & Paley bring forward the variety of moral customs as proof that no innate 'moral sense' exists.[23]

But the false step in the argument was to conclude from the fact that many different conventions of justice exist that, therefore, all that is contained in the idea of Justice is founded upon mere custom.

AR2[63]

V.vii.8

The Will constitutes Justice & Injustice in the Individual.[24]

AR2[67]

V.ix.15

To understand Justice is not to know a certain set of facts. It is a knowledge of principles.[25]

Laws are not just, except accidentally — i.e., when known & administered from certain motives & principles.[26]

---

[21] Oakeshott's note: 'Grant, *Ethics*, i.150. Cf. Bosanquet, *Philosophical Theory of the State*, 3rd edn, p. 33.'

[22] Oakeshott's note: 'Cf. Plato, *Minos*, 315e & d; cf. Herodotus, *Histories*, Bk III ch. 38.'

[23] Compare Grant, *Ethics*, ii.127.

[24] Compare Grant, *Ethics*, ii.129.

[25] Oakeshott's note: 'Cf. Aristotle, *Ethics*, Bk X ch. ix §20.'

[26] Oakeshott's note: 'Cf. Aristotle, *Ethics*, Bk V ch. viii §1.' Compare Stewart, *Notes*, i.523.

AR2[68]

V.ix.17

Justice is limited to a human sphere.

The idea of property cannot be connected with God who is & has all good nor with those outside the pale of society.[27] 'A God or a beast.'[28]
    Cf. Spinoza. Most modern writers concur in this. Kant etc.[29]

AR2[68–69]

V.x.2–6

Justice, like Ethics itself has its proper expression in action & not in words.[30] Words give to justice a kind of formality & rigidity which crushes from it that spontaneity & <u>life</u> which would enable it to adapt itself to circumstances. Law is a 'general statement' — a statement 'in outline' & so can never contain the whole of justice. Equity supplies this deficiency.

AR2[82]

VI.vii.3

We cannot say that <u>Politics</u> — practical wisdom — is supreme in an absolute sense unless our view of the universe is hopelessly anthropocentric. But 'all good Philosophy is Theocentric' (Inge).

---

27 Oakeshott's note: 'Cf. Aristotle, *Ethics*, Bk X ch. viii §7; Bk X ch. viii §7; Bk V ch. i §9.'
28 Oakeshott's note: 'Aristotle, *Politics*, Bk I ch. ii §14.' Compare Grant, *Ethics*, ii.138.
29 Oakeshott's note: 'Cf. Schweitzer's protest in A. Schweitzer, *Civilization and Ethics The Philosophy of Civilization Part II*, tr. J. Naish, 2 vols. (London: Adam and Charles Black, 1923), p. 239; Bosanquet, *Philosophical Theory of the State*, 3rd edn, p. 196.'
30 Oakeshott's note: 'Cf Aristotle, *Ethics*, Bk I ch. ii §3.'

AR3[01]

VI.viii.1

'πολιτική, the good sense of the citizen, & φρόνησις, the good sense of the man, are the same habit viewed from different points, as the citizen & the man are the same person viewed from different points.'[2]

This is rather an extraordinary position for a Greek to take up—so eminently was the man taken up into the citizen in the City-State.

πολιτική is here treated as a state of mind so that it may be compared with φρόνησις, whereas Aristotle had previously treated it as simply one of the divisions of the sciences.

AR3[11]

VII.ii.5

The Method of Ethics

1. State the phenomena.
2. State what men think on the subject.
3. Review the difficulties of the various opinions.

Not to overthrow any, wholly, but to wring from all a residuum of truth. Attempt to reconcile them all by drawing the necessary distinctions.[3]

AR3[13–14]

VII.iii.6

A man may have knowledge which is in abeyance because he does not apply a minor premise to his general principle.

A universal proposition has to go through a long process before it can be brought into immediate relation to a practical situation. There are no rules which can be slavishly applied.[4]

---

1   LSE 2/3/3. Hard cover, black and red marbling, 20 cm x 12.5 cm, blank. Recto folios numbered 1–77. Autograph, ink. Title page: 'Aristotle. / III / *Nicomachean Ethics*. VI.8 to End / [p. 72. Notes on Aristotle's *Ethics* / from Ferrier's *Lectures on Gk Philosophy* / (vol. 1 p. 367)] / January. 1924.'

2   Oakeshott's note: 'Stewart, *Notes*, ii.63.'

3   Oakeshott's note: 'Cf. Aristotle, *Ethics*, Bk VII ch. ii §12.'

4   Oakeshott's note: 'Cp. Bradley, *Ethical Studies*, p. 141 sqq.'

AR3[17]

VII.iv.4

It is more intemperate to pursue luxury in cold blood than under the influence of passion—it shows that the conduct is more essentially a part of the mind itself.[5]

AR3[21]

VII.vii.1

Most men are neither eminently good nor bad, but inclining to weakness & liable to the lesser excesses—imperfect self-control, & softness. This was a typically Greek view. Cf. the Hebrew view, that most men were desperately wicked; it is a more earnest view & finds a place in the Stoic teaching.[6]

AR3[22]

VII.viii.1

The greatest enemy to recovery or advance is satisfaction. There are many harmonies which are premature & so incomplete. The only true harmony of life & character is one which has developed a critical self-consciousness which is content with nothing less than perfection.

AR3[29]

VII.ii.2

Aristotle guards himself from admitting the Platonic theory that the absolute good is always the object of human desire.[7]

Friendship, he says, can exist on the basis of an apparent good—a good as conceived by an individual at any moment.

There can, however, be a kind of friendship which is not reciprocated—cf. Housman, *A Shropshire Lad*—'Soldier, I wish you well!'[8] This is fraternity, but perhaps not friendship.

AR3[30]

VII.iii.6

Aristotle here puts 'usefulness' & 'pleasure' in their right places—they are <u>results</u>, incidental to some extent, & not ends to be aimed at. Cf. R.L. Stevenson, *Weir of Hermiston*: 'Pleasure is a by-product of the singular chemistry of life, which only fools expect.'

---

5   Compare Grant, *Ethics*, ii.211.

6   Compare Grant, *Ethics*, ii.219–20.

7   Oakeshott's note: 'Cf. Aristotle, *Ethics*, Bk III ch. iv §1.' Compare Grant, *Ethics*, ii.254.

8   A.E. Housman, *A Shropshire Lad* (London: Kegan Paul and Co., 1896), no. XXII, l. 12.

The same process of distinction must be applied to 'The State' — but this many fail to do.

AR3[31]

VIII.v.1

The difference between the mere instinct of gregariousness & true fraternity — the latter is not affected by any physical separation, for it is a disposition of spirit.

AR3[33]

VIII.vii.3

The essential thing in Justice is that every man shall get his due, whatever it may be; the essential thing in Friendship is equality, or a certain degree of initial equality which will ensure that the gulf between the two men is not too great for the formation of a friendship.[9]

AR3[33]

VIII.vii.5

Cf. this with the Christian conception of God in Jesus Christ & we see how great a conception that brought into the world. God is not so far off that we cannot go unto him, or so exalted that we cannot be friends with him.

AR3[35]

VIII.ix.1

The basis of Communism — Friendship. Usually 'Communists' put the process the other way round, and instead of working for Friendship, think to introduce 'common ownership' first. Whereas if Friendship truly prevailed, common ownership & use would be a simple <u>fact</u> without more ado.

AR3[35–36]

VIII.ix.4

This is the meaning of 'the Sovereignty of the State.' When a state exists it throws its mantle over the whole of life — i.e. gives every activity an <u>end</u> which it did not have before, without necessarily changing the outward seeming of the activity in any respect. Cf. Spinoza's conception of state sovereignty.

---

9   Compare Grant, *Ethics*, ii.265.

VIII.ix.5–6

It is not doubted that some of these social clubs, etc., may have existed, historically, before the State came into actual existence. But the State, once having been inaugurated, necessarily gives the end & purpose for which these things shall exist in the future.

AR3[37]

VIII.x.4

Aristotle is not without the conception that <u>forms</u> of government & laws must be adapted to men & circumstances, though he tends to think of men as all in fundamentally similar circumstances. Montesquieu, of course, worked out the theory to its fullest extent.

AR3[39–40]

VIII.xiii.8

The General Will. Will is distinguished from actual momentary choice. Aristotle here departs from Plato, who would have held that to be honourable is finally more profitable than merely to seek & find profit. Cf. Spinoza — it is because all men's wills, in the last analysis, are directed towards the good that any hope of final agreement is held out for us.

AR3[39–40]

VIII.xiii.10

This is the meeting & parting point of Idealism & Utilitarianism.[10] Hitherto Aristotle has taken a middle position, saying that both motive & result are necessary criteria of goodness.

AR3[41]

VIII.xiv.1

Love does not reward merit. Love answers need. A true friendship exists for a mutual advantage — not by a mere adjustment of benefits, but because friends no longer live separate lives, but <u>one</u> life. Love yearns for oneness; not a mere leveling down, but a higher & yet higher oneness.

---

[10] Oakeshott's note: 'Cf. Aristotle, *Ethics*, Bk IV ch. I §12.'

AR3[42]

IX.i.3

True, moral friendship, based on character, does not require a medium of exchange, for it is not a matter of giving & receiving, for all things, all life, is common.

AR3[42–43]

IX.i.3

In his reverence & respect for philosophical teaching, Aristotle has, perhaps, in mind the twenty years he spent in the school of Plato. The highest friendship is, to Aristotle, in the nature of a philosophic communion – dialectic.[11]

AR3[43]

IX.i.8

Whatever other debts we have incurred & are obliged to repay, we have a standing debt to our parents (Plato would have put 'the state' on the same level) which we can never wholly repay. If, then, we are forced to choose whom we shall repay or ransom, we should consider this standing claim before all others.

AR3[46]

IX.iv.3

The psychology of the 'good will.' The good man is, as Plato said, the wise man, that is, not only desiring what he believes to be good – which all men do – but knowing what that good is.

AR3[46]

IX.iv.4

Willing is always directed towards states of the self, & not external objects, or rather, only to external objects in so far as they will satisfy or create the desired state of self.

AR3[48]

IX.vi.1

Fraternity – Unanimity is 'political friendship.'

---

[11]   Compare Stewart, *Notes*, ii.284.

AR3[49]

IX.vi.3

There is perfect agreement found with perfect wisdom. Spinoza, Plato, Rousseau — all hold this doctrine.

AR3[49]

IX.vii.4

The real cause of this is that 'a thing is its activities' — our self is extended in our work & above all in our self, & the loss of any is an actual loss of part of the real self. Cf. Hegelian view of property & see Bosanquet, 'Psychology of the Moral Self.'[12]

AR3[50]

IX.vii.6

Love is a power with an end to achieve (cf. the fact that the word 'Faith' in the N.T. is always followed by an accusative).

AR3[50]

IX.viii.2

One's feeling towards oneself are the only standard we know for one's feelings towards one's friend.

AR3[51]

IX.viii.8–10

The self-love of the good man leads him to all goodness & nobility, above all to self-sacrifice for his friends & country. But even this may be misunderstood, for in 'sacrificing' self — in dying — he attains a truer good — he lives more abundantly. In the self-sacrifice of the good man the highest good of all is attained. φιλαυτία is simply a passionate devotion to what is great & noble & enduring.[13]

AR3[53]

IX.ix.6–7

It is good to be alive.[14]

---

[12] Oakeshott's note: 'B. Bosanquet, *Psychology of the Moral Self* (London: Macmillan and Co. Limited, 1897), pp. 47–57, 89, etc.'

[13] Compare Grant, *Ethics*, ii.300.

[14] Oakeshott's note: 'Cf. *Politics*, Bk III ch. vi §5.'

In this the Greek view of life contrasts with some of the Indian philosophers—Hindu.

AR3[53]

IX.ix.9

Aristotle has the conception of the absolute unity of existence & thought; & in this respect anticipates Descartes' *Cogito; ergo sum*.[15]

AR3[54]

IX.x.4

The number of a man's real friends is limited by his capacity to feel the highest kind of affection (ὑπερβολή τις φιλίας) for many individuals, & the practical difficulties of close intercourse.

This question of <u>size</u> is one of the greatest importance. It is a problem in politics —most modern states are far too large to gain all the benefits of a common life. It is a problem in schools, universities, etc. Too small a number limits the common unity & experience, too large destroys it altogether.[16]

AR3[55]

IX.xii.2

There are many <u>means</u> of joining men—and the most useful is games.

AR3[59]

X.iv.4

Cf. the doctrine that art is play—it aims solely at pleasure (see Schiller etc.). Aesthetic appreciation is an act of 'sight,' & so 'immediate,' not considering comparisons etc., & for this reason is similar, psychologically, to pleasure. But psychology treats only mental states as such & can make no judgments of value or meaning.

AR3[59]

X.iv.10

Because all men grasp at pleasure, does not say that it is the <u>chief</u> good—it is, rather, something, in itself choiceworthy, which comes with an harmonious life of desire & function satisfied.

---

15   Compare Grant, *Ethics*, ii.305.
16   Compare Grant, *Ethics*, ii.306.

AR3[61]

X.v.9

This fact of everyday experience, that the good man is pained by many things which give pleasure to others, is one of the chief causes why the good life & the happy life cannot go together. Great poets & prophets suffer most. Yet, it may be said that they find pleasure in things which will give no pleasure to others. Yes, but to these higher things the common herd give no thought, they are not pained, in any sense, by them.[17]

AR3[62–63]

X.vi.5

We all find good in what we each take to be our own good. But this is no guarantee that it is good, really. The real good is the outcome of the general will – & this is most clearly exhibited in 'the good man'. Aristotle sees no benefit in the freedom which simply allows a man to follow his inclinations, or which allows a country to be ruled by a majority – goodness, conformity to the will of the 'good man,' is all that is finally worth attaining.

AR3[63–64]

X.vii.1

Happiness, in the highest sense, is found in the working of the intellectual faculty – philosophy.

(i) Because this is the most excellent part of our nature (§2).[18]

(ii) Because it most admits of continuance.

(iii) Because it affords most solid & lasting pleasure.[19]

Aristotle's statement suffers from that optimism (some call it pride)[20] which will believe in no limits to the possible attainments of the human mind.[21]

AR3[64]

X.vii.4

It may be supposed that the career of the man given up to contemplation is entirely divorced from the 'political' life. But the Savant, wise man, is rather to be considered as one who has little or nothing to learn from the world, but is not

---

17 Oakeshott's note: 'Cf. Plato, *Republic*, 409–end.'

18 Oakeshott's note: 'Cf. Aristotle, *Metaphysics*, Bk I ch. ii §14, Bk I ch. xiii §20.'

19 Compare Grant, *Ethics*, ii.334.

20 Oakeshott's note: 'Cf. Grant, *Ethics*, i.165.'

21 Oakeshott's note: 'Cf. Spinoza.'

averse from teaching men something. Has this emphasis on the retired life no cause in the contemporary history of Aristotle's time? Greece was about to enter upon its 'dark age.'[22] Contemplation has a soul-body relation. But the philosopher <u>learns</u> little from the inhabitants from the cave.

AR3[65]

X.vii.6

<u>Leisure.</u>[23]

It is a kind of leisure of mind which Aristotle aims at.[24]
   It is this leisure that we have lost in our industrial civilization.
   This doctrine of leisure is the corollary of the doctrine of the end.[25]

AR3[66]

X.vii.9

All ideals must be based upon the actual or they are false & useless (cf. §4.) We must take men as they <u>are</u> & put before them an ideal which can grow out of their truest nature. The best must develop out of the present state. Man's most real part is his best part, for it is a satisfaction for his higher & yet higher cravings & needs that he is always seeking.[26]

AR3[66]

X.viii.1–3

The life of practical morality holds a place second to the philosophic life.
   For it is bound up with man as an only partially achieved whole — with his passions and struggles.[27]
   Morality is made by the gradual struggle of man with his environment; it is evolved.

---

[22] Oakeshott's note: 'Cf. Boethius. Cf. Plato, *Republic*, 520a.' Compare Stewart, *Notes*, ii. 443.

[23] Oakeshott's note: 'See *Politics Of Aristotle Translated Into English With Introduction, Marginal Analysis Essays, Notes And Indices By B. Jowett, M.A. Master Of Balliol College Regius Professor Of Greek In The University Of Oxford Doctor In Theology Of The University Of Leyden*, 2 vols (Oxford: Clarendon Press, 1885), i.cxliv.'

[24] Oakeshott's note: 'Cf. B. Russell, *Roads to Freedom Socialism, Anarchism, and Syndicalism* (London: George Allen & Unwin Ltd., 1918), p. 188; B. Russell, *Principles of Social Reconstruction* (London: George Allen & Unwin Ltd., 1916), pp. 226, 230; *Prospects of Industrial Civilization*, p. 181.' See also Stewart, *Notes*, ii.446.

[25] Oakeshott's note: 'Aristotle, *Ethics*, Bk I ch. ii §1.'

[26] Oakeshott's note: 'See Bosanquet, *Psychology*, p. 107.'

[27] Oakeshott's note: 'Cf. Aristotle, *Ethics*, Bk X ch. vii §3.'

Philosophy 'is more than human.'[28]

AR3[67]

X.viii.7

Contemplation is clearly above the life of practical morality for it is the life we attribute to the gods.[29]

AR3[67]

X.viii.9

This complete happiness found in contemplative speculation is slightly anomalous in the case of men. Gods have no need of 'external prosperity' in order to exist, but man has, &, though it be little that he needs, yet he cannot cut himself entirely from these needs.

We may be away & off into the world of contemplation, but there are some who must rule & guide men's lives, & they need our help.

AR3[68]

X.ix.1

The end of morality is action, not mere knowledge.

AR3[69]

X.ix.4

Men are not free by <u>nature</u>, not born free, nor can they be made so by talking to them, for a man can only hear what he can understand; freedom is acquired by gradual teaching, & all teaching must be originally based on what a man can learn, not what the teacher can teach.[30]

AR3[69]

X.ix.8

The supreme task of the education of the young. Upon this everything depends – & so, it should be made a matter for legislation, or rather, the laws that govern the lives of men (especially the young) must be good laws.[31]

The reformer in Aristotle is far less evident than in Plato, but here he shows just that ardour which fell in love with Spartanism.

---

28 Compare Grant, *Ethics*, ii.338.
29 Compare Grant, *Ethics*, ii.340.
30 Compare Stewart, *Notes*, ii.459.
31 Oakeshott's note: 'Cf. Plato.'

AR3[69]

X.ix.11

Aristotle's view that knowledge is not power, as against Plato, comes out again & again when he is treating of practical questions.

AR3[70]

X.ix.12

The impersonal nature of law; its anger can only be the 'settled' anger of Bishop Butler, which has no part or lot with mere malice or caprice.

AR3[71]

X.ix.17

Aristotle holds that laws may improve, make good, because he holds that their value is educational. We should say — man's moral character can be educated.

AR3[76]

To sum up. Virtue is a habit.

There is — (i) An original power of acting rightly or wrongly — mere energy.

(ii) A *Προάιρεσισ,* a power of choice, involving freedom, deliberation, will.

(iii) The *ἐνέργεια* — i.e., the practice.

(iv) The *ἕξις,* or habit of virtue (or vice) — a disposition built on practice.

(v) The conduct resulting can alone be called virtuous, or moral.[32]

Kant made it clear that the will only can be good or bad. Aristotle says, rather, that it is the whole man, character, which can be good or bad, & not particular acts — and the two really mean the same thing.

---

32 Compare Ferrier, *Greek Philosophy,* i.398–9.

AR4[01]

I.ii

Who is the real 'statesman'? To-day, is it an M.P. (however ill-informed, traitorous, & bigoted) or a man who deeply influences the life of his country tho' not through 'politics'? Horatio Bottomley or Dean Inge?[2]

AR4[04]

1.ii.13

'Things are defined by their working & power.'[3]

A thing is a thing in virtue of some purpose; we have no other way of distinguishing one 'thing' from another except in terms of purpose, function (ἔργον) etc.

AR4[04]

1.ii.15

The idea of 'the legislator' or maker of states. It is found in Plato; & recurs in Spinoza ('the wise man') & Rousseau.

[1] LSE 2/3/4. Hard cover, black and red marbling, 20 cm x 12.5 cm, blank. Recto folios numbered 1–85. Autograph, ink. Title page: 'The Politics.—"It is an amazing book. It seems to me to show a Shakespearean understanding of human beings & their ways, together with a sublime good sense." Henry Jackson, in a letter (see Memoirs by Parry, p. 131). / Aristotle. / IV. / Politics. Bks. I, II, III, VII, VIII, IV, V, VI / VII & VIII. I & III (& II). IV. V. & VI. / February 1924.'

In addition to Jowett's translation, the notebooks on Aristotle's Politics make extensive use of Ἀριστοτέλους Τὰ Πολιτικά The Politics Of Aristotle With English Notes By Richard Congreve M.A. Late Fellow And Tutor Of Wadham College Oxford (London: John W. Parker And Son, 1855); and The Politics Of Aristotle With An Introduction, Two Prefatory Essays And Notes Critical And Explanatory By W.L. Newman, M.A., Fellow Of Balliol College, And Formerly Reader In Ancient History In The University Of Oxford, 4 vols. (Oxford: Clarendon Press, 1887). Quotations from Aristotle, Politics, are from Jowett's translation unless otherwise noted.

[2] Horatio Bottomley (1860–1933), MP for Hackney South 1918–22, lost his seat after a conviction for fraud; William Ralph Inge (1860–1954), Dean of St Paul's Cathedral, 1911–34.

[3] Oakeshott's note: 'Cf. Aristotle, Ethics, Bk II ch. v §2; Bk III ch. x §6 etc; ἀρετή. Cf. also R.L. Nettleship, Philosophical Remains of Richard Lewis Nettleship, ed. A.C. Bradley, 2 vols. (London: Macmillan and Co. Limited, 1897), on "Identity."'

AR4[06]

I.iii.3

'Looking to the needs of practical life and also seeking to attain some better theory of their relation than exists at present.'

The double aim of the *Politics*. To form a true theory, & at the same time be useful.

AR4[06]

I.iv.5

The relation of the master to the slave is different from the relation of the slave to the master.

Cf. Coleridge, who asserted that, for the Christian, the world minus God = 0, but God minus the world = God, while for Spinoza God minus the world = 0.[4]

AR4[08–09]

I.v.8

In the case of inferior men—cf. Carlyle, *Miscellaneous Essays*, 'The Nigger Question'—'Happy he who has found a master;—and now, farther I will say, having found, let him well keep him. In all human relations permanency is what I advocate, nomadism, continual change, is what I perceive to be prohibitory of any good whatsoever.'[5]

The same thought is expressed in Rousseau's idea of being forced to be free.

AR4[10]

I.vi.8

Perhaps a modern conclusion to be drawn from this is that Eugenics, tho' it may accomplish something, is not a solution to the greatest social problem; how to raise & enlighten men?

Cf. controversy between Edmund Holmes & Prof. Bateson.[6]

---

4 S.T. Coleridge, *Specimens Of The Table Talk Of The Late Samuel Taylor Coleridge*, 2 vols. (New York: Harper & Brothers, 1835), i.61–2.

5 T. Carlyle, 'The Nigger Question,' in *Critical And Miscellaneous Essays: Collected And Republished*, 7 vols. (London: Chapman & Hall, 1869), vii.79–110, at p. 96.

6 Oakeshott's note: 'Holmes, "The Real Basis Of Democracy" [not traced]. See also J.H. Oldham, *Christianity and the Race Problem* (London: Student Christian Movement, 1924), pp. 46–79.' Edmond Gore Alexander Holmes (1850–1936), educationalist, who argued that inequality was mostly the result of environmental factors, was criticized by William Bateson (1861–1926), geneticist, who held that it was innate.

AR4[11]

I.vii.1

Government differs with the difference of the governed.[7]

AR4[12–13]

I.ix.4

The point where trade becomes 'unnatural' is very difficult to determine, but Aristotle sees that it is the unforeseen consequence of the invention of a medium of exchange to which we must attribute many of the evils of society. Its evil nature is that it continually occupies men's minds with subjects not in themselves of value, & creates lives spent from false motives & for false ends.[8]

AR4[14]

I.x.1

'For political science does not make men, but takes them from nature and uses them.'

Political science deals with men as they are.[9] This is the whole basis of politics & social reform.

AR4[16]

I.xi.13

'A state is often as much in want of money and of such devices for obtaining it as a household, or even more so; hence some public men devote themselves entirely to finance.'

In our days finance is almost a fetish with politicians, more attention is paid to it than it deserves.[10]

AR4[16]

I.xii.3

Compare this idea of a father & therefore a king, & a king & therefore a father, to the Christian conception of God. The idea of God as a father differs greatly in its meaning for us when we have different conceptions of fatherhood. Aristotle here gives us a glance at the Greek conception.

---

7   Compare Congreve, *Politics*, p. 22.
8   Compare Congreve, *Politics*, p. 29.
9   Oakeshott's note: 'Cf. Plato, *Laws*, 889a.' Compare Jowett, *Politics*, i.18–19.
10   Oakeshott's note: 'Cf. Plato, *Laws*, 742d.' Compare Jowett, *Politics*, i.22.

Cf. also, this is the basis of all social reform—education. We can only understand something which is similar to us or what we already know. The social reformer must start with men as they are.

Christian conception of God in Christ. If Christ is not man he is of no use to use. If he is not God he is not true.

AR4[17]

I.xiii.7

'The freeman rules over the slave after another manner from that in which the male rules over the female, or the man over the child.'[11]

Note in this the whole theory & justification of education punishment in schools. 'Punishment' in schools differs fundamentally from punishment in the State. With Aristotle the same argument would apply to women & slaves.

AR4[19]

II.i.2

Aristotle treats the whole question of Communism in a quantitative manner—as to a large extent Plato had done before him. It is the triumph of modern political philosophy to have risen above this, & treated it qualitatively. Spinoza probably shows the first real attempt at this.

AR4[19-20]

II.ii.2

'Is it not obvious that a state may at length attain such a degree of unity as to be no longer a state.'[12]

Aristotle's point is that 'mere unity' is not a final aim. In a sense it is true, i.e., that unanimity is not necessarily truth. But Plato never uses unity = unanimity. It is the *volonté générale* & the *volonté de tous*.

The greatest unity is not the individual, for (i) the 'individual' is an abstraction, & (ii) if he did exist he could not be a 'whole.'

AR4[20]

II.ii.8

'A city only comes into being when the community is large enough to be self-sufficing.'

---

11 Jowett, *Politics*, i.24.
12 Jowett, *Politics*, i.28.

A 'whole' is surely the only truly self-sufficing thing (& a true whole must be compounded of opposites), so then the most self-sufficing thing is a unity, for a whole is a unity par excellence.[13]

AR4[21]

II.iii.6

The basis of Plato's doctrine was that he hoped that when the whole of the citizens spoke of the same person or thing as 'mine,' the State would be pervaded with a feeling of friendliness & brotherhood.[14]

AR4[22–23]

II.v.6

Aristotle has not the idea, so central in Hegel etc., that property should be common & private at the same time, <u>because</u> the general will is only fittingly expressed in the individual wills of good men. The conclusion is similar, but the reasons different.[15]

AR4[23]

II.v.8

'Property should be private, but the use of it common; the special business of the legislator is to create in men this benevolent disposition.'[16]

'The legislator': we should bear in mind the full Greek meaning. It was not a blind faith in 'law' as we know it, but rather the legislator was the moral, religious & legal teacher & possibly reformer.

AR4[23]

II.v.10

'No one, when men have all things in common, will any longer set an example of liberality, or do any liberal action.'[17]

Aristotle's point is that though the standard of moral action might be higher in Plato's state, yet it would cease to be <u>moral</u>, for morality is 'settled choice.' Plato emphasized habit almost to the exclusion of choice.

---

13 Jowett, *Politics*, i.29.
14 Compare Newman, *Politics*, ii.238.
15 Oakeshott's note: 'Cp. Plato, *Republic*, 424a.'
16 Jowett, *Politics*, i.34.
17 Jowett, *Politics*, i.34–5.

AR4[24]

II.v.19

'If, like the guardians, they are to have all things in common, in what do they differ from them?'[18]

Aristotle seems to assume that the <u>only</u> distinguishing mark between the Guardians & the rest was that of communal property, which was by no means the case. The Guardians were of a different <u>quality</u> altogether.

AR4[27–28]

II.vii.19

'We should bear in mind that a certain amount of wealth is an advantage. The best limit will probably be, not so much as will tempt a more powerful neighbour, or make it his interest to go to war with you.'[19]

If these were the only motives men ever had for war then Norman Angel's thesis would be right,—that war doesn't pay & therefore, if men can be persuaded of this truth, war will cease. Cf. the various 'economic' interpretations of history.

AR4[28]

II.vii.20

'The beginning of reform is not so much to equalize property as to train the nobler sort of natures not to desire more, and to prevent the lower from getting more; that is to say, they must be kept down, but not ill-treated.'[20]

The nature of all true reform is <u>education</u>; for which end persuasion moves the higher & better man, force, only, the lower. The great thing is to prevent the lower from influencing affairs, & at the same time to educate & train them.

AR4[30]

II.ix.24

'The law has no power to command obedience except that of habit, which can only be given by time.'[21]

Plato held that only old men should be allowed to draw attention to defects in law.[22]

---

18 Jowett, *Politics*, i.36.
19 Jowett, *Politics*, i.45.
20 Jowett, *Politics*, i 46.
21 Jowett, *Politics*, i.51.
22 Oakeshott's note: 'Plato, *Laws*, 634d, e.'

These remarks of Aristotle about laws & their nature are very acute. He sees that <u>law</u> must be a conservative force, & advance cannot originate in that quarter.

AR4[33-34]

II.xii.10

'It is surely a bad thing that the greatest offices, such as those of kings and generals, should be bought.'[23]

The error is making wealth a qualification for office. Wealth is necessary to office; but all wealthy people are not capable of holding office. If the 'governing class' (the 'gold' men of the *Republic*) were given sufficient wealth to secure leisure, then the actual rulers could be chosen from it easily.[24]

AR4[34]

II.xii.11

Aristotle has a view that the 'government' can absolutely direct opinion.[25]

But 'the chiefs of the State' may include other than the governors. But this is improbable in view of Aristotle's treatment of 'the Statesman.'[26]

This is perhaps the most important particular in which the modern world differs from the ancient city state. There, the men in the position of Socrates were few; the influential ones were all 'statesmen', politicians, public officials; here, almost, the reverse is the case.

AR4[36]

III.i.1

'What is a State? At present this is a disputed question.'[27]

It has since been disputed for 2000 years & we are not much nearer a consensus of opinion.

AR4[36-37]

III.i.2

The state is made up of citizens.[28]

---

23 Jowett, *Politics*, i.62.
24 Compare Jowett, *Politics*, ii.99.
25 Compare Congreve, *Politics*, p. 97.
26 Oakeshott's note: 'Cf. Aristotle, *Politics*, Bk I ch. I §2.'
27 Jowett, *Politics*, i.67.
28 Oakeshott's note: 'Cf. Thucydides, *History of the Peloponnesian War*, Bk VII ch. 77, & Rousseau, *Contrat Social*, Bk II ch. 7.'

Aristotle is forced to use 'citizen' in its narrow & technical sense, & the definition therefore depends on the nature of the constitution. Political practice has advanced immeasurably since that time, & the theorist is no longer bound by these restrictions. Citizenship does not depend upon government, it is a philosophic & not a legal term.

AR4[37]

III.ii.3

If we are to take origins into account we must accept the fact that there are many sources from which citizenship flows. It is more profitable, however, to take the citizen as he is & define him in terms of present states, rights & duties.

AR4[38]

III.iii.8

'When the form of the government changes and becomes different, then it may be supposed that the state is no longer the same.'[29]

Identity of a constitution forms the identity of the State.[30]

This is unsatisfactory because (i) identity consists in many things besides form of government, e.g. language, religion, history, etc. (ii) It is always changing & developing (iii) Its identity must be a matter of degree. How far, for instance, has the English constitution remained an identity? And how far does this question affect the identity of the State?

AR4[39]

III.iv.5

Aristotle's argument is that the State, having immediate power over, & immediate interest in, certain sides of man's nature, will count that perfect virtue which conforms to the standard, <u>in those activities</u> which it has set. In the main (cf. Green) it amounts to outward conformity. This is a restricted view, & we should rather hold (with Plato) that an immoral man was disloyal to the State in a way similar to the disloyalty of the political traitor.

AR4[40]

III.v.9

Citizenship is no status unchanged in history and unchangeable. It differs according to circumstances.

---

29   Jowett, *Politics*, i.71.
30   Compare Jowett, *Politics*, ii.112–13.

AR4[41]

III.vi.1

There is no real confusion here, but the extreme subtlety of the facts makes expression awkward.

πολίτευμα = the government, i.e. the administrative officers.

πολιτεία = government administering & being administered, i.e. the constitution.

πόλις = the State; which includes everything.

These meanings are, however, fluid, and constantly pass into one another.[31] Some (e.g. Congreve & Laski) have (erroneously) concluded from this that the State is the government.[32] This is neither true, nor Aristotelian.

AR4[41]

III.vi.8

'The trainer or the pilot considers the good of those committed to his care. But, when he is one of the persons taken care of, he accidentally participates in the advantage.'[33]

This is the key to all political philosophy, which is an attempt to theorize the harmony which life as we know it demands as a practical presupposition.[34]

AR4[43]

III.ix.2

'For all men cling to justice of some kind, but their conceptions are imperfect and they do not express the whole idea.'[35]

Men always consider themselves to be as good as others, & therefore claim equal political rights—e.g., they claim a vote without considering whether they are fit or not.

We might argue from practical experience that those who are wise enough to give consideration to their fitness or unfitness are usually wise enough to have a vote. From which follows that those who are unfit are those who give not con-

---

[31] Compare Jowett, *Politics*, ii.122.
[32] See Congreve, *Politics*, p. 122: 'more shortly, the state is its government.'
[33] Jowett, *Politics*, i.78–9.
[34] Oakeshott's note: 'Cf. F. Bastiat, *Harmonies économiques* (Paris: Guillaumin, 1850).'
[35] Jowett, *Politics*, i.81.

sideration to fitness & so can only be excluded by force & not by reasoned argument—for they would not understand argument.[36]

AR4[44]

III.ix.7

'There are no magistracies common to the contracting parties who will enforce their engagements; different states have each their own magistracies.'[37]

The sovereign state, & the problem of international relations. There is no international magistracy.

AR4[44]

III.ix.8

A true State is primarily a partnership in the good life. Cf. Burke, *French Revolution*. It should promote virtue. 'Still, even where the πόλις failed to do this, much was done for virtue by other agencies at work within it as we see from the address of Protagoras.[38] So that Aristotle's view that a πόλις omitting to make the promotion of virtue a matter of public concern becomes a mere "alliance" does not seem to be altogether true.'[39]

But the πόλις is the whole & there can be no such things as 'other agencies at work within it.' Newman confuses (like most political philosophy in England) πόλις & πολιτεία.

From this it would seem that we might develop a theory of degrees of statehood. It is a fallacy to suppose that a state is, any more than an individual is. All is growing or decaying. There are some men whom we can call 'individuals' only by courtesy; & so it is with States.

AR4[44]

III.ix.8

'A state is not a mere society, having a common place, established for the prevention of crime and for the sake of exchange. These are conditions without which a state cannot exist; but all of them together do not constitute a state.'[40]

There are certain minimum requirements for a state—a common area of territory etc:—just as 'living together' is a necessity of friendship.[41] But no amount of

---

[36] Oakeshott's note: 'Cf. Aristotle, *Politics*, Bk III ch. xvi §8.' Compare Jowett, *Politics*, ii.125.

[37] Jowett, *Politics*, i.83.

[38] Oakeshott's note: 'Plato, *Protagoras*, 325c sqq.'

[39] Oakeshott's note: 'Newman, iii.205.'

[40] Jowett, *Politics*, i.84.

[41] Oakeshott's note: 'Aristotle, *Ethics*,Bk IX ch. xii §1, etc.'

living together will produce, of itself, friendship, & no security on a piece of land will produce statehood. These things cannot enter into the definition.

AR4[45]

III.x.5

The rule of law.[42] Plato, of course, meant 'good' law. (Cf. Burke, speech on American taxation: 'bad laws are the worst sort of tyranny.')[43]

The only conclusion that can be drawn from this chapter is that all forms of government are equally baseless because they are not based on justice.[44]

AR4[46]

III.xi.14

Without saying *vox populi, vox dei*, it may be said of the people (i) they are free from sophism & hypercriticism (ii) they form conclusions on simple grounds (iii) their moral principles are generally sound (iv) susceptible to noble impulses & sacrifices (v) they retain human & national feeling.[45]

AR4[47]

III.xiii.11

Laws must all be 'general,' i.e., made with a view to the common good of all & not to the private good of any one section.[46]

AR4[47]

III.xiii.13

Law, to be just (that is, equal), must be made with a view to the needs of ordinary men, & must promote justice in ordinary circumstances. A god (or a beast) is outside their jurisdiction.

AR4[48]

III.xiii.25

'The only alternative is that all should joyfully obey such a ruler, according to what seems to be the order of nature, and that men like him should be kings in their state for life.'[47]

---

42 Oakeshott's note: 'Cf. Plato, *Laws*, 713e.'
43 Compare Newman, *Politics*, iii.212.
44 Compare Jowett, *Politics*, ii.127–8.
45 Compare Jowett, *Politics*, ii.131.
46 Compare Jowett, *Politics*, ii.135.
47 Jowett, *Politics*, i.95.

The tragedy of human history is that men's prejudices & pride have prevented them from recognizing a great leader & following him. Whether by law or merely by social custom, society <u>has</u> ostracized its great ones — laughed at them & not listened, rejected them & not followed. This difficulty that Aristotle presents is not one that merely affects a State with the peculiar laws of Athens, but it affects the relation between the great man & society under <u>all</u> circumstances.

It is characteristic of Aristotle that he always seizes upon those points in the make-up of the State & Society which are 'universal' or 'essential.' When treating a particular law he has his mind upon the necessity in human nature which made the law — the real problem in all political philosophy.

AR4[49]

III.xv.4

<u>Men</u> have always been more to men, than <u>laws</u> have — Augustine must find his Ambrose, the Christian Christ. Books, law, dead heroes — these avail nothing.[48]

AR4[49]

III.xv.13

Democracy accepted as inevitable, & not as good.

AR4[49–50]

III.xv.14

'Even supposing the principle to be maintained that kingly power is the best thing for states, how about the family of the king? Are his children to succeed him?'[49]

This has always been a great factor in history.[50] It is true that M. Aurelius refrained from giving the regency into the hands of his son Commodus, but most men cannot refrain from giving first thought to their friends & relations.[51] The popes of the later Middle Ages & Renaissance developed Nepotism to an unparalleled degree. But even English politics has been influenced by this e.g. Lord Salisbury's appointment of Mr. Balfour.[52] And in many cases it is not only to be excused, but recognized as a wise act.

---

[48]   Compare Jowett, ii.141.

[49]   Jowett, *Politics*, i.100.

[50]   Compare Congreve, pp. 154–5.

[51]   Oakeshott's note: 'See C. Merivale, *A History of the Romans Under The Empire*, 3rd edn, 8 vols. (London: Longman, Green, Longman, Roberts, & Green, 1865), viii.340.'

[52]   Arthur James Balfour, first Earl of Balfour (1848–1930), Prime Minister 1902–5, nephew of Robert Gascoyne-Cecil, third Marquess of Salisbury (1830–1903), Prime Minister 1885–92, 1895–1902, was given a succession of government appointments by his uncle including the office of Chief Secretary for Ireland in 1887.

AR4[50]

III.xvi.5

It is the aim of law, not to justify itself at all costs, but to bring justice about, & so a good law will, recognizing its own intrinsic limitations, atone for them by admitting the right of spirit over letter. Cf. Shakespeare, *Merchant of Venice*.

AR4[51]

III.xvii.2

Government did not come into being (as St Augustine etc. thought) because of man's wickedness, but because of the inequalities among men. If we were all equally bad or all equally good government would not be needed.

AR4[51]

III.xviii.1

The Good Man & the Good Citizen.[53]

(i) The good citizen is not the same as the good man, under ordinary circumstances, for virtue is relative to the constitution.

(ii) But in the perfect state he is the same.

(iii) Even in the perfect State, since each will have special duties, they will not all conform to a special type of perfection.

(iv) The good ruler alone can be <u>identified</u> with the good man.

(v) And yet the citizen, who knows both how to rule & how to obey is more complete.

(vi) So in the perfect state the citizens should take it in turn to rule & be ruled.

AR4[53]

VII.ii.6[54]

'For these two lives — the life of the philosopher and the life of the statesman — appear to have been preferred by those who have been most keen in the pursuit of virtue, both in our own and in other ages. Which is better is a question of no small moment.'

This is a practical question. There are many men, fitted for a 'life of contemplation,' who yet, because they feel it their duty, spend much of their strength in

---

[53]   Compare Jowett, *Politics*, ii.147.

[54]   Oakeshott's notes move directly from book III to book VII; at AR4[70] he cites the view of Ross, *Aristotle*, p. 265, that books IV–VI were 'Originally, it would appear, a separate treatise more technical in character than the rest of the work.'

the work of a 'statesman,' i.e., in practical work of helping their fellow men. In these, as Aristotle says, is a rough division of all that is best in life, of all that is worth living for; and many of the best have found their highest good in a combination of the two.

AR4[53]

VII.ii.12

Aristotle is never carried away by this thirst for power which history has always exhibited, on the contrary he wondered at it & saw how little it availed to satisfy man's true wants. If men could only be taught what the good life really is.

AR4[54]

VII.ii.18

Aristotle never imagines that the ordinary state can repudiate all thought of 'international relations,' but to make these, & conquest, its main end is wholly wrong.[55]

AR4[54–55]

VII.iii.2

Those who retire from active life & discard 'politics' are right in a certain way because there is nothing intrinsically good in commanding & governing. But they are wrong in supposing that the whole of 'political' activity is comprised in these things. There is another sort of rule, which is good & upon the exercise of which a good man might well spend his days. Those who remain in active life are wrong if they concern themselves merely with ruling but right if they are occupied with true 'statesmanship.'

It is a fact of common occurrence how often men whose lives are spent in action desire all the time to retire from the world for contemplation. The Emperor Charles V accomplished his wish in the end; Lord Strafford died in harness.

AR4[55]

VII.iii.3

Action is, after all, man's native expression of what he believes most surely & desires most ardently. 'The highest,' says Goethe, 'may not be spoken.' Drama is the only expression of our deepest thoughts & feelings, life of our truest ideals & longings.

---

[55] Compare Jowett, *Politics*, ii.258.

AR4[55]

VII.iii.5

A ruler must be in a position to better & enlighten his subjects, or he is merely 'governing' & spending his life in vain.

AR4[55]

VII.iii.7

There can be no real antagonism between the good of the individual & the good of the community.

AR4[56]

VII.iii.8

(i) Activity is not necessarily in relation to others.

(ii) It is not necessarily a means to something else; thoughts which are an end in themselves may be of an active type.

Cf. the common & erroneous idea that <u>fraternity</u> necessitates a physical pleasure & is equivalent to mere 'sociability' or 'gregariousness.'

AR4[57]

VII.iv.5

A city is great, not by its extent, but by its ability & success in fulfilling its station.[56]

AR4[57]

VII.vi.4

The city is not to make it an <u>end</u> to hold a great market.

AR4[58]

VII.viii.5

Governments are means to accomplish not their own ends, but the ends of the State. And as means have nothing in common with the end.

---

[56] Oakeshott's note: 'Cf. J. Ruskin, *Unto This Last and The Two Paths* (London: Collins Clear-Type Press, 1862).'

AR4[57]

VII.viii.8

'For a state is not a mere aggregate of persons, but a union of them sufficing for the purposes of life.'[57]

Fraternity — real unity is the key to the essence of the state.

AR4[59–60]

VII.xi.2

Would that our statesmen had half the wisdom of Aristotle about the establishment of cities. The difference lies in the fact that Aristotle is planning an ideal city, and one element in it, in his view, is that it should exist for the good life & not for commercial or military purposes. Cities in our own day grow up at the demand of economic <u>facts</u>, i.e., the establishment of industries. Population moves with employment. But it ought to be possible to regulate the establishment of industries, though just where they should be carried on is usually dictated by natural conditions.

AR4[61]

VII.xiii.6

'I use the term "conditional" to express that which is indispensable, and "absolute" to express that which is good in itself.'

'Conditional' = those minimum necessities which are good only as means & not ends. Punishment is a 'necessity' in our present state, but no-one can pretend that it has in it a power of real moral regeneration.[58]

AR4[61]

VII.xiii.9

External goods — themselves necessary, to a certain point, to the good life — are the gifts of fortune. Virtue comes from <u>knowledge</u> & <u>will</u>.

AR4[62]

VII.xiii.12

Reason can, & should, dominate man's impulses. For the manner of this domination, see, *Nicomachean Ethics* — the doctrine of 'pleasure.'

---

57   Jowett, *Politics*, i.220.
58   Jowett, *Politics*, i.230.

AR4[62]

VII.xiii.13

'We learn some things by habit and some by instruction.'[59]

Habit here = 'experience' in the sense of 'chance, everyday experience' — 'practice.' So, Aristotle's theory of education.

Habit ⎫
Instruction ⎬ Education
⎭

AR4[63]

VII.xiv.14

The training is to put first things first — to seek first the Kingdom of Heaven.

AR4[63]

VII.xiv.15

'Hellenes of the present day, and the legislators who gave them their constitutions, do not appear to have framed their government with a regard to the best end, or to have given them laws and education but in a vulgar spirit have fallen back on those which promised to be more useful and profitable.'[60]

Commercialization is Aristotle's *bête noire*. It is the curse of our own day — Industrialism.[61]

AR4[65]

VII.xvii.5

'The sports of children should be for the most part imitations of the occupation which they will hereafter pursue in earnest.'[62]

This has an element of truth in it when applied to physical education. But it is a fallacy to suppose that the best education is, in the widest sense, a technical one. Education of character must precede any instruction in particular businesses.

AR4[66]

VIII.i.1

The State, as much as an individual, has an end & a 'calling.'

---

59   Jowett, *Politics*, i.231.
60   Jowett, *Politics*, i.234.
61   Oakeshott's note: 'See R.H. Tawney, *The Sickness of an Acquisitive Society* (London: Fabian Society, 1920).'
62   Jowett, *Politics*, i.241.

AR4[66]

VIII.ii.5

'There are also some liberal arts quite proper for a freeman to acquire, but only in a certain degree.'[63]

Acquaintance, but not perfection in some arts is desirable. Cf. Bridge and other card games. Spencer's remark that perfection in billiards argues an ill-spent youth.[64]

AR4[66]

VIII.iii.13

'In education habit must go before reason, and the body before the mind.'[65]

Aristotle is very wise on the subject of <u>order</u> in education. Body must develop before the mind is too greatly taxed & burdened.

AR4[68]

VIII.v.22

The power that music may have over the minds of even the most unmusical is a matter of common experience. It may exert a power of good or of evil. I was once told by a man of great musical sensibility & of no narrow moral convictions that if a man & woman were on the brink of a moral crisis and they heard a perform-ance of Wagner's *Tristan & Isolde* they would have lost all hold over themselves before the evening was out.

AR4[68–69]

VIII.v.25

'There seems to be in us a sort of affinity to harmonies and rhythms.'[66]

Music is suitable in the education of the very youngest for its language is under-stood without being learned & its power the soul is unable to resist, for it creeps upon us and has stormed the heart before we realized its pleasure.

---

63 Jowett, *Politics*, i.245.
64 See D. Duncan, *The Life and Letters of Herbert Spencer* (London: Methuen & Co., 1908), pp. 298–9.
65 Jowett, *Politics*, i.248.
66 Jowett, *Politics*, i.253.

AR4[69]

VIII.vii.7

'A man receives pleasure from what is natural to him.'[67]

Pleasure is man's most disingenuous action. If a man really examines himself as to what he takes pleasure in he will find out more about himself than in any other way. Our actions are expressions of our beliefs & are often truer expressions than our words.

AR4[70]

IV.i

Aristotle sees that all advance must be built upon what the people can understand & not on what some prophet is able to tell them without them understanding.

   The principles of politics, like those of education, can be discovered by thought & experiment, but it is necessary to have some plan & method by which these principles are applied & adapted to varying stages of growth & development. This is the subject of Books IV, V, & VI.

AR4[73]

IV.iv.4

We must understand not that the rich are 'unfree' but that in oligarchy the fact of their 'freedom' is not taken into account, & see 'free' poor men are not admitted to office.

AR4[74]

IV.v.3

'In many states the constitution which is established by law, although not democratic, owing to the character and habits of the people, may be administered democractically.'[68]

Cp. Bryce, *American Commonwealth*: in England 'though the constitution has become democratic, the habits of the nation are still aristocratic.' (This is a change in the opposite direction to that contemplated by Aristotle.)[69]

   France has never become Republican at heart. Prussia has never become constitutional.

---

[67] Jowett, *Politics*, i.258.

[68] Jowett, *Politics*, i.118.

[69] Compare Jowett, ii.160 which refers to James Bryce, *The American Commonwealth*, 3 vols. (London: Macmillan, 1888), Ch. 76, 'The Nature of Public Opinion.'

AR4[74]

IV.vi.2

One of the uses of 'leisure' is political action.

AR4[74]

IV.vi.4

'Every one to whose birth there is no objection is eligible, and may share in the government if he can find leisure. And in such a democracy the supreme power is vested in the laws, because the state has no means of paying the citizens.'[70]

Something of this state of affairs obtained in England before the payment of M.Ps.

AR4[74]

IV.vii.2

One form of aristocracy is the perfect state. But there are others which are far from perfect.

AR4[75]

IV.viii.5

'Good laws, if they are not obeyed, do not constitute good government.'[71]

This was discovered by the Elizabethan legislators & to remedy it the whole English local government system grew up and with it police etc.

AR4[75]

IV.viii.6

'There are two parts of good government; one is the actual obedience of citizens to the laws, the other part is the goodness of the laws which they obey.'[72]

The division between the executive & the legislative for efficiency's sake. Cf. Montesquieu. There is no need to attribute to Montesquieu a deep knowledge of the English Constitution — as the inspiration he required is found in Aristotle.

---

[70] Jowett, *Politics*, i.119.
[71] Jowett, *Politics*, i.122.
[72] Jowett, *Politics*, i.122.

AR4[75]

IV.ix.3

'There are three modes in which fusions of government may be effected.'[73]

On the three modes of combination cf. Hobhouse, *The Rational Good*.[74] There is a fourth, to which both Aristotle & Hobhouse are blind, which is the key to the 'Idealist' position.

    The doctrine of the 'mean' was not meant by Aristotle to be a 'compromise' — it is something <u>new</u>, & <u>other</u> than either extreme, & the extremes find their fullest life in it. Aristotle seems to force political institutions into the frame which he made in the *Nicomachean Ethics*.

AR4[76]

IV.xi.17

'Whichever side gets the better...regards political supremacy as the prize of victory.'[75]

To assume that any class or party is, as a class or party, disinterested is absurd. They all desire power, & they all claim to desire good & democratic government.

AR4[79]

V.i.5

Revolution is the outcome of an internal dichotomy or lack of balance between the elements or parts of a State. There is a 'kind of 'justice' in the claims of each party, but they are party claims,[76] and not 'general,' & so lead to strife. Absolute justice is where all is ordered for the common good, & in this state no revolutions occur.

AR4[81]

V.vi.10

'An oligarchy which is at unity with itself is not easily destroyed from within.'[77]

Cf. the story told of Lord Melbourne when Prime Minister — he stood with his back to the door & said 'It does not much matter what we say so long as we all say the same thing' — (re: the Corn Laws).

---

[73] Jowett, *Politics*, i.124. Aristotle is discussing how to combine oligarchy and democracy.

[74] Oakeshott's note: 'L.T. Hobhouse, *The Rational Good: A Study in the Logic of Practice* (London: George Allen & Unwin Ltd, 1921), Ch. IV, notes, pp. 19–20.'

[75] Jowett, *Politics*, i.129.

[76] Oakeshott's note: 'Cf. Aristotle, *Politics*, Bk IV ch. ii §17.'

[77] Jowett, *Politics*, i.157.

AR4[82]

V.viii.5

How to control necessary change — this is the great problem of government.

AR4[83]

V.ix.2

'There may be a doubt, however, when all these qualities do not meet in the same person, how the selection is to be made.'[78]

Cf. Sᵗ Theresa's advice to choose a confessor both wise & pious, but if that is not possible, then prefer one who is wise.

---

[78] Jowett, *Politics*, i.166.

AR5[01–02]

VI.ii.2–4

'The basis of a democratic state is liberty.'[2]

Here are detailed several of the fallacies about liberty — fallacies still current in our own day.

(i) A person excluded from office is not free.
Cf. Rousseau — the English people are only free at elections. This is at the bottom of our belief in the <u>vote</u>.

Freedom identified with government by majority & permission to do what you like.[3]

(ii) <u>Numerical equality</u>.

(iii) <u>A man should do as he likes</u>. 'A desire of the individual to be let alone, to do as he pleases, indulge his impulses, follow out his projects' has been extremely strong in the U.S.A.[4] Cf. Lecky, *Democracy and Liberty*: 'in our own day no fact is more incontestable & conspicuous than the love of democracy for authoritative regulation.'[5]

Cf. also M. Arnold's strictures in *Culture & Anarchy*.

AR5[02]

VI.ii.9

Numerical equality is the great failure of democracy, but it is impossible to secure real freedom by this or any machinery.

AR5[02]

VI.iii.2

(i) Democracy is rule by <u>majority</u>.

(ii) Oligarchy is rule by <u>propertied class</u>.

---

1   LSE 2/3/4. Unlined loose sheets inserted at rear of Aristotle 4. Recto fos. numbered 1–5. Autograph, ink. Title page: 'ARISTOTLE. / V. / *Politics*. Book. VI. / April. 1924.'
2   Jowett, *Politics*, i.189.
3   Oakeshott's note: 'Sir J.R. Seeley, *Introduction to Political Science Two Series of Lectures* (London and New York: Macmillan and Co., 1896), pp. 119, 158.'
4   Oakeshott's note: 'Bryce, *American Commonwealth*, iii.269.'
5   Oakeshott's note: 'Cf. W.E.H. Lecky, *Democracy and Liberty*, 2 vols. (London: Longmans, Green, and Co., 1896), i.213, 462.'

But both are unjust for (i) will not care about the minority, & (ii) will disregard the poor.

AR5[03]

VI.iv.15

'Democracy…will not last long unless well regulated by laws and customs.'[6]

Aristotle again remarks upon the necessity for a sure-established custom & tradition where a greater independence of life is admitted. The law must be there — in the people's hearts, where it is absent from their circumstances.

AR5[03]

VI.iv.16

If every citizen is to have a share in the government we must take care not to make our citizen class too large. But democracies not only give every citizen a share in government, they make all men citizens.

AR5[03]

VI.iv.20

'Most persons would rather live in a disorderly than in a sober manner.'[7]

Aristotle's pessimistic view of 'human nature' as he saw it.[8]

AR5[04–05]

VI.vii.18

Religion is the basis of the State. & cf. the idea that men can only unite in a true unity when their end & aim for unison is the highest. We are only one with one another when we are one with the One. And Plotinus' idea of the harmony of the universe dependent upon the 'conducting' of the one. Spinoza, St Paul, and Aristotle (see *Nicomachean Ethics*) have this idea of the highest end & the only true ground of unity.

Greek 'religion' may have been very different from what we should recognize as such, & Aristotle's meaning may be repugnant to us. But he states in general terms such as have a meaning to us to-day.

Cf. 'maintenance of thy true religion' (Communion Service) meant something very different than it means today.

Cf. also Hooker & Rousseau on the place of religion in the State.

---

6   Jowett, *Politics*, i.195.
7   Jowett, *Politics*, i.196.
8   Oakeshott's note: 'Cf. Aristotle, *Ethics*, and Aristotle, *Politics*, Bk VI ch. iii §7 etc.'

Notebook 6 (September 1924)

06[02]

This novel puts before us the problem of <u>leadership</u>—education—in a simple, elemental & grand manner.[2] The Virginian is a born <u>leader</u>. Why? And we can see in the elements of his character just those qualities which give a man the mastery of men—for their own good. Not mere literary education; but a fundamental greatness of character. Here is collected, in a most admirable manner, the data which life affords for a true theory of education, leadership etc.

06[07–08]

Philosophers, as well as poets, have the elemental principle of childhood in them, are men who have never grown up, for, after all, they spend their lives enquiring where the candle flame went when it was 'blown out.' Their minds are unhardened by prejudice, they have not suffered from what Shelley calls the 'contagion of the world's slow stain,' & what St Paul calls being 'spotted' by the world.[3] It is the heart of religion that moves the mind of philosophy.

06[08]

A nation may be said to perish with its art & literature—its culture. Cf. modern Denmark & the fate of the Schleswig-Holstein provinces when bereft of Danish culture & before they acquired German—immorality, lawlessness increased 100% etc.[4]

---

[1] LSE 2/1/6. Soft cover, grey, exercise book, 20 cm x 16 cm, ruled. Recto folios numbered 1–46. Autograph, ink. Cover emblazoned 'KING EDWARD VII SCHOOL. LYTHAM,' endorsed: 'NOTES. VI. \ <u>Sept. 1924</u>.' Title page: 'Note Book. / VI. / September 1924.'

   Other works from which Oakeshott made excerpts in this notebook but which are not mentioned in the text include: Fos. 17–19, H.B. Walters, *The Art of the Greeks* (London: Methuen and Co., 1906); 26–7, J.J. Brousson, *Anatole France en pantoufles* (Paris: G. Cres, 1924); 32–3, T. Hardy, *The Return of the Native* (London: Smith, Elder, & Co., 1878); 34, T.B. Macaulay, *The History of England from the Accession of James II*, 5 vols. (London: Longman, Brown, Green, and Longmans, 1848–61); 40, H. Shipp, *The New Art. A Study of the Principles of Non-Representational Art and their Application in the Work of Lawrence Atkinson* (London: Cecil Palmer, 1922).

[2] Fos. 2–6 contain notes on Owen Wister, *The Virginian A Horseman Of The Plains* (New York: The Macmillan Company, 1902).

[3] See Percy Bysshe Shelley, 'An Elegy on the Death of John Keats,' ll. 14–15: 'From the contagion of the world's slow stain / He is secure'; James 1:27, 'Pure religion and undefiled before God and the Father is this, To visit the fatherless and widows in their affliction, and to keep himself unspotted from the world.'

[4] Fos. 8–12 contain notes on W.H. Prescott, *History of the Conquest of Mexico: With a Preliminary View of the Ancient Mexican Civilization and the Life of the Conquerer, Hernando*

06[09]

The realization of unity in Society & the universe is the last fruit of long experience.

06[09]

Cortés's methods — always divided responsibility by asking advice before action — but always had his own way. Eloquence. Explained everything first. Did nothing without calling attention to it in words.

The Greeks had a special style of rhetoric which they considered appropriate for the occasion of a general addressing troops before battle.[5]

Boldness. When in difficulty it is fruitless to ask, 'What is the wisest course?' Ask, 'What is the boldest?' & it will be the wisest.

06[10]

Clause in Cortés's will — 'It has long been a question whether one can conscientiously hold property in Indian slaves. Since this point has not yet been determined, I enjoin my son Martin & his heirs that they spare no pains to come to an exact knowledge of the truth.'[6]

Morality — its growth and development. So International Morality to-day; — to be followed by international <u>law</u>.

06[10]

Cortés's tireless activity.

'The mere excitement of exploring the strange & unknown was a sufficient compensation to the Spanish adventurer for all his toils & trials. It seems to have been ordered by Providence that such a race of man should exist contemporaneously with the discovery of the New World.'[7]

No! the discovery of the New World is evidence of the existence of such a race. Cf. Croce's view of history.

Cortés, ed. J.F. Kirk, 3 vols. (London: R. Bentley, 1843), but the edition Oakeshott was using has not been traced.

5   Oakeshott's note: 'See F.A. Wright, *Greek Athletics* (London: Jonathan Cape, 1925), p. 56.'

6   Oakeshott's note: 'Prescott, *History of the Conquest of Mexico*, VII, Ch. V, p. 622.'

7   Oakeshott's note: 'Prescott, *History of the Conquest of Mexico*, VII, Ch. III, p. 598.'

06[11]

'Nearly all fallacies & paradoxes depend upon a confusion of categories.'[8]

06[12]

Extremes are ever near to one another. Realism & Romanticism constantly merge with each other & they are the defect & excess of something truer – the 'Classic' – Idealism.

06[13]

(The artists) 'All set to work and strove to express nature as they saw her; but each saw her through the eyes of a master.[9] In a short time Philippe Dubois had knocked off in the style of Herbert Robert a deserted farm, a clump of storm-riven trees, a dried-up torrent. Evariste Gamelin found a landscape by Poussin ready made on the banks of the Yvette. Philippe Desmalins was at work before a pigeon-cote in the picaresque manner of Callot & Duplessis.'[10]

This is exactly the opposite process to that of the true artist, who sees things as they are.[11]

06[14]

The incomparable last scene between Maurice Brotteaux (with his love of man & his Lucretius), Father Longuemare (the priest who can see that the Atheist may be nearer God than he), & the girl Athenaïs.[12]

06[16]

'All this is metaphysics, you cry: That is enough: there needs nothing more to give a strong presumption of falsity.' Hume.

Science & Religion are seeing their way to reconciliation; but there is a more dangerous & subtle struggle going on between Science & Philosophy – dangerous, because largely unrecognized & unfaced.

---

[8] Oakeshott's note: 'B. Bosanquet, *Logic Or The Morphology Of Knowledge*, 2 vols. (Oxford: Clarendon Press, 1888), ii.156.'

[9] Fos. 13–14 contain notes on Anatole France, *The Gods Are Athirst*, tr. A. Allinson (London: John Lane, 1924).

[10] Oakeshott's note: 'France, *The Gods Are Athirst*, p. 114.'

[11] Oakeshott's note: 'Cf. Bergson.'

[12] Oakeshott's note: 'France, *The Gods Are Athirst*, Ch. XXIV.'

06[16]

Re: <u>Selective Breeding</u>

'To breed poets is quite possible, but it might cost us the adventure & enterprise that make a race worth writing about.'[13]

This denies the fact that, at bottom, it is the same kind of genius that makes e.g. a great explorer & a great philosopher. Cf. remark about Bradley, that had his health been better we might have lost a philosopher & gained an explorer of the first rank. Cf. poetry & soldiers — Raleigh's remark about Wordsworth. Wolfe, Nelson.

06[20]

<u>Truth & Coherence</u>

In literary judgments of value the standards are in the artists themselves — & not in the critics. Homer, Shakespeare, etc. possess the standards & the only standards by which they can be judged. It is the same as with truth — it cannot rest on any argument to uphold it, it rests solely upon itself — Coherence with the world of experience as the seeker knows it.

06[21]

<u>America</u>

In the letters of Walter Page there is constant reference to the American lack of 'foreign consciousness.' He notes their 'isolation.'[14]

Cf. President Wilson's career & his failure. It is nearly impossible for an American to be a great European statesman.

06[25]

Dancing to an audience.[15] All art commences with the individual practice, it is the immediate expression of motion with the object of making it more intense & more durable — (cf. Shelley's 'Defence'). But then, the audience comes in — & rightly. For it is no <u>exercise</u>, but an art. The artists aim, (e.g., as dancer etc.) is to produce in his audience the emotions he feels. This required faultless execution

---

[13] Oakeshott's note: 'A.E. Wiggam, *The New Decalogue of Science. Including the Corres-pondence Between the Author and George Bernard Shaw* (Indianapolis, IN: Bobbs-Merill Co., 1925).'

[14] Oakeshott's note: '*The Life and Letters of Walter H. Page*, ed. B.J. Hendrick , 2 vols. (London: Heinemann, 1922), ii.218.'

[15] Fos. 25–6 contain notes on Jehan Tabourot, aka Thoinot Arbeau, *Orchésographie. Et traicté en forme de dialogue, par lequel toutes personnes peuvent facilement apprendre et practiquer l'honneste exercice des dances* (Lengres: Lehan des Preyz, 1588).

on his part, & imagination of their part. He aims at producing similar emotion, not at merely describing. No art is merely descriptive.

06[26]

Most good dancers feel a rhythm that is more significant than the actual beats, and they follow its dictates rather than the absolute count of two, three or four.

People, generally, do not dance in time; the music plays in time, and stimulates the dancers' rhymic centres, and even though these respond in a very clumsy fashion, the music has done its work.

Jazz is a stimulant of this sort—not music in itself, but productive of rhythmic motion.

06[27]

F..M Forster has the double purpose of showing how miserably the Anglo-Indians fail to do the country any good, & also how extremely difficult it is to effect anything there however sympathetic you may be.[16]

06[28]

'We are not out here to be pleasant, we're here to do justice & keep the peace.'[17]

Then Forster goes on to show the immense difficulties which have to be faced to do even these things in India. The fundamental disregard for truth in the Indian's nature. To dispense justice fearlessly is very difficult there.

06[31]

'Religion needs science to save it from superstition.'
Principle Selbie, British Association, Sunday 30 August 1925.

On the contrary, Science has constructed an immense edifice of superstition in breaking down that which encumbered religion.[18]

06[33]

The Purpose of Life

The Germans have a theory that the world advances towards a single end & we are parts of that; this is so in a sense but it is misleading. In times of trouble we

---

[16] Fos. 27–30 contain notes on E.M. Forster, *A Passage to India* (London: Edward Arnold and Co., 1924).

[17] Oakeshott's note: 'Forster, *A Passage to India*, p. 48.'

[18] Oakeshott's note: 'See supra, p. 19.' At 06[19] Oakeshott quotes A. France, *L'Etui de Nacre* (Paris: Calmann-Lévy, 1892), p. 126: '*Une recherche d'ordre scientifique n'amènera jamais qu'un découverte du même ordre.*'

are apt to say, 'we must build for the future & remember that we cannot find in the present the end of life.' But this is not so.[19]

06[37]

How about adapting Pater's 'all art strives towards the condition of music' into 'all art strives towards the condition of dancing'?[20]

Terpsichore – the Muse of Dancing.

06[41]

'More can be said philosophically for an ornate ritual, symbolizing ideas regarded as valid now, than for a creed containing asssertions about matters of historical fact in the past.'[21]

The faith has suffered more from its defenders (apologetics – history etc.) than from those who have attacked it. Tho' it is true that the attackers have always chosen the ground of combat, & the defenders meekly followed them on to it.

06[41]

The doctrine of the Trinity is the greatest of all religio-speculative efforts to solve the most fundamental of all problems – the relation of the universal to the particular.

06[44]

The whole problem of the permissibility of divorce cannot be settled by casuistical arguments. It depends on the case – whereas a 'light' man or woman is rightly condemned, another may well perform the same acts without meriting a similar condemnation. We must judge only 'settled' character, not isolated acts.

06[46]

'It is indeed curious how ill-health, marriage, success in business, the birth of a child or change of neighbourhood will in turn drive in or divert all outward expression of religious interest.'[22]

This is questionable – the opposite contains greater truth.

---

[19] Oakeshott's note: 'But cf. R. Browning, *Rabbi Ben Ezra, and Prospice* (London: A.C. Fifield, 1906).'

[20] Fos 37–9 contain quotations from F.A. Wright, *The Arts in Greece. Three Essays* (London: Longmans, Green and Co., 1923).

[21] Oakeshott's note: 'D.G. Ritchie, *Philosophical Studies*, ed. R. Latta (London: Macmillan and Co., Limited, 1905), p. 119.'

[22] Oakeshott's note: 'A.C. Bouquet, *The Christian Religion and its Competitors To-day: Being the Hulsean Lectures for 1924–5 Delivered Before the University of Cambridge* (Cambridge: Cambridge University Press, 1925), p. 12.'

Cf. Schweitzer, *Edge of the Primeval Forest,* for a fine expression of 'what religion is.'[23]

06[46]

The beneficent part which an unprejudiced government (& government qua government must be unprejudiced & no respecter of persons) can play. How government rises above mere party & local prejudices. How it approaches the wisdom of the State.[24]

Religion — how much it is a practical affair of living, & how it grows & blossoms in a life of stress & anxiety — see Parkin, Thring's passion. His continual Θεῶ Δόξα.

06[A]

Aristotle, *Politics.* Leisure is the end of work. We must remember that the Greek while fully admiring the results of Phidias' labour, would have despised the labour itself. They never reached the notion of the creation of human personality as the end of labour — results to them were always visible, concrete results.[25]

---

[23] A. Schweitzer, *On the Edge of the Primeval Forest Experiences and Observations of a Doctor in Equatorial Africa,* tr. T. Campion (London: A. & C. Black, Ltd., 1924).

[24] Oakeshott's note: 'See G.R. Parkin, *Edward Thring Headmaster of Uppingham School: Life Diary and Letters,* 2 vols. (London: Macmillan and Co., Limited, 1898), p. 346 sq.'

[25] On the reverse of a half-sheet of typed minutes inserted at 06[22].

07[01]

Education

'When a certain quibbler asked him why he asked no questions of him, he replied, "Because I asked questions when I was a stripling; & it is not my business to ask questions now, but to teach other people what I have discovered." "How, then," the other asked him afresh, "O Appollonius, should the sage converse?" "Like a law-giver," he replied, "for it is the duty of the law-giver to deliver to the many the instructions of whose truth he has persuaded himself."'[2]

Consider the Socratic view of teaching — implying as it does a quite different view of what knowledge is & how it is reached.[3]

---

[1]   LSE 2/1/7. Hard cover, black and red marbling, 20 cm x 16 cm, blank. Recto pages numbered 1–64. Autograph, ink. Title page: 'κοινὰ τὰ τῶν φίλων. / *Republic*, 424a. / *O anima cortese!* / Notes / VII / November 1925.' ['Friends have all things in common,' tr. Jowett; 'O courteous shade!': *Dante's Inferno*, tr. H.F. Cary (New York, London and Paris: Cassell, Petter, Galpin & Co., [n.d.]), Canto II, l. 58, at p. 9.]
       Other works from which Oakeshott made excerpts in this notebook but which are not mentioned in the text include: Fo. 6, *Chance, Love and Logic Philosophical Essays By the late Charles S. Peirce*, ed. M.R. Cohen (London: Kegan Paul, Trench, Trübner & Co., Ltd; New York: Harcourt, Brace & Company, Ltd., 1923); 11, St John Ervine, *Parnell* (London: Ernest Benn, 1925); *The Letters of Paul Gauguin to Georges Daniel de Monfreid*, tr. R. Pielkovo (New York: Dodd, Mead and Company, 1922); 28–9, W. Macneile Dixon, *Tragedy* (London: Edward Arnold & Co., 1929); 30–1, C.K. Watson, 'The Life and Genius of Molière,' in *Cambridge Essays, contributed by Members of the University* (London: John W. Parker and Son, 1855), 1–56; 34, *Letters Written By The Earl of Chesterfield to his Son*, ed. E. Stanhope, 3 vols. (London: Thomas Tegg, 1827); 37–8, F.J.A. Hort, 'Coleridge,' in *Cambridge Essays, contributed by Members of the University* (London: John W. Parker and Son, 1856), 292–351; 50, *Virgil's Messianic Eclogue Its Meaning Occasion and Sources Three Studies By Joseph B. Mayor W. Warde Fowler R.S. Conway With The Text of the Eclogue, and a Verse Translation by R.S. Conway* (London: John Murray, 1907); 53–4, W.Y. Sellar, *The Roman Poets of the Augustan Age: Virgil* (Oxford: Clarendon Press, 1883); 55–9, *The Anabasis of Alexander; or, The history of the wars and conquests of Alexander the Great. Literally translated, with a commentary, from the Greek of Arrian, the Nicomedian*, tr. E.J. Chinnock (London: Hodder & Stoughton, 1884); 61–4, S. Johnson, *The Lives of the Most Eminent English Poets: With Critical Observations on Their Works* (London: Jones & Co., 1825 [1781]).
[2]   Oakeshott's note: 'Philostratus, *Life of Appollonius*, Bk I ch. xvii.' See *The Life of Apollonius of Tyana The Epistles of Apollonius and The Treatise of Eusebius*, tr. F.C. Conybeare, 2 vols. (London: William Heinemann; New York, The Macmillan Co., 1912).
[3]   Oakeshott's note: 'Cf. W. Pater, *Plato and Platonism: A Series of Lectures* (London and New York: Macmillan and Co., 1895).'

07[05]

Example of a man working for the State but against the government. Lord Fisher, by subterfuge & without the permission of Parliament, carried out a great submarine-building campaign in 1904 onwards.[4]

07[08]

'Professor Wobbermin of Breslau has tried to do it [express a necessary difference] by making a distinction between *Geschichte* & *Historie*...Professor Wobbermin uses *Geschichte* for the real Course of Events, the things, deeds, words, thoughts, that have made things what they are, while he defines *Historie* as that which we can reconstruct of the past times from our documents or other sources of information. *Historie* may therefore be false or imperfect: the Christian religion does not depend upon *Historie*, but it depends upon *Geschichte*... whether we happen to know it or be ignorant of it.'[5]

But just which our recorded events (*Historie*) are real *Geschichte*, & how are we to tell?

07[09]

'He was confident that, on the square, "on the square, mind!" there was nothing he couldn't meet. Ever since he had been "so high" — "quite a little chap" he had been preparing himself for all the difficulties that can beset one on land and water. He confessed proudly to this kind of foresight. He had been elaborating dangers & defences, expecting the worst, rehearsing his best.'[6]

(And Lord Jim was betrayed in the end! We must prepare not <u>for events</u>, but for a whole view of life. Education is not the presentation of a number of receipts for meeting different situations, it is the making of a prepared state of mind.)

07[10]

'Each blade of grass has its spot on earth whence it draws its life, its strength; & so is man rooted to the land from which he draws his faith together with his life.'[7]

(And that, written by a man who in youth left his native country to sail the sea & finally to settle among foreigners & contribute to their literature. It is either a God or a Beast who can leave his native land permanently without impairing his self.)

---

4   John Fisher, first Baron Fisher (1841–1920), First Sea Lord 1904–11, 1914.
5   Oakeshott's note: 'F.C. Burkitt, *Comments & Criticism*, 2.1 (May 1914), p. 28.'
6   Oakeshott's note: 'Joseph Conrad, *Lord Jim: A Tale* (Edinburgh: Blackwood, 1900), Ch. VIII.'
7   Oakeshott's note: 'Conrad, *Lord Jim*, Ch. XXI.'

07[13]

The necessary distinction between art as art & art as a teacher, between Homer qua poet-Homer, & Homer qua popular teacher of religion & mythology, is not sufficiently made in Plato. He condemns Homer on the second count, but says very little about him on the first.[8]

07[14]

Imaginative power in the realm of action means an aliveness to the social $\mathring{\eta}\theta o\varsigma$ as a whole & a power of placing particular events or persons within a whole of social tradition. More than this becomes casuistry, less than this is lack of sensibility & judgment. Cf. Dr Johnson's power of judgment.

07[15]

Hegel's philosophy of history is great history, but often poor philosophy. Hegel had that purely historical-literary interest in his work as well as the philosophical, & sometimes it gets the upper hand.

Cf. his literary criticisms in his *Aesthetic*.

07[17]

Ireland contains two cultures — cf. Canada in the Durham Report. And the position of Quebec with that of Ulster.[9]

Cf. the place of literature in politics. Yeats, Russell, Stephens etc.

Rough generalizations —

(i) All the great political leaders of Ireland have been Anglo-Irish (Protestants). Exception — Michael Davitt.[10]

(ii) All the great poets from Moore onwards, all greater writers, artists & playwrights have been Anglo-Irish (Protestants).[11]

(iii) All the great singers, actors, & movers in the renaissance of the Irish language have been of pure Irish stock (Roman Catholic) Gaelic League. Except: Douglas Hyde.[12]

---

[8] Fos. 13–16 contain quotation from W.P. Ker, 'On the Philosophy of Art,' in *Collected Essays*, ed. C. Whibley, 2 vols. (London: Macmillan & Co., 1925), vol. 2.

[9] Oakeshott's note: 'Stephen Gwynn, 'Ireland.''' Stephen Lucius Gwynn (1864–1950), Irish writer and politician, was author of a number of works on Ireland.

[10] Michael Davitt (1846–1906), Irish Catholic republican politician.

[11] Possibly George Augustus Moore (1852–1933), Irish novelist and poet who converted from Catholicism to Protestantism.

[12] Douglas Hyde (1860–1949), Irish Catholic Gaelic scholar and first President of Ireland, 1938–45.

'Citizenship' has always been a conscious force in the academic life of Ireland. Note the place which the Universities have taken in politics & public life. (Cf. Germany 1805 & 1919 & Egypt, 1923-4) Cf. also Greek Independence. Italian Independence.

07[19]

'To live as a <u>moral</u> being, the individual must look at himself & treat himself from the point of view of the family, of the state, or of humanity, giving to his own desires & interests just the weight which they deserve when regarded from such higher centre, & <u>not</u> the exclusive weight which they claim when they are allowed to speak for themselves.'[13]

And this <u>moral</u> life is not fully theorized till we see that by so doing we are obeying & fulfilling a self compared with which the 'individual self' is but a poor shadow of reality.

07[22]

(1) '"Natural objects always did, & now do, weaken, deaden, & obliterate imagination for me."[14]

"I assert for myself that I do not behold the outward creation & that to me it is hindrance & not action."

This doctrine, let it be said in all sincerity, may be good & true for the seer; it is certainly bad & false for the artist. It leaves Blake without a reason for drawing a man with two legs. His own pictorial art suffered from his belief that "nature is the work of the devil."'

(2) 'He taught his age to look <u>at</u> a picture, not <u>through</u> it, & the lesson was a needed one. But in his zeal to reprove the public for their preoccupation with incident & morality he was apt to deny to his pictures qualities which, after all, they have.'[15]

There is a subtle contradiction in these two statements. The 'thing' which Whistler looked at & painted was the same as what Blake saw — it was not the physical object *per se* — because no-one has ever seen <u>that</u>. To the artist the physical object has no meaning; the meaning is arrived at not by symbolism (which is the death of art), but by experience.

---

[13] Oakeshott's note: 'E. Caird, *Hegel* (London and Edinburgh: William Blackwood and Sons, 1883), pp. 151-2.'

[14] Oakeshott's note: 'Sir W. Raleigh on Blake.' Fos. 21-5 contain notes on Sir Walter Raleigh, *Some Authors A Collection of Literary Essays 1896–1916* (Oxford: Clarendon Press, 1923).

[15] Oakeshott's note: 'Raleigh on Whistler.'

07[24]

'Boccaccio describes so many kinds of lives that each of them is seen in relation to all humanity; & this is the truest criticism; it gives the right perspective.'[16]

(It is true logic too: the individual is not seen truly except as related to the whole — when he is seen as the whole.)

07[24–25]

'Don Quixote is a high-minded idealist, who sees all things by the light of his own lofty preconceptions...He shapes his behaviour in accordance with these ideas, and is laughed at for his pains.'[17]

To see things as they are, i.e., theoretically, is of no practical value. Life demands that we see things coming into being & help that growth & effort; philosophy sees things as existing.

cf. Don Quixote & leadership, Government, Social Reform.

07[25]

In the *Prometheus Unbound* the supreme suffering of Prometheus is brought about when he is led to doubt lest his age-long suffering is in vain. — The Christian Religion does not set out to explain the whole universe, but it does place this human suffering in relation to a larger whole — a whole of God, man & the world, & show it to be not in vain, but part of the system in which God shares.

07[26]

A certain university in America boasted a magnificent building led up to by an immense flight of steps, from the top of which, at the entrance to the building, a fine view was to be seen. For some purpose, it came about that the building was destroyed, but the flight of steps was left standing. And it occurred to some that this was no inappropriate figure by which to represent philosophy — an immense stair-way leading nowhere. The figure being put to the professor of philosophy he answered, 'Yes, but do not forget the view you may get from the top.'

07[30]

Controversy

The birds of which Fuller speaks who can only take wing against the wind.

---

16   Oakeshott's note: 'Raleigh.'
17   Oakeshott's note: 'Raleigh.'

07[33]

'School' Subjects & Education

'No study (pursued on intellectual grounds alone) is fit to be a general one, or a part of a scheme of education for all, in the manner in which most school education is carried on, unless it admits of being <u>mindless</u> without being positively nonsensical or hurtful; & most of the studies which are intellectually the highest will not admit of this.'[18]

The real point is that, even though some 'subjects' are common to both university & school education (for instance), they are treated from quite a different aspect at school, & for a different purpose. No subject is ever taught in a school for its own sake. So what appears as a single subject is, from the necessary diversity of treatment, two.[19]

07[33]

'Persons who would read Carlyle's *History of the French Revolution* unmoved, would not be proof against such books as *Uncle Tom's Cabin*, or the *Heir of Redclyffe*.'[20]

(This is hardly strange. The novel, as a work of art, is far more intense than ordinary life & its effect is naturally greater. This is just what it means to be a work of <u>art</u>.)

07[33]

Sentimentality denotes, not a capability of any sort of feeling, but the habitual indulgence of one particular class of feelings.

07[39]

'The *Compleat Angler* & the *Natural History of Selbourne* are types of a style of literature peculiar to this country (England).'[21]

---

[18] Oakeshott's note: 'J. Grote, "Old Studies and New," in *Cambridge Essays contributed by Members of the University* (London: John W. Parker and Son, 1856), p. 105.' Thomas Carlyle, *The French Revolution A History*, 3 vols. (London: James Fraser, 1837); Harriet Beecher Stowe, *Uncle Tom's Cabin: A Tale of Slave Life* (London: Clarke, Beeton & Co., 1853); Charlotte Mary Yonge, *The Heir of Redclyffe* (London: John W. Parker and son, 1853).

[19] Oakeshott's note: 'Cf. Burke on education in *French Revolution, Works*, i.418d.'

[20] Fos. 32–3 contain notes on Fitzjames Stephen, 'The Relation of Novels to Life,' in *Cambridge Essays* (1855), pp. 148–92.

[21] Oakeshott's note: 'A German Historian.' The quotation has not been traced. Izaak Walton, *The Compleat Angler or, The Contemplative Man's Recreation: Being a Discourse of Fish and Fishing, Not Unworthy the Perusal of Most Anglers* (London: Richard Marriot, 1653); Gilbert White, *The Natural History and Antiquities of Selborne, in the County of Southampton: With Engravings and an Appendix* (London: White and Son, 1789).

The English Mind

Cp. *Englishmen, Frenchmen & Spaniards.*[22]

Berkeley.
Cf. Nettleship.
John Grote.
Bradley, *Ethical Studies.*
F.C. Burkitt.
G.M. Trevelyan.
Pater.
Hort. Etc., etc.

07[39]

Lord Fisher was a great dancer till well over 70.

07[40]

Literature — poetry — is the result of life intensely experienced.[23]

07[41]

Societies are not overthrown because their foundations are tampered with, but because someone cries upon the house-tops & rocks the chimney-stacks. Foundations are out of sight, & in general out of mind. But question the superficialities of the social order, cry out against some trivial irregularity, but one which has the importance of something before our eyes, and men will destroy that social order, if not intentionally, at least inadvertently in their contentions.

07[41]

Morality

'A proper education would make it possible to live in accordance with instinct, but it would be a trained & cultivated instinct, not the crude, unformed impulse which is all that nature provides.'[24]

B. Russell means that a 'proper' education would give us not moral laws to be obeyed, but a 'law of the heart,' an 'instinct,' which would serve as a principle for action in life, a living principle ready to meet a diversity of circumstance. The

---

[22] Salvador de Madariaga, *Englishmen, Frenchmen, Spaniards: An Essay on Comparative Psychology* (Oxford: Oxford University Press, 1928).

[23] Fos. 39–40 contain quotations from a discussion of Samuel Johson in the *Times Literary Supplement*, 2 September 1926.

[24] Oakeshott's note: 'B. Russell, *On Education: Especially in Early Childhood* (London: George Allen & Unwin, 1926), p. 108.'

'casuistry' of the moral life is a kind of unconscious process which goes on on the 'instinctive' i.e., immediate, level – akin to a slow, invisible chemical change.

07[42]

The Self

In our earliest days & weeks of life our body is not (or parts of it are not) recognized as belonging to us more essentially than many other objects of perception. It is a definite stage of consciousness (or of conscious sensibility) when we recognize our toes as our own, & connect them with self – at least implicitly. This might suggest to us, that it is only a matter of sensibility that we do not more habitually give other 'objects of perception' a more personal quality & feel them to be parts of self. And indeed, it is a common experience with artists & poets & men of fine sensibility that all that they have 'met' is as truly a part of self as that which is physically joined to them – & that that which is physically a 'part' of them, is only a part of self through some intense experience of it.[25]

07[43]

'Why do sober scholars refuse to believe in the existence of a Baconian "cipher" in the works of Shakespeare? Not because the thing is an impossibility…but because of an unproved & unprovable conviction of the inherent craziness of the whole thing.'[26]

And this, in spite of the vague probability suggested by the fact that the ingenious Baconian can, by applying his 'key', extract some sort of coherent meaning.

We must distinguish between a rejection of the theory on the grounds of (i), the absurd arguments by which it is supported. And (ii), the improbability of finding any sound arguments to support it.

07[44]

'Since Christianity is a "positive" religion, which came into the world at a particular time & has & claims specific religious beliefs – it follows that Christianity is not anything which could be discovered or invented for himself by any person, however intellectually or spiritually gifted, in independence of historical tradition…It is a term which to the historian possesses a definite content, discoverable from history. And because Christianity is thus an historical and positive religion, it is impossible, in the first instance, for the individual to know anything about it at first hand. He must be content to derive his knowledge from

---

[25] Oakeshotts' note: 'Cf. A.E. Housman. Wordsworth etc.'

[26] Oakeshott's note: 'See A.E. Taylor, "The Vindication of Religion," in E.G. Selwyn (ed.), *Essays Catholic & Critical. By Members of the Anglican Communion* (London: S.P.C.K., 1926), pp. 35-6.'

authority, whether the authority in question be primarily that of a living teacher, or of past tradition.'[27]

The connection between Christianity & truth?

    The value of history?

    The necessity of interpretation.

    If this is true then Christianity, be what it will, is not a religion. No religion is founded, or can be founded ultimately upon 'history,' it is a contradiction in terms.

07[44]

'Wise men do not need to be reminded that the deliberate voluntary refusal of real good things is necessary, as a protection against the overvaluation of the secular, in any life they count worth living..."Good" is always recounced for the sake of some "better good." But the "better good" plainly cannot be any of the good things of this secular existence. For there is none of them whatever which it may not be a duty to renounce for some man at some time.'[28]

And this is true not merely of the 'good things' of the average man, but of the good things to which men of nobler mould are ready to sacrifice these other & obviously lesser 'goods.' There is nothing which we may not be called upon to give up.

    What then is the meaning of 'good'?

    What is the standard by which a 'better' good is judged?

    The only solution is that all 'goods' are good as far as they go, & that those which go furthest include everything of value in those beneath, so the sacrificing of the 'lesser' good to the greater is giving up nothing for something.

07[45]

'The church is not primarily a society for spiritual or intellectual research, but a society of which it belongs to the very essence to put forward the emphatic claim to be the bearer of a revelation, to have been put in trust with the Gospel as God's revealed message to mankind.'[29]

What is a revelation? What are the laws by which things are 'revealed' to men? etc.[30]

---

[27] Oakeshott's note: 'See A.E.J. Rawlinson, "Authority as a Ground of Belief," in *Essays Catholic and Critical*, pp. 85–6.'

[28] Oakeshott's note: 'Taylor, "Vindication of Religion," p. 60.'

[29] Oakeshott's note: 'Rawlinson, "Authority as a Ground of Belief," p. 87.'

[30] Oakeshott's note: 'J.W. Oman, *Grace and Personality* (Cambridge: Cambridge University Press, 1917).'

07[45–46]

'Aristotle was primarily a man not only of remarkable but universal intelligence; & universal intelligence means that he could apply his intelligence to anything. The ordinary intelligence is good for certain classes of objects; a brilliant man of science, if he is interested in poetry at all, may conceive grotesque judgments: like one poet because he reminds him of himself, or another because he expresses emotions which he admires; he may use art, in fact, as the outlet for the egotism which is suppressed in his own specialty. But Aristotle had none of these impure desires to satisfy; in whatever sphere of interest, he looked solely & steadfastly at the object.'[31]

Insistence on random tastes & desire.

The classical education, perhaps, may be said to foster this kind of intelligence more than any other. (Cf. Lord Fisher's saying that a 1st Class Greats Man was the best for the head of any government office.)

07[47]

Japan absorbed the civilization & culture of China 1000 years ago in the same way as it has recently absorbed that of the West.[32]

07[52–53]

Bossuet is said to have known the works of Virgil by heart. Renan knew the Psalms in Hebrew by heart.[33]

The pre-eminence of Virgil was unchallenged, from one point of view, throughout the Middle Ages, from another, his influence, as literature & as a poet, grew steadily till the second half of the 18th century. In France he continued to exercise great influence, but in Germany the 'romantic' spirit of its literature rejected him, & likewise in England. The only poet of that great age of English literature who was deeply influenced by him was Wordsworth. The rest, as with Goethe, turned to Greece. And together with the general disparagement of 'Augustan' poetry, the great original was condemned as one who had achieved merely technical perfection.

---

[31] Oakeshott's note: 'T.S. Eliot, *The Sacred Wood. Essays on Poetry and Criticism* (London: Methuen & Co., 1920), pp. 9–10.'

[32] Fos. 47–9 contain quotations from L. Binyon, *Painting in the Far East. An Introduction to the History of Pictorial Art in Asia, Especially China and Japan* (London: Edward Arnold, 1913).

[33] Fos. 50–4 contain notes on Virgil.

07[A]

Projected Labours[34]

The Logic of Political Philosophy.
A work on Political Philosophy — including Ethics. (Cf. Rousseau)
An edition of Spinoza, for the purposes of making clear his political philosophy.
A work on Aesthetic.
Essays on the English Prayer Book.
A work on the nature of Religion & the philosophy of the Christian Religion.
A volume on Coleridge.
Essays on Various Subjects.

Millet, Dancing, Thought in Art, Sleep, the Sea, Hegel, Spinoza, Plato, AE, Housman's poems, History, Pascal, Queen Christina of Sweden, Life and Letters of Lord Strafford.
Essays on the nature & meaning of Social Reform & Education.
A work on Historiography treated as a branch of epistemology.
An edition of the Psalms for schools, treated as religious poetry & compared with English religious poetry.
A life of Nelson.
A work on El Greco.
A work on Balzac.
The Portrait of a ~~Philosopher~~. Young Man.
The Lives of the Poets.

---

[34] In ink on both sides of a loose sheet inserted at the end of NB 7, letterhead: 'WADH / COLL / OXON.'

08[01]

Theology

Aristotle took this as the proper name of his primary philosophy, the philosophy of Being, which we perversely but inevitably call metaphysics, because of the accidental arrangement of his works by the Alexandrian editors.

08[01]

Truth & Pragmatism

Truth can be said to 'work' only within the discourse of the true. That is, a philosophy may be said to 'work' when it is consistent with itself. But by no theory of knowledge, or logic, can we suppose that truth will 'work' within a foreign discourse, e.g. the world as viewed by common sense.

One of the reasons why philosophy & 'the practical' are two different things, is that philosophy consists of certain reasons or grounds given for reaching certain conclusions, & 'the practical' takes account alone of the conclusions — which appear similar, & for its purposes <u>are</u> similar, even when they are reached for differing reasons.

08[03]

Law. <u>Knowledge v. ignorant action</u>.

'Blessed art thou, if thou knowest what thou doest; but if not, thou art accursed & a breaker of the law.'[2]

Jesus to the disciple plucking corn on the Sabbath.

---

[1]   LSE 2/1/8. Hard cover, black and red marbling, 20 cm x 16 cm, blank. Recto pages numbered 1–69. Autograph, ink. Title page: 'ἐφ' ὅσον ἐνδέχεται ἀθανατίζειν / So far as is possible live as an immortal. / Aristotle. *Nic. Eth.* / Notes. VIII / ἀγεωμέτρητος μηδεὶς εἰσίτω. / Let no-one who is not a geometrician enter these walls. / (wrongly attributed to Plato, but / put up at the Academy of Athens). / cf *Rep.* 502, 527. / ὁ Βιος ἐν τη κινήσει ἐστι . / [illegible] / 'To hunt the wind.' Cervantes. / Nov' 26.'

    Other works from which Oakeshott made excerpts in this notebook but which are not mentioned in the text include: Fos. 2–3, J. Galsworthy, *The Forsyte Saga* (London: William Heinemann, 1922); 10–11, F. Nietzsche, *Also sprach Zarathustra: Ein Buch für alle und keinen* (Leipzig: Insel-Verlag, 1908); 14, G. Keller, *Romeo und Julia auf dem Dorfe*, ed. W.A. Adams (Boston: D.C. Heath & Co., 1900); 19–20, I. Zangwill, *Dreamers of the Ghetto* (London: W. Heinemann, 1898); 51, C. O'Riordan, *Adam and Caroline Being the Sequel to Adam of Dublin* (London: W. Collins Sons & Co., 1921).

[2]   Luke 6:4, Codex.

08[03]

<u>General Will</u>

'Motto for Calvinists: – "Twenty wise men may easily add up into one fool."'[3]

(This, however, does not deny the reality of the 'general will' – it but demonstrates the *volonté de tous*.)

08[05]

<u>Statesmen & Leadership</u>

'When one of the children of light proves wiser in his generation than the children of this world, the powers of darkness may begin to tremble. Many of the great makers & emancipators have been supreme over the worldlings in worldly wiles – Cromwell, for instance, Cavour, & even Lincoln. As a rule the impatient idealists only win their victory when they get a man of this type to lead them, & a large part of his work consists in preventing them from ruining their cause by forcing his hands.'[4]

It is true that Lincoln, Cavour & Peel would have been nowhere without Lloyd Garrison, Mazzini & Garibaldi, & Cobden. We are often wrong when we blame statesmen for lack of enthusiasm, or cynicism, or scepticism – they ought to be sceptical & even cynical – a man without a measure of these qualities is without the basis of really sound judgment – blind enthusiasm never accomplished anything single-handed. A sceptical people is a sad spectacle, a sceptical statesman is a necessity.

08[06]

<u>Religion & the Kingdom of Heaven</u>

Religion may be divided into two classes.

(i) Mystical – treating the world as a veil between us & God – itself an evil.

(ii) Apocalyptic – this world has in itself the seeds of a change whereby God shall be revealed in it.[5]

Christianity is (ii). The world is to be changed. But this change is not to be identified with mere moral progress – the getting rid of one evil after another – but with looking at things from a new point of view & finding a new world <u>all at once</u>. John Oman.

---

3   Oakeshott's note: 'J.A. Spender, *The Comments of Bagshot* (London: Archibald Constable & Co., 1907), p. 24.'

4   Oakeshott's note: 'Spender, *Comments of Bagshot*, p. 230.'

5   Oakeshott's note: 'Cf. Plato, and Paul, Romans I.'

It is the rule that the originating mind is the spiritual & the later minds materialize—(cf. Plato's 'ideas')—Apply this to Christianity & what becomes of Schweitzer? Christ becomes less than St John?

08[07]

It is curious how some even of the best trained minds submit to the circumscription of genres. When I argue with my friends & am led to make some assertion, they are accustomed to cry out 'Instance! Instance!' (cf. *As You Like It*) for they say that my principal vice is hasty generalization. Sometimes I have turned to them & enquired what in their opinion would be the exact value of an instance supposing I were to produce one—for they are willing to be believe almost anything for which authority of this kind can be put forward. But this is treated as a mere subterfuge on my part (so small is their regard for my honesty), as a mere irrelevance. I have, they say, a diffuse & vague mind, & my thinking is undisciplined by a strict regard for facts. Some even hint at a certain lack of probity of thought. And yet, what <u>is</u> the value of an instance, what is the real nature of generalization? Does the mind always work in this fashion, or is it possible that what we take for a generalization is often an argument of a wholly different nature & value?

08[08]

The awful spectacle of the contempt of small minds for those a little smaller!

08[08]

The first condition for the improvement of the marriage relation is the economic freedom of women. ('Every woman who submits to-day to economic dependence on an individual is propping up parasitism & encouraging prostitution.'[6]

The second condition is a 'noviciate for marriage.'

08[09–10]

On the Teaching of Children

'It is well to remember that a "trailing cloud of glory," suddenly born into this world of flesh & blood, cannot grasp earthly conditions or secrets for some time. These conditions & secrets must be presented in terms of a possible different dimension or as near to it as human imagination can attain.'[7]

---

[6] Oakeshott's note: 'Edith Ellis, *The New Horizon in Love and Life* (London: Adam and Charles Black, 1921), p. 7.'

[7] Oakeshott's note: 'Ellis, *New Horizon*, p. 76.'

The illustrations afforded by botany, flowers, birds & beasts. There is no natural fact, told simply, that will shock a child – but it must be told as <u>it</u> can understand it. Our usual method is the one we follow with foreigners – to shout.[8]

Cf. Blake, 'Nothing can be told so as to be understood & not believed.'[9]

'Speaking the truth with love.'

Has Montessori studied the <u>mental attitude</u> of children towards sex? Psychologists tell us enough, nowadays, about the unconscious attitude; the teacher needs to know the <u>conscious</u> attitude. This is more difficult; vague, momentary, directed by conditions of body – but none the less important. We cannot answer questions aright till we understand this conscious attitude.

08[11]

The legend of the 'mad Englishman' still exists in Germany. They say *'Englischer Spleen,'* meaning thereby 'English impulsiveness & contradictoriness.' To them it is the predominating characteristic. Lord Byron is still the type.

They think of him, strangely enough, as an 'artistic' character, an 'original' character, full of whims and whimsicalities.[10]

08[11–12]

The Schwab or Würtemburger is the German 'Scotchman,' close fisted, *'all da,'* great colonizer, philosophic temperament & slightly inclined to pessimism. Schiller.

08[15]

'"Bow to the board," said Bumble. Oliver brushed away two or three tears that were lingering in his eyes, & seeing no board but the table, fortunately bowed to that.'

'He had been wondering, with his eyes fixed on the magistrate's powder, whether all boards were born with that white stuff on their heads, & were boards from thenceforth on that account.'[11]

(Argumentum – This element is present
    So far as I know it is common to this type of thing
     ∴ It is an account of this element that this thing is what it is.

---

[8] Oakeshott's note: 'Cf. E.T. Campagnac, *Society And Solitude* (Cambridge: Cambridge University Press, 1922).'

[9] See W. Blake, 'Proverbs of Hell,' in *The Marriage of Heaven and Hell.*

[10] Oakeshott's note: 'Cf. Hegel, *Philosophie der Geschichte,* p. 438.'

[11] Oakeshott's note: 'Charles Dickens, *Oliver Twist; or the Parish Boy's Progress* (London: Richard Bentley, 1838), Ch. 2.'

1. Psychological or Methodological Fallacy — That of looking for the 'essential' necessarily among the visible elements of the physical presentation.
2. Logical Fallacy — That the common or general is the essential.)[12]

08[16]

Was du ererbt von deinen Vätern hast,
Erwirb es, um es zu besitzen.[13]

And what shall we do to the Christianity we have inherited?

08[18]

'"In a little community like ours, my dear," said Fagin, "we have a general number one — that is, you can't consider yourself as number one without considering me too as the same, & all the other young people."'[14]

(The only real 'number one' is the Whole — because it is the only real thing in existence. It is according as we love & serve this that we follow that is best for our little 'number ones,' which appear as such, but really are not. That is the only difference between Fagin's political philosophy & a true political philosophy.)

(Because I am you, & you are I.)

08[22]

Make a comparison between *Faust* & *Hamlet* — *Faust*, I think, turns out an almost academic production, with its problems & their solution taken from an academic world, when set besides Shakespeare's play's character. Most Germans make the mistake of reading *Hamlet*, more or less unconsciously, in the light of *Faust*.[15]

Place *Faust* in relation to the spirit of the '*Aufklärung*.'
　　Cf. the 'Renaissance' & the '*Aufklärung*.' The latter was founded on 'books' — & so soon brought its own end upon itself; Goethe, in many respects, rose above it.
　　Cf. Also the '*Sentimentalität*' of the *Aufklärung* & its 'Romanticism,' with the spirit of the Renaissance.
　　Faust is the nemesis of the *Aufklärung*, cf. 'antiquarianism.'

---

[12] Oakeshott's note: 'Cf. William De Morgan, *Joseph Vance*.'
[13] Oakeshott's note: 'Goethe, *Faust*, Pt 1, ll. 682–3.'
[14] Oakeshott's note: 'Dickens, *Oliver Twist*, Ch. 43.'
[15] Fos. 22–9 contain notes in German on Theodor Meyer, *Der Ideengehalt von Goethe's Faust* [not traced].

08[31]

<u>Logic</u>

'He talks with angels.'
'How do you know that?'
'He admits it himself.'
'But suppose he lies!'
'What, a man who talks with angels be capable of a lie!'

08[31]

'Whatever is, is right!'[16]

(<u>Not</u> Hegel, you'll note!)

'Alles was ist, is vernünftig.'
'Die wirkliche Welt ist, wie sie sein soll.'[17]

08[31]

<u>The Comfort of God</u>

It is only in our weaker moments that we desire to live 'among the leaves' – & God does not encourage this weakness.[18]

08[32]

'The Victorians see the rolling ages pass as no other creators have seen them. Thackeray keeps his mayflies fluttering, half mournfully, but they die & are reborn from generation to generation; Carlyle sees the fiery lava-flow, with Jehova speaking in thunder above it; Dickens sees life's river growing deeper & kindlier; to George Eliot the law grows clearer as the ages pass, & Tennyson fixes his eyes on the forward march to the "divine event." These are of their age & time.'[19]

This they inherited in part from the 18th century. The idea of <u>Progress</u> (see Bury), of <u>Evolution</u>, became a new Philosophy by which to judge & systemize human life & the universe. But it was <u>new</u>, & it is not necessarily complete.

---

[16] Oakeshott's note: 'A. Pope, *An Essay on Man, being the first book of Ethic Epistles. To Henry S. John, L. Bolingbroke* (London: Lawton Gilliver, 1734), I. 289'.

[17] Oakeshott's note: 'Hegel, *Werke*, ix.45.'

[18] Oakeshott's note: 'Cf. supra 08[16], Nietzsche' presumably refers to the following quotation: '"Wenn ihr das Angenehme verachtet und das weiche Bett, und von den Weichlichen euch nicht weit genug betten könnt: da ist der Ursprung eurer Tugend." Nietzsche, *Zarathustra*, p. 81.'

[19] Oakeshott's note: 'M.P. Willcocks, *Between the Old World & the New Being Studies In Literary Personality From Goethe and Balzac to Anatole France and Thomas Hardy* (London: George Allen and Unwin Ltd, 1925), p. 162. Cp. G.E. Lessing, *Eine Duplik* (Baunschweig: Buchhandlug des Fürstl. Waisenhauses, 1778); Höffding, II, p. 18 sq, 80–1.'

Those who escaped Victorianism — Browning, Brontës & Meredith — different because they see that the value for human life, & so for religion, of this evolution idea is limited: & that what we must do is to live <u>our</u> lives, as entities. The value of the Evolution idea (which must be defined) for   (i) Religion.

　　　　　　　　　　　　　　　　　　　　　　　　　 (ii) Theology.

Its value for philosophy also — but that is negligible.

08[32]

The Last Judgment

Und eh man nur den halben Weg erreicht,
Muss wohl ein armer Teufel sterben.[20]

Were we to follow a philosophy in which 'accomplishment' were the aim, were we to live life in this faith, & to view the Last Judgment so — then suicide were only prevented because it were no remedy for what may come.

08[32]

Christianity

Whether we 'fall to rise' with Browning, or 'swim to sink' with Housman, Christianity does not claim to make us in any philosophical sense 'optimists' — only 'happy men.'[21]

08[33]

Accuracy

What is exactitude? The fitting of our standards of judgment to the subjects about which we judge.

So (i) It is <u>inexact</u> to fail to make a precise & categorical line between say acid & alkali in chemistry. Vagueness, meaning inexactness, is here lack of absolute precision.

But (ii) it is equally <u>in</u>exact to make a precise line between say one nation & another. In the realms of mind, & often in the realms of matter (e.g. organic & inorganic, solid & liquid etc.) precision is <u>in</u>accuracy, and, since vagueness means here inaccuracy, precision is vagueness.

Cf. with this the word 'ideal.' Instead of saying that a thing is 'too ideal' when it fails in respect of reality, we ought to say that it is 'not ideal enough' — it is not a unity in that characteristic which is its nature.

20　Oakeshott's note: 'Goethe, *Faust*, 150.'
21　R. Browning, 'Epilogue,' ll. 11–14: 'One who…Held we fall to rise'; A.E. Housman, *A Shropshire Lad*, XX, l. 2: 'Charge to fall and swim to drown.'

And so with 'scientific accuracy.' Or 'mathematical accuracy' —when wrongly applied, applied as a standard to subjects which are of a different nature to those strictly 'scientific' or 'mathematical' it is <u>in</u>accuracy.

08[34]

<u>Modernity & Antiquarianism</u>

Cf. old, & perhaps picturesque, forms of dress.

The German *Aufklärung*. Goethe's *Faust*.

Nietzsche's diatribe against the 'historicism' of the 19th century.

Some things are always modern—e.g. Plato.

Some things become modern after they have been in the world a considerable time—e.g. Spinoza.

Some things are never modern—e.g. Spencer?

For 'modern' means 'having meaning.'

P.S. Some things, also, grow old?

08[34–35]

<u>Religion</u>

Psychologically Taoism & Buddhism in China are as good as Christianity. The people come to pray either to ask a blessing on their life & work, or to give thanks. These religions make the people happy & contented.

By them they are calmed in times of trouble, & quieted in the hour of death. But what is this for a religion? (Cf. Gibbon's remark about Christianity in the Roman Empire).

Religion should awaken, not lull to sleep; should make discontented, not contented; should stir to newer effort, not breed quiescence.

The Chinese religion to-day is, naturally, an expression of their civilization. It has become hard, crystallized, & lacking movement. It, fundamentally, lacks life (ὁ Βιος ἐν τῃ κινήσει ἐστι), even though it plays a necessary part in the life of the people. It expresses the sleep which is there.

08[35–36]

<u>History (of philosophy)</u>

If we view this simply with regard to the ideas men have held, & the 'results' they have presented to the world, it appears, simply, as the repetition of a certain number of notions, at various intervals of time, & as, more or less, the result of a reaction to the culture & thought of a given period. But the 'real thing' in philosophy is never the result, but the reason we give for reaching the result. It is true of course that a given result held for two different reasons is, not, in any real sense, a <u>single</u> result at all—but it appears as such & historians treat it as such.

We must view the history of philosophy, not as a series of conclusions, but as a series of reasons given for reaching certain conclusions — for the reason is the conclusion, for philosophy.[22]

The same is true of all theoretical statements — e.g. the theory of Christianity.

When we do this, things which appear 'alike,' what appears a mere 'repetition,' will be seen as distinct — though we must not run away with the idea that there is any 'progress' to be found.

08[36]

Theory & Practice

Do you expect a theory of Humour to be funny?

08[37]

One of the things which Germans find it most difficult to understand in Englishmen is that they allow Shaw (& others) to say all sorts of insulting things about them — & then go & listen to his plays with enjoyment! One German I met supposed that these remarks were cut out in an English production of the plays. In the same way, it is an unheard of offense to caricature a professor or a leading Politician. When I explained that in England, on the contrary, many professors would take it as a compliment, delightful Fräulein Hauer remarked '*Ach! Für das bekommt man arrest in Deutschland!*'

Germany is even a little in the position of King Lear, often from among its people the good Kent speaks to it, but it will not listen — it is treason to speak the truth. But a healthy nation, in normal times, is prepared to hear anything about itself — only flippancy is abhorrent to it.

08[37–38]

One of the results of the war has been to make even the most thoughtless among us sensible to its horrors, and to cause us, also, in a way entirely foreign to our grandfathers, to question the morality of war. I sat this evening at the supper table with a dozen ordinary, normal young men & women, of six different nationalities — & not one of them had a good word to say for war: to everyone it was something immoral. But we may hardly conclude from this that our morality is changing in regard to this question — though, that it may change is by no means impossible — for this is more in the nature of a sentimental reaction, than a moral change. Twenty years ago the question of the morality of war was

---

22 Oakeshott's note: 'Cf. Coleridge's remark in S.T. Coleridge, *Aids to Reflection in the Formation of a Manly Character on the Several Grounds of Prudence, Morality, and Religion: Illustrated by Select Passages from our Elder Divines, especially from Archbishop Leighton* (London: Taylor and Hessey, 1825).'

debated & thought about by many — now it is not thought about at all; we <u>know</u>, it is said, that war is wrong. At any rate, we know that it is unchristian!

08[40]

The Historic Christ — to know Christ 'after the flesh'[23] — is not enough, & is not Christianity.

'After the flesh' — the imitation of the letter.[24]

08[41]

'Die Römischen Liturgie teilt mit der orientalischen den Mysteriencharakter.'[25]

(What is the *Mysteriencharakter*? Is it <u>essentially</u> lacking in the Protestant service?)[26]

08[42]

'Der Anglikanismus ist, wie es Friedrich von Hügel trufflich ausgedrückt hat, ein Kompromiz zwischen dem Calvinismus und dessen bête noire, dem römischen Katholizismus.'

The Oxford Movement & the modern Anglo-Catholics attempt to throw out the Calvinistic element.[27]

This may be a true account of the historical origins of Anglicanism — but it is a mere parody of Anglicanism itself. No-one who has really shared the spirit of an Anglican service could be guilty of so one-sided a conclusion.

08[43]

Conclusion — states how he has experienced the 'services' of all kinds of Christians & can find in each a peculiar & valuable experience.[28] Each has its contribution, each is a reflection of a strand in the 'service' of the early Christians.

'Ich freue mich darüber, dass es mir selbst immerlich möglich ist, am Gottesdienst der verschiedensten christlichen Bekenntsmuuse teilzunehmen.'[29]

His point of view is sane, but academic. It fails to grasp the fact that in matters of <u>life</u>, where a service is something inseparable from life, men can indeed recog-

---

23   Oakeshott's note: 'Romans 8:13.'
24   Fos. 39–43 contain notes in German on F. Heiler, *Katholischer und evangelischer Gottesdienst* (Munich: Ch. Kaiser, 1921).
25   Oakeshott's note: 'Heiler, *Gottesdienst*, p. 33.'
26   Oakeshott's note: 'Cf. Heiler, *Gottesdienst*, p. 37.'
27   Oakeshott's note: 'Heiler, *Gottesdienst*, pp. 57–8.'
28   Oakeshott's note: '1 Corinthians 12:4.'
29   Oakeshott's note: 'Heiler, *Gottesdienst*, p. 62.'

nize the validity of other forms than their own — but cannot share in them. It fails for the just the same reason that the Cosmpolitanism of the 18th century failed — it is academic.

The problem of 'Reunion' is just the problem of a 'world state' or some substitute for one — & it cannot be solved by some empty cosmopolitanism.

08[43]

Cuius regio, eijus religio — Though this, as a policy, may be repugnant to modern folk, yet as a principle of what is, there remains in it a fundamental truth. For what is a people's religion? Not, what creed do they officially subscribe to?, but What do they believe? What is the power which moves them in life? And when we have found out this, we shall see that it is ever, & essentially, closely bound up with the rest of its social life.

08[44]

Perhaps part of our unwillingness to hand 'morality' over to the ordinary judgment of humankind arises from our distrust of the capacity for judgment possessed by ordinary persons. But the ability of the 'ordinary' mind to win, by reflexion, from experience, is far greater than we imagine, & folk, innocent of all philosophy, who are yet accustomed to reflect upon events, sometimes develop a fineness of judgment in these matters that surprises us at every turn. Cf. the result of reflection on the 'war,' etc.

But why should we entrust 'morality' to the ordinary man? Why not to the 'moral seer'? Because it is only in so far as the teaching of the prophet is apprehended & digested by the ordinary man, that a 'morality,' in any true sense, exists. The judgments of ordinary people are a register for the morality of the whole — for morality is essentially a thing of community.

What is it that <u>often</u> incapacitates 'thinkers' & 'the learned' from being the best register? Irrelevant associations, and a lack of fineness of feeling for community sentiment.

08[45]

The course of philosophy is always to be making clear to itself the problems which belong properly to its sphere. The history of philosophy is not the history of so many riddles solved, but the history of so many problems, ever more clearly stated, so that in the end they are seen to be irrelevant. When are we going to arrive at the real problem? Who worries now about whether ideas are inside or outside the mind? And yet once, <u>that</u> was the whole of philosophy.

For this reason the great philosophers — Plato — never grow old: not because they solved a problem, but because they saw clearest the direction in which our thought must ever tend.

08[45]

Philosophers playing with analogies are like children playing with fire — it is pleasant, it is dangerous, & there's nothing to be gained by it.

Analogy is a <u>method of discovery</u> — not a proof.

08[46]

We, in these latter days, perhaps, do not hope to steal the fire of wisdom, & nor do we think of the gods as those who punish such presumption. The fire that we steal is this fire of freedom, of immortality, of the immortal life — ἐφ' ὅσον ενδέχεται αθανατίζειν — and it is the world which is ever ready to wreak its vengeance upon those who slight it in this manner.[30] This is what it is to 'overcome the world.'

08[49]

Physical 'fitness', physical strength, will often give us a sensation of power over ourselves which reacts upon the will in such a way as to strengthen resolve & even moral determination. This is a good illustration of an illogical & distinctively 'historical' relation. It is an illusion, & yet one that 'acts.' It has 'historical' existence, but lacks logical ground. We may sum up this kind of relation as 'suggestive' as opposed to 'logical.'

08[50]

'The arts of painting & of sculpture are wholly based upon imitation, & upon the reproduction with pigment upon canvas, or with chisel upon marble, of objects which have met the eye…Raphael & Rembrandt, Phidias & Michael Angelo, are only supreme masters of the perfection of imitation, or of idealization, by means of the setting & the treatment, of the various aspects of living figure & of nature's scenery.'[31]

An excellent illustration of the rubbish produced so often when an artist attempts to produce a theory of aesthetic. Artistic ability is <u>no</u> qualification for aesthetic theory, & lack of it <u>no</u> disqualification.

08[50]

'Interested judgments' i.e. those which have a psychological but no logical ground —

---

30   See Aristotle, *Nicomachean Ethics*, Bk X ch. vii §8.
31   Oakeshott's note: 'C.V. Stanford, "On the Study of Music," *Music & Letters*, 7 (1926), 229–35.'

(i) The man who refused to read *Paradise Lost* because he believed Milton to have composed his pamphlet on Divorce during his Honeymoon, & despised him for it.

(ii) The Norwegian philosopher, who, while single, stated in the first edition of his work that no important philosopher had been a married man, but having married in the interval, converted his dictum in the second edition to 'almost no important philosopher has been a married man.'

08[53]

English History[32]

Why was our Revolution so different from the French?

Why had England a Parliament long before other nations & still has a far better Parliament than any other.

Why have we never since 1688 suffered from monarchical tyranny or from mob anarchy?

Why have we a church which is neither Roman nor Calvinist?

Why did Presbyterianism fail in England & succeed in Scotland?

Why was England a nation a century or more before France or Spain, & many centuries before German?

08[54]

There is, perhaps, nothing so abstract as that which is at any particular moment.

08[54]

'I don't remember another night that I can at all compare with it since I was capable of suffering.'[33]

It is the same with everything — we confuse the thing as a real fact & something which looks like it. So, we are told, 'the family' is first & a number coming together make a 'state'; but the 'family' which existed before the 'state' is only one in appearance, it is only the embrio of the real institution, which cannot exist until the 'state,' i.e. some wider society, establishes, institutes it.

We know well that suffering has no unquestioned & easily distinguished & measured 'objective' existence. There are times in our lives when we are 'incapable' of suffering — we do not in fact become capable of it until we have outgrown the 'imperfect will' (Aristotle) of childhood; & we are increasingly

---

[32] Below this list of questions regarding English history Oakeshott pasted a cutting on Queen Elizabeth from G.M. Trevelyan, *History of England* (London: Longmans & Co., 1926).

[33] Oakeshott's note: 'Emily Brontë, *Wuthering Heights* (London: Smith, Elder and Co., 1850), Ch. 3.'

capable of it as we experience human life more completely & more deeply. What we call human suffering — the only suffering we know — because it is only children & men whose minds have never grown or become defunct who can 'experience' a purely 'sensational' suffering — mere physical pain — this human suffering, which is the reaction of a mind to a certain bodily (in the case of physical pain) circumstance, or to a certain mental experience, is attributable to animals only by some vague analogy — because it is not a quality common to sentient beings, but only to sentient beings capable of distinctively human experience & emotion. The problem of suffering which we have to face — the problem of Pain — is a problem of human, & not sentient, life as such.

08[56]

Much of what is called Pessimism & Optimism concerning human life may be described like this — Pessimism asserts that all is night (or Winter) & that the day (or Summer) comes & goes, is illusory or temporary. Optimism, that all is day (or Summer) & that the night (or Winter) comes & goes, is illusory or temporary. In these circumstances there clearly remains an alternative position, i.e., that 'good' & 'evil,' 'joy' & 'pain' are like, or may properly be compared with the day & night, the Summer & Winter of the world of nature. That one is not the absence of the other, that neither is more or less essential than the other, but that they are equally real, & equally permanent — that, in short, so far as human life is concerned Blake's poem — 'Joy & pain are woven fine' — express the truth. We have, then, not two alternative positions, but a choice between three.

This, of course, is not true of anything which is concerned with an ultimate optimism or pessimism.

08[57]

God & the Absolute

These the religious mind hardly distinguishes; & where religion takes on its intensest glow it merges into something which is more than the myths which tells us the truth in such a way as to put it into relation to the needs of human life, it takes on the being of a theoretic wholeness.

08[57]

Often the <u>wind</u> is in Emily Brontë's poems, this for instance,

> Yes; I could swear that glorious wind
> Has swept the world aside,
> Has dashed its memory from thy mind
> Like foam-bells from the tide.[34]

---

[34] Emily Brontë, 'The Night Wind', in *Poems of Emily Brontë*, ed. A. Symons (London: William Heinemann, 1906).

She knew the wind in all its moods – & they all meant for her, Liberty.

08[61]

On judging others. The World.

'Nicknames for the most part govern the world.'[35]

In practical life we are almost forced into this view of our fellows – but it is the world, & we should free ourselves of it. Religion seeks to free us from this – the world. It shows us that the partial view & judgments which we make every day, are views & judgments from a particular & often merely selfish standpoint. It is mere polemics – we speak, judge, deliver ourselves of views on other in order to attain a particular object – not in order to make a right judgment. But religion teaches to get above the world – to judge with the sole object of making a right judgment about the whole of a man or a circumstance.

08[61]

To deal justly (generously) with our fellow creatures, and courageously with our circumstances.

08[62]

Burke says that we should 'cherish our prejudices, because they are prejudices.' A prejudice which would pass itself off for reason is an unmitigated evil: – Burke was at the heart of the philosophy of modernity. See *French Revolution*.

08[63]

Savoir faire & savoir vivre.

08[63]

Romanticism, sentimentality & the 'business mind' of the Germans.

08[63]

'To trust people is a luxury in which only the wealthy can indulge; the poor cannot afford it.'[36]

But it is one of the ways of 'living beyond one's income' which is open to everyone; & has its own reward of quietness of mind.

---

[35] Oakeshott's note: 'William Hazlitt, *Sketches and Essays by William Hazlitt, now first Collected by his Son*, ed. W. Hazlitt (London: J. Templeman, 1839), p. 144.'

[36] Oakeshott's note: 'E.M. Forster, *Howard's End* (London: Edward Arnold, 1910), p. 33.'

08[64]

'Money is everything.'

'No, you're wrong, you've forgotten death. If we lived for ever, what you say would be true. But we have to die, we have to leave life presently. Injustice & greed would be the real thing if we lived for ever. As it is, we must hold to other things, because Death is coming. I love Death – not morbidly, but because He explains. He shows me the emptiness of Money. Death & Money are the eternal foes. Not Death & Life.'[37]

What is death? Only to be answered by, what is life. If life is existence, then death is its opposite. But 'human life' is not 'physical existence,' & death is not its cessation.

08[66]

<u>St Francis</u>

No cloistered saint. If you wish a restricted life go to Simon on his Pillar or Diogenes in his tub – not to Francis.

He more than any other Saint (since his re-discovery which began in the late 19th Century) has influenced the minds of ordinary English men & women. No other figure of the Calendar has approached his influence.

It is no odd chance that he is the first of the Renaissance poets – he was a poet from start to finish, without the hardness of 'ideas' or the harshness of the merely practical.

He it was who ended the tyranny of slavish belief, blind obedience & logic-less imitation which ruled the middle ages, & put Europe on the high road to a freedom which is religion.

Courage & religion – St Francis had the courage which 'goes on', not that which 'stands fast'. This latter is valuable – is, indeed, one of our chief natural characteristics – but it is of a lower order than the other, which requires wisdom before it is properly operative.

---

[37] Oakeshott's note: 'Forster, *Howard's End*, pp. 235–6.'

Notebook 9 (January 1927)

09[03]

'*Bis saltavit et placuit.*' — 'Danced Twice, & Pleased.'
Epitaph of a Roman dancing girl of the Early Roman Empire.

09[10]

Voltaire

The affair at Frankfurt. There is something almost sublime in his sitting down calmly to work at his *Annales de l'empire* as soon as the door closed on his tormentors.

09[12]

Though Voltaire despised men, he tried to help them:

'*Il vengea Calas, La Barre, Sirven et Monbailli. Poète, philosophe, historien, il a fait prendre un grand essor à l'esprit humain, et nous a préparés à être libres.*'[2]

---

[1] LSE 2/1/9. Hard cover, black and red marbling, 20 cm x 16 cm, blank. Recto pages numbered 1–72. Autograph, ink. Title page: 'O my soul, thou hast marched valiantly! / Song of Deborah / Proverbs. xxx. 9. / Notes. / IX. / *Memento vivere* / 'All sciences, indeed, are more necessary than this, / but none is better.' Arist. *Met.* 903a 10 / '*Die Wahrheit ist der Bacchantische Taumel, worin alle Gestalten trunken sind.*' Hegel. *Phän d. Geistes. Vorrede.* / '*Aimer et penser; c'est la véritable vie / des esprits.*' Voltaire. / Jan. 1927.'
   Other works from which Oakeshott made excerpts in this notebook but which are not mentioned in the text include: Fos. 2–3, *The Letters of Sir Walter Raleigh, 1879–1922*, ed. Lady Raleigh (London: Methuen & Co., 1926); 4–6 , L.R. Farnell, *The Attributes of God The Gifford Lectures Delivered in the University of St Andrews in the year 1924–25* (Oxford: Clarendon Press, 1925); 13, S. Johnson, *Rasselas* (London: R.and J. Dodsley; and W. Johnston, 1759); 21, Sir H.J.C. Grierson (ed.), *Metaphysical Lyrics & Poems of The Seventeenth Century* (Oxford: Clarendon Press, 1921); 24–5, Emily Dickinson, possibly *Poems of Emily Dickinson*, ed. M.L. Todd (London: Methuen and Co., 1904); 26–7, A.N. Whitehead, *Religion in the Making Lowell Lectures 1926* (New York: The Macmillan Company, 1926); 30–1, C.R. Leslie, *Memoirs of the Life of John Constable Composed Chiefly of his Letters* (London: James Carpenter, 1843); 33–4, H. Ford, *My Life and Work* (London: William Heinemann, 1922); 39–40, Oman, *Grace and Personality*; 41, W. Lewis, *Time and Western Man* (London: Chatto and Windus, 1927); 45–7, C.H. Cooley, *Life and the Student. Roadside Notes on Human Nature, Society, and Letters* (London and New York: Alfred A. Knopf, 1927); 62–3, G. Moore, *Modern Painting* (London: The Walter Scott Publishing Co., Ltd., 1906); 68, James Laver, *A Stitch in Time; or, Pride Prevents A Fall* (London: Nonesuch Press, 1927).
[2] This inscription appeared on the sarcophagus for Voltaire's funeral procession.

09[14]

'Poetry is not made with ideas, but with words.'
    Mallarmé.

09[14]

'Thought is abstract; & the intolerant use of abstractions is the major vice of the intellect.'[3]

But what kind of thinking are you speaking of?

09[15]

'There have been reactions & revivals. But on the whole, during many generations, there has been a gradual decay of religious influence in European civilization. Each revival touches a lower peak than its predecessor, & each period of slackness a lower depth.'[4]

Two causes:

(i) 'For over two centuries religion has been on the defensive.'[5] Each new development in thought has found religious thinkers unprepared.

    (But what is religion? How far does this unpreparedness show them to have been <u>not</u> 'religious thinkers'?)

(ii) 'The churches have put forward aspects of religion which are expressed in terms either suited to the emotional reactions of bygone times or directed to excite modern emotional interests of non-religious character.'[6]

'Conduct is a by-product of religion — an inevitable by-product but not the main point. Every great religious teacher has revolted against the presentation of religion as a mere sanction of rules of conduct.'[7]

(But what has 'a mere sanction etc': to do with conduct itself? Is conduct rules?)

09[16]

'In Philosophy itself investigation & reasoning are only preparatory & servile parts, means to an end. They terminate in insight, or what in the noblest sense of

---

3   Oakeshott's note: 'A.N. Whitehead, *Science and the Modern World* (New York and Cambridge: Macmillan, 1925), p. 26.'
4   Oakeshott's note: 'Whitehead, *Science*, p. 269.'
5   Oakeshott's note: 'Whitehead, *Scence*, p. 270.'
6   Oakeshott's note: 'Whitehead, *Science*, p. 273.'
7   Oakeshott's note: 'Whitehead, *Science*, p. 274.'

the word may be called <u>theory</u>, θεωρία, — a steady contemplation of all things in their order & worth. Such a contemplation is imaginative.'[8]

09[23]

Moby Dick is the *Paradise Lost* of Melville, *Billy Budd* his *Paradise Regained*.[9]

Moby Dick compared with *Paradise Lost*. Ahab sets out to conquer the whale, & in the end is slain by it. A parable of eternal strife. Cf. Dante's symbolism.

09[28]

<u>The World</u>

'As a people the Chinese possess a quality of extreme rarity even in European individuals, the power of enduring suffering or disaster without the compensation of metaphysical or religious dreams.'[10]

An English officer was ordered to burn a Chinese village; he went to the head-man to tell him. He was received with politeness, offered tea, which he refused & delivered his order. The Chinaman himself lighted a brand & without the smallest attempt to save any of his possessions, light his house, threw the brand into the middle of the village & walked away into the country.

09[28]

'Otherworldliness' — a new view of society.

09[29]

Lucian complained that history writing was, in his day, becoming an obsession. To-day historians have taken to writing — & a well schooled age to reading — history as an amusement, as a trade, as a means of grace & even as a new religion.[11]

09[35]

<u>Morality — Knowledge — Art</u>

> Our position — if we are not at all costs <u>ourselves</u>, —
> I have ventur'd

---

[8] Oakeshott's note: 'G. Santayana, *Three Philosophical Poets Lucretius Dante and Goethe* (Cambridge, MA: Harvard University, 1910), p. 10.'

[9] Fos. 22–3 contain quotations from J. Freeman, *Herman Melville* (London: Macmillan & Co., 1926).

[10] Oakeshott's note: 'D.W. Russell, *The Right to be Happy* (London: G. Routledge & Sons, 1927), p. 10.'

[11] Oakeshott's note: 'See E. Troeltsch, *"Der Historismus und seine Probleme"* in *Gesammelte Schriften*, 4 vols. (Tubingen: J.C.B. Mohr Paul Siebeck, 1912–25), iii.6, 26, 110.'

Like little wanton boys that swim on bladders,
This many summers in a sea of glory,
But far beyond my depth: my high-blown pride
At length broke under me.
    Wolsey.[12]

Gain the whole world & lose your soul.

Reputation, fame, working for 'humanity,' contributing to knowledge—
everything, if this is not added to it, is vanity.

09[36]

<u>The World & the Flesh</u>

The contrast has always been between the Spirit & Flesh & in a sense it is a
contrast which we experience vitally; but it has often & continually been misinterpreted—interpreted by prudish puritans—so as to make it something which
contradicts a full life—a life lived to its fullest. The great contrast, upon which
rests the whole of the true life of the mind is between spirit & the world. This,
too, is familiar & is misinterpreted so as to produce an indigent existence not
worth calling 'life.' But 'the Flesh' is not 'the world' except in so far as it means
'existence at any cost.'

All love poetry cries out against the identification of the Flesh & the World—
it is the world only which is the negation of love.

09[37]

Philosophy is to get rid of your phlegm.
Philosophieren ist dephlegmatisiren vivificium. Novalis.[13]

09[37–38]

'There is, thanks to our various communities & sects, a steady supply of religion
laid before the public, & a supply so varied that one would expect all tastes to
find satisfaction.'[14]

<u>A supply of religion</u>! As if it were water or bread & butter, instead of life itself.
How can there be <u>a supply of life</u> laid before the public?

'Every religion claims to tell us something which is not only true, but supremely
true, something that lets us into the secret of the universe.'[15]

---

12 Oakeshott's note: 'Shakespeare, *Henry VIII*, Act III sc. ii.'
13 For Oakeshott's use of this quotation see *SW*, v.147, n. 10.
14 Oakeshott's note: 'R.G. Collingwood, *Speculum Mentis or The Map of Knowledge*
(Oxford: Clarendon Press, 1924), p. 15.'
15 Oakeshott's note: 'Collingwood, *Speculum Mentis*, p. 40.'

? The religious consciousness does not understand 'the secret of the universe' – truth, strictly has little meaning for it: or else its object is religious truth – is a certain kind of truth, metaphorically called truth.

But 'the practical' must not be identified with 'the object of will,' because will is abstract, & nothing is the object of anything save mind as a whole. This is a common fallacy.

'Religion & science know their own business a great deal better than these impartial persons who attempt to "reconcile" them.'[16]

They do not. Religion & science, on your own showing, are not self-conscious knowledge, & therefore know nothing whatever of themselves, as a whole, as such.

09[38]

'When the philosopher devotes his attention to subjects with which other people are familiar, it often becomes possible to put down the book before finishing it. Thus treatises on aesthetics are mainly convincing to everybody but poets, painters & musicians, & philosophical writings on science are probably in great demand among classical scholars.'[17]

The fallacy being that the scientist as such is not familiar with science as such – it is not his subject.

09[42]

History tells us the when? of things: what could make more assumptions, what could be more abstract?

09[42]

It is often said that with women the chief business of life is love; but how much truer is this of men: & with them it appears to have less force simply because they are led into the 'world' & distracted with things lower, – & perhaps things higher.

09[45]

Sperry's conclusion[18] – Although the historical study of Jesus has no theological significance as far as its results are concerned, yet the discipline of historical study is one which is most calculated to produce religious-mindedness, because

---

16 Oakeshott's note: '*Speculum Mentis*, p. 49.'
17 Oakeshott's note: 'J.W.N. Sullivan, *Aspects of Science*, 2 vols. (London: R. Cobden-Sanderson and W. Collins Sons & Co., 1923-6), i.23.'
18 Fo. 45 contains quotations from W.L. Sperry, 'The Relation of Religion to Historical Fact', *Hibbert Journal*, 26 (1927), pp. 44-5.

it cannot be undertaken except religiously. Historical thinking requires faithfulness to objective fact and to personal interpretation – it is objective & subjective at once – and this is what religion requires also.

The notion is that Hellenism has not the 'time sense' of Hebraism. Is it true? How far were the Greek religions historical religions also?

09[49]

Nil nisi divinum stabile est; caetera fumus.

Nothing is lasting unless it is divine; the rest is smoke.

09[50]

'For myself...I had drawn the obvious deduction that since the fundamental instinct of life, in the savage as much as in the civilized man, is to hold on to life, that instinct must inevitably breed a belief in the continuance of life after its obvious cessation.'[19]

So much the worse for your logic!

09[52]

The aim of Dr Arnold at Rugby was to produce men who were Christians & Englishmen.[20] The two points at which reform was obviously demanded were (i) in the curriculum – the introduction of modern studies. (ii) in the moral tone. Arnold did more for (ii) than he did for (i).

Under (i) he introduced modern history – 1 hour a week: French, – purely grammatically – it was a failure. Mathematics. Indeed A. was convinced that the best education there was to be had was that to be obtained from Latin & Greek. But he did see that his object must be to teach 'not knowledge, but the means of gaining knowledge.' But he started out with certain prejudices – e.g. 'Boys do not like poetry' (cf. G.C. Armstrong on the poets vs the historians for boys); 'boys at a public school never will learn to speak or pronounce French well, under any circumstances.' His aim was 'to introduce a religious principle into education'; 'to make the school a place of really Christian education.'

(i) Religious & moral principle.

(ii) Gentlemanly conduct.

(iii) Intellectual ability.

---

19 Oakeshott's note: 'Beverley Nichols, *Are They They Same At Home? Being A Series of Bouquets Differently Distributed* (London: Jonathan Cape, 1927), p. 46.'

20 Fos. 51–3 contain notes on L. Strachey, *Eminent Victorians* (London: Chatto & Windus, 1918).

09[54]

The Philosophy of 'As If' & Theology

See Schleiermacher on Prayer etc.[21]

On Immortality.

Lipsius.

Immortality has been considered as a real thing i.e., an hypothesis, but it is really a fiction.

Dogma: hypothesis: fiction.[22]

09[54–55]

'The good man works towards the coming of a kingdom of God upon earth, the kingdom of truth's justice: but, at the end of his career, he sees it as far off as ever…what can he, a single individual, do against an immoral world? Shall he cease to struggle against the stream of wrong?…No—his good heart loudly admonishes him—you shall do good & never weary of it! Believe that virtue in the end will triumph…believe that the Kingdom of God, the Kingdom of truth & justice, will come on the earth; & do you but work for its coming. It is true that in all this you cannot scientifically demonstrate that it must be so. Enough that your heart bids you act <u>as if</u> it were so, & merely by so acting you will prove that you have religion.'[23]

(This can only be justified if it turns out that this notion of amelioration, progress is a fiction which, if followed, because of its power of inspiration & invigoration, will achieve the <u>real</u> end, the making of the individual soul. But there is such a thing as a decadent fiction, a fiction which has none of this power, & perhaps the idea of progress is one of this kind. At any rate the fiction of some kind of Kingdom of Heaven seems to be necessary for man's life to be lived to the fullest. But how far is it necessary that we should be unconscious that it is a fiction for it to do its work?)

---

[21] Oakeshott's note: 'Biedermann, *Christliche Dogmatik*, §§949–73.' Alois E. Biedermann, *Christliche Dogmatik* (Zurich: Orell, Füssli & Co., 1869).

[22] Oakeshott's note: 'See Lotze, *Logik*, E.T., p. 351.' Assuming 'E.T.' stands for 'English Translation,' probably a reference to Bosanquet's translation of H. Lotze, *Logik* (Leipzig: Weidmann'sche Buchhandlung, 1843) as *Logic in Three Books Of Thought, Of Investigation, And Of Knowledge* (Oxford: Clarendon Press, 1884).

[23] Oakeshott's note: 'F.K. Forberg, "*Entwicklung des Begriffs der Religion*" [Development of the Concept of Religion], *Philosophisches Journal einer Gesellschaft Teutscher Gelehrten*, 8 (1798), 21–46, quoted in H. Vaihinger, *The Philosophy of "As If,"* tr. C.K. Ogden (London: Kegan Paul & Co., 1924), p. 322.'

09[57]

Theology is concerned with setting forth the truth of God as He has revealed it in His Word to His Church. (All capitals!)

Cp. Bishop Wilson. 'Rule of Religion. When the Holy Scriptures are silent, the Church is my text; where the Holy Scripture speaks, the Church is my comment; where both are silent I follow reason.'[24]

(This, indeed, is the general view of theology. But what they don't see is that in any case they 'follow reason,' because everything is interpreted.[25] There can be no 'authority' in theology, except reason; though in religion there may be what appears to be an external authority — but even that is no more than an appearance.)

09[58]

'Afflictions bring us the nearest way to God.'

'Happy is the condition which forces us to trust only in God. Afflictions dispose us to pray.'
  Bishop Wilson.

This is a view of religion, undoubtedly true as far as it goes, but does it go far enough? What sort of religion is it which we feel most intensely only when in danger? The religion of most of us is like this, but is it the highest?

09[58]

'Religion only recommends modesty, and condemns singularity [in dress].'
  Bishop Wilson.

How well that speaks the mind of the makers of the Book of Common Prayer. E.g. the marriage Service etc.: 'Honesty' is the virtue commended, 'quietness,' 'sobriety.' There is no passion & wildness about this religion, no daring and venture. The apotheosis of dullness & provincialism.

09[59]

'The faith which was delivered once for all unto the Saints.'[26] — ἅπαξ.

This is the notion which is at the bottom of the total lack of logic in much Christian apologetic.

---

24 Oakeshott's note: 'Cf. Sir Thomas Browne, *Religio Medici* (London: A. Crooke, 1642), §5.'
25 Oakeshott's note: 'Cp. Hort.'
26 Oakeshott's note: 'Jude 3.'

09[59]

'Two things a Christian will do: Never go against the best light that he has; this will prove his sincerity: &, secondly, to take care that his light is not darkness.'
Bishop Wilson

But the <u>theoretical</u> problem of life is to see these as <u>one</u> & not as two; for if they <u>go together</u> they must be subsumable under a single principle of life.

09[60]

Lincoln (on a political platform, to his opponent)

'Mr So–&–so, suppose I called the tail of a mule a leg, how many legs would the mule then have?'
Mr So–&–so. 'Five legs, Sir.'
Lincoln. 'No, it would have only four. Calling a tail a leg does not make it one!'

<u>Three</u> possibilities.

(i) That the mule would still have only four legs.

(ii) That it would then have five.

(iii) That it would then have but one.

09[60]

Herbert Spencer was once confronted by a patient of a lunatic asylum who had heard him address an audience of convalescent inmates. The man was distraught with maniac laughter, but when calmed & asked to explain the joke to Spencer he remarked: 'To think of me in & you out!'

Wasn't he about right?

09[63]

The desire to organize art. Cp. Literature. The desire of some journalists to make their calling a 'profession.'
Cp. Schoolmasters, actors etc.
But is it not the death of literature & art to be made a 'profession'?[27]
A <u>planned</u> civilization!

09[63]

Emily Brontë projected all her unsatisfied emotion into one famous work of art: she made Heathcliff & Catherine out of the anger, beauty & pain of unsatisfied passion.

---

[27] Oakeshott's note: 'Cp. Raleigh in *Aesthetic Notes*, p. 60.'

How far is this true of all art? Comfort & reputation; ease & satisfied desire —
these kill art? Art is the product of dissatisfaction, of disharmony.

And how far is this true of <u>religion</u> also. And would not this explain the fact
that religion & danger are complementary?

09[64]

Human life, as Hegel says of the life of God, sinks into insipidity *'wenn der Ernst,
der Schmerz, die Geduld und Arbeit des Negativen darin fehlt.'*[28]

And this is the meaning both of Morality & Tragedy.

09[69–70]

Otherworldliness[29]

Sometimes said that primitive Christianity is wholly foreign to modern civilization.

It believed that the whole world-order was unstable, that shortly there would
be a great catastrophy which would change everything. The permanent things
were not the obviously permanent ones — the rich young man, the widow's mite.
They were living on the edge of a precipice; that, indeed, & the beliefs which
fostered that feeling, were the basis of the greatness of the religion & life of that
age. (Cp. the way in which Athenian social system accentuated & made man
conscious of the fact that it was <u>difficult</u> to be a real 'citizen.') They lived danger-
ously, & their religion answered to their life & vice versa.

<u>We</u> believe in Art & Literature & Patriotism & the pageant of history & the
growth of human life — evolution etc. (Cp. Pascal on 'Humanity'). Comfort. We
even believe in the progress of things such as Chemistry & Mathematics — <u>they</u>
go on, we it is who pass and are unstable elements.

Now, it is sometimes said that the sacredness of the individual is what
Christianity & particularly the Reformation gave Europe: but is this so?

Clearly the whole value of life is in the individual life to primitive Christianity; for that alone is stable; the <u>things</u> pass away, but the soul only passes on to
<u>life</u>. But our modern ideas are all against this; the individual is but a moment in
a process. The Reformation was nearer primitive Christianity in its beliefs about
the relative value of individuals & things, the Renaissance was also, & so were
the Greeks. (Yet cp. modern belief that the work of art is valued for the <u>work</u>, for
the artist.)

At all events; the ideas which governed primitive Christianity are different
from those which govern us. We believe in the fundamental stability of the
present order, or that it will merely evolve into another, & right or wrong this
belief has but small <u>religious</u> value. That is why the Gospels are & always will be

---

28 Oakeshott's note: 'Hegel, *Phänomenologie*, p. 13.'
29 Oakeshott's note: 'Cp. Green, *Prolegomena*, Bk VI, ch. 2, esp. §184.'

helpful; because Jesus & they express ideas, & a view of the world, — in a language perhaps which needs modernizing — which is higher & nobler than ours.

This belief which they express has been translated into the belief in a good time coming (Burkitt), but this I believe to be a mistranslation, which echoes our own beliefs in progress. It has also been said that we should live <u>as if</u> there were a good time coming, but that too, is too vague. What shall be our translation, what does, what can, otherworldliness mean to us?

09[72]

<u>Evolution</u>, the master principle of biological life, has been elevated into a principle of moral life — & causes only confusion & a false ideal.

09[72]

<u>Evolution</u>

The modern scholar's ideal. cp. Universal language; pooling of thought & learning.

Everything to contribute to a single end. Cp. Pascal on '*Humanité.*' Breaking down of barriers. The world state. The idea of humanity — civilization as a '<u>thing</u>.'

Cosmopolitanism. Intellectual intercourse. Esperanto. Conferences & congresses. And compare with it all the opposite ideal. — The value of life for me. Otherworldliness.

09[A][30]

<u>Voltaire, historian</u>[31]

Essai; Louis XIV; Louis XV; Annales de l'Empire; Charles XII; Russie.

New conception of history; after Clarendon & Bossuet, & before Hume & Gibbon. 'Rational' history.

Voltaire's prejudices — the Church, 'barbarous' absolutism. History devoid of fantastic 'theories.'

Desire to give more than a tale of kings — the people, the civilization.

Belief in the amelioration of human lot.

War & fanaticism his great enemies.

---

[30] On a loose sheet in ink numbered '10a.'

[31] Oakeshott's note 'See Saintsbury.' Possibly a reference to G.E.B. Saintsbury's article "Voltaire, Francois Marie Arouet de," in *Encylopaedia Britannica*, 11th edn (1911). The works listed by Voltaire are: *Essai sur l'Histoire Générale, et sur les Moeurs et l'Esprit des Nations, depuis Charlemagne jusqu'à nos jours*, 7 vols. (Geneva: Cramer, 1756); *Le siècle de Louis XIV*, 2 vols. (Berlin: C.F. Henning, 1751); *Précis du siècle de Louis XV*, 4 vols. (Geneva: Cramer, 1768); *Annales de l'empire depuis Charlemagne* (Geneva: Cramer, 1754); *Histoire de Charles XII. Roi de Suéde*, 2 vols. (Basle: C. Revis, 1731); *Histoire de l'empire de Russie sous Pierre le grand*, 2 vols. (Lyon: Bruyset, 1759–63).

Voltaire excels in rapid summaries of an age or a character.

Notebook 10 (September 1928)

10[02]

Shelley's total disregard of self-preservation. Cp. Trelawny's story of his throwing himself into the Arno, though he could not swim.[2]

10[05]

Christianity & History

Somehow we must get away from the meaningless dualism of 'what really happened' – the 'course of events' – and 'history' – an account of it. These are not two, but one – for our world is never one of 'things,' but always one of 'objects.'

Cp. in Christianity.

There is   (i) The Jesus of History.

(ii) The Christ.

But these are not two, but one.

(i) is Jesus as experienced in history, i.e., Jesus for history or historical thinking, and (ii) is Jesus as experienced in religion, i.e., Jesus for religion, or religious thinking.

---

[1]   LSE 2/1/10. Hard cover, blue, 17 cm x 11.5 cm, squared. Recto pages numbered 1–91. Autograph, ink. Title page: 'Notes. X. / 'Surtout point de zèle.' / Talleyrand. / Sept. 1928.'

Other works from which Oakeshott made excerpts in this notebook but which are not mentioned in the text include: Fos. 1–2, André Maurois, Ariel, ou la vie de Shelley (Paris: B. Grasset, 1923); 2–3, N. Douglas, South Wind (London: Martin Secker, 1922); 4, A. Huxley, Two or Three Graces and Other Stories (Leipzig: Bernard Tauchnitz, 1928); 6–7, Stendhal, On Love (London: Duckworth, 1915); 8–9, D.H. Lawrence, Kangaroo (London: Martin Secker, 1923); 11–12, T. Mann, Der Tod in Venedig (Munich: Hyperion-Verlag Hans von Weber, 1912); 13–14, Victoria Sackville-West, Heritage (London: W. Collins Sons & Co., 1919); 15, F. Nietzsche, Dawn of Day, tr. J. Votz (London: T. Fisher Unwin, 1902); 23–4, S. Sitwell, The Gothick North: A Study of Medieval Life, Art and Thought, 3 vols. (London: Duckworth, 1929); 27, G.E.B. Clemenceau, In the Evening of My Thought, tr. C.M. Thompson and J. Heard, 2 vols. (London: Constable & Co, 1929); 28, C. Bailey, Epicurus: The Extant Remains, tr. C. Bailey (Oxford: Clarendon Press, 1926); 32–3, D.H. Lawrence, The Plumed Serpent (London: Martin Secker, 1926); 38, Novalis, Christenheit oder Europa, possibly Christianity or Europe, tr. J. Dalton (London: J. Chapman, 1844); 72–4, F. Nietzsche, Human, All Too Human, tr. H. Zimmern (Edinburgh: T.N. Foulis, 1910); 78, Jean de La Bruyère, Les caractères de Théophraste, et de La Bruyère, avec des notes par M. Coste, 2 vols. (Dresden, G.C. Walther, 1769); 84–6, D.H. Lawrence, The Boy in the Bush (London: Martin Secker, 1924).

[2]   Oakeshott's note: 'E.J. Trelawny, Records of Shelley, Byron and the Author, 2 vols. (London: Basil Montagu Pickering, 1878), i.90.'

What is the relation of these two? That can only be answered when we know what is the essential nature of (i) history & (ii) religion. But we ought not to <u>assume</u> an obvious or a close relationship.

To know that something has happened brings it closer to us; to see it happening brings it closest.

10[06]

Stendhal says that love follows the stages of

(1) Admiration.

(2) One says to oneself: 'How delightful to kiss her, & be kissed in return.'

(3) Hope.

(4) Love is born.

A year may elapse between (1) & (2), a month between (2) & (3). Between (3) & (4) there is but the twinkling of an eye.

10[10]

Number of grains of sand spread over England would make a layer hundreds of yards in depth. 'Let us reflect that the earth is the millionth part of one such grain of sand, & our mundane affairs, our thoughts & our achievements, begin to appear in their correct proportion to the universe as a whole.'[3]

? Not, perhaps, when we realize that <u>this</u> universe of which Jeans is speaking is the creation of man. His comparison, because it leaves out so much, gives a wholly wrong impression.

It is anti-religious in the best sense.

10[16]

The *raison d'être* of marriage.

Its indissolubleness.

The exclusive legal responsibility of the man.

The necessity of descent.

The rights of property.

But 'by showing ever more & more favour to <u>love</u>-marriages, the very foundation of matrimony, that which alone makes it an institution, has been undermined...modern marriage has lost its meaning, consequently it is being abolished.'[4]

---

3 Oakeshott's note: 'J.H. Jeans, *EOS, or the Wider Aspects of Cosmogony* (London: Kegan Paul, Trench, Trübner & Co., Ltd.; New York: E.P. Dutton & Co., 1928), p. 21.'

4 Oakeshott's note: 'Nietzsche, *Twilight of the Idols*, p. 97 E.T.' is probably a reference to F. Nietzsche, *Twilight of the Idols*, tr. A.M. Ludovici (London: Allen & Uniwn, 1911).

10[18–19]

An examination & criticism of the 'mythology' of English Christianity. Cp. the criticism to which Socrates subjected the mythology of Greece.

English people do not readily personalize or materialize their beliefs, as the Greeks in their mythology; but none the less we have a 'mythology.' Many of the 'myths' of Hebrew religion we have inherited, many have been, in name, discarded—but they still haunt us. Book of Common Prayer a respository of English religious mythology.

Distinguish between mythology & theology.[5]

In Greece they were very much the same. — But their only theologians were the early scientists, Plato, Aristotle etc. — Homer & Hesiod were the creators of their myths; the scientists of their Theology. But the Greeks, until late in their history, were too religious a people to concern themselves much with theology.

Myth = a kind of practical thinking about religion. But must be distinguished from devotional thinking. It is creative.

Theology = theoretical thinking about religion — normally in the form of reflection upon myths already created and believed.

10[19–20]

God

'The man who demands a reality more solid than that of the religious consciousness seeks he knows not what.'[6]

What we must get away from is this notion that the religious man as such demands a proof of the existence of God. Nothing has less meaning than this for him. And to say, also, that he demands some 'objective' correspondent to his 'subjective' beliefs is equally misleading. What he demands is that he should know the object of his religious belief to be real, & 'real' does not mean 'objective.' Often he, & others, use the word 'objective' when they mean real; but we ought not to follow them in this mistake. And if 'objective' means 'independent of the religious consciousness,' then it has no meaning and no reality whatever.

---

[5] Oakeshott's note: 'Cp. Jane Harrison, *Myths of Greece & Rome* (London: Ernest Benn, 1927).'

[6] Oakeshott's note: 'Bradley, *Ethical Studies.*'

10[20]

The Prospects of Theology

'Modern Liberalism [in theology] is essentially based upon the critical study of the Old & New Testaments.'[7]

1. 'The discoveries of natural science — evolution — have knocked the bottom out of our traditional theology.'

2. 'The criticism of the Old & New Testament has knocked the bottom out of our traditional theology.'

What is science? What is history? Can they do this to Theology? What can they do to Theology?

'Attempts to deny that the synoptic gospels give us in the main a true historical picture of his character & teaching have altogether broken down.'[8]

Give who? Not the ordinary man, not the man who knows nothing but his Gospels. And is there any agreement about what that character is? And if not, how can it be said that we have a true picture?

10[21]

Gratitude

The effect of teaching children gratitude. They are voluble & communicative enough, charming & natural, until they are lead to be believe that they exist to glorify those 'who have done everything for them.' Then — reticence & an unavailing attempt to adjust their emotions to this new view.
  Children are egoistic.
  There is something distasteful in the notion of gratitude.

10[21]

Prospects of Theology

Distinguish these from the prospects of religion. Theology result of a decline of religion — not an historical statement, but resulting from the nature of theology, which is non-religious. Distinguish theological thinking from the effort to create a religious mythology, etc.

10[22]

The work of the higher critics. Its nature & conclusion.
  Theology is like this to a large extent. Why then is it important?

---

7 Oakeshott's note: 'H. Rashdall, *Ideas and Ideals: Selected by H.D.A. Major and F.L. Cross* (Oxford: Blackwell, 1928), p. 95.'

8 Oakeshott's note: 'Rashdall, *Ideas & Ideals*, p. 113.'

10[23]

'Religious experience must be made articulate & therefore needs a theology.'[9]

No; what it requires is not a <u>theology</u> but a <u>mythology</u>.

10[24]

<u>Religion</u>

Religion is 'a proposition or conciliation of powers superior to man, which are believed to direct & control the course of nature & of human life.'[10]

Religion the recognition of our duties as divine commands. Kant.

Religion is the consciousness of absolute dependence. Schleiermacher.

Feelings connected with religion — dependency, & independence, our insignificance & our significance, wonder & peace, admiration, far, awe, hope, joy, mystery.

Society is the primary object of religious devotion. Durkheim.

It is 'a system of ideas with which individuals represent to themselves the society of which they are members & the relations they have with it.'[11]

'The essence of religion is the strong & earnest dedication of the emotions & desires towards an ideal object, recognized as of the highest excellence, & as rightfully paramount over all selfish objects of desire.'[12]

Religion is an experience of God.

10[26]

'Popular theology has a positive appetite for absurdity.'[13]

(If 'popular religious myth' is meant, there is no reason why it should not be absurd. There is no such thing as 'popular <u>theology</u>.')

---

[9] Oakeshott's note: 'W.R. Smith, *Lectures on the Religion of the Semites*, ed. S.A. Cook, 3rd edn (London: Adam and Charles Black, 1927).'

[10] Oakeshott's note: 'J.G. Frazer, *The Golden Bough: A Study in Magic and Religion*, 2nd edn, 3 vols. (London: Macmillan, 1900), i.63.'

[11] Oakeshott's note: 'E. Durkheim, *The Elementary Forms of the Religious Life A Study in Religious Sociology*, tr. J.W. Swain (London: George Allen & Unwin, Ltd.; New York: The Macmillan Company, 1915), p. 225.'

[12] J.S. Mill, 'The Utility of Religion,' in *Three Essays on Religion Nature The Utility of Religion and Theism*, 2nd edn (London: Longmans, Green, Reader, and Dyer, 1874), p. 109. Reprinted in *Collected Works of John Stuart*, ed. J.M. Robson, 33 vols. (Toronto: University of Toronto Press, 1963–91), x.403–28.

[13] See D. Hume, 'The Natural History of Religion,' §11, 'With regard to Reason or Absurdity' in *Four dissertations. I. The Natural History of Religion. II. Of the Passions. III. Of Tragedy. IV. Of the Standard of Taste* (London: A. Millar, 1757), at p. 70.

10[28]

Λάθε βιώσασ — Live Unknown.
   Be unnoticed, having lived & died.
      Epicurus.

Live as far as possible without a following.

10[30]

'There is a curious illusion that a more complete culture was possible when there was less to know. Surely the only gain was, that it was more possible to remain unconscious of ignorance. It cannot have been a gain to Plato to have read neither Shakespeare, nor Newton, nor Darwin.'[14]

There are many other gains. When there is less to know we are less easily seduced by the ideal of culture as knowing as <u>much</u> as we can.[15]

10[30]

For Essays on Modern Religion

It seems essential that if worship has its chief effect on us — & not on God — we must somehow be unconscious of this fact if it is to be accomplished.[16]
   But the conclusion to be drawn from this is that theology does no good to religion.
   Cp. Santayana on how a philosophical attitude harms science.
   My object in these essays is to call attention to what I may call the Epicurean element in Christianity — Cp. Inge's work on the Platonic element in Christian theology.[17]

10[31]

On Saying What We Mean

A hero is never a hero to his valet, but as Hegel pointed out, that is not because the hero is not a hero, but because the valet is a valet.[18]

---

[14] Oakeshott's note: 'A.N. Whitehead, *The Aims of Education, and Other* Essays (London: Macmillan, 1929), p. 73.'

[15] Oakeshott's note: 'Cp. Conrad.'

[16] Oakeshott's note: 'Cp. J.B. Pratt, *The Religious Consciousness A Psychological Study* (New York: The Macmillan Company, 1921).'

[17] Oakeshott's note: 'See Inge, *Christianity & Personal Mysticism*; Bishop Paddock lectures.' Possibly W.R. Inge, *Christian Mysticism. Considered in Eight Lectures Delivered Before the University of Oxford* (London: Methuen & Co., 1899); and B.H. Paddock, *The Bishop Paddock Lectures*, 4 vols. (London: Griffith, Farran & Co., 1886–97).

[18] Oakeshott's note: 'Hegel, *Philosophy of History*, p. 33.'

10[31]

Saying What We Mean

Similes etc. The principle of them is pragmatic. The most usually associated things, not the most accurately associated. And further, what is 'telling'; what is unusual because it is unusual.[19]

10[32]

Christianity

The absurd suggestion that we should not try so much to alter or reform Christanity as to take it seriously, practice it.

But what is <u>it</u>?

10[33]

Religion, says Burke, should provide instruction in life & consolation in death.

What we must see is that these are not two tasks but <u>one</u>. To find a view of life which explains death — so that death & mortality & growing old are not contradictions — broken pillars — but part of the process of living. Life must be made to conform with death.

If we achieved this it is probable that we should deprive art & poetry of that vivid contrast between life & death which is at the heart of so many of the Elizabethans & 17th Century poets. But then poetry & art depend upon discomfort, mystery, unresolved contradictions, suffering & a feeling of not being at home in the universe.

10[34]

Myths & Superstitions

All myths tend to become superstitions, and in doing so they do not lose their force as myths, but they become dangerous. For a superstition is a myth taken literally, & when the belief or institution or way of living it supports no longer finds this support, it will dissolve not because of its inherent weakness, but because there is no evident reason, and no myth, to justify it.[20]

10[35]

'As a body everyone is single, as a soul never.'[21]

---

[19] Oakeshott's note: 'C. Morgan, *Portrait in a Mirror* (Leipzig: Bernard Tauchnitz, 1930), pp. 133, 258–66.'

[20] Oakeshott's note: 'Cp. J.G. Frazer, *Psyche's Task: A Discourse Concerning the Influence of Superstition on the Growth of Institutions* (London: Macmillan & Co., 1909), pp. 3–5, 154–6.'

[21] Oakeshott's note: 'H. Hesse, *Steppenwolf*, tr. B. Creighton (London: Martin Secker, 1929), p. 27.'

Body, 'matter,' 'physical' = what can be isolated.

10[35]

A long life, no less than a short, shows just as conclusively that we must all die in the end.

10[36]

'*L'histoire et la civilization marchant toujours du meme pied.*'[22]

One kind of civilization. Why should we not suppose history to be a qualification of civilization rather than an enhancement of it — or evidence of it.

10[38]

Napoleon found it difficult to believe in Christianity because it was not old enough.[23]

10[38]

Fantasy, terror, mystery are sought in a world of ghosts & shadows beyond the grave, or a world of fairies & goblins, only by a people which has not imagination enough to know that this life is mysterious enough, terrible enough, fantastic enough to supply all such needs.

Cp. Fairytales — children need them, because life is obvious to them & not mysterious or terrible?

The 'supernatural' in Shakespeare etc.

A 'practical' man understands all he sees — because he sees nothing save what he can explain to himself satisfactorily. It is another kind of man who sees all the while things he does not understand.

If we are looking for something which is difficult to understand — this life supplies the need, we require to invent no other.

10[39]

Otherworldliness

The period of life when the routine of life is just beginning to get hold of us, when we begin to fear it, because we feel it to be our master, or nearly so — that is a Shadow Line. We revolt against it; few succeed in that revolt. They leave it until too late; until they have committed themselves to the world, & cannot again be free of it. Life, then, for them will be full of regrets — until they also are forgotten & the world has mastered its own.

---

22   See Gabriel Hanotaux, *De l'histoire et des historiens* (Paris: Louis Conard, 1919), p. 47.
23   Oakeshott's note: 'Cp. A.P.P. Rosebery, *Napoleon: The Last Phase* (London: A.L. Humphreys, 1900), p. 257.'

When we are afraid of the routine of life — then is the hour to strike, or it will be too late.

10[40]

<u>Modernity</u> — the hate of anything that is not ourselves.[24]

10[40]

'He has overcome the sharpness of death.'

What is the sharpness of death?

(i) For ourselves.

(ii) For others.

10[40]

To 'turn our duties into doubts' — the weakness of the academic mind. We never believe any one thing strongly enough to lose consciousness of everything else.

10[41]

Schopenhauer asserts that death inspired philosophy.

It is more probable that poetry was inspired by death. The poetry & the mythology of the ancients are both taken up with the fear of death.

And why should we not fear death? To be tranquil in the face of death may be mere insensitiveness.

10[42]

'We see a man repent for his actions, and conclude that such actions should be avoided: an instance of false, but apparently irreproachable reasoning.'[25]

Alternative conclusions:

1. That to act & to repent are both valuable experiences — neither to be avoided, & certainly not the former on account of the latter.

2. Act, but never repent.

And either of these is better than the avoidance of actions merely because we know we shall repent for them.

---

[24] Oakeshott's note 'ibid., p. 131' may be to D.H. Lawrence, *The Lost Girl* (London: Martin Secker, 1920), notes on which appear on fos. 39–40.

[25] Oakeshott's note: 'L. Shestov, *All Things Are Possible, or, The Apotheosis of Groundlessness*, tr. S.S. Koteliansky (London: Martin Secker, 1920), p. 102.'

10[43]

Theological Studies

Religion, Christianity consists in problems — not in solutions. Or only in solutions in so far as these are restatements, reassessments of the problems.

But for so long has Christianity been concerned with the examination, the assertion & the exposition of solutions that we have forgotten what the problems are — we are even unaware that there are any.

Moreover, each new solution offered is not based upon, & does not spring from a sense & feeling of the problem, but merely upon & from the last or some previous solution.

The task always, & particularly now, is some restatement of the problems themselves. The greatness of the early fathers (some of them), of the greatest medieval theologians, of Luther & Melancthon, of the 17th century English Theologians was that they had not solutions before them, but problems. They began with problems, not mere solutions.

But it is impossible to restate problems unambiguously & freely unless we abandon altogether the language & the ideas of the traditional solutions. And this is not because these solutions are valueless, but because, whatever their value be, they must tend to obscure the problem itself.

What is required now is a free & unambiguous statement of the problems, which any & every solution has answered & must answer.

And these require restatement not because we have acquired new knowledge of ourselves & our world — that new knowledge may invalidate a solution that leaves the problem itself untouched. We must restate the problem because religion depends altogether for its vitality or a vivid consciousness of problems — & it is that which we have lost.

And also, not until we restate the problems shall we distinguish them from the solutions. e.g. sin is not a problem, it is a solution. God is not a problem, it is a solution. The current language of religion & of theology is quite inadequate for a restatement of problems.

10[45]

The old *'memento mori'* — & the new.[26]
The old — remember death because of what comes after it.
The new — remember death because it is the end.

10[46]

Sometimes the way back to a life of physical integrity, a life on the soil, undistracted by complicated, 'civilized' emotions, seems so much shorter & more

---

[26] Fos. 44–5 contain notes on Mrs Susannah Dobson, *Petrarch's View of Human Life* (London: John Stockdale, 1791).

inviting than the way forward to a higher order of consciousness. Both Rousseau & Tolstoy have felt its charm, & Tolstoy at least believed in it to the end. — To fly the world, to leave behind us all its complications, distractions, problems, pains, misery, & find a life of simple contentment in some distant spot of earth, cultivating one's own garden & living upon what one can produce for oneself. But there is so much that we must leave behind besides distraction & misery; & instead of leaving it we might perhaps to find a way of life which fosters & promotes that which we do not wish to & cannot leave behind. — friends, affections, art & poetry, & the fevers of love & hate.

How? Are we to pass an existence four fifths of which is the mere securing of the leisure to live?

10[47]

Death

'When you die the grass will grow on your grave, & that's all.'[27]

To become 'primitive,' to 'cease to be clever,' will that take the sting from death?

Death attracted Tolstoy under two aspects —

(i) When he was charged with the joy of living; death at the summit of consciousness.

(ii) When he was wearied by the strife of thought & desire — death the liberator.

What beauty can there be, if there be death?

Can Christianity overcome the sharpness of death? How?

10[49]

'There is nothing new in the fact that men have ceased to believe in the religion of their fathers.'[28]

But:

(i) Often when a generation thinks itself to have departed from the religion of its fathers it has done no such thing — e.g. Luther.

(ii) How far is this true of to-day?

(iii) What do the differences between the religion of a primitive community & a sophisticated man of to-day really amount to?

---

[27] Oakeshott's note: 'Tolstoy, *The Cossacks*, p. 129.' L. Tolstoy, *The Cossacks A Tale of the Caucasus in the Year 1852*, tr. N.H. Dole (New York: Thomas Y. Crowell & Co.).

[28] Oakeshott's note: 'W. Lippmann, *A Preface to Morals* (London: Allen & Unwin, 1929), p. 11.'

10[51]

'Progress—a visible & accelerated progress—is always a symptom of the end.'[29]

How could we take trouble about progress, or even believe in it, if we believed in death? Is not 'progress,' civilization etc: one answer to death? But how cogent an answer is it? And is it an answer, or merely an escape?

10[53]

The object—the sense of this life is to prepare for a future one—what argument have we against this? And in how many different forms is this believed?

How are we to achieve a rational scheme of life. To find the rules of moral life which (if any exist) correspond to rules of physical life, health. And to build up a scheme of life in accordance with these rules.

We must say more about death than merely that there is no use complaining about it—Dr Johnson—that it is a law of nature, that it is only individuals who die, the species lives on. We must moralize death. And that cannot be done except by giving it a place in the life of the individual. A philosophy of life must be a philosophy of death also.

10[54]

What is the attraction of suffering? That it is attractive, that it is often more attractive than what is called happiness, cannot be denied. It is a form of happiness, a form of satisfaction.

To be happy, to accomplish something, achievement—all this stands over against suffering, disappointment, sorrow. The satisfaction of sorrow is found in something other than achievement. And I think that its attraction & its <u>value</u> lies in this—that it directs our attention to an entirely different notion of life: otherworldliness: Epicureanism. It is only in the 'Epicurean' theory that suffering & disappointment can be seen to be positive goods—unless we believe in them as educative, & then they are only good as a <u>means</u>, not an end.

Goethe:—Christianity, the worship of sorrow—this is only another way of saying that Christianity is 'otherworldly,' is non-contributory.

10[56]

What is meant when it is said—

That few scholars accept the entire New Testament as authentic.[30]

---

29 Oakeshott's note: 'V. Soloviev, *War, Progress, and the End of History Including a Short Story of the Anti-Christ Three Discussions*, tr. A. Bakshy (London: University of London Press, 1915), p. 123.'

30 Fos. 55–6 contain notes on H.L. Mencken, *Treatise on the Gods* (London and New York: A.A. Knopf, 1930).

Or, that few of the elements of contemporary Christianity can be traced to its Founder?

The Renaissance was a bouleversement of all the principles of Christianity.

Christianity has rejected the ethical scheme propounded by Jesus.

E.g. the moral outlook of Jesus would for example have countenanced sexual intercourse, but not if it led to children. The <u>present</u>, but not the <u>future</u>.

10[57]

The intellectual life of the majority of men & women is cankered by a passion for indiscriminate knowledge. They not merely desert arguments for facts; they never enter upon argument at all. If a writer is to be popular he must pander to this taste. And the result has been the vast body of disconnected nonsense which is poured like an avalanche from our printing presses on every conceivable subject. Instead of considering the subject of religion, we are given numberless books on religious customs, rites, histories, anecdotes. Instead of love — we are given the histories of lovers. And this has penetrated even to our literature; it has indeed always infected literature; & most novelists are not less sinners in this respect than public lecturers. Some have escaped it; & their means of escape is by setting themselves to consider & master their own experience: In short, one has to become a poet or a philosopher to escape this disease. And neither poets or philosophers are loved of women or understood by men. Women, indeed, sometimes escape this disease — but rarely what are called educated women. For education with them has always been understood to require a stifling of oneself & ones own thoughts & feelings. Few women escape, but those who do escape usually escape more securely than men.

To be educated is to know how much one wishes to know & to have the courage not to be tempted beyond this limit.

10[58]

<u>Mortality</u>

I have sketched a view of life; I have tried to show it in as favourable a light as I can. But, besides those who will think it undesirable, a negation of all they have been taught to value, there will be some who will ask, is it possible? Is this pleasantness, this absolute aliveness, a possible state of mind? Or if possible for a time, does it take into account the fact that it will not be possible over a long life, or even throughout the life of a man who scarcely survives middle age?

And to this I must find some answer; for the whole tenor of my view is that it is in closer accord with the facts of human existence than other views, & certainly than the common view which is almost its opposite.

To the question, Is it possible for a long life? I answer, is a long life a sine qua non? Our length of life is not something absolute, much less something in itself good: it depends upon what we do with it. And a view of life which would make life impossible beyond middle age would not, for that reason, be discredited — except by those who embrace the naturalistic fallacy that what is, is good.

10[59]

To be cut off from communication with one's fellow creatures, from the sound of human voices, from the intercourse of minds & from love itself — is this to be cut off from everything, to be a prisoner?[31]

10[59–60]

Mortality

Dante met somewhere in hell a man whose crime was that he did not love the sweet light of day. It is the crime of our civilization. Instead of the sweetness of the present day, the light of today, we love what is gone or is to come. We despise all that is not productive, contributory: we do not understand what is simply for itself.

The consolation for defeat in this life that we get from the notion of a life hereafter. The doctrine that works alone are imperishable, cannot but breed despair in the hearts of the majority of men — for they have no works, or none which they would willingly see survive. We cannot live for the future. The doctrine of eternal works, the permanence of what is done & achieved. It is good enough for the few who create masterpieces; and we have built our view of the world to fit with these — but it cannot satisfy our hearts — we who have no talents, who leave nothing behind us. Some view must be found which explains those who are defeated, those who produce nothing.

We know well enough what it is to be defeated, unsuccessful: what is difficult is to understand the world from that standpoint. Many who are unsuccessful are not enough alive to despair; but some there are who are defeated & yet must find some way out. How are we to explain the attraction of lost causes? There are some men who will embrace any cause which is likely to fail; who are made for failure rather than success. What is the meaning of life to them? Mere activity? Or does their defeat refer merely to a part of their activity which to them is unimportant. They satisfy themselves — & that is enough, that is itself achievement.

Cf. the women's suffrage movement. No cause was more futile & misguided, & yet has given to people such satisfaction as this gave to the Pankhursts.

They lost themselves, & that is what we all desire.

---

[31] This passage is crossed out in the original.

10[60]

What will be our feeling about life when we come to die? — that is the test.

Shall we bear to die alone. If not we have misconceived life. But it is hard to die alone — harder than anything else.

What is it that would grace life & make death worth dying?

It is somehow to have lived an integrated life — to have integrity. But death is the last enemy — not because it comes at the end of life, but because it is the most difficult moment of life. If we could be convinced that we are, literally, 'full of immortality,' all would be well & death conquered. But instead, most convince themselves that immortality is 'to come,' & a few die with no sense of immortality at all.

10[61]

Anyone who is willing to die cannot feel himself entirely defeated. But for what reason willing to die? That is what matters. Mere disappointment & lassitude? It must be because we have understood death as a part of life. The business of life is the conquest of eternity, to master death. And often those have mastered death who think least about it. For we can master death only by a way of life which recognizes death. But most of those who do not frequently contemplate death have not mastered it — they have only thrust it aside for the moment.

10[61]

Show how the whole of our life & activity & achievement is just an attempt to master death. All religion, all philosophy, learning, science, business, poetry, literature, art, — everything we do or think or make. Love, the family, communities, the state.

10[61]

Besides gratitude, generosity also will go as a virtue. For generosity is essentially a feeling we have towards those whom we have little or no affection. When affection enters generosity becomes transformed. And in a life governed, dominated by affection, generosity can have no place.

Gratitude is a form of revenge — an attempt to re-establish oneself after one has suffered defeat.

People acquire no rights though gifts — but setting aside <u>rights</u>, is not a relationship inevitably set up, to refuse which we must refuse the gift, to accept which is to be grateful?

Gratitude — justice — compensation.

The 'Exchange' theory of life.

10[63]

Our eclectic culture —

*'Nous prenons tout ce que nous trouvons; ceci pour sa beauté, ceci pour sa commodité,
telle autre chose pour son antiquité, telle autre pour sa laideur même; en sorte que nous
ne vivons que de débris, comme si la fin du monde était proche.'*[32]

This ideal of culture will sometimes seize us with a sudden force, & the more
active our moods, the more certainly will it carry them away. We read, search,
pick up one book after another & life becomes a febrile pursuit of knowledge.

But culture is to know that there is much that one does not want to know.

No; if the end of the world were approaching we should, or we ought
logically, to abandon such a view of life & culture, & in order to prepare ourselves for the end, seek to establish the integrity of ourselves, but a vital
integrity.

Cp. the effect of:

(i) The early Christian doctrine of the end of the world.

(ii) The plague in Athens. Thucydides.
    Italy in Boccaccio.
    Rome. Lucretius.

(iii) *Zauberberg.*[33]

10[63]

We spend our lives trying to discover how to live, a perfect way of life, *sens de la
vie*. But we shall never find it. Life is the search for it; the successful life is that
which is given up to this search; & when we think we have found it, we are
farthest from it. Delude ourselves that we have found it, persuade ourselves that
here at least there is a point at which we can rest – and life has at once become
moribund. Just as to remain in love we must be continually falling in love, so to
remain living we must be continually striving to live.

10[64]

When we consider the accidents which may make an end to life, when we consider the thin thread of chance upon which the life of any one of us hangs – it is
impossible to believe that the purpose of life & its satisfaction is be found in the
production of some work, in achievement, in activity.

---

[32] Oakeshott's note: 'A. de Musset, *La confession d'un enfant du siècle*, 2 vols. (Paris: Félix
    Bonnaire, 1836), i.74.'
[33] Possibly a reference to T. Mann, *Der Zauberberg* [*The Magic Mountain*] (Berlin: S. Fischer
    Verlag, 1924).

10[64]

'When we are young the popular opinion sways us, & we are more solicitous to gain the esteem of others than of ourselves.'[34]

To be less anxious to gain the esteem of others than of ourselves – & here there is more often than not a contradiction. The esteem of the world is the death of the soul.

10[65]

The most & the least sensitive men will not be interested in what I have to say – they instinctively turn away from consecutive thought about the conditions of life – the most sensitive because they could not endure it; the least sensitive because the problem never presents itself to them. Both these classes engage in 'business' of one sort or another – it is their only course. It is we who live between who have no business but to consider life.

10[65]

I am no 'creator.'
   'I am he who dictates the values for a thousand years' – Zarathustra. But this is not a part I presume to play.

10[65]

Mihi ipse scripsi – for myself & one other. And yet since I cannot hope to persuade her, in the end it is for myself alone.

10[65]

Mortality

Most of us defend our ideas either as true or as our own. But in defending my ideas here against ideas which I take to be inimical to them, I do not surprise myself to be able to persuade any man of the truth of them. Poets alone can persuade us of the truths of such practical ideas of life as I am engaged in considering, and I do not pretend to be a poet. If I write to persuade anyone, it is myself. Every writer must preach to the converted for they alone will listen to what he has to say & understand it. And besides, as will become clear later on, were I to set out to persuade any man of the truth of my views, I should, in the very act, have abandoned the root idea I am anxious to elucidate. So then, my purpose is not to persuade, and it is extremely unlikely that I shall persuade.

---

[34] Oakeshott's note: 'St Évremond, *Letters.*' Possibly *Letters Supposed to have passed Between M. De St. Évremond and Mr. Waller*, ed. J. Langhorne, 2 vols. (London: T. Becket and P.A. de Hondt, 1769).

I have, then, no gospel which will make the Gospel forgotten. If I preach it is to persuade myself. It is not my ambition to dictate to the future the way of life it shall follow. All I have wished is to think out for myself a way of life, to make it clear to myself, so that I <u>must</u> follow it. And if it should not commend itself to anyone else, I shall not be shaken or disturbed on that account.

10[66–67]

The immense advantage it is to be free from extraneous interests. This alone allows a man to produce work which is homogenous, strong, relevant, & which will last.

But, if we reject the whole view of life which looks for the criterion of life in the production of such work, we do not require to reject also the benefits to be had from this freedom from extraneous interests, indeed we cannot reject them. For, on this other view of life, the production of such work is itself an extraneous interest of which we must free ourselves. It requires no less singleness of purpose, no less concentration of effort, no less discipline, to achieve a homogenous way of living, than to produce a homogenous piece of work. And if we are to embrace this view of life & follow it out to the end, life can be integrate, single, satisfying only when we have freed ourselves from the temptation to produce, to achieve, to accomplish anything whatsoever save an integrated life.

But, it will be replied, is it not possible, is it not, indeed, a universal experience, that an homogenous life, integrated and satisfying, can be achieved only by turning our attention elsewhere, by concentrating upon some definite & specific piece of work? Is not such a life as you desire to achieve always a <u>by-product</u> of the other kind of life, of 'the worlds' kind of life?

(i) It is certain that most who concentrate upon achievement miss life. If life is a byproduct of achievement, then it is certainly not a necessary byproduct.

(ii) And why should we suppose that life is the one thing in the world which can be satisfied by paying no attention to it, by neglecting it, by refusing to think of it? Everything else, we know, requires direct & specific effort, for what reason, save mere prejudice, is life itself excepted? Is it reasonable to expect that life can be lived in any conditions? And if there are conditions which promote life, shall we not seek them out; if there are conditions which are inimical to life, shall we not avoid them?

And some will say, 'My work, I know, is not my life; I do not pretend to stake my life upon contributing something to science or to history.'
What then is it?
It is an escape from life. And if we are determined not to escape from life, shall we not abandon this way of living? And if you say, 'I do it for my own satisfaction,' then you have already in principle abandoned the criterion which judges a work by what it actually achieves.

To how many of us is what we do an escape from living—the explorer, the scholar, the businessman, the soldier, the priest.

10[69]

I have wished to keep from my book the marks of those struggles, doubts, periods of waiting, experiments etc. by which I have reached the opinions I have expressed.

10[69]

Mortality

I want to consider the conduct of life. Our first business is, I suppose, to live, & the second to understand life. First easier than the second. But not to be divorced. I want to consider life in order to understand it, & to understand it in order to live it.

It is often thought that the defects of our way of living arose not so much from our ignorance as from the inferiority of our will. We know what we ought to do, but fail to do it. But this, I think, misrepresents our position. It is ignorance, it is the failure to think out & have clearly before us a view of life & a view of how such a life is to be achieved which stands in our way. For, I believe that if we saw clearly what it is we want we should find our flaccid wills replaced by a strong & steady purpose.

What I have to say might have been written in the form of an autobiography. I might have recounted the process by which I passed through a belief in these different views of the purpose & condition of life. But that would be too personal. And I have chosen instead to turn this story of my life into a more coherent account of the views of life which come before any man who thinks & the reasons which may persuade him to adopt one & reject the others.

10[71]

Nietzsche attacked Christianity not on the side of its myths, but its morality—& the ground of his attack was the conviction that Christian morality was contradictory of biological necessity or development. Here, then, is the crudest of naturalisms. It is the strength, not the weakness, of Christian morality that it does not pretend to promote what is biologically 'better.'

10[72]

The world of La Rochefoucauld & the world of Nietzsche—the former simpler, less elaborate, more complete & unified. The latter more individual, tentative; its data more extensive, <u>historical</u> attitude, more diffuse & less concentrated.

Less thought & more knowledge.

The advantages of less knowledge.

Nietzsche is more complete; but less effective.[35]

10[72]

Why is it more worthy for an old man, who feels his powers decline, to await his slow exhaustion & extinction than with full consciousness to set a limit to his life? And, if it be said that it is not necessarily more worthy, but it is anti-social, & that society must discourage it—why, again?

10[73]

Simonides advised his contemporaries to look upon life as a game; earnestness was too well known to them as pain.

10[75]

Criticism of the Epicurean view that we should live in the present.

So far as avoiding the future is concerned it is possible & fits the facts.

But the past we cannot escape. We can escape neither from our past selves, nor from the fact that having failed at one point in our lives, we can never have another opportunity.

10[75]

Suicide has not become universal. Why? Not because men have considered the conditions of life & found them tolerable. Very few have considered them at all.

The uselessness of suicide:—

For we only contemplate it, most of us, when the moment for it has passed. Death should come at the highest, not the lowest moment—& few, when at their highest moments, see clearly enough to kill themselves. And when the moment when suicide would have made life complete has passed, there seems no more point in killing oneself than in living on.

10[77]

Mortality

Perhaps, in the end, all I have done is to find reasons for what I believe by instinct.

Fundamentally I am quietist & indolent. And though I followed for some years an ideal of universal knowledge, I could not follow it for ever. The vanity of it, as of everything else, could not be excluded from my mind. What I write here, then, is merely a kind of justification of my temperament. If I wrote it to persuade others, I should be guilty of self-contradiction: I write it to persuade myself, & because no man can be said to be master of himself until he has made himself clear to himself.

---

[35] Oakeshott's note: 'cp. Nietzsche, *Human, all too Human*, §178'.

10[79]

Mortality

How then, shall we employ ourselves? What employment is there which will not distract us from this purpose to be without a purpose, this accomplishment to achieve nothing? No employment can save us. But cookery is better than most. Here is an art which can employ all that a man has of intellect & taste & ingenuity & invention. And yet he is still free: undogged by the past, whether failures or successes. Each day is new; each creation a thing of the moment & then gone. Perfect but fleeting. Here, if anywhere is the art which may be practised for art's sake: the contemporary life.

10[80]

D.H. Lawrence, *Fantasia of the Unconscious*.[36]

Compare all this, so like & yet so unlike the conventional view, with the Epicurean & the 'Christian' view.

Views:

(i) Sexual act is subsidiary to the procreation of children; to make children, to carry on the species—this is the work of woman; man may do something else besides.

(ii) Sexual act is parallel to the other activities of life: not the only activity. Subsidiary, but not subsidiary to procreation of children, but of works of art & the conquest of nature & knowledge.

(iii) Sexual act is not subsidiary to anything. It is an end in itself. A form, the most intense form of being, of being alive. Not for any ulterior purpose, but simply for the purpose of being alive.

10[82]

I want to consider, to write about, life from the standpoint of death. Death is the greatest, the all-pervading fact of life; if we can understand death, all our questions about life are answered already. Here then, in these meditations upon mortality & upon death, is all that I have come to think about life & living.

---

[36] Oakeshott's note: 'D.H. Lawrence, *Fantasia of the Unconscious* (New York: Thomas Seltzer, 1922), pp. 14, 96–7.'

10[82]

What is the meaning of the 'Christian' myth—derived from Genesis & expounded by Paul,—that God created not death, but the sin of man created it?[37]

There is a truth behind this—it is a 'true myth.' Death is the creation of a certain view of life—of sin. When there is no sin, death has no sting. And where there is no 'mortality,' there is no sin. But, somehow, death must be defeated, abolished without abolishing the moral world. And this is what Christianity offered—an abolition of death which did not entail the abolition of an ordered life.

10[82–83]

What is a 'Natural Death'?

(i) There is no 'normal' manner of dying.
   Anything may produce death. There are no accidents.
   We must first abolish this distinction between 'natural' & 'accidental.'

(ii) Natural death is not merely death which is <u>not procured</u>, because many die naturally as a result of some voluntary action.

(iii) Natural death is merely death which is not, as such, procured. If we bring about our own death by some action designed expressly for that purpose, our death is <u>unnatural</u>. A premeditated death, & a procured death is unnatural.

So, then, 'Natural death' has behind it the notion not of nature, but of providence. It implies the idea of a 'time' which is set. And 'natural death' means any death which is governed entirely by this providence (or chance or fatality). But:

(i) If natural Death is 'providential' luck—are we independent of this, are we stronger than God? And if not, how is any death unnatural.

(ii) If we await our destiny, anything that happens is our destiny & no death is unnatural.

(iii) So natural death can mean only death which is governed by <u>chance</u> alone.

And why should we deliver up to the hands of chance that event of our life which is the most momentous?
   Men have done this because, not knowing what comes after death they have shrunk from the responsibility of procuring their death. Just as the Athenians chose their governors by lot. But what Plato says to the Athenians, he says to us? Why leave it to chance? We may make mistakes, but surely that is better than allowing chance to make them. And if once we determined to decide for our-

---

37   Oakeshott's note 'Cp. Donne, *Devotions*, p. 97' may refer to J. Donne, *Devotions With Two Sermons 1. On the Deceease of Lady Danvers Mother of George Herbert 2. Deaths Duel – His Own Funeral Sermon* (London: William Pickering, 1860).

selves we should reflect upon the matter, & might, in time, achieve some wisdom which would guide us.

10[86]

'I suppose now you have come to see that the coming generation is the most important.'

No! No! No! This is a devastating, nihilist, doctrine. It cuts the roots of life, it saps vitality. Indeed, it is so far a denial of moral (as against merely natural) life, that even those who profess it most unreservedly never really believe it, & certainly do not act upon it. And yet how often it is professed. Posterity, the future, children, the coming generation — these are the gods: & they are gods which demand & are daily accorded the most loathsome of human sacrifices — the sacrifice of the mind & the soul — the sacrifice of the self itself.

10[87]

To assume complete responsibility for one's life is itself a life work — enough to occupy a man's whole energy & ingenuity. A man may engage upon all kinds of work besides this, but it will never be more than a mere by-product of his life. It breeds, also, a kind of spectator attitude to life.

Cp. the general attitude to life of the 'I' in *The White Peacock*.[38] Without profession, without work, engaged upon the complete assumption of responsibility for his own life.[39]

10[87]

It is difficult to be certain anything has been alive until it is dead. That is why the transitory seems so much more alive than the permanent & lasting.

10[89]

The owning of property has become boring to us — we want to be free from its incumbrances. And this is the first sign of life. And it is not merely property itself which disgusts us; it is the whole 'property attitude' to things. We want to experience, & ownership stands in the way of free experience. It is extraneous, it diverts our attention from what we want. It may be true that ownership need not stand in the way of experience; but the fact is that for us it does. It is permanent, settled, continuous; while experience is fleeting, momentary & dies with its death. Property exists when dead: experience perishes & disappears at the same moment — like the body of Alexander.

---

[38] Fo. 87 contains notes on D.H. Lawrence, *The White Peacock* (London: William Heinemann, 1911).

[39] Oakeshott's note: 'Cp. Birkin in D.H. Lawrence, *Women in Love* (London: Martin Secker, 1921).'

10[89–90]

How many 'causes' have I not adhered to in the belief that here was something enchanting, dangerous, liberating & something in which one could lose oneself? In the flush of youth I believed in socialism, because I thought it would be thrilling. I did not hate injustice, I merely wanted to escape from an existence without a purpose. Now I believe in love – & for the same reason. And by love I mean the adventure of a relationship which knows no bounds. Love is the greatest 'cause'. It is so much fuller & more satisfying than any other that it seems to be in an entirely different category. But love also is the most dangerous – unless you are content to be a mere Casanova.

10[91]

To sustain a heart against a world's reproof.

10[91]

To live, not as others think it proper that we should live, but as we think fit to live ourselves.

10[91]

Most of us have, at best, but a fitful hold on life; and our hold on death is no more sure.

10[91]

No experience is perfect & complete: to know this & to understand it, to accept this as life's loveliest grace is to have understood & to have accepted, & to have overcome death.

10[A]

'Truth conquers with itself.'[40]
    Epictetus.[41]
& for all I know he wrote better than he knew.

10[B]

Some problems in the life of Jesus.[42]

(i) Problems of interpretation of the New Testament & Gospels.

---

[40] On a loose sheet inserted at the front of Notebook 10.

[41] Oakeshott's note: 'G. Long (ed.), *The Discourses of Epictetus; with the Encheiridion and Fragments. Translated, with Notes, a Life of Epictetus, and a View of his Philosophy* (London: George Bell and Sons, 1890), p. 414.'

[42] On a loose sheet inserted at the front of Notebook 10.

(ii) Consider whether it is safe to base any belief upon the position that <u>any</u> of the sayings attributed to Jesus are his own. Do not necessarily disbelieve that <u>some</u> may be his own. But if it is not more than merely probable that any are his, should we base any belief on the position that they are 'his words.'

(iii) Supposing they are his words; what then? What authority? What meaning?

10[C]

Theological Studies[43]

The Historical Element in Christianity.

It is contended that if Christianity as a religion be really independent of the truth of certain historical facts, then it should remain unimpaired if we were to believe in the Christ-myth theory etc.[44] But:

(i) Consider how far a belief in historical facts does really enter into the Christianity of the majority of ordinary believers.

(ii) It is one thing to say – 'Suppose these events never happened'
And quite another to say –
   'These events happened, but it is not because they happened that I believe in the principles which have been attached to them.'

The distinction required is similar to the distinction between a psychological description of mental processes & a logical examination of the validity of the products of those processes. What we say is that history enters into the first, but not into the second when it is abstracted from the first.

---

43   On a loose sheet inserted at the front of Notebook 10.

44   Oakeshott's note: 'E.g. A.E. Taylor, *Faith of a Moralist Gifford Lectures Delivered in the University of St Andrews, 1926–28*, 2 vols. (London: Macmillan and Co., Limited), v. 2.' Oakeshott also noted 'Sorley, *J.T.S*,' but no article by W.R. Sorley in the *Journal of Theological Studies* has been traced. Oakeshott may have had in mind W.R. Sorley, 'Does Religion Need A Philosophy?,' *Hibbert Journal*, 11 (1913), 563–78.

Belle Dame Notebook 1 (1928–1929)

BD1[08]

Sometimes asked myself why this ideal should appear always in the form of a woman. Besides the appeal of sex; the feeling that here is the true life of the 'otherworld,' free from the cares & anxieties, fears & inhibitions of life as I have known it & transformed into its perfect self.[2]

BD1[10]

Solitude—divorce from the actual security of your desires actualized—induces life as a world of imagination, peopled by shadowy, ideal forms; memories assume an incredible value and importance.

BD1[10]

Beauty is what all men seek; some men so little that they are unconscious of the desire, some so passionately that they give up their whole lives to the pursuit.

BD1[12]

This desire to live a contemporary life, to live in the present. The hitch, the desire to escape from the present—into the personal past of youth. Perhaps the main temptation of the present generation to irreligion is this desire to retain a state of existence—youth—& not to move from it. It is a religious irreligion because this state desired is a vital state, & it desires the past, not for its own sake, but for the sake of its lost vitality.

BD1[13]

Some writers have attempted to give an expression of their actual feelings experiences as they come to them; the flood of sensation, the dizzy abyss of love, the quality of being outside time & space which belongs to union with the beloved — this I dare not attempt. Instead I choose to offer a mere description of these experiences as they seem to have been caught up in my character & become myself.

BD1[14]

What is age?—When the past & the future alike rule us.

---

[1]   LSE 20/1. Soft cover, black, 15.5 cm x 10 cm, squared. Recto folios numbered 1-22. Autograph, ink and pencil. Dated: '1928-1929 / Michael Oakeshott.' First page headed: 'La Belle Dame Sans Merci.'

[2]   Oakeshott's note: 'Cp. paper on "Religion & the World",' presumably a reference to M. Oakeshott, 'Religion and the World' (1929), in Religion, Politics and the Moral Life, ed. T. Fuller (New Haven, CT, and London: Yale University Press, 1993), pp. 27-38.

What is youth? — When all is present.

BD1[14–15]

<u>On Control</u>. — Early I learnt that I had to deny myself much in order to win what I most wanted. Sometimes forbid myself to touch, to speak, even to see her. Cp. Ulysses bound to the mast. Sometimes I have gone too far, grabbed & lost all. But in the end I learnt to look upon this as not a negative & difficult control, but as a positive condition of life, like

Cp. Aristotle — a pleasure, free activity; settled character — ease.

But that did not still my desire, or give rest to my longing. — <u>That</u> continued unabated.

BD1[15]

The feeling that my life began, began again with her — The days when I had not known her cease to exist.

BD1[15]

When one is in love one wishes above all to have her of whom one dreams aware that one dreams, but reason & common sense say what they like to the contrary. Yet I have hardly dared to provoke affection; she seemed a flower that to prick was to kill; & to lure her out of her own mysterious & charming world was like picking a wood flower to decorate a room.

BD1[16]

The excitement, which comes with the first word spoken in a relationship long secretly sustained, which concentrates all the past in the single moment of the present.

BD1[16]

Sometimes it seemed a kind of <u>hubris</u> to look at her, which would call down the swift revenge of jealous gods. And to defy the gods, the course always the most fascinating, in this case had no charm — for to defy them, though it might mean the winning of honour, the making of a self, would also mean the end of all possibility of seeing her again. So I dare not look, dare not touch, dare nothing save melt with longing.

BD1[16]

Not conscious of a specific change of affections, or change of object for affection. They were forms of one beauty, modes of one existence; and with each step I seemed to have reached a fuller & more perfect form. The sensation was of unity, of the one; not of the changing many.[3]

BD1[17]

1929. Ideas for a poem – The Spring is late: Persephone, as she leaves the underworld, is clutched at by Pluto – who is moved for once by genuine love of her beauty – but, because he could not really sustain it, her garment comes away in his hand & Persephone appears on earth, though delayed, more resplendent than ever before, because naked.

BD1[19]

Arranging my books & thinking all the while how Céline will like to look through them & her happiness in finding this or that. Putting those in front which I know will delight her.

BD1[20]

The <u>first</u> experience has a directness which is never repeated; but it has also an inadequacy which may be improved upon.

BD1[20]

The garden of Merton Lodge as a symbol of the unattainable life & beauty.

BD1[20]

Search for the faintest sign of response; desire to be kissed even greater than the desire to kiss. 'The knowledge of the lips' is true knowledge.

BD1[21]

Striving to get away from our past – an impossible task, yet 'life' is nothing else but this. The past – like a tattoo mark – which is ineradicable & brands us as a sailor whatever walk of life we may follow. Our effort to escape is like a fine spray of water, directed at a mark which, no sooner does it start on its way, than the wind dissipates it, & all is lost.

Cp. how certain words, expressions, gestures remind one of the past; likeness seen in the street to people & events I wished to forget.

---

3   Oakeshott's note: 'Cp. Plato, Bosanquet, p. 118. Shelley's translation.' 'Shelley's translation' may refer to P.B. Shelley, *The Banquet of Plato and Other Pieces Translated and Original* (London, Paris, New York, and Melbourne: Cassell & Company, Limited, 1887), which includes a translation of Plato's 'Symposium.'

BD1[21]

As I sat listening to them singing this song which I used to love & now hated, the whole burden of my past came upon me with such insistence that I cried out. How, how to get rid of it, how shall I form a contemporary life; how shall I throw off what ties me to what is no longer me? How can we live when each movement of mind & body is governed by a maniac inheritance? How one 'form' of *La Belle Dame* becomes intolerable, gradually, until at last we are forced to fly from it. Some will fly too early, some not at all; he understands life best who understands best the moment to fly.

BD1[21]

From one point of view life is but an illustration, in the form & the language of sense, of an 'eternal law' — 'So on our heels a fresh perfection treads' — but it is, I think, more than merely that.[4] To me, at least, it is more. For the so-called form & language of sense has a closeness & immediacy denied to all else, and when we dig down to it, there will be few of us who will not discover that the root of this 'eternal law' is not for them a root of sense — 'first in <u>beauty</u>.' This, at all events, if not our completest experience of the 'law', is our closest & most immediate experience.

---

[4]   John Keats, *Hyperion*, Bk II ll. 212–14: 'So on our heels a fresh perfection treads, / a power more strong in beauty, born of us / And fated to excel us.'

Belle Dame Notebook 2
(1929–January 1930)

BD2[01]

There is no burial for the past; different forms simply fade out of our lives.[2]

BD2[02]

As when we emerge from thought & seem to hear the clock striking, but when we look at our watches we find that it has struck five minutes ago just as we were losing ourselves in thought. A sort of delayed reminiscence which retains its sensual character long after the real moment of experience is past.

BD2[02]

What we love is a projection of ourselves, an ideal, something we imagine & then attach to somebody & persuade ourselves that we have discovered & not made it.

BD2[03]

Like someone who had read Jane Austen at school, but years after takes up *Emma* to find that she has grown along with him, & he has the uncanny feeling that he is pursued by a character which he can never outgrow.

BD2[03]

Note <u>how</u> the figure of *La Belle Dame* grows. The first vision — unconscious, unrealized — many later ones, & then the first fruit. Like a tree which blossoms for five seasons & then in the sixth bears fruit.

Cp. Proust on first hearing a piece of music. — *A l'ombre.*[3]

BD2[04]

No impression is wasted; & it requires many to produce a recognizable result.

---

[1] LSE 20/1. Soft cover, black, 13.5 cm x 8 cm. Ruled. Unnumbered. Autograph, ink and pencil. Title page: 'M. Oakeshott / 1929–Jan. 1930 / Gonville & Caius College / Cambridge. / *Die Schau sucht du, und was sie stellt* / When me they fly, I am the wings.'
   This notebook includes notes in German on Nietzsche, *Also sprach Zarathustra*, at fos. 24–5.

[2] Oakeshott's note: 'Cp. Arrian, vii.27. Rydberg. On Hadrian.' 'Arrian' may refer to *The Anabasis of Alexander*, tr. Chinnock, Bk VII ch. xxvii; 'Rydberg' may refer to Viktor Rydberg, *Roman Days*, tr. A.C. Clark (London: Sampson Low, Marston, Searle & Rivington, 1879).

[3] See M. Proust, *A l'ombre des jeunes filles en fleurs* (Paris: Editions de la nouvelle revue française, 1920), p. 95.

BD2[07]

Our anger when we are reminded of our past selves. We have no love for these selves: how, then, should we love the correlative world in which they lived — their attachments & their loves?

BD2[07]

Pangs of unwarranted emotion, unreasonable anxieties & anticipations, an unaccountable sense of expectation, suppressed excitement, violent disappoint-ments & jealousies, a trivial conversation becoming disproportionately signifi-cant, an absence absurdly disappointing, a report absurdly disquieting.

BD2[08]

An emotional experience is uncapturable at the moment of being intensely experienced. To be conscious of it & to master it as a whole we must wait for a later time. This 'second-experience' is as real & is certainly more lasting than the 'first.' In fact an experience is never complete until the second has been achieved.

BD2[09]

This intense attraction we call love lasts, in its intensity, for so short a time & is followed so frequently by a revulsion of feeling that we wonder whether it is worth all the attention we give it. Is it real? If the intensity could be permanent all would be well. If it is fleeting, what is its value? Cp. Keats' odes — the pro-gress from a passion for dead permanence to an understanding of living perma-nence in change. Identity — not mere absence of difference.

BD2[10]

The conversation of lovers hides a seething current of emotion. We talk of any-thing, say everything — but what we mean & are thinking.
　　Talk of sex often hides physical desire.

BD2[10]

What is the bliss of love? It is the bliss of annihilation — love is a foretaste of death. In the moment of love one loses the burden of consciousness, & tastes beforehand the pleasure of extinction, & when it is other the taste of individual existence is bitter.

BD2[15]

We fall in love with abstractions; like the coarse minds who distinguish only the dominant theme of an orchestral piece & have no ear for what is going on under-neath. What we are looking for is a whole person — any complete self, if only we could find it, would be oneself. But we succeed in flitting between abstractions.

BD2[17]

Accessibility & inaccessibility; the open & the hidden; laughter & tears; tenderness & passion — love deals with contraries & unites them.

BD2[20]

There is no difference between friendship & love between men & women.

BD2[26-27]

Can we be in love with more than one person at once — not at the same moment, but yet not successively so that one has finally gone?

We are on no surer ground than in the presence of an 'old flame' who has, for some reason or another, lost her charm for us.

BD2[27]

I distinguish clearly enough between those whom I am attracted to by appearance — almost an exclusively aesthetic attraction, & those with whom I am in love; but do I distinguish between those whose company I like & desire, whose conversation & mind attracts me, & those with whom I am in love?

BD2[30]

What I hate is to feel that the first sudden moment of love & its first wild response is gone for ever — there can never be a 'first' again, only a 'second' & a 'third.' And how I envy those whose first is still before them, & those, above all, who have it now!

BD2[30-31]

Apart from anyone for whom you have special affection, would you rather be in the company of those who have an obvious feeling of affection for you, or those who show no such feeling? Whose conversation is the most living? I do not mean of course, anyone whose affection is demonstrative.

BD2[33-34]

The remoteness of the faces which I passed in the street, the unapproachableness of those whose lives I longed to share, became for me a kind of symbol of the inaccessibility of all beauty, the heedlessness of the universe, the silence which answered all questioning, the blankness which met all desire.

BD2[34]

Whenever we feel ourselves to be less ourselves by living than by dying, suicide is not self-murder, but merely self-homicide.

BD2[34]

Incredulity at finding grief supportable.

BD2[36]

The imaginative importance of women. Men have always been willing to submerge the practical importance of women in the imaginative. We never look at them for themselves, but always in order to create from them a richer imaginative life for ourselves. Man the egoist.

BD2[36]

The <u>stimulus</u> of women. The fertilizing power of contact with women – in their natural difference of opinion.

BD2[37]

Sexual feeling towards men. Delight in physical characteristics. All the unreasonable intensities of love of women; the desire for companionship, disappointment in not meeting him where we expected him, delight at unexpected meeting, schemes for meeting, confusion at meeting, delight of touch, the sound of voice. Willingness to forgo everything for this companionship. Desire to penetrate that world which is his. Desire to spend onself & one's substance unreasonably on his behalf. – Martin Lloyd.

BD2[37]

How civilized life prevents the full expression of emotion – their intensity must always be veiled. Only when the emotions are reciprocated in intensity is an expression of them unaccompanied with discomfort, disharmony, absurdity.

BD2[39]

Distinguish the aesthetic and the sexual.

BD2[40]

The moments when love seems to wear the appearance of hate.

BD2[42]

Living in the belief of the imminence of the golden age; and then, one day, waking up to find eternity in the <u>Now</u>, the continuous present, the extemporary contemporary life.

Desire for spring always; until Autumn is revealed as Spring.

BD2[43]

The hypersensitiveness for youth. When I go into a room-full of men, my eye seeks out those who are the young—destined never to grow old, immortal & untouched by the hand of age. And among women I seek also those that live in an eternal spring-time of life.

BD2[45]

Is love some dull 'Evergreen'? And if it be not; shall it not fade with fading spring; hither with summer's heat & winter's frost?

Love is a Lent lily which must die before Easter.

BD2[47]

It is the unity in multiplicity of affection that satisfies our desires—but where can we find that for more than a moment? It must be intense, it must be conscious—but if it be these it cannot last.

BD2[47]

The lover like Prometheus—having stolen the fire, he must suffer unremitting pain. There is no release.

BD2[47]

The gloom of deep love: the Muses themselves approach it with a timid step.

Sappho, 'Ode to Anastasia.'

Landor, *Pericles & Aspasia*.[4]

BD2[48–49]

Love & the complete indifference to other people which comes with it. The others disappear: we abandon ourselves completely, reputation, position, ambition—everything to love. And if we do not—then we do not love.

The difficulty of loving like this. Moral considerations. Perhaps to abandon, to forget this person, who loves us but whom we do not love, will mean her death—she will sink back into a kind of dumb despair, the feeling of failure & inferiority will sweep over her & drown her soul. And yet, when love is elsewhere, what are we to do.

If it were real love elsewhere there might be no problem—all would disappear in face of it. But our moral nature clings to us & will not allow us that free flight into the life of love.

---

4   Oakeshott's note: 'W.S. Landor, *Pericles and Aspasia* (Boston: Roberts Bros, 1871), p. 41.'

BD2[49]

The feeling & desire of death in love. And the incongruity of it when looked at from the outside.[5]

BD2[51]

The woman's gift of making a world of her own wherever she is.

BD2[51]

The faithfulness, freeness & audacity of women. Absence of cynicism or scepticism.

BD2[51]

Is it simply a craving for intimacy? Or is intimacy something which kills itself. Is there perfect intimacy?

The charm & satisfaction of an intimacy which is not intimate — reserve, privacy, individuality.

---

5   Oakeshott's note: 'Cp. Virginia Woolf, *Mrs Dalloway* (L. & V. Woolf, 1925), p. 54.'

Belle Dame Notebook 3
(January–June 1930)

BD3[02–03]

Is there no progress? Is it just a passage from one vision to another? Are there no illusions destroyed so that they can never live again? Or must we be content with the dull monotony of a gallery of characters?

BD3[04]

Greece. The ideal & perfect age & civilization. Greek = perfect. What Greece means to us. Each of us endows Greece with the virtues which we desire to see flowering in the present. It has become almost a technical phrase (cp. Gothic = crude, vulgar). The imaginative value of Greece & ancient Greek civilization to subsequent ages — not dependent on detailed knowledge.[2]

BD3[05–06]

Shelley's 'Alastor.' The story of the poet who seeks ever what he finds to be unattainable, & when he finds it so, & because — dies.

Solitude = unsatisfied desire, homelessness.

See Shelley's 'Preface' to the Poem.

The Vision of the Desired comes in sleep — a dream vision, & the poet asks 'Does the dark gate of death / Conduct to thy mysterious paradise, / O sleep?'

Cp. 'Hymn to Intellectual Beauty.' Where the 'unseen power' is still sought in vain.

And *Epipsychidion*, where the poet finds an at least momentary satisfaction.[3]

---

[1] LSE 20/1. Soft cover, black, 13.5 cm x 8 cm. Ruled. Recto folios numbered 1–53. Autograph, ink and pencil. Dated: 'M. Oakeshott / Gonville & Caius College / Cambridge / Jan. 1930 / to June 1930.'

   This notebook includes quotations in German from the fragments of Novalis at fo. 40: see for example '*Fragmente über Ethisches, Philosophisches, und Wissentschaftliches*,' in *Sämmtliche Werke*, 3 vols. (Florence and Leipzig: Eugene Diederichs, 1898), iii.157.

[2] Oakeshott's note: 'Cp. Woolf, *Jacob's Room*.' Virginia Woolf, *Jacob's Room* (L. & V. Woolf, 1922).

[3] Percy Bysshe Shelley, 'Alastor, or the Spirit of Solitude,' in *Alastor; or, The Spirit of Solitude: and Other Poems* (London: Baldwin, Craddock & Joy and Carpenter & Son, 1816), pp. 1–49; 'Hymn to Intellectual Beauty,' in *Rosalind and Helen, A Modern Eclogue, with Other Poems* (London: C. and J. Ollier, 1819), pp. 87–91; *Epipsychidion Verses Addressed To The Noble And Unfortunate Lady Emila V___ Now Imprisoned in The Convent of ___* (London: C. and J. Ollier, 1821).

BD3[07]

How much of the beauty of the world is bound up with desire? Sometimes desire seems to stand in the way, & we say 'What beauty there would be on every hand if we did not kill it with desire.' But could we see it if we did not desire? Is desire the eye by which we see beauty?

BD3[07]

'Black laughter' — The African girl in the forest. The idea of there — far from civilization — making a home & living, free from the world, with her for the rest of one's life.

BD3[08]

The feeling — after a parting or some shattering disappointment or failure — of leading a <u>posthumous</u> life. And how this life turns into our true life.[4]

BD3[09]

'Remove sight, association & contact & the passion of love is at an end.'
  Epicurus, Fragment XVIII.

But why remove them?

BD3[09]

'Solitude is a certain condition of a helpless man.'[5]

The craving to be alone: & to be alone & yet not alone is to have grown, to have extended our being & our world.

BD3[10]

The abstractions we fall in love with are not always qualities. Sometimes they are features. We know nothing of this girl but her eyes, of this but her lips, of this her hair.

BD3[11]

De Quincey's Ann, whom he loved & lost & for whose face he looked into the face of women as long as he lived.

BD3[13]

Self-sympathy — sympathy with a past self — is rarer than sympathy with others. Sympathy of our age with our youth.

---

4 Oakeshott's note: 'Cp. Keats, *Letters*.'
5 See Long, *Discourses of Epictetus*, p. 228.

BD3[21]

Do not drink of the cup of love that holds far more of bitter than of sweet — but we may escape love only by escaping life itself.

BD3[22]

Women who loved strangers and were deserted.

Jason forsook Medea; Theseus forsook Ariadne & Dido died for love of Aeneas.

Men are always strangers — seeking *La Belle Dame*, finding her nowhere, they leave behind them a trail of suffering.

BD3[22]

The pleasure of love is brief, its sorrow very long; and when we suffer its sorrow we wonder at ourselves for desiring its pleasure.

BD3[23]

To throw all the stages & problems of life — its development & decay — into a metaphor of love. Love & sex being the most universal expression of these problems.

Cp. <u>Donne & Eliot</u>, & the way they give to the experience of love a new expression, freeing it from the associations of the past by using a new language.

BD3[23-24]

The sense of physical decay & the <u>intimations</u> of mortality, of death, of age in youth — passing semen, & the feeling of weakness following copulation.

Can the despair, which accompanies these experiences, be overcome — can we reach the state of mind of Keats' 'Ode to Autumn.'

BD3[25-26]

The value Montaigne places upon youth. Considers himself old at 40. Looks back with longing to the 'state full of lust, of prime & mirth.'

'The last fruit of health is voluptuousness.'

He likens old age to a state of small health & hates it because it imposes upon us a moderation which he refuses to call wisdom.

BD3[26]

Don Quixote. The story is played out in the lives of each of us. At the expense of Don Quixote, Sancho Panzo grows in each of us & comes to dominate us.

BD3[27]

As we go on knocking at the door of a house we now know to be empty, because the mind is unable to grasp at once the situation, because we do not know what to do next.

BD3[28]

The times when we cannot keep pace with the desires that arise in us, & cannot distinguish them.

BD3[29]

Effort to get free from my past. First sought that freedom in marriage, but did not find it. Found myself still tied & bound. Some more radical escape must be found, because it is not mere freedom from a past that I desired, but freedom from a past that had never been mine, freedom from a frozen environment. To break free & be myself above all things.

BD3[29]

How to free myself from the necessity of keeping up the myth that I have not changed, that I have not changed, that I am what I was or what I appear to be — the necessity of appearing to be what I was — or never was.

BD3[34–35]

This is to be a history of myself — & a history of mankind in so far as I recapitulate that history in myself. The period of extreme youth & the loves & desire of that time. The period of early youth, & its loves & desires.

Then the shadow-line — which must somehow be crossed, but not without pain & disenchantment. The books that this period has produced — Housman, *Shropshire Lad*.

And what beyond this line? That I do not know; is it to be a kind of devitalized, posthumous life, — a posthumous life like we feel ourselves to be living after every great parting only more acute, & this time permanent?

Or is it to be a *vita nuova*? That is almost impossible to believe, for we seem to be leaving behind all that is worth calling life. Is it a mere death-in-life?

BD3[36]

The great metaphors for life.
Love — D.H. Lawrence.
The Sea — Conrad. Melville.
Desert — Doughty.[6]

---

[6] C.M. Doughty, *Travels in Arabia Deserta*, 2 vols. (Cambridge: Cambridge University Press, 1888).

BD3[39]

Feeling that, if youth is not already passed, at any rate part of it is gone, and life can only be reformed by reforming what is already behind – which is imposs-ible. And to determine to live in the future in such a way as to cause no regrets avails nothing. That, indeed, is not impossible to accomplish, but it does nothing to still the frantic & vain regrets for what is gone. For it is myself which mislived the past, & a new self can never throw off that incubus – for it can never be entirely <u>new</u>.

BD3[39]

'Innocence' if lost can never be regained.[7] Anything else can be regained – but not this. And in so far as this appears what is most worth having, to lose it will appear least worth enduring.

But we may lose it before we know what it is, & find we have lost life. But have we? To believe this, is it not to be out of touch with life & its conditions?[8]

BD3[41–42]

Gifts as a kind of sublimation of affection. How I feel with Céline – I must find something to give her every time I see her. A kind of assertion of affection. And a feeling that I owe so much to her that I must be constantly giving in order not to be receiving. But is not 'giving & receiving' an inadequate antithesis – what we really experience is a <u>single</u> experience of giving & receiving at once – 'inter-course.' And perhaps this constant assertion of affection is unpleasant for her? And yet she knows how to take a gift so as to make it not 'giving & receiving' but 'intercourse.'

BD3[42]

The flattest of all lives is fighting for an attainable end. Despair is perhaps the last & greatest of all emotional experiences – Death. If it were abolished? And we no longer lived in fear of it. Death is a part of life – the most vital part.

BD3[43]

The girls who are unusually gifted in love; they are unable to do without it, they live for love – & they love greatly, passionately & without reserve, forethought or anxiety. The mistresses of revolutionaries. They understand everything with-out knowing anything. Every problem springs from their senses, & every doubt is stilled by their senses. Men are children to them.

---

7 Oakeshott's note: 'Innocence in *Romersholm*.' H. Ibsen, *Romersholm: Schauspiel in vier Auszugen* (Leipzig, Reclam, n.d. [1886?]).

8 Oakeshott's note 'Cf. James Thompson' may refer to James Thompson (1700–48), Scottish poet.

BD3[44–45]

May 16. 1930

Preparing lunch for Céline; waiting, watching from the window. And she not coming. Gradual realization of the groundlessness of my expectation as I laid the lunch. Waiting. And, then like a ship becalmed, sails flapping. The narcissi turned to ashes & the lilac to dust. Their scent no longer sweet, & poetry itself sour on my lips. The whole world about my ears because she did not come — when I had no reason to expect her. Waiting for her all the afternoon.

The incredibility of her not coming.

And the whole thing as a kind of symbol of the pursuit of *La Belle Dame*.

BD3[47]

Love and drunkenness cannot be concealed.

BD3[48]

Feeling that everyone who is not in love is in prison; feeling of freedom, of the emancipation from all the difficulties of life, the worries which the faces I pass in the street speak of.

BD3[48]

'A complicated love.' The future unknown, the present almost intolerable whether because of joy or despair.

BD3[49]

Love & friendship. If friendship is what knows no crisis, no waxing & waning of passion, no intense despair or hopeless joy — is it possible between men & women?

BD3[49]

We are not blind to her faults — we adore them.

BD3[50]

The adventure of that knight-errant, who thinking himself happy in the arms of a celestial nymph, found that he was the miserable slave of an infernal hag.

BD3[51]

Death rather than disillusion; death rather than the realization that what has been cannot be again or can no longer be. And why? Because, after all, the alternative is death of a more deadly sort — a living death.

BD3[51]

Parts of *La Belle Dame* to be written as dialogues, or a little play — a situation. Parts in verse. Parts in the form of reflections, parts as incidents in prose.

BD3[52]

Stories of women who disappear on the day when they are to be married.[9]

BD3[53]

Nature drives us to other living embraces; it cannot satisfy, it only urges us to what can satisfy.

In love there is both life and death.

BD3[53]

The five degrees of love —

Visus, colloquium, convictus, oscula, tactus. Lucian.

Sight, conversation, association, kisses, touch.

But sometimes — *non oculi sed mens videt*.[10] — Men & women fall in love with what they have never seen, only imagined or heard of. Is this not universally true?

---

[9] Oakeshott's note: 'Cp. Philostratus, *Apollonius*, IV.' This section of Philostratus contains several stories about marriage: see *The Life of Apollonius*, Bk IV chs xi, xxv, and xlv.

[10] Oakeshott appears to have been reading R. Burton, *The Anatomy of Melancholy*, 3 vols. (London: George Bell and Sons, 1904 [1621]), iii.72–3, where the Latin words *visus, colloquium, convictus, oscula, tactus* (ascribed to Lucian) and the phrase *non oculi sed mens videt* all occur.

BD4[01]

What is one more to one who has so many lovers offering her their devotion? If I ask something in return, she may not, perhaps cannot, give it. And, if I ask nothing, I am scarcely in love. The knowledge that she has lovers enough makes me feel — not hopeless, fainthearted — but an intruder. Were she to choose me all would be well, but if I choose her I am become a nuisance. And yet she may be waiting for me to 'choose' her.

BD4[01]

Why not be Epicurean — & seek not possessions but enjoyment? But without seeking possession we must seek more than a mere *cras amat*. I do not desire to possess, but there is no enjoyment without reciprocation — only desire & despair.

BD4[04]

You love like a woman — longing to be compromised, desiring only to spend, to give, to commit yourself without committing him — you love like Heloise.

BD4[07]

C. as the archetype — appearing & reappearing through the book, & on each appearance changed & glorified. Each time I meet her she has grown & means more than she meant before.

BD4[07]

She came to me like the wind which stirs in the trees after a thunderstorm, and touched my disconsolate leaves to life once more, bending me like a willow tree is bent in summer, and whispering as the wind whispers.

---

[1] LSE 20/1. Soft cover, dark green, metal ring binding, 12 cm x 8 cm. Squared. Recto folios numbered 1–34. Autograph, ink. Dated: 'M. Oakeshott / Gonville & Caius College / Cambridge. / June 1930.–Dec. 1930.'
    Other works from which Oakeshott made excerpts in this notebook but which are not mentioned in the text include: Fo. 25, G. Komai, *Fuji from Hampstead Heath* (London: W. Collins Sons & Co., 1925); 30–1, Sir A.R. Fraser, *Rose Anstey* (London: Jonathan Cape, 1930); 34, L. Tolstoy, *Childhood Boyhood and Youth*, tr. C.J. Hogarth (London and Toronto: J.M. Dent & Sons Ltd; New York, E.P. Dutton & Co., 1912).

BD4[08–09]

Jealousy & selfishness in love — Jealousy is usually considered a gross perversion of love. But there is a desire for exclusiveness, a desire to hide that which we love & to keep it to ourselves which is not purely selfish & it applies equally to a person or a thing that we love — a person or a place, a book, a piece of music, a play etc.: — It is the feeling that the person which other people will see in her whom we love is not the person we love & we fear being reminded of this. It appears to us a kind of sacrilege for something we love to be misunderstood & we feel unable to expose it wantonly to the possibility of being misunderstood. We cannot, in consequence, tell some people of the books we like, we hide them from them when they visit us, we lie about the delight a place has given us — we do all we can to cover up our real feelings — we will even go to the length of saying that we dislike that which has enchanted us & hate that which we love. — It is 'saying what we mean' — for what we mean is that all this is too precious to us for us to allow it to be misunderstood or perverted.

BD4[10]

How difficult it is to throw off a past of love. To have loved once is to leave behind one a past we shall not easily shake off. Something will remind us of her: a likeness seen in the street; the step of someone who walks for an instant in front of us; — and the whole past becomes alive once more, there is a resurrection of what was buried but never dead. We may even hate what we have loved, but if we have ever loved we shall never be entirely free from the possibility of those intense moments coming to life again — past selves haunt us like our shadows & who shall run the race with his shadow?

BD4[11–12]

The experience of complete newness, unbelievable freshness — which must be the feeling at the back of the notion of being born again. To walk abroad in the fields at dawn, to see the dew on the grass, to see virgin & untrodden snow in the dawn of a frosty day, to dress after a bathe & feel one's skin tight beneath one's clothes, to rise from one's bed refreshed and made new from intercourse with a lover — these all give that sensation of new birth which is one of the most precious life offers. It is to be had also in art, where the artist passes the scene through his mind and it becomes new & almost incredible to us. And in thought, when we dig & dig & come, at last, upon a beginning which clothes the whole argument with radiance. It is, perhaps, this sensation of newness which we get when we hear or see anything for the first time, & that is why the first time can never be repeated or replaced, no matter what depth of delight future & prolonged intercourse may bring. To live a life of these first sensations is the dream of every artist, the redemption of the world.

BD4[12]

The elements—earth, air & water, these will always remain the elements, so far as life is concerned, no matter what they are resolved into by science. They, in themselves, offer a complete life. To lie & let the earth <u>know</u> you—carnally; to leap & let the air <u>know</u> you—carnally; to swim & let the water <u>know</u> you—carnally. To <u>give</u> oneself to the elements. It is all sex; & sex is nothing but this.

BD4[13]

There is a love to which happiness belongs & harmony—when to be in each other's company is unbroken satisfaction.

And there is a love which a woman may have for a man who is cruel to her, who is hard, relentless, selfish, destructive; or what a man may have or a woman who is selfish. This love, in its essence, is the greater. And where it exists without these circumstances, where happiness is not denied but is not necessary, the greatest of all love exists. For the first love thrives on submission & domination, thrives on half-men & half-women. And the second, though it is a war, offers something more complete & less servile.

BD4[14]

That Southern preoccupation with the relations of men & women & the most important relations of life; the delight in love & in seeing a woman enveloped in the spell of a man, or a man abandoning himself to a woman—& all this is denied, fled from by the 'moderate' English.

BD4[15]

She had reached that brief period in her life which it is possible only to describe as a time of blossom. When to wake in the morning is to feel an inrush of sensetions, grave & gay; and to sleep at night is to be lapped with dreams as real to us as our waking moments. Every sense is alive, every moment a moment of intensest life. Soon it is over—with most it is over before they have realized its possibilities. And life dies away to its summer.

BD4[16]

Oh! If only I knew what I wanted! I lie back in my chair, & my mind is filled with flitting desires which will not, cannot blend. I pass from one to another, but without hope either of fulfilment or of release. My mind is a picture without a design; a chaos of warring desires. I know what I want. I want freedom. But since I can only grope for freedom blindly, not recognizing it when it appears, passing it closely but ignorantly by, I cannot be said to know what I want. I want merely all that I have not got—& until that is become more explicit, how can I find any release or any fulfilment? My life seems to be filled with duties which I do not recognize but I follow, with a weary round of frustration. Nothing I have do I want; everything I lack I desire. Oh! That I could recognize something I long for among the things that I have!

BD4[18]

That drying up of enthusiasm, that listless refusal of interest, that closing up of the whole self, shutting the doors of sympathy & understanding which the presence brings of one we have once loved but now no longer love. Here, here if anywhere in the universe is death – a contradiction of all that life means & should realize. This shutting of the self will take place always in the presence of people to whom we cannot show ourselves – to parents, to blood-relations & to the world – but nothing can equal the bitterness, the completeness of that closure when the cause of it is the one to whom we have shown all – to a lover.

BD4[19]

Moments of real happiness are very few – to awake from a conversation & to find oneself united with another mind, to lie with a woman one loves & lose oneself to her – these perhaps are the happiest moments. And how few! Happiness is somehow a combination of solitude & society; of society which belongs so much to ourselves that it is solitude; of solitude which is so magnificently and variously peopled that it is a society. Happiness is to possess one self, not the narrow self which we can possess by flying the world, but the real self which we can possess only by becoming the world. Happiness is to be with '*La Belle Dame Sans Merci*' – & that no man may do.[2]

BD4[20]

'How amazing are those moments when we really possess our possessions.'[3]

Never to understand what one has <u>escaped</u> in an unrequited affection – that is the secret character of youth.

BD4[23]

Those days, moments even, when we feel that life was made for them only, is complete in them, and to repeat, to go on, is to enter an imperfect world once more, to return from completeness to incompleteness.

But to try and live one's whole life for the sake of such moments? What then? An intensity it is impossible to sustain. Life then must be divided & the great part becomes a living death – a posthumous life, wretched & meaningless. And our days are spent seeking an opportunity to rekindle the fire; clutching at every

---

[2] Oakeshott's note: 'Cp. D.H. Lawrence, *The Plumed Serpent*, on closing up the gap between men and women.'

[3] Oakeshott's note: 'L.P. Smith, *Afterthoughts* (London: Archibald Constable & Co., 1931).' For Oakeshott's review see *SW*, iii.73–5.

relationship which appears to have the seeds of blossom in it — & suffering always disappointment.

BD4[24]

The necessity of suffering loss before our eyes are opened to what we really desire & really seek; the growth of estrangement — the mistaken desire for merely another love — the revelation that what we desire is ourselves completed.[4]

BD4[26]

La Belle Dame, like some lovely, inaccessible Geisha.

BD4[28]

It was as if a fire, long laid, had been lighted.

BD4[28]

'Death will annihilate love. Love is neither deep nor sweet, if it does not know this, and the kindness of it.'[5]

We speak of love & the Absolute. But love is a wild war of finite personalities. There is nothing absolute in it. It is, indeed, the closest to reality we can get; but it is too full of contradictions to last. It also must lose its life to gain it.

BD4[29]

'To Jean's Breasts'

> Loose now thy dress, dear Jean,
> And loose thy honey hair,
> And let those breasts be seen,
> That grow and blossom there.
> And let me lay my head,
> Where it has longed to lie,
> In that narcissus-bed.

BD4[32]

The morbid longing to recover an innocence which every human relationship seems to contaminate, & a liberty which every human attachment seems to restrict.

---

[4]   Oakeshott's note: 'P. Romanov, *Without Cherry Blossom and Other Stories*, tr. L. Zarine (London: Ernest Benn, 1930), p. 182.'

[5]   Oakeshott's note: 'Sir A.R. Fraser, *Flower Phantoms* (London: Jonathan Cape, 1926).'

BD4[32–33]

To love without limit, to abandon oneself completely & demand from oneself everything — this seems to be the least that love can & must be. For it appears the only hope of bliss, the only possibility of peace. But to follow such a purpose as this, to follow it seriously & without reserve, appears to involve me in so much misery & misunderstanding, so many impossible positions, so many inextricable contradictions — for to achieve it is, <u>at once</u>, to have found it unsatisfying. Somehow we must learn how 'to shun the heaven which leads men to this hell.' A heaven which leads to a hell is a mistaken heaven, an ideal which <u>must</u> perish when it is attained is no ideal. And yet how inviting, how impossibly attractive, is this vision of love!

Belle Dame Notebook 5
(December 1930–April 1931)

BD5[02–04]

Literature has always left out a part of 'life.' The 'life' of literature has always been an abstraction. Attempts have, indeed, been made to alter all that: but the result has been 'realism,' 'representationism' that is, the negation of art.

But exactly <u>what</u> has been left out—that has often changed. A large body of writers in the 18th & 19th Centuries left out everything that was obviously physical. But against this there has recently been a revolt. But the revolutionaries, no less than their predecessors, deal with abstractions—at least, those among them who know their business do so.

D.H. Lawrence, for example, does not abstract the non-physical, he abstracts from life what appears to him the most important part of life. His people follow no calling or trade, they are not concerned to eat & drink, they make no money—but they <u>live</u>. We hear little or nothing of their professions—much of their loves, their feelings, their desires, hopes & fears. His schoolmistresses do not teach, his miners do not mine. His 'world,' in short, is an 'other-world.'

But what is the result when we attempt to <u>live</u> such a life—when we count this world well lost for love, when we ignore our profession or neglect our career? Is it mere foolishness, an attempt to reduce life to art, no less preposterous than the attempt to reduce art to life? Or what? It is this 'life' which I live; the other, how little it means; how small is the actual sum of attention I give it.

BD5[07]

Sex as predominant in life—a sexless life being a living death.

Sexual activity comprising the symbol & the actuality of life. Age & impotence—death. The man who follows this to the end: in age & impotence turns to homosexuality: a eunuch.

---

1   LSE 20/1. Soft cover, blue, metal ring binding, 10.5 cm x 6.5 cm. Squared. Unnumbered. Autograph, ink and pencil. Dated: 'M. Oakeshott / December 1930 / to / April 1931.'

Other works from which Oakeshott made excerpts in this notebook but which are not mentioned in the text include: Fos. 8–9, Lady Murasaki, *The Sacred Tree: Being the Second Part of the 'Tale of Genji,'* tr. A. Waley (London: Allen & Unwin, 1927); 18–19, Lady Murasaki, *A Wreath of Cloud; Being the Third Part of 'The Tale of Genji,'* tr. A. Waley (London: Allen & Unwin, 1927); 36, notes in French on François de la Rochefoucauld, *Réflexions ou sentences et maximes morales* (Paris: Claude Barbin, 1665).

BD5[10–11]

The point in the course of each love affair in which any prolonged separation or lack of news produces the imagination of death. This imagination grows; until it almost begins to dominate the actual presence of she whom I love. So that when she is present I begin to imagine what life would be were she dead, to picture to myself the waste of life, the desert of existence without her, & to imagine by what philosophy, by what access of courage or insensitiveness I could go on living at all.

This somehow heightened with C., because I know that she has been near to dying, & carries about with her some of the seeds of death.

Should I have heard from her sister had she died? Or will her death leave only a silence which will never break until I break it?

BD5[12]

When we try to invade the integrity of those with whom we are passionately in love, when we attempt to tear away the inaccessibility with which she seems to be clothed, do we not merely exchange a life full of contemplative delights, for one of torture, disenchantment & despair?

And, even so, is not this torture happiness & this despair inseparable from all love?

BD5[13]

Like a comet, flashing its fiery way through space, & caught by the charms of the sun & lured from its path, lured even into the solar system & there held prisoner.

BD5[13]

As if some comet, passing close to our world, were to absorb the azote from our air & leave us an atmosphere so rich in oxygen that life would end in a few hours of delusions, intoxication & happiness — a happiness impossible to imagine, for it would be shared by all alike.

BD5[14]

As if his lost light were restored to Jupiter by some cosmic crash, & we, lighted by two suns, should enjoy continuous day.

BD5[14]

As if the thin crust of the earth's surface had become suddenly too thin to contain & shield us from the incandescent world beneath, which, breaking through, swallowed us instantly in a white-hot death, too sudden to be feared, too immense to be imagined, too tremendous to be enjoyed.

BD5[15]

Life as the beloved: the love of life, fear, hate, jealousy, despair, neglect, coldness, passion; the sexual relationship with life.

To abandon her is to abandon oneself. Suicide. To be abandoned by life.

BD5[17]

To have time for the things we really enjoy — flowers, autumn leaves, the sky, all those day-to-day changes & wonders that a single year brings forth.

Each person has his 'season.'

BD5[18]

The feeling that happiness is to be found only in the society of a few indispensable friends.

BD5[19]

How, when we become acquainted with some lovely creature, we imagine ourselves spending hours of enchanted bliss, not with her, but with someone in every respect exactly like her.

BD5[20]

Love begins with the assertion of a personality, an unsatisfied desire; it leads to the abandonment of that personality, but at the same time it assumes the continuous existence of the personality.

In love we seek to lose ourselves in another: but ourselves & the other must always remain distinct.

BD5[21–22]

We read in intimate letters & autobiographies of the remorse & torture suffered in later life by men who have spent their youth, or a period of it, in violence & fornication, lawless living, drunkenness, even murder — we read of such remorse in the *Confessions* of Tolstoy, for example. But what of the more subtle remorse, felt by a man who looks back upon an almost unconscious youth — years, which can never recover, passed in blindness, deafness, & inconsequence? And such years, not less than those spent in violence & lawlessness, carry their effects into later life. Perhaps we married during those years, or chose our profession, or undertook some obligation which still binds us. And we are not less lost & haunted than if our youth had been an orgy of excesses — indeed, we are more lost, more subject to a fruitless quenchless remorse than the greatest sinner imaginable.

BD5[22]

The envy of the old who have no harvest of youth for the young who have merely a harvest of wild oats.

BD5[23]

The old doctrine — live in such a way as to make you always fit for death. But this does not explain death; or put it in its place. It puts it outside life & makes life conform to this external principle.

BD5[27]

The construction of a scene or a conversation in advance. How everything falls into its place. Whatever is said is understood. But when we come to the scene itself; — all is different. That which we had planned to do & to say cannot be done or said. The person who we have met is not the person we have imagined: for she whom we imagined was a dream — was ourselves.

This takes place to a lesser extent when persons are not concerned. The actual accomplishment or experience falls short of what we had imagined.

BD5[28]

The sleeplessness of love cannot be compared with that of jealousy or disappointment.

SC[01]

Secularism = seeking human improvement by material means alone.
Morality based solely on the well-being of mankind in the present life.

SC[02]

'Kingdom' = an exclusive territory. This is misleading. 'Kingdom' = a rule, a way
of life, not a locus of life.

SC[02]

Christianity spiritual, not temporal. This not true of primitive Christianity: it was
temporal in the sense of belonging to the next age.

SC[03]

The world—'the lust of the flesh & the pride of life'—who is John writing to?[2]
Not Jesus—this is a new conception of the world—not temporal, but moral.
Foreign to the Jewish use. Church at Ephesus?

SC[03]

What is life without what one desires?

SC[03]

What is the forbidden world?

SC[03]

Something must be said about the nature of God = what we desire.
& Nature of Religion = the desire of communion with what we desire; God.[3]

SC[04]

Secularism. Taken to mean a love of the finite world & all that goes with it for its
own sake. The material world. But the love of this 'world'—material things,
wealth etc: is not anti-religious because these things are material in the moral
sense (but because they are material in the physical sense—mere abstractions)
but because attachment to them involves a belief in progress, setting our hopes
upon the future, & not satisfying them in the present—Evolution.

---

1   LSE 2/4/5. Soft cover, blue, exercise book, 22 cm x 14 cm. Ruled. Unnumbered.
Autograph, ink and pencil. Title page: 'SECULARISM.', undated.
2   Oakeshott's note: '1 John 2:15–17.'
3   Oakeshott's note: 'See 'D' Society Paper on "Deity."'

SC[04]

The idea of the Separation of Christians from the world most developed in 4th Gospel.[4]

SC[04]

Effect of abandoning the belief of the immediate *parousia*. Development of church organization. Drawing together of the church & the world. More settled character of Christian society — children etc.[5]

SC[04]

'The world' is not 'the secular power' for that is a pure abstraction and exists nowhere.

SC[05]

<u>Christianity & Civilization</u>

The only world we have is <u>this</u> world, & it is the only Christian world — to separate a part of it off & call it Christian, is to condemn religion to imprisonment in abstraction, & to make Christianity a fiction.[6]

SC[05]

'The chief rival to Christianity is secularism.'[7]

If we knew what secularism is, we should know what Christianity is & vice versa.

So in considering this subject, we may hope to get some clearer view of what <u>both</u> are: we shall be clear on the one only by being clear on the other. We shall not see the whole of religion by contrasting it with the 'world'; but an important aspect of it.

SC[05]

Do not imagine that this is an easy gospel with little to renounce & less to adhere to. There is plenty to renounce — & it is what we often value most; what is most ingrained in our senescent way of life.

---

4   Oakeshott's note: 'W. Hobhouse, *The Church and the World in Idea and in History Eight Lectures Preached Before the University of Oxford in the year 1909 on the Foundation of the Late Rev. John Bampton, M.A., Canon of Salisbury* (London: Macmillan and Co., Limited, 1910), p. 22.'

5   Oakeshott's note: 'Hobhouse, *The Church*, p. 364.'

6   Oakeshott's note: 'See end of "Religion and the Moral Life," in *Religion, Politics and the Moral Life*, pp. 39–45'.

7   Oakeshott's note: 'W.R. Inge, *Outspoken Essays* (London: Longmans, Green, and Co., 1919), p. 33.'

SC[06]

To stumble at the entrance of life.

SC[06]

Humanity

But it is humanity which dies.

Much modern 'humanism' is the worship of this perishing humanity. Show difference between humanism and otherworldliness.

SC[06]

There is no <u>other</u> world.[8]

SC[06]

Clogging Anglo-Saxon prosperity.

SC[06]

The danger of a derivative, non-contemporary life.[9]

SC[06]

The view of the Last Judgment which goes with 'humanism' — cumulative; not automatic.

SC[07]

Morality & the World

Ecclesiasticism always conservative.

Religion always revolutionary.

SC[08]

There is nothing secular except sin. Yet what is sin? It was the old view that there was nothing sinful except secularity & we get no further by transposing the proposition. E.g. To dance was sin & it was 'worldly.'[10]

---

8   Oakeshott's note: 'Nietzsche, *Zarathustra*, p. 9.'
9   Oakeshott's note: 'See Conrad, *Lord Jim*.'
10   Oakeshott's note: 'Goethe, *Faust*, 279.'

SC[09]

Religion to the Greek was made at home in his world.[11] Not the 'natural' world only, but society. 'The religion of the Greeks was the presupposition and bond of their political life.'[12]

Christianity cut itself off from the normal life of the 'the world' at the beginning for reasons of history (the end of the age), later for reasons of morality (evil & good), but I do not think it inherent in its nature to be so cut off, or to be cut off in exactly these ways.

The new synthesis of Christianity with civilization — which is a <u>fact</u> however little we recognize it — will not mean the destruction of Christianity. It is an illusion that it has ever been so cut off. Yet a fatal illusion, for it has bred a solitary theology which knows nothing of the learning of its contemporaries, & an abstract 'religion' knowing nothing of the life of its contemporaries.

SC[10]

'The Christian is that within us that is <u>not</u> ourselves but Christ in us.'[13]

Cp. the desire for <u>another</u> society, different, separate — the Kingdom of Heaven wholly separated from what we now know.

A discontinuous personality & universe, the aloofness of religion from the world is regarded as mere religious indigence.

God is something whole, complete in itself, a contrast to the world.

SC[10–11]

Introduction

§1. I wish to try & carry an old subject a little further than it has been carried. No originality: desire to speak for the present. '*Il faut être absolument moderne.*'[14] Limitations of the view from this standpoint. But it may help.

I can see, also, that whatever I say about religion & the world will involve views on many other subjects — Nature of religion, future life, kingdom of heaven, etc. — but while I cannot avoid these implications, I must avoid them in so far as they have immediate bearing on the subject in hand — This shows us how intimately related are all the topics of a theology. Our ideas in one affect those on another, & we are constructing a whole theology every time we build up our ideas on one topic.

---

11   Oakeshott's note: 'Lowes Dickinson, p. 4 sq.' See G. Lowes Dickinson, *The Greek View of Life*, 5th edn (London: Methuen & Co., 1906).
12   Oakeshott's note: 'Dickinson, *The Greek View of Life*, p. 11.'
13   Oakeshott's note: 'Barth, p. 273.' Possibly K. Barth, *The Christian Life*, tr. S.J. McNab (London: Student Christian Movement Press, 1930).
14   See A. Rimbaud, *Une saison en enfer* (Brussells: M.-J. Poot et compagnie, 1873), 'Adieu,' and cp. p. 293, below.

See 'D' Society papers.

§2. Two facts stand out.

(i) Religion implies some standing over against.

(ii) The particular standing over against which we are told it implies today does not satisfy us!

SC[11]

Why all the fuss & pother about Christianity, why cannot we let the thing go, as others have done before?

 Because it is an illusion that we can let it go. It is our civilization, our world & environment, our selves. We cannot escape it. We deny part of it only on the assumption of another part. It is the 'medium' through which all else reaches us & in which all else is embedded. It is that — & more. If Christianity were for us escapable, we should long ago have escaped from it.

SC[11]

Historicism & cosmopolitanism — worldliness

We listen to other people instead of thinking for ourselves. We appropriate but do not enjoy or use, we watch other people & forget that without action life perishes.

SC[11]

Moral notion of worldliness — i.e. matter = evil etc. Not Jewish & primitive Christian; Eastern in origin & only percolated gradually into medieval Christianity.

SC[12]

Distinguish my religion from humanism — progress.

SC[12]

It may be said that this 'world' is a very academic temptation — one which has little here for the ordinary man — & yet is it so? Show how our whole life is usually governed by this 'world' & its conventions — how when courage departs it swallows us up, when energy dies, it offers us rest, when sincerity is abandoned, it rules us, it is the attitude which we of the West naturally assume unless we assume any other.

SC[13]

'The characteristic feature of the age was not irreligion (the term would be too strong) but the religious indifference of the masses.'[15]

It is clear that the 'religion' opposed to this secularism is Puritanism, & not religion, & consequently this secularism is not that which opposes religion.

SC[13]

'Living like gypsies a life ignorant alike of permanence & stability, living, so speak, not on the products of civilization but upon the slender fruits of nature.'

The Early Christians literally 'temporized.'

SC[14]

We easily recognize the rights of other personalities & deplore the tragedies which result from tampering with them.[16]

But what of the results of tampering with our own?

SC[14]

The notion of <u>posterity</u>. When we speak of such & such an age, or such & such a people or person not contributing to civilization, we speak in an irreligious or non-religious manner. Cp. Inge on progress.

SC[14]

'Pot-hunting' is <u>the world</u>.

SC[14]

Whatever we say about <u>the world</u>, implies an idea of God; & just as everyone has his idea of God, so every man has his view of what the world is which stands over against God.

SC[14]

The doctrine of the world must necessarily be largely negative – for <u>the world is</u> what is to be negatived, denied, despised, escaped.

---

15 Oakeshott's note: 'Halévy, p. 380.' Possibly a reference to E. Halévy, *History of the English People in the Nineteenth Century*, tr. E.I Watkin, 6 vols. (London: Ernest Benn Ltd., 1931–2), but the quotation has not been traced.

16 Oakeshott's note: 'Cp. Hebbel.' Possibly Christian Friedrich Hebbel (1813–63), German poet and dramatist.

SC[15]

This is not a worship of what is transient—this passing sub-lunar life—it is an attachment to what is eternal—for what is actually achieved, enjoyed, won is eternal because it belongs neither to the past nor to the future but to a permanent present, a present at least as permanent as ourselves.[17]

SC[15]

Becoming as little children

Capacity of children for living in the present, so that life in company with them has neither hopes nor regrets. It is the life of the birds.

SC[15]

Living in the present—the difference between mere inconsequent flitting from one occupation indifferently pursued to the next as lazily followed—the present for the sake of the present—& the present for the sake of life, for the sake of freedom.

SC[16]

This is not a purely emotional religion—no religion which is wholly connected with a whole man is merely emotional, though of course it is personal in the fullest sense.

SC[16]

Secularism is on all hands acclaimed the enemy which religion in England today has most to fear, but I have seen little consideration of the question what that secularism really is? Conventional view usually assumed.[18]

SC[17]

Religion is always the highest which any individual or society knows. What matters is not so much whether it is better or worse, more primitive or more developed—for these are things which do not occur to the religious man—but whether it is the highest, whether it does actually make him at home in his world. And in order for religion to do this it must change—in order to remain the same it must change.

---

[17] Oakeshott's note: 'Atkins, p. 104 top.' Not traced.
[18] Oakeshott's note: 'Cp. Halévy.'

SC[18]

If the world is what the middle ages thought it does not stand over against our higher self absolutely. Always a conflict of which we can never permanently rid ourselves.

Cp. Keats on 'the world' & retirement from the world.[19]

It gives us two souls—M. Arnold, *Faust.* Our conception of the world must be something which will not dissipate our energies or divide our powers.

SC[18]

Religion makes us at home in <u>this</u> world, <u>this</u> life: & this may not mean that it will make us at home anywhere else. It is conditioned by <u>this</u> life.

E.g. an Englishman is not at home in China. And a cosmopolitan is at home nowhere.

SC[18]

<u>Eternal life</u>—the religious life—where the extemporary & the contemporary meet & are one.

SC[19]

<u>Integrity</u>

Whole secret of true education lies in the avoidance of this dichotomy or division of the child's self…So that the child grows up a single self.

SC[26]

Preface.
Primitive Christianity.
Medieval Christianity. ⎫
Modern Christianity. ⎭ More or less. See Hutton.[20]

Yet we are not satisfied with that: a religion which is the mere denial of that is nothing to us.

Examine the nature of the religion opposite to this—it is an abstraction—the soul.

So then we must start again.

But will we be producing <u>Christianity</u> in this way?

Two changes so far—why not a third?

---

[19] Oakeshott's note: 'in *Spirit of Man.*' Robert Bridges (ed.), *The Spirit of Man An Anthology in English & French from the Philosophers & Poets made by the Poet Laureate in 1915 & dedicated by gracious permission to His Majesty The King* (London, New York, Bombay, Calcutta and Madras: Longmans Green & Co, 1916), contains a section on 'Retirement' and selections from a number of poems by John Keats.

[20] Possibly Richard Holt Hutton (1826–97), journalist and religious writer.

Christianity as this given—this is impossible. There is no given save the whole.

BD6[03]

To those whose life is spent in love, death is a sweet sleep, passions consummation. Love & death explain one another: apart, life is without meaning.

BD6[05]

To be in love with love is to be in love with 'wandering shadows.' To be in love
is to have found 'the shadow of stability.'

BD6[07–08]

22/4/31

Like everyone else, I find myself full of contradictions. For example: how much I
desire to dominate those with whom I come into contact, how brutally do I wish
to deprive them of themselves, eat them up & include them in myself altogether
– & on the other hand, how little can I justify to myself this desire, how foreign
it is to some of my moods & all my principles. Like some others, also, I try to
resolve these contradictions, I try to curb what I dislike in myself, which (of
course) is not always, perhaps ever, what other people dislike or what the world
dislikes – this is no attempt at moral reformation. But, at the expense of one
impulse I try to develop another which I like better. Others, however, attempt no
such work upon themselves. Either their impulses are so strong that it were vain
to attempt it, or having attempted it, they have found themselves to fail so constantly that they have abandoned it altogether. D.H. Lawrence, for example,
again & again shows himself not as a unity of resolved contradictions, but as a
seething mass of unresolved contradictions, impulses which deny one another,
desires which oppose one another. This may be 'honesty,' an attempt to give us
himself as he is, or it may be mere inability to give to himself a unity in which
these contradictions are resolved, simply evidence of the overmastering strength
of his impulses. But, in any case, why should we attempt to unify our selves?
What is it bids us balance our impulses against one another? The man who
knows himself best, knows that, even if he has spent the greater part of his life in

---

[1] LSE 20/1. Soft cover, dark green, metal ring binding, 13.5 cm x 9 cm. Squared.
   Unnumbered. Autograph, ink. Dated: 'Michael Oakeshott / March 1931.–June 1931.'
     Other works from which Oakeshott made excerpts in this notebook but which are
   not mentioned in the text include: Fo. 1, notes in French on la Rochefoucauld, *Réflexions ou sentences et maximes morales*; 29, 32, notes in French on A. de Vigny, *Journal d'un
   poète*, ed. L. Ratisbonne (Paris: Michel Lévy frères, 1867); 33, quotations in French from
   de Musset, *La confession*.

this attempt, he has succeeded only because his impulses have with age became less insistent or he has failed altogether.

BD6[09]

23/4/31

Love is the most selfish thing on earth. How we imagine the beloved to be set about with enemies — that we may protect her. Ill, that we may nurse her; poor, that we may spend for her; unhappy, that we may comfort her; slighted, that we may fight for her; lonely, that we may be a comrade to her. In short, unsatisfied, — that we may love her.

BD6[09]

How, when we are in love, the ordinary business of life seems to go on independently of ourselves, or at times is merely transformed into material for our imaginations. Everything is referred to her whom we love, every letter we open we expect to be hers, every footstep, every knock at the door, the sound of every voice. She becomes the world, & the world is well lost in her.

BD6[11]

Must it fail? Is it absolutely impossible to find a relationship with another which satisfies? Must we always & inevitably & not merely by chance or incompetence — fall short of unity?

Yes; if we ask too much, if we ask that all relationship should be what any is at its highest moments, or that any can be for more than a moment what it is at its intensest moments, if we ask this, we are bound inevitably to be disappointed. And if we expect to find another who will understand & who knows how to accept the whole of ourselves which we want to give — there again, we shall be disappointed, probably. O Céline; why did I not meet you before!

BD6[12]

'The first thing one must make up one's mind to is that we will not be loved in the same way as we love'; — few, few, if any, will do that for us.

But can we be satisfied with any other love; can we understand any other? And if we find ourselves asking for something — is it not a sign that <u>our</u> love is withering? And if we find ourselves asking for something which is never given, how difficult it is to understand that what is given is love. For, in love more than in anything else, we understand only that which we have imagined or experienced, we want what we can give. For our very giving is a sign that we are seeking; & what we give, we give because it is what we desire most to have given us. And when, not this, but something else is given us, how difficult it is to recognize what is given as love. And, indeed, <u>is</u> it love?

BD6[14]

How is it possible to go on living conscious all the while of the gulf which separates my life from what I desire it to be? And how the imagination fails when I try to contemplate the waste of life which lies in the future: life & disappointment made one & indivisible.

BD6[15–16]

How I long for her whom I love to be ugly, deformed, to lose her beauty, to become, indeed, not even ugly, but to lose all outward charm & attraction.
And why?

So as to test my love? But it needs no testing.

So that the world shall know that my love is really love & not the passion which beauty provokes, the intoxication of what is fair? But what do I care for the world's thoughts & opinions?

Why, then? Because I believe that with this transformation might come a freer love, a love less tramelled with what is not love, less confused with what is not itself. A less limited, less obscure, clearer & more extreme love. Not a love less burdened with desire, not in that sense poorer; but poorer in the sense of being unadulterated with what is not love itself, absolute, separate & self-complete.

For, what have I now which promotes, which provokes, fosters, educates this unadulterated love? What have I which points & leads me away from the attraction of what is beautiful, the longing for what is fair? Yes, but I have something: & it is hard. For I love her who loves me not, a love without hope or prospect of satisfaction, a love which has had refined from it any tendency or instinct to ask for something in return.

Oh! But I am hiding my desires from myself. This is why I want her to be ugly & deformed — so that she should be <u>mine</u>, alone & utterly.

BD6[16]

Must, do love & jealousy always go together? Is one the complement, the implication, the part of the other? Or are love & jealousy parts of what is greater than either? Or are they contradictions, contraries? Are we jealous in proportion to our love? Or is it a modification of love?

BD6[17]

Feeling that I must reserve of my physical, sexual resources for that impossible event — when she whom I love comes to me. Feeling that I have worked out the necessity in me of finding satisfaction in what falls short of perfection, & henceforth reserve myself only for *La Belle Dame sans merci* — who can never come.

Perversion, yes! But who is not perverted? Where is the normal sexual life?

BD6[18]

Turn it all into an autobiography. Marriage & the discovery that what I wanted was something that marriage had not given me, something more dangerous, uncertain, alive. Seeing in marriage just that giving in to physical necessity, of taking a lower satisfaction in place of a higher.

And finding in this relationship with C. the shadow of what is wanted, & at the same time the impossibility of ever achieving it. Hopeless, frustrated, inaccessible love.

BD6[19]

The days when we are intensely, exclusively in love. Our feet scarcely touch the ground; it is something that belongs almost alone to adolescence. Or, it is as if our adolescence had followed us & become like a renewal of spring in the midst of summer.

BD6[19]

There is nothing to compare with the torture of seeing one with whom we have been intimate false to the idea we had formed of her.

BD6[19]

Feeling at the intense moment of love that life, even if in the future it had something comparable to this to offer, cannot be endured longer. This, this is the moment to die & so become *felix opportunitate mortis*. Life, after this, can only be posthumous.

BD6[20]

Love is found more often & more intensely in the pensive & the melancholy than in the lively and active.

BD6[20]

Love is sudden, eager, keen, exclusive & filled with jealousy.

BD6[21–27]

C. has been here this morning, and we have talked for an hour about our relationship. And, as we talked, I became more & more aware that somehow it must all end. But how & when? And then there flashed before me what a barren wilderness life without her would be. Underneath my consciousness I have known that everything I have done & everything I possess was done for her & valued for her. If she were to go, with her would go all the happiness of spring & summer, all the brightness of the sun & the beauty of the night. With her would go every delight I have in the flowers in my garden. For they were planted for her; this cherry tree is hers, the lettuces are hers, & every seed I sowed was sowed to produce an image of her. Money no longer would have for me any attraction or use, ambition would be dead, life extinct. What use a car? – it was bought for her – What use books or pictures? For two years she has been the centre & the limit of my life, and all shut up in my imagination. Everything I have done I have done for her; everything I have thought – she has been thought with it. Everything I have desired, has been a part of her. Every step I have heard, I have imagined to be hers, every letter I have received I have hoped was from her. She & beauty have been identified. She & life have been inseparable. Unless she were there, I preferred to be alone, so that I might be with her. No-one has ever been to me what she has been – & this without her ever showing to me more than the moderate affection of a friend. Life before I knew her is now impossible to imagine. Life when she goes is indistinguishable from death. I have never loved any save her: my life with her has shown me what love is. And what greater revolution could anyone create in the life of another? I know that she can do without me, I know that I am in no way indispensable to her. But she is utterly indispensable to me. What is there that I have done which I have not done for her? What is there that I have hated that I have not hated for her. Is there any country I have wanted to visit – I have thought of myself with her. Is there any life I have wanted to lead? It has been with her.

I know how I can keep her: – If I can succeed in concealing my real thoughts, if I were to keep under my real feelings, and appear only a friend or an acquaint-ance. But can I keep her on these false pretenses? Must she not inevitably dis-appear if I try to keep her by pretending my feelings are other than they are. Must I not say to her – 'This is what I am, & what I must ever remain; I ask from you nothing that you have not already given, no consideration you have not already shown, but I must not conceal from you what you are to me?' And I know that if I tell her all, she must decide to leave me, & the light of my life would be gone out.

And how long could I go on <u>asking</u> for nothing from her?

And dare I risk this utter blackness of death which must follow were she to go from me?

And I who have longed for youth; what use then would it be to me. I who have feared death; death would come as a release. For I have prized youth because you are young and I would share it with you. And I have feared death because it would take me from you. But now you are going – and what is that save the death I have feared?

But do not think when you go I shall be able to return with my affections to her from whom you think you have stolen them. For you have stolen none from anyone; they have been waiting, unawakened, for you since the day I was born. To love you less can never mean that I can love J. more.

Why redecorate my room? Why plant flowers or gather blossoms? Why write or think or act or live?

But why must it all end because I am in love? Why must this relationship end; this which has given to me everything I value, everything I desire. Cannot we be reasonable, cannot we be friends & forget our love? If it were our love, that would be impossible, but since it is only mine, & since I have kept it to myself so long & never desired any answer, cannot we continue friends?

Perhaps; but I have desired an answer — I have desired to see & to talk to you, to share your thoughts & feelings. And because I have not desired more than that can I say that I have asked for & desired nothing from you?

But oh! To think of never again seeing your writing in a letter.

O Céline, all I can think of is why did we not meet before; meet when I could ask your affection? Why did we not meet when I could give you everything of myself? And now that we have met, it is to give me the shadow of happiness & the body of misery.

The more it becomes clear that C's body is another's, that I must love her forever in vain, the more I find myself desiring to be master of her mind, to capture her soul. I am jealous not of him who has her body, but of her friends with whom she shares her mind. I am jealous not of those whom she loves, but of those she has intellectual intercourse with, those whom she understands & who understand her.

And, perhaps sexual intercourse, instead of being as I had always supposed, a kind of climax, end, completion of all other relationships, an act which includes & supersedes all other intercourse, is really a substitute for this communion of minds. Perhaps even, the one so far from finding its completion in the other, is actually contradictory of it. She may do what she will with her body; let me only be a necessity to her mind. But is this so? Whither our bodies go; there will our minds be also. But might we not dominate the body through the mind.

Where the intellectual life requires one for its existence, there is the beginning of love. My craving is to be always with her; to share everything with her, share myself; to give everything to her; do everything for her. I love like a woman. And oh! How jealous I am of those with whom she shares herself. Jealous of that intellectual intercourse with her friends; more jealous even of that than of the clothes she wears, the food which passes her lips, the bed she lies in.

BD6[28]

C. unwilling to see me because of Joyce. The war within the person of *La Belle Dame sans merci*. Cut off a part & treat it as if it were the whole & at once disharmony is created.

BD6[28–30]

Passing through all this whirl of life — life lived in the present, felt every moment, alive in every part — must we not, in the end, come out on the other side. To attempt to find in life something which corresponds with our imaginative desires, is vain. It is certain of disappointment.

Shall we not then, retire into our imagination, & there build freely, a life unrestricted by the conditions of the external world. And instead of tying our imagination to this world; rise freely above it, into a world where we can be master of our fate & not subject to the shattering disappointments & vain hopes of practical life?

Symbolise this: movement from my house, which signifies this 'present' life & the attempt to find satisfaction in the achievement of what I hope, to my room in college, which represents a retirement into the imagination, a retreat into the world of mind. Sense & the satisfactions of sense are abandoned; they give no satisfaction.

(Or, perhaps, to some other place; cp. *Portrait in a Mirror*, not the room in college.)[2]

But then, never being free from the seductions of sense. How a phrase of music, or the vision of a passing cloud in the April sky, will recall all that has been abandoned, and once more unsteady this life of the imagination. Is it possible to rest anywhere, to find *La Belle Dame* anywhere. Is there no world, no place, no time, no country of the mind, where satisfaction can be achieved? Or must we, to the end of our days, be thrown between satisfactions which do not satisfy?

BD6[30–31]

To be cut off from communication with one's fellow creatures, from the sweet sound of human voices, from the intercourse of minds, from love itself—is this to be utterly bereaved, to be cut off from everything, to be a prisoner?—or can the life of the imagination satisfy all the cravings of the mind & body? If it could, the satisfaction it would give would be surer & less random—but how intense?

But there will always be restlessness, gnawing desire, dark annihilation. Dante met somewhere in hell a man whose crime was that he did not love the sweet light of day—was he one who had retired into this life of the imagination?

BD6[31]

'Women worship a successful poet.'

Do they? They worship success; but it is a practical success, the success of a man of action which they most readily fall for.

---

2   Charles Morgan, *Portrait in a Mirror* (London: Macmillan, 1933).

BD6[34]

The contradictory feelings which love creates & intensifies in us—first the sensation of, for the first time, being an individual, of existing at all; but also the sensation of losing one's individual, separate existence, & the desire to lose it.

BD6[34]

To seek solace from the hopelessness of life between a woman's thighs.

BD6[34]

The Brothel

Why have I come? The consciousness, in this imitated play of love, in this false representation of love, of the futility of seeking satisfaction in what is merely physical. Know nothing of the mind of her with whom I am lying. No love: and now that I am here, I find no substitute for love either. Sordid.

BD6[37]

To be married is to awaken in a morning in early spring to find the sun shining, and to wonder whether it will last until midday.

BD6[37]

When her incompetence no longer delights you, it is time to take a holiday.

BD7[02–04]

My past, what I have experienced, is not endeared to me because it is my past — it is hateful. The things we have loved, no less than the persons, must be hated when they are no longer loved. I feel myself, all the time, growing out of myself, & what is behind I would fain leave behind — but I cannot. O to be free, free from this intolerable burthen of past selves! The self is not made of its past selves, it is made & maintained in spite of them. It is they which stand in the way of satisfaction — yesterday's self, no less than the self of ten years ago. And what are wives, children, possessions, save reminders of what we once were & desire to forget? And how, in each present moment we attempt to realize ourselves in these things which, a moment later, turn from things loved to fetters, from the instruments of freedom to chains. And life seems to consist in a continual emancipation which inevitably involves imprisonment. To be obsessed, to be enchanted, to be in love — this is the condition of freedom, & a moment later is the sign of bondage.

BD7[05]

To be alive we must be obsessed with something; to be alive fully we must be obsessed with a person. But all obsession is fruitless except it be with a creature of the imagination — & that is not obsession.

BD7[06–08]

How, when a period has been set to intimacy, when we know that in a few days or in a few weeks a friend is going away & there is little chance of seeing him or her again, or when we know that in a short while the whole character of the intercourse will be changed by him or her entering upon some fresh relationship elsewhere — marriage — how, when we know these things, present intimacy is intensified.

Sometimes we sense an acceleration of intimacy as a first premonition of the end. We draw together, flow together, the world grows brighter with a hectic glance & then the collision — & all is over, our life, our self falls in pieces about

---

1   LSE 20/1. Soft cover, black, 11 cm x 6.5 cm. Ruled. Unnumbered. Autograph, ink and pencil. Dated: 'Michael Oakeshott. / June. 1931. / to July 1931.'

    Other works from which Oakeshott made excerpts in this notebook but which are not mentioned in the text include: Fo. 16, notes in French on La Bruyère, possibly from *Les caractères de Théophraste*; 23–5, Lawrence, *Fantasia of the Unconscious*.

us. And the only foreknowledge we had of this end was the growing intensity of the intimacy. Press intimacy to its end – & it must end in a consuming fire.

What has taken a year to build up is surpassed in a few hours, each day, each hour & minute opens up fresh delights & life becomes accelerated – but not unbearably, except when we contemplate the end & wreck of it all that is to follow. Life becomes intensely aware of itself & our personalities grown in this summer sunshine of vivid intercourse. Like plants which have taken all the winter to root themselves & suddenly in early summer spring forward with rapid growth, our relationships wax & extend themselves.

Cp. all this to the end of the world. This is what early Christianity did for life, this is what any religion must do. It can be done for a short while, but when the event does not come, how impossible it is to readjust the intercourse, & bring it again within the bounds of time & place.

BD7[09–10]

The Caius Ball 1931. Now secure; it is mine, it is permanent, because it was never experienced. All that I imagined can stand, time cannot wreck or memory transform what belongs neither to time nor to memory but to mind & imagination. I suffered no disappointment; not only was it exquisitely suitable that this frustration should take place, not only was it of a piece with my relationship with Céline, that nothing should be brought to fruition, nothing achieved, nothing satisfied, but it is better so. This surely is the only satisfaction life has to offer – the imagination of satisfaction.

BD7[11–13]

To the man, after the pleasure of intercourse, comes coldness, indifference, remoteness. It is a physical reaction; to the woman there comes no such reaction, & often she cannot understand it, she does not forgive it. To her, if she is capable of deep feeling, it is cruelty. The man turns his back & loses himself in sleep; & this the woman neither can do nor desires to do.

To some women this appearance of cruelty is the most intolerable experience of their life. This, & this only, is the root of disenchantment, the poison of the affections.

And even when she can understand it, even when she can forgive it, it remains a qualification of delight, a mitigation of pleasure. She must remain for ever unsatisfied; the man alone has his full satisfaction. And consequently intercourse is happier, for her, in anticipation & in retrospect than in fact. For her the perfection of pleasure is followed always by, not oblivion & satisfaction, but by dissatisfaction. And here, as everywhere in love, unless cruelty can be turned to delight, unless love can find its pleasure in suffering, delight & pleasure can never be perfect.

BD7[14]

I am like the river Jordan, my course has ended in a Dead Sea — a sea in which nothing moves, beside which nothing can grow, & in which no memory can sink & be forgotten.

BD7[14]

I discovered her, though a stranger, as one discovers, at a glance, a friend in a crowd.

BD7[17]

Werther's suicide followed upon partial satisfaction, not upon complete denial. But this momentary satisfaction, which was isolated & consequently unreal, only made his disappointment more intense & his despair more complete. His death was an escape; but also a sacrifice, a consummation, a fulfilment. He died at the height, not in the depths.

BD7[18]

To make this book a series of pictures or studies of love. Types of love. The style of each study to be modeled upon the view it is presenting.

Cp. *Ulysses* by J. Joyce.

E.g. Romantic love.

Modern love; the unquiet, subtle, conflicting, self-criticizing love. Lawrence, Hebbel, etc.

BD7[19]

Those hours when our life & its activity seems to take on the actual character of time. Time does not wait for us. We sleep & we have grown older in our unconsciousness. So it is with moments in our life; with some of the things we do as well as with what we suffer. We cannot imagine ourselves getting to the end, but, as if we were suffering instead of doing, we arrive at the end almost without effort.

BD7[20–21]

The new birth, the resurrection which comes to most boys at puberty, came to me not until I was of age. I do not mean that it was not until then that I felt the sexual urge — I felt it younger than most. I can scarcely remember a time when I did not feel it — but that it was not until then that I recognized it, admitted it, welcomed it & made no attempt to sublimate it. All this sublimation is the devil. The impulse comes & we are taught to turn it into something else. And this is worse even than to be taught to stifle it. For if we attempt to stifle it, it will arise stronger than ever. If we sublimate it, it will perish — & we perish with it.

BD7[21–22]

And what is the use of all this knowledge about sex. The facts of sex. This is a side-track. A peculiarly Northern or Anglo-Saxon side-track. What we want is experience, not knowledge about the facts. And to substitute this knowledge for a free experience, is to sublimate & to kill. No harm in knowledge. What is dangerous, deadening, monstrous is knowledge <u>in place of</u> experience; knowledge as a means of precluding experience.

BD7[26]

I seem to have been in love, not with a star of benign influence, but with a bright consuming comet which has born down upon & has consumed me with its fire. And now that we have collided I am fallen altogether in pieces.

BD7[26–29]

14 July.

Goodbye to Céline. How I have felt this fatal moment drawing nearer for months past. And now it is come, & I do not realize what it means. Never to see her, talk with her, write to her again, never to know where or how she is living, never to know that she is married, never to see her children, never again to share or contribute to her happiness, never to know when she is ill, or sad, or disappointed — never, never, never.

'There is the seed of madness in every great parting,' says Goethe. And we are saved from madness only by the limits of our imagination. If at this moment I could realize what this parting means — more than just know what it entails, but realize all the bitter blankness of the future, realize what next Spring & Summer will be like without her, realize the loneliness of never being able to write to her — there would sweep over me such a wave of despair, that madness, even unconsciousness, must ensue. But I cannot yet realize this; the realization will come gradually, there will be moments of black despair, moments, days, nights of delirium — & then forgetfulness? Will that ever come? It was different when she was merely away — now she has gone & there is nothing more to hope for, nothing to expect. I am dead, perished, buried — oh that I could forget myself.

But that could be only if I lost myself — & now C. has gone I have nobody in whom I can lose myself. And a self can be lost only in another self — never in anything else.

BD7[33–34]

I am like one who suffering from an incipient disease is suddenly one day struck down with it. The fire is laid, the foundations are rotten, the earth is hollow — everything was there for the collapse. And now it has come. Perhaps it could have been warded off, by prudent living the disease might have remained latent, but (in any case) nothing could happen the materials for which were not already prepared within. These things do not befall any to whom they do not belong; where there is none laid, a fire cannot be lighted.

BD7[36–37]

I imagine to myself that because I love C. I want her to love me; but no. I have had enough of love—I want to love & be responded to with something else—what? I call it 'love' because that is what one is taught to expect in return for love; but to be loved is to be in bondage—unless one can be alone—& that I have found impossible. So then, I shower my affection upon C. whose affection is directed elsewhere.

And I want to continue like this for ever (though I imagine I want a consummation). But to C. that is impossible. I will give without taking—but cannot take without giving, & that she cannot do—to me I tell her—'You are free, free, free: no obligation, none at all.' And then set about building up a relationship in which I am free & she a slave.

BD7[38]

There is something wild in me to which my life gives no answer. One can fob it off by buying cars, spending money—spending more than one has—sleeping in the garden, climbing mountains, taking holidays—but not for ever, not for long. But what life will answer it? And how, now that I have committed myself to this life, can I free myself from my obligations. And yet the very sense of obligation belongs to this, & not that life.

BD7[39]

Craving for a perfect relationship, a perfect intimacy: & this symbolized in incest. To love one's own sister, one's own blood;—one's daughter.

BD7[39–40]

Oh, if I could somehow compromise myself with the world—show that I do not belong to it, show that what I value, it rejects, & that I reject what it values. Ruin my reputation. Love, affection, intimacy—these are what I value, & the world hates & qualifies them all. And yet the world's hold is strong. What it obliges me to, I feel an obligation for. Oh, to be free from the feeling of obligation. And because I have given myself so much to the world, it would seem that I could show an even greater contempt for it. I am obliged to it—throw off the obligation. I have got money: throw it away. And position & reputation. All these are weapons; if I had not them, I could not show my contempt so easily.

BD8[01–04]

All my life there has been this distrust of intimacy – at home, parents, brothers, friends. No frankness, openness. But all inside, seething & alone. I have always been alone. And when most alone I have wanted intimacy; when I have most distrusted it I have desired it. No freedom: only death & frustration.

Marriage: the attempt to free myself from the foreign world in which I lived & which I hated. But that too has failed. I am now as much a prisoner as ever.

Glimpses of freedom. With Céline. Moments of freedom with others – Beth. But nothing permanent, nothing lasting.

Freedom, I know, can be obtained either by finding an answer, or by refusing to ask. The first way I have tried. Asked & asked. Now, must I try the other; & retire for ever into myself & be alone there. It is a desperate remedy.

How difficult it is to live with other people – & how impossible not to. Intimacy, intimacy – & all I get is acquaintance. And when I press for intimacy – the world goes to pieces. If it is refused I am lost; if it is given, it turns to dust & ashes. Intimacy is impossible? Then why do we crave it? Is life a radical contradiction? Oneness, oneness; & always plurality. To be alone & yet to be intimate with another. To find one's aloneness with another.

Once it seemed as if life would offer what I asked of it – with Céline; but now that appearance of satisfaction has gone. Even this 'shadow of stability' is gone.

I want 'stability' & I want freedom. Intimacy & aloneness. A world & freedom. And these, it seems, can never be had together. Satisfied love? – but can love be satisfied. Love is ever unsatisfied.

BD8[05–06]

Revival of confidence since C's letter of parting. She belongs to me; I am her master. Previously, I had asked nothing of her, been dependent upon her. But now I know that she belongs to me – & I can wait. She must return, because she is mine. And even if she does not return, she is mine for ever. I am master of her

---

[1] LSE 20/1. Soft cover, black, 11 cm x 6.5 cm. Ruled. Unnumbered. Autograph, ink and pencil. Dated: 'M. Oakeshott. / July 1931.– / Dec 31st 1931.'

Other works from which Oakeshott made excerpts in this notebook but which are not mentioned in the text include: Fo. 16, quotations in French from La Bruyère, possibly from *Les caractères de Théophraste*; 23–5, Lawrence, *Fantasia of the Unconscious*; 28–9, G. D'Annunzio, *The Child of Pleasure*, tr. G. Harding (London: William Heinemann, 1898); 31, notes in French on F. Ponsard, *Les Charmettes – Souvenir de Chambéry* (Turin: Botta, 1856); 32–3, notes in French on Henri-Frédéric Amiel, *Journal intime*, ed. B. Gagnebin and P.M. Monnier, 12 vols. (Lausanne: L'Age d'Homme, 1976–94 [1882–4]).

dead, if not alive. R. may have her body; but I have her mind & soul. And some day she will awake & know it.

I shall go to her no longer as a servant, no longer to give myself to her, to abandon myself to her, but as a master. I am her home. And when I go to her again it will be to ask when she is coming to me. I can wait: wait for her to awake.

BD8[07]

A woman doesn't like being made love to except against her will.

BD8[08–10]

I want a relationship without a name. Something profound, dangerous, risky, incomplete & yet satisfying. Mother, sister, wife, mistress — we know what all these are.

I want something which has no name, is ruled by no convention. Something experimental. Something in which there is no routine. This is what I mean by love. I want a lover, someone with whom love — this unnamed relationship — can grow & blossom. I have often, continually sought this lover, & never found her. My life has been spent in seeking her; indeed, I believe the purpose of life is to seek her, & the satisfaction of life to find her. Is she a phantom, this *Belle Dame*? Is she a Chimera, a creature of fancy? And is this relationship merely an expression of dissatisfaction with all relationships? She gives me no peace; each year, each month I must set out again to find her. And if I did not identify this search with life itself, the number of my disappointments would long ago have made me hopeless. But, as with all lovers — I must have her or I die. For to be without her is not to be born, & to lose her is to die. For not until I have found her shall I have found myself.

BD8[11]

1. 'Secularism.'
2. *La Belle Dame Sans Merci.*

Two parts of the same work.

Two things — (i) to keep one's self whole, complete, untouched — to keep oneself free from the world. This is the otherworldliness which is essential to life.

(ii) To find a way of losing oneself in order to become oneself. And this is love. Hardness, imperviousness to the world. And a disintegrating love in which one can lose & find oneself.

BD8[12–16]

Each of us creates an 'ideal' woman, a type. & those with whom we are intimate begin to live up to this pattern. They become what we want them to be. And this ends in disaster. For they become part of ourselves & in the end they become a past self – a self which we look upon with distaste & loathing, something from which we wish to escape.

To identify a person with oneself leads in the end to identifying him or her with something which must perish. This is the mistake – or the inevitable contradiction of life. And the worst end is to marry such a past self – that brings with it only disenchantment.

But the fault is on both sides. Women love living up to the type we insist upon, the type we insist that they belong to – & they are in love with death. Neither men nor women know what belongs to their peace.

But all this is different with Elisabeth – I have tried to make her a pattern, to give her a type – & she has refused it. She has refused to become identified with a fleeting self of mine. She has insisted on being herself & no other: she is in love with life, not death, & knows what belongs to her peace.

It is a hard lesson for one to learn; the habits of the years of thought must be overcome & banished. Even Σ submitted to type, or nearly did so. Elizabeth never.

This does not mean that Elizabeth will not submit to my will, give in to me; it means far more. And it means that she could retain her own individuality even though she submitted to me & belonged to me. It is our habits of thought that are wrong: we think in terms of labels, names, types, classes, patterns – we do not think in terms of a clear view of what is there; we think in terms not of living experience but of dead, inherited habits.

BD8[17]

Oct. 1931.

Σ. How she came back to me, confessing her inability to stay away, confessing her affection. It was as if she belonged to me, & I to her, and we could not stay apart. Shall we in old age, when life has passed over us, when other relationships have perished, shall we come back to one another, and experience a relationship of spirit?

BD8[18–19]

24 Oct 1931.

To London to see Elisabeth. The whole scene. E's room. The firelight, the bed, the tea on the table & the candles. And all this sordidness, which love should transform, remaining sordid. The persuasion, the surrender. The promise, the expectation of happiness – & the result. The inherent impossibility of satisfaction, the impossibility of penetrating another self, & the foolishness & the misery of attempting. A symbol of this foolishness & misery; a symbol of the inherent impossibility of two meeting on earth. Surrender is no answer, no solution. It is a fence & not a way, a bar & not an entrance.

And all the misery following it. Fruition is death; & we must wait for a new life to blossom in spite of it.

BD8[20–21]

How we are satisfied with a low standard of friendship. It is so with everything which is universal. Friendship is a human need, & is found wherever men are found. But the standard of subtlety in a life of friendship is taken from what is commonly achieved, & not from what might be achieved & is inherent in it. It is a pass-time, a relief from the practical business of life, a thing for leisure hours, a parerga—instead of being the one thing in life worth achieving, instead of being the whole of life. This is the radical irreligion of our civilization, & of every civilization ever invented, that love & friendship are not life itself, but a part, a support, a by-product of life.

BD8[22–23]

How each relationship brings with it a new experience.

The freedom of Σ; the profundity of E.; & the light gentleness & simplicity of Effie.

But what does love mean to each of them?

Oh, that I could love without thinking of love; love without wondering what they think love is; love without talking of love. But always this contradiction, which arises from the attempt to achieve a relationship which is wholly satis-fying, instead of being content with the experiences of immediate satisfaction—which each offers—if only for a moment.

BD8[23–24]

The emblems of love.

The phases—moments—of love.

1. Man made for the mastery of the world, & woman for the delight of man. Man, wearied may find quiet & peace with woman, wash himself clean from the world, from toil & noise & renew himself for fresh endeavor.

2. A relationship—man & woman—toil, work, subordinate to this relationship. Love & friendship the being of life, not its recreation.

BD8[25]

Love is the element of dissatisfaction in life. And thus, it is the life of life. Routine, habit, profession—all these are the death of life; these offer & some-times afford satisfaction, quiet, certainty. Love offers only endless disquiet, war, dissatisfaction: but it offers a life which is complete though dissatisfied. Love is at once that which is limited & complete.

BD8[26]

Lust — the desire to dominate physically.

Rape. No intercourse; taking without what is taken being offered or given. But taking only a physical satisfaction.

Spiritual Lust: the desire to own, dominate, possess the mind, the person, the soul. The Rape of the soul. And this is the last death.

BD8[30–31]

In prospect, & increasingly as we draw near, love seems to answer all the questions of life, to cure all its maladies, solve all its riddles. And we go on believing this only because what we experience we will not admit to be love.

BD8[34]

With me friendship tends inevitably to become love.

BD8[34–35]

Love & death. These are together in our minds, because they are together in life. Love is always a self-immolation. And when it is not this, it is an attempt to escape from death. And when it is not this, it fears death most — death & parting.

BD8[35]

It is men who make women. And in order to please, women become what they are desired to be. Woman represents the customs of the times.

BD8[35–36]

1. Lust; the pure physical desire & its physical satisfaction. Here.

2. Romantic Love: *La Belle Dame sans merci.* Always somewhere else. There. A hopeless quest; but still a quest, a movement; & always unsatisfied. Beyond.
   Always somewhere else.

(a) Future.

(b) Past — satisfaction in a memory. Melancholy. Shelley. D'Annunzio. Heine. The end of Romantic love is death.

3. Nowhere. Despair, hopelessness. The death of desire. The abandonment of the Quest; but still a quest.

4. <u>The hermaphrodite ideal</u>. *Die Schau sucht du, & was sie stellt*.[2] The circle: satisfaction. Here, always <u>here</u>, but not in lust — of body or mind — but in communion & singleness. Not in the past, or in the future; but in the present, a continuing ever present, changeless present. No putting off; no hope to meet again — no craving to remember what is gone; but always in the present.

The end of this is the triumph of life over death.

BD8[36–37]

The escape from Romanticism — either to so-called Realism — or to satisfaction in dissatisfaction. The acceptance of life as incomplete.

BD8[37]

Is it possible, in the end, to escape from Romanticism? To be discontented with R. is inherent in Romanticism — to look <u>beyond</u>. <u>Beyond</u> is the word of Romanticism.

BD8[37]

Romanticism is sometimes represented as sentimentalism. But, it's not that. It is something stronger, & truer. The truth of Romanticism is profounder than that of sentimentalism — but both have <u>a</u> truth.

---

2   See p. 164 n. 1, above.

Notebook 11 (October 1931)

11[01]

Love is what is at once limited & complete — the whole & yet not all. Perfect love is to have lost & found oneself in another — not in everyone else. It is, then, at once imperfect & perfect. And a view of life which would take love as the symbol of the good life, would recognize the perfect life not as that which achieved most, nor as that which achieved a little, and that perfectly & as a contribution to the whole, but as that which achieved the whole of itself at every point; that which is limited but not a part, which is limited & yet the whole.

11[04]

We carry death within us as a lethal germ. Death is a part of our existence, an element of our life.

11[04]

The two necessities of life — love & loneliness.
  And the major problem — how to adjust them.

11[04]

I wish to substitute a view of life better adapted to the conditions of life than that which satisfies the majority of mankind.

---

[1] LSE 2/1/11. Hard cover, blue, 17 cm x 11.5 cm, squared. Recto folios numbered 1–91. Autograph, ink. Title page: 'Michael Oakeshott. / Notes. / XI / *La joie de l'esprit en marque la face* / Ninon de l'Enclos. / *Qui n'a pas l'esprit de son âge, / De son âge a tout le malheur.* / Amiel? Joubert? / *Nous perdons en projets les plus beaux / de nos jours.* / Voltaire. / October 1931.' [Ninon de l'Enclos (1620–1705), French courtesan and writer; the saying with a doubtful provenance is ascribed to Voltaire in Joseph Joubert, *Pensées, maximes, essais et correspondence*, ed. P. Raynal, 2 vols. (Paris: Didier et Co., 1861), i.229; the saying by Voltaire is quoted in Amiel, *Journal intime*, x.341.]
  Other works from which Oakeshott made excerpts in this notebook but which are not mentioned in the text include: Fo. 2, Lascalles Abercrombie, 'Emblems of Love'; 5, *The Note-Books of Samuel Butler Author of 'Erewhon'*, ed. H.F. Jones (London: A.C. Fifield, 1913); 6, notes on Sébastien-Roch Nicolas, aka Chamfort, possibly *The Cynic's Breviary Maxims and Anecdotes From Nicolas de Chamfort*, ed. W.G. Hutchinson (London: Elkin Mathews, 1902); 20, R.M. Scott, *Misogyny over the Weekend* (London: Macmillan & Co., 1931); 30, J. Maritain, *The Things That Are Not Caesar's*, tr. J.F. Scanlan (London: Sheed & Ward, 1930); 42–3, A.A. Cooper, third Earl of Shaftesbury, *Characteristicks of Men, Manners, Opinions, Times. In three volumes. Vol. I. I. A Letter concerning Enthusiasm. II. Sensus Communis, or an Essay on wit, &c. III. Soliloquy, or Advice to an author. Vol. II. IV. An Inquiry concerning Virtue and Merit. V. The Moralists: a philosophical rhapsody. Vol. III. VI. Miscellaneous Reflections on the said Treatises, and other critical subjects* (London: John Darby, 1711); 69–70, St Augustine, *Confessions*.

11[07]

Modern Christianity

By temperament I should be disposed to throw over what I could understand & build for myself a religion freed from the trammels of tradition. But the circumstances of my education set my feet upon another track, & prevented me from dismissing from my mind, what no one who is not taken up with prejudice or pride can altogether forget — the history of Christianity.

11[07]

Attempt to restate the doctrines of Christianity for the contemporary mind. And see where the Christian festivals, worship, prayer etc: fall into place.

Popular theology — to remove from it that appetite for absurdity which Hume found there.

The Hymns etc.

11[07]

Christianity is something which we have <u>made</u>.

11[07–08]

Note the entirely different approach of to-day from that of yesterday — both science & history have shot their bolt — Under their influence Christian doctrine has been cleansed from irrelevances — but, by the nature of these studies — it has not been reconstructed for the modern mind.

11[08]

Christian Evidences

The notion of establishing <u>Christian evidences</u>.

Cp. Paley. They were defended, not because they mattered, but because they were attacked.

Cp. Johnson on Hume — He admitted he had never studied the New Testament with attention.

Attempt to defend:

(i) Too much.

(ii) What was indefensible.

(iii) What was irrelevant.

11[08]

'Evidences'

The 'unbeliever' went with the 'free-thinker' — that most prejudiced of beings.

11[08]

Christianity will be stronger for the removal of what is not essential to it: not weaker.

11[08]

The notion of <u>defending</u> Christianity. This is out of date, but not entirely so. We should defend Christianity by defining it, by understanding it.

But perhaps beyond this, <u>defence</u> is still needed. But it must be a wise defence, not a conventional defence. We must defend it (i) where it is attacked <u>now</u>, not where it <u>was</u> attacked.

(ii) where it needs defence, even if it is not attacked there.

11[09]

'Either Jesus was the son of God, or He was not.' Butler, *Fair Haven*.[2]

This is the standpoint which is entirely out of date. We must get to the presuppositions of it. Find them, understand them, & defend them or reform them as we may find necessary.

'Faith is the "evidence of things not seen," but it is not "insufficient evidence for things alleged to have been seen."'[3]

To accept historical facts upon insufficient evidence is not faith; it is credulity.

Instead of asking about the reliability of this or that passage in the New Testament, we ought to enquire into the general character of the New Testament; what the New Testament says, & what it is silent about; & the value of these, depends upon its general character, the purpose for which its books were written, etc.

11[10]

We are told that Christianity rests upon or consists in, not a bare belief in facts, but a love of Jesus himself.

---

2   Oakeshott's note: 'p. 124.' See S. Butler, *The Fair Haven A Work in Defence of the Miraculous Element in our Lord's Ministry upon Earth, both as against Rationalistic Impugners and certain Orthodox Defenders, by the late John Pickard Owen, with a Memoir of the Authors by William Bickersteth Owen* (London: A.C. Fifield, 1913), p. 169.

3   Oakeshott's note: 'ibid. p. 137.' See Butler, *The Fair Haven* (1913), p. 180.

This was clearly possible to those who knew him. But in what sense is it possible to 'love' someone whom we have never seen in the flesh? Some kind of love is possible; but not the fullest. And it is always an uncertain love.

What we have is conclusive evidence of the love of those who knew him, & their picture of a man who, if we had known him, we could scarcely keep ourselves from loving.

But love cannot exist on 'Report'; and if it is said, 'Jesus lives; we love someone whom we have known.' What is the meaning of this? Do we know him, as we must know a person we <u>love</u>. We cannot love a merely perfect character. Perfection does not call forth love; & we can love only <u>persons</u>, not 'characters.'

11[11–14]

<u>Modern Christianity</u>

Whenever there is a change in our surroundings we must change ourselves, our ideas, desires, ideals, or remain in a state of chronic discomfort, contradiction, which ends by being self-contradiction. And it seems that Christianity is among those things which must change with circumstances. Christianity is what <u>we</u> think it is; it has always been what we thought it was. But <u>we</u> almost unique among the Christian generations, have submitted it to the principle that Christianity is what someone else thought it was — what Jesus, the Apostles, Paul, Augustine, Luther, thought it was.

This principle was tacitly accepted sometime in the last century, & more, it was acted upon. Other centuries had tacitly accepted, but none had acted upon it.

It received a severe testing when the evidences of Christianity began to be studied critically. But with various modifications it has survived that test. Indeed, there was nothing lethal in that test; it could never have shaken the general principle.

What we must do now is to follow, like good conservatives, the generations before us & make <u>our</u> Christianity, as they made <u>theirs</u>. There is no external test — an external test of truth is a figment of a false logic. A thing is what it develops into — & this development at this point is in our hands.

General principles of how Christianity can change & yet retain its identity.

Nothing <u>essential</u>, no detail, doctrine, moral or religious.

If we do this we shall be in one sense unique among the Christian generations — no other has consciously & systematically adapted what came to them. It has all been under the surface, & would have been denied if it had ever been brought to light.

But to do it consciously & systematically will save us from some mistakes. E.g. the mistake the middle ages made when it incorporated Aristotelian semantics into the Christian view of life.

This process of adaptation cannot, of course, be undertaken by every generation. It goes on under the surface all the time, but the moment for bringing this change to the surface, fixing it, defining its limits for the time being, crystallizing it—this must come but rarely. Indeed, with a religion, which must necessarily be conservative in its general view, however revolutionary its practices, this admission of change must be rare. But its seriousness, its apparent cataclysmic effect, the disorganization in which it is likely to result, is naturally proportional to its rareness.

This disorganization, however, is much lessened if the attempt to seek out the extent & nature of the change is not made until the change has been effected & established so firmly in our unconscious minds that to bring it to consciousness, though a serious step, will be or appear less revolutionary. A philosophy or theology must always follow, never precede a development in the religion itself.

Danger, however, in putting it off too long. Disorganized dissatisfaction; doubts unanswered, concealed, denied, stifled. Disharmony of life.

What I propose, then, falls into two independent, or semi-independent parts. First, an exposition of the general nature of religion & Christianity to show the necessity & the ground of <u>change</u>. And a consideration of the limits of change consistent with the retention of identity.

Secondly, a project for the reform of Christianity based (i) upon this view of Christianity; (ii) upon the present situation of Christian doctrine & practice.

I <u>may</u> be wrong in supposing that the time is ripe for this second project; and what I have to say under that head, depending as it does upon so many & so various contingencies, is less certain than what I have to say in the first part—which is a question of logic & of definition.

The second part should contain a review of the present situation; showing particularly how the attacks on Christianity of the last century have mainly been irrelevant, & the defences misconceived.

It is a work of <u>apologetic</u>; but with a new principle of apology—i.e., to admit everything that must be admitted, but to enquire into its bearing. To reconstruct rather than to buttress; to rebuild rather than to reconstruct; to reform rather than to rebuild.

One of our problems—by what criterion are we to decide whether a certain growth belongs to the main stem, or whether it is parasitic? For all religions & moral ideas which have currency in Western Europe are somehow attached to or derived from Christianity: ours is a Christian civilization in that its formative conceptions, its atmosphere etc are derived from Christianity. I do not meant that every idea we have can be traced to a definite source: I mean that the <u>whole</u> to which our ideas belong is dominated by the name Christianity. And those who have rejected the particular brand or phase of Christianity professed by their generation are not less influenced by it, than those who accept it.

But which is apple-tree & which is mistletoe?

The mistletoe feeds on the same sap—though it may modify it at the last moment—& is organically attached to the main stem.

Is Nietzsche mistletoe or apple-tree?

Or again, is there any mistletoe? Is this metaphor misplaced, misleading?

11[15]

Suicide is rare; compared to the miseries, pains, losses & complaints of men, it is surprisingly rare.

Why?

(i) Men, though they suffer and complain, really enjoy life more than they think they will enjoy death—whatever they believe about death.

We do not commit suicide because we enjoy life, rather than because we fear death.

(ii) Men fear death more than they love life.

(iii) Men are ignorant of methods by which death may be compassed easily.

(iv) Men remain alive because they think thereby to fulfil some responsibility to others, rather than from any desire to remain living.

11[16]

Love & death

Love as the attempt to overcome death. Indeed, love is all that can overcome death. It is the denial of death, because it is the assertion of the present.

11[16]

Love & justice

Love is the opposite of justice. Justice has no place in the comity of love. Love is always lavish or ungrateful. Where one has lost favour, one need not attempt to deserve it.

11[16]

A man who has a fatal taste for the useless, a scorn of worldly wisdom, an aversion from his own interests. Where profit offers itself, he flees. To think of a career appears base. Love of what is unproductive. Fear of personal interest. Passion for disinterestedness; horror of shrewdness. A Quixotic character. From the horror of one extreme he goes to the other.

11[17]

Modern Christianity

The conception of apostasy.

When does a change of faith amount to an apostasy?
What separates the apostate from the reformer?
Matter of <u>degree</u> — if we put aside the question of motive.
Cp. Bentham, *Fragment on Government*.

11[18]

<u>Death</u>

The connection between death & necessity is one which we have been slow to make.

For some primitive races, each death is a separate phenomenon, to be accounted for separately. This perhaps reflects the fact that one death does not, & never will, explain another — each is an experience which is overwhelming to those who survive.

But we have not yet fully grasped the notion of death & necessity. The idea of premature death is still current & still dominates.

11[18]

Eternal happiness is a compensation accorded to human sorrows.
The connexion between <u>justice</u> & <u>immortality</u>.

11[18]

Glory = posthumous reputation; & this must usually be infamy rather than fame if these later times were to take account of their own needs & not clutter themselves with what they have no need or use for.

11[19]

The fact that the women's freedom movement has followed in the steps, exactly, of the mens; shows the essential lack of initiative in women. A vote!!

11[20]

'True aesthetic satisfaction is not the satisfaction of the senses, for the senses are never satisfied; it is the satisfaction of the co-ordinating judgment of the intellect.'

Consider this tradition which connects the <u>senses</u> with art & aesthetic satisfaction. Not only are the senses never satisfied; but they do not exist; they are abstractions.

11[21]

Why are we less severe upon those who prostitute their minds than upon those who prostitute their bodies?

11[22]

The invulnerable philosophy of unambition.

11[22]

To be master of one's fate both in dying & living.

11[22]

The idea that it is 'morbid' to discuss or think about death.

11[22]

Death is thought to be suitable to a funeral sermon; & out of place elsewhere.

11[22]

Because we have left Death to be considered only by the elderly, our ideas of death are full of horror. He is old, the friend of Time, & forbidding.

11[22]

Because we have refused to think about death until somebody dies the thought has been disconnected, vague, directed toward winning comfort rather than truth.

11[22]

Mortality

'The man who has found the work that suits him & a wife whom he loves has squared his accounts with life.'
    Hegel.

Has he? Has he squared his accounts with death? And if not with death, then how with life?

11[22–23]

It is sometimes considered that while an elderly man may be permitted to think directly, even concentratedly about death, direct reflection upon death is out of place in a young man. His business is with life & how he is to love it; death he should leave to the moribund; to those who have already lived or who have reached the stage in their existence when they are obliged to admit that they have never lived.

    But this is a foolish notion, & moreover harmful. To leave our thinking about death to the elderly is to leave it to those who have least, not most, reason for thinking clearly, courageously & concentratedly about it.

And further, death is, so to speak, the natural subject for a young man to think of — to think of sometimes. For, when the elderly think of death it appears to them as something unavoidable, natural, inevitable, to be suffered even if not understood. But to the young man it appears either his greatest enemy, or his greatest friend. Something to be avoided, banished, thwarted; or something to be embraced. It is not the old who contemplate suicide. After a young man has experienced to the full what Hazlitt calls 'the feeling of immortality in youth,' after he has briefly considered death & dismissed it as impossible, unthinkable, a mistake which, though others have committed it, he will avoid, there comes to many the impulse & the necessity to consider more closely what had been hastily dismissed. And it is at this time, if ever, that he will consider the merits of suicide. The middle aged may commit suicide because they are tired of life; the young man will only abandon life because he is in love with death.

So then, to be young & to consider death, to reflect upon it, to attempt to understand it, so far from being contradictory, are correlative.

Moreover, if we wish for thoughts about death & mortality freed from senti-mentalism, clear-sighted, direct & without the prudery which is liable to attack, like a palsy, everything which is most important in life, we have to go (in England for example) to the most vital, youthful age of our literature, to the Elizabethans.

The Elizabethan's terror of youth's departure is felt & expressed without sentimentality.

11[23]

'The shadow line.'

11[23]

Religion, as I see it, must have some answer to the questions of youth, as well as some comforts for the fears of old age. It must have some suggestions for those who are beginning upon life, as well as some consolations for those whose life has been misspent — & whose life is not misspent?

11[23]

The forerunner of death is love. Love creates & separates. Death destroys & heals. It is love which marks out those who are the friends of death. Passionate love can have no other appropriate end, save death.

11[23]

We must see death as young & beautiful — this is how lovers see him. To others he is old, forbidding, full of horror. He is the friend, not of love, but of time. Only a lover knows death as beautiful. But lovers have not been influential in the moulding of the ideas which govern our civilization, & death consequently is dark & forbidding.

11[24]

Tragedy degenerates into mawkishness (sentimentality) through deficiency of intellectual content. This is the character of all sentimentality.

11[24]

The Anatomy of Romanticism/Sentimentality & Cant

Sentimentality is the cant of Love.
The origins & cause of Sentimentality.
Its forms, degrees & moods.
Mawkishness; immaturity; bogus & derivative sentiment; insincerity:
Sentimentality in art, in literature; in life.
Cp. D.H. Lawrence. 'My room is number 32.'[4]
Sentimentality & Romanticism.
Blindness to the facts of life: the Greek desire for youth?
Hoarding one's past as a form of sentimentality.
Unreality as the master principle of sentimentality – not that these feelings are not felt, but that they cannot stand the criticism & test of coherent feeling.
    Sentimentality as periphrasis – death; 'to pass over'; 'to pass away'; etc:

'If he had not heard of Love, he would never speak of it.'
    Tolstoy, *Anna Karenina*.

La Rochefoucauld.

11[25]

'Contemplative stillness is but the name for a state of invulnerability, & to be invulnerable is what all men desire.'[5]

    The desire for immortality is only part of the desire for invulnerability.

11[26]

Men stupidly say 'death is the answer of all things,' but they mean only that they are tired of thought. We cannot put off the answers to any of our questions, in the hope that they will be answered by God, when we meet him; if the questions are worth asking, they must be answered – somehow – this side of death.

---

4   See D.H. Lawrence, 'Do Women Change,' in *Late Essays and Articles*, ed. J.T. Boulton (Cambridge: Cambridge University Press, 2004), pp. 151–4, at 152.
5   Charles Morgan, *The Fountain* (London: Macmillan and Co., Limited, 1949 [1931]), p. 27.

But in another sense death is the <u>criterion</u> of all things. What does not stand the test of death is worthless for the purposes of life & living.

Death puts us in a 'second place' <u>absolutely</u>. It reduces everything in life to its proper level & importance.[6]

Cp. the vulgar saying, 'the best preparation for death is a good life.'

<u>What</u> is a 'good' life; — that depends on what we believe death to be.

11[27]

<u>Christianity</u>

To <u>defend</u> Christianity is always to transform it. Each defence has been a readjustment.[7]

11[27]

<u>Mortality</u>

In general, since the beginning of the Christian era, the way in which men have attempted to overcome death is by denying it — a doctrine of a future life.

Death, as even Spinoza said, is a thing which the good man thinks as little about as he can.[8]

This overcoming of Death may still be of value — but it has certainly lost its power. Even those who still believe in a future life are not so easily persuaded that this denial of death is a real overcoming.

And a new attempt must be made. In the past — in the 18th & 19th centuries e.g. — a great number of men asserted their disbelief in a future life — but they did not replace this belief with any other which could overcome death. Their disbelief was largely mere denial & negative. The positive implications of it were never thought out.

11[28]

<u>Immortality</u>

Is it possible to believe in a future life but to have no belief about the particular form of that life?

If not, what we have to consider is the forms which this life has been held to take & forms which it might be held to take.

---

6   Oakeshott's note: 'Cp. Morgan, *The Fountain*, pp. 317–8.'

7   Oakeshott's note: 'Cp. F. de Chateaubriand, *Le génie du Christianisme*, 2 vols. (Paris: Firmin Didot frères, 1844).'

8   Oakeshott's note: 'Cp. Bevan, *Christianity*.' Possibly E.R. Bevan (1870–1943), historian and religious writer, author of *Hellenism and Christianity* (London: George Allen & Unwin, 1921); *The World in which Christianity Arose* (London: Hodder and Stoughton, 1924); and *The Hope of a World to Come Underlying Judaism and Christianity* (London: George Allen & Unwin, 1930).

11[29]

'Human life' is not a constant to which all else must be related – it depends how it is lived. What we require is a way of living consonant with the facts of life.

A doctrine of 'after-life' is insufficient, in itself, to reconcile us with this life. We must be reconciled to this life by this life itself.[9]

11[30]

Sentimentality can be bona fide sentiment – To accuse a man of sentimentality does not entail a judgment about his motives; it is an objective judgment. He may feel this; but this feeling cannot maintain itself in the objective world of sentiment. Good & Right.

11[31]

We have not yet adjusted our view of life to our conception of the 'naturalness' of death. This is what I wish to attempt.

11[32]

Death

Primitive myths, customs & ideas about death seem all, in the first place, to recognize & emphasize its unnatural character. Death comes into the world by mistake.

Cp. Melanesia. The great foremother of their race sloughed her skin at intervals and remained eternally young. The catastrophe of death occurred because she was once disturbed in the operation by the screaming of her child & it was thus that death made its appearance.[10]

'No such thing as a natural death is realised by the native; a man who dies has of necessity been killed by some other man.'[11]

Death from old age first recognized as the only kind of 'natural' death.

Again – it is almost universal among primitive peoples to believe that unless a man's body is disposed of with an appropriate ceremony – the dead will 'walk.' The natural tendency of the deceased is to find his way back to the place in

---

9   Oakeshott's note: 'F.L. Lucas, p. 18.' See F.L. Lucas, *Thomas Lovell Beddoes: An Anthology* (Cambridge: Cambridge University Press, 1932).

10 Oakeshott's note: 'See A.C. Haddon, review of C. Ribbe, *Zwei Jahre unter den Kannibalen der Salamo-Inseln* (Dresden and Elgbau: H. Bayer, 1903), *Folkore*, 16 (1905), 113–16, at 115.'

11 Oakeshott's note: 'B. Spencer and F.J. Gillen, *The Native Tribes of Central Australia* (London and New York: Macmillan and Co. Limited, 1899), p. 48.'

which he lived. This is a corollary of the belief in the unnaturalness of death – & both may be seen as expressions of the will to live.

11[33]

Sentimentality & Romanticism

Romanticism, at variance with life & the conditions of life, proclaims the sovereign authority of dreams. Denial of any standard of coherence. The merely subjective. Pessimism.

How far is a life spent in clinging to an old, unsatisfied love sentimental? Just in so far as it is not avoidable. It is true & not sentimental when & only when this surrender of life is really (as it may be) an appropriation of life to its satisfaction.

11[33]

Romanticism as wedded to the <u>Infinite</u> (& the infinite mistaken for the Spiritual). Romanticism – Classicism as a part of the battle between spiritual & sensual – Cp. Heine, Jean Paul Richter.

11[33]

Two views

1. Life is an evil, the conditions of life are at variance with the necessities of life. To make them agree is impossible. To attempt it is itself defeat.

2. Life must conform to the conditions of life. All that we can <u>live</u> is a life according to these conditions. The Romanticist is the man who, trying to get outside these conditions, fails to live – e.g. the man intent on making a 'contribution,' dies before it is achieved: the man who lives in the future or the past. These are the Romantics; & our usual view of life is hopelessly romantic.

But this view (2) does not imply that we should <u>at all points</u> make our way of life conform to the <u>present</u> conditions of life. These so-called present conditions are often not conditions at all, but the results of our false view of life. The true life must be one which conforms not to what is merely present, but to what is inherent and unavoidable.

We ought to adapt ourselves to those conditions which are unalterable e.g. the fact of death.

But alterable conditions – e.g. the actual length of life – should be subject to our moral requirements & not to the blind operations of nature.

11[34]

A race of men who, when they had experienced the abyss of love, knowing that they had reached the climax of life, chose in that moment to die, rather than to experience that slow decline which is the lot of all who either do not know, or are afraid to admit that the natural term of life has no relation to the moral needs of men.

11[34]

It is the fortune of the philosopher to be an outcast, useless to men of business & troublesome to those of pleasure.

11[34]

The abstract thinker is like those Indians who believe the world to be supported by an elephant & the elephant by a tortoise, but when you ask them on what the tortoise rests, they can answer you no further.

11[35]

The only knowledge worth having – or rather, the only knowledge relevant to life is a knowledge of *'le vrai rapport des choses à l'homme.'*[12]

11[35]

The relation of the vulgar meaning of *'Savoir vivre'* with a more profound meaning. Is there a more profound meaning than the vulgar meaning pressed to its conclusion?

11[35]

Love & Marriage

Always the view that somehow there is something else & more important to do in life than to be in love. Love must be a mere recreation, a mere means for some ulterior end. It must not be allowed to interfere.[13]

11[36]

Otherworldliness

The invulnerable, untouched soul – the soul unimplicated.
    This is an abstraction. We must have something more than mere conscience.[14]

11[36]

Liars usually escape the vice of dogmatism.

---

12   Oakeshott's note: 'Rousseau, *Julie.*' J.J. Rousseau, *Julie, ou la nouvelle Héloïse* [*Lettres de deux amans habitans d'une petite ville au pied des Alpes*], 6 vols. (Amsterdam: Marc-Michel Rey, 1761).' The quotation is from Pt V, Letter I.

13   Oakeshott's note: 'Tolstoy, *Anna Karenina*, i.306.'

14   Oakeshott's note: 'Cp. Hegel, *Phänomenologie des Geistes; Philosophie des Rechts.'*
    H.A. Reyburn, *The Ethical Theory of Hegel A Study of the Philosophy of Right* (Oxford: Clarendon Press, 1921), p. 191 etc.'

11[36]

Why do we always attempt to make our passions appear other than they are? Why do we attempt to moralise them & to make them consistent?

11[37]

Gratitude

Men hate those to whom they owe an obligation, says La Rochefoucauld. We insist upon gratitude & are paid with hatred. Or is gratitude one of those virtues which we may insist upon only in ourselves & not in others? Are there any such virtues?

11[37]

Death

(1) 'Of all the enemies of human happiness none is so destructive, none is of so cussed & forward a disposition, as is death.'[15]

(2) 'It is the knowledge of death which gives a special tang to the taste of life...If we did not know our days were numbered then the water we drink & the bread we eat would lose something of their flavour.'[16]

How to reconcile 1 & 2? They are contradictory. We must become friends with death before we can be friends with life — *Mors janua vitae*, not in the old super-stitious sense; but as a real & present fact in life. We must overcome death before we can begin to live.

11[38]

To see that one has failed would create in some a desire to begin again & succeed; in me it creates the desire to prove to myself that failure is inevitable & therefore not failure at all, but the stuff of life which requires only be understood in order to be conquered.

11[38]

We may construct a view of life which shews that value does not & cannot belong to my world merely as mine — e.g. Powys, *The Meaning of Culture*, etc. — to shew that completeness rather than personalness is the only tenable criterion.[17]

---

[15] Oakeshott's note: 'L. Powys, *Impassioned Clay* (London: Longmans & Co., 1931), p. 100.'

[16] Oakeshott's note: 'Powys, *Impassioned Clay*, p. 101 sq.'

[17] J.C. Powys, *The Meaning of Culture* (London: Jonathan Cape, 1930). For Oakeshott's review see *SW* iii.58–60.

But when we have done it—there comes death. This view of life, & the view which takes the meaning of life to lie in extent of achievement, have no answer for death; & in so far as they have no answer for death, they have none for life.[18]

Freedom and Perfection—is there a contradiction; or how can it be resolved? Perhaps 'freedom' is an abstract, incomplete, idea when severed from perfection.

11[39]

The Apocalyptic or Eschatalogical expectation acts upon us by heightening our sensibility of present life.

It is the same as a consciousness of <u>death</u>.

It is like being aware of the seeds of death in one. It is like having consumption.

11[39]

Love gives intensity to life—but how far is it a false & exaggerated intensity. When we are in love we are dead & blind to everything else, nothing else exists, nothing exists except in relation to her whom we love.

Looking back, when love has passed—if it does pass—this intensity seems bogus. The scale of importance seems unreal—but then, life also becomes unreal when we are not in love. We are still animal through and through, and we touch the universe only in love. Love is what gives meaning to life, the world & everything in it. The man in love is the man who has found & understood the universe. The man who is not in love fails always to achieve a satisfactory experience.

But then—Bradley, *Aphorisms*.[19]

11[41]

Among the Stoics to despise ambition & to be free from the world had become a cult—a negative cult.

But with Epicurus it was a positive way of life—'Live Alone.' The freedom of the Stoic was an escape; that of the Epicurean a fulfilment.

11[44]

Consider how much of modern scholarship, learning etc. is expended not in a man making up his own mind upon a whole subject or a small portion of it, but in giving expositions of this or that subject (or part of it) for the sole benefit of other people—certain classes.

E.g. <u>popularization</u>.

---

[18] Oakeshott's note: 'Cp. Hegel, *Philosophie des Rechts.*'
[19] Oakeshott's note: 'F. Bradley, *Aphorisms* (Oxford: Clarendon Press, 1930), 100.' For Oakeshott's review see *SW* iii.73–5.

The aim here is not to make one's own mind clear, but to modify that clarity & completeness of experience for the benefit of somebody else – & what benefit? Is there any? Is it not all a delusion?

The scholar can do two things; he can make up his own mind; and he can give an exposition of his own views. Beyond this – all these expositions of other's views, these abridgments, resumés etc. – all is pointless & meaningless.

11[45]

Nil admirari

The positive value of disenchantment: disillusion as a principle, not a failure –
Turgenev, *Smoke*.[20]
Tennyson, 'Lotus Eaters.'[21]
Landor.

Romantic disillusion, i.e., disillusion as an end, as a principle. Not as what is negative & safe – (Cp. Horace), but as what is vital, positive, happy, successful.[22]

11[46]

The Homeric Greeks, & others, have tried to explain death, have tried to make death accord to life, & their way of life accord to the fact of death, by means of the notion of fate. We cannot die before our time. 'Our time' clearly does not mean, 'when we have achieved all that we believe we can achieve.' It is an attempt to understand life apart from achievement. They were not in complete possession of this notion – the notion of posthumous fame was something added & contradictory – another & different attempt to understand life.[23]

It is not the briefness of life which is disconcerting, but its uncertainty – & fate & fame are two notions which attempt to remove this uncertainty from life.

11[47]

A long life does not, itself, give happiness. And to be allowed to remain alive is not a sign of being valuable.
The Tower of Siloam.

11[47]

We must conceive mortality widely – it is not merely human mortality, but the death & passing away of every element in life. Mortality of affections, emotions,

---

20 I.S. Turgenev, *Smoke*, tr. C. Garnett (New York: The Macmillan Company; London: William Heinemann, 1906).
21 A. Tennyson, 'The Lotus Eaters' in *Poems* (London: Edward Moxon, 1832).
22 11[45] includes a quotation headed 'Disillusion' from Scott, *Misogyny over the Week-end*.
23 Oakeshott's note: 'Cp. Homer, *Iliad*, XXII, 300 sq.'

desires, achievements. It is these which leave us aghast, & not mere death. It is these we fear, & not mere death.

11[47]

<u>Mortality</u>

'Gloriously unprepared for the long littleness of life.'[24]

Not merely unprepared; but prepared to <u>refuse</u> the littleness of life. To lead a life devoid of the littleness of life. How shall we achieve this?

It is not great pains & great disappointments which cause us to contemplate suicide, which pollute life – it is the littleness of life. How to be content with the nauseous intimacies of ordinary life, the petty intimacies, when we have known what it is to be in love. Rather a life devoid of intimacy.

11[48]

Three Essays –

The prospects of Theology.

1. The present position in Theology.

2. What is Christianity?

3. The civilization of the Book of Common Prayer.[25]

11[48–49]

<u>Mortality</u>

1. Life is insufferable unless it is freed from <u>fear</u> and <u>care</u>. <u>Death</u>.[26]

1. Man is capable of living a godlike life & the life of a god is a life of peace & serenity & freedom from care.[27]

2. Epicurus was the first man to set about freeing mankind from this 'terror of the mind.'[28]

---

[24]   A misquotation from a poem by Frances Cornford (1886–1960) inspired by her fellow poet Rupert Brooke (1887–1915): 'A young Apollo, golden-haired, / stands dreaming on the verge of strife, / magnificently unprepared for the long littleness of life.'

[25]   Oakeshott's note: 'See L. Powys, "The Book of Common Prayer," *Cornhill Magazine* (159), 1934, 580–7, reprinted in *Essays of the Year, 1933–1934*, ed. F.J. Harvey Darton (London: Argonaut Press, 1934).'

[26]   Oakeshott's note: 'Lucretius, *De rerum natura*, Bk I, 31, 106, 111, 146; Bk II, 14, 45, 46, 48, 60–1, 343, 363; Bk III, 36–94; Bk IV, 908; Bk V, 1180, 1202, 1207; Bk VI, 14, 25 sq.'

[27]   Oakeshott's note: 'Lucretius, *De rerum natura*, Bk III, 319; Bk II, 343, 1093; Bk V, 58, 69.'

[28]   Oakeshott's note: 'Lucretius, *De rerum natura*, Bk III, 1 sq, 1042; Bk V 1 sq, Bk VI, 1 sq; Empedocles, Bk I, 716 sq.'

3. For the only thing which will give this freedom is <u>reason</u>, <u>knowledge</u>, knowledge of the nature of things, knowledge of <u>causes</u>.[29]

4. Not <u>religion</u> — that merely enslaves, & creates fear.[30]

5. Not <u>love</u> — this brings care with it. Like ambition, it is never satisfied.[31]

Sleep — insensibility — may banish care — but then:

(i) We may wake.

(ii) We may dream.

Dreams.
    Fear of Death.
    How does <u>knowledge</u> free us from care?[32]
    <u>Plato</u> believed that <u>knowledge</u> of the <u>Good</u> would give us life.
    <u>Lucretius</u> believed that what we need is a knowledge of the nature of things — causes.[33]
    Death must be shown to be natural & felt as a friend — Mortality is not to be fought against.[34]
    Ways in which we fight against death — mortality.

(i) Idea of Immortality.[35]

(ii) Ambition; the feverish life. Attempt to <u>complete</u> life.[36]

A <u>plan</u> of life — difficulty & importance.

11[49]

<u>Love & ambition</u>: the difference:

(i) Is to be satisfied at the moment. It lives in the present.

(ii) Is never satisfied. It lives always in the future.

Or is there no difference?

---

[29] Oakeshott's note: 'Lucretius, *De rerum natura*, Bk I, 130, 145, 368; Bk II, 169–183; Bk V, 1211; Bk VI, 54, 83; Bk V, 15, 43, 1455; Bk IV, 908.'

[30] Oakeshott's note: 'Lucretius, *De rerum natura*, Bk I, 62–101; 102 sq; Bk III, 36–94; Bk IV, 19; Bk V, 113, 116 sq.'

[31] Oakeshott's note: 'Lucretius, *De rerum natura*, Bk IV, 1060 sqq, etc.'

[32] Oakeshott's note: 'Lucretius, *De rerum natura*, e.g. Bk IV, 580.'

[33] Oakeshott's note: 'But cp. Augustine, *Confessions*, Bk V ch. iv.'

[34] Oakeshott's note: 'Lucretius, *De rerum natura*, Bk III, 530, 1091, 612.'

[35] Oakeshott's note: 'Lucretius, *De rerum natura*, Bk III, 612, 775, 851, 926. cp. Bk III, 830.'

[36] Oakeshott's note: 'Lucretius, *De rerum natura*, Bk III, 912, 956, 998, 1076; Bk V, 1118–35.'

11[49]

Of course, you will say, the Aswan Dam would never have been built if everyone lived on the principle I have suggested.[37] But what then? There would, also,
have been no Great War.

11[50]

Mortality

How can we outflank pessimism?

(i) Suicide.

(ii) By conceiving life as essentially mortal – by refusing to contrast it with what
does not belong to life. For pessimism can exist only if we contrast this life with
another.

What is this other life?
   It is a life given to us in our emotions & affections; if we abstract that feeling
of immortality which goes with every strongly felt emotion, or affection, &
make, on that basis a world – a perfect & eternal world – we have then something to contrast with this mortal life. But it is an abstraction: – whatever we feel,
emotions are not eternal. They will always appear so: love must always assume
its own immortality. But must it? And if it doesn't it becomes at once more
satisfactory – for it is on account of this assumption that it is always disappointing – & at the same time, this imaginary perfect world disappears – & with it
pessimism.
   Cp. Solipsism. Has meaning only when we assume two worlds. Abolish the
second, & solipsism goes with it.

11[51]

To appreciate, to love the gay appearances of the world, & to know them as
illusion. To experience at once the feeling of immortality in love & the mortality
of love. To yield neither of these; to hold fast to both. Can this be done? How can
this be done? But if it can be done it brings us within reach of the only sort of
certainty (a mortal certainty) & the only sort of happiness (a mortal happiness)
possible. All else is unprotected against disappointment & disenchantment. But
in this there can be no disappointment, for we expect nothing; no disenchantment, for we are never enchanted.

---

[37] Now known as the Aswan Low Dam in Egypt, completed in 1902.

11[53]

'Alas, we scarce live long enough to try
whether a true made clocke run right, or lie.'
Donne, An Anatomy of the World.[38]

It is not the briefness of life; but the fact that it ends.

'All casual joy doth loud & plainly say
Only by comming, that it can away.
Only in Heaven joyes strength is never spent;
And accidental things are permanent.'
Donne, ibid.[39]

Somehow, accidental things must be seen to be permanent <u>here</u>.

11[54]

<u>Mortality</u>

To become friends with mortality, to defeat death, it is necessary to live an extemporary life. In such a life there is no death, for there is no recognized change. Each moment, instead of being the successor to the last & the predecessor of the next, is complete in itself. Life becomes <u>continuous</u>, without breaks or <u>lacunae</u>. We no longer move from point to point, but are complete at every point.

Two things stand in the way of this.

(i) The future. How to free life from the despotism of the future. Take no thought for the morrow etc. This is comparatively easy. It may be difficult, but we can see <u>how</u> it can be done, & we know people who have achieved it.

(ii) The past. Is it possible to free life from the despotism of the past? This is the major & most difficult problem confronting anyone attempting to live an extemporary life. And Christianity (for example) has little to tell us which will help us.

To be continuously and certainly free from one's past? How? Each moment to be a genuine <u>beginning</u> as well as a genuine <u>end</u>. We can free ourselves temporarily from our past. But how can we be <u>certain</u> that the past will not break in upon our freedom?

Has Christianity no doctrine about freedom from the past as well as the future e.g. sin & freedom from sin, & its consequences.

Luther's attempt to free us from our past.

& the Doctrine of Divine forgiveness.

---

[38] Oakeshott's note: 'John Donne, *An Anatomy of the World. Wherein, by Occasion of the Untimely Death of Mistris Elizabeth Drury the Frailty and the Decay of this Whole World is Represented* (London: Samuel Macham: 1611), I. 235.'

[39] Oakeshott's note: 'Donne, *An Anatomy of the World*, I. 263, 265.'

To <u>forget</u> is no permanent solution.

11[55]

If we could not forget, & free ourselves from the past to that extent, our life would be short & mean. For wherever experience is dominated by the past, it is qualified, modified, distorted. For there to be a beginning there must be a forgetting—though not a total forgetting.

11[55]

The religion of all lovers is just their love. When we are in love & the world is in flower, when every action & every word & thought is thought of in relation to the beloved, when the whole world is simply the scene of our love—what religion could be superimposed upon that? There is no room for a religion; it is there already; & no man can have two religions.

11[55]

We feed upon the beloved.

11[56]

There is nothing so romantic as Hellenism.

11[56]

The relation between melancholy, sadism & masochism.

11[56]

To be invulnerable—with the single necessary exception of those whom we love—those, because we love them can always wound us. Is, then, love something to be avoided?

No: it is neither to be avoided, nor to be considered as something outside or contradictory of the good life—which is that of the invulnerable lover.

For the lover is vulnerable to the beloved, & on this account invulnerable to all the rest of the world. He who is vulnerable to one is more invulnerable to the rest, than if he were wholly invulnerable.

11[57]

Has the human race ever set itself seriously to follow any end which it knew to be spiritually desirable? Has it ever conceived that life should be lived for itself, thoroughly & without encumbrance?

Beauty, peace, happiness, health—have these ever been the <u>immediate</u> ends of human life?

Cp. Athens.

But, as a rule, these ends have always been put on one side, or thrown into the distance. And their place taken by material prosperity, fame, wealth, etc: —

The view of life implicated in our proverbs etc.

'A rolling stone gathers no moss.' But who wants to gather moss?

11[58]

Romanticism

Romanticism as the antithesis of classicism.

Romantic movement—an escape from restraint. The Romantic movement was something else besides Romantic: other characteristics: time & place & specific reaction against a particular classicism.

In literature; a new technique.

11[58]

Characteristic: of French Romanticism:

Anti French classicism.

Vitality.

Melancholy — fashion of sickness, consumption.[40]

Love of the grotesque; picturesque. The past — historical bric à brac.[41]

Enjoyment of crime, passion, cruelty, violence, outlaws, brigands.

French Romanticism coming after the Napoleonic Empire. A lost generation. Cp. de Musset.

Painting: influence of English painting — especially Constable on Delcacroix. etc:

The French Romantic movement began with painting.

Cp. The picture-writing — word-painting — of the Romantics — Gautier.[42]

The Romantic willingness to pursue an image.[43]

11[59]

Romantic love

To enjoy & to glory in the conflicts, the fire, the passions of love for their own sake. To be in love with love.

---

[40] Oakeshott's note: 'Cp. Carr, p. 129.' Possibly E.H. Carr, *The Romantic Exiles: A Nineteenth-century Portrait Gallery* (London: Victor Gollancz, 1933).

[41] Oakeshott's note: 'Cp. Scot.' Possibly a misspelling of the surname of historical novelist Sir Walter Scott (1771–1832).

[42] Possibly Théophile Gautier (1811–72), French poet, playwright, and critic noted for his defense of Romantic ideals.

[43] Oakeshott's note: 'Cp. Gérard de Nerval, *Les filles du feu* [*Sylvie*] (Paris: D. Giraud, 1854).'

Opposite to the 'classic' notion — love as a demon to be fled from & feared —
to be endured. Racine, *Phèdre*.[44]

11[59]

Romanticism & escape — two ways:

(i) To escape from life into poetry. To leave life behind & find a new life in
imagination.

(ii) To make life itself Romantic: to force life itself into the Romantic mould. —
Balzac.

11[59]

To die like a Greek runner, at the moment of reaching the goal. To die before the
disenchantment of success sets in.

11[61]

<u>Mortality</u>

Most men live as circumstances direct: a few live according to a plan.
    Cp. Bentham, Mill — Utility — a <u>principle</u>; & not mere chance, sympathy &
antipathy.

'All detached ethical precepts, all single & limited ethical ideas, all detailed
moral standards have in them elements arbitrary, provincial, temporary.'[45]

Some, however, who fail to live according to a plan, have a plan of life, a view.
They see life as a coherent whole, & fail to carry it out only through indolence or
lack of faith. They, however, lack the rigidity & hardness of those who practice,
& the inconsequence of those who do not think.

Plans of life —

(i) Strict code of morality: absolute. Cp. Cato.

(ii) Altruistic. St Francis.

(iii) The man of the world. Chesterfield.

(iv) Nature — Rousseau. Day.

(v) Freedom — Georges Sand.

(vi) Withdrawal. Buddha.

---

[44] J. Racine, *Phèdre: tragédie* (Paris: Bordas, 1966).
[45] Oakeshott's note: 'Cp. Nietzsche, *Zarathustra*; cp. M. Jaeger, *Experimental Lives from
      Cato to George Sand* (London: George Bell & Sons, 1932).' See William Wallace,
      'Nietzsche's *Thus Spake Zarathustra*,' in *Lectures and Essays on Natural Theology and
      Ethics*, ed. E. Caird (Oxford: Clarendon Press, 1898), pp. 530–41, at 533.

(These are not absolutely exclusive of one another — or, not all of them.)

The man of the world, intent upon succeeding, who knows he must use every advantage he can get, or else go under. And the man who happily goes under because it bores him to be clinging always to his advantages; who throws them away because they nauseate him; the man who does not care whether he 'succeeds' or not, so long as he remains happy in himself.

11[62]

Two opposing impulses —

(i) To make and keep oneself independent of circumstances. To preserve oneself. To regard circumstances as hindrances, as enemies. Nature the enemy. An absolute standard.

(ii) To live a 'natural' life; to conform, to find oneself in conformity. To discover that one's plan & way of life is actual self-realization. To make one's life conform to the conditions of life. A life opposed to the conditions of life is dissipated. But what conditions?

Reconciliation —
Some 'conditions of life' are real & unchangeable conditions.
E.g. mortality.
Others are circumstances which our actual way of life creates.
We must conform to the first; & be free of the second, whenever these conflict with the first. Our life, will, then, be at once free, self-centred, other-worldly; and in conformity with the conditions of life which belong to living itself & are inseparable from it.
E.g. To be true to one's love for someone whom one can never possess & who does not return it. This would appear foolish; but does it actually contradict the conditions of mortality?
The bitterness of love not returned; is it even love?[46]

11[65]

Who is *felix opportunitate mortis*?
Cp. Parnell's father, a devotee of cricket who died from a chill contracted while playing.
The beau who died rescuing his favourite pair of boots.
The Greek athlete who died at the moment of victory.
The bride who dies on her wedding night.
Ovid's wish to die in the act of love.

---

[46] Oakeshott's note: 'Alan Porter, *The Signature of Pain, and Other Poems* (London: Cobden-Sanderson, 1930).'

11[66]

Romanticism

Nature. This romantic feeling for Nature is probably possible only in conjunction with a feeling of separation from nature.[47]

Tolstoy & Goethe, both children of nature — sensual, elemental; & their problem is how to become children of spirit. A moralizing problem.

Schiller & Dostoevsky, both children of spirit & content to remain so.

What happens when a child of spirit wants to be joined to nature?

11[66]

Mortality

'Life requires discipline & rules, but the thoughts which underlie & determine the discipline & the rules must in the last resort have been extracted from life.'

Harold Höffding.[48]

Yes; & if we listened to life — what sort of discipline & what rules should we follow?

But we must escape 'Naturalism.'

11[67]

Mortality

The conception of man as a 'stage,' a 'bridge' & not a 'goal' (Nietzsche), unsatisfactory. Human life must be seen to be complete in every moment before it can be conceived to be tolerable. A stage in a process, a means that is not an end, is not merely immoral, but <u>death</u>.

11[67]

Romanticism

Rousseau's marriage to Thérèse la Vasseur. He did not take as a mistress some brilliant member of Parisian society, but this child of the people. Something untouched by the corruption of that society — or so he thought.

To us Rousseau, especially in his relations to women, may strike us as sentimental. But sentimentality is the attempt to follow an old, outworn fashion in feeling; & of this Romanticism Rousseau was the originator — in revolt against the sophistication of Parisian society of the 18th century.

But Rousseau is less out of place to-day than then; for it is the sophistication of France in the 18th century which is the sentimentality of to-day, it is

---

[47] Oakeshott's note: 'Cp. T. Mann, "Goethe & Tolstoy," p. 31 sq.' See T. Mann, *Three Essays*, tr. H.T. Lowe-Porter (London: Secker and Warburg, 1932).

[48] Harold Höffding (1843–1931), Danish philosopher and theologian.

classicism which is Romantic. There is more genuine Romanticism, & less genuine classicism, than ever before.

There is doubt, criticism, complexity — the ingredients of the Romantic outlook.

11[68]

Irving Babbitt. Modern Romanticism[49]

The attempt to recreate the disillusion of Horace in place of the faith & vigour of Rousseau. He does not see that the disillusion of to-day must <u>include</u> the Romantic spirit & not merely <u>deny</u> it. We must have a Romantic disillusion — all else is derivative, dead, sentimental, bogus.

11[68]

It is impossible to get happiness by following a plan. Everything about us, & we ourselves change continually. To attempt to <u>capture</u> happiness & keep it is foolish. To put away this illusion is to be disillusioned; but at the same time happy. For then only can we enjoy the happiness which comes to us, without regret or pain.[50]

11[72]

The Philosopher & the Moralist

The one engaged in the analysis of the moral consciousness & its acts & the ideas of value, good, & right.

The other concerned with, 'What things are good?', 'What in detail & in fact is valuable?'

Nietzsche — warning us that we have never yet known what good & evil are.

The re-valuation of values.

An inspection of our values.

Cp. Romanticism of the 19th century & how it it has silently created a world of value for us — innocence etc. Virginity.

That is the way our values get changed — silently, surreptitiously.

What we want is to become conscious of our values, & then forget them.

'The moralist' — misleading; the abstract meaning attached to it. — The preacher & evangelist. Get away from this; something less noisy than a gospel, something more complete than a creed. Not aiming to convince & persuade, but to see clearly & to speak unambiguously.

---

[49] Irving Babbitt (1865–1933), American critic of Romanticism, author of *Rousseau and Romanticism* (Boston; New York: Houghton Mifflin Co., 1919).

[50] Oakeshott's note: 'Cp. J.J. Rousseau, *Rêveries du promeneur solitaire*, in *Confessions de J.J. Rousseau, suivi des rêveries du promeneur solitaire*, 2 vols. (Geneva: 1782), Ch. IX (beginning).'

11[74]

There are various possible retreats. The safest of them is death. This is too drastic. What people want is a 'death-surrogate' — a state of being that combines the advantages of being alive with those of being dead.

Drink, sensuality, dreams — None of these is a perfect refuge.

Religious meditation, science, knowledge, philosophy.

But what of the life which refuses <u>substitutes</u>? This, that & the other — business, learning, hobbies, religion, drink — are all substitutes, good & bad. Adolescence is distinguished by the refusal of all substitutes, it must have all or nothing. And those who never rise out of that state, go on refusing substitutes. The end, I suppose must be suicide; for we must die or find some substitute for death. The poet, I suppose, finds his substitute in poetry, & that perhaps is the least qualified of all substitutes.

11[77]

<u>Romanticism</u>

Romanticism & liberalism. [51]

View that besides the pathological element in R. there was an urge towards liberty, humanitarianism, justice, purity. But that is a superficial view.

'Approximate terms such as "baroque," "romantic," "decadent," have their origins in definite revolutions of sensibility, and it serves no purpose to detach them from their historical foundations & apply them generously to artists of varied types.'[52]

Classic & Romantic.[53]

Hellenism a form of romanticism.

Nothing so romantic as 'classicism.'[54]

The inseparability of pleasure & pain — especially in love; & the search for tormented beauty. Beauty is not beautiful except it be sad, tormented, painful, ugly, accursed.[55]

Medusa.

Beauty tainted with corruption and death.

---

[51] Oakeshott's note: 'P. Lasserre, *Le romantisme français: essai sur la révolution dans les sentiments et dans les idées au XIXe siècle* (Paris: Mercure de France, 1907).'

[52] Oakeshott's note: 'Praz, *Romantic Agony*, pp. 6–7.' Mario Praz, *The Romantic Agony. A Study of the Morbid Tendencies of Romantic Literature, 1800–1900*, tr. A. Davidson (Oxford: Oxford University Press, 1933).

[53] Oakeshott's note: 'Cp. Sir H.J.C. Grierson, *The Background of English Literature, and Other Collected Essays & Addresses* (London: Chatto & Windus, 1925).'

[54] Oakeshott's note: 'Praz, *Romantic Agony*, pp. 10–11.'

[55] Oakeshott's note: 'Praz, *Romantic Agony*, p. 28.'

11[77]

What in the 17th century — e.g. Donne — are conceits, literary devices, in the 18th & 19th centuries with the Romantics, are real feelings.

11[77]

'Ennui is not only the most generic aspect of the *mal du siècle*; its specific aspect is — sadism.'[56]

Masochism & sadism.

11[77]

Exotic & erotic ideals go together.
    The fatal woman — Spain: Carmen.
    Russia.
    A love of the exotic is usually an imaginative projection of a sexual desire.
    How far was the fatal woman the projection of a <u>fear</u> of lack of potency in the male — fear & pride. The masochistic attitude is a defence against fear.

11[77]

Romanticism — fury of frenzied action.
Decadence — sterile contemplation.

11[78]

The modern Epicurean — the spectator — disillusioned.[57]
    Positive disillusion — happiness something not to be <u>expected</u>.[58]

11[79]

<u>Mortality</u>[59]

If you are interested only in the destinies of yourself & your friends — you will live a purposeless old age — friends gone & your own aims either already achieved; or, what is more probable, failure.
    ∴ For a happy life, it is necessary to have at heart the destinies of <u>the race</u>, of mankind in general.
    But what, & all that is necessary, is to be <u>without</u> this sense of purpose. To banish the word 'achievement' banishes also 'failure.' If your life is taken up entirely with the immediate joys & sorrows of your friends & yourself; old age

---

56   Oakeshott's note: 'Praz, *Romantic* Agony, p. 144.'
57   Oakeshott's note: 'p. 147.' I.S. Turgenev, *A House of Gentlefolk*, tr. C. Garnett (London: William Heinemann; New York, The Macmillan Company, 1915).
58   Oakeshott's note: 'Turgenev, *House of Gentlefolk*, pp. 264–5.'
59   Oakeshott's note: 'Mill, *Utilitarianism*, p. 13.' J.S. Mill, *Utilitarianism*, first published in *Fraser's Magazine*, 64 (1861), 391–406, reprinted in *CW*, x.203–59.

will not be subject to the lack of interest Mill predicts. For <u>this</u> is a continuous & unexamined interest, whereas all others may work themselves out before the end. This is the only <u>invulnerable</u> state. Interest centered upon nobody's <u>destiny</u>, upon no future <u>aim</u>, no <u>purpose</u>.

A life unimpeded by this fatal, but seductive, mistress — achievement, purpose, destiny, progress.

Cp. <u>Liberalism</u>: progress.

11[80]

<u>Mortality</u>

It is said that the fact of immortality is so clear & obvious, that not to take it as the criterion of value in life would be foolish & stupid.

E.g. Shakespeare <u>is</u> immortal.

But this is merely a question of fact — which may be left to look after itself.

The point for us is not how to reconcile the fact that Shakespeare is immortal with our view of life. But whether to make this so-called fact the central belief results in a happy life or not.

Or, in other words, are we, because of our immortality, to govern our own lives by this concept?

E.g. Shakespeare is immortal: but did he live <u>as</u> an immortal?

Many men have lived as immortals —

Expressly: (a) fame, name, reputation etc:

Anonymously: (b) Descendants, the next generation, etc:

This can be <u>done</u>; it has been done: but the question is whether or not it enables us to 'overcome' life?

Put it another way — <u>immortality</u> is the name we give for the principle by which we 'overcome' life. How is it to be attained?

(i) By seeking it in its most obvious form — the future, the race etc.

(ii) By seeking it in the present — <u>in</u> mortality. <u>Positive mortality</u> is a form of Immortality different from mere negative mortality. Cf. positive & negative disillusion.

11[80]

The idea of 'innocence,' 'virginity' & the principle of keeping yourself pure for the one great & satisfying event.

This is true & genuine — the 'first' time may well be the greatest & most profound. But knowledge & practice essential — best perhaps if knowledge can be had without practice, but no enjoyment without knowledge.

Sometimes those who prize the 'first' beyond everything else & are (consequently) disappointed, never try again. It is these who lose their lives *'par délicatesse.'*[60]

11[80]

We are always either surprised or kept waiting by death — (as birth). Birth & death are alike unexpected; and our view of life should take this into account.

Live each day as if it were your last.

11[80]

Perhaps it is the 'sting of life' rather than of death — the sharpness of life — which is most difficult to overcome. But if we have overcome that of death, the sting of life is also overcome.

11[82]

It has been said that a religion must suit & recognize both good & bad times, times of adversity & times of prosperity, peace & trouble, progress & decadence.

But there is something more profound than these; there are the universal & unvarying conditions of human life common to both adversity & prosperity & of which these are merely superficial variations. It is these which a successful religion must recognize, and when it recognizes them it will be more than a consolation in times of adversity or an encouragement & a sobering influence in times of prosperity. And Mortality is what I mean by these universal conditions.

11[82]

Epicureanism

Epicureanism represents a way of looking at the world & human life which possesses permanent interest for the human race.

Cp. Zélide.[61] How she 'lived alone' — contempt of pretention, display. Preference for simple people, and close, personal relationships. A private life.

11[82]

The mixture of melancholy & gaiety in Epicureanism; the response both to adversity & prosperity.

This is, at first sight, contradictory; but it is the contradiction of life itself — the contradiction of activity.

---

60 See A. Rimbaud, *'Chanson de la plus haute tour'*: *'Par délicatesse j'ai perdu ma vie.'* Cp. p. 325, below.

61 Possibly Isabelle Agnès Élizabeth de Charrière, aka Zélide (1740–1805), Swiss novelist. Oakeshott may have been reading *Four Tales by Zélide*, tr. Sybil Scott-Cutting (London: Archibald Constable & Co., 1925).

See *Experience & its Modes*.

Encouragement in the face of adversity; stability in the face of prosperity. (The second the more difficult.)

11[83]

Two questions to be answered, two related & inseparable questions.

(i) What to believe about the world.

(ii) How to live.

11[83]

Stoicism & Epicureanism

What really matters depends upon you yourself alone — Stoicism — Everything else is external & negligible — pleasure & pain, health, wealth & position. The abstract, separate, invulnerable self.

Epicureanism — What really matters depends upon you alone — & your friends. The self is not isolated: what is isolated, or whole & stands out against the universe is self & friends. A man & his friends are complete, free, inviolable, invulnerable. A man can be wounded only by his friends. This is a concrete self; Stoicism tends, at least, towards the worship of an abstract self, a self which can never be self-complete, a self created merely by separation, subtraction, isolation.

To be invulnerable — but without the crass armour of self-esteem.

11[84]

Physical death is an instance of mutability — it is mutability itself which has to be overcome.

11[84]

How to be reconciled to mutability's theft of all beautiful things? —

Keats — each moment is fulfilled of beauty, and we must live in each moment. cp. his life of sensations rather than of thought.

With Keats this was first an emotional solution; which later he attempts to make philosophical in the 'Ode to Autumn.' But the great thing for Keats is that he was able to feel it, & so find happiness. Shelley never really felt it; his faith in the future — gradually waning.

11[85]

Mortality & humour

Humour is the attitude which a full realization of mortality induces, and which is the only answer to mortality. Humour — the maturity of sentiment. Impossible in adolescence — age impossible without it. The only substitute which has a positive quality.

11[86]

The Suicide of the lover — the last consummate flattery of the beloved.

11[86]

Love & desire are signs of the insufficiency of the self for itself. <u>Stoic</u>: we must school ourselves to self-sufficiency & become independent of what is outside us. But this denies human nature. 'We are too weak to live without love': Spinoza. But that again is an error; it takes mortality not to belong to human nature. We must love & desire, but we must conquer desire not by denying it & withdrawing from it as much as possible, but by admitting its inevitable unsatisfactoriness.[62]

11[87]

The moral courage which permits us to recognize what does not coincide with the purpose of our lives — a moral courage which, if followed, may lead to the disintegration of that purpose.

11[87]

'Man lives between two desires — his desire of spiritual peace & happiness, & his desire of earthly experience.'[63]

And somehow we have got to get our spiritual peace & happiness out of this earthly experience. To let it remain something extraneous to that experience — e.g., in a religion or religious belief unrelated to, perhaps in contrast to experience — is to leave it always insecure.

11[88]

Death is like the virus of leprosy, which lies within a man for years before it becomes active. We are born with this germ within us, in childhood & youth it is unrealized, in early manhood we become acutely aware of it, as age advances we get used to it, & if we are wise & fortunate, master it. Its terrors are controlled, its horror mastered.

Period of incubation of leprosy can be as much as 20 or 30 years.

11[89]

The transformation of <u>moral values</u> into <u>facts</u>.

---

[62] Oakeshott's note: 'Duff, p. 114.'
[63] Oakeshott's note: 'George Moore, *Evelyn Innes* (London: T. Fisher Unwin, 1898), p. 237.'

Good & evil — moral.

Yin & Yang — non-moral.

11[89]

Confucianism

The central concept — '*jen*': humanity, mankind, kindness, sympathy.

The feeling of one man for another.

This '*jen*' is the original gift of nature; it is the spirit which man has received in order to live. It is what is common & most fundamental in all men.

Public service insisted upon by Confucianism — the reaction of Taoism.

The 'superior man' of Confucius.

Cp. The '*homme habile*' of La Rochefoucauld.

The 'wise man' of the Stoic.

_____ of the Epicurean.

and Nietzsche? & other moralists.

The 'free' man.

The 'righteous' man.

11[90]

Reaction to disillusion, to the troubled state of the world, to failure & to despondency.

To find a life which is expressed & satisfied in some intensely personal experience.[64]

11[A]

Social substance of religion[65] — yes, but society itself is a particular attempt to answer these questions about life, & it is an attempt rather to be subsumed under religion, rather than religion under it. For religion is the force which makes society as well as that which reforms or destroys it.

The view that nature makes, & religion destroys is meaningless.

We must see religion as the ground of both:

(i) The disruptive forces in society;

(ii) The integrative & conservative forces in society.

It is something much more fundamental than either of these taken alone. It is energy itself, the manifestation of energy for whatever purpose — & these are the two great conflicting purposes — rather than a peculiar type of energy. It is

---

[64] Oakeshott's note: 'J.B. Leishman, *The Metaphysical Poets: Donne, Herbert, Vaughan, Traherne* (Oxford: Clarendon Press, 1934), p. 3.'

[65] On a loose sheet inserted at 11[16], numbered 11[16a].

energy—mental & physical—directed towards a practical union with life, towards finding the world a home & giving life a meaning.

11[A]

Rationalization—Heard sees in it only something 'after the fact.' But it is inherent in self-conciousness.[66] Self-consciousness, experience, makes the 'fact'; & Rationalization is merely carrying this process to its conclusion—The determination to satisfy self-conscious experience for its own sake.

The normal, civilized man to-day does nothing but rationalize—experience is itself rationalization—& the trouble is that he stops too soon.

Man has made many mistakes in his rationalizing e.g. when he mistakes his thirst for immortality for a desire for a life hereafter, rather than as a desire for a life harmonious here.

And, perhaps, one of these mistakes is that he mistakes the 'sense of the group' & the satisfaction he hopes to get from that, for a desire for something beyond the group—the group, so to speak is the symbol for something beyond the threshold of explicit experience, but inside his world of volitional experience.[67]

11[B]

Mortality[68]

To overturn & abolish the criterion of life which prizes what has been accomplished, the static world of what is achieved, possessed, won; to which the flower is merely the promise of a fruit. To overturn it because it is out of touch with the real facts of life; to abolish it, because to retain it involves the abolition of life.

The superiority of present, extemporary experience over knowledge which has already been acquired—'classed & done-with.' The superiority which we recognize belongs to one who has just now discovered, for the first time, something which to me, as I stood by, was merely already known, remembered. He is living in the May-morning of creation; I, in the drowsy decline of afternoon. The superiority which belongs to what is <u>first</u> experienced. To recognize this superiority, & to plan our criteria of life to be consistent with that recognition, instead of, as now, inconsistent & contradictory.

---

[66] Oakeshott's note: 'G. Heard, *Social Substance of Religion: An Essay on the Evolution of Religion* (London: George Allen & Unwin, 1931), pp. 120–1.'
[67] Oakeshott's note: 'Cp. Heard, *Social Substance of Religion*, p. 94.'
[68] On a loose sheet inserted at 11[16], numbered 11[16b].

11[C]

Ibsen[69]

Subject of his plays —

The sacrifice of the natural good to some ideal — dead or living.

E.g. *Ghosts* — respectability.

Brand — all or nothing Religion.

    ↖ Kierkegaard.

'The jury of life,' 'the love of life in the individual' — this must be asserted & maintained at all costs.

Ibsen is not simply the idealist critic who castigates a Peer Gynt or a Berkman; *Brand* also denies what Ibsen asserts — or wants to assert. On which side is he in *Romersholm*?

Conflict — how unreal any cause is beside a human being.

How trivial a human being is beside a cause.

The solution lies only in a unification of these: — the cause seen as the self realization of the human being.

Both are abstractions.

11[D]

What I want to achieve is a view of life which has got rid of everything doctrinaire.[70] Most of us live with a doctrinaire view of life, a view which is not in correspondence with the facts of actual life, but with the facts of an imaginary life. Life & death we see through a haze of inherited & half-understood conceptions & words. Let us get back to the facts & construct our conceptions anew. But to get away from what is doctrinaire is not to do without a doctrine. Nor does it mean that life is lived without a doctrine.[71]

Even the view of life which is 'pagan' has an aim, a doctrine, a logic.

11[E]

Mortality[72]

The question used to be put in the form, What am I here for? But this form makes too many presuppositions for it to be satisfactory or radical.

The position to-day.

The good life wanted by everybody. Mass.

Cp. 18th century civilization.

Organization; large communities; prosperity.

---

[69] On a loose sheet inserted at 11[19], stamped: 'GONVILLE AND CAIUS COLLEGE / CAMBRIDGE,' numbered 11[19a].

[70] On a loose sheet inserted at 11[19], numbered 11[19e].

[71] Oakeshott's note: 'Brewster, pp. 43 sq.'

[72] In pencil on a loose sheet inserted at 11[19]. Numbered 11[19f].

Everything infected with this 'achievement.'
Ideal — And nothing can be abolished.
Culture, education, etc.

Answers —

(i) Drugs. Our whole way of life a drug. The problem insoluble: so it must be avoided or forgotten. Enter the system & forget what lies outside it.

(ii) Revolution. But is this possible? And what do we want? Our needs complex; would be better if simplified. Can they be simplified. We want some things that civilization provides — & we must take the rest with them.

(iii) Suicide.

11[F]

What do we want?[73]
　　What is satisfying?
　　Certain physical enjoyments; what more?
　　Bondage — we are tied　& bound. We have no freedom to plan our lives, deaths.
　　There is no consonance between our desires & our circumstances. Only disharmony.
　　Is this at the root of life? Should we be always like this?
　　Powerless to alter our circumstances.
　　Frustration everywhere. Forget it?
　　Nostalgia.
　　Monasticism.

11[G]

The Prospects of Christian Theology[74]

The Catholic Reaction. Cp. Gore's Commentary.[75] But this is less significant than it would have been 20 years ago, because we no longer think of Christianity as resting upon the Scriptures in the old way.

Introduction

Wherever I have become conscious of a presupposition I have questioned it.

73　In pencil on a loose sheet inserted at [11.19]. Numbered 11[19g].
74　On a loose sheet inserted at 11[19], numbered 11[19h].
75　Possibly C. Gore et al. (eds), *A New Commentary on Holy Scripture, including the Apocrypha* (London: S.P.C.K., 1929).

Belle Dame Notebook 9
(January–October 1932)

BD9[01]

C's poise of manner. Superiority, mastery, confidence, integrity. Clothes contribute to this poise. Balanced, not rooted, growing, resilient, ready & yet specifically unprepared—extemporary. A virtuouso.

Slow, fashionable indifference.

C's hardness—eye for the main chance—money—'you'll <u>pay</u> for that'—venom. How it can slip out under the appearance of friendship. Ruthless in a quarrel.

BD9[03]

The moments when memory breaks in & ruins everything. Just as we are setting out upon some new life, memory steps in & lays it waste before we can begin to enjoy it. Never, never, never can we begin again. Always ourselves, & always what we <u>were</u> haunts us, hinders us, makes us impotent.

BD9[04]

First stage—

To lie with a beautiful girl because she is beautiful. To have the pleasure of beauty. To realize the desire of the eye & the happiness of the body. To delight in her lips, her cheeks, her hair, her skin, her thighs. This is beyond the primitive, animal desire.

BD9[04–05]

<u>Letters to the unknown</u>. Attempts to satisfy desire by denying it. To be free by suppressing desire.

<u>Margaret</u>—the red-haired girl. Her grey eyes, solitude, self-completeness.
This is to follow Romanticism; it arises from a failure of Romanticism, but is, itself, a form of Romanticism. It lies between the 'Beyond' & the 'Nowhere' as the satisfaction of desire.

---

[1] LSE 20/1. Paper cover, brown, exercise book, 13.5 cm x 8 cm. Ruled. Unnumbered. Autograph, ink. Dated: 'M. Oakeshott. / Gonville & Caius College / Cambridge. / Jan 1. 1932–Oct 1. 1932.'

Other works from which Oakeshott made excerpts in this notebook but which are not mentioned in the text include: Fo. 2, Lawrence, *Women in Love*; 15, Rousseau, *Julie*.

BD9[05]

In these last months before C. is married & goes to Greece, I seem to be like a man who knows accurately the date of his death. Not merely a moribund man, who may hang on to life for an indefinite period & the end of whose life will come as unexpectedly as anyone else's; but a condemned man, to whom reprieve is impossible. And this experience gives a new standpoint to life, a new intensity to the enjoyments with C. I am on a 'magic mountain.'

BD9[06]

The awakening of love is accidental. One may marry, one may lust, one may lie with a girl & have pleasure from her – without love ever awakening. Two may lie together, but love is not always there.

But when love is awakened, then the world is transformed, & every item of life blossoms.

BD9[07]

The Pattern of Mortality

To see love as the middle moment of a search for completeness, realization.

First: disinclination, refusal to be drawn into the world. To remain untouched. Desire to be stilled by refusal. Ascetic religions.

Second: out into the world: the love of women, in all its phases. Attempt at completeness. Positive freedom sought.

First failure of love owing to having taken into this new attempt the old conceptions of asceticism. First love the love of a dead self & so, when the fact that the self is dead is realized, the love perishes also.

The possibility of completeness, revealed, seen – but refused – Céline. But, in this second moment, completeness is possible to see; & that vision must be a vision of disquiet for the rest of life.

Third: Retirement: failure of completeness: & adoption of an ideal in invulnerability instead. Negative freedom. Nothing more than this is possible in life.[2]

Fourth: War – unending strife between second & third. But always a reluctance to leave the second moment – love – that seemed to offer completeness – the rest is the admission of failure. The perpetual war between the third & the second is the pattern of life.

BD9[08]

Qualities of mind are more stable than the beauties of the body – I have not found it so. I am a different person from the person who married four years ago.

---

[2]   Oakeshott's note: 'Cp. *The Fountain*, p. 148.' Probably C. Morgan, *The Fountain*: see p. 224 n. 5, above.

The change has not been a physical change – it has been a change of the mind. The mind is the least enduring of all the stuffs of men.

BD9[08]

The intimations of mortality

The fingers become hard, the skin less supple, the nails dry up & become brittle. The mouth no longer waters at the sight of food.

BD9[11]

The parting of lovers has been compared with death – but it is not that. The death of the beloved is final, complete; it has meaning. But there is no realized finality in mere parting. It has the feverishness of life & the emptiness of death in one.

BD9[11]

Love & friendship & every intimate association has a kind of underlying substance, to preserve which & to maintain it every activity is directed.

BD9[12]

I had a wife, & now I have a mistress – but where is happiness? Where is love?

BD9[12-13]

March 1932.

C. gradually slipping from me. The time drawing near when I shall neither see her nor be able to write to her: when I shall neither hear her voice nor see her writing. Like a man condemned to death; believing always that a last minute reprieve will come but believing without either ground or hope.

And, with it all, the presentiment of the loneliness which will follow her departure. How I make plans to avoid that loneliness; beg C. to find out the name of the girl with the red hair – all the while knowing that no new relationship can ever relieve the loneliness or mitigate it. The pathetic illusion that we can banish this awful solitude by making fresh acquaintances or friends.

BD9[13-14]

The discontent inherent in every satisfaction. The desire always to oppose, to strive against, to hate in the midst of loving. The only satisfaction lies in being denied, continually denied, but denied in such a way as to be led on. A continual, subtle movement to & fro. A warfare, a struggle. Continual temptation, continually overcome. A relationship which is never formulated, or established. Fluid, moving, flowing & ebbing, ceaseless, unsatisfied, but final in its dissatisfaction, & absolute in it.

BD9[14]

We fall in love with a friend; we lie with her, & wake to find beside us a stranger.

BD9[16]

To be in love is heaven itself — to be loved is hell, or at least insufferable boredom.

BD9[23]

I married, not <u>without</u> love, but not knowing what love was.

BD9[23]

I wanted a disciple, a follower, someone to teach, to enthuse, to lead. But if you love anyone it is only for what they are and not for what you want them to be.

BD9[23]

To be *primesautière* — to expend terrific energy, or to do nothing at all.

BD9[24]

Times, 8 August 1932.

'Σ is dead — No; I mean she's been married.'
   'Which do you mean?'
   'Both.'

BD9[25]

The symbolic failure, lack of complete success, in all my relations with Σ. E.g The Ball, 1931. The growth of the notion that she is mine because I have never possessed her. Lack of achievement.

BD9[26-27]

My conscious life came into being like a late & sudden spring. One day all was hidden; the next I was overwhelmed with an inconceivable wealth of sensations. Sensibilities in every direction — nature, style, love. What previously had been ideas, now were experiences. The torrents of spring! It was like a Russian spring; a sudden & complete change. Cp. Persian spring.

BD9[27]

The notion of parallel lives, which never meet, but are never very far distant from one another.

BD9[28]

I was happy in those few months — if happiness consists in a swift life, in a strong, all-obscuring love, without anything to regret, or anything to hope for.

BD9[28-29]

The quiet, strong self-possession with which Σ met me always. Full of sympathy, frankness, abandon; nothing withheld, yet nothing given: everything given, yet no encouragement. It was as if she knew what she had to give, what she could give, knew its limits, but gave what she had always & without reserve. No promises, but all fulfilment. No fulfilment, but nothing promised. She raised between us a wall of glass: cold, impenetrable, inexorable — yet intimate, sympathetic — concealing nothing.

BD9[29]

Like Marpessa, she chose the mortal, fearing lest the god should prove faithless.[3]

BD9[30]

A history of how love found me & what she did with me. Each has this history; with some it is simple, & they are happy. With others it is complex. Venus brings to some peace, & to others war: to some satisfaction & to others endless unrest.

BD9[31]

Love & care are insperable: it is always mixed with pain, always unsatisfied. Successful love is never free from pain; unsuccessful love is worse.[4]

We must then avoid love: intercourse without love is at once less disappointing & free from care.[5]

BD9[32]

Nature arouses in us the need for love; but it cannot satisfy it.

BD9[32-33]

Suddenly he became aware of all the frustration & insignificance of his life. Frequently this sense of frustration had almost overwhelmed him, but now it overtook him altogether. The lack of fulfilment, the failure — the love unsatisfied

---

3   Oakeshott's note: 'Homer, *Illiad*, Bk IX, l. 560 & Lang's note.' See *The Illiad of Homer Done Into English Prose*, tr. A. Lang, W. Leaf, and E. Myers (London: Macmillan and Co., 1883). According to Leaf's note at p. 513, 'Idas son of Aphareus carried off Marpessa from her father Euenos; and Apolla wished to take her from Idas. So the two came to fighting, until Zeus separated them, and bade Marpessa choose which she would have. And she chose the mortal, fearing least the god should prove faithless.'

4   Oakeshott's note: 'Lucretius, *De rerum natura*, Bk IV, 1057–1087.'

5   Oakeshott's note: 'Lucretius, *De rerum natura*, Bk IV, 1073.'

which filled his life. And in a sudden fit of utter exasperation, he drove the car at the gate post.

Fire; nothing left. He had disappeared.

BD9[33]

She is dead. The end of the world. What was looked for & has been dreaded has happened. No more debate — by heat? By cold? It is by heat & cold. The world ends with her death.

BD9[33]

Death is no more: she, being dead, has killed death. There is no more death for there is no one more to die.[6] The world has gone. Life is now posthumous. And to know only the empty kisses of whores.

BD9[34]

To die like Alcibiades — protected by a whore. Timandra.

BD9[35]

If I went with a prostitute I should want to bring her flowers.

BD9[35]

The man who has no lust will have no intense love. Lust & love may be different; there may be very many different kinds or degrees of love, but they are not entirely separable. Lust is not love, nor love lust; but they cannot be separated absolutely.

BD9[37]

Love: obligation: gratitude: — the irreconcilable.

BD9[37]

Love and desert: 'He won her & he deserves her.' The notion of a long labour, the performance of some great task in order to prove desert. This often a myth for wooing: but where it is not, it contains an entirely false notion of love.

BD9[39]

Any profound, jealous, exclusive indiscreet sympathy is <u>love</u>. Love is the desire and the sensation of living in another person more than in ourselves.

---

6 Oakeshott's note: 'Cp. 1 Corinthians & Amiel, *Sa vie.*'

BD9[39]

E.g. love of God. What we desire in that, as in all love, is happiness. And the happiness which the beloved has to give is not a fixed quantity, & is not a fund attached to her person or belonging to her—it is something created in the intercourse of love—it is the *Einheit von du und ich*.

BD9[40]

'A single person is missing, & the whole world is unpeopled.'[7]

The streets are empty & colourless, the air dull & heavy, the sun clouded & there is delight neither for the eye nor the ear.

BD9[41]

1. The Frenzy of love.
   Love which knows nothing save itself & desires nothing else.

2. The Peace of love—flowers, smiles, fine clothes, happy feasts, etc.

BD9[42]

Love & the desire to find oneself and to be alone.

'O last delight; I know I am alone.' Mallarmé, *Herodias*.[8]

BD9[42]

Dante called upon all beautiful women to praise his lady—I would hide my beloved in myself: the praises of another are impertinent; they add nothing & they break into that absolute invulnerability which comes with love. We are not interested in the world's opinion: we are free from the world.

---

7 See Alphonse de Lamartine, '*L'isolement*', in *Méditations poétiques*, 2 vols. (Paris: Librairie Hachette), i.13: '*Un seul être vous manque, et tout est dépeuplé.*'
8 S. Mallarmé, *Herodias*, tr. C. Mills (New York: AMS Press, 1940).

Belle Dame Notebook 10
(October 1932–March 1934)

BD10[02]

Love as the absolute category of experience; as perfection.[2]

Is not love essentially unstable, practical, mortal, inseparable from pain, movement, change?

BD10[03]

See, I have pricked my finger picking roses for you; & my feet are wet with the dew.

BD10[03]

October 1932.

Oh Σ, how empty is this place without you. The streets are deserted, it is a city of the dead — a desert & deserted place.

Now is the time when I should be sending flowers to you. Your room should be filled with daisies & chrysanthemums; and soon the beech leaves will turn red — but there is no-one here for whom I may gather them.

Komm süsse Tod.

BD10[04]

L'amour et la mort, c'est la même chose.[3]

BD10[04]

Oh love! Who gave thee thy superfluous name?
Loving & dying — is it not the same?

Japanese.

BD10[04]

The moments in life when we have to choose whether we shall live or die.

---

[1]   LSE 20/1. Paper cover, brown, exercise book, 13.5 cm x 8 cm. Ruled. Unnumbered. Autograph, ink. Dated: 'M. Oakeshott. / Oct 1. 1932. / to March 1934.'

Other works from which Oakeshott made excerpts in this notebook but which are not mentioned in the text include: Fo. 5–6, T. Mann, *Death in Venice*, tr. K. Burke (New York: Knopf, 1925); 12, St. Augustine, *Confessions*; 13, R.M. Rilke, *Advent* (Leipzig: Friesenhahn, 1898) and *Das Buch der Bilder* (Leipzig: Insel Verlag, 1913); 32–3, L.-F. Céline, *Voyage au bout de la nuit* (Paris: Deonël et Steele, 1932).

[2]   Oakeshott's note: 'Cp. Plato, McTaggart, & cp. Bradley, *Essays*, p. 10 note.'

[3]   Octave Mirbeau, *Le jardin des supplices* (Paris: Bibliothèque Charpentier, 1899), p. 158.

BD10[06]

The passionate desire to be compromised, to lose everything the world regards & values—reputation, wealth, health—everything—this is inseparable from passionate love.

BD10[06]

Passion paralyses good taste—the door is open to sentimentality & he must have a very firm-rooted taste who is to avoid it.

BD10[07]

To be in love is to be tortured; not to be in love is to be bored.

BD10[07]

Like a weak swimmer—not out of his depth, but in shallow water.
    I swam in shallow water.

BD10[08]

The primacy of the 'first' experience. But the incomparable intensity of a first experience for which one has somehow been prepared—but prepared without the actual experience itself. This was my experience of love with Σ.

BD10[08]

The heavenly early morning freshness of the Elizabethans.

BD10[11]

It is that force of sensuality which overcomes boredom—the great enemy of life. Sensuality perhaps, alone produces a fundamental aversion from death. Ambition may easily fail; but it is only when sensuality fails that life goes with it. The life of a man or the life of a relationship. This aversion from death is felt, is a matter of emotion—the rest are matters of principle.
    The actual & felt satisfactoriness of one's present existence may also breed an aversion from death.

BD10[11]

What has kept me alive during these last few weeks is the sheer force of sensuality, a meaningless but strong vitality. The nervous energy of youth. How long can it last?

BD10[12]

Brought up as a child of spirit, ascetic etc: sublimation of natural & physical impulses. Sensitive to this upbringing. But with a fully awakened self-consciousness finding it barren & empty.

Goethe & Tolstoy were children of nature who tried to find spirit—to moralize their impulses or to deny them.

Schiller & Dostoevsky were children of spirit & content in the main.

I am a child of spirit attempting to become a child of nature. Spirit is education in me; nature is impulse & myself.

Marriage while under the dominance of spirit. And it was that which awakened this slumbering, merely sublimated self, the strongest self in me.

BD10[14]

I confided my ambitions, my ideas, my self—& when they & this changed, I must leave her with whom I confided them.

A young man in love should not too readily confide anything save his love.

BD10[14]

I thought that to be in love was to confide myself; & that to confide myself was to be in love. I dreamed that the sweetest thing in love was to give myself up, freely to my beloved, to express my devotion at any moment. But to do this is to play one's part badly: love exists upon pretence, duplicity. To let oneself go is to be a clumsy lover.

BD10[16]

The attraction of incest.

The regenerate, beautiful prostitute.

Beauty tortured, spoiled, killed.

Sacrilege, profanity, blasphemy.

Death in love.

BD10[17]

I loved her, & my love destroyed her.

BD10[17]

'Each man kills the thing he loves'[4] & perhaps also the thing that loves him.

Terrifying desire for depredation, squalor, humiliation, vagabondage: outcast.

---

4   Oscar Wilde, *The Ballad of Reading Gaol* (London: Leonard Smithers, 1898), l. 37.

BD10[17]

Sexual intercourse with a dead body: like you to be cold so that I can imagine you dead.

Death-coldness of a body after bathing.

BD10[17]

I should like her to beat me, to kill me — no, better to ruin me — morally, in reputation, financially — completely.

BD10[17]

Botticelli's *Primavera* — Satanic, terrifying.

_____ *Venus* — cold, distant, unapproachable.

BD10[18]

Black narcissi.

BD10[18]

To reach the turning point in life when a man has ceased to think of his own happiness, personal ambitions. To have let the heart grow old with the head & the body.

But is this the real turning point? — the shadow-line?

BD10[19]

Looking back at it now I can see the whole of this period of my life dominated & unified by Céline. If I were unfaithful to her — it was on account of my relationship to her. If I forgot her, it was because she made it unbearable for me to remember her. If I tried to escape from her, it was because my relationship with her was intolerable. If I flew from her, it was not because I wanted somebody else, or to be somewhere else, but merely to be away from her. Positive & negative alike — she dominated all my life & actions.

BD10[19]

Our actions, even our ideas & feelings have only a symptomatic value.
It seemed to me that I was forgetting Σ, when I decided to seek elsewhere someone to love, whereas it meant that I loved her still. The desire for love was part of my regret, was an expression of it.

Perhaps we can only love once, & one person; even though we fall in love many times, & even though we find satisfaction in the end, with a person other than she who first awakened love in us.

It is not as a balm or a consolation that these other 'loves' should be regarded; they are a fulfilment, a partial response.

BD10[20]

A relationship must be kept at a certain speed, or, like a gramophone which is running down as it plays, it goes out of tune. And when the relationship is one of love, the speed is more difficult to keep, and the least falling-off is at once evident & disastrous.

BD10[20]

How a relationship gradually cools. Without any sudden break or calamity, without any crisis or catastrophe, it goes through that painful process which, we are told, will overtake this planet, until an age of icy-death finally overtakes it.

BD10[21]

When Elizabeth & I made love together, when she would slide (as I taught her) her tongue between my lips, it was to me, as if were enjoying these delights with Céline, & at the same time as if I were betraying her; and my delight lay in both these feelings.

BD10[22-24]

Σ asleep

Description of how she lay on her side, with her face towards me. Summer; she had taken off her frock, but not shoes or stockings.

Feeling that she at this moment belonged to me more fully than ever before. All that resistance was gone, the coldness which she assumed towards me, the intentional withdrawal of herself which was evident whenever we were together — all this was gone. And in its place, passivity, an almost welcoming passivity. Her personality & her relationships no longer stood as a barrier between us. It was my desires & my affections & love which counted, because nothing save that was positive & present. She was to me, then, the same as she was in the first moment that I saw her, before she was conscious of me, before I had made any impression upon her, before she was obliged to take up an attitude towards me. By shutting her eyes, & losing consciousness, she had become mine again, as she was before she knew me.

The rain outside seemed like a curtain cutting us off from the rest of the world, a barrier against disturbance, a sea which surrounded us excluding sight & sound — everything but ourselves. An island. This was the first, perhaps, the only moment when I found her brought down to my own level. She could become mine; I possessed her because her spirit could no longer resist me.

BD10[25]

Sometimes when we have committed the madness of having thought at all, we wonder whether we are in love at all; and it is futile to attempt to prove love by the idea we form of our lover. Love is proved by action. Are you ready to give up everything you have – your wealth, health, reputation, work, friends – everything for her, simply because she asked you to do so? & for nothing in return, not even her approval. If not, you are not in love.

BD10[25]

Love without possession must remain a cruel bondage, a horrible, painful, disintegrating pleasure. But in love, where possession & realization destroys the faculty of imagination, the pleasure becomes at once insipid.

BD10[26]

To be in love with one, makes it possible to admire many without the torture of desire – restores to us a world of beauty & calm delight.

BD10[26]

At parting, it is the one who is not in love who makes the tender speeches: pity has succeeded to love – or perhaps merely fear.

BD10[27]

In my relations with Céline I never had to overcome the passion of jealousy. It was as if I had got beyond jealousy at one stride, without even recognizing it or knowing what it was. Only later, & in relation to another girl, did I come to feel the force of jealousy. With Céline my love was at once unsatisfied & free from jealousy – & it has remained both to this day.

BD10[28]

If what we seek is freedom from suffering, then we know where it is to be found – in oblivion, in forgetfulness. While there is memory there will remain desire, and desire is never stilled by possession. Eradicate desire, extinguish it, for it can never be satisfied.

But in order to extinguish love, one must extinguish oneself. To forget one with whom one is in love, is to forget oneself. A new self, a new world, a new universe must be created & grow. The death of oneself is neither impossible nor extraordinary; but it is not easy to learn the world again.

BD10[29]

The world seen in grief.

BD10[29]

Like the elderly husband of a young girl, I thought only of the 'kindness' which she showed me; & I interpreted everything she said to me in terms of this kindness. And as such a husband will be satisfied with 'kindness' & will scarcely expect faithfulness, & will moreover find added reasons for gratefulness for kindness where he is betrayed, I limited my ambitions to those of senility.

BD10[29]

To read the newspaper & find everything in it insignificant. Sympathy extinguished. The greatest calamities are reduced to insignificance; the greatest triumphs are at once petty & insignificant.

BD10[30]

No despair; for to feel despair is still to be attached to a life which has not ended but to which we anticipate a disastrous end. When we have left that life altogether, there can be no despair. Disillusion.

BD10[30]

To imitate age, and allow our griefs to beget our attachments & loves, rather than our joys & desires.

BD10[32]

Love is not blind; it searches out imperfections, & each defect is an added reason & impulse for loving. There is no love which does not include a love of defect as well as an admiration of goodness — there is no love which is not immoral.

Indeed, it would appear that women in love search always for the 'eternal bounder' — virtue is far less an incentive for love than vice.

BD10[34–35]

Love is desire; and mine was love to the end, for desire was never satisfied.

It was love too, in a kind of generic, essential sense, because it was accepted defeat from the very beginning. This gave it a certain flavor of disinterestedness; but not a genuine, moral disinterestedness; but a disinterestedness arising not from an absence of personal desire, but from acceptance of defeat. I desired & simultaneously qualified desire by recognizing the impossibility of its satisfaction. It was love in a kind of immaterial, generic, essential sense, also because it was at once <u>first</u> love, and a love for which I was <u>prepared</u>, which was anticipated & understood: Like a candle, lately lighted but extinguished is prepared for the flame which relights it, as love itself can be said to anticipate death.

BD10[36]

As we grow more mature & experienced in human relationships, one thing we lose is the sense of disintegration, sometimes amounting to an actual loss of consciousness, but always depriving the occasion of normality (etc.) which is felt when one is first brought into contact with another human being. Physical sensation; rush of blood to the head, loss of control of speech & limbs, etc:

The sensations on first <u>touching</u> a person with whom one is in love. Great waves of blood surge through the body.

The world floats around us; or we float in a stable, but strange world.

Movement is floating.

Cp. the sensation which, as a boy or young man, we receive praise for first successes — or on the sudden assumption of a new responsibility or office — or when some half-unexpected honour or office is offered — the world turns round, speechlessness, pleasure, bewilderment, giving place to wild excitement or to unconsciousness.

Reading examination results, receiving news of an appointment, or a legacy, or a death, an unexpected meeting — anything, however expected, which brings to the system a shock. Astonishment.

All this belongs to 'falling in love'; and it is something which can scarcely happen twice: & can only happen with a stranger.

Replaced later by calm self-possession, command of the situation, calculation of chances, choice of tactics. Shockproof: balance.

BD10[38]

Les filles que vous ont presque aimé.

The condition of being 'nearly in love' — possible only after having been completely in love with another person — not possible in extreme youth — not possible after having been in love. Tantilizing. Desire to find oneself in love and yet being unable to fall in love. More unsettling, more disintegrating than the condition of being in love. Without any positive satisfaction; a negative condition.

BD10[39]

1. Begin by describing present position — all that is left is to write about this love. The reasons for writing — <u>exorcism</u>. Cp. Goethe, *Werther's Leiden*. Impossible to live until this life has been put behind me — the effort to throw off the sense that the life I live is a <u>posthumous</u> life.

2. Then; my position at the beginning — marriage & married life, & my character then.

3. The four years. The continual contrast of:

(a) The dying relationship.

(b) The living relationship.

BD11[01]

Carrying adolescence into later life—the intensity of adolescent feeling, its unreasonableness, its overwhelming power, blotting out experience, extinguishing sense and humour—this is the fountain of poetry, the source at once of the intensest happiness & the intensest misery, melancholy.

BD11[02]

To see a door close which has been opened is a far more devastating experience than to beat for a lifetime upon a door which never opens.

BD11[02]

A love affair which ends in death is one which has not ended, & is therefore satisfying & complete.

BD11[02]

Second adolescence.

BD11[02]

Adolescence—the refusal of <u>substitutes</u>; the demand for <u>complete</u> satisfaction.

BD11[03]

Self-centred love.[2]

BD11[03–04]

What is unsatisfied love? What does love require to satisfy itself? If love, in its extreme treats its own devotion as worthless, if it prostitutes itself to its object, then it can never be unsatisfied—it is always one & self-complete. It requires neither expression nor reply. But love is a relationship, and the lover must & does make demands—what are they? Not for sympathy or understanding—these he might like, but as a lover does not require. Does he demand love. Yes, I suppose so—he demands somehow to find himself in his beloved, & this is the sole element of self in his love. And it is difficult to see either how love can be satisfied without this, or how this can be unless his love is returned.

It is not love, it is something else which demands no return, & which, consequently, is never from beginning to end unsatisfied.

---

[1]   LSE 20/1. Paper cover, brown, exercise book, 13.5 cm x 8 cm. Ruled. Unnumbered. Autograph, ink. Dated: 'M. Oakeshott. / 18 March 1934.'
[2]   Oakeshott's note: 'Goethe, *Werther*, LVII, p. 148.'

BD11[05]

Werther's love for Charlotte was his second love; the first had died before the book begins.

BD11[05]

Love & the world.[3]

BD11[05]

The desire for insensibility.[4]

BD11[05]

The impossibility of describing the person with whom you have fallen in love — the kind of things you say — all irrelevant. What are the relevant things?[5]

BD11[05]

Werther heard of the girl before he met her; heard she was beautiful.

BD11[05]

Love is a very dangerous state to be in, you must control it. It is no compliment to the girl to be in love with her. You are thinking only of yourself — 'your little emotions' — instead of thinking of her; you are still entirely self-centred; you have made a great picture to yourself of your emotions, you exaggerate them, & they have blotted out everything else — including W.[6]

BD11[06]

A relationship in which jealousy can scarcely enter.

BD11[06]

How, against our intentions, our steps turn towards the place where she whom we love is — even when it is impossible to see her, even when we are afraid of meeting her.

BD11[07–08]

While we are in love, there may be disappointment if plans go wrong, or have to be abandoned, if we are hindered from meeting her, or are separated for a short while, but, afterwards, there is no real regret, there is no room for regret. We live as much, almost, in the future as in the present, 'time's winged chariots' go

---

3   Oakeshott's note: 'Goethe, *Werther*, pp. 19–20.'
4   Oakeshott's note: 'Goethe, *Werther*, p. 32.'
5   Oakeshott's note: 'Goethe, *Werther*, pp. 24–5.'
6   Oakeshott's note: 'Cp. George's advice. Goethe, *Werther*, pp. 79–80.'

unheard, & we are unconscious of the passing days. For while we are in love we are satisfied completely with that state of mutual understanding. But when an end comes in sight, then a tide of regret begins to flow in our minds, and every opportunity lost seems to be more important, to have held out the possibility of greater happiness, than those actually enjoyed. And melancholy takes the place of joy. So it was with my proposal to visit Winifred early in the morning on her birthday—at the time there was no acute regret & little disappointment; but now it seems as though that occasion held out a more intense happiness than any we enjoyed.

How I pictured the whole thing to myself in advance—how I actually experienced it. And I wonder now if the actual event could have added more.

Creeping toward the house, avoidance of noise, the window, the climb, the flowers in my hands, entering the room, W. waking—her smile—or frown—her welcome, throwing off my clothes & getting into her bed—& then; yes, the rest. Whatever the force of imagination, the rest because it was not physically enjoyed was not experienced, but only that.

BD11[09]

'R. might die'—suggested to me, but I was unable to entertain the idea. It did not fit into my world—I knew Σ was happier with R. than ever I could make her happy. And besides, the notion that my love for Σ would never be fulfilled was so firmly fixed, was so to speak so much an axiom or postulate of our entire relationship, that even if R. were to die, I could not imagine myself as taking his place as her actual lover.

BD11[10]

The peculiar & bitter sweet sensation of spring—for the young a sensation of expectation, for the old, regret. This, indeed, is the difference between youth & age—age has arrived when the spring brings with it regret rather than anticipation.

BD11[10]

Love & gratitude—these are the incompatibles. Love demands love or nothing: gratitude is an insult, a form of insensitiveness. But does love demand love?[7]

BD11[11]

Suddenly to wake up & find ourselves bound to another person by chains stronger than even ourselves, chains so strong that sooner than break, they tear themselves free from their moorings & carry a part of ourselves with them.

---

7   Oakeshott's note: 'I.S. Turgenev, *Virgin Soil*, tr. C. Garnet, 2 vols. (London: William Heinemann, 1913–15), ii.85.'

BD11[12]

To love is not merely to subject oneself to another's personality, to refer every-thing to that person's tastes & desires, but it is to subject oneself to another's moods. And no man is genuinely in love who finds hardship in this slavery to the mood of another. To the learner this subjection appears more difficult than anything else he has to encounter: it is more wholly immoral, it more completely places the relationship outside & beyond the conditions of reasonable social relationship. Indeed, this perhaps is impossible to learn; the lover, in this respect, is born, not made.

BD11[13]

Love, perhaps, is not a relationship, & that is why, as love, it is satisfied & never satisfied.

BD11[14–15]

Σ.

Sometimes I was conscious that my love was too much like the love of a woman to be welcomed or even appreciated by a woman. This desire to perform the simple services of life, to welcome her, to find her tired & wait upon her, to listen to her, to sympathize with her tenderly, to admire her, to comfort her — was too feminine a desire to satisfy a woman's emotions. And yet it was often so strong in me that to attempt to replace it, at these times, with something more accept-able must have failed even if it could have been made. The occasions when this mood & these emotions held me seemed to become more frequent. And before long I came to regard it as just one more symptom of that emasculation which the tacit conditions of our relationship involved. If C. had dictated those condi-tions, it might have been said that in insisting upon them she was insisting upon a form of conduct in me which must inherently leave her unsatisfied & which, in the end, must become tedious & intolerable to her; that she was insisting upon a form of conduct in me which must before long lessen her affection & respect for me: For she would have been demanding from a man an emotional response which she must more readily & more appropriately find in other women. But, in fact, it was not her insistence which created & fed these emotions in me, & this form of behavior; they appeared in me independently of any conscious desire or effort on my part, and independently of my character, but merely as an intuitive response to the situation in which we found ourselves. A desire to win her for myself, a desire, even, to insist upon my own desires would have made their appearance impossible.

BD11[17]

C: 'Looking back on it now the thing I am ashamed of is my lack of response. I had affection for you, but I refused you any demonstration of your affection, &

that, after all, is unpardonable. It is all very well to refuse it to a man whom one dislikes, however much he may desire it or be in need of it; but to refuse it simply from lack of courage is a mistake. We must help one another; & I could have helped you & I am sorry now that I didn't.'

'But you did help me. To have given me a little would have been worse than to give me nothing. After all, you made me feel that I was in something of a privileged position with regard to you – I was a person to whom you would not stoop to give a little. You gave me happiness because you gave me great pain.'

BD11[18]

The wild desire for amusement & pleasure which is one of the symptoms of the onset of leprosy.

BD11[18]

Don Juan & Werther?

BD11[18]

Like a leper, condemned never again to see the girl he loves & condemned always to think of her with an ever intensifying desire & longing. Leprosy, the disease of which we cannot be cured & of which one cannot die.

BD11[19]

The legend that if one can infect another one will be cured of leprosy – if we can infect another of this disease of love one will be cured oneself.

BD11[20]

An idealized, complicated love, enriched by a thousand embellishments of subtle feeling & motive; magnanimous affections, unwillingness to conquer, disquieting, ever-unsatisfied love: sensitive, imaginative, egoistic, expecting, requiring no reply; refined, indulgent of every character & quality of the beloved, unindulgent of itself. Universal comprehension & compassion, morbid: complete, egotistic alienation of one's own person; sublime, imaginative devotion.
    Is this the first growth of the seed of impotence?

BD11[21]

Not the absolute ennui of René; I was not chaste as Werther, nor as ruthless as Don Juan – I had neither the purity, nor the strength.

BD11[21]

Love & life ill agree. Life is at once too short & too long for love.

BD11[22]

<u>The first experience</u>[8]

No experience is a first experience: the experience of infancy we forget, & perhaps of the race, and when we meet it again it is new & yet not strange.

E.g. sex knowledge.

BD11[25]

Mother of God, how lucky you were having the Holy Ghost for a lover.

BD11[27]

To make abstinence easy by making life hateful.

BD11[27]

Anhedonia.

BD11[28]

<u>Marriage</u>

Two stags with their antlers locked together dying in a knowledge of one another that they never wanted, dying of starvation.

---

8   Oakeshott's note: 'Leopardi, *Parini on Glory*, pp. 92–5.' See G. Leopardi, 'Parini, or Concerning Fame,' in *Moral Tales*, tr. P. Creagh (Manchester: Carcanet New Press, 1983).

Notebook 12 (December 1934)

12[01]

The sailor's life contains in itself a paradox which enables it to satisfy the contradictory needs of human beings. A death surrogate.[2]

12[01]

To spend one's life for another person because we know his need of us. To believe in him more than anyone else, more than himself. To spend one's life treasuring up every word, glance, sigh, sign.

12[01]

To feel the need of 'the illusion of affairs.' Not to feel it is to triumph over death; the illusion of affairs is a way of putting off mortality, forgetting it.

12[02]

Attempts to banish the principle of failure: –

(i) In practice – social reform. Communism.

(ii) By a new comprehension of mortality.

12[02]

'It is only in degree that any improvement in society could prevent wastage of human powers.'[3]

If it is <u>accepted</u>, then it is no longer waste. The negative is turned into a positive. It cannot be accepted so long as it is seen as mere waste – failure.

---

[1] LSE 2/1/12. Soft cover, green cotton, 16 cm x 10 cm, ruled. Recto folios numbered 1–35. Autograph, ink. Title page: 'Michael Oakeshott. / Notes. / XII. / December 1934 / *denn liebend gibt der Sterbliche vom Besten* / It is in love that mortal man gives his best. / Hölderlin.' [See Friedrich Hölderlin, *Der Tod des Empedokles*, Act II sc. iv.]

Other works from which Oakeshott made excerpts in this notebook but which are not mentioned in the text include: Fo. 7, F. Dostoevsky, *The Possessed*, tr. C. Garnett (London: Dent, 1931); 11–12, G. Leopardi, *Parini on Glory*; 19, V. Woolf, *The Common Reader* (London: L. & V. Woolf, 1925); 26–8, F. Nietzsche, *The Joyful Wisdom*, tr. T. Common (Edinburgh: T.N. Foulis, 1910) and *Human, All Too Human*.

[2] Fo. 1 contains notes on Joseph Conrad, 'Heart of Darkness,' first published in *Blackwood's Magazine* (1899), reprinted in *Youth: A Narrative, and Two Other Stories* (London: William Blackwood, 1902).

[3] Oakeshott's note: 'W. Empson, "Proletarian Literature," *Scrutiny*, 3 (1935), p. 333.'

12[03]

Men have become aware —

(i) That they exist in a physical world which, in the physical universe, is insignificant.

17th century astronomy: but the length of time taken for this idea to penetrate.[4]

(ii) That they exist in a period of time, insignificant in the whole length of history. Ice age.

Conclusions they are tempted to draw from this — the insignificance of:

(i) Man;

(ii) The present.

But these conclusions false.

Previous awareness — Religion: the insignificance of man compared with God. This on a different basis from the others; & relevant to human life. But still capable of being falsely construed.

12[04]

When love finds one weary & disillusioned & hopeless, enduring a life without sympathy or meaning, with people who awake no spark, it gives, suddenly, a meaning & a vision of freedom and it gives the strength to throw the past behind & to begin life, not again, but for the first time — to begin a life which is one's own. Everyone is born twice — once from his mother, & once from his lover. *Incipit vita nuova.*

12[05]

Different beliefs in immortality

Belief in a future life because of a belief in immortality.
Belief in immortality because of a belief in a future life.
    E.g. Japanese.
Belief in personal immortality. Memory.
    Das Fortleben der Personen.
Belief in the immortality of Spirit or mind.
    Ewigkeit des Geistes e.g. Plato.

12[05]

There is only one absolute certainty in human life — & that certainty is death.
The future of a man may be obscure; but one thing is clearly before him — death.

---

4   Oakeshott's note: 'Cp. Jeans.' Probably J.H. Jeans, *EOS*: see p. 136 n. 3, above.

12[08]

'To any individual the evil of his own death lies in the present dread of his future annihiliation, & the good of a future life lies in his present relief from this dreaded prospect.'[5]

That is, the question of immortality is a question which must be considered even by those determined to life only in the present.

12[08]

Does, in fact, a belief in immortality take from life the sting & pain of mortality?

Death; & parting. He lives elsewhere — but what of that? We must live without him.

Death is <u>always</u> a palpable & certain loss.

12[08]

The death of <u>others</u>. If death is the end, then the death of others is insupportable, the worst of evils.

But here again, does it relieve the loneliness, the desolation of parting, to believe, or to know, that the dead lives elsewhere, another life? How is the feeling of a mutilation relieved?

12[09]

Is it good that men who die should live again?

'Whatever philosophy praises the creation of man must deplore his annihilation'

Is this true? It depends upon the view taken of creation.

A mature person is the result of time, effort, discipline etc. — he is unique. Is it not <u>waste</u>, intolerable waste that this should be destroyed? Futility.

'A personality cannot be transmitted to posterity merely through the fact of <u>having been</u>.'

Memory, history. Tangible works, ideas, deeds — these can remain; but they are all perishable, & in any case something different from the survival of the <u>person</u>.

'Our normal sense of the fitness of things is based upon the assumption that death <u>is</u> the end.' — i.e. we divide life into youth, middle age, & senescence — a pattern of mortality.

12[10]

The *terzo incomodo*; a third person when two are in company.

---

5   Oakeshott's note: 'R.B. Perry, "The Meaning of Death," *Hibbert Journal*, 34 (1935).'

12[14]

'It was a delightful visit — perfect in being much too short.'
   Jane Austen, *Emma*.

Mortality

And what contentment can I have, & how shall I order my conduct, when I
know not how long my visit is to last?

12[15]

Theory follows practice.[6] Not suggested that to think out reasonably from the
beginning will make much difference to how we behave. We behave from
instinct. But instincts change in time. But our *Weltanschauung* has to be instinctive before it will affect practice.

12[17]

Mortality

What have we to put in place of the belief in Immortality & its implications?
Very little that will attract those still satisfied, or if not still satisfied, still encumbered with the tradition of a 1000 years and a civilization. For it is something
simpler, less grandiose, almost prosaic, though the soul of poetry —

> Long fed on boundless hopes, O race of man,
> How angrily thou spurn'st all simpler fare![7]

12[17]

Mortality

It is not death which is dismaying, but that which is more mortal than ourselves.
We die, & there is an end; but our life is filled with death & decay. Death, in the
ordinary sense, is endurable; which is difficult to endure is the deaths we suffer
before we die.

12[18]

Mortality

View of life based upon the 7 Cardinal Virtues:
   Natural: (i) Pagan: Plato — Prudence, Courage (Fortitude), Temperance,
Justice.
   Theological: (ii) Christian: Faith, Hope, Charity.

---

6   Fos. 15–16 contain notes on M. Scheler, *Philosophische Weltanschauung* (Bonn: F. Cohen,
    1929).
7   Oakeshott's note: 'M. Arnold, 396.' See M. Arnold, 'The Better Part,' in *Poems*, 3 vols.
    (London: Macmillan and Co., 1877), i.260–1 and p. 305, below.

7 Deadly Sins: — Pride, Avarice, Anger, Gluttony, Unchastity, Envy, Vain-glory, Gloominess (*tristitia*), Languid Indifference (*acedia*).

12[19]

Mortality

Changes of appearance — not merely ageing. On marriage, or change of occupation or company changes for better or worse.

Growth: but growth in human beings mean <u>death</u>, implies it.

There may be the same person there, in spite of the changes, as there may be the same tree there, in spite of growth, or lopping; but with the man, a change in appearance is a death, or loss.

Usual to welcome or to regret these changes. But to master mortality there must be no regret. Each present appearance must be appreciated for itself.

12[19]

The most wonderful experience — to discover a virginity in oneself which we believed to have been lost. To know & feel for the second time as if it were for the first. And to discover this in another.

Some people are always virgin until they meet what they are looking for: they preserve their integrity of feeling in spite of anything circumstances obliges them to undergo.

12[21]

A battle with this established society, which kills all that is lifegiving in us. But with no conception of winning, of reforming; only now & then to score.

12[22]

Mortality

End with a myth: gods give to man the desire of immortal life — why?

12[23]

Mortality

Integrity (*Redlichkeit*): a refusal to be deceived about the significance of human existence, & personal existence.[8]

12[23]

The abominable cult of culture.

---

[8] Oakeshott's note: 'See Nietzsche, *Schopenhauer als Erzieher*, Kap. 2.' Fos. 24–5 contain notes on F. Nietzsche, *Schopenhauer als Erzieher* (Schloss-Chemnitz: Steffen Dietzsch, 1874).

12[25]

When the lover finds that his rival is a love of solitude, surrender is his only chance of victory. In some women a love of solitude is so deep a part of their character, that not to respect it is to win their lasting hatred.

12[30]

But whether death is sweet or bitter, sought or avoided, loved or hated, it is misunderstood.[9] It is not part of life, but the end of life. It is the opposite of life, not an element of life.

12[31]

My Physiology   1. Physical autobiography.

2. My physiological theories & ideas.

The old wound.
The Parts.
The Roughage Theory.
The Germ Theory.
The central nervous system.

Most autobiographies are abstracts, in the sense that they leave much untold. Cp. Montaigne; Rousseau; G. Moore; Pepys.

What a man's body has done for him, its history & the history of his health & sickness; and what a man has thought & thinks about his body — both highly important.

12[32]

Mortality[10]

Mortality is not a 'fact' — in that sense there are no 'facts' — it is an experience, an invention of the human mind, it is a statement of what experience signifies. Some never experience mortality. It requires a high degree of self-consciousness before the idea of mortality has any meaning.

We may see the seasons change, we may suffer the loss of friends & the death of affections, & yet never know the experience of mortality.

The deadness of death.

---

9   12[30] is headed 'Mortality' and contains a list of 'The epithets by which Death has been described,' including the phrase 'Sweet death. *Süsse Tod.*' Cp. p. 259, above.

10 Oakeshott's note: 'Cp. Hopkins, Margaret.' Presumably Gerard Manley Hopkins, 'Margaret Clitheroe.'

12[32]

Death in Life

The most comprehensive experience of death in life is in 'dejection.' The death of desire; utter inability to exert desire or mind.

The sharpest experience of death in the sexual act; but that is death with the hope of <u>resurrection</u>: that is sweet death — not sweet because it ends all finally, but because it is death & yet doesn't end all.

12[33]

Mortality

Shakespeare's '<u>Negative Capability</u>.'

'When a man is capable of being in uncertainties, mysteries, doubts, without any unstable reaching after facts & reason…remaining content with half-knowledge.'[11]

'Half-knowledge' conceived positively — & ∴ not half-knowledge, but complete knowledge in relation to the total situation.

12[33]

Mortality & Humour

Humour: being satisfied that you are right.
    Irony: being satisfied that they should think you wrong.
    Humour takes away all apprehension & dread: courage.
    'Humour is like a silly vow of virginity.'
    A hard surface, our habitual reaction, which takes the sting out of experience.
    The humourlessness of the young & adolescent.

12[34]

Epicurus

His attitude to science. No <u>value</u> except in relation to human conduct.[12]

This does not mean that science is <u>nothing</u> except in relation to human conduct, has no <u>meaning</u> (cp. Pragmatism); but just that it has no <u>value</u> — value being relative to human conduct & the end in human life.

Epicurus tended towards the doctrine of pragmatism, judging the <u>truth</u> of science but its contribution to human conduct, not merely its <u>value</u>.

---

[11] Oakeshott's note: 'Keats, *Letters*, p. 48.'
[12] Oakeshott's note: 'A.E. Taylor, *Epicurus* (London: Archibald Constable & Co., 1911), pp. 1, 67, 80.'

12[34]

Secularism

(i) Rejection of a belief in a god-ruled world.

(ii) Rejection of a life lived for the sake of illusions & in the guidance of false doctrines.[13]

12[35]

Mortality

The world — the Western world, for example, has already settled its way of living, its standards, its values — of what use is it to propose another; of what use to any save oneself? None. If one proposes another way of living it must be for oneself & for any others only who find it attractive.

But the way of living which the Western world has settled for itself, is by no means fixed. And, if it is nothing more, this way of living has produced this criticism of itself. There is discontent. Nobody imagines that we will be thanked for pointing out inconsistencies in this way of living: & to point out failures is futile, failure is what everyone can observe. No: this must be a personal expression of a personal faith, a reasoned expression, but neither a dogma, nor a gospel.

12[35]

Ways of living, sets of values, standards are the product of a civilization, of a social experience — what does a single individual imagine he is doing in questioning those of his civilization & suggesting others? He too is a product of that civilization; in him the civilization observes & examines itself. No man can hope to devise a way of living wholly different from & better than (& livable) the way of living which belongs to his civilization. The most he can do is to apprehend some of the failures & inconsistencies of his civilization & set them right in his own mind — &, if he is fortunate, in his own life.

12[A]

Spectator attitude.[14]

Money has always come to me; I never seek it, scarcely expect it.

Cp. *Le Neveu de Rameau*.[15]

---

[13] Oakeshott's note: 'Taylor, *Epicurus*, pp. 97, 104–5.'
[14] On a loose sheet inserted at 11[23], stamped: 'GONVILLE AND CAIUS COLLEGE / CAMBRIDGE,' numbered 11[23a].
[15] D. Diderot, *Le neveu de Rameau satyre publiée pour la première fois sur le manuscrit orginal autographe*, ed. G. Monval (Paris: Librairie Plon, 1891).

The modern parasite.

The necessity of <u>some</u> object, but complete indifference <u>what</u> object in life.

Cp. Votes for women.

The careerist: the denial of a 'career.'

Denial of the value of 'knowledge.' Cp. Novalis. All books in the end disappear except 'literature.'

D.H. Lawrence.

The position of a non-careerist in a careerist civilization. Secularism.

<u>Absurd</u> notion of progress.

Cp. The 'Christian' view of life. Otherworldliness. Death. Love. The life given over to love. <u>Bradley</u>.

Gratitude. — (see Santayana in *Life & Letters*).[16]

How you <u>spend</u> matters, not how you get.

Those who know how to spend.

The disparity between the natural term of life & the moral. Suicide.

The Beloved so inaccessible that we must find our satisfaction in what is less.

The conception of <u>Good</u>: as against that of desire & satisfaction.

Do you not sometimes wonder if your moral, sober life is not really all a waste? Do you not wonder whether it is all fruitless.

The notion that our past <u>dogs</u> us — 'B.V.'

Life for (i) future life. (ii) the generation to come.

12[A]

After all, is not an increase in income, more money, as good a thing to work for as anything else. Compare the life & satisfaction of a business-man whose criterion of success is money (to be used for fulfilling his satisfactions) with that, say, of a writer or a teacher, whose success is in his work, or in the future, in other people or humanity in general. The one has a life of immediate satisfactions; the other a life of ever deferred satisfactions bound up with a belief in progress or in general enlightenment. The man who works for himself, & he does not work for money, is rare; but his, perhaps, is the perfect life.

---

[16] Possibly G. Santayana, 'Proust on Essences,' *Life and Letters*, 2 (1929), pp. 455–9.

13[02]

'That faith in the purity of his motive which is to self-confidence what genius is to talent.'[2]

No man can have absolute faith in the purity of his motive — not even the man who knows himself best. But he can have a sense of the absolute <u>integrity</u> of his life & character in his actions & words — & that is to self-confidence what genius is to talent.

'To make up one's life as one goes along.'[3]

This requires not a <u>less</u> firm hold upon principle than a life lived according to rule, but a <u>more</u> firm hold.

---

[1] LSE 2/1/13. Stiff card cover, turquoise cotton, 17 cm x 11 cm, unruled. Recto folios numbered 1–86. Autograph, ink with occasional pencil. Title page: 'Notes. / XIII. / April 1936.'
   Other works from which Oakeshott made excerpts in this notebook but which are not mentioned in the text include: Fo. 12, poems by Margot Ruddock (1907–51), lover of W.B. Yeats; 13, L.A.G. Strong, *The Brothers* (London: Victor Gollancz, 1932); 17–18, M. Granet, *Festivals and Songs of Ancient China*, tr. E.D. Edwards (London: G. Routledge & Sons, 1932); 21, R. Wilhelm, *Confucius and Confucianism*, tr. G.H. Danton and A.P. Danton (London: Harcourt, Brace, 1931); 22, W. Bagehot, *Estimates of Some Englishmen and Scotchmen A Series of Articles Reprinted By Permission Principally From The National Review* (London: Chapman and Hall, 1858); 23, S. Butler, *Hudibras. In Three Parts* (London: H. Herringman et al., 1684); 25, T.S. Eliot, *Murder in the Cathedral* (London: Faber and Faber, 1935); 41, A. Huxley, *Ends and Means. A Enquiry Into the Nature of Ideals and Into the Methods Employed for their Realization* (London: Chatto & Windus, 1937); 48, G.C. Lichtenberg, *Reflections*, tr. N. Alliston (London: Swan Sonnenschein & Co., 1908); 59, W.B. Yeats, 'Come Let Us Mock At The Great,' in *Seven Poems and a Fragment* (Dublin: Cuala Press, 1922); 60, B. Croce, *History as the Story of Liberty*, tr. S. Sprigge (London: George Allen and Unwin Limited, 1941); 61, W. Starkie, *Spanish Raggle-Taggle: Adventures with a Fiddle in North Spain* (London: John Murray, 1934); 62, W.H. Auden, *New Year Letter* (London: Faber and Faber, 1941); 64, R.M. Rilke, *The Notebook of Malte Laurids Brigge*, tr. J. Linton (London: Hogarth Press, 1930); 69, Florence Margaret Smith, aka Stevie Smith, *Over the Frontier* (London: Jonathan Cape, 1938); 74-5, C.P. Duclos, *Considérations sur les mœurs de ce siècle* (Amsterdam: [n.p.], 1751).
[2] Oakeshott's note: 'C. Morgan, *Sparkenbroke* (London: MacMillan and Co. Ltd, 1936), p. 335.'
[3] Oakeshott's note: 'Morgan, *Sparkenbroke*, p. 364.'

13[04]

Sentimentality

1. Inappropriate emotions; e.g. too large for the occasion. This is to judge by 'the occasion.' But what is 'the occasion'? Nothing at all.

2. Insincere emotions. Many people when they say that an emotion is inappropriate, they mean that, in their view of the occasion, it must be insincere. But how to tell?

Does this mean that 'sentimentality' is not a fact of observation at all, but merely 'somebody else's sentiment when it differs in feeling or expression from mine.'

13[04]

Mortality and Property

Many Christian writers (& others) have found a dissonance between property & the immortal soul of man. How can a man whose soul is immortal take up with the tedium & the distraction involved in the ownership of property? they have asked.

I find the dissonance between property and the mortality of man's soul. I ask, how can a man who has the few years of youth, of manhood & of old age in which to enjoy the world and taste all its sweetness — how can this mortal man take up with the tedium & the distraction involved in the ownership of property?

'Possession is one with loss.' Dante.

'The expense of spirit in a waste of shame' — lust, & property.

13[05]

What would life be like if men determined to organize it (or not to organize it) so as to get as much happiness as possible?

13[06]

'To wrestle with life as an equal' — but why these pugnacious similes? We & 'life' are not two combatants, but a simple whole. Life becomes conscious of itself in us and is self-mastered.

13[07]

(i) We must have the will to live.

(ii) We must have the will to die.

And we must, somehow, have them both at once & without contradiction.

Nonchalant.

13[07–08]

Mortality

'That philosophy is to learn how to die.'[4]

Montaigne collects together a number of notions, mostly Epicurean, about death, but they do not form a consistent whole; he does not present a logical argument. He triumphs over death empirically, by a number of arguments & attitudes which are not self-consistent.

1. Death <u>must</u> be thought about & conquered emotionally & intellectually.[5]

2. Death always comes suddenly & unexpectedly ∴ we must master it in advance: 'fore-see it.'

3. First, death must be seen as 'natural', not strange; we must make ourselves familiar with it. We must expect it always & everywhere.
    A <u>constant meditation</u> on death conquers it.
    Nothing should be allowed to put death out of our minds.

4. Reaction of this upon our way of life.[6] No long views: no putting off: no saving for another day.

5. The contradiction at the heart of mortality —
    (i) We are all born to be <u>doing</u>.
    (ii) Doing must not be made an end, or we shall fail, for death comes before accomplishment.
    ? 'Let death take me planting my cabbages, but careless of <u>her</u> & of my imperfect garden.'

6. Montaigne's necrophilia.[7]
    Death has an emotional & intellectual fascination for him.

7. Death leads to a contempt of life.
    Epicurean argument — since after death we shall not feel the loss of what death makes us lose — why worry.[8]

8. Many kinds of death: mortality is in everything.[9]
    Death is the condition of your creation: death is a part of yourselves: fly from death & you fly from yourselves.

---

[4]   Oakeshott's note: 'Montaigne, *Essais*, I. xiv.'
[5]   Oakeshott's note: 'Montaigne, *Essais*, p. 92.'
[6]   Oakeshott's note: 'Montaigne, *Essais*, p. 102.'
[7]   Oakeshott's note: 'Montaigne, *Essais*, p. 103.'
[8]   Oakeshott's note: 'Montaigne, *Essais*, p. 107.'
[9]   Oakeshott's note: 'Montaigne, *Essais*, p. 107.'

9. The 'profit' of life must be something that death does not touch & cannot destroy — otherwise there is no profit.

(Perhaps — life exists; there is no absolute profit in it; but it is better to live it so as to get some profit from it than to live it in another way: & this is possible if we observe its conditions — death.)

13[09]

Mortality

The relevant fact is not that some people escape the pains & the perplexities of mortality — until the end. It is that human life is always subject to them & can never be certain of avoiding them. We have to be very lucky to escape them all; most suffer them frequently. The relevant fact is that life & mortality are inseparable. It is not pain or suffering that is the enigma; it is mortality itself. And that somehow must be understood.

13[09]

'De toutes les aberrations sexuelles, la plus singulière, c'est la chastité.' [10]

Is it? It would appear to be, but is it?

13[10]

The Past

'Once poor always poor' — what rescues us from this? — imagination; the power of mastering the past & creating a new life, a life of a different sort with new principles & fresh conventions.

13[10]

'Death is a defeat: an interruption of our life's work.' This is just what it must <u>not</u> be thought of as.

Mortality 'a disease' — so some fanciful writers: but its not. Mortality isn't a disease, poisoning the very roots of our life, it is the condition & essence of that life itself.

13[11]

A future life — Do not deny the possibility, but the <u>relevance</u>. At all events it is grotesque to let it influence our way of living <u>now</u>. We do know something about this life, & we must live it in the <u>light</u> of that knowledge. It is absurd to throw that knowledge away & live it in the <u>darkness</u> of supposition & ignorance.

---

[10] Oakeshott's note: 'Anatole France.' Actually Remy de Gourmont, *Physique de l'amour essai sur l'instinct sexuel* (Paris: Société du Mercure de France: 1903), Ch. XVIII, 'La question des aberrations', p. 233.

13[14]

The place of ambition in mortality?

The mortality of ambition; how a man finds that he has payed away his life for nothing at all. Ambition must have a place similar to that of all relationships.

But love? Is this not a break-down of mortality; or denial of mortality? Immortality in life, & its danger & pleasure. Live as an immortal.

Omsk.

13[14]

Sentimentality

The sentimental are those who have neither the intellectual consciousness nor the feeling of mortality. To be sentimental is to have succumbed to standards & values other than those of mortality.

13[15]

Mortality

'We shall never get to Omsk.' A specific end, an external goal to be achieved — these contradict Mortality. If our life is to comprehend its own mortality, these must be replaced by something else. A different scale of values & a different scale of desires.

13[15]

'It takes a nature of great genius (like St Francis of Assisi) to be determined for ever by a single experience. The ordinary human being, when his way is blocked in one direction by some dreadful experience, will move in the other direction.'[11]

To be determined for ever by a single experience...is that mortality? It is immortality, true & timeless. It is immortal mortality.

13[16]

Mortality

To most people some conditions of life, some periods & places in history, seem more desirable than others; to many people the hope of progress, the hope that the future will be better than the past or the present, is some sort of an inspiration, & they allow this faith to determine their values — but, every time, every place, every actual condition of life leaves something to be desired. No man since the world began has ever found his condition of life wholly satisfactory, & no man, in spite of progress or anything else, ever will. The actual conditions of

---

11   Oakeshott's note: 'Hofmannsthal, *Andreas.*' H. von Hofmannsthal, *Andreas or the United*, tr. M.D. Hottinger (London: J.M. Dent and Sons Ltd, 1936).

life are always more or less unsatisfactory. This is the condition of mortality — what are we to do about it. A belief in progress does not help, clearly; an imaginative projection of ourselves into a more desirable condition, does not help.

We must admit this condition, admit it as the actual essence & character of human life, & from it we must derive our values; they must be the values of mortality.

13[19]

Anyone who has been touched at all deeply by the instinct for life must love 'fashion' & find a peculiar fascination in it. Wantonness & fashion — the spirit awake in the body & not yet experienced enough to know how to live in its wakefulness: the spirit alive to mortality & grasping at the first wild expression of mortality. And those first expressions are inexpressibly touching.

13[24]

Mortality

Not the first to attempt a consideration of life from the standpoint of death.

Cp. Epicurus.

Hobbes on death.[12]

Christian tradition, from New Testament onwards.

Now, perhaps, out of fashion; but it has a long & vital enough tradition to make certain that it will never be entirely out of fashion.

13[24]

Jealousy, in fact, has nothing to do with sex. It is purely egoistic.

13[26]

Not to be content to go through life without inheriting what the past life of the world, & of one's civilization, has left to us. To avoid the feverish acquisition of a knowledge of things past & dead; but, at the same time, to enter into the present life of the world, a present life which has its meaning only its place in the tradition to which it belongs.

E.g for an Englishman to be content with an ignorance of the civilization, the literature, the arts to which he belongs — to allow his life to be taken up with business, the business of living, without entering into that common world of experience, is barely to be alive — is to have wasted one's life on things without significance.

The 'business' man.

---

[12] Oakeshott's note: 'Cp. L. Strauss, *The Political Philosophy of Hobbes, its Basis and Genesis*, tr. E.M. Sinclair (Oxford: Clarendon Press, 1936), p. 16.'

The feeling that what one is forced to do daily 'interferes' with one's 'living one's own life.'

13[27]

In each human life there is a crisis, a decision point. Sometimes it is reached early – this is the case with lives lived against a fixed background, or with temperaments in which there is little or no instability. Sometimes it is reached late; sometimes, it almost seems, not at all. Once the decisive point is reached, this development is virtually ended; change, if there is change at all, is within a narrow & narrowing limit. The crisis, too, may attach itself to different elements in different lives – a profession entered upon, marriage, an experience which determines the whole future.

To reach this crisis too early (sometimes it comes so early that it loses its character as a crisis, it is unappreciated) is the sign of a low degree of vitality, an unconsciousness of life; to reach it too late is disintegrating; to reach it not at all is unhappiness.

There is in some a fear of reaching the crisis – cp. Shelley's fear of habits. – it seems to them inseparable from death. But it is a death which the living must have died – it is part of the mortality of life.

False crises – crises which work themselves out & fail to accomplish the change & the equilibrium – this is to live in pain without dying, the vulture which gnaws the liver of Prometheus. Romantic Agony.

13[28]

Mortality – Time – Eternity –

Sub specie momenti; sub specie aeternitatis.

13[28–29]

'The necessary ignorance of man explains to us much; it shows that we could not be what we might be, if we lived in the sort of universe we should expect. It shows us that a latent Providence, a confused life, an odd material world, an existence broken short in the midst are not real difficulties, but real helps; that they, or something like them, are essential conditions of a moral life to a subordinate being.'[13]

That is one reaction to mortality – 'a subordinate being,' this gives meaning, makes satisfaction possible in spite of mortality.

But it is not the only reaction; & it is not one which appeals to or convinces us to-day. 'An existence broken short in the midst' must be shown to be, not some-

---

13   Oakeshott's note: 'W. Bagehot, "The Ignorance of Man," in *The Works of Walter Bagehot*, ed. F. Morgan, 5 vols. (Hartford: The Travelers Insurance Company, 1891), ii.297–325, at p. 319.'

thing for which this is compensation & meaning in the compensation, but an inaccurate analysis of the situation. Only when 'existence' is conceived in a certain way, a way which implies a denial of mortality, can it be thought of as 'broken off in the midst.' It must be shown to be something other than this, something with a meaning in its own self & not in what may come after, before one can claim to understand our mortal life. The doctrine of immortality, of a 'subordinate being,' of a 'latent Providence,' explain mortality only by denying it — we must explain it by admitting it.

13[29]

To set men free from <u>fear</u> & <u>greed</u>.

13[30]

Mortality

'When a man realizes his own insignificance, by that act he becomes more than insignificant.' Santayana.

But 'insignificance' compared to what? The physical universe (Jeans)? The history of the world — ice age (Balfour). Insignificance as a <u>moral</u> attitude.

13[30]

Mortality

Everything is irreparable — that is, the idea of 'repair' doesn't apply.

Ideas of repair, forgiveness.

13[31]

<u>The Mortal's hunger for Immortality: Eternity</u>

Eternity is a condition that cannot vary, a habit, a safety, & changeless certainty. The desire in marriage. But a marriage which does not give this?

There is a certain necessity in mortality for immortality; but we must live as if we were mortals, for there is no real immortality, only mortal immortalities. To achieve a mortal immortality, a temporal eternity is the greatest achievement open to mortals — but it may be a death, & what we want is a immortal <u>life</u>.

13[32]

Mortality

'There is no point. Life & love are life & love, a bunch of violets is a bunch of violets, & to drag in the idea of a point is to ruin everything. Live & let live, love

& let love, flowers & fade, & follow the natural curve, which flows on, pointless.'[14]

Lawrence's hatred & suspicion of *divertissements*: (i) Work; the vice of work. The
gospel of work; it is really only idle amusement. Frivolous view of life. (ii)
Spirituality; i.e. forgetting the delights & occupations of mortality by pretending
that you are an immortal.

The true doctrine of the immortality of man never blinked the fact of mortality; its mistake was not pretending that man was, in one sense, mortal, or in
asserting that mortality did not matter, but in making it subordinate & a means
to an end beyond itself, & other than itself. It refused the immortality of mortal
life.

13[33]

Intimations of Immortality

Have we, apart from our hunger for it, any intimation of immortality, that is
anything in us which, conflicting with our mortality, gives us, not a hope of
another life, but another life itself?

The binding of mortal love — cp. Blake, it is love itself, in its very nature
which is binding — this is to be accepted. But we cannot accept it. There is something in us which cries out against it — our loneliness. And this refusal to accept a
condition of mortality is not merely a defect in the realization of our mortality, it
is an intimation of mortality — no, not even an 'intimation,' for that suggests
something to come which is not here, but a suggestion of an immortal character
in us — immortal merely in the sense that it conflicts with our own mortality.

But what is it? A romantic unreality — a creation of our own mortality? Is it
anything more significant than the desire for a future life? Even if we find &
assert a personality which protests against the binding of mortal love, do we do
more than assert a personality which protests against the mortality of love?

13[34]

The Courage of Women

It is not a moral phenomenon, but almost physiological. It comes from not being
obliged to look very far ahead, not having to consider what life will be like after
the risk has been taken & the situation won or lost. It is not optimism, a feeling
of the certainty of winning; it is a complete carelessness about the future. This is
clear from the fact that when they are obliged to consider the future that miraculous courage vanishes. But it is not physiological, rather sociological — it arises
from the arrangements of our & other civilizations by which responsibility for
the future, which makes cowards of us, has been the duty of men rather than

---

14   D.H. Lawrence, 'Do Women Change,' p. 153.

women. And women, by this chance, have kept alive an attitude & an irresponsibility which is bright & clear in this dullness of the masculine world.

Nerve.

13[35]

Mortality

The unwanted child – some of us are this, literally; all of us are this, metaphorically. The product of an instinct, a passion, an emotion which is complete in itself & yet finds this added to it. It is a symbol of our mortality. Mortality is a natural fact; we have not yet moralized it – or only a few poets have succeeded in moralizing it; the world has merely tried to escape from it.

13[37]

The notion of a task, and finding the meaning of life in the fulfilment of a task – an attempt to circumvent mortality, but a clumsy & ill-conceived attempt, an empty formalism – what task? Duty for duty's sake.

13[38]

Mortality

Mortality & Civilization – the connection. The sense of mortality as the great civilizing force. Cp. Chinese civilization; the sense of mortality in Chinese poetry.

Freedom from unreal loyalties.

Freedom from power complex, & power motive.

Poverty – the limitation of the desire for money & property to what can be used for the purposes of a good life. Cp. capitalism, where unlimited money making is the aim, & no longer the simple satisfaction of material wants. Building bigger & bigger barns. But this conflicts with the spirit of mortality, it is out of relation with a mortal life. The immortal family or community.

Chastity; refusal to sell your life for something which is less valuable.

Sense of Mortality as the giver of a true scale of values.

13[40]

Mortality

'The individual felt dwarfed by the mass of population; the vast urban cemeteries with their labyrinths of tombstones seemed fit end for a life as crowded, blurred, & impersonal as that of the old villages had been detached & distinct.'[15]

---

[15] Oakeshott's note: 'R.C.K. Ensor, *England: 1870–1914* (Oxford: Claredon Press, 1936), p. 553.'

But:

(i) This was the result of a new <u>consciousness</u>: the new fact was a knowledge of the world, a sense of the world, & not a world or a population <u>in fact</u> vaster than before.

(ii) Cp. similar sense derived from the new astronomical knowledge.

13[42]

A sense of mortality is a sense of the deserts of vast eternity.

13[43]

<u>Mortality</u> — negative & positive, as an escape from doubt or unhappiness or as a positive, active attitude, as a <u>doubt</u> or a <u>faith</u>, as a defence against confusion or a source of power & happiness.

13[43]

Philosophy — the knowledge of what is certain.
    Viz. — all we can know for certain is something about the character of knowledge.

13[43]

Hume: civility not truth.

13[43]

The value & importance of philosophy in the modern world —

(i) Freedom of opinion (as against <u>truth</u>. Science).

(ii) Belief in reason.

(iii) Something for its own sake; freer from the contagion of the world than anything else can be — (cp. Science).

'Philosophy needs neither protection, attention, nor sympathy from the masses. It maintains its character of complete inutility, & thereby frees itself from subservience to the average man.'[16]

Recognizes itself as essentially problematic. Does not live on the profit it brings to others. If it <u>happens</u> to help the world, it is a matter for joy from simple human sympathy. Not serious.[17]

---

16 José Ortega y Gasset, *The Revolt of the Masses* (London and New York: W.W. Norton & Company, 1957), p. 86.
17 Oakeshott's note: 'Cp. Pascal.'

Philosophy does not rule by making philosophers kings, but by being itself: philosophers need only be philosophers in order to rule. What is wrong with philosophy is that it has left behind its true character in order to rule in another way — philosophers becoming scientists, politicians, pedagogues.

13[44]

Mortality

The unavoidableness of contingency — time.

I am born here, live here, die here; I am born, live, & die at <u>this</u> time. My life is here & now — nowhere and nowhen else.

The meaning of modernity; the meaning & necessity.

'Il faut être absolument moderne.'[18]

So we cannot escape; and to try to escape is to defeat oneself — escape to another time or another place.

We must sink down, deep into our time & place — for these are ourselves.

13[44]

'All primitive races, without exception, believe that there is an after life for mankind.'[19]

This perhaps should lead us to suspect that this belief is a primitive and probably inadequate rationalization of human experience.

13[45]

Life is neither for ever, nor for a very short while: its positive character derives from its limit; neither long nor short.

The plague in Athens.[20]

13[45]

Fear of death does not appear in societies in which sudden death is common — e.g. a society engaged in military conquest, but in societies where life is comparatively secure & is directed towards creative activities. There life becomes valuable & men are sensitive to its sweetness &, if they fear anything, fear to give it up.

---

[18] Rimbaud, *Une saison en enfer*: see p. 190, above.

[19] Oakeshott's note: 'Eyre, *History of Civilization*, i.67.' Probably Edward Eyre (ed.), *European Civilization: Its Origin and Development*, 7 vols. (London: Oxford University Press, 1935-9).

[20] Oakeshott's note: 'Eyre, ii.53.'

13[46]

A hiatus between his total personality & his cultivated powers.

E.g. his art not an expression of his whole personality but an interest, known & felt to be less than the whole.

13[46]

There is no hope or joy except in human relationships. One by one our comrades slip away & deprive us of their shade.[21]

Death in its proper place & time. It becomes part of the order of things — e.g. when the old peasant of Provence, at the end of his reign, remits into the hands of his sons his parcel of goats & olive-trees…When one is part of a peasant lineage, one's death is only half a death.[22]

Death can be in its right place; a civilization which had got death into its right place.

13[47]

The actual precariousness of human life on the earth. How easily it is destroyed — destroyed in bulk, even whole civilizations. Earthquake, volcano, tidal wave. This earth is a scarcely cooled bed of lava, upon which human beings build their civilizations in spite of the rumblings which go on underneath.[23]

13[48]

Schopenhauer: —

Thinkers:

(i) Who think for themselves: philosophers: for its own sake.

(ii) Who think for others: Sophists: for the sake of what can come of it.

13[48]

Personal identity   A mode of mortality, the ever perishing self

'Time heals griefs and quarrels, for we change & are no longer the same persons.'[24]

It is a short step from this to Blake's doctrine of 'states,' & with it the complete destruction of the moral personality & moral responsibility. Somehow we must

---

21 Oakeshott's note: 'A. de Saint-Exupéry, *Wind, Sand and Stars*, tr. L. Galantière (London: William Heinemann, 1939).'

22 Oakeshott's note: 'Thucydides, *Peloponnesian War*, p. 273.'

23 Oakeshott's note: 'Exupéry, *Wind Sand & Stars*, pp. 87–8.'

24 Oakeshott's note: 'Pascal, *Pensées*, 122.'

hold on to the truth in Pascal's observation without involving ourselves in a false doctrine of 'states.'

13[49–50]

The view that the most important thing is personal relationships.

But note the way in which these relationships go bad if they are made an end in themselves, if everything else is subordinated to them.

Answer—'Personal relationships are satisfactory when the people who enjoy them have a satisfactory relationship with society'—i.e., when they are a source of inspiration for some <u>work</u> in the outside world. Then a personal relationship is an alliance between two people who form a united front to deal with the problems of the outside world.

But this is no answer in the end. True, personal relationships exist within society & directly they become a kind of conspiracy against society they are perverted. But, what is this 'work,' this 'outside world'? It is a world in which personal relationships are the most important things in. By insisting upon this importance we are, not disowning society, or cutting ourselves off from it & making a purely personal world of our own, we are asserting the supreme value of a certain sort of society. That is, the importance of personal relationships becomes the law of society & not the exclusive view or feeling of a single person; it becomes the basis of a system of rights & duties, & not a denial of rights & duties in favour of a single personal relationship.

People who put personal relationships before their work, it is said, become parasites on each other, form mutual admiration societies, agree to do nothing that may make one jealous of the success in the world of the other. But this is only true when we agree to separate 'work' & 'personal relationships'—that is, when we assert the prime importance of personal relationships without making it a principle of the life & structure of a society.

And why should I prefer to please the world rather than my lover? Posterity —illusion.

13[51]

Mortality

The mortality peculiar to this age—for a great part of the 19th century there was a <u>future</u> in which they had confidence. Mortality was not brought home to them because the life they lived they could think of as going on. To-day there is no future to which we can look forward with confidence, & consequently our life is peculiarly & desperately mortal. Or rather, we are aware of the actual mortality of human life because we have been relieved of a false confidence that the future will be continuous and similar to the present. To us the present is mortal because the future, unknown & difficult to control, is something in which the present appears to die, & not in which the present is represented.

13[52]

'The belief in progress & that in transubstantiation are alike superstitions.'[25]

But what I want to show is not merely that the belief in progress is a super-stition, but that this belief is a misstatement of, misrepresentation of the cond-itions of human life—that as a doctrine it may or may not be true (in some sense), but is certainly irrelevant. Like the belief in immortality, the belief in progress aims at supplying an answer to one of the questions which being alive presents: both these answers are really no answers at all because they are based on a misconception of the question. That is, they answer a question, but not the important question. Consequently, we can leave behind all discussion about their truth & falsehood, & turn to re-examine the question & to answer it.

13[53]

'When all is done, human life is, at the greatest & best, but like a froward child, that must be played with & humoured a little to keep it quiet till it falls asleep, & then the care is over.'[26]

But this is a hoax—it is a false sentiment about life—words without meaning—no-one could have felt like this except in a mood. This is no <u>doctrine</u>.

13[53]

All the troubles of the world come from men wanting what they can only get with violence.

13[53]

'Surely God will soon close down the human show with its misery.'[27]

The erroneous assumption is that the human show is a means to some end—an end which it fails to advance, or which is not worth the apparent price. Misery is the price paid for something—too great misery is too great a price for anything; & the doubt always remains whether the something is worth having, or indeed what exactly it is.

But remove from our minds this assumption of a something beyond, & the problem changes its character. This assumption is gratuitous, & nothing that we know of in human life justifies it. The misery is insupportable only when it is considered as a price paid for something else, possibly not worth the misery.

---

[25] Oakeshott's note: 'Cp. Crossman, *Government and The Governed*, p. 204.' R.H.S. Crossman, *Government and The Governed: A History of Political Ideas and Political Practice* (London: Basis Books, 1940).

[26] Oakeshott's note: 'Sir William Temple, "Of Poetry," in *Essays on Ancient & Modern Learning*, ed. J.E. Spingarn (Oxford: Clarendon Press, 1909), p. 79.'

[27] Oakeshott's note: 'T. Hardy.'

Keats' 'vale of soul-making' suggests, but not quite satisfactorily, an entirely different & better approach.

13[54]

Human fulfilment is not another state, following upon the conduct of life, as wages follow work.

13[54]

Each man is different from every other man, but ordinary men find no difference between men. The tyrant, the megalomaniac, the man conditioned by a desire for power, by ambition, is an ordinary man because, though he may find differences between men, he does not recognize them and denies their value.

13[54]

Pascal & Epicurus[28]

Pascal's social & political doctrine; its blend of Epicureanism & Stoicism, coming near to the truth of Hegel — Will & Reason.[29]

Restlessness / curiosity / power: 17th century mental atmosphere?

Cp. Hobbes — restless desire for power after power, which can never be satisfied ∴ the Leviathan — a common 'error.'[30]

Glory & curiosity the scourge of mankind. Montaigne.

13[56]

Mortality

'It is certain that the mortality or immortality of the soul must make an entire difference to morality.'[31]

This is profoundly true; but what do we mean by soul?

What is Pascal's relation between the self & the soul?

He can't have a continuously perishing self and an immortal soul, unless he is prepared to separate self from soul.[32]

It makes all the difference to morality whether the self is mortal or permanent.

---

[28] Oakeshott's note: 'Pascal, *Pensées*, i.18: "When we do not know the truth of a thing, it is of advantage that there should exist a common error which determines the mind of man."'

[29] Oakeshott's note: 'Pascal, *Pensées*, 291–338.'

[30] Oakeshott's note: 'Cp. Pascal, *Pensées*, 451.'

[31] Oakeshott's note: 'Pascal, *Pensées*, 219.'

[32] Oakeshott's note: 'Pascal, *Pensées*, 122.'

'We must live differently in the world, according to these different assumptions: — (i) that we could always remain in it; (ii) that it is certain that we shall not remain long, & uncertain if we shall remain here one hour. This last assumption is our condition.'[33]

This is the assumption of <u>mortality</u> — a different assumption from the one Pascal elsewhere urges — i.e. that we shall not remain here long, but <u>that the soul is immortal</u>. This is a <u>third</u> assumption, different from the other two.

Note two things about Pascal —

(i) The invalid's closesness to death & contemplation of it, is ever before his mind.

(ii) <u>Fear;</u> religious fear.[34] This belongs to the Christian tradition — St Paul, Augustine, et seq.

13[57]

'I wonder how people in a condition so wretched do not fall into despair. I see other persons around me of a like nature. I ask them if they are better informed than I am. They tell me that they are not. And thereupon these wretched & lost beings, having looked around them, and seen some pleasing objects, have given & attached themselves to them.'[35]

This last is perhaps truer to-day than in 17th century. Indifferentism to human life as a puzzle & a problem has become our normal way of thinking or failing to think. Few now are terrified, few even bewildered; few fall into despair about <u>this</u>.

Perhaps this has come about because we have accustomed ourselves to live with questions unanswered; & instead of trying to answer them we go in for politics, science or business. Those who might think have made for themselves a misologic philosophy which excuses them the necessity of beginning to think from the bottom upwards: a philosophy of indifferentism is now the partner of a natural, thoughtless indifferentism & they divide between themselves the majority of mankind.

13[57]

'We have frequently printed the word Democracy. Yet I cannot too often repeat that it is a word the gist of which still sleeps, quite unawakened, notwithstanding the resonance and the many angry tempests out of which its syllables have

---

33   Oakeshott's note: 'Pascal , *Pensées*, 237.'
34   Oakeshott's note: 'Cp. Pascal, *Pensées*, 205, 241, 693.'
35   Oakeshott's note: 'Pascal, *Pensées*, 693.'

come, from pen & tongue. It is a great word whose history, I suppose, remains unwritten, because that history has yet to be enacted.'[36]

The real gist of 'democracy' is that it is the expression of <u>mortality</u>.

13[58]

'Democracy requires three conditions for its fulfilment —

1. All production should be for use, & not for profit.

2. Each should give according to his abilities, & each receive according to his needs.

3. The workers in each industry should collectively own & control that industry.'[37]

Tripe: these conditions may be desirable, they may even have some meaning (which isn't at all certain), but they could exist without even the beginning of democracy being in sight. They are, in fact, nothing whatever to do with democracy, which, fundamentally, is the social & political expression of the sense of mortality, & nothing else. These conditions don't express this sense; indeed, to lay them down in this manner is possible only when we forget or neglect the fact of mortality.

13[63]

Somehow to detach Democracy from the doctrine of progress with its false implication of the evanescence of imperfection. Not progress is the heart of democracy, but love & the sense of mortality.

Eternal change — no *summum bonum*, never ask the end; Croce.

13[65]

On the conduct of mortals; mortality the principle of conduct in individual life, in the life of societies, states & societies of states.

Characters; the believer in immortality; eternal youth.*

Progress.

Violence; power.

The mysologist:* believes that the 'eternal truth' cannot be ascertained.

---

36 Oakeshott's note: 'Walt Whitman, *Democratic Vistas* (New York: Smith & McDougal, 1871), p. 37.'

37 Oakeshott's note: 'H. Read, *To Hell With Culture: Democratic Values Are New Values* (London: Kegan Paul, Trench, Trübner, 1941), p. 19.'

13[65]

'It is doubtful whether the eternal truth that exists in the democratic ideal can ever be perfectly distilled & formulated as a dogma for all time.'[38]

(i) Why not?

(ii) What do you mean by 'eternal truth'? Degrees of truth.

This is a 'practical truth,' a truth of conduct, & therefore only a mode.
   Philosophical truths alone can be 'eternal.'
   Show first what quality of truth belongs to truths of conduct & then draw out the truth of conduct which belongs to the democratic ideal.
   Democratic ideal – 'a society which shall give the greatest degree of freedom & happiness to the ordinary citizen.'[39]
   A society which conforms to the conditions of human life & human nature.
   Cp. Plato's plan in the *Republic* & Hobbes in the *Leviathan*.

13[66]

Will and Reason

Burke, Address to Bristol Electors 1774.

'If government were a matter of will upon any side, yours, without question, ought to be superior. But government & legislation are matters of reason & judgment & not of inclination.'

Note Burke's equation of will & inclination. He belongs to the school of Reason, but has a faulty philosophy of Will.

13[67]

Pride & Sensuality – the two extremes between which human life must be conducted if it is to be conducted rationally – that is, in accordance with its nature.
   Pride – the 'too-much' – the immortal man, the mere soul – living 'for ever.' Immortality.
   Sensuality – the 'too-little' – the moment – death in life.
   Mortality – stands for the mean, the conduct of human life in accordance with its unique nature.
   This – not only of the individual life, but the life of a society & the conduct of man in society.
   Natural Law = Pride; the immortal, absolute law & the making absolute of what is really only finite.

---

[38] Oakeshott's note: 'Preface, Thomson, *Democratic Ideal in France & England.*' D. Thomson, *The Democratic Ideal in France and England* (Cambridge: Cambridge University Press, 1940).

[39] Oakeshott's note: 'Thomson, *The Democratic Ideal*, p. 5.'

<u>Natural Right</u> = Sensuality; the no-law, the rule of the momentary sensation, the finite <u>will</u>.

Hegel's synthesis of these.

13[68]

Democracy based upon <u>individualism</u>, & equality.[40]

Not based upon the 'goodness' of the people.[41]

13[68]

'Be the mind never so full of facts, the education of the heart is incomplete if no time has been left for Sir Philip Sidney at Zutphen.'[42]

The <u>education of the heart</u>, this not less necessary than the education of the mind.

13[69]

The lovely decadence of Athens.

13[69]

Everything is penultimate.

13[70]

What causes one to fall in love?
  A sense of personality.
  Love & hatred are its extreme intensifications.

13[72]

'Deep down each one of us feels he has an historical mission to fulfil, that he has to leave some mark on the world, so that he will be remembered after death. This wish gives rise to daydreaming & fantasies. Fascism allows & encourages the daydream to become fact…the feeling of being important…these things do away with, at least temporarily, the feeling of inferiority in each individual.'[43]

---

[40] Oakeshott's note: 'Whitman, *Democratic Vistas*, pp. 311–13, 317–19, 329–30.' W. Whitman, *Leaves of Grass (1) & Democratic Vistas* (London, Toronto, and Paris: J.M. Dent and Sons; New York, E.P. Dutton: 1912).

[41] Oakeshott's note: 'Whitman, *Democratic Vistas*, p. 318.'

[42] Oakeshott's note: 'C.V. Wedgwood.' Possibly C.V. Wedgwood, *The Thirty Years War* (London: Jonathan Cape, 1938).

[43] Oakeshott's note: 'P. Nathan, *Psychology of Fascism.*' P.W. Nathan, *The Psychology of Fascism* (London: Faber and Faber, 1943).

This feeling of inferiority, where it exists, arises from our past history etc. To be sublimated: it is false; 'fear & care' of which Lucretius spoke etc. How free ourselves? An emotional insight into the conditions of human life.

Evil: ambition, desire to excel, mission, etc. 'Live unknown': Epicurus to the rescue.

What has 'democracy' to put in the place of this feeling of satisfaction & fulfilment which Fascism gives to souls in search of freedom from their feelings of inferiority?

Democracy, the social order for those who are free from 'fear & care.' It gives, instead of a temporary fulfilment, a rational denial of the need of such fulfilment: it dispels the illusion, & can exist only where there is a society of men no longer under the power of illusion.

Christianity: –

13[73]

The supreme need of Western civilization to-day is to be made conscious of its virtue by being made conscious of its true character. What is required is a synthesis of insight. When all was shaken, Plato's *Republic* did this for Greece. Aquinas did it for the Christian civilization of medieval Europe.

But why is it required? Will a synthesis, a system, a corpus, teach, when we have failed to learn from those who given us insight into our civilization already? No. Academic – yet worth trying.

Its small value; not pretentious.

The part more clearly seen than the whole – no man will reveal the whole as clearly as Montaigne or Nietzsche revealed the part.

Lucretius – a body of knowledge which should form the basis of belief.

Not knowledge; but insight into character & condition.

13[77]

Mortality

The young enthusiast – Now we know what we want, let us set about making the world conform – let us make our Plan of Society and put it into operation –

But no; even that consolation is denied us – show why 'plan' does not belong to mortality.

Society – Democracy.

13[78]

To know the future is no more desirable in the life of mankind than in the life of the individual – a confusion of all desire & endeavour follows.

13[78]

Of all the struggles of mankind, the most appalling have been the wars of religion – those between religions in which the thought of a future life predominates.

13[78]

The modern world & its emphasis on <u>security</u>, & plan.[44]

13[78]

<u>Power</u>[45]

Evil. Why is power in itself evil? Because it involves a false valuation of everything: it denies mortality & the values of mortality.

The corruption of him who exercises it.[46]

13[79]

The human good as a state to be attained & achieved & rested in – to <u>stop</u> there, having nothing further to wish for.[47]

Desire 'in some fashion to escape' from death and the condition of mortality.[48]

Disenchantment with the whole of human life.

13[80]

The manner in which we are accustomed to look back to early life – with its privations & struggle – as something nevertheless better than later achievement, gives a hint of the mortality to which all living is subject. The highest pinnacle of fame, the greatest achievements, the most solid gains – these lack the life & excitement which belongs to early struggle. An actors first part, an author's first achievement, a poet's first poem – these live in the memory. Later achievements are a decline from these.

13[80]

Politics are an inferior form of human activity.

---

[44] Oakeshott's note: 'J. Burckhardt, *Reflections on History*, tr. M.D. Hottinger (London: George Allen and Unwin, 1944), pp. 60–3, 106–9–17, 120–1, 143, 158–9, 204–19.'

[45] Oakeshott's note: 'Burckhardt, *Reflections*, pp. 85, 86, 113, 118, 120–1, 213, 215.'

[46] Oakeshott's note: 'R.G. Collingwood, *The New Leviathan: Or, Man, Society, Civilization, and Barbarism* (Oxford: Clarendon Press, 1942).'

[47] Oakeshott's note: 'John Comenius, *The Labyrinth of the World and the Paradise of the Heart*, tr. Count Lutzow (London: J.M. Dent and Co., 1905), p. 5.'

[48] Oakeshott's note: 'Comenius, *Labyrinth*, p. 31.'

13[80]

It was always impossible to draw Isaac Butt into an argument, always he had other things to think about.

13[81]

An inconsequent life — how make it consequent? Rather — life is inconsequent — how endure the inconsequence?

'Never ask the end.'

13[84]

Not a struggle between ambition and the Absolute (tho' consider this: George Herbert) but one between ambition and a life in conformity to the principle of mortality, between ambition & self-realization. Ambition — external: ∴ only a means, & not a good one.

13[85]

'These first sweet moments, why could one not live an eternal, undying life in them?'[49]

That is why men seek in somebody or something <u>new</u> the recreation of what is dead.

13[A]

Neither a rebel nor a slave.[50]

13[A]

1) The times when the need for a sympathetic gesture is so great that we care not what exactly it signifies or how much we may have to pay for it afterward.

2) The ability to supply the sympathetic gesture as an action without consequences, a gift that implies no obligation, a 'good work' not asking for gratitude or even recognition.

13[B]

You, Sir, alas, are not old enough to remember a world not dominated by the scientist, nor, alas, am I. Our civilization a civilization of the scientist. — Not, thankfully, all & everything that he would desire; nevertheless a civilization. created by the scientist. Difficult to imagine anything different from this science-

---

[49] Oakeshott's note: 'Turgenev, *Fathers & Children.*' I.S. Turgenev, *Fathers and Children*, tr. C. Garnett (London: William Heinemann, 1905).

[50] On a loose sheet, numbered 12[86a].

ridden civilization — it is all that we know — have known — or are likely to know.[51]

How can we speak of the scientist as a menace to civilization? Has he not conceived it, brought it to birth, nurtured it? Is a parent a menace to his off-spring? Yes; such is the case. How? — not for me to say. But this unnatural parent, dead to pity & devoid of affection, is now in process of strangling what he has created. Stung, perhaps, by some guilty, but unnatural, conscience, science is now engaged upon the removal of its early indiscretion, it is destroy-ing what it has created.

That, one would imagine, is menace enough. But I do not propose to confine myself to so superficial a view of the activity of the scientist — indeed, if the scientist were to perish along with the civilization he has created, nobody could regret this loss. No, my view of the menace of the scientist is more profoundly shocking than this. My case is that this science-ridden civilization is a menace to civilized life. Worse than a menace; it has already removed from mankind both the hope & the desire for a civilized mode of existence.

If the scientist had kept himself & his knowledge to himself, he would have merited only our pity & contempt — not our reproach. Not trouble you with a review of the uselessness of all scientific knowledge — it is well enough known. But the scientist doesn't keep himself to himself — he is an evangelist, a preacher with a gospel that is anything but good news. He has imposed upon mankind; imposed a civilization. He has persuaded mankind of his benevolence; but little — nothing — in the history of folly to be compared with the infatuation which the modern mind has conceived for science.

What has the scientist given us? False hopes — desires — values.

1. False hopes: — The evanescence of imperfection. Lucretius; banish fear, fear of the gods; but it has put a thousand fears in place of the few it has removed. The scientist came before the world with a magnificent programme.

2. False desires — And what it has made us hope for, it has made us desire. And what is our condition — long fed on boundless hopes, O race of men How angrily thou spurnest all simple fare.[52]

3. False values — Perverted our standard of importance. It has organized the world into larger & larger & less manageable communities. Made us think that the value of life is increased merely by making life <u>longer</u>. It has perverted our moral sense so that we believe in nothing but productivity. It has made us believe that our sole purpose of existence is to contribute to some present evo-lution or development: It has removed from us our capacity for merely pleasant enjoyment of life. By its crass insensitiveness it has pretended to deprive the

---

51   On a loose sheet, stamped: 'GONVILLE AND CAIUS COLLEGE / CAMBRIDGE,' numbered 12[92].

52   See p. 276 n. 7, above.

natural world of its mystery & has driven our poets to the supernatural, to a world of ghosts & shadows, in order to satisfy their sense of the mystery of life. It has made what is negligible important; & what is valueless valuable. It has created a civilization which is a menace to civilized life.

Two objections.[53]

1. Not the scientist, but science. Who is responsible for this science ridden civilization but the scientist? It is he who has liberated the evil genie from the jar in which he was safely confined. Who was the first scientist? Ah! I see you know the answer. I need only remind you. A woman. No not Eve: Pandora.

What is more, the scientist is a blackmailer: he trades upon the stupidity of mankind. First he whets our desires & flatters our hopes, then he lets loose a civilization more horrible than we could have imagined, & then he says 'you can't do without me.' But he does nothing to rescue us. Trust me; wait & see; if my lips were not sealed.

2. Not science, but the misapplication of scientific knowledge. Science, it will be said, has lessened our misery & relieved our pains. But the misery & pain which it has removed are the creations of this scientific civilization. Medical science is scarcely more than a vain attempt to relieve the miseries which science has created; it is one more example of the attempt of the scientist to remove what he has been indiscrete enough to bring into being. And he's unsuccessful. I am willing to concede few benefits from science. The misapplication of scientific discoveries is not merely regrettable; it is inevitable. The price we have paid for allowing the scientist to do what he likes with the world is a civilization based upon false hopes, desires & values: a radical perversion of human life. It is too dear. And things that we buy too dear we always turn to bad use, because we have no love for them, but only a painful recollection, the recollection of being swindled.

'The whole universe is about 1000 million times as big as the part of space which is visible in a telescope, which reveals about 2 million nebulae. Let us multiply 1000 million by 2 million & the product by 1000 million. The answer (2×10^{24}) gives some indication of the probable number of stars in the universe; & the same number of grains of sand spread over England would make a layer hundreds of yards in depth. Let us reflect that our earth is one millionth part of such a grain of sand, & our mundane affairs begin to appear in their correct proportions.'

That, Sir, is science & I submit is a wholly false standard of importance; it is nonsense; it is the magna charta of stupidity.

---

[53]   Oakeshott added four lines at the top of 13[92] in pencil: 'Ridicule unnecessary / Misapplication of science + / Given the present civilization — science necessary. / More people — .'

A Conversation (1944)

Characters?

'The soldier' — unnamed.
The philosopher & poet. Academic profession.
The doctrinaire: Rationalist.
The poet.
The man of the world (Peter Newall). Elastic, non-doctrinaire, but worldly & commonsensical. + 'Public man.'
The politician; the 'public man.'
The scientist. Russell — Haldane — Jeans, Hogben, Needham.[2] Doctrinaire Rationalist in politics. Planner.
The religious man — lack of interest in everything topical or transitory.

No 'detail' of participants or their characters or occupation: information to come out in the course of the conversation. As little machinery as possible, & as little scenery.

1) The scene. Any occasion that makes conversation the only thing available. Books not available; thrown together for the time being. Opening with a con-

---

[1]   LSE 2/4/3. Hard cover, grey marbling, cloth covered spine, 35 cm x 20 cm, ruled. Autograph, Ink and occasional pencil. Recto folios numbered 1–62; the first two folios are unnumbered and include the title page and CV[00]. Title page: 'A Conversation / *Somnia sunt non docentis, sed optantis* / Pauso's horse. Burton III.249 / 'All men say "I know," but they are driven into nets, caught in traps, fall / in pitfalls, and not one knows how to avoid this. All men say "I know," but, should they / choose the mean in action, they could not persist in it for a round month.' / Tzu Ssu, *The Doctrine of the Mean*, VII.I / 'Now that Lucius Gellius is dead,' Cicero, *Laws*, I. 53 / 'It is all one where I begin, for I shall come back there again' / Parmenides of Elea. Diels 3. / As soon as we have destroyed the enemy, let us banish steel, & destroy iron. / In perishable wood & with immortal souls let us construct a world of freedom.' Undated, but the inside front cover bears a paper sticker in Dutch, suggesting Oakeshott acquired this notebook when in Holland on military service in 1944. This dating is reinforced by the insertion at CV[30b] of a page from the *Times Literary Supplement*, 20 May 1944. [Possibly an adaptation of Cicero, *Academica priora*, Bk II ch. xxxviii: *Somnia censet haec esse Democriti non docentis, sed optantis*; Burton, *The Anatomy of Melancholy*, iii.249; Tzu Ssu, *The Conduct of Life, or, the Universal Order of Confucius. A Translation of One of the Four Confucian Books, Hitherto Known as the Doctrine of the Mean*, tr. Gu Hongming aka Ku Hung-ming (London: John Murray, 1912); *Die Fragmente der Vorsokratiker Griechisch und Deutsch*, ed. H. Diels, 3 vols. (Berlin: Weidmannische Buchhandlung, 1922 [1903]), i.116; not traced.]

[2]   Probably Bertrand Russell (1872–1970), philosopher and logician; John Burdon Sanderson Haldane (1892–1964), geneticist; James Hopwood Jeans (1877–1946), physicist and mathematician; Lancelot Hogben (1895–1975), zoologist and statistician; and Noel Joseph Terence Montgomery Needham (1900–95), biologist and sinologist.

versation on conversation. Prison, country house? The pub, the dinner table (the visitor) (Henry Brandon).

2) The characters. How well known should they be to one another? Not too well known; acquaintance of 2 months. But two of them close friends. Not more than three or four. Similarity of education, but not the same. Same civilization.

Les soirées de Saint-Pétersburg.[3] Begins on a boat in the evening on the Neva. The company lands and begins conversation. Comte, Chevalier, Senateur.

CV[01]

Conversation

A philosophy of conversation; & conversation as a philosophy of life.
The nature of a conversation   — knowledge of self
                                                 — knowledge of truth?

The art of conversation: its destruction. No place in the modern world. B.B.C.
    The topics of conversation: love & death — the two fatalities of human life.[4]
    The man averse from conversation — from talk nothing comes. We know what we know, & neither thought nor talk make things clearer.[5] Keep the common path & avoid subtleties.
    Avoid the suggestion of 'disputants' — or let it enter only occasionally, when passion is aroused. This is a conversation within oneself. No central figure. A recorder or commentator? Not victory, not agreement or persuasion.

CV[01]

Conversation as the microcosm of life and as an interpretation of human life. That is, human life conceived in terms of conversation — not of war, or struggle, or commerce or even of a card game or a racehorse or the acquisition of learning, but of a conversation. The idiom of conversation.
    A type of life: an ideal of life.
    Open 'A Conversation' with a conversation on conversation: the ideal human relationship, the relationship that expresses best at once the character of man & the character of human life. Springing from this will be 'mortality' — death — and love, as the two topics of conversation.

---

3   Joseph de Maistre, *Les soirées de Saint-Pétersbourg, ou entretiens sur le gouvernement temporel de la providence: suivis d'un traité sur les sacrifices*, 2 vols. (Paris: Cosson, 1821).
4   Oakeshott's note: 'Berdyaev, pp. 83–4, 317 sq.' Possibly Nikolai Berdyaev, *The Destiny of Man*, tr. N. Duddington (London: Geoffrey Bles, 1937), referred to at p. 314 n. 15 below. For Oakeshott's review of Berdyaev, *The Meaning of History* (London: Centenary Press, 1936), see *SW* iii.137.
5   Oakeshott's note: 'Montaigne, *Essais*, iii.144, 404–5.'

Dialectic of conversation: a Penelope's web — a doing & an undoing: a circle.

CV[01]

The spirit of conversation opposed to the *pièce à thèse*.

Not to be in the habit of discussing general topics does not mean that one has not the spirit of conversation in one. Scepticism of a sort is its essence. And toleration.

CV[01]

Conversation like a meal — a breakfast at some wealthy friend's house where the sideboard is covered with dishes & one can take one's choice. Not a set meal with a menu where one must go through and either eat each course or refuse & wait for the next.

(Cp. the carefully designed & planned meal).

Certain conventions observed — one would not start with an ice and go on to a roast. A restaurant meal, where one can choose at will, and where what one chooses is determined partly by one's tastes, but partly also by one's companions' tastes.

CV[01]

Conversation dialectic not eristic.[6]

CV[01]

The participants in a conversation must, one might say, have everything in common except their opinions. There must be a common civilization, certain common tastes. The notion that a contribution to a conversation can be made by a dogmatic savage is an error: for conversation consists in being able to understand what others say better than they understand it themselves; and being able to speak not only so as to express one's own opinions, but so as to[7]

CV[01]

We live in an age of dogmatism, which has only to continue in the way it is going, to bring us to a new dark age of enlightenment: what may save us is conversation. Cp. the degeneration of debate in Parliament — debate replaced by the statement of dogma.

---

6 Oakeshott's note: 'Plato, *Meno*, 75c–d; cp. Collingwood, *New Leviathan*, 24:57.'
7 The sentence is unfinished in the original.

CV[02]

Conversation as the form of social relationship: its criterion. Exclusion of power & force. Exclusion of plan. Toleration. A natural following of the mood of the argument: there is nothing which, from the start, is 'to be proved.'

CV[02]

The value of discussing a question, & the pleasure, with two or three others – with food & wine and the feeling of unlimited time.

'I would rather make love than talk.': I cannot see the distinction. A distinction without a difference.

The participants must all be persuaded of the <u>pleasure</u> of conversation. Symposium?

The dialectic of conversation – continually returning to the same points only on a different level.

A participant may win <u>a point</u>, may disarm his opponents, but nobody 'wins' the conversation as a whole.

Defects of conversation – the right reply escapes us at the time, & afterwards, in the night, we would return to the argument – but the others are not there. But this is relevant only when the conversation is thought of as a matter of 'winning'; if it is not thought of in this way – then, if the right reply comes when too late for that conversation, it is not too late for the conversation that our ideas always have with one another. (*Esprit de l'escalier.* In a dispute this may be a matter of regret, but not in a conversation.)

CV[02]

A conversation does <u>not</u> require all possible opinions to be represented: in Plato's *Republic* a variety of opinions is represented, but there is plenty of foolishness that makes no appearance; several people appear, but no <u>fool</u>.

CV[03]

<u>The Criterion</u>

Cp. the Stoic doctrine of the 'Criterion.'

Things are interesting because we care about them & important because we need them. There is no other true criterion. The universe is significant to us only as it belongs to us in feeling: its size, its longevity, its multiplicity – are not in themselves significant, but only as they affect our lives, our ideas & emotions. Man & his world <u>is</u> the centre. The false 'Copernican Revolution.'[8]

Contrast: The Stars and Astronomy.

---

8   Oakeshott's note: 'See R.G. Collingwood, *The Idea of Nature* (Oxford: Clarendon Press, 1945), p. 96.'

Again: to know that the earth is spinning through space at some incredible speed is to know nothing significant, because it cannot be heard or felt.

What answer to—'<u>God</u> is the centre.'

The three sided argument: 1. The Poet.

                                     2. The Scientist. Jeans etc.

                                     3. The Religious Man. Cp Pascal.

                                     4. The 'Philosophe'—the believer in the practical value of philosophic truth: amateur philosophy. To be answered by 1–3.

What <u>is</u> relevant to, significant in, human life?

The value is the thing itself: but the thing itself is never devoid of conjunctions.

Cp. Friendship—value, a relation.

Comradeship—a means to an end: a 'political' relation. Palinurus.[9]

CV[03]

Somehow not to allow the universe to impose its false values on mankind.

When man (by the Copernican revolution, since continued by modern science, cp. Jeans) was deposed from his place in the centre, the individual degenerated into a means to an end, and all the enormities of modern society were made intellectually possible.

If the Copernican revolution had any moral significance, what it took away from the earth & its inhabitants should be given to the sun & the moon—which is absurd. Because you happen to inhabit a fixed star does not make you more important.

CV[03]

The one all-pervading principle—is there such? Confucius, *Analects*.[10]

'Conscientiousness within, and consideration for others.' But not occult.[11]

The one principle (Confucius), the main thought (Pascal) = Tao. The way.[12]

The implication of the <u>Way</u>. Not a law or a principle or an end. Cp. 'The English <u>Way</u>.' Maitland.

---

9   Palinurus was the helmsman in Virgil's *Aeneid*, but see p. 351 n. 89, below.

10 Oakeshott's note: 'Confucius, *Analects*, Bk IV ch. xv; Bk VII ch. xxiv; Bk XV ch. ii.'

11 Oakeshott's note: 'Confucius, *Analects*, Bk VII ch. xxii.'

12 Oakeshott's note: 'Cp. Hughes, pp. 261, 263.' Possibly E.R. Hughes (ed.), *Chinese Philosophy in Classical Times* (London: J.M. Dent & Sons; New York, E.P. Dutton & Co., 1942).

CV[03]

The absolute value of man, human personality. How established?[13]
    Its meaning. Egoism. Cp. Hobbes.
    Personality the root because it is the source of all values.[14]
    The necessity of a criterion.[15]

CV[05]

The Present

The force & relevance of the present. Exemplified by the limitation of <u>memory</u> to comfort, console or even to relate to a present circumstance. The memory of a satisfied love, of the resilience of youth, the rapture of passion — of sight or sound: these have no relevance to present melancholy or frustration. Present evil requires present joy to heal it. In this sense we certainly live in the present.[16]

CV[05]

Spontaneity of conduct. ∴ Habit rather than ideas, tradition rather than doctrine: habit & tradition are less deadly to spontaneity than ideas & doctrine. Spontaneity: extemporary — full aliveness to the present. The Artist. 'We are never wise but by present learning.'[17]

CV[05]

Each present has its politics: all true politics are politics of the present — but not too short or too long.

CV[06]

A Time For Everything

To know the four seasons: that is the sum of practical knowledge.[18]
    The seasons & their emotions.[19]

CV[06]

Every man has a fit of madness once in his life, if it does not run upon love or money, it takes the direction of politics or of religion.

---

[13] Oakeshott's note: 'V. Soloviev, *The Meaning of Love,* tr. J. Marshall (London: Geoffrey Bles, 1945), pp. 17–22, 23, 59.'
[14] Oakeshott's note: 'Hughes, *Chinese Philosophy,* pp. 57, 172.'
[15] Oakeshott's note: 'Berdyaev, *Destiny of Man,* p. 44.'
[16] Oakeshott's note: 'Santayana, pp. 97–8.' Possibly Santayana, *Persons and Places,* referred to at p. 324 n. 43, below.
[17] Oakeshott's note: 'Montaigne, *Essais,* i.188, 190.'
[18] Oakeshott's note: 'Cp. Hughes, *Chinese Philosophy,* p. 216.'
[19] Oakeshott's note: 'Cp. Hughes, *Chinese Philosophy,* p. 282.'

CV[06]

The characteristics of life — we come upon them ignorant, not knowing what is suitable for our age, victims of necessary inexperience.

CV[06]

'The sixth age is ascribed to Jupiter…the sorrow only abideth.'
  Sir Walter Raleigh.

1) All is in vain & only sorrow abideth.

2) The desire to have again or to enjoy permanently what was once so sweet is a false desire: refuse disillusion by the limitation of expectation. The sorrow in which all ends is, also, an experience, if not to be enjoyed, at least to be accepted in its place.

CV[06]

Neither Dionysius nor Apollo — but both in their places. But these two must be seen as one: they unite in mortality.

CV[06]

Everything in its own place; but not a place for quite everything.
  Let the glare of passion pass its meridian & we have entered upon a new life — live it without desiring to return.
  The Seasons: Palinurus.
  Keats: Odes are odes to mortality.

CV[07]

The Small Opposed to the Large

Principle — the only real goods spring from actual personal relationships. What we cannot enter into a personal relationship with has only a fiction's value for us.
  The local & the close — opposed to the global & the distant.
  Friends as opposed to 'humanity.'
  Ideal ∴ close personal relationships with a few.
  The fiction's value of 'contacts', acquaintance, knowledge gained from travel etc.

CV[07]

Piety — faithfulness to what is close to us & a part of ourselves, not because of its intrinsic worth, but because the fortune of living has placed us on earth together.[20]

CV[07]

The western European tradition of the mean. Cp. Confucius.
  Aristotle; Burton.

CV[07]

To cultivate & find satisfaction in little things enables us to keep contact with the world, with nature & with ourselves. It also saves us from hubris. Do this; but avoid niggling.
  Importance & size not related: avoid the grandiose & the niggling.
  The art of the miniature &c.

CV[07]

Local as against national. But avoid the parochial.[21]
  National as against world.
  Modern communities first destroy local culture & then seek to resurrect it by compulsion or encouragement. Cp. Russia.

CV[07]

The evil infinite.

CV[07]

Contrast the limited with the unlimited — cp. Horse race & motor race.
  Cp. Greek civilization — a horse race. This is the immortal quality of Greek civilization.[22]

CV[09]

Politics and Government, Law

The false notion of 'destiny' in politics. Destiny — man has only one destiny — death. To speak of these childish plans for the immediate future of a mortal society as its 'destiny' is absurd.

---

[20] Oakeshott's note: 'Santayana, p. 83; Hayek, p. 174.'
[21] Oakeshott's note: 'Vauvenargues, 382.' A reference at CV[15] to 'Vauvenargues, *Pensées*' suggests Oakeshott may have been using *Pensées, maximes et réflexions de Pascal, La Rochefoucauld, Vauvenargues*, ed. A.T. Baker (London: Macmillan and Co., 1937).
[22] Oakeshott's note: 'K.B. Smellie, *Why We Read History* (London: Paul Elek, 1947), p. 29.' For Oakeshott's review see *SW* iii.228–9.

CV[09]

How does it come about that a policy (party or national) acquires a sort of moral halo? This happens, but there is no substance in it. It is a trick — not conscious, but a trick of circumstance.[23] Cp.

1) The case of the North in the American Civil War.

2) The case of Socialism in England for 40 years.

3) The case of Russian policy, 1944–5.

And how difficult it is to disperse this false moral sanctity. Socialists think they have a corner in ideas — & this reveals the defect of their mentality.

CV[09]

Let me be reconciled to my childhood — but this is not difficult: what is difficult is for the middle aged to be reconciled with their youth: for childhood is outside his control, while youth is something for which he can blame himself.

CV[09]

Society & the artist: the necessity of being an 'outcast,' necessity of rejection by society. Art flourishes only when it is slightly discreditable to be an artist, for then only is it free.

CV[09]

Each society has its own life — the doctrinaire misses this and falls down. 'Democracy' does not & could not exist: an abstraction. Same with Fascism.

CV[09]

Continuity of the history of a nation — the inspiration & the guide to politics. The good fortune of those nations that possess & value continuity. A nation reconciled with its past, as an individual reconciled with his past, is sane in a way no other can be sane: — not subject to the impediments of morbid compulsions and neurotic fears.

England made peace with its middle ages by misconstruing them.

CV[10]

A general interest & preoccupation with politics is the surest sign of a general decay in a society. A universal preoccupation with rights, interests, affairs of government, political questions in general is fatal to the public peace & individual happiness.

---

[23] Oakeshott's note: 'Cp. Pickthorn, *Prejudice.*' Probably K. Pickthorn, *Principles or Prejudices* (London: Signpost Press, 1943).

CV[10]

The politician's attitude to men — 'use': i.e., he sees 'qualities,' not individuals.[24]

CV[10]

Not to break the grand affirmative flow of things.

CV[10]

Revolution. 'When the springs dry up the fish are all together on dry land. They will moisten each other with their dampness and keep each other wet with their slime. But this is not to be compared with their forgetting each other in a river or a lake.'[25]

CV[10]

Our non-doctrinaire view of politics has enabled us to escape the error of putting too high a value on political action, too high a hope on political achievement, to escape the error imbedded in the belief in the evanescence of imperfection.[26]

England with its non-doctrinaire system of politics benefited more by the French Revolution than France, or Germany or any country that accepted the revolution as a new beginning. Stimulated instead of intoxicated by the abstractions & perfections it asserted.

CV[10]

Politics seen as a struggle for power — is it more than this?

CV[10]

Each day, each period, has its 'politics' — its major political problem. This is important, but no more important than politics itself. The politician alive to his day is he who apprehends the politics of his day and applies his art to its solution.

The problem to-day:

1) Germany?

2) How to protect the individual against mass despotism.[27]

3) The protection of society against the 'gangster.'

---

24   Oakeshott's note: 'See J.A. Stewart, *Plato's Doctrine of Ideas* (Oxford: Clarendon Press, 1909), pp. 132–4.'
25   Oakeshott's note: 'Chuang Chou, in Hughes, *Chinese Philosophy*, p. 193.'
26   Oakeshott's note: 'Cp. Halifax, *Maxims*.'
27   Oakeshott's note: 'Maillaud, pp. 78–9.' Probably Pierre Maillaud, *The English Way* (New York: Oxford University Press, 1946).

4) How to encourage in an industrial society the social virtues which were achieved in other simpler forms of society.

CV[10]

Rationale of second chamber —

1) The majority — the mass against the individual. Equality.

2) The individual against the mass. Liberty.

The ideal second chamber — an impoverished aristocracy.[28]

CV[11]

<u>The Psychic and the Supernatural</u>

The error of supposing that we could lead better lives if we knew the future. Blessedness of ignorance. Divination; fortune telling. A detailed knowledge of our future life would be fatal to living. Is this true of knowledge of a life after death?

Bagehot.

Even if there is survival, proved, it does not get over the fact that <u>now</u> we have to live without those who have died: — <u>that</u> is the sharpness of death, not the possibility of extinction, but the fact of loss.[29]

But does this not put psychic communication on the map again? Is it not a means of <u>not</u> doing without those who have died? A false means? A refusal of mortality, a refusal to experience.

CV[11]

Personal immortality: the evidence of psychical research might become overwhelming. But survival of bodily death is different from personal immortality. Ability to communicate. Evidence can never be more than to show the postponement of psychical death.

CV[12]

The common man more dangerous to civilization than the atomic bomb.

CV[12]

Democracy not relieved of the imperfections & partiality that belongs to political arrangements.[30]

---

28 Oakeshott's note: 'Maillaud, p. 95.'
29 Oakeshott's note: 'B.E. Dugdale, *Arthur James Balfour, First Earl of Balfour*, 2 vols. (London: Hutchinson, 1936), ii.297.'
30 Oakeshott's note: 'Berdyaev, p. 249.'

The fundamental problem still remains the State and the Individual.[31]

CV[12]

Democracy is politics without the idea of perfection. All government involves error; democracy alone admits this. The least scientific of all government.

CV[12]

Democracy is politics become conversible.

CV[12]

Those who mistake a sort of pelagianism for democracy – identifying the two.[32]

CV[12]

The principle in democracy. *Que sais-je?* Montaigne. Humility & not presumption; enquiry & not scepticism.

CV[12]

Montaigne's doctrine of the fallibility of human judgment, wisdom, & experience. No man is ever free from it – & the arrangement of the world should be based upon it as the finest & most certain foundation we have.[33]

This is not so much an imperfection in human character as the very stuff & structure of human character – it is 'imperfection' only because in rare spirits it is, not absent, but curtailed & modified. What is required in the world's arrangement is not perfection, the total absence of fallibility – because that is impossible – but the absence of certain types of fallibility in certain men – e.g. injustice & partiality in judges, pusillanimity in soldiers, etc.

CV[12]

All systems of government fail, & must fail. The important question then is, not What system is the best, abstractly & if it succeeds entirely? But, What system of government is the best when it fails? The failure of absolutism is worse than the failure of democracy.

CV[12]

Democracy and a contempt for human beings not inconsistent.

---

31 Oakeshott's note: 'Berdyaev, p. 251.'
32 Oakeshott's note: 'R.B. Perry, *Puritanism and Democracy* (New York: Vanguard Press, 1944), p. 424 sq.'
33 Oakeshott's note: 'Montaigne, *Essais*, v.1–2.'

CV[12]

The 'radical' insistence on the primacy of the 'man': e.g. monarchy valuable only when the king is personally a good & able man. The primacy of personal worth & ability. It seems so reasonable, so undeniable. But it ignores more than it comprehends. The 'tradition,' the 'system' is, in fact, more than the man. If life were in an immediate present only, then 'the man' would comprehend all. But it is neither in an immediate present, nor in an eternity, but in a middle stretch of time, which requires both 'the man' and 'the system.'

CV[13]

Sense of space and time; the foolishness of undue haste.

Sense of <u>impersonal factors</u> — Tradition, the past, the inability to see far into the future or to control beyond a certain point the consequences of our actions. E.g. the way in which man's plans turn out differently from what was intended — either better or worse. The incalculability of remote consequences of action. Chance & fortune. Impersonal factor in <u>law</u> & in competitive commerce — Hayek. The ease with which circumstances deflect the results of human endeavour: e.g. the romantic concept of nationality containing the seeds of the malignant nationalism of fascism. We have no sovereignty in the face of destiny.

Sense of the past & the importance of continuity: preservation of identity in change.

Respect for the other man's personality; the sense of the improbability of any rigid doctrine being 'right.' The refusal to see the political world in simple black & white.

Pursuit of the good that can be seen and grasped, not of the 'highest good.' Limitation — self-limitation — of those in power; for power is something transitory and to be exercised only within the limits of a tradition.

Apprehension that no man can be certain of not making a mistake, and the determination to put no man in a position where a single mistake will overturn the world.

Scepticism of political genius; a sense of relative values that discourages the attempt to achieve great ends quickly when the cost is disproportionate to the ends achieved.

Scepticism of the 'all or nothing' attitude.

So far from this system of politics being merely empirical, it requires far greater subtlety & elasticity of mind than a doctrinaire system.

Love of one's neighbour rather than love of mankind.

CV[13]

The error of transposing the ideas & traditions of English democracy in the doctrines of continental politics.[34]

CV[13]

When everyone can read and write, there is an end of good taste.

CV[13]

Democracy? substituted progress for civilization. Progress means failure to appreciate, living always in a world not yet inhabited. It involves a doctrinaire attitude to human life, and takes away the foundation from which the great creations of art arise. But progress is a euphemism for the perpetual readjustments that are going on: it is designed to give an importance to these readjustments by attributing to them a direction; but it is a false importance; their true importance is concealed. <u>Progress leads to planning</u>. Civilization is humbler, tolerant, permits the recognition of the circular movement of human life & institutions; it asserts personality. The individual emerges in civilization & is submerged in progress. That is why progress is inconsistent with democracy: they are in fact mutually exclusive and incompatible. Democracy — mortality — civilization.

CV[13]

Democracy cannot be 'introduced' into a society ∴ it <u>must</u> grow there. A democracy less than say 200 years old is impossible. Democracy can be developed only by the practice of democracy.[35]

CV[14]

Philosophy and Life

Pater, 'Sebastian van Storck': the confusion of philosophy with life.[36]

Romanticism is this confusion of philosophy & life: Classicism as the distinction. But yet there remains — either a <u>preference </u>for life or for philosophy (death). The pursuit of perfection, the unconditioned, the absolute. In practice it is an error, for this perfection does not belong to the world of practice, to human life, whose ideals must be as mortal as that life itself.

---

[34] Oakeshott's note: 'C. Brogan, *Who Are "The People"? Some Thoughts on Our Present Malcontents* (London: Hollis & Carter, 1943), pp. 85–7.'

[35] Oakeshott's note: 'Swartzchild, pp. 150 sq.' Possibly Leopold Schwarzschild (1891–1950), author of *End to Illusion. A Study of Post-War Europe*, tr. M. Meiklejohn (London: John Lane, 1934); *World in Trance* (London: Hamish Hamilton, 1943); and *Primer of the Coming World* (New York: Alfred A. Knopf, 1944).

[36] W. Pater, 'Sebastian van Storck,' *Macmillan's Magazine*, 53 (1886), 348–60, reprinted in W. Pater, *Miscellaneous Studies A Series Of Essays* (London: Macmillan and Co, 1895).

It takes two forms in life:

1) Mysticism, which is both the pursuit & the achievement of perfection.

2) Sebastian van Storck or M. Teste (Valéry).[37]

CV[14]

To love the earth & hate the world — Rationalism, Naturalism: not knowing that all the most valuable things of life are great concrete human achievements, not abstractions or the gifts of nature.

CV[15]

Values — What is Valuable

Charm compensates for the lack of everything else: charm that comes from a sincere and generous spirit. Those who ignore charm & fix their appreciation upon what they consider more solid virtues are, in fact, ignoring mortality. Mortality is the rationale of the primacy of charm.

CV[15]

To desire is better than to possess — i.e., it is more in accord with the happiness possible to the human condition. Desire may be mortal, but possession is more frail. Indeed, desire is an intimation of immortality; the acceptance & the defeat of mortality.

CV[15]

The enjoyment of what is best is, in some cases, impossible because the majority seizing the best makes it unenjoyable. In these cases the rule is never to have the best, but only the second best. In this way enjoyment is at least secured, if what is enjoyed is less than what might be enjoyed.

Modifications of this principle:

1) Where the best is not wanted by the majority — then one is safe in fixing one's enjoyment in the best.

2) Where the best can be enjoyed (e.g. books etc.) without interference.

If, by chance, the majority desire the best (mostly without appreciating it), then the wise man will surrender the best for the second best, because what is selected by the majority is rapidly destroyed.

---

[37] P. Valéry, *An Evening with Monsieur Teste*, tr. M. Gould (London: Besant & Co., 1936).

CV[15]

'Quand l'universe considère avec indifférence l'être que nous aimons, qui est la vérité?'[38]

The question should not be, 'what is the truth,' because that isn't relevant: it should be, what shall we think? Or what shall we do? And the answer <u>must</u> be 'ignore the universe.'[39]

CV[15]

We must take account of the fact that the love of the good and constant striving for it may make a man spiteful, hard & merciless. Indifference to good & evil in one extreme, a too great insistence on good & evil in the other. The true life of man lies between. <u>Tolerance</u>, <u>mercy</u>, 'consideration for others' (Confucius), i.e. love. Freedom from obsession.[40]

CV[15]

To be second is better than to be first: —

1) To be first requires & implies extraneous qualities, worldly qualities, that mislead. It requires not only merit in whatever one is first in, but also ability to be 'first.' It carries with it the penalty of success.

Perhaps it implies the extraneous will to success.

To be full to the brim is not so good as to know when to stop — to have a limit of one's own; to control.

2) It avoids hubris.

CV[15]

If there are no realities, appearances rise in value.

CV[15]

The falseness of the idea of perfection: — It is an intellectual, philosophical ideal improperly carried over into life — Democracy — the removal of the idea of perfection from politics.

CV[16]

The baseness of the mercantile & the military ideals: & note how they merge into one another. The Germans were apt to contrast their military & heroic civilization with the mercantile: but the contrast can't be maintained in the end, and the true military ideal is something that has no place in modern civilization: vide

---

[38] Oakeshott's note: 'Jouhandeau.' Presumably Marcel Jouhandeau (1888–1979), French Catholic novelist and moralist.

[39] Oakeshott's note: 'Cp. Homer, *Odyssey*, X.70–7.'

[40] Oakeshott's note: 'Berdyaev, 231.'

'War.' The German military idea degenerated in a struggle in which the acquisition of patents & the management of currencies were more important than the military character.

CV[16]

'The old qualitative civilizations had as their aim perfection, not power, & are our Paradise Lost.'[41]

No, not <u>perfection</u>, for that would dismiss what is strongest in these civilizations — their perception of mortality, of balance. It is the West that has destroyed them in the search for perfection — power after power. The loss of the power to let well alone. The thoughtless exploitation of invention.

CV[16]

What of the innumerable joys, struggles, thoughts, sorrows, hopes & desires that are of no account to the world? The emotions of the individual whom one sees in a city crowd? One may either be oppressed when one thinks of the absolute reality to themselves of these emotions; or one may reject their not being of any account to the world and take them as they are valued by those who feel them. An illusion is real to those who suffer it — it is the reality. But psychological states are not valuable simply in themselves; there is another criteria — that which distinguishes between illusion & reality. Nevertheless, in human intercourse, & above all in close relationships, illusion even known as such must be accepted as reality.

CV[16]

<u>Lost causes</u>

Jacobites; the South in the American Civil War; Cavaliers & Roundheads.

Often the great moments of history; often, because they are fixed & finished, more permanent than that which succeeded & therefore tends to be lost in further achievements.

The value of loss itself.

The moments of success tend to lose their individuality in a general development; the moments of loss retain their individuality and power.

The same true of decay — it is freed from the dissolving power of success.

<u>Loss</u>.[42]

---

[41] Oakeshott's note: 'Ferrero.' Guglielmo Ferrero (1871-1942), Italian historian and novelist.

[42] Oakeshott's note: 'Maillaud, p. 214.'

CV[16]

The cultivation of life in a world of mechanization & mass labour involves a form of escapism. This in itself is a criterion of our civilization; though the true sweetness of life was, perhaps, always something involving an escape from the current & conventional life belonging to any civilization. It is the quality & the direction of the escape that matters. The English tradition encourages an individual escape, & that is an escape of the highest quality. Continental societies, especially Germany, tend to make it a communal, almost mass escape; this is of the lowest quality. E.g. sports clubs etc.

Democracy & escape. Democracy implies the encouragement of individual escape: mass escape is not democratic.[43]

CV[17]

The Ideal Human Character

The necessity of belonging to a time & a place. Equally, the necessity of not being wholly governed by that time & place. The representative of a civilization.

The nature of an ideal. A possible form of being, expressive of the will. Expressive of a consistent moral attitude towards all things in human experience, a coordination of our interests, a criterion, a means of valuing things & persons – a logical-imaginative perception of what is important & what is trivial. Ideal – the voice of love & hate, hope & desire.

Ideal a function of reality. Imaginary, only because more complete.
Independent of any possibility of its realization – does not even imply that it would be better if it were realized. An ideal has authority, not by reason of its prophetic content, but because of its insight into the conditions of human life. Not necessarily good that all should conform to the ideal.

By its nature, full conformity to the ideal is impossible. It deserves & wins imaginative allegiance because it expresses what the will demands. It does not require to wait for realization for its validity to be proved.

An ideal character implies an ideal world; i.e. that part of the world controlled by will must be in accord with the character itself.

An ideal has no force. It is explanatory rather than creative. It is a creature of the imagination & it creates only images. Ideal – a principle & example of comprehension. An extrapolation.

CV[17]

The ideal is the expression of a temperament, a realization of a character. Does it ever get beyond this? Get to reason?[44] It is susceptible of no proof; it belongs to ourself, never a true universal.

---

43 Oakeshott's note: 'Santayana, *Persons & Places*, p. 215.'
44 Oakeshott's note: 'Montaigne, *Essais*, iv.13.'

CV[17]

To be contented with oneself, reconciled, without being self-satisfied.
  Wisdom's content with that which is present.

CV[17]

An ideal human character must assent with and express a civilization: it is always the 'ideal of a civilization.'

CV[17]

The <u>form</u> & the <u>content</u> of the ideal character.

1) Integrity

2) Inheritor of his civilization

3) Charm

These joined in <u>piety</u>.

CV[17]

The ideal not something abstract, a set of principles embodied in a mechanical man. <u>This</u> ideal has been learnt from my society, from England. It matters not that it is not exactly the ideal of my society — everything in it has sprung from seeds that find this social soil not inimical: it <u>could</u> be the ideal of my society.[45]

CV[17]

Perfection: — not belonging to life at all. Not required by love, not required in ourselves.

CV[18]

The 'Thruster'!
  The Irish character: decadence.
  Par délicatesse j'ai perdu ma vie.[46]
  How shall we follow Montaigne & escape the Left Book Club.
  The ideal human character as the myth of a civilization.
  Confucius & Epicurus joined: not the false synthesis of Taoism.

CV[18]

The myth of Palinurus: will-to-failure, repugnance-of-success, desire to give up at the last moment. Not a suitable criterion for external activity itself, for it denies the value in external achievement; but considering the inappropriateness of external achievement to human life, it becomes a suitable condition for a good

---

[45] Oakeshott's note: 'Berdyaev, pp. 306–10.'
[46] Cp. p. 245, above.

life. Entering into the promised land seems to put everything on a false foundation—not that in itself it is evil, but it is false as the motive of desire. A demonstration to oneself that one's motive of desire is true to human life. The dis-
engagement with anything that is not an end in itself. Serve flow of life: austere.

CV[18]

Is 'live unknown'? anything more than the natural prejudice of a temperament?
Has it any universal significance?
E.g. the natural prejudice of the Englishman against ostentation in habit,
speech or appearance. The English, unemphatic, undemonstrative in work &
leisure. Not frivolous.

CV[19]

The implication of 'consideration for others'—avoidance of interference with
others or using them for our own ends. Always the good man thinks himself at
once not called upon to tell others what they should do and under obligation to
do whatever he can for others.[47]

CV[19]

To discover <u>yourself</u>. Sometimes this is achieved only formally—the discovery of
a vocation, or a skill. But to discover yourself fully is to find freedom; and until
this discovery is made all freedom is frivolity.

CV[20]

<u>War</u>

The object of any war is power—increase or preservation of power.
This war—the modification introduced by liberation.

CV[20]

War produces the worst in everyone; no man is as bad at other times as he is in
the army—as selfish, as stupidly insistent on his rights, as impervious to reason,
as dishonest.

CV[20]

The similarity of war & the life of pleasure—the sense of the shortness of life, the
life from day to day, without more than daily responsibilities—surely the military life is itself a fair example of the life of pleasure? No; because war is not the
same as the circumstances of military life—at least not the circumstances that
make it akin to the life of pleasure. Wars can be conducted only because they

---

47   Oakeshott's note: 'A. Wingate, *The Golden Phoenix: Essays on Chinese Art and Culture*
(London: J. Jenkins, 1930), p. 182.'

create circumstances agreeable to those who desire a life of pleasure, but they appear because a mere life of pleasure has ceased to attract: a new background at least is required, an illusion of destiny, an illusion of affairs, even an illusion of action that has some object beyond the moment & some motive other than pursued pleasure. Ambition, glory — these have no place in the life of pleasure.

CV[20]

War & the military life contrasted: a prolonged war destroys the virtue of the military life. The function of <u>military power</u>; the military life as the agent of military power.[48]

CV[20]

War and its false standard of <u>immediacy</u> & the necessity for <u>speed</u>: standards that mislead in peace. A politics of peace conceived in the categories of war & recommended in the terms of war — 'labour front' — 'D-day in the schools' — 'five year plan' — tactics & strategy — is a false politics: Germany; Russia.

CV[20]

War 1) its folly 2) its possibility. How much of history is, in fact, taken up with war? On any count it must be one of the major facts of human life: and one so deeply & so frequently experienced, that we might have expected that the human mind would have distilled from it some essence, its idea.

CV[20]

War & love. Does war give the catharsis of love? Or does war perhaps give the opportunity of that catharsis? A people that desires war & embraces it with relief or enthusiasm is almost certainly a people whose sexual life is unhappy.

CV[21]

Imagination not powerful enough to forsee all the conditions created by a plan.[49] The evils we design to avoid, when we fail to avoid them, are not experienced as we imagined them. They become conditions that, when accepted, are transformed by acceptance. Imagination to be complete must comprehend not only fact, conditions, but also what these conditions will appear as when they are seen to be unavoidable.

Liberalism & planning.[50]

---

48 Oakeshott's note: 'Swartzchild, p. 33.'
49 Oakeshott's note: 'Montaigne, *Essais*, iii.69–70, 73.'
50 Oakeshott's note: 'Croce, *Morals & Politics*, p. 147 sq.' Probably B. Croce, *Politics and Morals*, tr. S.J. Castiglione (London: George Allen & Unwin, 1946).

CV[21]

Planning is the interjection of philosophy into life — a *confusion des genres,* *ignoratio elenchi.*

CV[21]

The <u>feeling</u> of the Russian revolution, cp. Wordsworth & the French Revolution. I was 17 and in 1917 felt it all. Illusions. But saw dimly even then the value of what was being destroyed — the civilization of Tolstoy & Turgenev. The intellectual grandeur of the Eastern church.

CV[21]

The idea of Christian unity — the unity of the churches — doctrinaire; an early example of the 'planned' religion.

CV[21]

<u>Planning and Millenarism</u>

The perfect society; a society from which all vulgar & extraneous elements have been excluded; other ideals — a society in which production is organized throughout on the most economical plan, from which all rules of inefficiency & tradition have been excluded:

All such ideals, & one or other of them or a combination of them is certainly implied in a planned society, are false.

Compare the notion of a literature <u>only</u> of masterpieces.

A society that is <u>unmixed</u>, no discordant element as well as no imperfection.

This perhaps is an ideal (though also perhaps a false one) for a man's own personal narrow society.

But if our aim is <u>persons</u> & our politics are the <u>politics of the person</u>, none of these ideals appear even for consideration. What sort of society is implied in the politics of the person?

CV[22]

<u>Science and the Modern World</u>

The inventions of 'science' — what do people want with all this electricity rushing up & down the country — telephone & telegraph.

Argument: the gifts of science cannot be separated from one another: it is impossible to have modern surgery without the rest of the modern world. This true only if you suppose that these inventions spring from an energy which <u>can't</u> be directed selectively. Why should not a civilization say 'yes' to some and 'NO' to others? We feel that it ought to do so when this energy of the scientific mind spends itself on destruction; but we don't do it & don't know how to do it. The only <u>way</u> to do it: not 'authoritatively', from above, by law or order, but by the presence of the values the civilization embodies. Since these are forgotten, perverted, or not appreciated there remains no selective principle to govern this activity.

CV[22]

The terrorism of science in the modern world.

CV[22]

Science — the factory ideal of culture. Division of labour — the result only matters — speed — each must specialize. When science dominates, then culture becomes pseudo-culture because science & journalism divide the field between them.

CV[23]

'Creation' in art — always conditioned by the 'material' = craft. Acceptance combined with rejection.

CV[23]

Only the supreme artist is perfectly simple, perfectly balanced — arising out of such an excess of energy that discipline alone would save it from disintegration. Weaker imaginations can allow themselves full play. Classic & Romantic.

CV[23]

The artist — at once an outcast and adored, idolized, commanded devotion.

CV[23]

Without actual physical embodiment — words, sounds, stone, pigment — even if actual embodiment is only imagined, the artistic experience does not exist.

In no sense is a poem the translation into words of the state of mind of the poet, for he does not know till he has said it either what he wants to say or how he shall say it — two things that are admittedly one. The artist is driven by a passion, an excitement, his expression may be at once representative of that passion or it may become so after much change & correction — but 'correction' is not to make it correspond with images in his mind, but to make it a more satisfying expression of his passion. A work of art is the expression of the artistic passion or excitement, & not of any imaginative artistic experience. That experience is generated in & through the expression itself. <u>Creation</u>; rather a recreation & a practical creation — acceptance of the material & the creation of the experience…the subject chooses the material and the material chooses & modifies the images & the artist finds himself compelled by his material to fresh or altered imagination. Creation & acceptance.

CV[23]

The business of the writer is to produce a masterpiece. Literature as a library of masterpieces — is it possible? The place of the second rate?

(i) As <u>contemporary</u>.

(ii) As the condition of the <u>masterpiece</u>.

CV[23]

Perfectionism in <u>art</u>, but not in life.

CV[23]

The place of the artist in his society is one of the definitive characteristics of both the art & the society.

CV[23]

<u>The modified ivory-tower</u>

To be an artist is a high calling, demanding patience and a certain self-sacrifice, a sacrifice of certain other ordinarily enjoyed activities & enjoyments.

Artist inherently isolated; should not seek admission to the organized body of society. He is an outcast, or alternatively, an aristocrat. An outcast by calling: but more by temperament & necessity.

Flaubertian conception of art & the artist.

This view, it is true, belonged characteristically to the nineties. But it has a universal aspect — the theory & the practice of the nineties was only one mode of its existence, one avatar.

Our question is: Is this universal aspect valid? Not, is this mode valid?

CV[23]

<u>Art & Life</u>

If we assume that art represents what we want in life — that the literature of Europe is Europe's expression of its longings & desires — then certain conclusions about the civilization of Europe will follow.[51]

But this perhaps is not so; art may represent something else but desires; it may represent an understanding of life. And if this is so, our conclusions about the civilization will be different.

---

51 Oakeshott's note: 'Cp. D. de Rougemont, *Passion and Society*, tr. M. Belgion (London: Faber and Faber, 1940).'

CV[23]

Let us give up the fruitless, meaningless question of the relation of art & society, & consider the relation of art & society <u>now</u>.

The best is corrupted by the mob.

CV[24]

The discipline of adaption to circumstances. We are so ready to consider everything as a construction & therefore as subject to the exercise of the human will, that we forget that we live in a world in which not everything can be changed, & possess natures whose characters cannot wholly be recreated. We would rather destroy & recreate than adapt. But adaptation belongs much more to the fallible human character & judgment; it is more in accord with our actual powers. We are not 'gods.'

CV[24]

Creation v. Acceptance

We undertake to <u>decide</u> everything e.g. death — suicide. Birth — contraception. And yet we do not possess the necessary wisdom to make half these decisions. A <u>planned</u> life.

CV[24]

The value of something beyond our control — something we accept.

Marriage — arranged.[52]

CV[24]

<u>Language</u>. Each has its own range of possibilities, its own arbitrary euphony & prosody, its own strength & weakness. The poet does not reject these; he does not even feel them as limitations; they are his material, they belong to his experience, & the habit of his ear. So mortality is the material of human life — <u>things that do not last for ever</u>.

CV[24]

You can't have a good wine without a long tradition — principle of minimum time. And the best speak to us now of a passion, an experience, a life & a wisdom more serene than can now be enjoyed. Even the worst remind us of something better, in closer touch with the ancient realities, than our present world. Like poetry from a world ignorant of newspapers & advertisements & the other prostitution of the magic of words — & even when it is not poetry of the highest class — even when it is a little sentimental — we are in partnership with it; our

---

[52] Oakeshott's note: 'Montaigne, *Essais*, v.102–86.'

age, alas, will be one that the future will skip over as its roots strike down for the earth that nourishes.

CV[25]

<u>Suicide</u>

Part of suicide is no more than the readiness to die if what makes life worth living is denied. What sure distinction can we draw between the suicide and the man who is prepared to die because he knows that nothing he can lose by dying is half so precious as the readiness to die for what he prizes most?

Suicide as the escape from mortality and as the recognition of mortality.

CV[26]

<u>Death</u>

Delight increased by rareness & by precariousness: a life surrounded by death, a mortal life, has delights that an immortal life could never possess.

The fact that one can do some things only <u>once</u> makes them infinitely precious: & if by misjudgment the value is lost, it can never be regained.

Indeed, everything in life is 'once.' External acts—e.g. marriage etc.—can take place more than once, but that is only because they are generalizations, abstractions; the thing itself is only & always <u>once</u>.

Everything is irreparable: the notion of repair inapplicable to human life.

CV[26]

Epicurus—why should we fear to lose something that being lost we no longer remain to experience the loss? Death not to be feared because it is at once the end of life & the self. But this does not touch the lesser deaths—only the last death. And these lesser deaths—the mortal material of our life—are the worst.

To lose youth, vitality, power, love, a friend—all are deaths & they are felt & suffered as deaths. Hence, not death, but transience, old age is the crucial predicament of life. The lesser deaths are the greater because they are not final.

How to overcome death—& these lesser deaths? The sharpness of death?

Not overcome by another life.

1) If we are the same person, personal immortality. Because if we are the same, then the last death is like the lesser deaths, we have to feel it. And the sudden transition, without depriving ourselves of ourselves, makes us exiles until we become naturized to the new world: there must be felt loss.

2) If we are not the same person. Because then death really is the end.
No doctrine of another world can overcome the sharpness of death: only 1) tiredness, willingness to die, or 2) a mastery of death by acceptance.

Not death, but this <u>fear</u> of death, the enemy.

One death cannot explain or prepare for another: the lesser deaths are not a school teaching how to die finally. One loss does not prepare for another. And a series of suffered & felt losses has nothing in common with a final loss in which we ourselves also are lost.

How to overcome the fear of death?

CV[26]

How much thought do we normally give to death?

The evidence suggests:

1) That children think much about it

2) That adults may think often & deeply of it or may hardly think of it at all — matter of temperament.

CV[26]

Our reactions to death are the most civilized of our reactions. Sex still remains a reflection of a dim & distant part of human history, taking us back to the childhood of the race — to its infancy. But in death our conscious ideas about death, and our childish reactions to death, are mirrored the struggle & intellectual pains of those ages when the religions of the civilized world were being born and when the Greeks shed the clear, compassionate light of their intellect upon the human predicament.

CV[26]

To leap from being (even ill-being) to not being is neither so great nor so revolutionary as to leap from one state of being to another in which the first is lost but remembered, felt & may be lamented.[53]

CV[27]

Death belongs to life: part of it. We could not remove death without transforming the whole character of our life. But we can remove the <u>fear</u> of death.

1) Forget it: do not think of it.

2) Consider it closely, expect it, forsee it, live with it continuously in mind. Cp. Pascal. But this prepares us for the death of <u>others</u> rather than our own: & the idea of others is one of the lesser deaths we have to suffer.

Remove the strangeness of death by close acquaintance with it. Conversation. Friendliness with death. But no mastery of death in the abstract will console for an actual death. One death does not explain another; one loss cannot reconcile us to another.

---

53 Oakeshott's note: 'Cp. Homer, *Odyssey*, X.237–41.'

'He who has learned to die has unlearned to serve...To know how to die doth free us from all subjection & constraint.'[54]

But this can apply only to the last death — which is the least.

The most we can learn is how not to fear death.

'The deadest deaths are the best.' Montaigne, *Essais* — i.e., the last.[55]

Permitting death to influence our way of living. E.g. not attempting what we do not think we shall live to complete.

Death should find us — cultivating our garden, prepared, but not dominated by death.

No man dies before his time — not that his death is predetermined, but because the time you leave behind is no more yours than the years before you were born. No man dies <u>too</u> late, no man is cut off in the middle of his life — except in the irrelevant sense that there is an average span of life that (being an average) some do not attain & others exceed.

As long as one is not forgotten one is not dead?

Birth presents many of the same problems as death. S. Butler, Pascal.

The practical importance of a doctrine of death. What makes extinction tolerable or intolerable.

(a) Intolerable: selfishness, ambition, glory, desire not to be cheated, purpose, failure, subject to disappointment.

(b) Tolerable: detachment, unambition, failure, present enjoyment, absence of contempt for life.

Suicide more appropriate to (a).[56]

'If death ends my career, then I should decide that this earth-life, taken as a whole, is not worth living':[57] i.e. only the evanescence of imperfection satisfies.

Doctrines of survival.[58]

The argument that only the immortality of the soul can substantiate individualism, because it makes the soul outlast everything in the worldly scene — state, society, civilization, etc. But a soul separable from its world is nothing: an empty shell.[59]

---

[54] Oakeshott's note: 'Montaigne, *Essais*, i.98.'

[55] Oakeshott's note: 'Montaigne, *Essais*, i.101.'

[56] Oakeshott's note: 'McDougal, *Body & Mind*, "Preface," p. xiii; Faucett, *Zermatt*, pp. 4, 51, 94.' W. McDougal, *Body & Mind A History And A Defense Of Animism* (London: Methuen & Co. Ltd., 1911); E.D. Fawcett, *The Zermatt Dialogues, Constituting the Outlines of a Philosophy of Mysticism* (London: Macmillan & Co., 1931).

[57] Oakeshott's note: '*Oberland*, pp. 201–2.' Possibly D.M. Richardson, *Oberland* (London: Duckworth, 1927).

[58] Oakeshott's note: '*Oberland*, p. 205.'

[59] Oakeshott's note: '*Oberland*, p. 378 sq.'

'Neither at the sun nor at death can one look steadily.' La Rochefoucauld.

CV[27]

Socrates refused to grieve over his own death, saying that it would set his soul free, but he could not keep his friends from weeping.

CV[27]

The mental acceptance of death is difficult — so difficult that the effort may cloud our whole life — consciously or unconsciously. This is deeply written in the records of mankind. Religion — by its doctrines & by its rites — has helped to ease this difficulty & everything it has done in this direction is good: whether it is by way of a doctrine of life after death, or merely by the consolations it offers when the farewell is felt as final.

Brings death into a grand & positive relation with life. Religion — a social organization of human reactions relating them to a culture.

Religion & its offer of relief from anxiety — even suttee, martyrdom or sacrifice.

A true religion is the integration in each individual of his attitude to death.

CV[28]

Death defeated by propagation. This is an important element in Eastern culture — e.g. Chinese, but has never been important in Western civilization.[60]

Hatred of death, and fear of death. Death universal & inevitable, but an evil.

This felt sometimes by those in love with life, but also by those who have no strong feeling or reason to attach themselves to life.

CV[28]

Since it is <u>fear</u> of death that is evil, what is required to combat it, is not reason, but <u>courage</u>. Cp. Lucretius who gave man a <u>reason</u>. Relation of reason and courage, what is it.

If fear of death is the father of all fear, then courage is no answer to death — or rather courage can answer death only when it has answered all lesser fears.

Fear of death — a child hoping that he would be an exception to the general rule: children only gradually come to see death as a natural & universal event, connecting it first with human ill-will or accident. But when they see it as a natural event it is difficult to accept it.

---

[60] Oakeshott's note: 'Plato, *Symposium*, 206c–207d. Cp. "Come let us make love deathless" — sexual love and not its <u>result</u>. Shakespeare, Sonnet 12.'

CV[28]

To take death's part in life—any great casting away of ambition or worldly goods, any retirement from the normal competition of one's profession, any overcriticalness that prevents production or inhibits result, certainly any philosophy of failure or non-success—is taking death's part—is an accommodation to death in life. But a too complete anticipation of death and what death will do to us, will turn life into death. Here again, a <u>mean</u> is the only avoidance of the unreality & madness of the extreme.

CV[28]

The Christian tradition that death came into the world with sin. Somehow death did not belong to man as he was created. Bodily immortality was one of the special privileges belonging to man that he lost with the *vitium originis*.

CV[29]

<u>Life. Mortality—Transience</u>

Human character: a middle.

    Not a god nor a child.

    Not living for ever, nor for a very short while. Not like day-flies. Thucydides.

    Not wholly bound by mortality because able to transcend by comprehension some elements of mortality (defeat it), nor immortal, but it must accept.[61]

CV[29]

We have both to accept & defeat mortality.

    Shakespeare, the poet of mortality: what he leaves out: cp. Homer, Lucretius, Dante, Goethe, Santayana.

CV[29]

Life is a barmecide feast: know it as such. 'Patience & shuffle the cards.'[62] The point is, not whether we have rational grounds for believing in survival, continuance or immortality, but that however firmly we are convinced of any of these, we are still subject to the conditions of mortality. Even if we are in some sense immortal, yet we cannot avoid the sufferings of mortals. Mortality still the prime fact. Immortality & survival only touch the last death.

---

[61] Oakeshott's note: 'Montaigne, *Essais*, vi.314–15.'

[62] M. de. Cervantes, *El Ingenioso Hidalgo Don Quixote De La Mancha* [*The Ingenious Gentleman Don Quixote of La Mancha*] (Madrid: Juan de la Cuesta, 1605), Pt II Bk III ch. xxiii. Cp. pp. 388–9, below.

CV[29]

To 'admit' mortality is familiar to us as a mood, an attitude of mind, a mood peculiar perhaps to a certain period in life when the mind has become adult. But the admission of mortality is also more than a mood; it is a philosophy, or at least what Pascal called the 'hidden thought' that gives coherence to the parts of a philosophy.

CV[30]

The charm & pleasure of the suggestion of immortality that youth contains. A man whose body remains young past its time; a girl *en fleur* in the hey-day of her youth — these make us forget mortality for a moment. But they are not intimations of immortality: they are a momentary suspension of the law of mortality that, for a moment, lifts the weight of death from the shoulders of those who yet must surely die.

CV[30]

Tedium vitae.

To avoid:

1) The 'American' fear of never having lived — leading to febrile nervous activity, continual, unguided experiment: losing your head about living.

2) Never in fact having lived.

CV[30]

To avoid regret that hinders life. Not to mourn over wasted years that cannot be recalled.

CV[30]

Having conceived a discontent on account of the conditions of human life — its sorrows or even just its shortness, we then go for comfort to the philosophers. Three great doctrines:

1) Stoic: — it is inevitable, so do not allow it to worry you. *Grave nihil est homini quod fert necessitas.*[63]

2) Epicurean: — dismissal.

3) Christian: — Life a warfare; suffering temporary; the new world is at hand.

None of these accept.

---

[63] Oakeshott's note: 'Cicero; Burton, ii.148–9 sq., 180.' Probably Burton, *The Anatomy of Melancholy*: see p. 176, above.

CV[30]

Manichaeism

The denial of mortality: perfectionism—and a heresy. The feeling for mortality that has always lain at the root of Christianity (at least from the 4th century A.D.)

CV[31]

How can we come to feel and know that the troubles & happiness of this transient life justify themselves. There is nothing else, beyond or outside, to which they can be referred for justification. They must be known as their own reward. And <u>we</u> can feel & know this if we give up searching for some ulterior meaning & justification & apply our minds to what is known to us. This life is a 'stumble' only when we compare it with a perfection that does not belong to its character, a perfection that is not <u>its</u> perfection.

Let us, by all means, distinguish & hold before us clearly the imperfections that belong to this life; but do not let us attribute to it as imperfections what belongs to its character. (Cp. Spinoza. Nothing must be attributed as an imperfection that belongs to the nature of the thing.)

What do we <u>know</u> of human life? That it is neither long nor short, that we do <u>not</u> know what, if anything, comes after it. That every detail of it is subject to mortality. That we are ignorant of any ulterior purpose or meaning. That it is made of joy and sorrow. That it is governed by a chance that, if it is accepted, may be understood as a necessity.

CV[32]

That the nature of our emotions change & have changed is as certain as that the institutions under which we live have changed and our ideas have changed. If our conception of nature is radically different from that of the Greeks, it is not less certain that the emotions we connect with <u>love</u> and e.g. external nature, are different from what they were 500 years ago. There is, in fact, no absolute stability. The important question is, what may be inferred from this instability? The first inference, when this transience was recognized in the 18th century, was that no one stage or thing is more valuable than another—absolute relativity. That this is a false inference we know—but knowing this, we have ceased to infer. But there <u>is</u> a true inference.

CV[33]

Chance; Fortune; Necessity

In another age I should never have known what it was to be a soldier.

In another generation, five years of my life would not have been spent in the army.

There is no <u>natural</u> course of life. Life is a predicament in which circumstances command, and in which we become what can be made from circumstances.

Nothing inevitable. E.g. This move towards planning.[64]

Turning points in history: —

1) Reformation.

2) Victory of North over the South in USA.

At both these points the life of the Western world took a turn for the worse: the one produced the modern German character; the other the modern American character: both menaces to civilization.

To entertain the possibility that Western civilization has taken a <u>wrong</u> turning: what do we mean by wrong? Perhaps a denial of its central character, or a malignant as opposed to a healthy growth.[65]

Remedy —

1) Not to go back.

2) Not to go on.

3) But to catch up by a short cut; & meanwhile not to lose what is not already lost.

CV[33]

Progress?[66]

Why do we need to <u>believe</u> in progress?

Progress, in some sense, may be a fact but it isn't a relevant fact because 1) it does not bring the <u>present</u> release from imperfection that we demand, it is a not a surrogate salvation, and 2) it assumes the evanescence of imperfection and therefore puts us on the wrong track. Unless we leave this track we shall never find salvation in mortal life.

The appearance of a faith in progress carried with it an exuberant optimism and a febrile impatience — tempting men to tear themselves adrift from their historic past and to set sail after utopias & perfectibilities conceived not in terms of the society & time to which they belonged, but in terms of abstractions, doctrinaire 'rights of man', eternal orders, new orders etc. Only those societies which had a firm hold on their past & a deep affection for it escape: perhaps only England: Progress & continuity. So firmly grounded in our non-doctrinaire system of politics, we were not tempted.

---

64   Oakeshott's note: 'Hayek, p. 16 & Ch. IV.'
65   Oakeshott's note: 'Hayek, p. 8.'
66   Oakeshott's note: 'Montaigne, *Essais*, v.251–4; *Essais*, vi.71, 102, 122.'

CV[33]

The conception of Trumps — divine or quasi-divine intervention: a degeneracy in the game. A Joker even more degenerate. Did card games originally contain either?

CV[33]

'The science of life consists in seizing every chance that presents itself.'[67]

1) <u>Every</u> chance?

2) How to avoid the dissipation of personality, & the fear of never having lived at all?

CV[33]

No inevitable cause of events; also, what has happened is not necessarily the best — and even if we decide that there is no going back, we need not assert that what has happened is good, or that, if it is not good, going on will cure it. There is no cure. The world is henceforth different — worse than it might have been — if this cause or that had not been lost. The fact that it <u>was</u> lost does not mean that what was lost was not good & better perhaps than what prevailed. E.g. <u>population</u>. The fall in the death rate and the extended expectation of life means an older population — unless there is a rapidly increasing population due to a rising birth rate. But even with a rising birth rate — which might keep the age proportion in the population stable — the gross number of old people would have increased & be increasing. Is this good? Yet, if it isn't we can't undo it, for most of the things that have made us live longer have also made those who are younger live less painfully.

CV[34]

What responsibility can we accept for our actions, the consequences of which, or what might appear to be the consequences, are, from the very beginning modified and conditioned by what is out of our control?[68]

CV[34]

The anatomy of hope. What is the place of hope? 'Patience is the art of hoping.'[69]
    Gambling as the expression of optimism.

---

67 Oakeshott's note: 'Joseph Conrad, *Chance: A Tale in Two Parts* (London: Methuen & Co., 1913).'

68 Oakeshott's note: 'Cp. Lord Salisbury.'

69 Oakeshott's note: 'Vauvenargues, 251.'

CV[34]

Often small mistakes bring great misfortunes; a man may break his leg walking in his room. It is only good luck that prevents a man's errors bringing him ill consequences.

CV[34]

Misfortune = lack of external achievement that might be expected to be achieved.

Suffering external circumstances that might be expected to be avoided.

Its relation to personality: we think of it as merely hindering, but if this is so, then the whole world must be regarded as a potential hindrance to the achievement of personality.

CV[34]

A man without a sense of chance or fortune is a man liable to the defect of pride. A sense of fortune is part of humility. Hubris implies the lack of it.

CV[34]

Why are there years without spring or autumn, when the fruits of the season wither in their bloom? Years without summer? Useless questions. Yet this may happen in years when to us personally it is most important that the full sweetness of the seasons should appear. A lost year.

CV[34]

All particular stations in life are, at bottom, accidental; and inequalities which they indicate will trouble only those in whose mind a theory has completely effaced experience. To see these as the result of chance, reinforces rather than removes the responsibilities which go with them: but they are not responsibilities to abolish that which gives meaning to responsibility.

CV[35]

Religion

What determined our religious beliefs & their intensity & importance? The influence of circumstance: adolescence, marriage, etc: This true particularly of mystical religion. Social religious beliefs: Piety, sympathy with simple believers.[70]

CV[35]

The 'herd creeds' — but why not?[71]

---

[70] Oakeshott's note: 'H. Wodehouse, *One Kind of Religion* (Cambridge: Cambridge University Press, 1944).'

[71] Oakeshott's note: 'Fawcett, *Zermatt*, pp. 138–59.'

Two great periods in a religion —

1) The near-beginning; archaic; first customs & ceremonials established.

2) The high summer: the creation of a theology.

CV[35]

'The appalling possibilities of a world uncontrolled by the divine' — this is the beginning of Fascism, which creates a god so as to eliminate the possibility that there may not be one.

CV[35]

A blind God — but do you trust blind pilots? But what if God isn't a pilot?

CV[35]

Belief in God — what does the common man believe? How far can we follow him?[72]

Religion is devotion — God the organizing centre of devotion.

Have I any experience, similar to the apparent experience of the disciples, that forces one to attribute divinity to somebody or something I know? Can we know something & then later come to know it to be divine?[73]

CV[35]

The comforting Greek religion in which, if one god is against you, it is always possible to find another to help you. It is a kind of personification of the Christian God who is at once secure & loving.[74]

CV[35]

For the Greek men & gods inhabited the same world; they walked hand in hand over the earth. Direct contact. For the Hebrew, God was an overseer; a supervisor; the <u>dossier</u> business. A superior to control human affairs. Christianity, the incarnation, introduced into the Hebrew religion an intimacy, but it did not succeed in overcoming the overseer & the dossier. Protestantism reintroduced an added Hebrew element into Medieval Christianity. A bridge between man & god — Christianity — incarnation — a cumbersome contrivance to overcome a defect that (whatever its other defects) Greek religion never suffered from.

---

72 Oakeshott's note: 'Fawcett, *Zermatt*, p. 65.'
73 Oakeshott's note: 'Fawcett, *Zermatt*, p. 193.'
74 Oakeshott's note: 'Cp. Homer, *Odyssey*, V.333–54.'

CV[35]

Religion as an attempt to explain away & modify the felt insignificance of the life of the individual by creating a God everlastingly occupied in watching every single one of us & engrossed in the welfare of each. We add to our own importance. What is the alternative? Accept insignificance or transform it in some other way.

CV[36]

Religion in England. Diversity in institutional religion. No advantage in theoretic unity.

Unity of the churches a false ideal.[75]

Churchgoing in England.[76]

CV[36]

Fear is the basis of religious dogma: fear of nature — B. Russell.

Primus in orbe deos fecit timor. Petronius?[77]

But are not the gods, from earliest times, associated with dancing, feasting, laughter, poetry, holiday, joy, gifts?

Yes; but how far were these things autosuggestive? Appeasement? Sacrifices.

CV[36]

In religion to ask for something other than what the religious consciousness provides is to ask for something that does not exist. True religion is the outflow of an uncorrupt religious consciousness — & is nothing else beyond this.

CV[36]

Religious observance.[78]

What matters is the range of human need & aspiration focused in the observance.[79]

CV[36]

We may suppose, like the anthropologist, that mankind is somehow, & perhaps in spite of elements tending in the opposite direction, on the whole better for its religion. There is a certain survival value — value in living & dealing with life, in a religion.

---

[75] Oakeshott's note: 'Maillaud, pp. 205–6.'

[76] Oakeshott's note: 'Maillaud, pp. 35–6, 211.'

[77] The phrase occurs in a fragment of poetry by Petronius (*c*.27–66 CE), Roman satirist, and also in the *Thebaid* by Publius Papinius Statius (*c*.45–96 CE), Roman poet.

[78] Oakeshott's note: 'Santayana, *Persons & Places*, pp. 107–9, 121, 172.'

[79] Oakeshott's note: 'Laurence Whistler, *The English Festivals* (London: William Heinemann, 1947).' For Oakeshott's review see *SW* iii.222–3.

Religion = religious <u>feeling</u>, with which is allied action of a sort, formalized action, rather than thought. A developed religion, perhaps, must have dogma: but the primitive religion is almost without it.

God – beginning perhaps as an implication of a ritual, who answers only when he is called, becomes something that cannot be denied – becomes 'the conditionality which the religious man comes more & more to feel in his efforts to adjust himself to this universe by means of rites.'[80]

CV[36]

Religion gives a feeling of expectation, of <u>power</u> which may turn into the false intoxication of the *non posse peccare* – a sort of <u>hubris</u>. Religious license usually an indication of a religious prohibition in normal times. Cp. carnival, Dionsyiac rites.[81] Gives a dynamical mood. The thrill of the obscene to quicken the sense of life. If religion is taken as an intensified expression of the will to live, a positive <u>hopefulness</u> must be a basic element in it. To give nerve to the nervous strain entailed in the great enterprise of living. Those who do without a religion are those who have no sense of nervous <u>apprehension</u> in meeting life (cp. Robinson Crusoe). Relation of <u>hope</u> & <u>fear</u>.

CV[37]

<u>Education</u>

A true education of the spirit for the first time in the history of Western civilization is not to be found without great difficulty. Because we no longer have a true civilization.

Gadgets: science: specialization: eclecticism.
Music; dancing.
What shall we aim at? Cp. The eclectic life as against the unified life.

1) Variety of information; so-called 'knowledge of the world we live in.'

2) Travel – seeing how others live.[82]

3) Understanding other people.

4) Cosmopolitanism.

5) Insularity; parochialism.[83]

Cp. with this – Custom and plan; nature & art; growth & construction.

---

[80] Oakeshott's note: 'p. 11.' Probably a reference to Whistler, *English Festivals*.
[81] Oakeshott's note: 'R.R. Marett, *Faith, Hope and Charity in Primitive Religion* (Oxford: Clarendon Press, 1932), p. 78.'
[82] Oakeshott's note: 'Montaigne, *Essais*, vi.54, 79–81.'
[83] Oakeshott's note: 'Montaigne, *Essais*, vi.78–9.'

CV[37]

Education as the preparation of the mind for the enjoyment of the fruits of one's civilization. Civilization a partnership of the living & the dead: education making real this partnership to the individual.

CV[37]

The best environment for the young child: country, gardens, orchards, meadows, forests, snow in winter, the snow of the countryside, rock, river, sea, peasants, hills, flowers, trees. The town, its pavements, over-stimulate children. Change is too rapid; the impermanence of everything is founded upon no permanent ground. As proof: an intelligent countryman can quickly grasp the life of a town, its complexity; no townsman can <u>ever</u> fill the gap caused by the failure to know the country & grow up in it. The life of cities may be the true life of a civilized man (though that is doubtful), but it is not the best education for civilized children. Who knows only towns does not know the real secret of the life of cities.

CV[37]

'The secret of happiness is curiosity.'[84]

This is the great lie of the modern world. Curiosity to Aristotle was a defect, to Aquinas a sin & Burton recognizes it as a cause of madness. Curiosity = a mind filled with bric à brac = this is <u>not</u> the enjoyment & appreciation of the fruits of our civilization, of human experience. A prying mind.

CV[37]

Mathematics; Not desirable beyond the elements of arithmetic, algebra, & geometry. It affords no, or a harmful, training of the intelligence. There are no nuances & *la verité reste dans les nuances.*
   Chemistry: its entertainment value. Physiology & biology?
   Enough should be acquired of these sciences to save a man from being at the mercy of bogus science. Astronomy: — rather the appreciation of the stars as they have become part of human experience. Mythology.

CV[37]

Education should safeguard the world against the crafty egoists who will always dominate it by making them value craftiness less highly and modifying their natural egoism.

---

84 Oakeshott's note: 'N. Douglas, *South Wind.*'

CV[37]

Give a serenity to life to counterbalance the febrile mercantile activity that surrounds us.

CV[37]

Don't let us bog ourselves talking about education in general — what we should talk about is education <u>now</u>. And the most obvious thing to say is that the whole force & pressure of the contemporary western world is <u>against</u> education. It is a world of violent stimuli — film, radio, newspapers, magazines — & a mind early adapted to these stimuli will be a mind so much less capable of suffering that slow permeation of the personality that is characteristic of great literature. The world once, undesignedly, offered no positive opposition to this: the walk to school, the relatively slow moving days, long days without movement, time for enjoyment, time for recollection, time for doing nothing. Indeed, such a world is a frame of friendliness to the requirements of cultivation. Time for loneliness. Now the frame is unfriendly and we have to tear our opportunities 'through the iron gates of life'[85] — a life that has been created, not the 'mortality' which, in its character of a mean (neither short not long) itself gives the appropriate wider frame — appropriate because our education <u>must</u> conform to <u>that</u> frame.

CV[37]

Education and <u>a rite of initiation</u>; why are those rites so severe? The necessity of remembering, the importance of preservation of tradition where tradition is only oral. How many lost arts have savages had to deplore owing simply to the precariousness of the means of transmission at a stage in society when continuous participation in a ritual is the only way of keeping truth alive. And how many lost arts & values have <u>we</u> to deplore.

CV[37]

<u>The predicament of paternity</u>

Cp. Lord Chesterfield & his son. Desire that the new generation shall redress the balance of the old. Indeed, a failure to treat the child as a <u>person</u>; using him as a means to an end: — to exact successes that we have desired & missed. To insist on perfection.[86]

---

85 Andrew Marvell, 'To His Coy Mistress,' ll. 41–4: 'Let us roll all our strength and all / Our sweetness up into one ball, / And tear our pleasures with rough strife / Through the iron gates of life.'

86 Oakeshott's note: 'Connolly, *The Forbidden Playground*, p. 33.' Possibly C. Connolly, *The Condemned Playground. Essays: 1927–44* (London: Routledge, 1945).

CV[37]

There are two things about which we can have knowledge — the natural world & the civilized world. Knowledge of the second is the object of education.

CV[38]

Alas, in a mercantile world we must expect a mercantile education — just as we must take chemical warfare with the benefits of modern medicine — a civilization is a single piece, if we wish to change any part of it, that change will be reflected throughout — no change in any part without change in every part.

CV[38]

Variety of schools/education — why? No single psychologically correct system of education; the burden is always on the individual teacher. But he must know the civilization he is imparting. Dangers of a rational system of education: power, uniformity.

CV[38]

Books & the decline of 1) memory 2) power of extemporary composition. The human mind has never been so loaded with useless & superficial knowledge as it is to-day. Real erudition is called pedantry, and the values of learning have been turned upside down.

CV[38]

Education in the myths/legends of 1) the civilization 2) the country. This should be the 'history' of the young. The young mind should enter the world filled with myth & legend.

CV[38]

Culture[87]

The Culture-Philistine; the pseudo-culture.

The governing principle is <u>curiosity</u> without judgment — taste never formed; style never achieved. What should we say of such people if their morals were like their culture?

Knowledge <u>about</u> culture.

---

[87] Oakeshott's note: 'Cp. Nietzsche, *Thoughts Out of Season; The Future of Our Educational Institutions; Twilight of the Idols; Schopenhauer as Educator.*' F. Nietzsche, *Thoughts Out Of Season*, tr. A.M. Ludovici and A. Collins, 2 vols. (Edinburgh and London: Foulis Press, 1909); F. Nietzsche, *On The Future Of Our Educational Institutions. Homer And Classical Philology*, tr. J.M. Kennedy (Edinburgh and London: Foulis Press, 1909); F. Nietzsche, *The Twilight of the Idols; Or, How To Philosophize With The Hammer. The Antichrist. Notes to Zarathustra, and Eternal Recurrence*, tr. A.M. Ludovici (Edinburgh and London: Foulis Press, 1911).

The culture of the encyclopedia. Alexandrine culture.

The Philistine is better than the culture-philistine.

For Nietzsche the production of genius was the aim of culture. Cp. The business of the writer is to produce a masterpiece. Culture implies <u>cultivation</u>; its not to be acquired in a seed shop.

CV[38]

Education not <u>accommodation</u> to the culture of a civilization, nor the <u>acceptance</u>, but the <u>understanding & appropriation</u> of a living culture. We must <u>possess</u> what we have come to inherit (Goethe). What education has to do is to offer something coherent: what it tends to do now is to fit the learner only to accommodate himself to many cultures without fitting him to the appropriate one. Religion.

We can overrate the importance of understanding the child – what is more important is to have something (a coherent culture) to give. It will always remain a mystery how knowledge & understanding of a cultural tradition is acquired; but we tend to pay a lot too much attention to the way we impart that knowledge – always endeavouring to tell the child only what we know he can understand – instead of leaving to him the problem of understanding & telling him what is true & relevant. All learning is trying to understand what we are not yet quite fitted to understand. With the adult it is a problem that solves itself: the great effort of modern education is to circumvent it, if possible, with the child. But it is not possible, and our lack of faith here only reflects our general lack of faith in learning.

Montaigne – whatever we do it will be wrong.

CV[38]

The Economics of Education: how a system of education could have come about by private enterprise in the 19th century, if, by a system of family allowances, a demand could have been made for it. Instead, the state system came into being, with all its evils.

CV[39]

Love

The phenomenon of love, perhaps, more than anything else, shows the secondary place of justice and morality in human life. We live suspended in an unstable solution; only for immediate purposes of practical life a certain stability is introduced – called justice & morality. The rest is favour & affection.

CV[39]

The stirrings of love can be felt, like those of ambition, before we have an object. This true particularly of the young. The potentiality felt in advance of any choice of object. In love with love. What does this imply about the nature of love?

CV[39]

It would appear from Soloviev's argument that to love without being loved in return is enough.

Does being loved add anything to love? If so, what?

Love not dependent upon being requited. But requited love has something.

1) Love, the supersession of egoism.

2) Being loved in return – the return of modified egoism.

The self not fully achieved except in requited love.

CV[39]

Love & Death

Tristan a 'fatal' love. Passion is linked with death.

Preference for what thwarts passion, hinders the happiness of love, parts lovers.

Tristan & Iseult never miss an opportunity to be parted; creation of reasons for parting; preference for pains over pleasure. It is a romance about the parting of lovers in the name of passion in order that the love shall be intensified. What they love is love itself or being in love. The partings are dictated by the passion itself. The love of love is the love of death. The longing for what annihilates us.

CV[39]

'Happy love has no history – in European literature.'[88]

Assumes too readily that art represents what we want in life.

Love & perfection: an immortal love – not a 'poise in imperfection.'

CV[39]

European culture has known two myths of love – Tristan & Don Juan – both are myths of excess.

CV[39]

Is not the contrast between courtly love & marriage only one instance of the necessary contrast between love & morality?

---

88 Oakeshott's note: 'De Rougemont, *Passion and Society*, p. 63.'

CV[40]

In pretty girls moral qualities are not so awfully relevant.

CV[40]

Virginity — loss of virginity — its significance: the loss of that original egoism which, in its way, was complete: the loss of one coherent personality in the attempt to find one more coherent.

CV[40]

Why is love the most violent of our emotions?

1) Is the violence in it really belonging not to love but to what so often it is connected with — sexual hunger?

2) Love is a birth & a death: it is revolutionary, but not in essence violent.

CV[40]

Love & morality

Love never demands perfection: it is false to say we love only the ideal in those whom we love, or love them in spite of their recognized imperfections. Love is to be pleased by something other than perfection. Indeed, two may be more surely bound by their failings than by their virtues.

CV[40]

Parents who do not observe a strict impartiality towards all their children, are generally inflicted with an impartiality for the least deserving.

CV[40]

When hunger is the root of love, love becomes the tension of two egoisms, or merely the expression of one; because properly speaking love begins where egoism ends.

CV[41]

Power

It is as difficult to wield power and not come to make the exercise of power an end as it is to follow a profitable occupation and not make profit one's aim.

CV[41]

Power as the crudest denial of death.

CV[41]

A taste of political power, supreme political power, is like hashish, giving a wild, unnatural energy in its further pursuit, fatal to peace of mind, destructive of personality — & in the end they drop dead, worn out by this drugged activity. It is the most excessive, insatiable thing upon earth.

CV[41]

Power makes men stupid. It corrupts because it intoxicates.

CV[41]

Of all our appetites the love of power is the most unsociable, for it requires the silent submission of those with whom we associate.

CV[43]

Myth

The necessity of myth. Science cannot substitute for it, & in so far as it destroys myth it destroys a human necessity. Epicurus.

The necessity of a myth about the beginning of the world & the cause of what belongs to the character of human life. This different from the 'scientific' explanation, which cannot take its place.

Myth & poetry.

The myth of original sin — scientific explanation (e.g. Freud) does not take its place.

The expression of a civilization or of an ideal in a human character is a myth — without that myth the civilization is inarticulate.

The corn goddess or the tractor? The womb or the bulldozer?[89]

CV[43]

The Tower of Babel: how the gods prevent a premature ascent into heaven.

CV[43]

Myth is rooted in the collective subconscious.

CV[43]

Myth and story; myth belongs to the esoteric tradition; it holds a more concentrated meaning than story, and a more universal meaning — it is connected with rite, it is the oral part of the rite. But more, it contains also the representation of the gesticulating part of the rite; dance & movement.

---

[89] Oakeshott's note: 'Palinurus, p. 75.' Possibly C. Connolly ['Palinurus'], *The Unquiet Grave A Word Cycle By Palinurus* (London: Horizon, 1944); see p. 311 n. 9, above.

CV[43]

Myth not typically aetiological or explanatory in its aim. Does not answer the question <u>why</u> myth gives <u>faith</u>, is <u>fidejussive</u>; not to satisfy curiosity but to confirm faith. No aesthetic.[90]

CV[45]

<u>The Life of Pleasure</u>

Analysis of pleasure; not as a moral end but as a practical way.

The true life of pleasure is the life of the <u>instant</u>: the day-flies life.

The power of pleasure.[91]

Ennui of pleasure — Pascal.[92]

Cp. Montaigne's 'Life of voluptuousness': the middle between pleasure & ambition.[93]

War & the life of pleasure as opposites: the extremes. War = eternity, Pleasure = the point instant.

Rational human life lies between. The extremes must always be passing over into each other — the tedium of war leads to 'pleasure'; the ennui of pleasure leads to 'war.'

CV[45]

Christianity assumed a <u>short</u> life, but since the end was the 'good time,' it did not need to adopt a philosophy of the moment. The *interimsethik* avoided the problem of mortality, that is why the fact of mortality — in spite of its pressure — is not in the front of Christian teachings. Christianity sidestepped the main issue by its doctrine of the new world; Western civilization has nevertheless had this problem at the back of its mind ever since the second-coming failed to take place. Life neither short nor long.

CV[45]

The <u>direct opposite</u> of the life of politics.

CV[45]

A life littered with cards & stained with drink.

---

[90] Oakeshott's note: 'See B. Malinowski, *Myth in Primitive Psychology* (London: Kegan Paul, 1926).'

[91] Oakeshott's note: 'Palinurus, pp. 4, 6.'

[92] Oakeshott's note: 'Palinurus, p. 16.'

[93] Oakeshott's note: 'Palinurus, p. 86.'

CV[45]

Paganism

1) Cyrenaicsm: the active 'pagan' life, the life without moderation or limit. Cp. Rochester. Frantic.

2) Chesterfield: mellow, without frenzy or excess.[94]

CV[45]

The life of pleasure seems the good life because it has the <u>form</u> of the good life — i.e. it is a life desired for its own sake. And this is the secret of its charm and its truth.[95] Amusement <u>is</u> desired for its own sake — but it is not itself desirable for its own sake.

CV[47]

Sin. Guilt and Redemption

Statement of the problem of mortality in terms of sin, guilt & redemption.

The necessity of <u>feeling</u> that salvation is possible, that there is an escape from guilt.

Luther.

The confession & its purpose of absolution: in tune with mortality.

Salvation — not in the future & in another world, but here & now: Christianity offers, in its theology, a rationale of present salvation.[96]

CV[48]

Epicureanism

Epicureanism — the philosophy of waning powers: pleasure the absence of pain, happiness to be found in practising moderation. Passionless. Favouring mild eccentricities & holding within it a fear of life. — How can we answer this — the accusation that our doctrine of the mean, our philosophy of unsuccess and non-ambition, our creed of non-competition, our gospel of acceptance, is, after all, nothing but the expression of a temperament, & the expression of spent passion and exhausted vitality?

Because the case <u>against</u> this doctrine is the more than plausible case that whether or not it conforms to the grand 'conditions of human life,' it certainly is out of tune with the crude vitality of human character: the plausible case that it is the philosophy of the half-man. Somehow this crude vitality must be shown to be comprehended, not merely rejected — or if rejected, then rejected because it

---

[94] Oakeshott's note: 'Cp. R. Murray, *The Good Pagan's Failure. A Defence of Christianity* (London: Longmans, Green & Co., 1939).'

[95] Oakeshott's note: 'Cp. Aristotle, *Nicomachean Ethics*, X, ad init.'

[96] Oakeshott's note: 'Palinurus, p. 5.'

belongs not to 'human character' but to a restricted, non-adult human character which because it is there to be grown out of in fact rejects itself when it comes to know itself.

CV[51]

The Mean

Mortality a doctrine of the Mean.

Mortal life neither too long nor short.

The mean between 1) The unexamined life (Plato) & 2) The psycho-analysed life.

To think clearly & soberly about oneself — that is enough to destroy hypocrisy & self-deception, without destroying joy & confidence.

Let your mind alone.

Tradition & the new: a middle way.

Civilization a partnership between the living & the dead — Burke.

CV[51]

Avoidance of importunity or excess. But what is the truth in 'the way of excess leads to the palace of wisdom' (Blake). Is not excess involved in all greatness?

The Chinese concealment of feeing and avoidance of excessive expression. Understatement. It is their social sense; it belongs to a truly social life.

Is not a certain frigidity — a certain foreignness to enthusiasm — involved in the mean? And if so, can it be the whole truth?

We can more easily understand the pleasures of others than their excesses.

CV[51]

The value of a limit: e.g. why horse racing is more interesting than motor racing because you can't go away & make a horse that can do double the speed of any known horse.

CV[51]

Extremes abnormal — e.g. impulse to kill animals, excessive tenderness to animals.

CV[51]

Behaviour determined by others — A balance sought.

The excesses of the French Revolution killed in some all enthusiasm for liberty.

To be the one sober man in the party, not because of a love of sobriety but because everyone else is drunk.

To live on understatement because one's companion lives on superlatives.

CV[51]

'The Mean' a morality for the civilized only — not the savage and primitive. Not because the civilized lack energy (cp. Epicureanism q.v.) but because he can be more discriminating. Savage conditions require savage virtues — & these are virtues of <u>excess</u>: bravado rather than courage — because everything is <u>in front</u>. Civilized man has something to <u>lose</u>; the savage has something to <u>win</u>. Savage society lives on positive, aggressive virtue: to tackle fire, to go to sea on a log, to ride the wild horse, to fly the Atlantic — imagination & courage required — <u>nerve</u> rather than <u>patience</u>. The greatest hero of all time was <u>Prometheus</u> — who <u>stole</u> the fire — fire which had till then terrorized the world — to touch was agony, to embrace death.[97] A sort of justified megalomania required in savage society.

CV[53]

<u>Women</u>

In face of a man's desire a girl is excusable if she thinks herself priceless.

CV[53]

Women are pleased with small things — this is right, because it is in small things that the deepest loyalty, the loyalty of the passing moment, is expressed.

CV[53]

It is a principle of society established in the earliest history of the world, on the best authority, that woman should rule man, & the Devil rule her.

CV[55]

<u>Marriage</u>

Marriage —

1) The ceremony.

2) The social institution in general.

3) The human relation.

The ordinary marital quarrel — a difference about nothing: a thing of nerves. An idle sense of wrong.

Words of perfidious compassion.

CV[55]

Of all the forms offered us by life it is the one demanding a couple to realize it fully, which is the most imperative. Pairing off is the fate of mankind. And if two

---

97 Oakeshott's note: 'See Marrett, *Faith, Hope and Charity*, pp. 23–4.'

beings, thrown together, mutually attracted, resist the necessity, fail in understanding & voluntarily stop short of — the embrace, in the noblest meaning of the word, then they are committing a sin against life, the call of which is simple. Perhaps sacred. And the punishment of it is an invasion of complexity, a tormenting, forcibly tortuous involution of feelings, the deepest form of suffering from which indeed something significant may come at last.

CV[55]

The late 17th century & early 18th century is the high point in European civilization in the history of marriage. Just as the late 12th century & the 20th century are low points. Marriage a basic institution: stability. Formality. Nothing to do with <u>love</u>. Diplomacy of 'family' alliances. Rationality. Manners exist on their own, severed from religious beliefs & supported by religious ceremonies. <u>Worth</u> decided a union; <u>worth</u> alone rendered agreeable a prospective partner. Scrupulous weighing of pros and cons.

CV[55]

The modern honeymoon — wish to escape from habitual social environment: an insistence on the <u>private</u> nature of married life. Contrast earlier when 'the semipublicity of the nuptial bed' emphasized the social character.

CV[57]

<u>Personality</u>

Our experience never gets into our blood & bones. It always remains outside of us. That is why we look with wonder at the past. It is the cause of our surprise — when mere ignorance & inexperience is not the cause.

CV[57]

Personality is a partnership of the present & the past & the future — of what we have seen, see and desire to see. Always ideal, never fully realized.

CV[57]

The collapse of personality — taking place when society collapses. The mechanism. What gives some personalities the power to resist collapse?

CV[57]

Somehow personality must be freed from the burden of history. For personality is something of value in itself and the only source of values. If it is tied to history then, for example, those who lived during the long warm spell beginning in the 5th century AD had the opportunity of a perfectibility denied to others; & this must not be. Cp. wealth and poverty. It can be freed only by the recognition of mortality—i.e. independence of personality of <u>particular</u> circumstances and its utter dependence on actual circumstances. Not better or worse because of greater or less achievement. Its achievement, the only one that counts, is <u>itself</u>. What favourable circumstances allow is merely external achievement. This is not the old crux, is virtue independent of external circumstances.

CV[57]

A mercantile age has interpreted the parable of the talents in a mercantile manner—but it is significant <u>morally</u>, in the world of values.

CV[57]

Personal unity & identity. Relative. But no personality without some degree of coherence and continuous conscious existence (memory?).

Coherence as the fulfilment of personality.

CV[59]

Spirit. Courage and Fear. Will

All fear is bad & should be overcome—by 1) courage 2) rational reflection.
Combatting fear by 1) increasing security 2) cultivating courage.

Is courage really physiological? Intrepidity/Nerve: the aristocratic quality of nerve is a remedy against fear—at least a practical & temporary remedy. Women. It may even overcome fear of death. Courage can never be 'democratized'.[98]

CV[59]

Fear is its own father & a most prolific self-propagator.

CV[59]

Courage not reducible to Reason; an answer to situations to which Reason has no compelling answer. Cp. Plato.

CV[59]

All fears have one parentage—fear of death.[99]

CV[59]

The relation of courage & rationalism e.g. in Voltaire rationalism was an expression of courage rather than intellect: he is a man of nerve rather than sensibility.[100]

---

[98] Oakeshott's note: 'Cp. B. Russell, *What I Believe*, p. 81.'

[99] Oakeshott's note: 'Marrett, *Faith Hope & Charity in Primitive Religion*, p. 41.'

[100] Oakeshott's note: 'Connolly, *Forbidden Playground*, p. 82': see p. 346 n. 86, above.

CV[59]

Christian moralists regarded fortitude as the corrective of accidie. Courage one of the 'natural'/'cardinal' virtues, with wisdom, justice & temperance.

CV[60]

Man & Society

See, Ideal Character.
    Politics.
    Democracy.
    Planning.
    Personality.
    The ideal society & the ideal character correlations.
    Relation of man & his society: personality.
    A man's society <u>is</u> his civilization.

CV[60]

A community rooted in the land, whatever privileged classes it may have, whatever hierarchy or hereditary positions, is a society—the relations between the aristocracy & the peasant are more successful & more social than those yet achieved between the industrialist & his employee.

    We are still looking for an emotional substitute for feudalism.

CV[60]

Conversation as the form of social relationship.

CV[60]

<u>Personalism</u>. A transformed <u>individualism</u>.

    Individual = ego. Cp. Aquinas; individuality is rooted in matter.

    Personality = interiority to oneself. I.e. a redeemed individuality. Redemption is by love—but redemption does not mean extinction.

    Personality tends towards communion. Society a society of <u>persons</u>. The state must recognize the 'rights' not of <u>individuals</u> but of <u>persons</u>, and maintain a condition in which the rights of persons can be exercised & enjoyed.

    The <u>person</u>, as such, is a <u>whole</u>. The human person is not a pure person; corrupted by individuality, & ∴ so far, <u>not</u> a whole.

CV[62]

The Non-Political End in Politics

Plato—*Republic*.
    Aristotle—the Contemplative life. Doctrine of 'rest': Leisure.
    Augustine—the supernatural end of man & the doctrine of contemplation.

Aquinas.

Spinoza. The Freedom of the Intellect.

Hobbes.

'The ideal of volition is rather the experience of perfect harmony between our-selves and our environment which excludes alike action and choice.'[101]

Yes; and besides those who can create, Oh for a Voltaire who with his rich, aggressive gaiety will destroy the superstition of politics.

CV[64]

The effort of the historical imagination to go beyond those hypothetically pene-trating judgments of persons & events, which show only what they <u>might</u> be, to something that can maintain itself as what they <u>were</u>. The criterion of this: *die Prüfstein ist die Zeit*. To know the person in the context, & the context in the person. & to know them as they <u>are</u>.

    The application of dialectic to history.[102]

CV[A]

This nonsense about seeing the world. The 'world' is a very dull place and there is not much to be learned from it. I was in the world for a short time & I was glad to get out of it again, back to my village: I didn't care for the world.[103]

CV[A]

African tribe: Although God is good & wishes good for everybody, unfortun-ately he has a half-witted brother who keeps on obtruding himself & doesn't give God a chance.

CV[B]

Theme: we live now in a similar position to Athens in the 3rd & 2nd centuries B.C.[104] What shall be our reaction—Stoic or Epicurean—or have the intervening centuries provided us with some third attitude which will better fit the times?

    The vulgar crowd: how escape.[105]

---

[101] Oakeshott's note: 'J.M.E. McTaggart, *Studies in Hegelian Cosmology* (Cambridge: Cambridge University Press, 1918), p. 259.'

[102] Oakeshott's note: 'Santayana, *Persons & Places*, p. 253.'

[103] Inserted inside front cover, numbered [1a].

[104] Inserted inside front cover, numbered [1b].

[105] Oakeshott's note: 'Grant, Aristotle, *Nichomachean Ethics*, vol. I, Essay IV.'

CV[C]

1. Politicians are scoundrels.[106]

2. No society is new.

3. Omniscience impossible. Cp. remarks made about Peace in 1914. Laski. Foresight limited. Experience limited.

4. Imperfection is <u>not</u> evanescent.

5. Men are not certainly either good or bad.

6. Men are often self-interested & always credulous.

7. Power corrupts.

8. Speed: & limited time.

9. There are men who desire power.

10. Men erratic. ∴ government by law is more wise than man, it is product of man – but because it is more disinterested than its administrators.

CV[D]

'Recreation, and not improvement, is the proper object of conversation.'[107]

That is, conversation, as such, is an end in itself. Speech & the exchange of ideas takes place for all kinds of purposes; but <u>conversation</u> exists when they are an end in themselves. Information not the object, but sometimes part of the irrelevance of conversation.[108]

Bad talkers – tedious, pertinacious, noisy, quarrelsome, contentious. The meaningless repetition of catchwords & phrases – like a kind of physical contortions. The inability to progress in thought – to move on. Tact to know when a topic has been sufficiently discussed – cp. the essay; conversation not exhaustive.

Conversation – its connection with Western civilization. Or is it connected with any cultivated civilization? E.g. China; Persia & Arabia.

The expression of a social habit, or even instinct.

CV[D]

Tone of voice – a soft & sweet tone, like personal beauty, disarms prejudice and disposes the mind in favour of the speaker. Voice as the voice of temperament. The secret power of personal beauty – securing sympathy.

---

[106] Inserted at CV[09].

[107] Oakeshott's note: 'J.P. Mahaffy, *The Principles of the Art of Conversation* (London and New York: Macmillan and Co., 1887), p. 106.'

[108] Inserted inside front cover, numbered [1d].

CV[D]

Sympathy — the common agreement not to talk at cross-purposes.

Tact, sympathy in conscious operation to remedy a possible breach.

The moment the company has grasped his meaning, the good talker passes on to something else, without regard to the form of his sentence.

No emphasis on the particular <u>value</u> of any argument; argument taking what effect it can in the company.

Equality the ground of conversation — an established or natural equality.

CV[D]

The enhanced stimulus of conversation with a stranger — two things taking place, exploring a character & discussing a topic, the one subordinate to the other? & if so which is which?

But even with a stranger, there must be a common ground.

CV[D]

Politics is a suitable subject of conversation — indeed perhaps that is all it is suitable for.

CV[D]

Neither too many nor too few — *tête à tête* not conversation.

The Mean — between the Muses & the Graces.

Length of time on one topic.

Number.

Modesty & confidence.

Sympathy and self.

CV[E]

In conversation freedom & intelligence are both at a premium — cp. Acton: How to have reason & freedom at once.[109]

CV[F]

The oblique character of the conclusions of conversation — not what the argument <u>ends</u> with; but the effect it has.[110]

CV[F]

The <u>quality</u> of ideas. Function of their <u>context</u> in the contents of a mind — not always a <u>system</u>, but nonetheless, a whole.

Conversation as discourse round the <u>quality</u> of ideas.

---

[109] Inserted inside front cover, numbered [1e].
[110] Inserted inside front cover, numbered [1f].

CV[G]

If it is true that the major achievements of mankind have not been the offspring of war or even of force; it is not true that so predominating a part of man's time & energy has been spent in peaceful pursuits? War always associated with the <u>expansion</u> of a civilization—Hellenic, Roman, Islamic, West-European. War & the <u>triumph</u> of a society, a point of view.[111]

The hold of war on the imagination—& what gets as far as the common imagination of a civilization is thereby indicated to be pretty deep. Even wars of conquest. Why this holds—of Alexander the Great, of Roland & Charlemagne, of the Trojan wars, of Cortés & Pizarro. Tolstoy's *War & Peace*.

War belongs to evil—not in the sense that all wars are always evil, but in the sense that one of the <u>taproots</u> of war is the evil that lies in man.

War and a supposed fighting instinct. No real comparison. 1) War a conflict between organized communities. 2) War does not necessarily imply 'fighting.'

Darwinian struggle not a war—does not follow that there must be a struggle between peoples. A competition, not involving fighting, & certainly not the cooperative conflict of peoples.

Belief in the inevitability of war a cause of war.

War a conflict between organized communities, not a conflict between individuals. It is <u>one</u> type of conflict.

Modern war different: merely a quantitative & technical difference? "Total." Previous totality of war has only been for one side—the totality of total destruction.

CV[G]

The psychological roots of European war in the belief in the <u>fruitfulness of suffering</u>—allied to the belief in passionate love. War and eroticism.

The common <u>language</u> of love & war from the 12th century to to-day. The language of love changes with the language of war;[112] and the character of love (making love) & war (making war) change together. 'All's fair in love & war.'

CV[G]

It is not the fighting that makes war the enemy of liberty, but the organization—the perversion of a society. That is why modern war is so much more dangerous. It is not the devastation cp. Thirty Years War—but the organization. Liberty in Greece—always modified by war.

CV[G]

The false urgency that war gives to post-war politics.

---

[111] Inserted at CV[20], numbered [20b].

[112] Oakeshott's note: 'De Rougemont, *Passion & Society*, p. 248 sq.'

CV[H]

Christianity did not take account of mortality: human life to be <u>short</u>. ∴ while combating 'eat drink & be merry,' the true intermediary state of life — neither long nor short — is not appreciated.[113]

Interimsethik.

---

[113] Inserted at CV[29], numbered [29a].

NE[04]

'What would Nelson have done' (Cp. what would Wolfe have done?) No man can be a proper model for another man; the natural egoism of human character steps in to prevent it. Model for an occasion. Just as we can never really bring ourselves to wish that we were anyone else on earth than ourselves (though we may often wish we enjoyed some detail of the character or circumstances of another), so no man can ever be the model for another.

NE[06]

Ambition. Nelson's not unlimited; not for power after power. Indeed, all this talk of exterior success is really only an expression for interior success. Not for tangible ends — wealth, power, position. But honour, reputation, fame.

Cincinnatus.

NE[07]

Of few men do we know anything like what we know of Nelson. Every detail.

Letters.

Words.

Self-analysis; self-consciousness which comes into writing.

NE[07]

Action for no ulterior motive — Honour, glory, fame.

Not so uncommon as is sometimes supposed; exploration, mountaineering, etc. The poetry of action. Ideas of 'service,' the plausible ethics of productivity absent.

Productivity — the protection of England with Nelson — a by-product of something intensely personal.

Sponzia. 'Purposeless' we say, meaning not without purpose, but without a tangible ulterior purpose. The morality that is preached to us now is the death of this.

Cp. Aristotle — all activity is for leisure.

Cp. academic world — 1) to produce something, to make a contribution. 2) to win fame & glory.

---

1 LSE 3/10. Hard cover, green cotton overlay with brown leather spine and corners, 17 cm x 11 cm, blank. Recto folios numbered 1–11. Autograph, ink and pencil. No title page, no date. The folder also includes notes on loose sheets, given alphabetic references here.

NE[08–09]

Naval Tactics

Nelson inherited principles which were admirably suited to the prevailing conditions.

There are no absolutely superior tactics; success is the only criterion.

The tactics which had been developed by Rodney & Howe could be successful only if those who practised them commanded superior vessels & more skilful seamen. They were inherently <u>daring</u> tactics; the risk in each engagement was considerable.

What Nelson added – a <u>touch</u>.

1) By temperament suited to a daring tactic. But such a daring tactic depended upon <u>training</u> and skill in manoeuvre, & Nelson knew it.

2) Determination. The chase. Annihilation the aim.

But how short a time was spent in battle.

The landing engagement.

NE[A]

We can understand or can think we understand the past only by virtue of a tradition which joins us to the past. Any past from which we have broken away completely becomes incomprehensible to us.

Cp. Greek philosophy.

Contrast Chinese philosophy.

NE[B]

Dilthey on biography.[2]

The experience of being able to discern character. Lessing. Novalis.

Confidence in reliability of insight: no infallible method proposed.

Obscures scepticism: never considers the validity of these insights – they might be complete misconceptions.

<u>Convincingness</u> of biography – character study.

NE[C]

The interpretation (investigation) of human character in history.

1. History

2. Biography.

3. Investigation/Interpretation of character.

---

[2] Oakeshott's note: 'Lucas, p. 49.' Not traced.

(i) The enterprise: to detect the historical individual & disclose his historical individuality. Elaborate a little.

Cp. to history & biography: 'a mental portrait.' Travel over the mind. Mind, character.

(ii) How this enterprise is carried out usually; inference from action. Historian's character sketches; their terms. This a common enterprise; every historian attempts it. But not all successfully. The results of this (a) too general; not individual. Fails to be properly historical. Why? (b) hit & miss — unscientific. Depends upon the insight of the particular historian.

(iii) How improved?
    1) Science of character.
    2) Typology of character.

(iv) Examination of presuppositions.
    What do we mean by character?
    Expression in action. No.

(v) Method of investigation of character in history.
    The purpose, & the criterion of success.

NE[D]

We are told that a man is an 'individualist' — a type of human character; but what we want to know is, what sort of an individualist?

And when we look closer, the historian has merely translated an anecdote into an abstraction: no attempt has been made to interpret <u>character</u>.

NE[D]

What so often starts from the pages of history is not an individual at all, but a type. And often it is not even an historical type, but a universal type. And even where it is an historical type, it is anachronistic, a 20th century type projected into the 16th century.

NE[D]

La Bruyère has some sense of historical type, but none of historical individual.

NE[D]

'To travel over a man's mind' — a phrase of the Druid.

NE[E]

Character & temperament.

The necessity of distinguishing character & temperament.[3]

NE[F]

Biography & History

1. Belief that History & biography are not the same thing.

2. When we know little history it degenerates into biography — e.g. Prussia & Russia. Text books.

3. The historian feels this to be defective — Why?

4. The nature of history.

5. ∴ biography not history, <u>not</u> because true history is impersonal — e.g. Marx, e.g. Hegel. Ideas.

6. Why then?[4]

NE[G]

<u>Psychology</u>

1) Positivisitic — i.e., in terms of natural sciences.
  E.g. Chemistry — elements etc.

2) Types. Descriptive 'real' psychology (Dilthey).

3) <u>Historical</u>, i.e. the historical person — the person in the world — the person as a whole.

Dilthey's Hermeneutic.
  Not psychological, but <u>historical</u>.

NE[H]

<u>Biography</u>. The study of a <u>person</u>.
  The inner connections of the personality, which may be expected (& must be allowed) to cut across <u>logical</u> distinctions —
  E.g. idea & emotion; science & religion; total interaction. And abstractions of all sorts — virtue & vice.
  A personality is, philosophically (? logically) a vast confusion. Biography is the enterprise of exhibiting the nature of <u>this</u> confusion. The whole is in every part.
  Cp. relation to history.

---

3 Oakeshott's note: 'W.T. Jones, *Masters of Political Thought. Vol. 2. Machiavelli to Bentham* (London: Harrap & Co. Ltd, 1942), p. 25.'
4 Oakeshott's note: 'Collingwood, p. 304.' Possibly R.G. Collingwood, *The Idea of History*, ed. T.M. Knox (Oxford: Clarendon Press, 1946).

NE[I]

Style is a magic wand that turns everything it touches to gold.

NE[J]

In a writer (e.g. Goethe) we often have a record of change in character; but because we have no written record in the case of others, does not mean that such change did not take place.

Cp. Nelson. Introvert & extrovert.

NE[K]

Idea that we must find something that cannot be doubted on which to build our historical investigation of character – false – cp. Dilthey's psychology.

It does not invalidate a method if it grow with its use.

NE[L]

The ideological courage which inspires men to risk death for a great cause – and the <u>nerve</u> of the aristocrat; death in the hunting field.

NE[M]

Nothing new to be said about Nelson. The vocab of eulogy has been exhausted; – Nelson & Shakespeare. Even a bad book on Nelson...

But I think there is something new to be said of him.

The psychologists, thank God, have so far let him rest in peace.

Interest in human character – how provoked.

Temperament & character: how defined. The nature of character – cp. Forecasting actions.

Nelson; the model.

The inadequacy of any human character to be a model; nevertheless something to be learned from the study of human character. What?

Nelson's character: unreflective, unphilosophical, simple & direct. Seems to offer little opportunity for analysis. But this is not so.

True his was a remarkably unphilosophical character; but not unself-conscious. Indeed, the first thing to be noted is the complication of a highly self-conscious character with an unreflective character. Not the unexamined life; & not the life frittered away in self-examination. A mean between extremes, & an unusual mean.

NE[N]

Quo Fas et Gloria ducunt.

1) It can be assumed that all English audiences know the facts of Nelson's career. This in itself remarkable; true of no other Englishman.

2) One supposes that before 1800 boys had heroes, but one wonders who those heroes were before Nelson caught up into himself about 99% of hero worship.

3) His place in public affection in 1804 – before Trafalgar. At his burial. Half god. The Norfolk Hero. Lord Nelson. Never been superseded in this character.

4) My own hero-worship.
   'The Victory.'
   St. Paul's.
   Nelson's Father.

5) Our knowledge of Nelson. Its completeness. Letters; every one of them expressing naively his personality. Cp. Letters of women.

6) Nothing new to be said about Nelson. And yet scarcely a year passes without somebody writing a new book on him: 1947 – <u>two</u>.[5]

7) What I have undertaken to do is to say something about his <u>character</u>: this, in spite of all that has been written is still relatively unexplored.

8) The problem of investigating an historical character, opened up, – but laid aside. The character sketches of historians – their inadequacy. Cp. i) Clarendon,[6] ii) Gibbon.

9) The true aim of an investigation of character i) an individual ii) an historical indvidual.

10)   (a) Temperament $\left.\right\}$ the nature of these

      (b) Character

11) <u>Physiognomy</u>: 'the pouting lower lip of the spoilt school boy.' Cp. The Italian painter's remark after the battle of the Nile.

12) Courage; Nerve; Self-confidence.

13) Glory; Honour; Ambition.

14) Charm.

NE[O]

Nelson the hero – to his own generation he was a saviour, half-divine, to ours he is still a hero, but of a different sort. What he is to us is still something to swell the heart & catch the breath.

---

[5]   Possibly C. Oman, *Nelson* (London: Hodder & Stoughton, 1947), and C.J. Britton, *New Chronicles of the Life of Lord Nelson* (Birmingham: Cornish Brothers, 1947).

[6]   Oakeshott's note: 'See Stroud.' Possibly William Strode (*c*.1599–1645), anti-royalist politician, described in E. Hyde, Earl of Clarendon, *The History of the Rebellion and Civil Wars in England*, 8 vols. (1826) at ii.26 as 'one of those ephori who most avowed curbing and suppressing of majesty.'

No debunking Nelson.

Blind devotees — not blind, but still devoted.

NE[P]

<u>Nerve</u>

In a sea fight 150 years ago it was often all or nothing, success or failure — certainly this was so with Nelson's tactics. The indecisive had no charm for him, & he ruled it out before he began. Risks.[7]

Religious resignation is an expression of nerve, rather than <u>vice versa</u>. By itself, the idea could never give nerve. Nerve is the <u>habit</u> of resignation.[8]

---

7   Oakeshott's note: 'Mahan, p. 107.' Possibly A.T. Mahan, *The Life of Nelson The Embodiment of the Sea Power of Great Britain* (London: Sampson Low, 1897).

8   Oakeshott's note: 'Mahan, p. 306.'

Notebook 14 (February 1955)

14[01]

<u>Montaigne</u>

'Those innumerable differences, mental & physical, of which men had always been aware, on which they had so largely fed their vanity, were ultimate.'[2]

The practical truth in the philosophical error of scepticism – diversities that are ultimate, because we do not & cannot <u>know</u>. Opinion master of the realm of the practical, in the end.[3]

The practical self: practical reason.
    Balance, equilibrium, in place of certainty.

14[02]

The need of the time (expressed, but ill expressed in Fascism) – the creation of a non-economic society striving for the freedom & equality of the individual (cp. the society of the late middle ages, & its survival in rural England & elsewhere – the organic society of the village.)[4]

---

[1] LSE 2/1/14. Soft cover, brown canvas overlay, 18 cm x 12 cm, blank. Recto folios numbered 1–68 (continues for three more unnumbered folios). Autograph, ink. Title page: 'Notes XIV. / *Amour, folie aimable; ambition, sottise sérieuse.* / Chamfort l. 6. / *Je hais la grandeur qui m'a fait fuir ce que j'amais, ou ce que j'aurois aimé.* / Montaigne.' Dated: 'Feb 1955.'
    Other works from which Oakeshott made excerpts in this notebook but which are not mentioned in the text include: Fo. 5, G. Santayana, *Little Essays Drawn From The Writings Of George Santayana*, ed. L.P. Smith (London and New York: Charles Scribner's Sons); 23, notes on George Savile, first Marquess of Halifax (1633–95), possibly from *The Complete Works Of George Savile First Marquess Of Halifax*, ed. W. Raleigh (Oxford: Clarendon Press, 1912); 31–2, Joseph Conrad, *An Outcast Of The Islands* (London: T. Fisher Unwin, 1896); 35, Pádraic H. Pearse, 'The Wayfarer', in *Collected Works of Pádraic H. Pearse* (Dublin: Phoenix, 1917), 341; 37, *The Note-Books of Samuel Butler*; 41, C.J. Lever, *Arthur O'Leary: His Wanderings and Ponderings In Many Lands*, 3 vols. (London: Henry Colburn, 1844).

[2] Oakeshott's note: 'Pater, *Gaston De Latour*, p. 91.' Fo. 1 contains notes on W. Pater, *Gaston De Latour An Unfinished Romance*, ed. C.L. Shadwell (London: Macmillan and Co., 1896).

[3] Oakeshott's note: 'Pater, *Gaston De Latour*, pp. 92–3 q.v.'

[4] Fo. 2 contains notes on P. Drucker, *The End of Economic Man A Study Of The New Totalitarianism* (London: William Heinemann, 1939).

14[08]

'*D'obscures nécessités nous gouvernent à toute heure, depuis avant notre naissance jusqu'après notre mort.*'[5]

The ambitious regard this as slavery; but they live in the illusion that they control their destiny. Ambition is the belief that the transformation of the world is a worthy end in itself.

14[08–09]

Pascal—'*Il ne faut pas avoir l'âme fort élevée pour comprendre qu'il n'y a point ici de satisfaction véritable et solide; que tous nos plaisirs ne sont que vanité; que nos maux sont infinis; et qu'enfin la mort qui nous menace à chaque instant, doit nous mettre dans peu d'années...infailliblement dans l'horrible nécessité d'être eternellement ou anéantis ou malhereux. Il n'y a rien de plus réel que cela, ni de plus terrible.*'

This is all taken as evil; it is not simply admitted as the condition of human life. It is true that there is something in human nature that revolts against it; but nevertheless it is not in itself evil, but something to be moralized. The diagnosis is correct, but the prognosis is false. What is required is 'insouciance.' Death is not a spectre haunting us; it is the prime condition of human life.

14[10]

'*De tous les hommes à programme, le plus surprenant est l'avocat de l'avenir.*'[6]

L'avocats de l'avenir are better than those who are concerned solely with ultimate ends: they stand between the sensualist and the perfectionist; they look further than the one and less far than the other. In human life we must look neither too close nor too far; for human life is neither short nor for ever.

14[11]

Society — Living and Planned. Revolution.

The necessity of the organic view.
    Massingham. *Men of Earth.*[7]
    Pickthorn. *Prejudices or principles.*
    Burke.
    Halifax.

---

5   Oakeshottt's note: 'Brewster, *L'ame païenne*, p. 20.' Fos. 8–11 contains notes on H.B. Brewster, *L'ame païenne* (Paris: Société du Mercure de France, 1902).

6   Oakeshott's note: 'Brewster, *L'ame païenne*, p. 147.'

7   Oakeshott's note: 'H.J. Massingham, *Men of Earth* (London: Chapman & Hall, Ltd., 1943), pp. 6–9, 163–6, Ch. V.'

14[12]

Mortality

'Man has a prejudice against himself: anything which is a product of his mind*[8] seems to him to be unreal or comparatively insignificant. We are satisfied only when we fancy ourselves surrounded by objects and laws independent of our nature.'[9]

This is what makes democracy difficult. Not only, or not so much, the stupidity of the mass, but their superstition.

14[12]

To love the earth & hate the world.
There is no earth that is not the world — experience.

14[14]

Comradeship — 'When men are in the same boat together, when a common anxiety, occupation or spirit unites them, they feel their human kinship in an intensified form without any greater personal affinity subsisting between them.'[10]

Circumstance, & not animal contagion, makes comrades.
Friendship — is impossible without animal contagion. It lasts when the circumstances which might create comradeship have disappeared. A friend is not primarily someone whom one trusts, it is someone who, by the power of affinity, charms, someone who engages the imagination.

14[17]

Atheists are the creation of accident & circumstance.
Their rebellion is against a religion alien to their nature: in another place or time, they would be believers & the interpreters of an orthodoxy.

'Religions, like languages, are necessarily rivals. What religion a man has is an historical accident, quite as much as what language he speaks. In rare circumstances, where choice is possible, he may, with some difficulty, make an exchange.'[11]

Moreover, it is an illusion that one may easily change one's religious nationality, or that the change is ever quite radical. Roman Catholicism is an abstraction, like

---

8   Oakeshott's note: '* imagination' on the verso.
9   Oakeshott's note: 'Santayana, *The Sense of Beauty*, p. 3.' G. Santayana, *The Sense of Beauty Being The Outlines of Aesthetic Theory* (New York: Charles Scribner's Sons, 1896).
10 Oakeshott's note: 'Santayana, *The Sense of Beauty*, ibid., p. 147.'
11 Oakeshott's note: 'Santayana, *Reason in Society*, p. 121.'

any other religion—in each society it speaks a different language & has a different imaginative content.[12]

14[19]

'Many a man dies too soon and some are born in the wrong age or station. Could these persons drink at the fountain of youth at least once more they might do themselves fuller justice…But how should a future life be constituted if it is to satisfy this demand, & how long need it last?'[13]

It must be my life, and it must be in this world, this world with the necessary connections of circumstance.

'Were I transformed into a cherub or transported into a timeless ecstasy, it is hard to see in what sense I should continue to exist…it would not prolong my life or retrieve my disasters.'[14]

But does not the magic of immortality vanish when the immortal life is seen in this way? And is such a reduplication of earthly life & society possible?

14[20]

'The glory of life exists in accepting the knowledge of natural death [which is peculiar to man] as an opportunity to live in the spirit.'

Nothing is eternal in its duration…the sort of immortality that belongs to us, is the ability to find joy in the flying moment, the ability to accept the limitations of mortality & to reserve ourselves from the foreign & disruptive influence of what does not belong to our nature.[15]

14[21]

The end of Faust—the Politics of Planning.[16]

14[22]

Morality—not concerned with the attainment of happiness, but with the prevention of suffering. This is duty; when & if it is achieved duty gives place to freedom, & happiness.

---

[12] Oakeshott's note: 'Cp. Santayana, *Winds of Doctrine*, p. 33 sq.; *Poetry & Religion*; *Reason in Religion*, p. 99.' G. Santayana, *Interpretations of Poetry and Religion* (London: Adam and Charles Black, 1900); G. Santayana, *The Life of Reason Or The Phases Of Human Progress Reason in Religion* (London: Archibald Constable and Co., 1905).

[13] Oakeshott's note: 'Santayana, *Reason in Religion*, p. 243.'

[14] Santayana, *Reason in Religion*, p. 244.

[15] Oakeshott's note: 'See Brewster, *L'ame païenne*, p. 172: "*Mourir avant d'avoir réussi' — ce ne sont pas les passionnés qui parlent ainsi, ce sont les infatués. Ils n'aiment pas la chasse, ils aiment le gibier.*"'

[16] Oakeshott's note: 'Santayana, *Three Poets*, pp. 181–5.'

14[22]

'We cannot venerate anyone in whom appreciation is not divorced from desire.'[17]

The character of a god. Not as the result of disappointment, but in a man a rational detachment arising from the experience of many and deep affections.

14[24]

Mortality

A conversation that is sometimes a dialogue, sometimes even a monologue (cp. an essay read to the conversationists). A conversation in which friends are made, and like recognizes like as well as unlike, unlike.

    A conversation in which no one person is always right — i.e. is always intended to 'win.'

    Sometimes an internal dialogue (cp. Halifax) — indeed, an internal dialogue all the time.

14[24]

That sweet softening of the heart which, going along with a less firm purpose & less wilful ambition, is called decadence. No glory here, perhaps; but sweetness and light. Disenchantment; lowered vitality, perhaps; but a gentleness that could not exist in the 'great' ages of a civilization. This is the time when a man might free his slave because, for a moment, he saw into the heart of slavery & was not turned from gratifying a whim. Great ages, like great men, are apt to be hard; they are out of touch with mortality — they are bathed in an alluring light of immortality, confidence.

14[25]

Some will die for a cause, some for a faith, or for a person — but those who die climbing a mountain or exploring a sea, represent the immortal mortality of human endeavour, they are the overplus, in whom life has become art.

14[25]

Three religions: —

1) Of activity — Christianity, Shinto, Islam.

2) Of passivity — Buddhism, Taoism.

3) Of mortality — Confucianism, the religions of Greece, what humanism might & should be.

---

[17] Santayana, *Sense of Beauty*, p. 242.

14[25]

There is no substitute for youth.

14[26]

Très séparatiste — without this, intimacy is impossible, for it is impossible to be equally intimate with all friends on all subjects. Indeed the character to whom intimacy is a pleasure will always be *très séparatiste*.

'*Le don terrible de la familiarité.*'[18]

14[27]

ἐφ' ὅσον ἐνδέχεται ἀθανατίζειν.[19]

So far as possible to live as an immortal.

Whatever one believes of another world and a personal survival.

But how far will this lead us from finding a home in this world — what does one do, how does one behave, if one lives as an immortal, as one who has no part in death?

Keeping a sense of the future — a sense that there is still something to come — a practical substitute for a belief in a future life after death. If we never lose this sense of the future until the day of death, we never experience death — & yet, after all, death does catch up.

And in any case, with the smaller, recurrent deaths which happen to us every day, keeping a sense of the future — e.g. a new love — takes away the power to experience deeply what we go through.

Problem of immortality is the problem of memory. Shall I remember? For unless I remember I do not survive. Lethe is fatal to a life in another world.

The condition of mortality — the irony of life.

Achievement defeats itself in the moment of victory.

The seeds of death are always there.

There is no moment that can be made to stay fixed.

14[28]

Government

A sure test — all types of society & sorts of government are, in practice, less than perfect.

The question to ask is — is not life more tolerable in a democracy which fails than in another sort of community — e.g. a despotism — which succeeds? Or rather, all types fail, the best is not that which gives the greatest or easiest pros-

---

18 Oakeshott's note: 'de Retz.' Jean François Paul de Gondi, Cardinal de Retz (1613–79), French churchman and memoirist, but the quotation has not been traced.

19 Aristotle, *Nicomachean Ethics*, Bk X ch. vii.

pect of succeeding (for that is largely illusion), but that which is most tolerable in failure.

14[28]

The Extensive Mind

The more we know of the world, the more we travel about, the more we make contrasts, so the more we divide & dissipate our minds among a hundred imperfectly realized images. This is the condition of the modern intelligence, and it is also the <u>ideal</u> encouraged by modern civilization—the man at home everywhere who is really never at home anywhere. The sharp, shallow, pseudo-sympathetic mind. Preferring many contacts to few intimacies; preferring quantity to quality, preferring fact to thought. The quiz mentality. The article rather than the book, the paragraph to the article, the headline to the paragraph.

If we go out of ourselves, if we travel & make contacts, it must never be for its own sake, but in order to make deeper our intimacies—we go away to find home, we make acquaintances to understand friends, we converse in order to enrich our conversation with ourselves.

14[29]

Science and Living

1) We are the inhabitants of one of the meaner planets—microscopic parasites on the surface of an atom.

Size: we are swallowed up in the vastness of the universe. Cp. Jeans.

2) Time: our world, & this universe is in its infancy. Its entire history is comprised within 10,000 years. And this planet may be habitable for at least 15 million years. The significance of the individual life is contracted to something negligible.

Yet these facts have no more moral significance—i.e., they give no more guidance for living—than, for instance, the knowledge that our world is whirling through space at 60 miles a second. The individual, in fact, defies this universe, and lives untouched by this knowledge. All this matters nothing whatever to me if I am happy & in love, and less if I am unhappy and frustrated. These are facts without moral significance. They give no guide whatever to the determination of the <u>importance</u> of individual life, feeling, emotion. Emotion dwarfs the physical universe rather than the other way about. Cp. Pascal. And one death never explains another, one parting never consoles another.

Pain, privation, bereavement.

14[29]

The chief human malady is fear.
   Lucretius.

14[30]

<u>Politics</u> are necessarily opportunist. The politician works under conditions that make this unavoidable. The necessary toleration of evil. What a politician does or can do for 40 million people <u>must</u> be second best.
   Using bad arguments in a good cause.
   The gross oversimplification necessary in politics.

14[30]

Never ask the end. Never let the corruption of winter stand in the way of the enjoyment of spring. To everything its time, and exclude only that which is out of its place.

14[30]

The litany as a microcosm of human life; a superb appreciation of its grandeurs & miseries.

14[30]

The demand that fire should warm but not burn, water should bless, but not drown. Against mortality.

14[30]

The worst thing about life is that the worst part comes last. How enchanting to work back from old age to youth.

14[32]

The feeling for mortality that runs through Elizabethan poetry – it is the other side of that age of activity, not in contradiction to the vitality of the age, but providing the scepticism which saved that vitality from an easy optimism. 'Time' – no man can escape.
   Life's a play.[20]

---

20 Oakeshott's note: 'Stephen Hawes, 'Epitaph of Grande Amour,' *Oxford Book Of Six-teenth Century Verse*, p. 14; Richard Barnfield, "A Comparison of the Life of Man," ibid. p. 728; Fulke Greville.' *Oxford Book Of Sixteenth Century Verse*, ed. E.K. Chambers (Oxford: Clarendon Press, 1932); Fulke Greville, first Baron Brooke (1554–1628), poet and politician.

14[33]

'On what grand and luminous figure does contemporary humanity attempt to model itself?'[21]

Middle Ages — Contemplative Saint.
Renaissance — Free Individual.
16th century — Rationalist.
17th century — Christian Stoic.

Too great a simplification: We should ask on what 'figures,' for each age admits of several, disparate models, several alternative ideal characters.

14[33]

Sub specie momenti is, for the artist, *sub specie aeternitas*: and no *aeternitas* that is not known as a moment.

14[33]

Just as man craves for infinity as an escape from the difficulty of living in time, so he supposes the gods to crave mortality as an escape from the tedium of infinity: man seeks the condition of divinity & god that of mortality.[22]

14[34]

The poetry of transience: its differing moods — mournful, sad, resigned, exasperated, plaintive, rejecting, accepting, understanding.

14[34]

The indifference & apathy of old age.[23]

14[34]

Folly is infinite.

14[36]

Ireland

'There is no nation under the sun that doth love equal & indifferent justice better than the Irish; or will rest better satisfied with the execution thereof, although it

---

21 Oakeshott's note: 'Aldous Huxley, *Texts & Pretexts*, p. 4.' A. Huxley, *Texts and Pretexts: An Anthology With Commentaries* (London: Chatto & Windus, 1932).

22 Oakeshott's note: 'Christianity?' immediately beneath this passage in a different ink.

23 Oakeshott's note: 'Maine de Biran, *Journal intime: de l'année 1792 a l'année 1824*, ed. A. de la Valette-Mobrun, 2 vols. (Paris: Plon, 1927–31).'

be against themselves; so as they may have the protection and benefit of the law, when upon just cause, they do desire it.'[24]

The Irish passion for the truth; their intellectual curiosity & power: their intellectual tradition.

But now 'agin the government.'

The change is the product of several centuries of experience & suffering.

An example of a real change in national character.

14[36]

The scepticism of Montaigne

'I always call reason, that appearance or show of discourse, which every man deviseth or forgeth in himself.'[25]

14[36]

'It is only when our feelings are imaginary that we analyse them.'[26]

It is only when our feelings become images of contemplation that they may be the stuff of poetry.

14[38]

'Cunning is circuitous folly.'[27]

Like most men who cultivate mere cunning, he underrated all who do not place the greatest reliance upon it.

14[39]

Confucianism is a system of ethics, incorporating the primeval cult, assimilating all other religions & nationalizing the earliest devout instinct.

Confucianism & Taoism — the first, open, ancient, primitive, rational, traditional.

---

[24] Oakeshott's note: 'Sir John Davies, Attorney-General — James I.' See Sir John Davies, 'A Discovery of the True Causes Why Ireland Was Never Entirely Subdued And Brought Under Obedience to the Crown of England, Until the Beginning of His Majesty's Happy Reign [1612],' in *Ireland Under Elizabeth and James the First*, ed. H. Morley (London, Glasgow, Manchester and New York: George Routledge and Sons, Limited, 1890), p. 342.

[25] Oakeshott's note: 'Montaigne, *Essais*, iv.13.'

[26] See H.S. Merriman, *The Slave of the Lamp* (London: Smith, Elder, & Co., 1897 [1892]), p. 188.

[27] Oakeshott's note: 'Coleridge, *The Friend*.' See S.T. Coleridge, *The Friend: A Series Of Essays, In Three Volumes, To Aid In The Formation Of Fixed Principles In Politics, Morals, and Religion, With Literary Amusements Interspersed*, 3 vols. (London: Rest Fenner, 1818), i.257.

The second, hidden, esoteric, exotic, revolutionary, new, arbitrary. Nihilism, superstition.

Jen = consideration for others: sympathy: love.

14[39]

Τέχνη χρηματιστική – the craft of getting on: practised in addition to a man's proper τέχνη.[28]

14[40]

Perversion always appears when he who pays the piper calls the tune.

14[40]

The sons of god were probably priests, and lived in celibacy, until by a protestant reformation they were allowed to take the fair daughters of men.

14[41]

To change one's allegiance is often necessary, but it should be avoided at those moments when to change involves personal profit: that is too much like changing fealty in return for life.

14[42]

The composure, but not the depression of solitude.

14[43]

A philosophy of failure – the will not to succeed – is a philosophy of personal life – Epicurus's 'live alone.'

This philosophy springs from the belief that personal happiness alone is valuable in the end; success = a reassurance of oneself because personal happiness is impossible or elusive.

14[44]

Man is an animal delicately balanced. He has one prime necessity – to survive. To advance too quickly is as fatal as to lag behind.

14[44]

Ambition, the desire to succeed, to have power, leads to most ills of the human soul. If the desire is realized it leads to arrogance, violence & final satiety – & if it is denied – all the asylums for the insane are filled with human beings who were unable to face being mediocre, insignificant, ineffective, & who therefore created

---

[28] Oakeshott's note: 'Plato, *Republic*.'

for themselves ways of escape from reality so as to be shut off from life itself for ever.

14[44]

'Pour être heureux, il ne faut avoir rien à oublier.'[29]

Hence, 'to admire without desiring', for to desire is to give a hostage to regret.

14[45]

One can never tell what the effect of a satisfied desire will be.

14[45]

A long acquaintanceship does not necessarily mean friendship — one being the result of circumstance, the other of choice.

14[45]

To follow tradition does not mean doing 'what was done last time,' 'last time' is only a moment in the tradition, with no more weight than any other moment taken by itself.

14[45a]

In a young country events move by jerks — the man who is nobody to-day may be somebody tomorrow.[30]

14[45a]

One does not catch rabbits with a dead ferret.

14[45a]

Happiness is a dangerous thing to meddle with. There is so little of it in the world, & it lasts so short a time.

14[46]

The advantage of a soldier's life — his duty is so often clearly defined. The ultimate success of policy, the bona fide, even, of the master one serves — these lie below his horizon, and have no power to break into his unity of spirit. The military life as a circumscribed life: the cause to which he is committed is limited & temporary, it may even be known as a lost cause, but it remains his duty to achieve the temporary success which is military victory.

---

[29] This quotation appears at the head of Merriman, *The Slave of the Lamp*, Ch. IV.

[30] Oakeshott numbered two consecutive folios [45]; to distinguish them the second is referred to here as [45a].

14[51]

To know, not oneself, but only one's appetites (as the French say).

14[51]

To treat each day as if it were our life & not a prologue.

14[52]

An indecent revelation of a nauseating mind.

14[52]

The belief in progress is more cruel than a belief in predestination; it arouses cupidity without satisfying it.

14[52]

Mass in San Marco—so distant, so remote that the whole world seemed to have returned into the eleventh century.[31]

14[55]

Ideals in politics = Omsk—we are haunted rather than directed by them, & they turn activity into an eternally frustrated enterprise.

14[55]

Air de famille—a character which distinguishes a family.

14[55]

Aristotle: Diogenes Laertius

'Some men live so sparingly as if they were to live always, others so prodigally, as if they were to die tomorrow.'

The important part of mortality is not merely the inevitability of death, but not knowing <u>when</u>.

14[56]

'Such courage accounted for the extraordinary feats they had performed.'[32]

Substantialism—an activity translated into an entity & the entity made a cause of the activity.

---

[31] Oakeshott had recently visited Venice.
[32] Oakeshott's note: 'Caesar, *De bello Gallico*, Bk II ch. xxvii.'

14[57]

The <u>historic</u> & the <u>practical</u> past.[33]

History — a world in which there are no illegitimate children (therefore different from the practical world.) Cp. science.

To consider misfortunes as legitimate children.

14[57]

The 'democratic' hatred of everything that is not commonplace.

14[61]

'The history of a soldier's wound beguiles the pain of it.'[34]

14[63]

As secure as a man who has led the ace of trumps for the last trick.

14[64]

The soldier's conception of honour.

Soldiers have the supreme virtue of fidelity, though they are not always clear about what they are being faithful <u>to</u>.

A soldier if he is any good cannot be without virtue. In other trades you offer your services in a limited contract. Not in soldiering — there you put your life at the disposal of your fellow creatures.

You get the commands you don't ask for, they find the dullest theatres for you to serve in.

14[64a][35]

Love at first sight: but not first love at first sight.

The significance of the <u>second</u> performance.

14[64a]

Two desires — to travel & that no-one should know me. To travel & to be unknown.

To see the world & remain unknown.

---

33 Oakeshott's note: 'Valéry: *On the world to-day*, pp. 12–13.' P. Valéry, *Reflections On The World Today*, tr. F. Scarfe (New York: Panteon, 1948).

34 Oakeshott's note: '*Shandy*.' See Laurence Sterne, *The Life and Opinions of Tristram Shandy Gentleman*, 9 vols. (London: R. & J. Dodsley, 1760–7), vol. I, ch. XXV.

35 Oakeshott numbered two consecutive folios [64]; to distinguish them the second is referred to here as [64a].

14[65]

Genius reconciles one to anything.

14[66]

Scientists — they do their cumulative best.

14[67]

He made no major concession to life.

Notebook 15 (March 1955)

15[01]

The forms of religion engage our thoughts & affections long after disbelief has transformed them. Indeed, disbelief can do no more than transform. The mysteries become one mystery. And to trace legends & images back to events does nothing to deprive them of their interest & power. Athena, St Michael, each no doubt has some connection with event; but each remains a marvel of imagination.

'There is a constant turn & return from nature to religion, and from religion to nature.'[2]

To have this moment reproduced in oneself is the glory & the difficulty of the religious man.

Abstractions back to events.

Characters—such as Faust, Don Juan, etc.—undergo the same process of elaboration & detachment from events.

15[01]

Nelson was seasick from the first time to the last time he was afloat: what would a vocational director make of that?

---

[1] LSE 2/1/15. Soft cover, green, 18 cm x 11.5 cm, lined. Recto folios numbered 1–61. Autograph, ink. Title page: 'XV./ Mar.1955. / Sept 1958 / *Paciencia y barajar.'* [Cervantes: see p. 336, above].

Other works from which Oakeshott made excerpts in this notebook but which are not mentioned in the text include: Fo. 9, *Contes des fées*, a collection of French fairy tales, but the English translation attributed by Oakeshott to 'Anthony Greene, 1929' has not been traced; 11–12, Ovid, *Metamorphoses*; 12–13, Cervantes, *Don Quixote*; 15–16, C.C. Colton, *Lacon; Or Many Things In Few Words: Addressed To Those Who Think* (New York: E. Kearny, *c.*1836); 30–1, notes on Antoine Rivarol (1753–1801), French aphorist: see for example *Notes, maximes et pensées de A. Rivarol*, 2 vols. (Paris: J. Haumont, 1941); 32, B. Disraeli, *Tancred: Or, The New Crusade*, 3 vols. (Henry Colburn, 1947); 36–7, Thomas Aquinas, *Summa theologica*; 48–9, Guillaume de Lorris, *Le roman de la rose*; 54, excerpts on Mark Antony and Cleopatra from Plutarch, *Lives*; 61, I.S. Turgenev, 'An Unhappy Girl,' in *The Jew and Other Stories*, tr. C. Garnett (London: William Heinemann, 1899).

[2] Oakeshott's note: 'St-Evremond, *Reflections on Religion, Misc. Essays*. In Dryden 1692, p. 334.' Charles de Marguetel de Saint Denis, seigneur de Saint-Evremond, *Miscellaneous Essays. Translated out of the French. With a Character, by a Person of Honour here in England; Continued by Mr. Dryden* (London: John Everingham, 1692).

15[01–02]

There is an inextinguishable hope in mankind that, in the end, their ephemeral affairs will be regulated by reason…An orderly procession from conception to death. Even vast power is looked upon as beneficent when it is regarded as an opportunity for the achievement of this.

But it is absurd to expect men to define their objectives in terms of their capacities, & govern themselves accordingly. How should our artless ancestor have known that he desired to become an astronomer, a bootlegger, an architect or an aviator? There were no such animals; it was necessary to invent them. Nor indeed were they invented; they emerged as activities before they became professions, & as professions before they became desires or ambitions.

15[02]

Fame is a vulgar affair at best. It is like being caught in the rush-hour crowd.

15[02]

There are infinite odds against even the most transient pleasure. The exact conjunction of individuation & circumstance. The marvel of the best moments is enhanced by their fortuitous occurrence.

15[02]

To be always young, & light-footed, and in love.

15[02]

Love, even first love, is a mingling of old aspiration & present desire.

15[03]

'*Paciencia y barajar.*'[3]
   Patience & shuffle the cards.

15[03]

Poetry is nothing whatever to do with nature. The poet is a poet in virtue of his penetration of nature (of life).

   The impossible is the true domain of poetry. Poetry as the present. The conquest of time.[4]

15[03]

Attention means as much as love.

---

3   Cervantes: see n. 1 and p. 336, above.
4   Oakeshott's note: 'Von Hofmannsthal, *Andreas.*'

15[03]

Concupiscence of experience, boundless curiosity to set our foot everywhere, to enter every possible situation. Montaigne.

15[04]

Hunger is desire without delight and its satisfaction is relief without pleasure.

15[04]

The sweet madness of love & the ties of friendship, both may be eternal if, even intermittently, they reach the level of poetry. This quality of poetry may be absent when, on account of a lack of imagination, they remain fixed in the commonplace; or when, being enjoyed, they reflect only immediate desires. But what forbids its appearance absolutely is egotism; where the impulse is only hunger and the satisfaction only the satisfaction of hunger. For there greed meets greed, and desire & satisfaction are alike devoid of pleasure. And always two egotisms are worse than one – they are sterile, incapable of flower or fruit. It is with love as with eating & talking: unless there is more than the impulse of hunger & something other than the desire to convince or persuade, there is neither pleasure nor conversation.

15[05]

June:

> We resembled one another in some respects,
> And seeing more than each other's need,
> We recognized each other across the room &
> Entered each other's lives without knowing

15[05]

'The road is better than the inn.'[5]

15[05]

To be young – is not to be absolved from obligations, but is not have any, or to have fewer. It is to inhabit a world not yet made. It is to live on credit, & to be recognized to have a right to do so. It is not to be committed, not to have recognized the fixed price of things & always to make a bargain with events. Fluid; elastic. Words are poetry, used for the first time. Actions are poetry, done for the first time. It is not to keep accounts; nothing is specified in advance; everything is what it can be made into. No fixed shapes.

---

5   Oakeshott's note: 'Cervantes.'

And all this means that the activity of <u>politics</u> is supremely unsuitable for the young: <u>anything</u> but politics. For politics is essentially regulative & not creative.

15[06]

From a biological point of view human history is a story of regress. Self-consciousness, reflection etc. have weakened the power of instinct & diminished the power of survival. Physical organs have been impaired by civilization. Something has been acquired as a substitute for what has been lost, but it does not replace it. New defences have been built up; but while they promote survival, they promote only the survival of what human beings have become — biologically they are less efficient, & there is a net loss.

We perceive this when, on rare occasions, we meet a person who has remained biologically unimpaired. Such persons, usually women, display an egoism which conflicts with every civilized achievement. They are masterfully insensitive to everything but their own desires. Without hesitation, they ignore every fine distinction; their conduct is supremely unselfconscious; they feel, but the world in which they live is invisible to them. They recognize only friends & enemies.

15[06]

Women get on very well without any serious respect for rules, without any great aversion to lies or to sharp practice etc. To enjoy without responsibilities. Ineptitude for justice, inconsistency. Keeping secrets.

But they can do so only because the prosaic rectitude of men holds the world together.

The bourgeois holds the world together for the poet.

15[08]

The doctrine of 'more or less.'

The 'logic of imperfection': in practical matters one must not strive for perfection.

The second best; stopping short of the mountain top.

The jealousy of the gods; the jealousy of 'the people.'

15[10]

'Sadness' is a feeling possible only to the young: or, perhaps, it is a word which should be used to express this feeling which is possible only to the young — the emotion of unhappiness in those who do not yet know the transience of unhappiness. After our eyes have been opened, & we know how comparatively easy it is to recover from even the most intense unhappiness, we can never again be 'sad.' *'Tristesse'* — the sadness of those who imagine that there is no end & no recovery: the sadness of those to whom every sadness is irreparable.

15[17]

The only thing tolerable would be to be married to a great man; genius reconciles us to anything, & the trouble is that there are not enough great men to go round.

15[17]

I think it would be difficult to find a conservative in politics who had not some passionate interest other than politics: and any man who has a passionate interest other than politics will be disposed to be a conservative in politics.

15[17]

Anyone touched with the sense of mortality will be apt to be a conservative in politics.

15[18]

To be afraid of conversation.

15[18]

An image should surprise us without making us incredulous.

15[19]

A politician should never discuss hypothetical cases or he will lose his freedom of choice when an actual situation appears.

15[19]

There ought to be something that ought to be done.

15[19]

And sometimes, briefly, we become aware what the camel thinks of the camel driver: democratic politics.

15[19]

Whose only notion of importance is urgency.

15[20]

To be found out is not the same thing as being understood. And to be self-conscious is not the same thing as self-knowledge.

15[20]

When we see a motorcyclist dressed up in an over-all & a helmet we say: 'like a Martian.' But the truth is that Martians are like motor-cyclists.

15[20]

The 'geisha,' a hired conversational companion.

15[20]

The emotional groundswell of good conversation.

15[20]

The sage & the bore—equally averse from conversation.

15[20]

There is no greater sin in politics than to be *trop prononcé.*

15[21]

The art of haircutting is to send your client away <u>not</u> looking as if he'd just had his hair cut.

15[21]

You need to be well-mounted for leaping the hedge of custom.

15[21]

To respect the sleep of friendship.

15[22]

Guarding against the worst; competitive examinations—at any rate they keep out the half-witted.

15[22]

In politics the excited amateur of passion must die before the artist can be born.

15[22]

To have subjects, but not followers, as a good schoolmaster desires pupils & not disciples.

15[22]

A fine imperviousness to mere gentility.

15[23]

Perhaps the chief thing one may learn at school & at a university is something about one's own mental character (as well as something about one's own mental powers).

One's mental character is partly a question of the size & consequently of the sort of ideas it can accommodate & use. Living is exploring & using & enjoying & accommodating oneself to one's own mental character. This, I believe, is formed at a fairly early stage in life—not of course fixed, but its main lines acquired & laid out. One has to explore it, to know what it can do, rather than develop it. And develop it rather than change it or try to acquire some quite new mental character: Knowing how to follow one's own thoughts to their end & being to explore one's own thoughts clearly. And to be humble about them as well as to enjoy them.[6]

15[23]

Be assured that you have & can have nothing but your own thoughts—your own understandings of what others have thought.

15[24]

It is possible to forget everything else in the world. The death of your parents, the loss of all your money, the unfaithfulness of your wife…You forget your mistresses, even the most charming. But a desire that has not been satisfied…an overwhelming desire…that always remains in your heart, even if you live to be a hundred.

15[24]

Ont hi la pel, hi ha alegria.

Where there is hair there is pleasure.
    Catalan proverb.

15[24]

Expensive simplicity.

15[25]

Everybody's youth is a dream, a brief, sweet insanity, a confusion of life & art in which all human activities save love are dissolved into infinite possibilities, in which there are no obligations & nothing is forbidden. No concessions to life. In this dream politics alone has no place. For politics is concerned with things, not dreams, with things as they are & not with our own feelings & emotions but respect for other people's feelings & emotions. The young never feel the balance of a thing in their hands—unless it be a cricket bat—because they recognize no

---

6   On the verso of 15[23]; the recto folio contains a lengthy quotation from William Johnson Cory (1823–92), master at Eton College 1845–72, which Oakeshott used as a footnote in 'The Voice of Poetry in the Conversation of Mankind': see *Rationalism in Politics*, ed. T. Fuller (Indianapolis: Liberty Press, 1991), pp. 491–2 n. 1.

obligation to accept anything save their own emotions. Self & world undistinguished. It is the sign that what Conrad called the 'shadow line' has been passed, that the young man has become an adult when he has accepted things enough to have acquired some skill in using them, when things & people are no longer infinite possibilities, when self & world distinguish themselves from one another, when the sweet solipsism of youth itself dissolves, the 'selfishness.'

When one is young nothing seems more desirable than to take risks.

15[26]

Omnes eodem cogimur.[7] When we are no longer light-footed, we find a place for ourselves in the band.

15[26]

The carefree gaiety of first embraces.

15[26]

…to have sympathy for all happy loves, all desperate matings, all profound frustrations, all slavery…for this is love.

15[27]

One likes those whom one is hurting to be gay. It is less upsetting.

15[27]

Not love, not affection, but a sweet harmony, without obsession, without calculation, without sadness, without constraint: neither comedy nor tragedy. No regrets; not asking for more than there is. Nothing hidden. Admiration & desire balanced with one another.

And thus to make love.[8]

15[27]

To be strong enough, free enough, happy enough to have a happy love affair.

15[28]

The girl in the advertisement urging us to drink more milk is not a 'real' girl. She does not hold a glass of milk up in front of one eye while she looks at us with the other — she has only one eye. The artist did not paint a face with two eyes & then put a glass of milk in front of one of them; he painted a one-eyed girl. It is as perverse to ask what she is doing with her other eye as it is to ask what Hamlet is doing when he is off stage.

---

7   Horace, *Odes*, Bk II ch. iii, 'To Dellius': 'we are all driven to the same end.'
8   A question mark has been placed at the end of the sentence in a different ink.

15[35]

'Religion is an art of self-encouragement in the face of the uncertainties of life.'[9]

The occasional & *ad hoc* gives place to the periodic — ceremony, ritual, etc.
   The harvest festival etc.
   Religion is the art of procuring courage.
   But by 'thought.'[10]

15[35]

Why there cannot be another religion.

15[37]

Poetic experience is sometimes momentary and leaves the impression of a visitation. There are no settled conditions for this visitation. Opium.

15[37]

The feeling of recollection, of having seen it before.
   Déjà vu.

15[37]

There is a likeness, an analogy between loving & poetic experience — both entail delight — but it is a mistake to identify them.[11]

15[38]

A disillusion with the world as it is has commonly lead to a search for relief in three different directions — retirement from the world, the amelioration of the world by practical enterprise, and the transformation of the world in art: religion, moral endeavour & poetry.

15[39–40]

Art in the Middle Ages was 'wrapped up in life.' Its function was to <u>decorate</u>, to convince, to move. 'The Middle Ages knew only applied art.'[12]

The love of art for its own sake did not spring from a new craving for beauty — but was its result. It sprang from <u>a superabundance of artistic production</u>.

---

9   Oakeshott's note: 'Marrett.' See R.R. Marett, *Head, Heart and Hands in Human Evolution* (London: Hutchinson, 1935), p. 145.
10 Oakeshott added this sentence in pencil.
11 Oakeshott's note: 'Cp Aquinas.'
12 Oakeshott's note: 'J. Huizinga, *The Waning of the Middle Ages. A Study of the Forms of Life, Thought and Art in France and the Netherlands in the Fourteenth and Fifteenth Centuries*, tr. F. Hopman (London: Edward Arnold & Co., 1924),p. 246.'

'In the treasuries of princes & nobles objects of art were accumulated so as to form collections. No longer serving a practical use, they were admired as articles of beauty & of curiosity; thus taste for art was born which the Renaissance developed consciously.'[13]

Thus <u>modern art</u> was born.

Art of the Middle Ages for decoration, for record, portraits, ecclesiastical art etc:. The practical use of portraits — betrothal.

'Art' was learned & we ourselves learn to look at pictures — lead on by what is irrelevant, an interest in the subject etc., to what belongs to the picture as a work of art — or a poem.

15[41]

The Christian when he sins, injures God; if he is penitent he may find forgiveness and absolution. But where sin or wrong-doing is recognized only as injury to others, the effects of that wrong-doing can never be expunged: everything is irreparable, and even if there is forgiveness there can never be absolution.

15[42]

It is a great misfortune not to be loved when you love, but it is a much greater to be loved passionately when you no longer love.

15[42]

Love is proof against anger, injustice, forgetfulness, even dissimulation; what poisons it is having something important to dissimulate about.

15[42]

Most of the people we see here are dead.

15[42]

Love is two dreams of love which do their best to spare each other.

15[43]

The charm of love.

The sudden illumination of life; the illusion that the greatest mystery — why we have been born — is solved; the new value that attaches itself to the most insignificant things; the dissolution of things that had become fixed immovable shapes and their resolution into new shapes; surprise, astonishment but without any incredulity; desire & contemplation for a moment united; invulnerability — neither adverse opinion, nor misfortune, nor death itself can touch us; passion &

---

[13] Oakeshott's note: 'Huizinga, *Waning of the Middle Ages*, p. 246.'

tenderness joined; infinite possibility; a world that is always at its end but perpetually renewed; a present without a past; movement untied from direction;
lightness; peace without immobility; alertness; a tension that is always relaxed;
the absence of calculation; freedom.

15[45]

A good horse is never of a bad colour.

15[45]

I want to stand in a thing as big as a mind.

15[47]

Things of the past:
    Dusty Roads
    The inky fingers of children.
    Trouser clips.
    Sweets at 4 oz a 1$^{d.}$

15[50]

He liked to imagine that life was a kind of adventure in which nothing happened that was fixed or irreparable.

15[50]

His boredom came from a complete scepticism about the destiny of humanity…
Scepticism was not merely a mode of thought, but a duty. It seemed to him that
just as he had to evacuate his body every day so that it should not become pois-
oned, so he must preserve his mind from being burdened or obstructed by
beliefs.

15[50]

The ease, the grace, which love imparts to the movements of a girl, and the
manner in which it softens every contour of the face & body & smoothes out
every line. Maturity is given the grace of youth again.

15[51]

The True Believer

Before he became a member of the Party he felt himself to be merely an isolated
individual, lonely & lost, tormented, helpless, vindictive, but quite incapable of
forming judgments either about himself or about the affairs of the world. He
held no standard of values; he felt himself to be a pariah. All he knew for certain

was that he was not a man at peace with himself & could not be at peace with other men. He sought an authority to obey; in the party he found release.

15[51a]

To be capable of *tendresse* as well as of love; to know the difference between them.[14]

15[51a]

Carelessness may govern our lives, but it does not provide us with any arguments in its defence.

15[52]

There is a time, between childhood and manhood, when one has become aware of oneself and become aware also of the hostility of the world which is claiming us for itself — the world where things have fixed shapes, where everything has its price, where imagination is no longer sovereign. Fact & obligation are about to drive out image & poetry. Some people rush forward, eager to assume their appointed place in this new world; others hesitate, draw back from its threshold, clinging to what is threatened with destruction and loving it with the passionate love which everything both lovely & evanescent generates; others again, go forward, reluctantly believing themselves to have a talisman which will deprive the hostile world of its power to transform them — and are, nevertheless, in the end, engulfed; others, a few, manage to live in the world, but never come to belong to it. Others find in poetry what they have lost in life.

This moment is the <u>shadow-line</u>.

This, it should be noted, is <u>not</u> the contrast between art & life, or an attempt to approximate life to art.[15]

Life, an adventure.

15[53]

'There was so much youthful pride about him that all the madness in the world was right for him.'[16]

What we know when we really know another person is how <u>he</u> should behave — that is, his character, what belongs to him, what <u>he</u> can manage without self-destruction.

---

[14] Oakeshott numbered two consecutive folios [51]; to distinguish them the second is referred to here as [51a].

[15] Oakeshott's note: 'Cp. Alain-Fournier, *Le grand Meaulnes.*' Alain Fournier, *Le grand Meaulnes* (Paris: Emile-Paul frères, 1913).

[16] Oakeshott's note: 'Fournier, *Le grand Meaulnes.*'

15[55]

The soul of a lover lives in somebody else's body.

15[56]

The homogeneity of the left — Clemenceau — no enemies on the left.

15[56]

Attachment, friendship may be founded on a common interest in some activity, such as music; and then it is often as profound as the interest is profound; and if it is profound it may generate the dramatic relationship which is the heart of friendship. And it may be profound without being passionate, the link being devoid of violence, frenzy, anguish, envy, emulation.

Love, on the other hand, subsists upon a less specific bond: it is delight & enjoyment of another's vision of the world; and love is requited when this delight is reciprocal. To make love is to celebrate this delight, to speak of it in the language of the body, to know why one is alive and to be glad of being alive.

15[57]

What mischief you've done us, you who would have us believe in nothing…

15[57]

Decadence, Venice as it is now, is not a defect, it is the fruit of which power & glory were only the flower.

15[57]

The copy is not the idea corrupted, it is all there is, & it is nothing apart from its fortunes.

15[57]

Life is like a huge expanse of virgin sand which we must get over without leaving a foot-print.

15[57]

There are girls who get more pleasure out of being talked about & becoming notorious for having given up a lover or one who might have been supposed to be a lover than they get from enjoying the attentions of the sweetest lover. The pleasures of being loved are best when they are intermittent; the pleasure of having the eye of the world on them is a permanent need. And to have the attention of the world for having given up a lover is greater to them than having it for having taken a lover.

15[58]

Some girls take everything as flattery.

15[58]

Sometimes with a look or a word one finds one has sounded the A and there is an instrument tuned to it; sometimes one hears the A and finds oneself in tune – either way, there is peace & happiness & the longing to play a tune.

15[59]

To be young, to believe that happiness is near and that one has only to set out in order to find it.

15[59]

When you are alone you are nothing & you are restless to escape from this nothingness. You like being petted & flattered because this gives you the illusion of being something. You are afraid of being loved because this might make you something & you cling to your nothingness relieved by distractions.

15[59]

God is not a being or a person, it is a way of thinking about human life.

15[60]

Children are great conversationalists.

15[60]

To be either light or serious is to play one's part badly in love. Happy love is a tension between the two in which each opposes the other and each keeps the other alive. The unhappiness of unhappy love is that one is left only with the serious: grief is heavy.

It is to mourn a lost lightness, & mourning was never very graceful.

There can be no lightness when there is no confidence.

To the one (R) I had to teach lightness; & she never learned. To the other (P) I had to teach seriousness; & she never learned.

She had neither Reason nor Passion, only a miraculous lightness.

15[A][17]

Unrequited Love:

---

[17] On a loose sheet inserted at 15[48].

1. Love that never was returned and never looked like being returned. Narouz's love for Clea.

(a) Unspoken love.

(b) Spoken love which received no reply.

(c) Spoken love which received some reply, but not the reply to love—e.g. marriage in the hope that love will be answered, but knowing it is not answered.

2. Love that was returned, but died in one sooner than in the other. In the one in whom it did not die this is unrequited love—in time. The answer was less, because shorter, than that which was desired. —I loved you once—

3. Love that is half-answered, and remains half-answered. Pierot & Pierette. Love that is answered but in such a manner that the answer is not recognized as an answer. Love oblique.

4. Unhappy love—great variety.

5. Love not returned to one, but given to another.

15[B][18]

The full score, immanent, though perverted in its actual manifestation, but intelligible in its eternal character = the <u>idea of the good</u>.

The permanent parts = 'ideas.' Their actual performance = copies.

Orchestra also represents <u>the Republic</u>, the 'ideal' state.

Conductor = the philosopher king, the instrumentalists = citizens.

Each born to his part, can only be educated appropriately—finding in his part his complete self-expression, i.e. as a <u>flautist</u>. Relatively undeveloped compared with the Conductor. The conductor alone knows the full score. The hierarchy of instrumentalists.

<u>Orchestral performance</u>—Necessaries—

1) Full score—held in the memory of the conductor.

2) Instrumentalists, each playing parts, as provided in the full score, & obeying the conductor.

(a) As played, each part is temporary & imperfect; but the part itself is eternal (& Perfect).

(b) The significance of each part lies in the composition as a whole, the unwritten score immanent in the Orchestral performance. Therefore:

---

[18] On a loose printed form in pencil headed 'ARMY FORM C 2136 (Large) MESSAGE FORM' inserted at 15[48].

(c) each performer can copy (on his instrument) accurately his own part if he follows the conductor's guidance, but only the conductor can give that guidance, either to the parts as parts, or to the parts as parts of the whole; & the power to guide comes from his knowledge of the ultimate idea/character of each part, that is the part as an aspect of the whole i.e. — his knowledge of the full score.

This knowledge is purely <u>intellectual</u> — it is in his memory — it is not <u>one</u> of the parts & cannot be played on an instrument.

Rivalry between the instrumentalists is impossible — flutes cannot play the parts of triangles — but each instrumentalist can fully realize himself along his appropriate & specialized line.

Yet there is a hierarchy of unequal development from timpani to strings — the leader of the violins has a greater directive power & larger conception of the whole performance than anyone else under the conductor. But the conductor alone is fully developed. His function is universal — he is, in a sense, in a purely intellectual sense, the whole orchestra.

Notebook 16 (September 1958)

16[01]

Ginginare—a verb meaning everything that passes at a distance between two people who might be in love with one another before they have spoken. 'Love comes in at the eyes.' It is what follows a sort of visual (& perhaps mutual) recognition: perhaps it simply <u>is</u> that recognition. Chance and choice.

16[01]

When we love somebody we wish, in the first place, simply to share our time with her and all time not shared is time lost.

16[01]

The nearest approach to passion in her was the passion that springs from complicity in deception.

16[03]

Statements which, if they were true, things would be as they are.

16[03]

Tired, not with age, but with supporting the burden of a secret existence.

16[04]

Some people need a great deal more courage to live than others, not because they have greater or more frequent misfortunes, but merely because they feel being alive more acutely. So when we tell a man to be brave, we do not know just how much bravery he needs, & he may need much more than someone else in his situation would need.

16[05]

The endearing, gentle imperfection of all living things.

---

1   LSE 2/1/16. Hard cover, red, 17 cm x 12 cm, ruled. Recto folios numbered 1–64. Autograph, ink with occasional pencil. Inside front cover: 'M. Oakeshott / 16 New Row / London WC 2.' Title page: 'XVI. / To see the world & live unknown. / ignotos / We are children & we have done a / foolish thing: do not follow me. / Sept 1958 / *O monde! Je veux ce que tu veux.'*

    Other works from which Oakeshott made excerpts in this notebook but which are not mentioned in the text include: Fo. 12, Leonhard Frank, *Karl and Anna*, tr. C. Brooks (London: Peter Davies, 1929); 67–8, Karen Blixen aka Isak Dinesen, *Shadows On The Grass* (London: M. Joseph, 1960).

16[05]

Trust is necessary. Everything rests on confidence. To live is always to live on credit.

16[05]

Where there is no choice we are for ever at the mercy of chance.

16[07]

'The world is like a cucumber — to-day it's in your hand, tomorrow up your arse.'

Arabic proverb.

16[07]

A man is a seismograph — Nietzsche or Burckhardt, for example. Better than thinking of them as diagnosticians.

16[07]

For most people living is a hobby; the <u>business</u> of life is elsewhere in ambitions & achievements. This, perhaps, is wise; at least it shows appropriate caution, for to make living one's *grande passion* gives too many hostages to fortune. However, this is not a matter of choice.

16[08]

Nibbling at the edge of stale ideas.

16[08]

'The lion shall eat straw like the ox.'[2]

The tame world of universal mediocrity.

16[08]

There are many ways of loving. The word may be given the absolute meaning it has for young lovers, or rather the absolute meaning which young lovers have conferred upon it & which speaks not only to them but sometimes to others also. But, apart from this, which belongs to 'loving & being in love' at the same time; there are other meanings. The passion of 'being in love' without any profound emotion of love; the gentleness of 'loving' without 'being in love.' Love too is complete without reciprocation: the intransitive 'I love' which proclaims merely an experience, a discovery in oneself. And love that seeks to be requited.

---

2   Oakeshott's note: 'Isaiah 11:9.'

16[08]

The desire to give her an experience of pleasure which she did not pretend to feel; the feeling that possession is lacking until this is done.

'The lineaments of gratified desire.'[3]

16[08]

Not everybody loves, though most people have an intimation of it. With some it is a brilliant firework which flares up in the night & is gone; with others it is a promise which is never fulfilled, the power to give & forget is absent; with others it is devouring & inescapable. The first may, sometime or other, know the last; but the second will never know either of the others, only guess.

16[09]

<u>Documentation</u>

A man has <u>become</u> a collection of documents: identity cards, employment card, health service card, employers certificates, party card, etc. This is the mass man.
    What provoked it?
    Increase in population, writing, printing, literacy, techniques acquired by government, photography, hollerith machines.

16[09]

She lived as if she were blind, aware only (& that imperfectly) of the objects she came into contact with, but knowing nothing of the general aspect of things.

16[10]

The love of adventure, stranger than all other loves.

16[10]

It requires wisdom to be happy in love, and it requires wisdom to do without love — & it is the same wisdom.

16[11]

Someone to whom he could be life and who could be life to him.

16[11]

Shone like a star in hell.

---

3   See William Blake, 'The Question Answered,' in *The Poetical Works of William Blake*, ed. E.J. Ellis, 2 vols. (London: Chatto & Windus, 1906), i.152.

16[11]

Nothing in the whole world is so cruel as love—centred upon one, all others, no matter what they have been, are nothing; tied to one all other ties are obliterated; self-surrender to one & fierce egoism in the face of all others.

16[11]

In love we grow acquainted because we are already attached.

16[11]

Loneliness is not living alone; it is loving alone.

16[13]

To love is to have a faithful memory.

16[13]

The Beeches.

In this sweet house Patricia lived & moved;
Was loved, and lovely was; but never loved.

16[13]

What one loves in a woman is her life:
Je veux une femme à son gré: not perfection, but *une femme telle qu'elle est, une femme libre.*

16[14]

No one is more particular about the conventions than a woman who is tired of her love.

16[14]

Love is a condition which reveals what one has to give and what one is able to take: apart from love one never knows.

16[14]

What is love—to be enchanted by whatever is happening, to forget oneself completely; it is an air of surprise, a joy which is visible in the eyes & can never be counterfeited.
An adventure.

16[14]

Innocence & generosity.

16[14]

It is only when one's lover is also *une amie* that everything becomes possible —
the greatest happiness & the greatest pain. Love & *amitié* joined, the most vital of
all mixtures. The greatest adventure.

16[15]

How strange is the determination to succeed in the circus of life.

16[15]

Fear in young girls is an emotion which a man can hardly understand; it springs
from a feeling of helplessness.

16[15]

One forgives a woman one loves, forgives everything, & that is what makes
one's love stifling.

16[15]

It is not time, or satiety or neglect that is to be feared in love, but an impression
of security. They wish to be certain but hate anyone they can be certain of.

16[15]

Love is not really a human feeling until it is over.

16[15]

The lottery of great passions.

16[16]

The idiotic heroism of sublime delicacy.

16[16]

I felt torn up by the roots & thrown away.

16[17]

The secret of success — get into the queue in life. One's moment always comes if
one has patience & if one doesn't change queues!!

16[17]

Certain circumstances generate rapid advance — e.g. war generated rapid
advance in aeronautics, in chemistry, in the treatment of wounds & diseases, etc
etc. And the argument is that we should make these circumstances permanent &
thus enjoy continuous rapid advance. If we can do it in war why not in peace.

Warships generate liners; ferroconcrete fortifications generate new styles of building, etc etc: why surrender these means in peace? But this is merely the technological argument. 'We were pushed into doing, inventing, contriving it; we succeeded in finding out how to do or contrive it; therefore let us go on doing so.' Surrender of choice.

16[18]

Glory: the poetry of reputation.

16[18]

We are constantly trying to recover in happiness the imaginative expense which the invention of our love has cost us.

16[18]

Between love & the dream of love there is no common measure: to love is two dreams of love which do their best to spare one another.

16[18]

To hate tenderly.

16[19]

The legendary & the historical. Their different structure.

In legend, all that is casual, secondary, unresolved, truncated, obscure or uncertain is absent. There is a clear outline; men act from few & simple motives; there is a unity of feeling. It is a pattern; there are repetitions, types. Exact time & place are absent, but everything else is exact & nothing is confused.

In history, there is confusion, contradiction, individuality, lack of arrangement, uncertainty, events which lead nowhere & complicated motives & circumstances; obscurity, variety — & yet a kind of intelligibility. To write history is so difficult that most historians are forced to make concessions to the technique of legend.

16[20]

In the romances of the 12th century, the means by which the courtly virtues are proved & established & preserved is *avanture*: the surmounting of perils, encounters with enemies, demons, spirits, magical powers, 'natural' vicissitudes, requiring strength, resolution, courage, fortitude, cunning, etc.

But *avanture* differs from 'adventure' in not being fortuitous: they are the structure of the world of courtly conduct. They are possible only to a knight. The world of knighthood contains nothing but the requisites of *avanture*. The world is specially adapted to prove the virtues of knighthood.

Don Quixote's 'adventures' are true parodies of knightly *avanture*: they are chance encounters in the ordinary world with ordinary circumstances & people, but transformed into moments of self-enactment.

16[21]

Those who think that the world isn't good enough for them, to whom it is an adversity to be alive.

16[21]

The victims of activity.

16[21]

Chance & courage (choice) – Love. Love is our high idea of courage: courage is our high idea of love.

16[21]

The horror of all compulsion, of getting or keeping anything by force or subterfuge or importunity.

16[21]

The world of art – a world where only the unforeseen can happen and where conduct is understood only by children.

16[23]

Utopian ideals have always turned to blood when they have touched the earth – & they <u>must</u> always do so. 'Truths' always kill; errors are better, they are sometimes merciful.

   Of all such truths one must ask – who does it strike & who does it save? Who will it kill or poison? What will grow from it? Does it smell of rotting corpses? What will happen to those who taste it? What will happen to those who swallow it?

16[23]

Some people are both inert and unstable at the same time.

16[23]

Her lack of self-confidence showed itself in her leaning towards complicated & equivocal situations & relationships.

16[24]

<u>Our</u> fears are all mundane. The fear of spirits & demons, which is still the most important thing to savage people, has disappeared from our world. The fear of the gods, which Lucretius designed to rescue his contemporaries from, has gone also. The last fear, which lasted until a generation ago & still lingers, is the fear of hell.

We are, in this sense, unbelievers. To us the day is the day & the night is the night — nothing more. The dead do not speak or threaten. Every man is wise and alone.

But, with fear, belief has also disappeared: we understand everything & despise what we do not understand. Beliefs, too, have become mundane, because thoughts are mundane.

'Freedom from fear.' Was this not what Lucretius designed to give his contemporaries — 'fear of the gods.'

16[25]

Poseidon

The world of the sea and men on the sea. Simplified: its demands are simple & cannot be evaded. A world that can be understood by those who inhabit it who, at the same time are entirely lost on land, and among men on land.

16[25]

How much of our 'morality,' what we think it is right & wrong to do, comes from looking into the future — of which heaven & hell are the extremes. If men & women were accustomed to die, not worn out, or with passion spent, but at the height of their energy, say about thirty or thirty-five, would not this transform our 'morality'? Morality always distinguishes between feelings, but it reflects feelings & distinguishes only between actual feelings.

Passions interrogate values.

16[26]

Men handicap themselves with all kinds of 'virtues,' like honour, decency, moderation, honesty, consistency, sincerity, detachment, compunction, justice, which women do very well without. And yet they can do without these 'virtues' only because men recognize them — that is to say, the world of women is not a viable world and they have the supreme joy in living in a world which is viable but to whose viability they have to contribute nothing. <u>They</u> contribute 'movement,' instability, madness, laughter, pleasure & pain. And they will have to engage in masculine occupations for many generations before they will <u>commonly</u> acquire masculine virtues. Fortunately, 'women' as they are will outlast my time.

16[26]

The warmth of patience.

16[26]

To have imagined every detail; for it all to have been different & yet unmistakable.

16[27]

The lower middle class may be defined as that class which approves only of its own ways & manners & dispositions; the class which has sympathy only for itself.

16[27]

'My dear husban, I would like to wash your dirty shirts again.'
    Letter to a soldier 1808.

16[27]

You have neither a just nor a compassionate mind.

16[28]

You have everything but happiness to offer those who love you. If you look for anything it is for what you would be afraid to find.

16[28]

Personality — a settled collection of dispositions & attributes — is an illusion, but if we are to love, it is a necessary illusion. What we love is the flavour of a personality.

16[28]

Without reason or passion; unable to give or to take; neither to be raised up nor cast down; incapable of life or of death. She had never experienced pleasure, which is impossible to be entirely self-centred.

16[28]

There was no break on the surface, only a gradual sinking of the level.

16[29–30]

Ad Patriciam.

All these experiences: of desire and frustration and fulfilment; of longing & denial & release; of violence & contentment; of affection, tenderness, sadness, elation, misery, closeness & remoteness, loneliness, hope, fear, wonder, expectation, jealousy, forbearance, forgiveness, serenity, remorse, disappointment, anger, bitterness, suspicion, delight; of joy and defeat; of security & insecurity; of resolution & irresolution; of alienation & friendship; of uncertainty, confidence, doubt, faith, patience & impatience; of freedom & bondage; of life, death & resurrection; of sympathy & estrangement; of kindness & cruelty & rebellion & submission; of compassion & extenuation & obstinacy; of warmth & coldness; of generosity & meanness; of gentleness & hardness; of shame & guilt & absolution; of imprisonment & liberation; of contention & peace; of doing & suffering & waiting; of pursuit, deception & evasion; of coming & going & returning; of giving & taking and surrendering; of intimacy & understanding & misunderstanding; of blindness & recognition, acceptance & rejection; of hurt & healing; of devotion & blasphemy; of losing & finding & being lost; of creation & destruction & recreaction, making & unmaking; the red, the black, the green & the blue; spring & summer & winter; the sun, moon, & stars; the earth, the air & the sea; the dark, the light & the half-light—all these are the components of the adventure of loving & being loved by you, in which only indifference & satiety have found no place. A night without darkness. A magic circle in which every embrace is a rejection & every rejection an embrace; every entrance an exit & every exit an entrance. A circle that holds us part-owners of one another. A reality and an illusion.

16[30]

Loving is two people who are in flower giving shade to one another; there is no fruit.

16[31]

Loving & being loved is to live in a world in flower. The egoism of being in love is to believe that you can make the world flower for the person you love. But many things can stand in the way. I never succeeded in doing this for Patricia; tho there was often promise of it & some moments of fulfilment. She loved me enough to spare my dream of love; but she had no dream herself & was therefore invulnerable.

  If only she could have extorted compliance from me. But she was not positive or great enough to do this; & I am not naturally compliant. In any case it is difficult for a lover to be compliant: I should have done better as a husband for then love might have engendered compliance without the feeling of loss.

16[33]

Love is a fearful struggle to give oneself to another. To be happy in love one must either find one's love answered in the manner one desires it to be answered, or one must love in so unpremeditated a manner (without any preconceived image of how it needs to be answered) that disappointment is impossible.

The first is a miracle, the miracle that every lover desires to perform; but deep love which seeks a premeditated answer is difficult because the miracle of being able to answer it seems impossible to perform. The second is to love like a god or a child — something that passionate men have to learn & find difficulty in learning.

Perhaps, in love, depth and this kind of unpremeditation go together; or perhaps deep love cannot easily avoid unhappiness, the unhappiness of not being answered? These things cannot be arranged. Every man has his special coin in which he wishes to be paid.

16[34]

I would have thought I had succeeded if she had stopped biting her nails.

16[34]

Every art of fortification has its own art of siege.

16[35]

Loving is like gambling — winning & losing are equally irrelevant; what matters is wagering, the adventure.

'Gamblers & lovers really play to lose.' How much truth is there in this?

16[35]

Love is a human invention, the invention of a new pain & a new pleasure of which only those who know themselves & others as individuals are capable.

16[35]

Images which sometimes will provoke a paroxysm of jealousy at others provoke only jealous thoughts. The images are the same, but the mood is different. Is the indifference only tiredness?

16[35]

Our dreams are as much a part of our life as our waking thoughts: there is <u>one</u> life, dreaming & waking.

16[36]

The world is a set of conditions which must be accepted if we are to be happy. In order to make them acceptable we invent stories of how they came into being & theories about their character. The most foolish of these inventions is that they are the creation of a god and represent part of a process in which human beings are perfected, a period of education & probation. This makes the creator all too human. The Manichean theory is much more convincing.

16[36]

When we are young 'love' is self-centred — we drink from thirst or to get drunk. Later we are concerned with the individuality of who is loved; love is an attachment to individuality. In old age we are, perhaps, young again.

16[37]

For the poet and those who read what he has made in its proper, poetic, character, 'poetry' does not exist. He does not know what he is doing and they only know what he provokes in them. 'Poetry' was invented in an enquiring mood, the mood of the critic, the philosopher, the historian. A poem is something different.[4]

16[37]

What we do is largely determined by our inventions — what we find out how to do. But our inventions mirror our secret wishes.

16[37]

Two fatalities: to fall in love with a girl who turns out to be a bitch; to be charmed & delighted by a light & wanton, careless unloving character, & then to find one has fallen in love with her. Perhaps the second is the worse because the love one would have would be deeper & less destructible.

16[37]

October 1st 1959: the longest day of my life.

16[38]

In love, as in some other connections, knowledge does not generate power, but is only the sign of a lost innocence: it is only in defeat that one knows for certain whether it is love or egoism. For love is surrounded & penetrated by so many egoisms — the egoism of desire, of want, of need; the egoism entailed in imposing one's own dream of love upon another; the egoism of giving as well as of taking; the egoism of wanting to lose oneself; the egoism of devoting oneself entirely to another's pleasure, and there is even detectable egoism in the willingness to die for another. And love may be mistaken for the passion & the peace which springs up when the needs of two are requited in each other. This is happiness, & we need enquire no further. But while egoism unrequited may dissolve into

---

4   The last sentence has been added in a different ink.

hatred, love unrequited remains or is forgotten. Hamlet: 'I did love you once' —
yes, it is possible; the test is in what it turned into.

16[38]

'The classic in art is what marches by intention with the cosmology of the age.' I
am sure this must be Santayana, bless him.

16[38]

People of various degrees of nothing.

16[38]

Love is a condition of intense concentration: desires, cares, thoughts, pleasures,
pains, hopes, fears — all revolve round one centre. It is a revolution which destroys all that is trifling — or a revolution which gives one the illusion of knowing
why one is alive.

16[40]

The woman whom love & youth have deserted takes offence at everything.

16[40]

It must be difficult not to feel some degree of contempt for somebody with
whom you can play a part with impunity. It you need to deceive, it should be a
little difficult to deceive.

16[40]

In the past when I fished in my head for bright ideas I usually caught something;
nowadays the fish don't come so easily & never look as attractive as they used to
look.

16[40]

Convives.

16[40]

Savoir-mourir.

16[40]

'*Dieu, que le son du cor est triste au fond du bois.*'[5]

---

5   See Alfred de Vigny, 'Le Cor,' in *Alfred de Vigny collection des plus belles pages,* 2nd
     edition (Paris: Mercure de France, 1914), 58. The quotation recurs at pp. 503 n. 1 and
     520, below.

16[41]

Do not allow the star to be put out.

16[41]

The feeling of trudging through life incognito and in shoes of lead.

16[41]

Nothing stirred in her except a vague & intermittent desire to be stirred.

16[41]

People who dance, not because they are happy but because they are musical.

16[41]

To care nothing for one's enemies & all for one's friends.

16[42]

Some people love life, others are in love with life, but the rare few make love with life in every moment.

16[42]

I don't know whether I believe in God, but I believe in the Virgin Mary, Jesus Christ, St Michael & the devil.

16[42]

It was like making love with somebody in the dark who never answers.

16[43]

The complexity of the world & of the interrelation of its components is such that our control over it never lifts us above being gamblers in a lottery. One of the conclusions is that we waste time in refining too much on how children are brought up.

16[43]

To have confidence independent of success.

16[43]

When we conceive of the possibility of being in the same difficult situations as others, youth is over.

16[44]

I was not hostile to him, nor was I friendly; I never dreamed of him.

16[44]

Every man has his own sphere of knowledge and he knows his way about it better than most philosophers know their way about theirs: The cook, the seaman, the accountant, the journalist, the actor, the carpenter; each knows at once what will work & what won't, what is absurd & what is possible & what is probable & what is certain. Our aim is to know our way about our sphere of knowledge as well as these know their way about theirs. This is the way F.C. Burkitt knew the first four centuries of the Christian era.

16[45]

Enthusiasm provokes large views and opens up long vistas. But there is a kind of negative enthusiasm where we see little but in immense detail.

16[45]

A book is a mirror; we see only ourselves.

16[45]

Works of art are works of an artist.

16[46]

To love & to cherish the pride of your adversary as highly as your own – or it may be not an adversary, but a partner or one whom we encounter.

16[46]

We are now brought up on a system of examinations & promotions, we look for merit & value 'justice'; and this has bitten into us so deeply that we hardly understand a way of life in which luck & favour are pre-eminent – the adjustment to the unforeseen & the unexpected which it entails, a way of life in which to be safe or to be saved seems to be the least necessary of all things.

16[47]

'By thy mask I shall know thee': we choose a mask that reveals what is usually concealed; its ugliness says, 'Do not regard my beauty; there is something else.'

16[47]

What is staggering is God's imagination: no human inventor could possibly have imagined relationships such as love. There is nothing humane about this imagination, it is pure fantasy.

16[47]

It is only a very courageous people who will impose responsibility for the evil & misery in the world upon their gods; alternatively, it is only by imposing this responsibility upon gods that evil & misery (which is unavoidable) is made tolerable.

16[48]

Si libet licet — if you want to, why not?

16[48]

I am a small incident in your life. Do not say those things which a girl says to a man when she wishes to spare his feelings.

16[49]

Prudent men cannot be argued out of their prudence, but they may find it suddenly deprived of its weight & solidity when they see a friend engaged upon a risky enterprise. Then it is like being reminded by a flute-player in the street, that there is such a thing as music & there is such a thing as folly: gilt-edged security seems a shade less attractive.

16[49]

There are unshed tears between my eyes & what I see.

16[49]

An outlook not jaundiced but simplified.

16[50–51]

To be a wanderer, that is, one with no destination or only interim destinations, is to make a world utterly different from the world of those who have a home & live in it or those who go somewhere for an ulterior purpose; this is the world of poetry.

If the way is unfamiliar, everything is seen from the outside, & unexpectedly: Medina will rise suddenly from the plain, St Marks appear as the alley takes its last turn before the piazza, the white cliffs emerge from the mist — none was sought because none was known about in advance; and each is for its own sake, is what it appears & is nothing more. And the same experience may take place in books & plays & pictures & operas, & dances. A stopping place for the eyes.

But the same can happen if the way is familiar; we may anticipate what we are to see, imagine a glint in the sky before it appears (the white cliffs), or a happening on the stage, know what we shall see round the next corner. But it is not a home, or a resting place; it is not how a tired traveller thinks who is on his way to a destination, it is not what a man at home sees & thinks. For these, things are symbols; for the wanderer they 'mean' nothing, whether or not he has wandered this way before. They are not 'land-marks', they do not indicate where he has got on his way, they have no history, they cannot be 'used', they do not tell him the time of day; they tell him nothing in this sense. Perhaps it is impossible to enter this world with a companion: when we want a companion to see the world with we anticipate an emotional experience & seek it, not a contemplative experience.

Everything is superficial.

16[52]

The most successful politicians are those who do not pretend to be serious: no undertaker is a success in a music hall.

16[52]

The real grievances of mankind are incurable; politics consists in manufacturing curable grievances.

16[52]

Love is what happens between <u>two</u> people who love one another.

16[52]

Stendhal isn't interested in love — only in ambition & conquest. Julian Sorel actually didn't love Mathilde de la Mole. Did Fabrice love Clélia? or did he revenge himself on her? Lucien Luewen doesn't go to bed with Mme de Chasteller.

16[53]

Agreement/Silence may be an expression of contempt.
Wellington's 'Ha' is the best reply to most remarks.

16[53]

The course of obstacles etc. in the field gun competition at the annual Royal Tournament is based upon the obstacles which had to be overcome by the Royal Naval Field Gun Battery on its way to the relief of Ladysmith.

16[53]

Politics is an uninteresting form of activity to anyone who has no desire to rule others.

16[54]

'The excellence of things is their undoing.'
Han Yü

Everything that diverges from the Mean is vulnerable. Everything, in the end, is 'undone,' but that which is excellent is more of a thing and its undoing is a great undoing & unmistakeable.

16[54–55]

It is a mistaken feeling one has when one gets older that one cannot afford to dream. When one is young one may waste time dreaming because there seems time enough to spare; there is time to make mistakes & recover from them; whole years may be spent in dreaming. Thus, one thinks; but the reasoning is mistaken. It is based upon the false assumption that there is something else, other than making mistakes, to do, & the false assumption that waking & dreaming are not all one. There is in fact nothing discreditable even in dying in a mistake. And yet all the force of one's up-bringing goes against this. The pressure to accomplish something; the horror of a life spent in dead-ends. And this pressure, instead of relaxing, as it should, when one gets older, seems to increase. One has to jerk oneself out of the view that one should not still be waiting & still have time to dream away the days. And it seems all right for the young to dream because we imagine that there is time for <u>something</u> to 'come true.'

16[55]

First cut and then polish.

16[55]

Eyes too easily understood.

16[55]

Some people confuse love with an insight into virtues & failings.

16[56]

Confucius, like all profoundly reflective men, <u>concentrated</u> a civilization in his thoughts. Out of three thousand songs he selected three hundred; out of a vast variety of customs & behaviour he chose a few; out of concrete morality he made one abstract, universal morality; out of various philosophies he made one. For example, *Jen*, consideration for others, is a universal abstraction from filial piety and respect for elders: these were the primitive virtues of the Chinese, the roots of their moral conduct. What Confucius did was to universalize them. This is also what Aristotle did with the native morality of the Athenians.

In short, what Confucius did was to give a sharp outline to what was thitherto vague, and having found his 'one thought' he made it the principle of a

world of ideas – but in doing so, much was lost. When we move from 'possibilities' to this sort of finality, we seem to have gained, but we have also lost.[6]

16[57]

What slips through the net of moral finality is the poetry of conduct, and no
amount of subsequent qualification will get it back. A too critical anthologist.

16[57]

The conversations & actions of lovers have to be construed differently from the
similar words & actions of other people. Actions & words in both cases may be
commonplace & banal, but with lovers they mean always: 'No matter what I say
or do I cannot express my delight in you, so I am trying it this way now & you
must try to understand.'

16[58]

Some people's judgment is acute in respect of the current value of things; they
know what is fashionable & what is unfashionable; they are 'in touch.' And
some historians have this quality of judgment also about the past. But such
people are rarely able to escape from this sort of acuteness; they don't even
consider the intrinsic value of things. And, in the case of the historian, he doesn't
get beyond the 'feel' of the time. It is the faculty of journalists, good journalists,
& salesmen – the man who knows what currently an artist's pictures will fetch.

16[59]

The tenderness of making love is the hope that in penetrating each other's
bodies that a secret other than the secret of lust will be revealed.

16[59]

To have the dignity of time without the disabilities of time.

16[59]

'Values' are what people parade who have neither settled habits of behaviour
nor religious beliefs to suggest to them what they should do.

16[61]

The Masai when they were moved from their old country to the present Masai
Reserve took with them the names of their hills, plains & rivers and gave them to

---

6   Oakeshott's note: 'Cp. J. Huizinga, *Men and Ideas: History, the Middle Ages, the
    Renaissance* (tr. J.S. Holmes and H. van Marle) London: Eyre & Spottiswoode, 1959), p.
    205.'

the hills, plains & rivers in the new country…they were trying, in exile, to keep their past by a formula.

And to keep one's past is a necessary component of keeping one's identity. It is self-preservation. If you must inhabit a new country, then the tribe must not be split up. How to avoid the shame of extinction?

This is primitive; we feel it less, for our own identity is more concerned with personal memories, than tribal or community: but it is still something we cannot do without.

16[63]

Curious as a concierge.

16[63]

Dum vivimus vivamus: you've gotta live it up boy.

16[63]

Civil association concerned with people whom we do not particularly like, with whom we do not agree, whom we may even despise or even hate, but with whom we must have a relationship because we live near them or have come to be concerned with them in common undertakings.

16[64]

With attention narrowed down to listening for *faux pas*.

16[64]

Teeming with second-hand dealings with life.

Notebook 17 (April 1961)

17[01]

One who turns away from no-one but the one who loves her.

17[02–03]

A man's 'system' is usually of very little interest except to himself: it is his own particular & exclusive 'modernity.'

We should look for 'something else'; and often the great systematizers (like Hegel) are great because they have more of the 'something else' than others.

The 'something else' is difficult to define, except that it has a casualness & a contingency about it. At bottom it is the reminiscences of the intellectual folk-tunes of Europe; it is what connects a man to the roots, which are always contingent.

Comte would be a good subject to study in this manner, because these reminiscences are so over-laid. But they are there. This absurd worship of 'humanity' & the Comtian 'heroes' — it is an ancient perception that gods & heroes have little to separate them. Ancient taboos; the practice of sacrifice. And the trauma which the replacement of matriarchy by patriarchy has left with us.

17[03]

The past is past only for history; elsewhere it is present. The event has gone; but it lives on in fable, in gesture, in turns of speech, in habit, and above all in myth.

17[03]

Speed may not be the essence of justice, but it has a virtue of its own.

17[04]

'Your enjoyment of the world is never right till every morning you awake in Heaven.'[2]

---

1   LSE 2/1/17. Soft cover, black with gold trim, 18 cm x 12 cm, ruled. Recto folios numbered 1–74. Autograph, ink with occasional pencil. Title page: 'XVII /April 1961. / Mar. 1964 / To cherish the pride / of those with whom you / are associated, as / partner or adversary, as highly as your own.'

Other works from which Oakeshott made excerpts in this notebook but which are not mentioned in the text include: Fo. 19, Joseph Conrad, *The Mirror of the Sea: Memories and Impressions* (London: J.M. Dent and Sons Ltd, 1906); 52–3, A. Schopenhauer, *Parerga and Paralipomena*, tr. E.F.J. Payne, 2 vols. (Oxford: Clarendon Press, 1974), §§399–400; 65, Henry James, *Washington Square* (New York: Harper & Bros, 1881).

2   Oakeshott's note: 'Thomas Traherne.' Thomas Traherne, *Centuries of Meditations*, ed. B. Dobell (London: B. Dobell, 1908), p. 20.

('Heaven' here means — 'not as a "natural" world but as God's artefact & dwelling place.')

17[05]

Philosophy à la Hume

'Do not strive to seek after the true, only cease to cherish opinions.'
A Zen Master.[3]

17[05]

'It was when the Great Way declined that human kindness & morality arose.'
Lao Tzu.

i.e. with the rise of self-consciousness, animal grace is no longer sufficient for the conduct of life & must be supplemented by conscious & deliberate choices between right & wrong.

17[06]

'Turning to God without turning from Self.'[4]

i.e. pursuing personal ends with religious passion. Imposing our 'ideals' with religious conviction and passion.

17[06]

The morality of ideals is 'idolatry' — the worship of what we desire; objects recognized as Gods.

17[07]

The 'individualism' of Chuang Tzu; its conditions. Belief in the supreme importance of cultivating <u>one's own powers</u>. No pursuing 'goodness,' or obeying the law. Freedom from reputation & a desire to exploit life.

17[08]

Confucius' belief in a moral tradition saved him from extreme moral positivism.
Filial piety & brotherly obedience.
The value of <u>ritual</u>. 'When the heart is uneasy we support it with ritual.'

---

[3] See Jianzhi Sengcan, aka Chien-chih Seng-ts'an, 'On Believing in Mind,' in D.T. Suzuki, *Manual of Zen Buddhism* (Kyoto: Eastern Buddhist Society, 1935).

[4] Oakeshott's note: 'William Law.' The quotation has not been traced, but William Law (1686–1761), Anglican mystical theologian, typically argued that 'all turning to self is so far turning from God': see *Selected Mystical Writings of William Law Edited With Notes And Twenty-Four Studies In The Mystical Theology Of William Law And Jacob Boehme* (London: C.W. Daniel Company Ltd, 1938), p. 97.

17[09]

The Sages of old: all that was worth handing on died with them; the rest they put in their books.

17[09]

The Platonic tradition of political philosophy; the government of a state is a reflection of the self-government of a ruler.

17[09]

The Sages – they are the <u>inventors</u> of goodness and duty and of the laws which embody morality. Perhaps, in the circumstances, it was a useful invention: it was a remedy for a disease, but it left its own mark.

Schools of moral instruction.

17[09]

Rulers cannot rule without a Sage counselor (*hsien*). Mencius.

The Stoic notion of government in the 16th century.

17[11]

<u>Chuang Tzu</u>

Dim your light. The importance of seeming unimportant.

No man can be both admired and at peace.

Live unknown: Epicurus.

17[12]

Nimrod was a tyrant who conquered the whole earth; heaven alone defied him. Many of his subjects, including his son Abraham, still worshipped the God of Heaven & were aghast at his iniquities. He therefore decided to make war upon God & became the King of Heaven as well as of earth. He built a great tower (the Tower of Babel) from the top of which he shot an arrow at God. The arrow fell down again, dripping with blood. But Nimrod suddenly became grey & old. Too feeble to move, he lay till a host of ants devoured him.[5]

17[12]

For one thing to become as good as another is death.

17[13]

When knowledge is the recognition of something absent.

---

[5] Oakeshott's note 'See p. 44' refers to p. 434, below.

17[14]

It is said that in China those who live in the North speak a language incomprehensible to those who live in the South, and a Southerner is unable to understand a Northerner; but the inhabitants of every village which lies between the North and the South understand the speech of the villages which lie immediately to the north & the south of them.

It is the same with nearly all words: the gradual change of meaning mediates the change, but what the 16th century understood is quite different (sometimes) the opposite of what the 19th century understood.

17[14]

I had nothing to offer to her vanity.

17[15]

There is nothing intrusive in 'history'; no 'intruders.'[6]

17[15]

The experiences & the achievements of the 16th century explorers & voyagers seldom entered the poetry of the time, were seldom the theme of imaginative writers. It is only when they were receding, when they were <u>remembered</u>, that they became poetic themes. They were more important to Drayton than to Shakespeare, and more important to Milton & Donne than to Drayton. The themes of imagination — ancient Greece & Rome, Italy, English history & legend, Arcadia.

17[16]

Racine & Milton are the only poets who thoroughly followed out the humanist ideal of style & were not destroyed by it.

17[17]

<u>Courage</u>

'Moral constancy' and 'philosophy.'[7] To endure the toothache with patience — this is 'philosophy.'

The 'superior man' (Confucius); 'the Magnanimous Man' the *sapiens*/ἀπάθεια of the Stoic — the good will of Kant; the elect of the Calvinist, the importance of

---

6   This remark occurs beneath a quotation from C.S. Lewis, *English Literature in the Sixteenth Century, Excluding Drama* (Oxford: Clarendon Press, 1954), pp. 4–5.

7   Oakeshott's note: 'Donne, Sermon 75.' See *The Works of John Donne, D.D., Dean of Saint Paul's, 1621–1631. With a Memoir of His Life*, ed. H. Alford, 6 vols. (London: John W. Parker, 1839), iii.356: 'moral constancy…is somewhat above the carnal man, but yet far below the man truly Christian.'

'living alone' (Epicurus, Chuang Tzu) — to be <u>free</u> (Spinoza); 'courage' of Vauvenargues: all manners of being superior to fortune, invulnerable; of being a 'mortal god': Milton's Christ & his Satan. Unconquerable. Not by Platonic wisdom (contemplation, the *vita contemplativa*, Aristotle); and not by succeeding — by having <u>good</u> fortune; but by something else — the Platonic courage; the Hobbesian 'pride'. The hardness of it all; that is only Vauvenargues — '*coeur <u>tendre</u> et stoique*' hits the right note.

17[18]

<u>Public</u> and <u>Private</u> — two spheres of activity, each with its own character, separate; Home & the State.   <u>Society</u> on the other hand confuses them; 'Private' becomes 'public' and together they are 'social.' Public gardens.

17[18]

One of the most remarkable happenings of modern times was the way in which old soldiers, retired after a generation of war, got out their uniforms, saddled their horses and took flight into a dream world when Napoleon landed from Elba. A triumph of poetic imagination over reason and *bon sens*.
   '*Il se lève.*'

17[20]

The military-man. The relics of chivalry in professionalism. Conrad: *Mirror of the Sea*.
   The heroic age.

17[20]

People have a great passion for happiness; they seek it & consider that it is their right. This is an invasion of lower-middle class morality.

17[21]

On Living Abroad

A world of contemplative images; detached & framed by their unfamiliarity. Cp. the Romans & Greek sculpture.
   To live abroad is to live a more detached life, unless one were to try to seem to be a native.
   A sense of escape from all that is homely & habitual, from the dust of vain associations. Being born again to youth; the world as fresh as it seemed at twenty.

17[21]

The only new world is the past.

17[22]

Prejudice is knowing the answer to a question without knowing that it is an answer to a question.

Loss of prejudice is loss of answers without realizing that they were answers to questions.

17[23]

Pugnacity is an almost unimportant feature of the character of the military man; indeed, he may be almost devoid of it.

Though Nelson had his pugnacious streak, Wellington, very little.

17[23]

To have a head so full of ideas that there is no room for sense.

17[23]

The dreamers are those who let the world form itself around them, enchanted with whatever appears. They have no problems, they live in a world of happenings. Those who imagine the world different from what it is & who try to impose their imaginings upon the world as it is—these we call 'dreamers.' But they are not, they are incapable of dreaming.

17[24]

Misfortune sometimes makes us wicked; but then 'misfortune' happens only to a certain sort of man—I mean happenings which are recognized as 'misfortunes.'

17[24]

Historical explanation—the reference of the circumstantial to circumstances—a whole in which everything is contingent—even the whole. Explanation of what is recognized to be circumstantial (contingent) without recourse to the necessary.

'History' is concerned with occasions, not causes.

17[25]

What not to say:

Of a book called *A Grief Observed* in which a man recollects a deeply felt grief in tranquility & makes of it a poetic image—'it is safe to recommend this rather unusual book to anyone who has recently suffered bereavement.'[8]

17[26]

The fall of aristocracy. Dragged down by the fear of being conspicuous. The worst the lower-middle-class did for themselves was to generate in others a fear

---

8   C.S. Lewis, *A Grief Observed* (London: Faber & Faber, 1961).

of being unlike themselves—inconspicuousness on account of mediocrity.
Mediocracy. The rule of the insignificant.

17[26]

It may be hoped that God is a Neapolitan rather than a Mancunian or a Boston-
ian. But it does not follow that Naples is the better place to live: God may not be
so desirable as a neighbour.

17[26]

Every great man treats the earth as if it were the boards of a stage; but one has to
be a great man.

17[27]

Every norm is an artificial construction, an approximation to which is never
wholly desirable.
    The importance of 'norms' is not their correctness/comprehensiveness but
their integrity.

17[27]

'Nature' for practical purposes does not exist. What exists everywhere (except
for negligible parts of the world) is the world of 'objective mind.' For scientific
purposes, 'nature' (what the scientist studies) is wholly 'mind.'
    The world is a world of 'facts' not things.

17[27]

Government imposes uniformity—most profitably a negative uniformity of
abstention from certain conduct. Uniformity, as such, is ugly, boring, 'natural,' &
undesirable. Some is necessary, unavoidable; there should be as little as possible.
Uniformities which emerge (i.e. in electrical fittings or in the pitch of nuts &
bolts) are better than those which are imposed. Law (as distinct from taboo or
direction) is the least restricting & the most desirable manner of imposing uniformity.

17[28]

Artifice:

(1) Artificial flowers; statue (different material).

(2) A cathedral (nothing to correspond in 'nature').

(3) A cox's orange pippin (Same material modified).

A field of wheat.

17[28]

The aristocrat is 'detached' in a strange, often non-poetic, manner, from both 'nature' & 'other people.' He does not seem to depend.

17[28]

'Charm' & 'faith' & 'grace.'

17[29]

The 'law': —
    'Slavery, feudalism, individualism, collectivism.'

This 'idealistic' conception of legality belongs only to the politics of scepticism — the politics in which what you do is much less important than how you do it.

17[29]

To him the world was a bride, each unveiling a surprise and a delight, each a joy — a pain.

17[29]

The sweetest success cannot entirely obliterate the taste of that doubt which is inseparable from every human enterprise.

17[30]

'When you know what things are really like, you can make no poems about them.'

To know what things are really like is an accomplishment from which it is difficult to escape again into the world of possibilities.

17[30]

As 'Imperialists' the British have never been disposed to condescend to their subjects by an exercise of understanding. This is at once their modesty & their strength; it is in this that they left their subjects 'free.' It is because of this that they have been hated more than tyrants are hated.

17[31]

Poetic images — characters, situations, scenes, phrases — inhabit a common world together, the world of aesthetic creatures (images). Ulysses, Faust, Anna Karenina, Don Quixote, Cherubims, Celia, Bovary, Lord Jim; the death of Hamlet, the death of Boris, the death of Insarov; etc. etc: — are <u>comparable</u> with one another, because they inhabit a common world, in a manner in which they are <u>not</u> comparable with any real person, scene, or situation. With some poetic images it may be said that they are <u>related</u> to one another — cousins, brothers, parents. This is the <u>world</u> of art, autonomous <u>and</u> articulated.

17[32]

When, because you are a philosopher (i.e. engaged in explaining things), you find that many, perhaps most, of the activities of the human race have ceased to have relevance for you, you have yourself succumbed to irrelevance. There is no reason why you should not lose sympathy with many, perhaps most, of the activities of the human race, but you are guilty of an *ignoratio elenchi* if you think it is because you have found an explanation for them.

17[33]

The difference between moral dispositions which are part of one's *amour-propre* and those which are 'principles' or 'ideals' or are recognized as independent virtues of a certain character. Is morality entirely itself if its precepts are not part of one's *amour-propre*? The morality of 'honour,' of 'pride.'

17[33]

Fatalism can be immensely powerful, but it is something learnt, acquired; and consequently it can put to sleep, but it cannot kill, desire, the thought of the future, the pain of frustration. It is a medicine, not a food.

17[34]

For exactly 50 years (1814–1864) the British ruled in Corfu. What did they leave behind? Traces of habits (picnics), fashions (side-whiskers & top-boots), rock cakes, chutney, dignity, bookkeeping, virtue, Church bazaars, hunting, eccentricity. Some legends attached to persons whose names have become corrupted. Some traces of duty & of the military man's character. A saying or two. A modification of the landscape. Cricket (the chalked stumps against the walls of the alleys of Corfu). Was it things like these that the Romans left in Britain?

17[35]

νοσταλγία, what did it mean?

17[35]

There was a species of mischievous sprite which succeeded on the death of Pan as the representation of disorder in the world, of minor evil. They could be placated with food (a saucer of milk or a cake), but only temporarily. But they were capable of no final destructiveness.

There is a story of them in Corfu (where they are called Kallikantzaroi): during the ten days before Good Friday they are all engaged in the underworld upon the task of sawing through the giant plane-tree whose trunk upholds the world. Every year they almost succeed, but the cry 'Christ is Risen' saves us all by restoring the tree & driving the malicious spirits up into the world again for another year.

17[35]

How nearly we are all continually destroyed.
No certain salvation.

17[36]

Sea & land are different worlds which generate different sorts of inhabitants. To each belongs a life of a different intensity. They never really touch one another: the life long-shore is a mixture which deceives. It is not, therefore, surprising that anyone who, like Nelson, was at home on the sea, should not know how to behave on land.

17[37]

'The birth of the founder of our religion.' Queen's Xmas broadcast 1961.

How strangely positivistic & <u>un</u>christian an expression to come from an acknowledged 'believer': 'The Birth of God.'

17[37]

The titles of so many books give one the feeling of *déjà vu*.

17[37]

The chief interest: man, his conduct & the excuses & explanations he offers for it.

17[38–48]

The History of Creation

Before the creation of the world, God made angels: free intelligences & free wills. He made them so that he should not be alone. It is the image of a restless, discontented God. He gave the angels freedom because the praise & the companionship of slaves is not worth having.

Some of the angels rebelled; they rebelled against their subordinate status. Satan desired to be as great as God himself—to be an independent God. 'I will be like the Most High.'[9]

---

[9] Oakeshott's note: 'Isaiah 14:14.'

Satan & those whom he suborned from their obedience were cast of out of heaven by Michael & the faithful angels. He fell, 'like lightning from the heavens.'[10]

After his fall (according to the Talmudists) he had four wives: Lilith, Naamah (daughter of Lamech), Iggereth & Mahalath, & raised a brood of devils. According to some Lilith is identical with Eve.

The character of Satan is like the character of God — he desires & longs to be worshipped: this is the significance of the Temptation of Christ.

As a result of his fall, Satan was lame — like Hephaestus, Typhon, Loki, Wayland Smith, Vulcan.

Human Beings

God made man for the same reason as he had made the angels.

1a. He created man & woman.[11] They were created from dust gathered from the four corners of the world. The woman created at the same time as Adam was Lilith & was Adam's first wife. She was expelled from Eden & afterwards Eve was created. She was expelled because she became proud & vexatious to Adam.

1b. The first human creation was a man-woman — male-female.[12] They were joined, back to back at the shoulder, & were hewn apart with a hatchet.

2. God created Adam out of dust, and, after the expulsion of Lilith, Eve was created from a rib of Adam's.[13] This 'subordinate' Eve was recognized by God & by Adam as a proper mate for Adam because she was 'Bone of my bone, flesh of my flesh.'[14]

Lilith, after she was expelled from Eden, married Satan.

Eden

Two special trees: the tree of life & the tree of the knowledge of good & evil (Genesis 2:9). Adam forbidden to eat of the second.

The world & everything in it at the disposal of Adam.

The Fall

1. Disobedience.

2. Satan tempted Eve
   (a) with the promise that to eat would give eternal youth & beauty, immunity from disease, old age, and death. Vanity.

---

10   Oakeshott's note: 'Luke 10:18.'
11   Oakeshott's note: 'Genesis 1:27.'
12   Oakeshott's note: 'Genesis 1:27, v. 2.'
13   Oakeshott's note: 'Genesis 2:18.'
14   Oakeshott's note: 'Genesis 2:23.'

(b) with the promise that she & Adam would 'be like Gods.'[15] She gave Adam to eat in order that he also should be ageless.

3. The result was 'self-consciousness' — they 'knew that they were naked.'[16] The fall of man, then, follows the pattern of the fall of Satan: a desire to be God-like. Pride.

Cp. Lao Tzu: man, born innocent & obedient & recognizing his part as that of glorifying god, fell because of an immoderate desire to be 'wise,' and from a desire 'to eat.'

The burden of original sin is 'self-consciousness.' Adam & Eve were expelled from Eden, 'lest they should also eat of the tree of life.'[17]

There is a contradiction here: the story should run — they ate of the tree of knowledge & desired to be ageless by eating of the tree of life, but they were expelled from Eden before they could do so.

After the Fall

Adam & Eve wandered disconsolate over the face of the earth. There was darkness everywhere & they were in despair. But God did not abandon them; their penitence touched Him, & he sent the angel Gabriel, who said to them: God has accepted your penitence; pray to Him and after a certain time you will even be allowed to return to Paradise. The current conditions of their life were to be: —

For Eve to bear children with pain, & for both to have their desires met by the things of the earth but only by work.[18]

Each time Eve bore children she bore twins, a boy & a girl, and each of these twins were given to one another as man & wife.

Of the many children the most notable were: 1. Cain. 2. Abel, & 3. (later) Seth.

Cain & Abel

Their rivalry:

(1) Because each wanted the land of the other — Cain a cultivator & Abel a shepherd. And this dispute was not ended when the earth was divided between them, Cain having the earth & all that was stationary & Abel all that was movable.

(2) Because Cain was given Abel's twin sister for his wife & he wanted his own, better looking, twin sister. Cain's sister was Calmana & Abel's Deborah.

And Cain killed Abel because Abel had been given Cain's twin sister.

---

[15] Oakeshott's note: 'Genesis 3:5.'
[16] Oakeshott's note: 'Genesis 3:7.'
[17] Oakeshott's note: 'Genesis 3:23.'
[18] Oakeshott's note: 'Genesis 3:16–21.'

The first-born of Cain & his wife was <u>Enoch</u>. Lamech was his great, great grandson, who by his two wives (Adah & Zillah) got—Jabal & Jubal; and Tubal-Cain
& (a girl) Naamah. Later he begat Noah, who begat Shem, Ham, & Japheth.

<u>Seth</u>, the last-born of Adam & Eve, begat 'the race of prophets.' His first born
was Enos.

The progeny of Cain & Seth seem to join in Enoch who is alternatively said to
be the son of <u>Cain</u> & to have as his descendants Irad, Mehujael, Methusael &
Lamech, and the great great grandson of <u>Seth</u> & to have as his forbears Enos (the
son of Seth) & Mahaleel, & as his descendants Methuselah & Lamech (the father
of Noah).[19]

(Ham was said also to have earned Noah's displeasure by making love to his
wife when he was in the Ark.)

Nimrod & the Tower of Babel[20]

Noah cursed <u>Ham</u> because Ham had seen his nakedness when he lay drunk and
uncovered in his tent.[21] (Shem & Japheth, who went to cover their father with a
garment 'went backwards' & did not see his nakedness.[22] Noah blessed them &
their descendants.)

Shem assumed the leadership on Noah's death; he was pious & feared a
repetition of God's wrath.

But Ham, a more adventurous character, displaced Shem. Ham begat Cush,
& Cush in his old age begat Nimrod.[23] Nimrod was the spirit child of his father's
old age. Cush gave Nimrod the garment which God made for Adam when he
was expelled from Paradise. (Adam had given it to Enoch, the reputed inventor
of tailoring, Enoch gave it to Methuselah, Methuselah left it to Noah who took it
into the Ark & while it was in the Ark Ham stole it & gave it later to Cush.)
Vested in his garment Nimrod became invincible.

Nimrod rejected God & trusted to his own might, & he gained a following.
But he was uneasy because he feared that somebody, empowered by God,
would overthrow him. So he said to his followers: 'Come let us build a city & let
us settle therein, that we may not be scattered over the face of the earth & be destroyed once more by a deluge. And in the midst of our own city, let us build a
high tower, so lofty that it will overlap any flood, & so strong that it will resist
any fire. Yea, let us do further, let us prop up the heavens on all sides from the
top of the tower that it may not again fall & inundate us. Then let us climb up
into heaven, & break it up with axes, & drain its water away where it can do no
injury. Thus shall we avenge the death of our ancestors. And at the summit of

---

[19] Oakeshott's note: 'Genesis 4:18; Genesis 5.'
[20] Oakeshot's note: 'See 17[12].' See p. 424, above.
[21] Oakeshot's note: 'Genesis 9:21–2.'
[22] Oakeshot's note: 'Genesis 9:23.'
[23] Oakeshot's note: 'Genesis 10:8.'

our tower we will place the image of our God with a sword in his hand, & he shall fight for us. Thus shall we obtain a great name, and reign over the universe.'

Even if all were not inspired by so large a presumption, they fell in with the proposal of Nimrod, & saw in the tower a refuge from a future deluge. They built with passion & energy; if a man in the process fell & was killed, nobody took any notice; but if the bricks gave way there was an outcry. Some shot arrows into the sky & they came down tinged with blood & it was said: 'See, we have killed everyone in heaven.'

(There is a Chinese legend that one of their early kings thought himself so great as to make war on heaven. He shot an arrow into the sky & a drop of blood fell. The king said: 'See, I have killed God.')

At this time Abraham (son of Shem) was forty-eight & he was filled with grief at the impiety of the followers of Nimrod & prayed: 'O Lord, confound their tongues for I have seen unrighteousness in the city.'

And God commanded the seventy angels who surround his throne that they should confuse the language of the builders so that no man should understand his neighbour.

The angels did as they were commanded, & seventy languages sprang up among the subjects of Nimrod. So they separated from one another & were spread over the face of the earth. The tower itself was, in part, destroyed.

Nimrod & his followers were incensed by the preaching of Abraham and they cast him into a furnace (from which he issued unhurt). And Nimrod, in his arrogance said, 'I will go to heaven and see this God whom Abraham preaches & who protects him.'

His wise men told Nimrod that heaven is very high, so he ordered the erection of a tower. His followers laboured for three years, & every day Nimrod ascended it; but the sky seemed, from the summit, not to be appreciably closer.

One morning he found his tower collapsed. But he refused to be defeated & ordered firmer foundations to be laid & a second tower was constructed; but it, also, seemed not to carry him appreciably nearer to heaven. So he decided to get there by another means. He had a large box made & to its four corners he attached gigantic birds, Rocs. They bore him in the box high in the air, but the box was upset by the winds & Nimrod fell out on to a mountain top, without however hurting himself. He returned to the project of the tower, & God confounded his followers by a confusion of languages. A word from God overthrew the tower & Nimrod was buried in the ruins.

17[48]

Nimrod persuaded his subjects that when the tower was built he would bring down heaven to earth for them.

For this he urged them never to be idle; idleness was punishable by death — idleness in building.

The tower was a device for <u>unifying his subjects</u>.

When a Tower workman died at his work he was believed to go straight to paradise.

Everything was subordinated to the Tower; Nimrod's subjects became 'Tower builders.'

Replicas of the Tower were compulsory ornaments in every house. The 'Tower-motiv' alone appeared in the life of Babel. Postage stamps.

They spoke <u>one</u> language, & said but one thing.

Build, not for Nimrod but for the people's paradise.

Students, as the Tower grew higher, formed 'Heaven parties,' groups who would enter paradise together.

As the Tower grew higher it had to be re-enforced with <u>iron</u>.

As it grew higher, farmers sowed no more crops in expectation of paradise.

As it grew higher, Nimrod spent days at the top of it, and the workmen below began to be suspicious that Nimrod was already talking with angels & they were left out of it. He was suspected of playing them false, tricking them. And they downed tools & rushed to the summit to see if Nimrod were sneaking into heaven & leaving them behind – pretending when they reached the top to have come to praise Nimrod.

But this invasion of the summit overbalanced the Tower, which crashed to the ground.

17[48]

A confusion of tongues & a separation of the nations is connected with a presumptuous building of a tower or an attack upon heaven in the mythology of both the Greeks (Titans) & the Chaldeans & also among the Incas.

17[48]

Bridges are built where there have been fords or ferries; it is to these that the roads lead.

'Water' streets are usually those which run 'beside' water.

17[48]

I spoke to you of yourself; he spoke to you of himself; you loved him.

17[49]

The difference between the belief that 'everything is possible' – i.e., nothing fixed, irreversible, that evil can be turned into good etc; which is attributed (H. Arendt) to nihilists & totalitarian dictators (Hitler), and the belief, held by a man who feels the mystery of existence, that everything is possible, that there is nothing that may not fall in with the beautiful & harmonious & mysterious scheme of things.

Is not this belief only an extension of the belief in government as a sovereign activity?

17[49]

Courage is more nearly an hereditary virtue than any other.

17[49]

Perhaps the greatest principle in politics is that people love to be frightened.

17[50]

'The consolations of the vulgar are bitter in the royal ear.'[24]

—for the royal depend upon what they <u>are</u> & not what they have done or suffered.

This is the reason why it was thought that <u>tragedy</u> is the representation of the life of a prince, & <u>comedy</u> that of an ordinary man.[25]

17[50]

None of humanity's most vulgar ideas are left unsatisfied. We have discovered the secret of power: to generate desires & to promise to satisfy them miraculously.

17[51]

In the early design of motor cars the radiator was not 'purely functional'—i.e. size, shape, position etc were not determined purely in respect of its 'function' as a 'cooler.' Later they have become purely functional & are now hidden behind a façade.

But may they not be said to have had originally two functions?—'cooling' & 'appearance.' And may we not reduce everything to a collection of 'functions.' Not without depriving 'function' of any specific significance.

17[51]

<u>'Functional analysis'; 'Rôle'</u>

What is the 'function' of the <u>National Gallery</u>?

To exhibit, free of charge, a collection of paintings which has been purchased by public money (or bequeathed or given to 'the nation') so that all may have the opportunity of seeing them?

---

[24] See K. Blixen aka I. Dinesen, 'The Dreamers,' in *Seven Gothic Tales* (London: Putnam, 1934).

[25] Oakeshott's note: 'Butcher, *Poetics of Aristotle*, pp. 232 seq.' See S.H. Butcher, *Aristotle's Theory of Poetry And Fine Art With A Critical Text And Translation Of The Poetics*, 2nd edn (London: Macmillan and Co. Limited, 1898).

But how little this tells us of the actual place occupied in London life of the National Gallery.

Its expression of national 'pride.' It is a place where people go in winter to be warm, where Indians go to try to pick up girls, where Ban the Bombers assemble before a Trafalgar square demonstration — its actual 'function' is multifarious & is no 'function' at all.

17[54]

Compare the words 'function' and 'meaning.' If for 'meaning' we prefer 'use,' we should for the same reasons (i.e., context gives use) prefer 'use' for 'function.' Though 'use' has a 'functional' usage — e.g. 'What is the use of?'

But 'How is X used?' is not functional.

17[54]

'The function of poetry.'

Newspapers to wrap up fish and chips.

Cp. What happened in the newspaper strike in the USA.

Those most hard hit — those who used newspapers to keep warm & those who used them for training dogs for the house.

17[54–55]

Function

1. To fulfil some specific need; or related to some specific end.

The ends & needs may be variously understood; differences of scale. E.g. The 'function' of man is to glorify God (Calvin).

The life-process.

A social order.

2. To relate to a whole or system or organization. E.g. 'The function of the liver' or lungs etc.

'The function of the entrepreneur'

'The function of the Trade Unions'

But here it becomes significant only when the system is specifically defined eg. Trade Unions in England.

The 'function' of 'language' — communication? This is the defect. Poetry.

To apply the concept of 'function' indiscriminately brings things together which are unlike.

Human actions, personalities, historical events: these have no 'functions.' To 'function' is not the same thing as to 'act' or 'to happen.' A man 'acts,' it is only a 'functionaire' who 'functions.' If we attribute a 'function' to events & happenings we speak in a historicist manner.

'Functional analysis,' then, tells us something abstract about human beings, events etc. The concrete is missed. That surrender of personality which comes with the the performance of function. House of Commons, a 'function.'

3. 'Design' may or may not belong to a functional analysis. The world of 'fabrication.'

4. 'Office'; 'purpose'; means & end. 'Functional.' 'A function of.'

5. The difficulty of determining the 'end,' 'need,' 'whole.'
  E.g. Cathedrals – 'religious function,' but what?
  Sociological or religious. *Ad majorem gloriam dei*. But this passes out of the sphere of 'function.'

17[56]

Everything is to be considered in respect of its nearness to or its distance from Love. Thus blackmail is worse than murder, gluttony than drunkenness.

17[56]

Australian 'grace': For what we have received, thank God & the British Navy.

17[58]

Function

What is the 'function' of a passport? This is like asking what is the 'meaning' of a word, whereas the question, if it is to reveal anything important, should be 'what are the uses of a passport'? How is it used? What may it do? Its current character, like the current character of all such things, is a palimpsest in which it is not merely the latest writing that is significant.

1. Licence to leave the country, an act as a rule prohibited because it deprived the king of a man's military services.

2. Licence to an alien to travel in the country (now, visa).

3. Demand that the holder shall be respected when travelling abroad.

4. Voucher of respectability, demanded by the state he is visiting – precaution against crime & political conspiracy.

5. A source of revenue, like all licenses.

To think of a man as 'performing a function' is to think of an abstraction – an abstraction easily generated in urban life. There men are known only for what they do in an 'economic system' – a baker, a miner, a lorry-driver, a chemist. They are not members of a local society which knows them as 'men' – no 'baker' has a wife, as he does e.g. in a French village, who may be supremely important in the making of bread. In these circumstances, we think of people as being 'simple,' 'functional' — which in fact they are not.

Just as philosophers have long ago ceased to ask what is 'the meaning' of a word, so it is time sociologists ceased to ask what is the function of an institution.

17[59]

An 'intellectual' is a person governed by a false conception of the relation between theoretical & practical reason, between explanation & action, explaining & doing. His forte is explanation, & on the strength of this he claims to be the custodian of morality.

Further, if he is a 'scientist,' he believes he has the technical knowledge necessary for government; what he really believes is that by virtue of his technical knowledge he is necessary to his society (which is a technological society) & may therefore dictate.

17[60]

We are children of the machine. This means we have forgotten, lost almost all sense of process — at least of process which is not declared upon the surface.

A loaf of bread is something one buys; one does not think (one has no knowledge of) the earth, the seed, the corn field, the weather, the plough, the harvest, the threshing machine, the mill — almost the bakery is concealed from us. Light we get from turning down a switch — the process above all the mental process behind the switch is concealed.

Therefore we believe that all benefits can come from small efforts — the turning down of a switch — full employment, high wages, free medical service. And we believe in the man who says he can give us everything because we do not think his claims to be beyond reason & because we want what he offers more than we want anything else.

17[61]

Religion, even if it does not begin in naïve ancestor-worship, always returns to ancestor-worship. All religion is 'family' religion. Perhaps it may be said that Christianity did not establish itself as a significant religion until it became a form of ancestor-worship. God a father.

17[61]

θαρσέω the Greeks connected with breathing — breathing <u>out</u> something the Gods had breathed <u>into</u> one. <u>It</u> was a sort of <u>energy</u>.[26] It depended upon a man's spirit

---

26   Oakeshott's note: 'Cp. Homer, *Iliad*, X.482.'

θυμός, his 'breath-soul.' Similarly the Gods put 'boldness' or 'high-spirit' θαρσέω with a man's θυμός.[27]

χόλοσ—'anger.'[28]

17[62]

My physiology.[29] Every people has its 'physiology' except ourselves who have become both ignorant & rationalistic.

17[63]

Africa

The liquidation of colonial government is an incident overshadowed by a revolution with which it is not very closely connected—a revolution in which Africans have learned to <u>want</u>. What they want they are utterly unable to provide for themselves: they lack skill, habits of industry, organization and capital. That is to say, this revolution in which tribal societies, based upon subsistence farming & magic, are turned into the replica of a modern society based upon materialism & technology, is inspired from the outside. Besides farming of a primitive sort & magic the only asset the African himself has is a certain commercial experience—which he has also acquired from the outside, from Asia & the middle East.

17[64]

Democritus. The *aidos* (respect or revererence) which a man feels for himself is the root of morality.[30] Similar to the *aidos* that a man feels for the law. 'Secret shame.'

Cp. Gyges & his ring.[31]

17[64]

Morality—'honour'—*amour propre*.

---

27 Oakeshott's note: 'Cp. Homer, *Odyssey*, IX.380.'

28 Oakeshott's note: 'R.B. Onians, *The Origins Of European Thought About The Body, The Mind, The Soul, The World, Time, and Fate New Interpretations of Greek, Roman and kindred evidence also of some basic Jewish and Christian beliefs* (Cambridge: Cambridge University Press, 1951), pp. 52, 56.'

29 Oakeshott's note: 'Cp. Onions, *Origins.*'

30 Oakeshott's note: 'Diels, Fragment 264.' See Diels, *Die Fragmente der Vorsokratiker*, ii. 114. 'Feel shame before others no more than before yourself: do wrong no more if no-one is to know about it than if all men are: feel shame above all before yourself and set this up as a law in your soul so that you may do nothing unsuitable,' tr. J. Barnes, *Early Greek Philosophy* (London, Penguin, 1987), p. 278.

31 Oakeshott's note: 'Plato, *Republic*, 359d; Jaeger, *Paideia*, i.328, etc.' W.W. Jaeger, *Padeia: The Ideals of Greek Culture*, tr. H. Highet, 3 vols. (Oxford: Blackwell, 1939–45).

Honour is the life & soul of a military man.

17[64]

Law must have authority.

In a system of laws, the authority of each must be the same.

In no system of law could <u>every</u> law have moral authority, therefore <u>no</u> law has moral authority, i.e. authority based upon approval of what is commanded, i.e. desirability.

The authority of law must be independent of an approval of what it commands. The error of Liberalism is that it has no idea of legitimacy.

17[65]

The 'theory' is neither the disease, nor the prescription. But it is related to both.

17[66]

The worst crime —

For the French: *parricide de la patrie.*

For the English: treason.

17[66]

For centuries, indeed at all times in the history of Western Europe (except in the Greek polis) 'Education' has meant a release from the current vulgarities of the world. A good education & 'upbringing' was an entry into a world, not timeless, but relieved from merely current ambitions or occupations. It was a defence, a stronghold, an emancipation. To have enjoyed it was not only to be armoured, but free, invulnerable.

Now, education is merely instruction in the current vulgarities.

17[67]

'Good and ill fortune are to my mind sovereign powers. It is ignorance to deem that human knowledge can play the part of fortune; and vain is the undertaking of him who presumes to embrace cause & consequences.'[32]

In other words, every designed action has undesigned consequences, and it is these which compose the world of events.

17[67]

If 'analysis' were a process of taking to pieces it could be productive of some result — here are the components; although this is not obviously relevant to anything but a machine. But normally what is called 'analysis' is a process of taking

---

[32] Oakeshott's note: 'Montaigne, *Essais*, i.118.'

to pieces & <u>discarding</u> what does not belong to the <u>essence</u>: & this is a worthless activity, because there is no essence.

17[68]

<u>'Democratic' (modern) politics & religion</u>

'Grace is a feeling that God is inside you helping. You tell sinners that they have that feeling, & they'll soon find it—just as if you tell a man he has a pain he'll soon find one. Having told them they've got the feeling (Grace), they'll find it; and you've only got to tell them what it is saying, & they're yours, in your power & you're their "representative."'

The assumption here is that you have to do with those who feel themselves to be sinners & therefore need Grace; all <u>they</u> need to have for you to work on is a feeling of inadequacy, not a want, but a lack of something unspecified, an anxiety, a worry.

17[69]

I don't want to understand it, I only want to know how it works.

17[69]

The great defect of most politicians is that they never learned how to play a *misère* hand. They don't understand that this is one of the ways of <u>winning</u>.

17[70]

<u>Ambitions</u>

To be a wonderful old lady of ninety-five & to have been the mistress of Robert E. Lee.

17[71]

The world that the 'intellectual' has imposed upon us. A world where everything is known by its 'function'; and where 'function' is judged to be good—all else is forgotten or dismissed as of no account. All the unintended by-products are neglected—whereas, these are larger & more important than any 'function.'

A world where desire is to be fulfilled—no place for frustrated desire, no value. Indeed, 'frustration' is only frustration of supposed 'function.'

A world where every reward should be adjusted to merit; where everything is subjected to this crushing uniformity of 'function.'

17[72]

Lord Leicester, when told that the Education Act had been passed: 'The game's up.'

17[72]

Love is imagination before it is feeling.

17[72]

Rape is the typical crime of modern politics; politicians rape their victims, rulers rape their subjects; technology is the rape of the earth.

17[72]

The hold which a man may have on another man is now based upon the guilty feelings of the subordinate. The ruling class is that class of society which does not, for the moment, feel itself guilty. But to rule is to acquire guilt. The only chance of breaking the chain is the dispersal of guilt. Guilt came into Europe about 1650.

17[73]

Documenti – identity card, unemployment card, army record card, employer's certificates, insurance card, etc etc: – these compose the identity of the modern man, together with photographs & numbers etc. – these constitute his legal existence.

17[73]

How to be the enemy of superstition without being the friend of 'truth' – a problem never solved by J.S. Mill or any 'liberal.'

17[74]

The <u>moral</u> virtue which contains all others is courage. Courage is to rely solely upon onself.

17[74]

<u>Civil Association</u>

Politics is the art of living together & of being 'just' to one another – <u>not</u> of imposing a way of life, but of organizing a common life. The art of peace; the art of accommodating moralities to one another.

    Methods – various.

(1) A 'Law'

(2) An arrangement. Cp. the Key to the Holy Sepulchre in Jerusalem is kept by a Moslem – because of the disputes between Christian sects.

18[01]

I have to talk about doing & being.

We are apt to judge human endeavours in terms of 'result,' their success & failure. We think of Christabel Pankhurst in terms of the current right of women to vote & sit in Parliament. And when we do so we think of human conduct as contributing, successfully or unsuccessfully, to a stream of happenings & events in the world.

But this is only one side of the matter, & often the least interesting. A man's endeavours & conduct are also his attempts to pass his own life with some sort of satisfaction; sometimes, even, to be judged in respect of how they allow him to get through the day, as pass-times.

These endeavours are human beings <u>living</u>. Their 'products' are insignificant; to fail is as good as to succeed, sometimes better. It's not the 'promised land' that counts, it's the way there. A whole generation wandered in the wilderness; that was their <u>life</u>.

This is why 'courage' is the only moral virtue completely compatible with the circumstances of human life.

For example, we are apt to think of the contraction of civilized living which took place in the 8th century A.D. as a period of quiescence, of 'waiting.' We interpret it in terms of what it did, of the future. But it wasn't like that at all. This is simply what civilized life <u>became</u> by reason of the impact of the invaders — Goths, Avars, Norsemen, Muslims. Nobody was waiting to enter a 'promised land.' The sagas are epics of defeat.[2]

---

[1] LSE 2/1/18. Hardback book, red cover, 22 cm x 14 cm, blank. Spine: IVO LAPENNA: State and Law: Soviet and Yugoslav Theory. The book appears to have been mis-printed and the pages left blank; Oakeshott may have seen the humour in this but the volume was genuine, published by Yale University Press, 1964. Recto folios numbered 1–38, 124–46. Autograph, ink. Title page: '<u>XVIII</u> / March / 1964 / All things hang like a drop of dew / Upon a blade of grass. / Yeats / Gratitude to the Unknown Instructors / The art of being in the world. / The art of mortality.'

Other works from which Oakeshott made excerpts in this notebook but which are not mentioned in the text include: Fo. 129, S. Bligh, *The Direction of Desire: Suggestions for the Application of Psychology to Everyday Life* (London and Edinburgh: Henry Frowde, 1910); 135–6, Jean François Paul de Gondi, *Memoirs of the Cardinal de Retz, Containing all the Great Events During the Minority of Louis XIV, and Administration of Cardinal Mazarin. To Which are Added Some other Pieces Written by the Cardinal de Retz, or Explanatory to these Memoirs*, tr. P. Davall, 4 vols. (London: 1723).

[2] The last sentence has been added in a different ink.

18[02]

The Romans made the coastal strip of North Africa, from Tripoli to Tangier, a cultivated land of cities & villages & shady groves. It had peace, security, & prosperity.

But it can't last. People sometimes look for some special reason for throwing away peace & security, but often they merely get tired of it. <u>Change</u> is what people long for, not better or worse. In this they are like God.

18[02]

'Speak now, or forever hold your peace.' This is a great principle of civilized life. Where there are wrongs which can be righted only at too great a cost; there must be an Act of Oblivion. We must stay reconciled with our past, & if we can do this only by forgetting, then we should forget.

It is like the fiction that a married woman's children are all legitimate.

No government should require its subjects to approve of the manner in which its original came to power.[3]

Or a government must invent a legend about its advent which corresponds to current moral approval—like the Americans.

18[02]

Lord Harewood, editor of *Opera*, a director of Covent Garden, boss of the Edinburgh Festival: 'I'd be prepared to see more control if we get proper subsidies from the government.' The longing for the concept of lordship.

18[02]

With two people who love one another the pain & the cruelty they may cause each other grieves but does not humiliate.

18[03]

The S-type Jaguar originated as a gap-filler, in both size & price, between the Mark 10 & Mark 2 Jaguar saloon ranges. Both these cars descended from the XK120 which, 15 years ago, reshaped the concept of British sports car design & led both to the Jaguar series of saloon cars & to the present E-type. The historical perspective is important, because in design the Jaguar S owes something to every Jaguar since the XK120.

The six-cylinder 3.4 litre engine dates back directly to those days, while the alternative 3.8 litre unit is an enlarged version of the same engine. The four-speed manual gearbox has been in used in almost every Jaguar model from the XK-120 onwards. The independent rear suspension was developed for the E-

---

[3]   Oakeshott's note: '*Leviathan*, Review & Conclusion.'

type, then used on the Mark 10, while the body shape is an amalgam of Mark 2 & Mark 10.

Surprisingly enough, this mixture of Jaguars adds up in the S-type to an extremely pleasant vehicle…

The gear-box is dated.

Motor Correspondent, *The Sunday Times*

A 'constitution.'

Anyone who could write about the five futile republics of France in this manner may be said to understand them in the only way they may be understood.

18[04]

Fay ce que vouldras. This, in Rabelais, was a maxim, not an axiom. It was one of the 'admitted goods' of European civilization which had become neglected. A plea for a little more play between the working parts of a society, not a gospel of anarchy. How agreeable the world would be if there were a little more variety & a little less uniformity in the human species. And how much more agreeable if we did not find this variety frustrating, but recognized it as we recognized variety in birds & flowers.

From Rabelais, through Montaigne, to Pascal — the deepest concern was with what had been <u>neglected</u>. Their 'Rationalism' was opposed to 'dogma,' & therefore it was a sceptical rationalism.

Their arguments, of course, were all aimed to 'universalize' what they pleaded for, but this is just the nature of argument.

18[04]

<u>Irony</u>

Some writers about the past spend their efforts in getting up a demonstration against it — & call it 'history.' The one thing which there is absolutely no point in demonstrating against is the past.

18[04]

It should be 'the Curragh Incident,' not 'the Curragh Mutiny.'

18[04]

The remarkable thing about Mrs Ruth Harrison's book *Animal Machines* is that it shows us to be treating animals just about the same as we treat human beings.[4]

---

[4]   R. Harrison, *Animal Machines: The New Factory Farming Industry* (London: V. Stuart, 1964).

18[05]

All great works of art have a touch of lightness, happiness, almost inconsequence, & this saves us from being oppressed & having to turn away from
them. This is true also of great intellectual constructions, like those of Plato, or
Hegel, or Leibniz. It must not be understood as an imperfection; it is one of their
virtues.[5]

Where 'finish' appears, it should be a natural facility, a correctness which is
recognizable as a form of carelessness.

Everything is an 'idiom,' nothing an 'essence.'

18[05]

In Mexico the country people, as they go to mass, throw a kiss to the sun as they
enter the church, a relic of Aztec sun-worship.

18[05]

The daemon of Socrates, according to the *Apology*, would sometimes hold him
back, but it never urged him forward.[6]

18[05]

Making allowances. Most people, if you allow them three faults, show themselves as tolerable human beings. Why three? Because it is a magic number.

18[06]

One view: barbaric —

Art is reactionary in its essence; like alcohol, it merely tends to make people
forget their unhappiness & forget their ideals and purposes.

18[06]

'Come back to us in dreams, if you will; but not as a ghost.' Australian native to
his dead kinsman.[7]

---

5   Oakeshott's note: 'Cp. Hobbes, *Leviathan*, Ch. 43, Molesworth, p. 602.' *Leviathan* was
     published as vol. 3 of *The English Works of Thomas Hobbes of Malmesbury*, ed. W. Moles-
     worth, 11 vols. (vols. 1–6, 8, 9, London, John Bohn, 1839–41; vols. 7, 10–11, London:
     Longman, Brown, Green, and Longmans).

6   Oakeshott's note: 'Plato, *Apology*, 31.'

7   See p. 511, below.

18[06]

The trouble is that I can't bring myself to take a scientific interest in Lionel Robbins.[8]

When this is lost, all is lost.

18[06]

'Felix'; the Romans bestowed this epithet with exquisite perception. 'Fortunate,' rather than 'happy.'

18[07]

In a ritual an item or a passage does not need to be intelligible so long as it is duly performed or enacted. There is no 'plot' to which any item may be considered to be extraneous or superogatory.

18[07]

Modes of human experience.

'Knowing' — various sorts.

'Doing.'

'Contemplating.'

'Feeling.' This need not be in the service of any of the others. To feel 'right with the world' may be 'make believe,' but it is something quite different from an hypothesis about the results of action. Religion, or one aspect of it. Release.[9]

18[07]

For Aristotle clansmen are not so much men of the same blood as men of the same milk — homogalacts.[10] Blood-brotherhood & milk-brotherhood are ultimately the same.

For Aristotle the 'friendship' which distinguished the early πόλις was 'watery' — as compared with the blood & milk of the tribe.

18[07]

'Ada Spelvexit was one of those naturally stagnant souls who take infinite pleasure in what are called "movements."'[11]

---

8   Lionel Robbins (1898–1984), Professor of Economics at the London School of Economics 1929–61.

9   A question mark has been placed next to the passage on 'feeling.'

10   See Marrett, *Faith, Hope, and Charity*, p. 171.

11   The character of Ada Spelvexit appears in H.H. Munro, aka Saki, *The Unbearable Bassington* (London: John Lane The Bodley Head, 1912), Ch. VII: 'Ada Spelvexit was one of those naturally stagnant souls who take infinite pleasure in what are called "movements." "Most of the really great lessons I have learned have been taught me by the Poor," was one of her favourite statements. The one great lesson that the Poor in

18[08]

Taboo—the act generates its own 'punishment' which is a consequence of the act. 'Punishment' has nothing to do with desert, or with intention. It is like catching an infectious disease.

Law—the act is judged, & the punishment is assigned—& it does not matter if it is pre-assigned.

18[08]

'Progress' is an affection for the new. It may be connected with the mere multiplication of the human race. For this has greatly increased the variability of human 'pro-feelings,' that is, 'the new,' & thus the 'pro-feeling' for 'the new.'

18[08]

The difference between a communal & an individualistic morality:

(1) 'Conscience is self-judgment in the name of the tribe.'[12]

(2) Conscience is one's own good opinion of what one has done or intends. (Hobbes) αιδοσ.

And then (3) Hegel: conscience is the subjective recognition of *Recht*.

18[08]

The story about the ape may be told without embarrassment to each member of the party privately, but not to the whole party at once.

A. says: This 'proves' that the whole is something other than the sum of its parts.

B. says: This is 'explained' by the proposition that the whole is something other than the sum of its parts.

But:

(1) A's 'proof' is not an explanation.

(2) It 'proves' nothing.

(3) It <u>may</u> be explained by this proposition, but it is susceptible of other & less extravagant propositions. 'Is an example of.'

---

general would have liked to have taught her, that their kitchens and sickrooms were not unreservedly at her disposal as private lecture halls, she had never been able to assimilate.'

12 Oakeshott's note: 'Clifford.' See W.K. Clifford, 'On the Scientific Basis of Morals,' in *Lectures and Essays*, ed. L. Stephen and F. Pollock, 2 vols. (London: Macmillan and Co., 1879), i.116.

18[09]

'A "reasonable" character is one who has a store of stable & worthy ends, & who does not decide about any action till he has calmly ascertained whether it be ministerial or detrimental to any one of these.'[13]

Add:

(1) That 'ascertaining' this is a matter of conjecture, not proof.

(2) That having 'ascertained' that it is 'ministerial' to one of these, it also has to be decided whether the end concerned is that which is, <u>on this occasion,</u> to be preferred to any other—because this 'store of stable & worthy ends' is not necessarily, or usually, self-consistent, & action which may promote one may be detrimental to others.

In any case, this is how one <u>might</u> behave, but not how we usually behave. In most cases the answer to the sum has been ascertained long ago & is followed by custom, even habit, but not without choice.

Is it possible to <u>prove</u> the worthiness of any end? What does 'prove' mean? And if we had 'proof' what would this entail? 'Ends' could not be <u>separately proved</u> to be worthy, they may be conjectured to be worthy of pursuit on <u>this</u> occasion.

18[10]

'In the ordinary, the indifferent affairs of life we content ourselves with much less than demonstration. We content ourselves, & have to be content with the balance of <u>probabilities</u>: & then we act reasonably, because in the ordinary affairs of life no passion distorts our judgment…The balance of <u>probabilities</u>, in short, is the truth.'[14]

Not 'probabilities' (which concern frequencies in a finite series), but 'likelihoods.'

<u>Add</u>: this is true not only of the ordinary & the indifferent, but in the fundamental. Cp. Pascal's wager.

<u>Also</u>, 'passion' enters at an earlier stage & is not to be merely excluded. What determines the end in relation to which this calculation is undertaken? Passion, prejudice, custom, etc. etc.?

To the convinced Jacobite, his duty to rally to the standard raised by one of the Pretenders would be self-evident.

---

[13] Oakeshott's note: 'William James, *The Principles of Psychology*, 2 vols. (New York: Henry Holt and Company, 1890), ii.532.'

[14] Oakeshott's note: 'C.F. Keary, *The Pursuit of Reason* (Cambridge: Cambridge University Press, 1910), pp. 9–10.'

18[10]

A 'criterion' is something that 'settles' the question.

18[11]

Pragmatism — 'our beliefs are really rules for action…to develop a thought's meaning, we need only determine what conduct it is fitted to produce' etc.[15]

This neglects the distinction between practical & explanatory beliefs, and it neglects the fact that most practical beliefs are 'fitted' to produce a great variety of conduct. E.g. 'Fatalism'; 'predestination' etc.

It <u>explains</u> nothing to call it an 'atrocity,' but it displays & recommends a certain attitude towards it.

18[11]

Not enough has been said about the love of adventure. It is different from every other love. God, clearly, has a great love of adventure.

18[11]

In pragmatism theory & practice are made to coincide. It is the counterpart of the current assimilation of political & social activity.

The only writer I know who understood the virtues of pragmatism & distinguished them from its vices, is Bradley.

18[12]

Amour-cameraderie (Camille Bos).[16] This was the notion of marriage which, for a short time in England, in the Edwardian era, was the ideal of a certain sort of 'progressives' — the sort which Rebecca West so admirably depicts in *Treason*.[17] It went with early suburban life, electric light, 'progressive' education, hobbies, etc. It was admirable in its sincerity, but its correspondence with life was exiguous. Chintz. Life, in fact, is much more like Ibsen, & this was the escape from Ibsen. The remarkable fact that the relations of those who were thought of as exemplifying it — J.S. Mill, Shaw, the Webbs, etc. etc. bore next to no correspondence with it. Most of the 'Fellowships' & 'Communities' of the time which were designed to exemplify it in fact broke on it. It was unknown to Stendhal.

---

[15] W. James, *Pragmatism A New Name For Some Old Ways Of Thinking Popular Lectures On Philosophy* (London, New York, Bombay, and Calcutta: Longmans, Green, and Co., 1916), p. 46.

[16] Camille Bos (1868–1907), author of *Psychologie de la croyance* (Paris: F. Alcan, 1901), and *Pessimisme, féminisme, moralisme* (Paris: F. Alcan, 1907).

[17] R. West, *The Meaning of Treason* (New York: Viking Press, 1947).

18[12]

Tolstoy thought that no 'sincere & serious man' could possibly disagree with the proposition that sexual intercourse was giving way to a 'weakness' & should never be thought of as a pleasure. Epicurus, of course, agreed with the proposition.[18]

18[13]

Teleocratic politicians are wiley. Knowing the opposition there is among civilized people to living in a zoo (security maximum, & all found) they have invented the political counterparts of the Mappin Terraces and Whipsnade. This creates the illusion that they are not teleocrats at all, & that their 'subjects' are 'free.'

18[13]

The 'renegade priest' became an 'art type'; it then began to be copied in real life. It had the cachet of an art-type.

18[13]

The remarkable thing about the age we live in is that beliefs & opinions are <u>favourably</u> influenced by considerations based upon statistics: the more who believe the truer it seems to be.

Gresham's law has it that the dilute drives out the more concentrated, but it doesn't assert that the dilute is more valuable.

We live among people who tend to vote for the side they believe to be winning. The pollsters determine who is going up & who is going down, & the vote follows the pollster. The nemesis.

But it was long ago that Christians took it as a sign of the 'truth' of their faith that millions were converted to it. They should have seen this as a sign of usefulness, not 'truth.' And that, after all, is a recommendation for a religion.

Cp. Marxism — a farrago of nonsense said to be important because a third of the world's population believes it to be sense. But <u>what</u> a third? And do they believe it?

18[14]

'Mr Alexander Balmain Bruce Valentine, chairman of London transport, woke his two daughters to-day & told them he had received a knighthood in to-day's Birthday Honours List...

'He had been attending the international railway Congress in Dublin, & hurried back to his nine-roomed neo-georgian house...'

---

[18] Oakeshott's note: 'Tolstoy, *The Relations of the Sexes*, p. 27.' L. Tolstoy, *The Relations of the Sexes*, ed. V. Tchertkoff (London: C.W. Daniel, 1901).

How vulgar can you get? Why not remind us once again of the salary he gets, that he buys his suits at Burton & his cheese at the Co-op & that he's a scholarship-boy?

18[15]

How much of what in medieval times was believed about the world was a combination of the attribution of *auctoritas* to classical writers and the mere contingency of what they knew of classical writers — what had happened to have survived & be available.

18[15]

Evidence is what is elicited in cross-examination; other questions, other answers.

18[15]

The barrister's role — enough is enough, do not ask too many questions.

Claughton Scott cross-examining a farmer claiming damages for cattle having flattened his corn. After a number of questions designed to cast doubt on the cause of the damage: 'This was in September wasn't it?'

'Yes.'

'It was rather a wet September wasn't it?'

'Yes.'

'Rain is apt to beat down corn at that time of year, isn't it?'

'Yes, but it couldn't have shat on it.'

18[15]

I was wrong about 'fictitious persons in fictitious love'; its familiarity is not accounted for by experience. 'Falling in love' & 'passionate love' (taking the whole population of the world) are exceedingly rare experiences.

18[15]

A cure for a disease which does not exist.

18[15]

The gleam & glitter that only candle-light gives to eyes; even the dullest become stars.

18[16]

When excommunication, expulsion, or indeed any other penalty, is understood to be the decision of the 'whole community' a severity is introduced which is absent when penalties are understood to be the decisions of rulers or governments. Those who suffer these penalties have no refuge; every man's hand is assumed to be against him.

A Russian banished to Siberia by the Tzar found in Siberia a welcome; those among whom he lived, even the Governors of Provinces, did not think of themselves as having participated in the ban.

That is why, in idea at least, a King's Court is less severe than a People's Court. Where 'the People' is the prosecutor, those convicted have no refuge. There are no interstices in such a society where a man might hide.

Calvinist & Papal excommunication: the Pastor is the perpetual executor of the congregational decision; but the parish priest who does his duty in refusing 'communion' remains a friend. There is no total excommunication.

18[17]

'Insult,' 'injustice,' 'injury.'

Three attitudes to a happening (to ourselves or to another); three interpretations. We reveal ourselves in our interpretation – or, perhaps, in our <u>first</u> interpretation, because reflection may always generate an interpretation in which all three are recognized.

'Injury,' I suppose, is the least sophisticated of the three; 'insult' is aristocratic; 'injustice' is somewhere between.

18[17]

La belle laide. One of those <u>nuances</u> – so many of them – which we owe to the genius of the French. All absolutes are abstractions.

18[17]

One may renounce the world, disregard it. But if you want to fight it, do not suppose that you can be successful without cheating.

The Stoic of the 16th century was presented with the choice – retirement from the world, or reform. But he thought that he could reform the world (when he did think it) by his own <u>virtue</u>.

18[18]

In criminal investigations, what is called 'motive' is, properly speaking, 'intention'; & 'intention' is the result which it is desired to achieve. 'Motives' 'explain'; intentions indicate who done it.

18[18]

A lorry broke down on a lonely road in Abyssinia. The driver could not get it going again, & set off to walk to the nearest town to help.

The rocks were full of baboons who had climbed down to watch the driver's efforts. When he got back with a mechanic & a break-down truck, he found that the baboons had mastered the use of the spanner & were busy unscrewing the lorry, nut by nut.

Politicians; clever & willing to learn.

18[18]

A life too thickly orchestrated, in which the melody is lost in elaboration. A life like Brahms or Wagner, not like Mozart.

18[19]

A mind that deals in symbols, catchwords & large abstractions, unconfused by concrete reality.

18[19]

His only use for thought was to contrive what he had intended & to justify what he had done.

18[19]

The human race reduced to a race of ants hurrying obediently from school to work, from work to pension, so painless a living that they will not know when they are dead.

18[19]

'Higher education': its range & scope must be increased 'to meet the ever increasing need for trained minds.' Would you believe it?

18[19]

αιδοσ—the only thing a man can <u>betray</u> is himself. Sometimes it is said: 'his own conscience' — but this is merely an unfortunate way of theorizing it.

18[20]

'A "Ministry of Care" should be created: children now the concern of the Health Service, the Education Service, the Home Office should be brought within one orbit.'
 Mr Menday, Warden of a Boys Training School.

Yes; there should be somebody 'in charge' of everything & everybody. I wonder where 'parents' come in?

18[20]

'Many so-called criminal offences are nothing more than the expression of a desire to be orientated.'

This may be an explanation, but it tells us nothing about what to do with the delinquent.

18[20]

One of the remarkable things about courage is that it can be communicated so easily. One can almost procure courage from a courageous man.

18[20]

The world being what it is, we must know what to give up to it in order to keep it quiet—the sea-captain who threw his coat into the stormy sea & said, 'Take that.'

18[21]

'Non est tanti.' Ovid.[19] An emotion foreign to the young & the very old alike: the one cannot feel it, & for the other it is indiscriminate. The confidence of experience.

18[21]

The greed for the spectacular.

18[21]

People who have no selves other than those created by 'experts' who tell them what they are.

18[21]

The diagnosis of schizophrenia: always in the concepts of one or other the 'schools.' And schizophrenia is so multiple a disease that each can make a plausible diagnosis. Diagnosis & 'explanation.'

One of the interests of schizophrenia is that those who suffer from it make worlds of their own in a more obvious way than normal people. The oddity of the worlds is not, in fact, much greater than the oddity of the worlds created by other maniacs—bureaucrats, for example; though perhaps it is more individual & personal. Kafka. 'Facts' & 'fantasies.'

The schizophrenic's world remains a little less organized & a little more fragmentary, & a little more shapeless.

18[22]

I have never liked to see a man ashamed; which is odd, because I am as near as damit 'shameless' myself.[20]

---

[19]   Possibly an allusion to Ovid, *Fasti*, Bk VI, l. 701: '*ars mihi non tanti est.*'

[20]   18[22] contains an anecdote about a lie told to Louis XIV by Boileau from S. Johnson, 'Congreve': see *Lives of the Poets*, p. 188.

18[22]

Care for the hearer's pride!

18[23]

The Cromwellian parliament in which it was proposed to burn all the records in the Tower so that all memory of kings past should be effaced, & that the whole system of life should commence anew.

18[23]

'Goodness' is not an object of desire or aversion, it is not the 'aim' of endeavour, it is simply the general name for the whole class of things we approve.

And so 'truth'; 'justice'; 'liberty.'

18[24]

Politics is not determined by abstract ideas but by memories. Every nation seeks a great wrong in its past by which to govern its movements; England, perhaps alone, never found a convincing wrong large enough to move it, although serious attempts were made to write the Norman Conquest up into such a wrong. England, on the whole, has come to terms with its memories of wrongs. Not so Scotland or Ireland.

20th century England has discovered the 'guilt' which has so long eluded it — the 'empire.'

18[24]

'Freedom' for a man in prison is escape or release.

18[24]

'All land belongs to the king.'
'Lordship.'
'Nationalization.'
'Crown hold.'

18[24]

The French have acquired a strangely ambiguous character. Their tendency to mix irony with intensely felt emotions; their political stupidity.

18[25]

Once 'the king' was a *tertium quid*, the authority which stood between the noble & the common mass & the custodian of a common law. The redresser of wrongs. *Jurisdictio*: 'the crown.'

But when *rex in parliamento* became 'the crown,' its position as a *tertium quid* was compromised. And the compromise has been subsequently increased. 'Government' is now 'one.' *Gubernaculum* has swallowed up *jurisdictio.*

The rule of law = *jurisdictio.*

18[25]

'Socialism' had within it, from its emergence, a tension between a disposition to redistribute wealth & a disposition to create it more abundantly. The second is the 'Baconian' inheritance, a technological civilization, & was always joined with the notion that 'government' should manage the production of wealth — not because this would ensure its appropriate (equal?) distribution, but because 'efficiency' called for a single manager.

18[26]

Some people talk as if they thought desirable a world without nostalgia, ennui, indolence, a world of <u>normal</u> people, a world without frustrations, a world of 'virtue' without 'vice.' But this is both impossible & undesirable.

We should acknowledge our debt to the 'vicious'; they suffer, we have the benefit.

Only an <u>army</u> is better without vice because (unlike 'life') it has a 'function' to perform — victory.

18[27]

When 'politics' was regarded as the duty of those born to a certain station in society, together with a few who entered the political world by choice but who never gave it its tone, because most became recognizably honorary members of the 'political' class — in these circumstances, 'politics' was never over-valued. Few of those who engaged in it had political 'ambitions,' like the Duke of Devonshire who (although a 'political' Duke) felt that the proudest moment in his life was when his pig won first prize at Skipton Fair, their 'ambitions' lay elsewhere, if they were ambitious men.

Politics as an 'hereditary duty' carries with it a certain notion of what politics is about, & it is only absurd when it is allied with another notion of politics. Nobody would seriously mind being 'ruled' by those who knew it to be their hereditary duty to rule — but nobody would tolerate being 'managed' by such people.

And for the most part 'politics' in these circumstances was the activity of keeping the ambition of rulers in bounds.

18[28]

'I've become a production manager, not a scientist.' But there are those who tell us that this is just a 'science' of another sort.

18[28]

Political discourse. 'Mary ate her steak. "Cheese?" William suggested when she had finished. He was in no way hopeful that Mary would agree to cheese, but he was exercising a simple cunning. Strawberries & cream were what he had arranged, but offer them directly & they might be refused. Whereas, if something else been declined..."Cheese?" he suggested again. Mary shook her head. "Then strawberries," William said, "& cream." He intended the impression that the idea had come to him suddenly. "Thank you," Mary said quickly, "I should love some."'

18[29]

'There is no best MS. of Propertius.' There are a number of different MSS, each of which has its virtues — virtues of 'purity,' 'integrity' — not age. None is 'correct'; each can be made to criticize the others. Their value is their differences. If two agree, one is redundant, & we would rather have something in its place. A MS which lacks 'integrity' — i.e., which blends others, does not help. A MS which represents a certain tradition pure, is supremely valuable.[21]

What is the 'criterion': 'intrinsic probability.' You must know your author; but your author remains only imperfectly known until you have made his text.

18[29]

Politics is concerned with deliberating what shall be done, or what shall be recommended to be done.

This, beyond considerations of mere survival (which may be taken to be agreed, or probably agreed), is not a question of determining the best means of achieving an agreed end. As Adam Smith observed, civilized people do not wish merely to live, but to 'live well,' live in a certain manner.

There are, then, on every occasion many competing goods, no one of which is demonstrably, & in all circumstances, better than any possible alternative, as the end to be pursued.

How are we to deliberate? How are we to argue in support of what we reasoned?

The situation is analogous to the situation of a textual critic constructing the 'best' text out of a variety of MSS.

---

[21] The verso bears a quotation ascribed by Oakeshott to 'Housman, "Preface" to *Manilius*': 'An editor of no judgment, perpetually confronted with a couple of MSS to choose from, cannot but feel in every fibre of his being that he is a donkey between two bundles of hay. What shall he do now? Leave criticism to critics, you may say, and betake himself to any honest trade for which he is less unfit. But he prefers a more flattering solution: he confusedly imagines that if one bundle of hay is removed he will cease to be a donkey.' See A.E. Housman, 'Preface' to *M. Manilii Astronomica. Editio Minor* (Cambridge: Cambridge University Press, 1932), p. xxxi.

The 'rationalist' believes that one of their MSS is 'more correct' than others, & he may decide this upon some general principle, not concerning the contents of the MS, but concerning its provenance, its age, etc.

But this is absurdity, preposterous! As Housman says, 'the legitimate glory of a MS is not its correctness, but its integrity, & a MS which adulterates its text forfeits integrity in direct proportion as it achieves correctness.'

'Give us,' he says, 'our ingredients pure: we will mix the salad: we will not take it ready made from any other cook if we can help it.'[22]

The point is that we have got to make a decision; & the materials upon which this decision is to be made are none of them valuable in virtue of their 'correctness,' but only in virtue of their integrity, their purity.[23]

18[30]

Prud'homie

The moral characteristic of 'integrity,' 'probity.' It is a word frequently employed by the Troubadours of the 12th century & de Joinville (*Memoirs*) attributes it to his master, St Louis.[24]

It was made the focal point of the moral & the intellectual life by Charron.[25]

'True *Prud'homie*...is free, candid, manly, generous, cheerful, pleasant, self-possessed, constant, it walks with a firm tread, is bold and confident, pursuing its own path...not changing its gait & pace for wind or weather or any other circumstance.'[26]

It is this, in Charron's opinion, which makes it possible for God's grace to operate in a man, not the Augustinian 'will.'

Cp. φρόνησις. *Sagesse.* [27]
αιδοσ.
Savoir — Sophia.

It seems to be the intellectual counterpart to 'courage.'

---

[22] Oakeshott's note: 'A.E. Housman, "The Manuscripts of Propertius," *Classical Review*, 9 (1895), 19–29, at 22.'

[23] Oakeshott's note: 'A.E. Housman, *Selected Prose*, ed. J. Carter (Cambridge: Cambridge University Press), pp. 88, 94.'

[24] Oakeshott's note: 'Cp. *Roman de la Rose*.' Jean de Joinville, *The Memoirs of the Lord of Joinville*, tr. E. Wedgwood (London: John Murray, 1906).

[25] Pierre Charron (1541–1603), French theologian.

[26] Oakeshott's note: 'P. Charron, *De la sagesse, trois livres*, ed. A. Duval, 3 vols. (Paris: Chassériau: 1824), ii.78.'

[27] Oakeshott's note: 'See *Littré*, ad vol.' Possibly E. Littré, *Dictionnaire de la langue française*, 5 vols. (Paris and London: Hachette, 1863–77).

Michelet called it an *'ideal faible et negative, qui ne pas faire encore le héros et le citoyen.'* [28]

Cp. Montaigne: *L'honnête homme.*
Rabelais: & at a more formal level Fénelon. Rousseau has something of it.
Pompanozzi. [29]
Ochino. [30]
Pascal.
And, a long, long way off, Sartre.

'Honour' — de Vigny. Self-sufficient. Disinterested. Vauvenargues — 'courage.'
A rediscovery of the Democritian *aidos*. [31]
Amour propre. [32]

Cp. the current adoration of 'freedom' & 'toleration.'

18[31]

Insouciance.
Cp. the *Nonchaloir* of Charles d'Orléans — detached resignation.

The ability to console oneself for having failed is a most important part of the art of being in the world.

18[31]

Ataraxia.
The 'sceptic's' 'faith.'
The consciousness of a human certitude which is less than complete certitude; an acquiescence in unavoidable ignorance.
Its emotional ally, *Metriopatheia*: equanimity.
The Pyrrhonism of Charron: *'C'est à peu près et en quelque sense l'ateraxie des Pyrrhoniens, qu'ils appellent le souverain bien.'* [33]

18[31]

What else can move the mass in one direction? Only a single purpose.

---

[28] Oakeshott's note: 'Michelet, *Histoire de la France*, viii.422.' See J. Michelet, *Histoire de France*, 2nd edn, 17 vols. (Paris: Chamerot, 1857), viii.349.

[29] Probably Pietro Pompanozzi (1462–1525), Italian philosopher.

[30] Probably Bernadino Ochino (1487–1564), Italian Franciscan and later a Protestant convert.

[31] Oakeshott's note: 'Diels, *Fragments*, 264.' See p. 441, above.

[32] Oakeshott's note: 'Jaeger, *Paideia*, i.328; Plato, *Republic*, 359a.'

[33] Oakeshott's note: '*Sagesse*, 321.' See Charron, *De la sagesse*, ii.28 n.

18[32]

<u>Pascal & Hobbes</u>

What Pascal is concerned with is the fallibility of <u>practical argument</u> & <u>practical judgment</u>.

He was aware of geometrical argument & the possibility of <u>demonstration</u>. But he understood that its demonstrative possibility sprang from its abstraction.

What is the certainty of practical judgment? For the existence of God, immortality & the virtuous life are all matters of <u>practice</u>. The wager.

Hobbes's argument is also in the form of a <u>wager</u> — but his problem is that of a peaceful & civilized life on earth, whereas Pascal's problem is that of the ultimate destiny of human beings.

Hobbes asks, What is the bet that a man must make to live a peaceful life, & what is the degree of reasonableness in making this bet?

Pascal asks, What are the odds in favour of a virtuous life being the best?

18[32]

'Probability' = relative frequency of occurrence where occurrences are finite in number & mutually exclusive. ∴ Pascal & Hobbes are not concerned, strictly, with probability, in the actuarial sense? Or are they, & is this the defect in their thinking?

18[32]

How I wish I had now all those oddities which made up my childhood. That bound volume of the Canadian boy's magazine, for example.

18[33]

Note the change that takes place in the idea of <u>Enlightenment</u>.

The *illuminati* of the Italian Renaissance; the *éclairé* of Jansenism; the *Aufklärung* & the <u>Enlightenment</u> of the 18th century.

The half of 16th century 'science' was <u>magic</u>. 'Enlightenment' is the child of 'magic.' Faust.

Cp. *Libertins.*

Libertins spirituels.

18[33]

Revolutions design to demolish cathedrals, but like earthquakes, they are apt also to fracture the main drain.

18[33]

People whose lives are spent fruitlessly are always fascinating. Not the fruit but the flower.[34]

18[33]

The odd appearance of 'sanctity' which belongs to Russia — alike to its autocrats & its revolutionaries. Much too profound to be mistaken for sanctimoniousness. When will the Sovietologists pay attention to <u>Russia</u>. Conrad understood it better than anyone else. A sort of detestation of life on earth, a corroding simplicity. And, deepest of all, the belief that the Saviour of the world will be a Russian. Guilt for being alive. Gnosticism.

'Wherever two Russians come together, the shadow of autocracy is with them.'[35]
   Russia's gift to the world.

18[34]

'Loyal' is an innovation on 'legal.'

18[34]

To understand a people's politics is like understanding its language. Grammar, yes; & perhaps some very general principles; but the language is only intelligible in the light of its past, & often of its very remote past. For both language & politics are <u>concrete</u>, 'historic'; the so-called anomalies which logic detects are not 'anomalies' but what in fact is the case.

   Every politics & every language may be said to have 'latent' capabilities, eligibilities, & to understand it is to understand these. Intimations.

   A language <u>is</u> its vicissitudes.

18[34]

A <u>dictionary</u> is a language at <u>rest</u>.
   <u>Sentences</u>, speech, is a language <u>in motion</u>.

18[34]

Languages are <u>composite</u> only in vocabulary, not in grammar & syntax. E.g., English <u>construction</u> is Anglo-Saxon; its vocabulary is Anglo-Saxon, French, Latin, etc. etc. It is its grammar that has 'latent' possibilities.

---

34 Oakeshott's note: 'See E.E. Coxhead, *Daughters of Erin: Five Women of the Irish Renaissance* (London: Secker & Warburg, 1965).'
35 Joseph Conrad, *Under Western Eyes* (London: Methuen & Co., 1911), p. 105.

'Languages, though mixed in their dictionaries, can never be mixed in their grammar.'

Max Müller.[36]

18[35]

But for the Norman Conquest (or for some other extensive connection between Anglo-Saxon & the Romance languages) English would be very like German. The Conquest not only introduced a new language, the language of the conquerors, but it imposed modifications upon Anglo-Saxon which became a 'utility' language losing its inflections etc. A vast simplifying process.

There is a period during which a language generates new 'roots,' but this is over long before people begin by a reflective act to take notice of what is happening to their language. After this pure productive energy has subsided, the history of the language is a history of change conditioned by a settled character.

Many later enrichments of a vocabulary are really recoveries of what had fallen out of use. The language of Spenser & of Shakespeare is easier for us today than it was for the early 18th century.

A language may be said, after a time, to have become 'set on a course'; there is much that may happen to it, but its 'course' does not change.[37]

There is something which 'presides' over all subsequent changes.

18[36]

'English' was constructed out of 3 Anglo-Saxon dialects, one of which was predominant — the language of the 'Middle' of England, the place where the Northern & the Southern met.

18[36]

One piece of evidence about changes in pronunciation comes from observing the words which poets rhyme.

Pope rhymes: <u>great</u> & <u>complete</u>, <u>obey</u> & <u>tea</u>.

Dryden rhymes: <u>unbought</u> & <u>draught</u>.

Shakespeare: <u>should</u> & <u>cooled</u>.

How do we tell <u>which</u> of the words has changed? There is no <u>principle</u>, yet we are in never in doubt that it is '<u>tea</u>' and not '<u>obey</u>' which has changed; <u>draught</u> & not <u>unbought</u>.

Shakespeare: *Julius Caesar*, I.ii. <u>Rome</u> & <u>room</u>. 'Rome' has changed.

---

[36] Max Müller (1823–1900), German philologist and Orientalist.
[37] Oakeshott's note: 'R.C. Trench, *English, Past and Present. Five Lectures* (London: John W. Parker and Son, 1855), pp. 143, 156, 191, 194–5.'

18[36]

There is a craving to have a meaning <u>in</u> a word, & where a word has become inert, a meaning is given it by finding it a <u>lineage</u>, a past-relationship, by spelling it differently.[38]

18[37]

'A skilled psychiatrist, using his scientific knowledge & experience gained in his counseling room, is in a fairly good position to understand his fellow human beings. But it is possible, especially if he allows himself to be influenced by theories, that he will understand them less perfectly than a good schoolmaster, a novelist or a detective.'[39]

Why? Because the understanding of the psychiatrist is in terms of generalities, which illuminates, no doubt, human conduct in general — but not what <u>this</u> man did.

18[37]

'It's possible, but it's only an hypothesis.'[40]

Poirot speaks the language properly; others use the vulgarism 'theory' when they mean 'hypothesis.'
    But why should an hypothesis not be a 'theory'?
    It could be a theory if it had some 'generality' about it, but it would not be a theory if it were merely an hypothesis about what happened in a particular situation.
    'Biological evolution' is a long way towards being a 'theory,' though it began as an hypothesis. But the proposition: 'It was X and not Y who murdered Z,' may be an hypothesis, but gets no distance at all to being a 'theory.'

18[37]

A fit of ambulatory madness.

18[38]

This appalling <u>drive</u> to impose uniformity everywhere. Why cannot it be recognized that Spain is unique, utterly unlike any other European country? This destructive, nationalistic, *philosophe* notion that there is a perfect condition of things, & the later identification of it with something called 'democracy.'

---

38 Oakeshott's note: 'Trench, *English Past & Present*, p. 355.'
39 Oakeshott's note: 'Dr Richard Fox, in the *Lancet*.'
40 Oakeshott's note: 'Agatha Christie.'

18[38]

The current lunacy—decision theory—putting the 'facts' into a computer & accepting the result: it is only the latest idiom of the destructive pursuit of certainty.

18[38]

Living abroad; its quality as a <u>second</u> life, chosen & therefore we are apt to expect more from it. But it is an imaginary life, or the opportunity for an imaginary life. It is like <u>living</u> in the theatre; nothing is quite real. It is partly because what we see & what we hear have never been seen or heard in childhood, & therefore it is a <u>second</u> childhood.

Newness in adult life—a prize not to be missed.

18[124]

The strength that lies in an energetic 'No.'

The supreme word, 'No'; the essence of morality; the defiance of human unhappiness.

'Yes' is a crawling, corrupt symbol of dependence, of surrender. 'No' is upright, fine, dry, superb. 'Yes' is soft, dishonoured, pliable, the symbol of defeat.

All great religions are 'No' religions: Buddhism, Christianity.

18[124]

The greatest mistake that has been made in the interpretation of moral theory since the 17th century is the identification of 'self interest' with 'selfishness.' Nonsense about 'psychological hedonism'—there can be no such thing. <u>None</u> of these writers attributed 'selfishness'[41] to human beings; they all attributed 'self-interest.' This emphasis was on the <u>self</u>, in answer to the question: Who is to be satisfied in moral conduct? When 'God' was rejected, when 'humanity' was rejected, when 'the social conscience' was rejected, the answer was 'the self.' This is what Kant was saying as much as Hobbes. It is the morality of 'honour,' αιδοσ. One's own good opinion of oneself. Self-respect.

They were not talking about <u>motives</u>, what could be appealed to in order to get a response—that was quite a different discussion.[42] They were concerned with moral theory as such. And this is the direction in which the 'intuitionist' moral theory moved—or one of them. J.S. Mill writes on the assumption that the current dominant moral theory is 'intuitionist.'

---

[41] Oakeshott wrote 'egoism' above 'selfishness' and 'self-respect' in the margin.

[42] Oakeshott's note: 'Cp. *Guesses at Truth*, p. 118 ff.' A.W. Hare and J.C. Hare, *Guesses At Truth, By Two Brothers* (London: John Taylor, 1827).

Even James Mill, who was not a subtle thinker, distinguished between 'self-interest' & 'egoism.'

18[125]

What the revolutionary agitator sees, intensely, is something wrong which must be abolished. It is intensely, but dimly seen. What he does not see is the deadliness of doing, the passionate levity of action & the illusion of what will appear when the wrong has been banished. He <u>cannot</u> be justified in terms of what he <u>does</u>; he can be justified only as his particular flowering. But he can never think of it in these terms; he must have fruit, & demand to be judged by it.

18[125]

There is, perhaps, a characteristically <u>youthful</u> courage; good nerves.

18[125]

What is astonishing is that Lao Tzu & Confucius should have belonged to the same civilization; the one wholly inward & the other wholly outward.

18[125]

If the universe is explicable in terms of mathematics it does not follow that God is a mathematician.

18[126]

'Achievement' is the 'diabolical' element in human life; and the symbol of our vulgarization of human life is our near exclusive concern with achievements. Not scientific thinking, but the gifts of 'science': the motor-car, the telephone, radar, getting to the moon, breaking the sound-barrier, flying the Atlantic, generating electricity, anti-biotics, penicillin, telstar, the bomb. Baconian. Whereas the only <u>human</u> value lies in the adventure & the excitement of discovery. Not standing on the top of Everest, but getting there. Not the 'conquests' but the 'battles' not the 'victory' but the 'play.' It is our non-recognition of this, our rejection of it, which makes our civilization a non-religious civilization. At least, non-Christian; Christianity is the religion of 'non-achievement.'

The 'welfare-state.'

This has to be combined with an understanding of 'art' as non-achievement.

18[127]

Aristotle was wrong (& for a Greek characteristically wrong) when he said that the τι ἐστι of 'politics,' what it <u>is</u> and what makes it possible, is the power of speech. Polis-life is certainly impossible without 'speech,' but this is not its sufficient condition. Polis-life is not deciding what to do by deliberating about what to do, it is doing this within a tradition of beliefs about what is better &

worse, what Hegel called "an ethical world." What makes a man a *zoon politikon* is not merely *logos*, but *phronesis*; & *phronesis* is having pro- & con-feelings, having 'standards' in terms of which *boulesis*, deliberation, is carried on. *Logos* is without content; *phronesis* entails 'experience.' What makes a man *phronimos* is not merely being able to deliberate & to speak, but having something to say. What distinguishes 'men' from 'animals' is not speech but a *geistige Welt*. And this entails a past relationship. Men, & not animals, live in a world which is past, present, & future; men have a civilization to inherit, & they become <u>men</u> in so far as they possess what they have inherited, not merely in so far as they can communicate with one another in words.

18[128]

'Social enquiry' (so-called) where it is not the unacknowledged servant of despotism, is like boys taking down the numbers of railway engines as they pass. A good day's work may cover many pages.

18[128]

'*Institutions libres*' means '<u>private</u> schools.'

18[128]

The Athenian who voted for the ostracism of Aristides because he was tired of hearing him called 'the Just.'

18[128]

The 'complacency' of the perpetually self-critical is the worst.

18[130]

<u>May 1453. Byzantium; during the siege</u>.

Ships from Venice, financed by the Papacy, were expected & were known to have set sail.

A brigantine of the Venetian fleet at Byzantium was sent out to make contact with the relieving fleet; it sailed across the Marmora & out into the Aegean (3 May).

On the 23rd May it returned, having failed to make contact with the Venetian fleet, which, in fact, had been delayed.

When it had seemed that no contact would be made, the captain of the Brigantine asked his crew what they wished to do. One made said that it was foolish to return to a city that was probably already in Turkish hands. But the others silenced him. It was their duty, they said, to go back & tell the Emperor, whether it was to life or to death.

When they reached Byzantium & reported to the Emperor, he wept & thanked them for returning.

18[130]

'Until you understand an author's ignorance, presume yourself ignorant of his understanding.'[43]

18[131]

Administration under the Sung dynasty was not a utilitarian, but an aesthetic activity; it had no relationship with practical progressive results, but was the exercise of refinement in mental sensitiveness. This was true also of calligraphy.

18[132]

Human Relationships

1) Equal or unequal.

2) Directed to some external purpose, not so directed.[44]

3) Dramatic or utilitarian.

4) Moral or instrumental.

Friend.
Comrade.
Partner.
Ally.
Companion.
Accomplice.
Convive.

18[133]

Fidelity: *Mutabilitie*

It seems that the only fidelity one should expect is that things & people should remain faithful to themselves.

But this must be distinguished from remaining faithful to the first impression they gave us of themselves – & this distinction is terribly difficult to make.

For oneself, all that matters is that everything should remain faithful to the first impression it gave – or at least to the impression (perhaps a little later than the first) which it came to give, what one took for its identity.

---

[43]   S.T. Coleridge, *Biographia Literaria or Biographical Sketches of My Literary Life and Opinions*, ed. G. Watson (London: J.M. Dent & Sons Ltd, 1991), p. 134.

[44]   Oakeshott's note: 'Cp. Aristotle, *Nicomachean Ethics*, Bk I.'

This 'identity' is imagined; it is something that we <u>give</u> to things & people. And for oneself all that matters is that the world should be faithful to our imaginings. But this is impossible.

This is the root of 'nostalgia.' Persons & places are always unfaithful; and our own fidelity is the illusion that we, alone, are faithful.

In short, faithfulness is the triumph of imagination over experience. In order to live, we have to forgive the unfaithfulness of things & persons: living is forgiving unfaithfulness, & perhaps forgiving unfaithfulness is itself the only possible fidelity.

Absolute faithfulness belongs only to those persons & places we never meet again: Petrarch's Laura & Dante's Beatrice.

Fidelity is a dream; it requires not the absence of imperfection, but the absence of change. What we seek is not something that keeps up with the flow of our imaginings, but something which remains always we had imagined it, & wanting this is the evidence of our not having acquired 'the art of being in the world.'

18[134]

Fourier, & I do not know how many others, belong not to the history of political thought, but to the history of dreams. Their thoughts are endless & often banal variations on a single theme: *Schlaraffenland*.

18[134]

A fifth-rate dictatorship of political neurotics.

18[134]

University Students

½ of them do not know why they have come to a university. Of the other half, about a half know very well why they have come — it is to manage other students & to help to make them at home in a university. (These are worse than the truly lost: they are saved by the vicarious suffering of the lost.) This leaves ¼ (about) who know that they have come in order to be shown-round their human inheritance — to be students.

18[136]

'Intellectual freedom' — the big, meaningless words.

18[136]

It is beyond the power of governments to deprive us of the great things — thoughts & imaginings. Nor can they either give or assure us of them. By their nature, these cannot be the subject of rights or duties.

What we look to government to assure us of are the little things: to go where we like & when; having paid my taxes, to spend my money on what I wish.

It is when we look to government for the great things, that we deprive it of the power to give us the little things.

Hölderlin: In trying to make a State heaven we make it hell.

18[137]

How have we learned what has become characteristic of every generation for the last few centuries — to laugh at the beliefs, the habits, the customs, the dress of our fathers? And, what is more puzzling, how have we learned it so well that we can teach it so convincingly to Orientals?

18[137]

The ambivalence of modern politics

'Most of us are gathered at Congress in the faith of Democratic Socialism.

We desire a fully planned economy, greater & better social services, industrial democracy, a classless society, an educational system which eliminates the barriers of class — and all this within the framework of a free society.'

Mr Gunter, Trade Unions Congress 1965.

18[137]

The impossibility of denunciation from the lips of a man of honour. De Thou.

18[137]

'*Mon Dieu, qu'est-ce que ce monde.*'
    Cinq-Mars, *dernières paroles*.[45]

18[138]

To be a poet is to be lost in wonder.

18[138]

Of some things we love we are allowed no presentiment of love because they are there before we have imagined them: the moon, the sun. Of others we are allowed, & may have, a presentiment of love. I doubt whether such a presentiment is ever disappointed — not, at least, when it is overwhelmingly strong; the imagined, in these circumstances, defeats the fact. Although one sometimes fears that this will not be so and one is reluctant to encounter the fact. The truth is, I suppose, that love attaches itself only to creatures of the imagination, to a dream; and a presentiment of love is a distinction without a difference.

---

[45] Henri Coiffier de Ruzé, Marquis de Cinq-Mars (1620–42), was executed for plotting against Cardinal Richelieu.

But it is something which occurs: I had a presentiment of love with regard to the sea, Dublin, the forests of Schwabenland, Rome (but not Florence), Spain, Yucatan, New England, Cambridge, the Chateau de Montaigne, the Loire, the sister I never had, the circus. The condition of such a presentiment is the opportunity to imagine often & in detail, before the fact. That is why one can rarely if ever have it of books, writers, poems, pieces of music, though I suppose one might dwell in imagination on the *Magic Flute* after being familiar with *Figaro*.

18[139]

In Galicia it is believed that ghosts are the spirits of those who, in life, <u>loved</u> too well the places that they haunt.

18[139]

'The cowboy costume remains mysteriously sexy.' Yes, but how much better it was when it was <u>felt</u> but not <u>recognized</u> to be so.

18[139]

'*Hamur.*' A Viennese word, meaning 'Nerve' & something more; what?

18[140]

One sort of 'despotism' is doulocracy.

18[140]

Dogs & cats, *per se*, have no 'history.' They have a 'history' only when they are understood as human inventions (which they are), & then they belong to human history. There is no history but human history.

18[140]

There are some events, some of one's own actions, about which one feels that if one understood them the whole universe would at once become intelligible.

18[140]

The 'best' undergraduates, even the cleverest & the most serious, seem only to be concerned with learning what it will be useful for them to know.

18[141]

One is often told about the meeting of the East & the West. Sometimes it is located at Suez; sometimes it is said to be impossible.

But there are two places where there has been a genuine meeting, where East & West have coalesced to generate an alloy; Spain & Vienna. One should recognize the uniqueness of these places; they are neither European nor Oriental.

18[141]

I, who hate practically every change in the world since I was old enough to notice, consort with progressives & am unable myself to leave alone the things I am concerned with. What do you make of this paradox? Mostly I suppose it is undoing the work of progressives.[46]

18[141]

The knowledge which enables a connoisseur tasting an unseasoned wine to guess what it will be like when it has matured.

18[142]

The world belongs, has always belonged & always will belong to the powerful (*potentia*), the activists, the controllers, the doers; the real men can hope for nothing more than a place to hide.

Potentate, not a political word. Used of a man who so clearly disposes of notable *potentia* that it seems almost irrelevant to ask about his *potestas*.

What is the worst is when the powerful enter an appearance as the protectors & benefactors of the real men, and set about making their hiding places comfortable, even building special hiding places for them according to the benefactors' standards & specifications.

18[142]

The love of inanimate things whose virtue is their familiarity. They do not, cannot, last; their fragility itself makes them loved.

All this is destroyed, overwhelmed by a striving for redemption at every moment, the introduction of eternity into mortality. Let redemption come; do not seek it, forget it, it is not our business, it is God's business.

18[142]

It is surprising that humour, laughter, which is the lightest thing in the world, can also be the thickest armour; gallows humour.

18[143]

The world is not a disfigured copy of an 'ideal' world—it is what it is. It has within itself the distinctions of better & worse, beauty & ugliness, slime and clear running water, & they are not the distinctions of a closer or a less close approximation to an 'ideal.' What is, & what ought to be, both belong wholly to this world.

---

[46] The last sentence is in a different ink.

18[143]

In ancient times men and animals were not distinguished as they are now (though there are still relics of their ancient relationship).

Men recognized animals as almost their equals. Wild animals competed with men for the resources of the world, and between them there existed a strange sort of relationship — friendly & hostile, sympathy & antipathy, admiration, fear & worship.

This was all caught up in the cult of Diana or Artemis: the human amity & enormity to wild creatures. Diana was the protectoress of all new-born creatures; & it was as if men recognized themselves to be in a common predicament with the wild.

All this disappeared when animals were domesticated & became slaves. It was only domesticated animal which were 'sacrificed' as surrogates for human beings.

18[144]

The chief point of consideration is 'the experience' as it becomes known in memory — that is, when it is recollected & comes to compose an element in the identity of the experient: when it joins a *geistige welt*. Recollection.

18[144]

The moral life is <u>never</u> simple. The moral world is made up of the pro- and con-feelings of the young, the getting old & the old, & each makes its contribution to the complex manifold, which can be expressed only in a paradox e.g. Vauvenargues: *un coeur tendre et stoique*.

The contribution of the young is an acute sense of the brevity & the wonder of life — a spring, melancholy with an anticipation of winter, but no experience of it. Warmth, generosity, golden, lyric, unworldly. A generation, a moral world, without this contribution is sadly depleted — & this is our own present condition. The older are made to do the 'youngness' of the young (& they can't do it very well), for the young are born old. The metamorphosis of the generations nowhere more clearly seen than in a modern university.

18[144]

The strange passion of the current young for uniformity: to be lost in a uniformity.

18[144]

The 'generation gap' — ours is the gap between the old who are young, & the young who are already senile.

18[144]

Amenity — *amaenitas, amoenus* — the lovable, the comely, the pleasant.

(Amen: so let it be.)

18[145]

'Principles' are not <u>criteria</u>, they are formulae of protest against what is currently neglected; and as 'protests' they are apt to be exaggerated even where they do not appear as <u>criteria</u>. They indicate what should be preferred <u>now</u>, in the circumstances.

They should always be servants; when they become masters they become corrupt. To the uninitiated they become masters.

They are not axioms, but maxims. As servants they are always 'in use' & apart from 'use' they are nothing. They are not targets to be aimed at, or destinations to be sought; they are breezes to open one's sails to. As 'fruit' they are tasteless, or even poisonous. They are flowers.

Every 'principle' has its opposite, no less valuable.

The Stoic denial of patriotism & friendship is given a false absoluteness.

Blasphemy is not possible without 'faith.' If the 'libertarian' had his way he would destroy 'liberty': the young do not know how they have become impoverished by the absence of parental frustration, it's what gave them their youngness.

The only moral life we have ever known, if we would only admit it, is one in which 'principles' are continuously bouncing off one another.

18[146]

Theory & Practice

θεωρία; an 'understanding,' represented by Plato as an 'intuition.'

The translation of philosophical ideas into sentiments & then into practical conduct: this is represented, sometimes, as finding the 'moral' or sentimental '<u>equivalent</u>' of the philosophical idea. (This is quite a different notion from that of a moral entailment or implication of a philosophical idea.)

But there is no 'equivalence'; it is merely what it appears <u>would</u> correspond, if there could be any correspondence.

Cp. The use of the Stoic doctrine of the imperceptibility of pain to justify or excuse the infliction of pain, or the belief that the infliction of pain doesn't matter.

The moral or the sentimental belief <u>cannot</u> look to the philosophical idea for support, justification, or confirmation. *Ignoratio elenchi.*

A whole series of pretended 'equivalents' which are not equivalents. E.g.:

1. Aristippus of Cyrene: the philosophical theory.

2. Horace: the poetic image.

3. The devotee of 'pleasure': the practical sentiment or conduct.

Philosophy cannot be the theoretical equivalent of practice; it does not provide a 'moral <u>world</u>' (i.e., a complete conspectus) for individual beliefs & acts, it provides a theoretical explanation.

What determines conduct is 'sympathies,' pro- & con-feelings, not 'theories.' All morality is <u>specific</u>, & this cannot be <u>justified</u> by writing it up in more general & less specific terms.

The philosopher's attitude to 'practice' is, really, ironical – his 'practical' attitude. He can recognize the moral world only with a kind of irony. The cave.

Philosophers must be understood by what they <u>say</u>, not by what they do.

The judges of the Areopagus who tried their causes in the darkness of the night because they were concerned only with what was said, were guilty of an *ignoratio elenchi*. They behaved like philosophers; but as judges they were concerned with <u>persuasion</u> & thus not merely what is said.

18[A]

Universitas[47]

Middle ages – John of Salisbury speaks of a realm (*provincia*) as a *universitas* and of course his writings are famous for his so-called 'organic' analogies, e.g. *Policraticus*. And speaks almost as if a king were a 'lord' – an organizer of an estate.

A realm a *universitas* = a realm as a multitude of people joined in the pursuit of purposes which they could not achieve separately – necessity.

But the divergence & irrationality (sin) of men made a ruler necessary to achieve a *universitas*.

A ruled *universitas*.

Union of 'members' – members are members in respect of their common not individual characters cp. 'subjects.'[48]

Even the Church for which it was sometimes claimed that it was a <u>mystical body</u>, was thought of as a multitude united in a single faith.

'United,' rather than a 'one.'[49]

The reluctance to accord 'real personality' to a corporation.

---

[47] Loose sheet inserted at the rear, numbered '146d.'

[48] Oakeshott's note: 'E. Lewis, *Medieval Political Ideas*, 2 vols. (London: Routledge & Kegan Paul, 1954), p. 347 n. 18.' Lewis quotes Aquinas, *Summa contra gentes*, Bk 3 Ch. XXX: 'In human affairs there is a common good, which is the good of a city or people…There is also a human good which does not consist in the community but pertains to each individual as a self.'

[49] Oakeshott's note: 'Lewis, *Medieval Political Ideas*, pp. 228–9.'

Notebook 19 (January 1966)

Morality and Identity

A man's identity is what he understands himself to be. Morality is not obedience to rules, but a man's loyalty to his identity. All morality is 'loyalty,' 'honour,' 'pride.' A moralist's originality and distinction lies in the identity he offers to mankind. Relation of this to 'conscience.'

Identities: 'A servant of God'
'I belong to Christ'
'The member of a family'
'A man responsible for his own actions'
'A station'
'The servant of an ideal'
'A man bound to a law — of god, nature, etc.'

The 'liberal' identity: what? 'A human being.' But this is very abstract. '*Humanitas*' was something more! A past.

Name.
Race.
Family.
Society.
Colour.

A man's identity is not to be confused with his 'better self,' though the morality of the 'better self' was an attempt to formulate an identity. It is more like his

---

1   LSE 2/1/19. Soft cover, black, 17 cm x 12 cm, ruled. Recto folios numbered 1–76. Autograph, ink. Title page: 'XIX. / Jan 1966 / Much of modern European "political thought," / so-called, belongs, not to the history of / political reflection, but to the history of dreams. / It is a set of, often banal variations, on / the theme: *Schlaraffenland*. / *Et ego in Arcadia fui*. <u>Death</u>. / *Mon Dieu, qu'est-ce que ce monde* / Cinq-Mars, *dernières paroles* / *Nous n'irons plus aux bois, les lauriers sont coupés*.' [Compare p. 473; the popular title of a pair of paintings by Nicolas Poussin, (1594–1665); compare p. 474; Théodore Faullain de Banville, '*Nous n'irons plus au bois*,' in *Les stalactites* (Paris: Michel Levy frères, 1846), pp. 9–10.]
   Other works from which Oakeshott made excerpts in this notebook but which are not mentioned in the text include: Fos. 21–3, Flora Thompson, *Lark Rise* (London: Oxford University Press, 1939); *Over to Candleford* (London: Oxford University Press, 1941); *Candleford Green* (London: Oxford University Press, 1943); 33, Henry James, *The Pupil* (London: Martin Secker, 1916); 34–5, notes on anecdotes of Arthur Wellesley, first Duke of Wellington (1769–1852), from an unidentified source; 49, H. Bosco, *The Farm Théotime*, tr. M. Savill (London: Francis Aldor, 1946); 61, Kai Iskandar Kā'ūs Ibn, *A Mirror for Princes. The Qābus nāma*, tr. R. Levy (London: Cressel Press, 1951).

'more important self,' a more 'entire' self. An identity may be achieved by exclusion, denial, unsympathy: the 'identity' of puritan morality.

An 'identity' is not an individual achievement, it is the achievement of a civilization. Education = learning to participate in an identity, learning the structure & convolutions of an identity – & this is quite different from learning to play a part in a current social order.

Identity = the sympathies which determine conduct.

Part of our 'identity' is care for the identity of others, care for their pride.

Few, in these days, have a <u>simple</u> identity: mostly it is complex, made up of tensions, conflicting or partly conflicting sympathies.

To be 'immoral' is, in the first place, to commit offenses against our own affections, our own identity.

The current confusion between what is called 'image' & 'identity.' To be concerned with one's 'image' is to be concerned with a surrogate 'identity.' This is usually the case with those who have no proper sense of their own identity. 'Image' is the 'poor' man's identity.

'Image' is the figure one acts before 'others,' & mere contemporaries. It sanctions appeals to what is called 'world opinion' which = the opinion of those who have never achieved an 'identity.' A 'majority' opinion. Where a 'majority' is relevant and where it is not.

'Image' is the short cut to being 'something,' the artificial respiration given to 'nonentities' in order to make them appear to be alive.

This is a very radical doctrine. It convicts 'utilitarianism' of non-moral rationality. The utilitarian reference to the <u>consequences</u> of action is 'rational,' consequences <u>are</u> significant, but they have no <u>moral</u> significance. The consequences of actions may be used as a <u>sign</u> of the morality of actions but they do not specify it.

My station & its duties is a representation of an 'identity.'

What constitutes a 'superior' & an 'inferior' identity? A human identity must be consonant with the conditions of human life, but the 'conditions of human life' are themselves a statement of an identity.

Pascal: our 'identity' is that of a creature who does not know, & cannot know, for certain that he is merely a mortal.

19[04]

<u>Self-interest</u>

'Self-interest' is <u>not</u> a psychological, but a moral doctrine. It does not require 'egoism' or a psychological theory of 'egoism,' 'selfishness.' This is clear in Hobbes, whose moral doctrine does not depend upon a belief in psychological egoism. 'Self-interest' is an identification of morality with 'honour.' When 'honour' went out of our moral vocabulary (in the late 17th century), 'self-interest' took its place in the formula.

It has been misinterpreted in the same manner as the formula *laissez-faire* has been misinterpreted.

19[05]

<u>Loyal-legal</u>

The morality of faithfulness to an 'identity,' & the morality of obedience to a law. One's identity can be understood as that of man who comes under a law. But a 'law' cannot be <u>merely</u> obeyed.

19[06]

The effort to endow oneself, one's relations with another person, or any of one's activities, with significance, importance, e.g. the devouring passion to search for beginnings, previous encounters, earlier remote connections & relationship, to which lovers are prone. Indeed, this is one of the things which distinguishes a profound love relationship from a superficial adventure. The reconstruction of occasions when earlier meetings might have taken place, but did not. The effort to establish the relationship as not purely fortuitous, as something in which chance is modified not only by choice but by the course of events or even the necessary character of the universe. To detect a moving towards, a close passing by, common friends. To make the actual meeting and its consequences seem not fortuitous. To establish a relationship or a pre-relationship, even in terms of experiences which each had enjoyed but at different times: people, places, sights, sounds, etc.

The present is so fragile; it needs a past to make it substantial or even credible.

19[07]

The understanding of an experience which comes when one has to <u>recount</u> it for the first time.

19[07]

The things one puts out of one's mind — like sights seen in battle.

19[07]

'A seminal mind.'

A gift of seeds, however mysterious and wonderful, is less mysterious & wonderful than a gift of thoughts. A packet of seeds is a garden of petunias; a packet of thoughts, Hegel's *Phänomenologie des Geistes* — who knows the flower?

Perhaps one should settle for a packet of seeds.

19[08]

A coat of arms: A sword lying upon a heart. And the motto: *El me manda*: My heart rules my life.

19[08]

Courage. Hegel, *Philosophie des Rechts*.

19[08]

Strangely enough, I have always preferred practice to theory. But that does not mean that I prefer the executions of justice to the announcement of justice. Perhaps this means that I am, by temperament, a judge—which is a middle, between a philosopher & an executioner: not enough intellect to be a philosopher, not enough stomach to be an executioner. An <u>interested</u> spectator.

19[09]

Our concern with a philosopher, says Augustine, is not with his eloquence (his rhetoric), but with his evidence—not, that is, with what he can persuade us of, but with what he can prove.

19[09]

Mens regalis: a royal mind, a mind which is master of itself.

19[10]

The occasions of death have been fully explored, they repeat themselves *ad lib*, and they are insignificant. What matters is the circumstances of death; these change slowly & never return to what they were. One may die in a relatively old-fashioned way, or in a relatively modern way, but the difference is slight. There is always a certain range of deaths available at any time. This is sad, because one envies an impossibly old-fashioned death. Who could now say, with the same meaning, what Alcuin said: 'The time draws near when I must leave the hospice of the body, & go out into things unknown'?[2] And yet the intellectual circumstances of death change so slowly that we can still recognize this as <u>a</u> death. Every man is disposed to be a bit conservative when he comes to die; we are naturally a little less self-confident in death than in life. But, even so, innovation has not been absent.

19[10]

How brilliant some titles of books are:

---

[2]   Alcuin of York (*c*.735–804), English theologian and member of the court of Charlemagne (742–814), King of the Franks from 768, was Abbot of Tours from 796.

Cur deus homo?[3]
Sic et non.[4]
De rerum natura.[5]
Voyages.[6]

There are more, but it is a nearly lost art.

19[11–12]

Raymond Sebond, *Book of Creatures, or Natural Theology* (1484).[7]

The originality of this work lies in its attempt to <u>deduce</u> the 'truths of Christianity' from the 'facts' of the natural world, or the 'evidence' of the natural world. It is an 'ontological' argument, concerned with the necessary <u>existence</u> & nature of God and the obligations etc. of human beings to God to be <u>deduced</u> from this existence & nature; but God is deduced from 'man' (or from 'creation' or the 'natural' world).

Now, Montaigne clearly perceived the original design of the work, & his main criticism of it is directed to showing that human beings by the power of their 'natural reason' cannot acquire certain knowledge about God's existence & character. It is a 'fideist' argument.

But Montaigne was on the verge of something else which he never quite achieved; that is, an enquiry into the nature of 'religious beliefs' designed to show that they are not concerned with demonstrable 'truth' at all, but with 'pragmatic' intelligibility. Sebond's argument is, almost, *more geometrico*.

Montaigne sees that this will not do; and he almost sees that this will not do, not because deductive argument is always impossible, & that certain knowledge is always out of reach, but because it is impossible in all practical affairs. But not quite. What he can't quite get over is, as he sees it, the impossibility of practical truth if absolute 'truth' is denied: if we do not know *le vraiy* we cannot know what resembles it, *le vraysemblable*, that the 'probable' depends upon the 'absolute.' The <u>probable</u> depends on the certain, but the <u>likely</u> does not.' But he had in his hands the means for getting over this: his conception of 'human <u>judgment</u>,' i.e. 'understanding' the world without knowing its 'necessity.'

---

3   St Anselm, *'Cur deus homo?'*, in *Basic Writings*, tr. S.N. Deane, 2nd edn (Illinois: Open Court Publishing, 1962), pp. 191–302.
4   Pierre Abélard aka Peter Abailard, *Sic et non: A Critical Edition*, ed. B.B. Boyer and R. McKeon (London and Chicago: Chicago University Press, 1977 [c.1121]).
5   Lucretius, *On the Nature of Things*, tr. J.S. Watson (London: H.G. Bohn, 1851).
6   Not identified.
7   Raymundus de Sabunde aka Raymond Sebond, *Theologia naturalis: sive liber creaturarum* (Deventer: Richard Parfraet, c.1480–85), translated by M. de Montaigne as *La théologie naturelle de Raymond Sebon, docteur excellent entre les modernes, en laquelle par l'ordre de nature est demonstrée la vérité de la foy Chrestienne et Catholique* (Paris: Guillaume Chaudiere, 1569).

19[13]

Le Prudhomme. Integrity: identity: honour.

'I have kept myself intact.' Montaigne, *Apology.*[8]

To have affection, though not esteem, for himself.

'Morality' nothing to do with accomplishment—accomplishment is not within our power, we cannot control it. It has to do with 'will,' & 'all rules of duty are necessarily founded upon our will.'[9]

Impervious to the contempt of others; 'Without shame.' 'The greatest thing in the world is to know how to belong to oneself.'[10]

De la Boëtie—Montaigne called him the 'witness' of his life who, when he had gone, Montaigne might live less carelessly.[11] An alter ego.

19[14]

Individuality

The non-individual is one who does not know how to belong to himself.

The insistence on diversity, difference, variety. Montaigne.[12]

The individual *manqué*: business for business sake.[13]

Men who, being nothing, try to do something in order to convince themselves that they exist: they 'push in indiscriminately wherever there is business and involvement & are without life when they are without tumultuous agitation.'[14]

When they are not 'public.' Lord Mellifont.[15]

19[15]

Character. Montaigne on Repentance.[16]

Every man has his own 'ruling pattern,' *une forme sienne, une forme maîtresse,* which opposes itself even to 'education' and against sudden 'passions.' The impossibility of condemning or departing from my 'whole nature.' Whatever I

---

[8] Oakeshott's note: 'Montaigne, "Apology For Sebond," F. p. 428.' M. de Montaigne, *Apology for Raymond Sebond* (Indianapolis, Hackett, 2003), was included in the *Essais*, but the edition Oakeshott was using has not been traced although the 'F' may stand for 'Florio', i.e. John Florio (1553–1625), Montaigne's translator.

[9] Oakeshott's note: 'Montaigne, *Essais*, "That Intention is the Judge of our Actions"; "Of Experience," ad fin.'

[10] Oakeshott's note: 'Montaigne, *Essais*, F., 178–9.'

[11] Etienne de la Boétie (1530–63), French nobleman and judge, close friend of Montaigne.

[12] Oakeshott's note: 'Montaigne, *Essais*, F., 597–8.'

[13] Oakeshott's note: 'Montaigne, *Essais*, F., 767.'

[14] Oakeshott's note: 'Montaigne, *Essais*, F., 767.'

[15] The character of Lord Mellifont, who only exists in public, appears in Henry James's 'The Private Life.' See Henry James, *The Private Life. The Wheel of Time. Lord Beaupré. The Visits. Collaboration. Owen Wingrave* (London: Osgood and McIlvaine, 1893).

[16] Oakeshott's note: 'Montaigne, *Essais*, ii.2.'

do, 'my actions are in order & conformity with what I am & with my condition.' We are full of 'inanity and nonsense' which we cannot get rid of without getting rid of ourselves.[17]

'A pattern established within us <u>by which to test our actions</u>.'

The nature of a 'character,' as a kind of practical identity, is not its 'coherence,' but the manner in which contraries are balanced with one another. It does not follow a principle of 'non-contradiction' but of contraries assimilated to one another: it is a 'resultant,' not a 'result'; a 'resolution' of forces.

The 'character' of modern politics.

19[16]

An ironical study of the idea of irony — example of the abortive mixture of universes of discourse, in this case, rhetoric & philosophy.

19[16]

An adventure in verbiage.

19[16]

'Riding shot-gun.' The government.

19[17]

It is the reason given, & not the judgment, which reveals the thought.

(1) The London magistrate who gave as a reason for being severe to a man convicted of theft & damage to a telephone box — that the telephone might have been needed to call an ambulance in an emergency.

(2) The ex-Archbishop of Canterbury objecting to having received an invitation to join the new Playboy Club — this club is objectionable because it promoted 'luxury spending' unsuitable in 'the present economic condition of our country' which calls for 'more productive forms of national service.'

Both these 'reasons' are eccentric, but their particular form of eccentricity reveals the current moral persuasion. Both reveal how far *jurisdictio* has been superseded by a vague *salus populi*.

19[18]

A great deal of 'explanation,' literary criticism etc. is like merely comparing & relating different features of the scenery of a landscape.

---

17 Oakeshott's note: 'Montaigne, "On Vanity," *Essais*, iii.9 ad fin. Cp. F., 749, 758.'

But 'explanation' does not properly begin until the visible scenery is related to what is <u>not</u> seen — e.g. the geological structure, or the impress upon it of human artifice.

A century ago the *Landes* had no pine trees; 2000 years ago North Africa was not desert.

19[18]

The stubborn stupidity of the pseudo-intellectual.

19[19]

Two occasions lately when arguments of another sort have been substituted for 'political' arguments.

1. The opponents of the compulsory fluoridation of water have been slapped down on the ground that it has been 'proved' that the fluoridation of water is beneficial to children's teeth. What does not seem to be understood is that this is the point at which 'political' argument <u>begins</u>, not ends. Supposing the 'proof' to have been provided, or supposing that we have information which amounts to something less than proof — then, we <u>begin</u> to place the proposal alongside our other admitted goods & consider whether or not the disturbance of them is too great to allow the proposal.

2. The advocates of compulsory finger-printing think they have <u>made their case</u> if they have demonstrated that it will help the police in combating crime. It is only when we have some plausible information of this kind that we can <u>begin</u> to argue it.

Cp. Cards of Identity.

19[20]

'If we are not prepared drastically to reorganize we shall not have the modern instruments with which to carry out the policies we want.'
     Crossman.[18]

'How can we press a programme of modernization in industry if we refuse to modernize the procedures of the House of Commons?'

The difference between political institutions and factories ignored. A procedure which <u>prevents</u> something being done which someone might want to do is in place in politics & out of place in business.

---

[18] Probably Richard Howard Stafford Crossman (1907–74), Labour MP 1947–74 and editor of the *New Statesman*, 1970–2.

19[25]

The writer never lies. The art of reading is the art of detecting the truth in what he writes.

This is a hard saying. For the truth in what he writes is his self-revelation; and to seek <u>that</u> is to reject him either as an artist or as a 'scientific' writer.

19[25]

The 'abstract' & the 'concrete' universal:

The 'abstract' is a genus with different species; the 'concrete' is an individual with different potentialities. The genus must exist in one or other of its species; but the individual does not exist in this or that of its potentialities, but in all of them taken together.

Per genus et differentiam.

19[26]

The belief that most men are evil is a kind of moral fallacy; the conception of 'good' it involves is a *petitio principii*.

Our notion of 'good' must recognize the incommensurability of goodness & happiness, between a 'good' life & a life which achieves its purposes. To be successful is not the same thing as being 'good.' The life of the man & the woman in 'Freya of the Seven Isles' was frustrated in all its hopes & designs, but it could not have been nobler or better than it was.[19]

Fortuna.

19[27–29]

Tout comprendre, c'est tout pardonner.

There is a truth in this saying, but it emerges only when a great deal of confusion has been sorted out.

1. It suggests a recognition of guilt, or at least wrong (otherwise there would be nothing to forgive), & it suggests that a full understanding of the situation will generate a readiness to overlook the wrong. In short, it seems to be the recommendation of a way of getting rid of guilt or wrong, not by generosity of heart, but by intellectual perception. This, in the first place, is misleading because 'forgiveness' does not have the effect of banishing wrong (except God's forgiveness).

2. It purports to be a recommendation of what ought to be done – a maxim of conduct. And if this is so, it is clearly immoral: the suggestion that, by an

---

[19] See Joseph Conrad, 'Freya of the Seven Isles,' in *'Twixt Land and Sea* (New York: Hodder & Stoughton, 1912), pp. 179–287.

intellectual process of understanding, we should deprive ourselves of the possibility of judging conduct to be wrong.

This is the muddle. The truth is somewhat different.

It suggests that there is an intellectual situation (that of understanding) in which right & wrong, guilt & innocence, do not & cannot appear upon the scene — a point of view in relation to which 'judgment' & 'justification' are irrelevant. But it does not suggest that to take this point of view is a duty.

From what point of view do 'guilt' & 'innocence,' right & wrong, not appear upon the scene?

1. If human behavior is regarded as an ineluctable process of cause & effect. This is crude, because the categories of cause & effect are crude.

2. If, from contemplating human conduct (which as such is always judgeable) we go on to consider it in terms of necessity — that is, if we think no longer of the tune made by the notes and transfer our attention to the principles of sound. Here the possibility of moral differentiation between one action & another is negated.

In short, this is not a maxim of good conduct, it is a statement of fact — the fact that the point of view of moral differentiation is not the only point of view.

It points out <u>one</u> of the points at which practice becoming theory has nothing more to do with practice. Irony & a theory of irony. This shall go along side rhetoric & the theory of rhetoric. Comedy & the theory of comedy, etc: as examples of the real break.

'Guilt' & 'innocence,' & the obligation of interpreting human conduct in these terms — that is, the terms of approval & disapproval — disappears only when the intellectual world we have transferred ourselves into is one which has no place for approving or disapproving.

19[30]

'Honour' is the reference of conduct to the pro- and con-feelings which constitute a moral personality. Like everything else, it is social in content but individual in form. Its counterpoint is 'shame'; 'shameful' conduct is conduct which conflicts in some way with the approvals which constitute a moral personality.

This allows for the moral personality to be self-understood in varying degrees of concreteness. Mandy Rice-Davis was, perhaps, not mistaken when she asserts that she never lost her 'honour' because what she meant by her 'honour' was her sexual independence — her aversion to 'prostituting' herself.[20] And by 'prostitution' she meant offering oneself as an object of sexual gratification. It is fair to say that she asserts, also, that she has never needed to do this overtly; but that is another matter.

---

[20] Mandy Rice-Davies (b.1944), British model involved in the Profumo scandal of 1963.

19[32]

An order which produces confusion in our minds we call chaos. For example, history is a chaos if we try to understand it in terms of our moral sentiments. If we seek an overall purpose we induce chaos.

19[32]

Self-consciousness is not self-knowledge.

19[32]

Her elegance was intermittent.

19[37]

The world really is a stage, & all the men and women merely players. Only the producers of plays imagine that this World Theatre has any connection with reality.

19[38]

Politics

Augustus considered discontinuing the distribution of free grain because he believed the practice to be injurious to Italian agriculture. He did not, however, do so, & said: 'I did not carry out my purpose because I was sure that one day the practice would be restored by someone ambitious of popular favour.'[21]

19[38]

Henry Ford wanted his car to give men of small means easy access to 'God's great open spaces.' The net result, however, has been to turn 'God's great open spaces' into trivial carscapes, suburban wastes & junkyards.

19[39]

For some people 'politics' is an invitation to inventiveness, and their desire not to be out-bid by others. Their proposals have only to be unusual, drastic, & unexpected. It is not always a bid for 'power'; it is an exhibition of what they think of as 'intelligence.'

19[39]

To write a book which a soldier or an explorer might, centuries later, carry in his knapsack.

---

[21] Oaksehott's note: 'Suetonius.' See C. Suetonius Tranquillus, *The Lives of the Twelve Caesars To Which Are Added His Lives Of The Grammarians, Rhetoricians, and Poets*, tr. A. Thomson and T. Forester (London: George Bell & Sons, 1896), p. 105.

19[41]

What distinguishes war from a criminal adventure?

Duty & honour. The adversary is a comrade.

Abnegation, loyalty.

The mask of almost deliberate thoughtlessness on a soldier's face; the knowledge that he is always betrayed except by his comrades & his army.

War, properly speaking, has disappeared from the world; it went with aristocracy, dedicated to bear arms & to military honour.[22]

What people don't easily understand is that soldiers do not have enemies — only politicians have enemies. At least this was so until war was abolished in the twentieth century.

The military condition entails its own sins, but they are spiritual sins, like drunkenness; not like gluttony. A relative asceticism. Soldiers, priests.

The ruins & the graves.

Magnanimity, disinterestedness, good manners. Ascetic.

The soldier does not fight for his political masters. He obeys them, but he fights to defend his imaginary world — or sometimes, with more difficulty, to praise & honour his imaginary world.

19[42]

The military intellect: to reduce a complex situation to its simple elements & deal with it directly. Never to be distracted by going beyond the limits. Death always near.

19[42]

'The war against crime' — the expression marks the corruption which has destroyed war. One does not fight criminals; one fights moral equals.

19[42]

War is a world apart. The military condition is an autonomous condition.

19[42]

The quite extraordinary activities of people in an industrial civilization.

19[43]

In the late '30s Stephen Spender in a book called *Forward from Liberalism* argued that the Communists & Communism were the natural heirs of Liberalism.[23]

---

[22] Oakeshott's note: 'Péguy.' Possibly Charles Péguy (1873–1914), French poet and essayist, killed in the First World War.

[23] Stephen Spender, *Forward From Liberalism* (London: Victor Gollancz, 1937).

19[43]

It sometimes seems that governments are playing roulette with their subjects' money.

19[44]

'As raw material for scientific history the gospels have the gravest deficiencies. They are incomplete and, in places, inconsistent.'

This is a misconception. What makes 'material' valuable for 'history' is not its alleged truth, but its <u>integrity</u>.

19[45]

We say that 'Nature' has no concern for the individual except as the member of a species, the race. Perhaps, what we should say is that, from one point of view, we live in a world in which all individuality is episodic, evanescent, is unrecognized except as an episode in reproduction. We call the world seen from this point of view the 'natural world.' We belong to it in respect of thinking of ourselves in terms of 'human nature.'

When it is said that a man may have a 'history' as well as a 'nature' we [are] not only asserting a different point of view in respect of human beings, but in respect of everything else. It is the point of view in which <u>everything</u> has an 'individuality'; the world of proper names. The organization of this world is 'morality.'

If we think of it in this way we avoid the fatal ambiguity of the 'conquest of nature': Descartes' 'conquest' or that of Confucius.

19[46]

The story of 'Nam-Bok the unveracious' is the story of the philosopher & the Cave, on a lower level.[24]

19[46]

The drug addict—particularly the young & particularly those who are under 20 —'exposes at its most painful point not only his own personal disorder but the sickness of our society…We are confronting those whom a violent society has wounded, we are confronting our own sickness.'

But 'drugs' are not like an influenza epidemic in which a lowered vitality makes way for an infection, and if you catch the disease it has its natural course to run. Nor is there this sort of connection between 'violence' & 'drug addiction.' The

---

[24] Oakeshott's note: 'J. London, "Nam-Bok the Unveracious," in *Children of the Frost* (New York: The McMillan Co., 1902), pp. 53–80.'

reason why we are not all drug addicts is not the same sort of reason why, in an influenza epidemic, some escape infection.

19[47]

Courage. T. Traherne, *Christian Ethics*.[25]

19[48]

Of J.M.W. Turner.

'The contrast between the man and his work is awe-inspiring. He concealed within a down-at-heels little physical frame a poetic & visionary temperament unequalled in British art.'

'All his life he remained taciturn & gauche & he could never look anyone in the face while talking (his drawings of faces are uncertain).'
    Nigel Gosling

What sort of observations are these? Why should there be a connection between figure & imagination? Could he not look at a face when not talking to it?

19[48]

The 'incommensurability' 'beginnings' & 'ends.'

'Nothing great has great beginnings.'[26]

19[49]

Principles are tents in which to pass the night. Build a house of them & you will find that you have built your tomb.
    After A.J. Balfour.

19[49–50]

The materials of 'history' are the components of the world in which we at present live understood as evidence for a 'past' condition of things.
    The selection, the classification & the identification of what in our present world we should attend to in this respect is often fortuitous, often dictated by a current turn of events, normally at the mercy of our habits & traditional modes of thought & speech — arbitrary & accidental.

---

[25] Thomas Traherne, *Christian Ethics: or, Divine Morality: Opening the Way to Blessedness, by the Rules of Vertue and Reason* (London: Jonathan Edwin, 1675).

[26] Oakeshott's note: 'De Maistre, *Principe generatif*, XXIII.' See J. de Maistre, '*Essai sur le principe générateur des constitutions politiques, et des autres institutions humaines*', in *Oeuvres du comte Maistre, ancien ministre plenipotentiaire de s. m. le roi de Sardaigne prés s. m. l'empereur de Russie* (Montrouge: Jacques-Paul Migne, 1841), p. 123: '*Rien de grand n'a de grands commencemens.*'

But we know that no enquiry (if we identify 'history' as an enquiry) can get off the ground & make progress until specific notions are substituted for ordinary language. And if we are to make a beginning with this enquiry, our first move must be to divest ourselves of this 'natural' present & to think of what is before us (& therefore of what it is evidence of) in a manner, at any rate, less at the mercy of chance & current happenings.

19[50]

Love betrays itself in a suggestion of connivance, an unmistakable complicity.

19[50]

The animal quality of childhood.

19[51–52]

Tristan & Sir Gallahad were both bastards, & King Arthur escaped being one only by a subterfuge; in his case, the important thing was the royal blood of his father.

<u>Merlin</u>

In Malory, Arthur's knights are constantly recorded as giving him 'advice' — 'and every man said his advice.'[27] Merlin, also, is said to give 'advice' — e.g., on an approach to King Ban & King Bors — but his 'advice' was clearly of a different quality from that of the others.[28]

(1) Merlin knew in advance that if his 'advice' was followed, success would ensue, i.e. he had 'certain' fore-knowledge of the results of actions. Not merely astute.

(2) Merlin knew that the two yet unborn sons of Sir Pellinor would be distinguished knights.[29]

(3) He tells King Mark of Cornwall (& puts it in writing) that there would be a battle between two armed knights, at a certain place, & neither would be killed. This is called 'prophesy.'[30]

(4) Merlin knew that Guenever would not turn out well & that Launcelot would love her & she him.[31]
Nevertheless, Arthur married her at Camelot.

---

27 Oakeshott's note: 'Malory, *Morte d'Arthur*, Bk I, ch. xxi.' Sir Thomas Malory, *Le morte d'Arthur* (London: William Caxton, 1485).

28 Oakeshott's note: 'Malory, *Morte d'Arthur*, Bk I, ch. x.'

29 Oakeshott's note: 'Malory, *Morte d'Arthur*, Bk I, ch. xxiv.'

30 Oakeshott's note: 'Malory, *Morte d'Arthur*, Bk II, ch. viii.'

31 Oakeshott's note: 'Malory, *Morte d'Arthur*, Bk III, ch. i.'

(5) Merlin's foreknowledge was said to be 'by the devil's craft.' He was 'a devil's son.'[32]

(6) None of this deprived him of human weakness so far as his own affairs were concerned. 'He fell into a dotage on a damosel that King Pellinore brought to court' — Nemue. When reminded by Arthur that he had the gift of prophecy & knew he was going to the bad, he answered that he couldn't help it.

19[52]

One of Rabelais' most passionate rejections was the art of astrology, especially when used in making political decisions — the *sortes virgilianae*[33] & all the current modes of presaging the future. He was content with human uncertainty.

Merlin, Nostradamus, Ruggieri.

19[53]

Sir Tristram & La Beale Isoud easily win our admiration, but Isoud la Blanche Mains is an ill-used character, & her wedding night is a pathetic story.[34]

19[53]

The subtle difference between the relationships of Lancelot & Guenever, & Tristam & Isoud; the uncertainty of the one and the trustfulness of the other.[35]

19[54]

Sir Dinadan is an odd & attractive character. He is said to be 'the merriest knight that ever ye spake withal & the maddest talker.'[36] He is 'disillusioned' but remains very human. In some ways he is a 'loner,' but with a great sense of loyalty. He says, 'the joy of love is too short, & the sorrows thereof, & what cometh thereof, dureth over long.' And he could refuse to 'fight for a lady' with such grace that Isoud was bound to 'laugh.' He has more self-possession than the other knights — *un coeur tendre et stoique*?

---

[32] Oakeshott's note: 'Malory, *Morte d'Arthur*, Bk III, ch. xiv; Bk IV, ch. i.'

[33] A form of divination practised in medieval and early modern Europe, based on randomly opening Virgil's *Aeneid* and interpreting prophetically whichever passage struck the reader.

[34] Oakeshott's note: 'Malory, *Morte d'Arthur*, Bk VIII ch xxxvi' probably refers to the following passage: 'And so upon a time Sir Tristram agreed to wed Isoud la Blanche Mains. And at the last they were wedded, and solemnly held their marriage. And so when they were abed both Sir Tristram remembered him of his old lady La Beale Isoud. And then he took such a thought suddenly that he was all dismayed, and other cheer made he none but with clipping and kissing; as for other fleshly lusts Sir Tristram never thought nor had ado with her.'

[35] Oakeshott's note: 'Cp. Malory, *Morte d'Arthur*, Bk XI, ch. i, where Guenever becomes less shrewish.'

[36] Oakeshott's note: 'Malory, *Morte d'Arthur*, Bk X, ch. lvi.'

19[54]

The Sangreal has an element of the *cornucopia* in it. When it appeared 'the hall was filled with good odours, & every knight had such meats & drinks as he best loved in this world.'[37]

19[55]

<u>Bk XIV, ch. ii</u>

To join the Fellowship of the Round Table meant that a man lost his father, his mother, his kin, his wife & his children. It was an exclusive 'fellowship' which a man joined by choice & election. Not a 'religious' fellowship; altogether different from an 'earthly' society.

The Round Table was temporarily broken up by the quest of the Sangreal – a similarly exclusive engagement. This angered Arthur, & he was relieved when the Knights returned from the quest.[38]

<u>Bks XX–XXI</u>

How 'the flower of chivalry of all the world was destroyed & slain.'

This is unlike tragedy because the collapse is neither inherent in the situation nor is it represented as an unavoidable fate imposed from the outside. It is a nemesis set in motion by blameworthy conduct. But it is exceedingly complicated, a convergence of many different characters & responses, any of which might have been different. Who is to blame? And what vice generated it?

The envy & 'public spirit' of Agravaine & Mordred, the 'simplicity' of Arthur, the indiscretion of Lancelot & Guenever, the misfortune of the accidental death of Gareth, the implacability of Gawaine?[39]

And, finally, the 'misadventure of an adder.'[40]

19[56]

There is a fish which 'haunteth the flood of Euphrates.' It is called Ertanax, 'and his bones be of such a manner of kind that who that handleth them shall have so much will that he shall never be weary, & he shall not think on joy nor sorrow that he hath had, but only that thing that he beholdeth before him.'[41]

All too like '*La Bonheure.*'

---

[37] Oakeshott's note: 'Malory, *Morte d'Arthur*, Bk XIII, ch. vii.'
[38] Oakeshott's note: 'Malory, *Morte d'Arthur*, Bk XIII, chs iv, vii; Bk XVIII.'
[39] Oakeshott's note: 'Malory, *Morte d'Arthur*, Bk XXI, ch. ix.'
[40] Oakeshott's note: 'Malory, *Morte d'Arthur*, Bk XXI, ch. iv.'
[41] Oakeshott's note: 'Malory, *Morte d'Arthur*, Bk XVII, ch. iii.'

19[55]

'How true love is likened to summer.'[42] A strange chapter, in praise of constancy. The theme of 'mutability,' likened to 'modernity.'

19[55–56]

Arthur's first response to Mordred's assertion that Lancelot & Guinever had been taken *in flagrante* & that Lancelot had fought his way out, was one of admiration: 'Jesu mercy, he is a marvelous Knight of prowess.'[43] And as Arthur says later, a Queen can be got easily, but not a fellowship of Knights.[44]

Lancelot's subsequent conduct is impeccable. He submits to authority in everything except the condemnation of Guenever to be burnt.

19[58–59]

'All policy is but circumstantial dissembling; pretending one thing, intending another.'[45]

This is a common reputation. It may be agreed that it is exaggerated; indeed, Feltham admits that 'there is an honest policy.' But what is the truth which is here exaggerated?

'Policy' is the pursuit of ends by means other than the observance of rules. There are rules, but in 'policy' they tell us less than is usually the case.

In 'policy,' then, it is the end that is to be achieved which is important; & the pursuit of 'policy' beings when the argument about the desirability of the end has come to an affirmative end. In this argument the desirability of <u>this</u> end may have been balanced against the desirability of some <u>other</u> end; but we may take it that a conclusion has been reached that this end is, now, desirable, the cost of pursuing it (in terms of what has to be foregone) having been weighed & found not too great to be tolerated.

The chosen 'end' in 'policy' is, then, the important thing; & it is a chosen end which <u>cannot</u> be pursued merely by observing rules of conduct.

The end in 'policy' is a condition of human circumstance – that is, it concerns human conduct & not (for example) the 'earth' as such. It entails mobilizing the support of human beings & the imposition upon human beings of some pattern of conduct. It entails overcoming opposition.

'Dissembling' is, or may be, the most economical manner of overcoming opposition. Consequently, the policy <u>may</u> be pursued by dissimulation, while (for example) the administration of justice cannot be pursued in this manner.

---

42 Oakeshott's note: 'Malory, *Morte d'Arthur*, Bk XVIII, ch. xxv.'

43 Oakeshott's note: 'Malory, *Morte d'Arthur*, Bk XX, ch. vii.'

44 Oakesholtt's note: 'Malory, *Morte d'Arthur*, Bk XX, ch. ix.'

45 Oakeshott's note: 'Owen Feltham, *Resolves*, p. 42.' The edition Oakeshott was using has not been traced, but see Owen Feltham, *Resolves Divine, Morall, Politicall* (London: J.H. Parker, 1840 [*c.*1620]), 114.

In short, as Machiavelli says, where there are no rules what governs conduct is the end pursued. One cannot give a rule as a reason for pursuing an end or performing an action.

Alternatively, in the pursuit of 'policy,' words are used persuasively, because they cannot be used dialectically.

19[60]

'As policy is taken in general, we hold it but a kind of crafty wisdom, which boweth everything to self-profit. And therefore a politician is one of the worst sorts of man, to make a friend of.'[46]

The 'self-profit' is unnecessary and not even characteristic. What is necessary & characteristic is the pursuit of an end in respect of which human beings are merely valued for their usefulness to one another.

19[60]

In Rabelais, when the Franciscan monastery is invaded by marauders, the monks ring the bell & go to pray. Picrochole's army lays waste the vineyard. It was Friar John (a not very admirable, but a realistic character) who recalled the monks from their folly. Cp. Machiavelli's remark about meeting an enemy with prayer.[47]

19[62a][48]

The use of the word 'syndrome' in connection with human conduct is all part of the 'abolition of man' which has been afoot for the last four centuries; it assimilates thought to reflex movement, action to 'behaviour.'

The fantasy of some in the eighteenth century was to turn all physical movement into mental process — to make life 'rational' by turning the circulation of the blood into conduct; the outcome was to turn conduct into behaviour. Love becomes copulation. Relation becomes correlation.

The Stevens-Johnson syndrome.

The Stoics knew better than this.

19[63]

In ancient China the profession of actor was despised; the actor was a social outcast.

---

[46] Oakeshott's note: 'Feltham, *Resolves*, p. 83.' See Feltham, *Resolves*, p. 216.

[47] See François Rabelais, *The Lives, Heroic Deeds & Sayings of GARGANTUA & his Son PANTAGRUEL*, tr. Sir T. Urquhart and P. Le Motteux, 3 vols. (London: Chatto & Windus, 1921 [*c.*1532–65]), i.84–5.

[48] Oakeshott numbered two consecutive folios [62]; to distinguish them the second is referred to here as 19[62a].

This was also so for a long time in Europe. And it may be said that when actors became socially acceptable the life went out of drama.

19[64]

Both Napoleon & Frederick the Great recognized 'chance' as sovereign in human affairs. But 'chance' for them was <u>not</u> *fortuna*. It is the relative unlikelihood that the responses made by others to your actions will be the responses you hoped they might make.

19[64]

Politics the art of the possible — but is this not true of <u>all</u> practical conduct whatever? And the possible is not given; it is made.

19[64]

The common error that the steps in which we retrace where we have been before leave no footprints.

19[65]

The old-fashioned reproof to children: 'You forget yourself.' A relic of the morality of honour: a utilitarian could never forget (or remember) himself.

19[65]

The *libido dominandi*, the 'will to power.' One of the problems has always been how to extricate 'government' from this. For if to rule is merely to exercise the *libido dominandi* then rules are, *eo ipso*, wedded to evil. St Augustine solved this problem in his own way. But it is worth noticing that the person whom we are apt to call a 'born leader' is almost without any 'will to power'; & there have been some 'aristocracies' (a few) brought up to the duty of 'ruling' who, as nearly as may be, ruled without any 'will to power.' The private-enterprise, democratic politician is, almost inevitably, a slave to the *libido dominandi*.

19[66]

Most people are always wondering what other people will think, and they rule their conduct by what they guess its consequences will be.

But there are some who don't bother at all about what others think of them, & whose conduct is determined not by its likely consequences but by what they think is appropriate for them to do. They often do the first thing that comes into their heads to do; but if they are asked for a reason for not doing something they are not disposed to say more than that it is not the sort of thing they do. These are the tramps & the aristocrats: consequences are nothing to them. They are fearless, truthful & often extraordinarily foolish. And, if the truth were told, while they give to life all the savour it has, they live on the first kind of person who holds the world together.

19[67]

Some people seem never to be quite sure that they are alive unless life deals them a blow or unless they become involved in some unusual (preferably disagreeable) happening.

19[67]

The revolutionary impulse may spring from many different sources: 'revolutionaries' are less alike than we often suppose. In a weak mind it may be no more than a desire to have one's frustrations removed by magic, or even to see the world in chaos to match one's own inner chaos or to match a destructive misfortune. These, however, are more likely to welcome a revolution than to make one.

19[67]

'I set fire to the building because I wanted to be famous.'

No distinction between 'fame' and 'infamy.'

19[68]

Men without a dominant passion who set themselves moral problems all the more fascinating because they are insoluble.

19[68]

Rationalism

The project of turning the 'public schools' into special boarding schools for children from broken homes, in need of psychiatric attention, deprived children, etc. What the 'rationalist' does not understand is that this is the <u>complete destruction</u> of 'public schools'; he thinks of it as a useful adaptation.

The public schools are a product of a certain sort of culture. Their distinctive virtues spring from a certain sort of education related to the children who come to them from a certain sort of home. These are counterparts of one another: the school would not exist with, at any rate, a dominant child of this sort.

It is like supposing that if you have '<u>popular</u>' newspapers, you still have 'newspapers'; you don't, you have something <u>else</u>.

Cp. the project of admitting women to Caius.

19[69]

<u>Sicily under the Norman rule of Roger Guiscard</u>

Elsewhere in the Mediterranean the Normans were mainly destroyers. They were men of war who happened upon a Byzantine & a Saracen culture which was weak, perhaps decadent, & they destroyed it.

But in Sicily they made the first modern European state — a multiracial, polyglot state in which Greek, Saracen & Norman, Christian, Jew & Moslem each followed their own cultural traditions under a central Norman rule. 'Rule' was keeping the peace in a manifold, <u>not</u> imposing a single solidarity.

19[70–71]

<u>Individuality</u>

The 'modern' pro-feeling for individuality which flowered in the theory of the morally autonomous personality, was a confluence of many tributaries of thought & feeling & was composed of a great variety of idioms of thought & feeling. It expressed itself sometimes in the idioms of the ancient world — Stoicism, Epicureanism — & sometimes in contemporary vernacular ideas. Its vocabulary is confused. It invaded every corner of European life: the business of getting a living, religion, law, art, etc. But fundamentally it was a moral sentiment. Its earlier expressions were apt to be extreme; it first emerged as a protest — a choice, a rejection — and, until the word became corrupted, it all revolved round the notion of 'freedom.'

Its least spectacular emergence was, probably, in Italy in the late fourteenth century, for here it was preceded with many intimations. But elsewhere this pro-feeling acquired 'prophets': the greatest of whom were Rabelais, Luther, and Montaigne. It generated many different idioms of human character; part of the greatness of Rabelais is that he recognized this variety. If Pantagruel is the central character, the same pro-feeling appears, at different levels, in Friar John & Panurge. The Abbey of Thélème was perhaps, the first of the utopias of individuality.

Its reflection is, in some respects, strongest in the writers on education.

'Puritanism' & the 'Enlightenment' were both on the other side: the new superstitions.

The only <u>moral</u> utopia; the only utopia which wasn't a corporation.

Appropriately, Rabelais remained an Aristotelian.

Kant, Fichte, Hegel — 'freedom' = being in control of one's own world & destiny — choosing.

19[71]

One of the most remarkable differences between the 20th & the 15th century is that it was the <u>obscenities</u> of Rabelais which <u>protected</u> him from immediate prosecution & censorship.

19[72]

The vulgar is the opposite of the corrupt, the perverse & the uncharitable.

19[73]

(1) Minds are forms of matter. Popper: organic matter. Thought & reasoning are elaborations of sense experience.

'*Penser, c'est sentir*': Destutt de Tracy.[49]

Thought is not a response to circumstances, it is determined by circumstances.

'Behaviour.'

Religion is the product of desire—'God' is a wish-fulfilment (cp. Hobbes)—not 'thought.'

(2) In virtue of being able to 'think' men are 'free'—i.e. they can formulate their own response to circumstances. Choice. 'Will' is 'thinking'—choosing a response. *Sentir, c'est penser—un peu.*

'Conduct.'

Yes, men create their gods, but by taking 'thought.'

19[74]

The past as a succession of 'phases' was the product of geology (geognosis). And the periodization of the human past which was the work of archaeologists was in terms of the tools which human beings had used—Stone Age, Iron Age, Bronze Age: man presented as a 'tool-using' animal.

19[74]

Not to worry about death is a maxim for soldiers for whom death is one of the fulfilments. For others it is important, but it means something different. Glory.

19[75–76]

In a sacred liturgy the words & gestures are only symbols of the beatitude.

Religion <u>is</u> 'eternal life'—a note of timelessness, of the unconditioned, of the absolute which may be heard in the hubbub of the transitory & the conditional:

---

[49] See Antoine Louis Claude Destutt de Tracy, *Eléments d'idéologie: projets d'éléments d'idéologie à l'usage des écoles centrales*, 4 vols. (Paris: Levi, 1804–15), vol. 1 ch. 1, '*Qu'est-ce que penser?*'

human beings recognized as immortal souls. This appears almost unqualified in the life of a 'saint'; in others, it is a mood which may come & go. The 'saint' is a human being capable of being determined almost entirely by his character as an immortal soul. He is not concerned with a 'future' because he is not concerned with time; it is not 'the life to come,' or the 'next' world — these are analogies, approximations.

This is something very sophisticated; it is not more than intimated in the 'religious' customs, rituals, festivals etc. of the world. But these <u>are</u> 'religions' in virtue of their intimation of 'eternity,' just as heroic self-sacrifice is an intimation of eternity.

The virgin Mary, Jesus, the saints are there to collect the offerings, the prayers, the kisses & to safeguard the inaccessible solitude of God. God is not a ruler or a commander; he is remote, untouched, caring nothing for suffering, for the desires & the longings of men, for their life or death. He cares only about good & evil.

19[A]

Education — to impart the power of distinguishing within our everyday life the elements of distinction, and of living with them. An 'idealizing' power.[50]

19[A]

To translate, not into practice, but into sentiment, the abstract ideas of a metaphysics; translate them into precepts about how to feel & so to act. The sentimental equivalent of the ethical theory.

Cp. the Aristotelian mean.

Happiness; pleasure.

To transform theory into practice.

E.g. idealism & a non-valuing of materialities.

19[B]

Bourgeois. A disposition; a kind of person; a social class.[51]

The 'Mean' & the virtues of the absence of extremes — these particular virtues. A pro-feeling for a 'balance,' an equilibrium. Not distinguished by any particular amount of wealth; but, on the whole, this is a disposition absent from the very poor & perhaps from the very rich. But it is not, essentially, anything to do with wealth.

The extremes to be avoided are religious, cultural, emotional etc., not essentially economic.

A middle road. Temperate.

---

[50] On a loose sheet inserted at 19[26].
[51] On a loose sheet inserted at 19[66].

The extremes are what they are in any civilization: piety, profligacy, asceticism, lust.

Pro-feeling for maintaining his own identity. Security. Law, rules.

His defects — prone to anxiety — the world (of extremes) is hostile & is always pressing upon him. But always avoids the extremes, self-hatred, guilt, mad joy.

The puritan is <u>not</u> of this disposition.

The reason why he should <u>rule</u> in a society, & not the extremist.

The <u>value</u> of the bourgeois to the extremist: he keeps the world going, a world in which to be extremist is not absolute disaster.

The bourgeois & the bohemian — they exist in virtue of one another.
'Tame'; not 'wild'; common-sense.

They easily attract contempt — the contempt of the young, the eager, the strong, the unconditioned.

The 'self' he has to 'please,' the 'conscience' he has to follow, is not very grand, but it is not offensive or barbaric.

Irony, humour, both spring from the contact of mean & extremes.

The bourgeois does the scepticism of the world for it; its extremists the moral magnificence — faith.

20[01]

The title of a book seen in a bookshop: *Ten Fund-raising Sermons.*

20[01]

The Red Guards broke into the Peking Foreign Office, stole confidential documents and copied them into their note-books, shouting 'What's so terrific about secrets anyway?'

Kafka's 'King's messengers.'[2]

20[02]

1. When one is alone one loses one's head and ends by loving too much.

2. Great separations defeat fidelity.

The first is the condition of the religious man; the second is that of one who feels he 'has to live.'

What happens, happens. Who is to say what <u>should</u> happen in such an encounter between mortality and immortality?

---

[1]   LSE 2/1/20. Soft cover, light brown canvas over card, 23 cm x 13 cm, ruled. Recto folios numbered 1–139. Autograph, ink. Title page: 'XX. / April 1967 / *Que vivre est difficile, o mon coeur fatigué* / Amiel / *Dieu, que le son du cor est triste au fond du bois.* Vigny / In the 14th century the hunting horn had but one / note / No, not Jack Buchanan; Fred Astaire.'

   Other works from which Oakeshott made excerpts in this notebook but which are not mentioned in the text include: Fo. 5, G.R. Gleig, *The Subaltern* (Edinburgh: William Blackwood; London: T. Cadell, 1825); 9, Lady Gwendolen Cecil, *Life of Robert, Marquis of Salisbury*, 4 vols. (London: Hodder and Stoughton, 1921–32); 34–5, L. Tolstoy, 'The Wood-Felling A Junker's Tale,' in *Sevastopol and Other Military Tales*, tr. L. Maude and A. Maude (New York: Funk & Wagnalls Company, 1903), 154–205, 36, L. Tolstoy, *The Cossacks*; 58, H. Fielding, *Don Quixote in England. A Comedy* (London: George Faulkner, 1734); 67, Thomas Love Peacock, *Crochet Castle* (London, Paris, New York, and Melbourne: Cassell & Company Limited, 1887); 88, Freya Stark, *Traveller's Prelude: An Autobiography*, 3 vols. (London: John Murray, 1950–3); 94, Vauvenargues, *Pensées*; 95, E.S. Kuznetsov, *Prison Diaries*, tr. H. Spier (London: Vallentine, Mitchell, 1975).

[2]   Possibly an allusion to Franz Kafka, *The Blue Octavo Notebooks*, ed. M. Brod, tr. E. Kaier and E. Wilkins (Cambridge, MA: Exact Change, 1991 [1954]), Notebook 3, 2 December 1917: 'They were given the choice of becoming kings or the kings' messengers. As is the way with children, they all wanted to be messengers. That is why there are only messengers, racing through the world and, since there are no kings, calling out to each other the messages that have now become meaningless.'

20[02]

'Men' and 'women' are not different sorts of beings; 'masculine' and 'feminine' are tendencies or dispositions common to both 'men' and 'women.'

20[02]

ἐφ᾽ ὅσον ἐνδέχεται ἀθανατίζειν.

So far as is possible, live as an immortal. Not 'as if there were another life.' Not a wager, not a prognostication, and certainly not a prediction.

20[02]

Identity: As children we used to write elaborate names and addresses into our school books: X–, Y–, the room, the house, the street, the town, the country – & then, Europe, the Western Hemisphere, the World, the Universe. Oddly enough, none of them human relationships. Not, mother, father, grandfather etc: up to Adam & then to God. Space, not time.

20[03]

A peasant saying his *Ave Maria* and *Requiem aeternam* aloud to himself at the door of his hut, turning towards the moon hanging low over the trees of his hut.
    Leopardi.

20[03]

Generals who are said to have chained *Fortuna* to the wheels of their chariots.
    Virtus.

20[03]

Religion is the way-side Calvary, decorated with a twist of wheat and a sprig of flowers. This is the religion of the civilized; in earlier times it was appropriately more violent.

20[03]

The doctrine of the Trinity is a wonderful baroque or even rococo construction. The most impressive image of it is in the Graben in Wien.[3]
    But consider Burkitt on the Athanasian creed.[4] Theory & practice.

20[03]

'Dumb animals': not incapable of uttering a sound (as some are, or nearly so) but incapable of speech. The mute swan.

---

[3]   i.e. the sculpture known as the Trinity column or the plague column in Vienna.
[4]   F.C. Burkitt, *Some Thoughts on the Athanasian Creed* (London: S.P.C.K., 1916).

20[03]

The Sexual Offences Bill (No. 2) 1967.

Mr Abse (Labour), its initiator, said that 'the Bill was socially useful & would help a group that had for long been alienated to become integrated in the community.'

20[03]

The Pleades was shining brightly in the west & it was very cold.

20[04]

Medicine is concerned with alleviation or cure; diagnosis is 'understanding' in relation to cure or alleviation.

The so-called 'principle' of modern medicine — 'the physical causation of all phenomena material and mental' — is neither a principle, nor an hypothesis: it is merely a method of diagnosis and treatment.

It is therefore an intellectual muddle to speak of certain kinds of 'mental deficiency' as 'traceable to the lack of a specific enzyme,' or to speak of the 'biochemical basis' of schizophrenia. To ascertain that to correct a chemical deficiency will remove, or suppress, the symptoms is to ascertain this, and nothing more than this. It says nothing whatever about the cause of the condition. And if something which could be represented as the 'cause' were discovered, it would not follow that we had at our disposal superior methods of cure.

Medical practice is not at all concerned with the 'nature' of disease: it is concerned solely with the relief of symptoms. To the patient it is only 'symptoms' which matter. Indeed, there is nothing of which a 'symptom' can be said to be a sign or an 'effect.'

Drugs in so-called psychiatric treatment: it is said 'the drugs are not curing the disease but only suppressing the symptoms.' But what is wrong with this? It is no argument against a treatment that it only relieves the symptoms. If a man of 40 is relieved of this distress (the symptoms) for the rest of his life, what more can he ask? There are, of course, symptoms of symptoms.

There is, in short, no such thing as 'mental disease.' There is, on the one side, 'physical disease,' for which cure may perhaps be found (i.e., means of suppressing the symptoms); and on the other side, there are mental conditions which are not susceptible of therapeutic treatment because they are understood to be conditions, not of 'the mind' (there is no such thing), but of thought. These are failures in self-understanding for which 'education,' not 'therapy,' is appropriate.

Do people who prescribe group therapy & what-not imagine that they are doing something for their patients' immortal soul?

20[05]

The old relationship (it is gone now) between a soldier & the commander of the army was a strange personal loyalty, trust often mixed with admiration. As a boy I worked on a farm and my companion in the fields was a man named Ted Blaber who had fought in the Boer War, twenty years before. But this was not how he thought of it; what he said was that he had been in 'General Buller's army.' And I don't believe he had ever seen General Buller. He was proud of having 'been with General Buller.'

20[06]

The insatiable curiosity, the passion to know all about the world, to explore it in haste, which belongs to some children; sometimes it is a sign that they are not destined to live long.

20[06]

The difference between the kind of 'organic' fidelity of which some animals are capable, & human friendship.

20[06]

Sometimes love is the gift of an impetus towards fantasy.

20[07]

To lose somebody one loves is to be deprived of the opportunity to express a tenderness.

20[07]

Any activity has a certain semblance of integrity when it is engaged in, not for profit, nor for any practical purpose, but for the glory of doing it, as play.

20[08]

The New Atlantis

'Professor Sir Gordon Sutherland, Master of Emmanuel College, addressing the meeting of Pugwash in Sweden, Sept 1967, on the "brain drain." He suggested fuller immigration statistics & intensified training by "importing" countries (especially the USA) to produce a surplus of scientists & technologists for export. He also wanted the highly developed countries to introduce legislation which would ensure that the less developed countries could not lose more than 5 to 10 percent of their annual output of scientists and engineers. In the case of the underdeveloped countries, he wanted legislation by the hosts to compel the return home of those sent by their governments to study abroad.'

Sunday Times, 10 September.

The reduction of human beings to the status of battery-hens proceeds apace. And we actually have the gall to criticize the 'inhumanity' of the Bourbon auto-cracies. This is a million times more inhumane that a life-time in prison in 18th century Naples.

20[09]

Lytton Strachey confessed that he would willingly surrender all his literary talent & success for the gift of physical beauty.

20[09]

I have wasted a lot of time living.

20[10]

Every man needs a country besides his own, a chosen as well as a native land. It is the opportunity of knowing better all that one may have learned at home by hearing it in another idiom. The difficulty is that it must be chosen when one is comparatively young, & thus, like all adventures in love, it is very much a union of chance and choice. But it is not a choice to be dissipated, &, in most cases, there are clearly eligible partners and & less eligible.

It is different from choosing a wife; for one thing one cannot be refused. I made the mistake of never making a choice, one choice; & consequently, I have never managed a deep, dramatic relationship of this sort. I have frittered away my affections; France, Germany, Austria, Italy, Ireland. If I had known then what I know now, I should have chosen Spain.

20[11]

'Physical' courage, nerve, respect for tradition & contempt for convention, a proud sense of personal honour, an indifference to death: an aristocrat.

20[11]

These young Americans: they are third generation Lt. Pinkertons having their identity crises & convinced that they are interesting.[5]

20[11]

'No man's dignity can be asserted without being impaired':[6] & this goes, also, for the 'dignity of man' — 'human dignity,' so-called.

---

[5] The character of Lieutenant Pinkerton appears in the opera *Madama Butterfly* by Giacomo Puccini (1858–1924).

[6] Henry Taylor, *The Statesman* (London: Longman, Rees, Orme, Brown, Green, & Longman, 1836), Ch. XV, 'On Quarrelling,' at p. 107.

20[11]

At the Russian embassy. About the cat.

Journalist: Do people have many pets in Russia?
Official: Yes, like you, we are great lovers of domestic animals.
Journalist: Are cats the most popular pets?
Official: In Russia, all pets have an equal opportunity to be popular.
  February 1968.

20[12]

'A mind is a fortuitous arrangement of vermicular appetites.'
'A painting is a certain interaction of electrons & nuclei.'

These are the great false truths.

20[13]

An odd contrast, more or less contemporaries, Tolstoy & Amiel. (I recollect that I came across them both at the same time, when I was about 17 ½, & both have remained with me.)

Tolstoy (except in regard to whom he would marry; when he dithered) never had any difficulty in deciding. His only difficulty was his aptitude for making half a dozen 'irrevocable' & contradictory decisions in as many days.

Amiel could never decide anything. But he managed to live in indecision, to make it a way of life. (Keats has something about this.)

They were both fascinated with themselves. But whereas Tolstoy's self-consciousness never, or rarely, reached the level of self-knowledge, Amiel was self-knowledgeable as well as self-conscious.

On the other hand, Tolstoy, by a wonderful intuition, knew an enormous amount about other people; & Amiel — some people (women) believed that they had never been so profoundly understood, but I doubt if he ever understood anyone but himself.

Tolstoy upsets the classification of extrovert & introvert; & he denies also 'man' & 'woman.'

20[14]

Our historic situation

It is reason enough to profess to being a Christian & to support the Church because if we lost all our culture we would cease to exist.

20[14]

A 'compromise' is not a 'position'; it can only be defended pragmatically.

20[15]

'The sailor's consciousness of complete independence from all land affairs.'
  Conrad, *The Shadow Line*.[7]

The feeling of isolation, relieved by a tradition of conduct with peculiarly severe & absolute rules e.g. for the conduct of the Master of the ship. Nelson. Poseidon.

20[15]

Those who look for only one thing when they look for 'meaning.' Meaning is what it means to somebody.

20[15]

The writer never lies; even if he does not mean what he says, he says what he means.

20[16]

The unhappiness, the frustration & the immorality of the age is its morbid hankering after virtue.

20[16]

An exaggerated notion of the importance of every human soul but one's own — the proud belief that only you can do without being in some manner important — dispense with it & still be a man.

20[17]

Theory and Practice

The counterpart of philosophy in actual feeling. The Stoic analysis of human nature — action & passion. Cp. Bernard Longueville in Henry James, *Confidence*.[8]

20[19]

For understanding politics there is more to be got from reflecting upon Hazlitt's four essays on Chatham, Burke, Fox & Pitt than from all the enquiries into voting behaviour & rôle perceptions.[9]

---

[7] Joseph Conrad, *The Shadow Line: A Confession* (New York: DoubleDay, Page, & Company, 1917), p. 27.

[8] Oakeshott's note: 'Henry James, *Confidence* (London: Chatto & Windus, 1879), Ch. XV.'

[9] See W. Hazlitt, 'Character of Lord Chatham'; 'Character of Mr. Burke'; 'Character of Mr. Fox'; and 'Character of Mr. Pitt,' in *Political Essays, With Sketches of Public Characters* (London: William Hone, 1819), pp. 356–93.

20[20]

The superiority & the inferiority of Christianity: it must be made (remade) by every believer. This was not so of the only other religion of the western world — the nature religion of the Romans — which is, say, ½ of Christianity: we live, & for two millennia have lived, in a Roman world. The twentieth century is distinguished by the large number of people who do not think it worthwhile to remake Christianity for themselves. But I doubt if its eligibility to be remade has come to an end. Needless to say, I do not think of the Bishop of Woolwich[10] etc as 'remakers'; they are merely soft in the head.

20[20]

We have substituted universal pauperization for poverty.

20[20]

Edison to his son when his workshop caught on fire: 'Go and fetch your mother, she'll never see anything like this again.'

20[20]

What the plague effected in Athens, inflation is effecting in European states. Of course, it need not do so, but the response made & likely to be continued to be made is moral collapse. Honest men become rare; honour & self-respect diminish. Universal pauperization is quite a different thing than poverty.

20[20]

My father's atheism was based chiefly on the insufficiencies of persons, as if the fact that so many clocks are out of order had made him lose faith in Time.

20[20]

When we lose a friend in war, he never seems quite gone.

20[23]

Both men & women may love a man because of his misfortunes, but no man or woman can ever love a woman on this account.

20[23]

Karl Marx is a remarkable writer. No other can turn possible truths into superstitions so rapidly & so conclusively. Every truth that came to him he turned into a falsehood. He is, possibly, the most corrupt writer who ever lived. It is not, therefore, surprising that he has become the apostle of the illiterate masses of the

---

10 Presumably John Robinson (1919–83), Bishop of Woolwich 1959–69, author of numerous popular Christian works including *Honest to God* (London: SCM, 1963).

world — by 'illiterate' I mean those who can accept nothing but what has been endowed with the quality of superstition.

20[24]

In my dream I had in front of me a book of the seventeenth century, & at the bottom of a page I read: Faith is a fruit; lyric flowers grow on other trees. And I knew this to be both true and false. And I turned the page & found there a sentence in which all the conflicting truths about religion were reconciled. But when I woke I could not recall it.

20[24]

I was born under a wandering star.

20[24]

The human world is composed of gestures. The language of gestures may change, but it may also become impoverished. Nothing in our world has replaced the peasant crossing himself in the hay-field when he hears the angelus bell, & this is far older than Christianity.

20[25]

Cecil King was voted out of the Chairmanship of the Daily Mirror Publishing Company by his fellow Directors. When asked whether he had been surprised, he answered that his only surprise was that the vote was unanimous. 'After all,' he said, 'there were some on the board to whom he had not done favours.'

Tacitus, Pascal, La Rochefoucauld, Hobbes.

20[25]

If I were asked what constituted the decadence of our current life, I would say it was having lost the opportunity of noticing. To whom, now, has the expression 'the bloom of the fruit' any direct meaning?

And the destruction of distinctions. When all men are brothers & all men friends, there is an end of brotherhood & friendship.

20[25]

A writer, a thinker, may 'haunt' us, or 'haunt' a whole subsequent generation of thinkers. But to these we should say, as the Australian native said to his dead kinsman, 'Come back to us in our dreams, if you will; but not as a ghost.'[11]

---

[11] See p. 448, above.

20[27]

They want to arrive without having travelled, to have learned without learning. Teaching is initiating into the difficulties & pleasures of travel, therefore they abhor a teacher. What they look for is a drug from which they may awake having arrived, a magic incantation which will open the door, a formula which contains all truth. And what they look for is supplied: the gnostic word which breaks the spell which has hitherto held prisoner the human race. It is supplied by 'progressive education' whose message is that it is better to arrive than to travel. It is supplied by Karl Marx & Sigmund Freud. It is received by those who do not know the difference between Mao & Confucius.

20[28]

Query: How to deprive death of its sting without depriving life of its sweetness.

20[28]

Repentance is not an attempt to cancel what has been; that is impossible. It is a new experience to be added. It does not mean that we should have avoided what we did. There are actions which are both proper to be done & proper to repent of doing.

20[28]

Arletty.[12]

20[29]

Le don terrible de la familiarité:[13] the power of awakening new thoughts, feelings, emotions in another so that she becomes almost a stranger to herself, & then recognizes herself. Unmaking & remaking.

20[29]

What Plato lacked was the *amicitia rerum mortalium*.[14]

20[29]

The worst comes last.

20[30]

'It is not enough to end the misery of poverty, we must also end what has been described as the "misery of unimportance." In the work place, in the schools & universities & in government at every level we have got to reflect our belief in

---

[12]   Léonie Bathiat (1898–1992), aka 'Arletty,' French actress, singer, and model.
[13]   See p. 376, above.
[14]   Oakeshott's note: 'Augustine, *Confessions*, Bk IV ch. vi.'

the individual value of every man & woman: their right to be heard, to express their personalities, to control their own environment, to be taken into account as individuals.'

Mr B. Castle at Cambridge, October 1969.

Oh, what rubbish.

20[30]

How to reconcile adventure & fidelity.

20[31]

'Many so-called criminal offenses are nothing more than the expression of a desire to be orientated.'

'Nothing' more?

20[31]

Defending Counsel: 'In this permissive society no great harm was done except that he broke the law.'

20[31]

Every objection to an enormity is called a 'backlash.' Every firm stand is called an 'over-reaction.'

Only Halifax knew how to release us.[15]

20[32]

The custom in French country churches to distribute to the congregation at high Mass pieces of *brioche, pain bénit*; a symbolic communion.

Christian doctrine is a vast collection of heresies; Christian worship a vast collection of local inventions. It will die only when it ceases to be inventive.

20[33]

Leave much to time & little to argument.

20[33]

Life imitates art. 'Nature' is the invention of poets & painters; 'human nature' is the invention of poets. The office of inventor has now been usurped by 'scientists,' & they have invented a human being who is a 'gene-structure.'

---

[15] The last sentence is in a different ink.

20[33]

The art of a nation is the model available for the life of a nation to imitate. But then most of what is called 'art' is not the work of artists.

20[37]

The work criticizes itself unnoticed, for the most part, by the author. But there are authors who notice, but who do not know how to bring their noticings to bear. The masterpiece is a criticism of everything else.

20[37]

'Fact finding.' Facts are not 'found,' they are 'made.' Every 'fact' in a court of law has nine lives.

20[37]

The ends of a court of law are 'relative,' limited — the best that can be made, the best that can be got, here & now.

20[37]

The fatal 'materialism' in morals which relies upon 'facts' more than feelings, sentiments, loves.

20[39]

The 'justification' of 'comprehensive education' — 'the fact that society has a right to the fully developed talents of all its children'!

20[39]

Every man is an attempt on the part of God to make a human being — that is, one whose life is a self-enactment. Some never become human, they remain frogs & and ants. But, somehow, they must all be treated as if they were human.

20[40]

Goethe, & I have no doubt others, believed that civilized human beings might be restrained in their relentless exploitation of the world, & perhaps even saved from the ultimate disaster of a barbarism worse than savagery, by a 'principle' in human nature called 'feminine,' not because it was exclusive to women but because it was apt to be preponderant in their characters. But with every year that passes this preponderance diminishes; the vocation to 'save' no longer calls or is even understood. The urge of every emancipated woman is to become a man. Unisex is not our predicament; it is the triumph of the 'male.'

20[41]

For those who talk most about it, the revolt against 'alienation' is a longing to be <u>given</u> an indestructible identity. It is not a flight from loneliness but a yearning to be lost in a 'solidarity.' It is a revolt against multiplicity, against *humanitas*.

20[41]

Agnes Sorèl dominates the history of Charles VII's reign; Joan of Arc was but an episode in it, a camp legend destined to raise the sinking courage of soldiers.[16]

20[42]

The Rolls of Honour & dishonour; the man of integrity and his counterfeiters; to be continued.

Goethe.   Marx.
Burckhardt.   St Simon.
Nietzsche.
Kierkegaard.
Schopenhauer.
Karl Kraus.
Valéry.
Swift.

20[43]

But how could the 'popular press' be anything other than a vast corruption of language?

20[43]

'A generation bred on syllabuses can hardly understand the inspiration of the medieval schools in their prime.' — The first rapture of walking or riding hundreds of miles to sit at Abelard's feet — before this was converted into the formal university 'course' of the 13th century. And even then it survived. Ramus was sought as Abelard had been sought.

20[44]

That fresh exploration of the resources of the Latin language — an exploration in which the language lived again — by the lyricists of the 12th century. Brief — swallowed up by the vernacular.

---

16   Agnès Sorel (1422–50), mistress of Charles VII (1403–61), King of France from 1422.

20[44]

We make the mistake of counting as ours only what we experience differently from others or recognize as being divergent. Or we make the mistake of recognizing ourselves as mere reflections of a 'society' to which we owe everything.

20[44]

A statement which in the mouth of another would be ironical is transformed when it is, in fact, naïve. It has a double meaning. 'It all helped to pass the time,' said naively of a life of domestic tragedy.

20[45]

'Community spirit' everywhere, sitting about together everywhere, communicating everywhere, but with less and less to communicate. To be out of touch is to be extinguished; and it matters not at all what is said so long as the silence which is equated with extinction is broken.

20[45]

The unforced integrity of an educated mind.

20[48]

'The observation of species so close to our own [apes & monkeys] throws serious doubt as to whether the way we rear our infants in the West is the best possible. Contact between mother & infant is vital for security in monkeys & apes; yet we are content to let our infants lie out in prams for large portions of their early lives.'

Anthony Storr, *Sunday Times*, 11 October 1970!

What rot. We're not apes but good Christians.

20[49]

'In Paris one should either have everything or want nothing.' Yes, but that was the lost sweet Paris of 40 years ago.

20[50]

'When I was a child,' writes Julian Green, 'owing to a misapprehension of a picture in a history book, I got it into my head that France was a real person, a woman with a crown which she doffed at certain times to wear a Phrygian cap, & one of my main sources of worry was that, sooner or later, this person with whom I was in love would grow old & eventually die.' Perhaps she has died.

France: a person whose failings were surpassed by her generosity & courage; a creature of whims & sudden fancies, which led her astray, but with a great power of recovery; a soul of great spiritual wealth; proud, valiant, courageous.

Really a family of persons, the Parisian branch of which was flighty, talkative, euphoric, and which was not taken much notice of by the cousins in the Dordogne.

France, a land every square foot of which is cultivated, a land without forests or hedges.

Which is my France? The France in whom choice & chance are one at last? The France of the *Chanson de Roland*, of St Bernard & Abélard, of Rabelais & Villan & Louise Labé & Ronsard, of Montaigne & de la Boétie & Charron & Michel de l'Hôpital, of de Thou & Cinq-Mars, Pascal, Vauvenargues & Chamfort, of Balzac, Racine, Rachel, of the Chartreuse de Parme, Verlaine, Péguy, de Vigny, Manet & Poussin, Cézanne, Braque & Valéry.

20[50]

That famous 'Oak' in whose shade democracy is said to have been born — it was not the scene of political deliberation; it was a court of law, or it was the tree upon which the grandees fixed their shields in proclamation of their loyalty or it was a totem.

The half of the corruption which 'democracy' has imposed upon the past in its search for a lineage has not yet been spoken. There are French writers who trace 'democracy' to Joan of Arc.

20[52]

To be happy for the first time & to be surprised at being happy — it must have happened if only one could recollect.

20[52]

The *ex-votos* that can be seen in a country church in France, giving thanks for miraculous recoveries, safe returns, narrow escapes from death & disaster, little worldly successes & happinesses: a sweet, wonderful, pathetic gratitude. In Winchester Cathedral it is different. Besides the ancient monuments, two centuries of imperial adventure, memorials to boys drowned in shipwrecks, killed in battle in India, Africa, China & on the plains of Europe, a strange mixture of pride & gratitude.

20[53]

In 1917, after a great bombardment, an attack having been ordered, a French soldier clambered out of his trench to meet the enemy. Finding himself alone on the parapet he looked back & saw that almost his companions were lying dead or dying in the trench. He uttered a strange & magnificent cry which soon became known all over the country & did more than all the soixante-quinze to save the French nation from destruction: *Debout les morts!* It took many centuries to breed a man capable of this exclamation.

His ancestors were de Thou & Cinq-Mars.

20[54]

The most important change in European civilization which marks the twentieth century is the disappearance of 'war.' It came slowly, with many set-backs; Wellington noticed it. And it was intimated earlier in the 'religious wars' of the 16th century; although it has no counterpart in the wars of the middle-ages, not even in the Crusades. Soon after 1918 Europe entered upon a period of 'gnostic' war; 'democratic' war, which is not 'war.'

20[54]

One would have thought that if Scott Fitzgerald & his wife could remain together, any couple could do so; but this discounts the sheer genius for misery of those two.

20[55]

There is much less love in the world to-day than there was fifty years ago, & much more ill-temper. We are living the fifties of the seventeenth century over again.

20[55]

I arrived & passed the midway of the journey of life without recognizing it, without enough introspection to recognize it. Where Dante stood at the beginning of the *Divina Comedia*, I never stood. It is a great loss, or is it? I passed that 'shadow line' in a dream; the sweet dream of June, *si bleu, si calme*.

20[56]

From that day to this every Spanish soldier carries under his tunic a holy relic & a pack of cards.

20[59]

Vera Lynn: 'Where have all the flowers gone?'
Marlene Dietrich: '*Wo sind alle die Männer?*'

The German song is just that much more profound because it is the song of a people deeply, extravagantly in love with death.

20[59]

His conduct was founded upon the foolish hope that his opponents would not have the sense to take advantage of his errors.

20[59]

I too have tried to be a philosopher, but happiness keeps breaking in.

20[59]

Love touched her, but found her without courage.

20[60]

'Only this morning when I got up I said to myself, where are the good old days when I was unhappy?'[17]

Ah, those dear vanished days when I was so unhappy.

20[60]

It was not 'social change' which brought the Labour party into a Parliament hitherto dominated by the Liberal and Tory parties — it was the bargain made in 1903 between the officials of the Liberal party and the ILP to allow the ILP a straight fight with a conservative in thirty-odd constituencies.

20[61]

When pop music provides anything half as good as Ronald Burge's 'Take a look at Ireland'…

The indescribable vulgarity of 'Sergeant Pepper.'

20[61]

The Immortals: the reveller who, when asked by a railway ticket-collector 'Do you belong to Glasgow,' replied 'No, Glasgow belongs to me!'

20[61]

In everything he had his own way of doing it.

20[62]

Wyat resteth here, that
Quick could never rest

Inscription on Wyatt's memorial in Sherborne Priory.[18]

---

[17] Oakeshott's note: 'Delacroix.' Possibly Eugène Delacroix (1798–1863), French painter, but the quotation has not been traced.

[18] Sir Thomas Wyatt (1503–42), English diplomat and poet. The first two lines of the poem 'Wyatt Resteth Here,' composed by Henry Howard, Earl of Surrey (c.1516–47), were used for the inscription on Wyatt's memorial in the Wykeham chapel of Sherborne Abbey.

20[62]

'*Dieu, que le son du cor est triste au fond des bois.*' Vigny.[19]

It is the horn of Roland.

The world we inhabit to-day emerged in those marvelous ambiguous centuries of the early Christian era, which carried with them reminiscences of ancient Athens & Sparta, & the realities of Rome. This is <u>my world</u>; it is not past, it is present. I & Charlemagne & Roland & Oliver are contemporaries. O rich wild world into which to be born. And it comes to us as it was imagined & put together, for the most part, in the 12th century. This is the century in which we are all born.

20[63]

The lyre of Apollo cannot silence the pipes of Pan, but as their sound becomes fainter it becomes more human, more melancholy. If one lived long enough, perhaps they would become one music.

20[63]

In love and friendship we take each other *à son gré*. This is difficult to learn.

20[63]

In Conrad places are often magic states which explain the actions performed in them. And of how many 'gardens' in Henry James is this not also true?

20[63]

She was incapable of sadness, only of resentment.

20[64]

The ancient, living, miscellaneous world — the world of Gloucestershire which Maitland resurrected — dies slowly. On the morning of 3 September 1939 the outbreak of war was announced in Chipping Camden by the town crier in tricorne hat & cape, with his bell & parchment.

It was not Marx who portended the new, deadly uniformity; it was Francis Bacon & St Simon, the Faustian progenitors of a world where everything is organized. The world where law has ceased to be lore.

20[64]

This is a sort of *Zibaldone*: a written chaos.[20]

---

[19] See p. 414, above.

[20] See Giacomo Leopardi, *Zibaldone*, ed. M. Caesar and F. D'Intino (New York: Farrar, Straus, and Giroux, 2013 [1898]).

20[65]

You may be bored, but you are quite certain of not being bored by decency.

20[65]

Religion: no doubt it is an *affaire des moeurs*, & if it were not more it would be something. But, like everything else, it may be something more, much more.

20[66]

'*Tous les comédiens ne sont pas au théâtre.*'

Yes, they <u>are</u>: those others have not a jot of the true comedy which reconciles us to life; they are *farceurs*.

20[67]

The National Association for the promotion of Social Science![21]

20[68]

'We all know that young men must go to the devil, but it is intolerable that they should make a theory of it.'[22]

Even then! Perhaps the only difference is that now there are more of them & their 'theories' are more pretentious.

20[68]

The peculiarly graceful & not merely detached attention that a man whose affections are anchored may give to attractive women.

20[69]

Pascal misunderstood Montaigne (as Montaigne had mistaken Rabelais); and Montaigne would never have understood Pascal. But there is a land, an island, where they meet & understand one another. I have not found it; but this is what I have looked for, without knowing what I looked for.

20[69]

One is under an obligation to be happy with the here & now.

---

[21] The National Association for the Promotion of Social Science campaigned for social reform in the mid-Victorian era: see Lawrence Goldman, *Science, Reform and Politics in Victorian Britain. The Social Science Association 1857–1886* (Cambridge, 2002).

[22] Oakeshott's note: 'Jowett.' Probably Benjamin Jowett (1817–93), Master of Balliol College, Oxford University, 1870–93, and Vice-Chancellor of Oxford University, 1882–6, but the quotation has not been traced.

20[70]

Unforgettable, but not memorable.

20[70]

One of the great charms of children to adults is their great faith in the imminence of the unlikely. Of course, this is not how the children themselves think of it; they merely imagine the world to be less set in its ways than it is.

20[70]

How much of love is a 'will to love'? Heavenly love is love without a 'will to love'; peace.

20[70]

O the wide, wide inviolate spaces of the recollected past.

20[70]

The eyes of adolescents which show everything.

20[71]

A memory. I went to see Llewelyn Powys as he lay dying in his garden hut in Chaldon Herring.[23] He could not speak above a whisper, but after a time he pushed a book towards me; it was lying on his bed. It was *Leviathan*. And he whispered to me: 'Read to me about the Kingdom of the Fairies.' And I read until the sun went down.

20[72]

I often read the *In Memoriam* column in the newspaper. It revives one's confidence in love, devotion & faithfulness & it is a small window through which one can see a happy world. Of course, people rarely know how to express their love & their loss. One has to to wait many weeks, but then comes: 'Figg, Gerald. Darling, unforgettable Figgy. Diana.' And if it does not speak with the *gravitas* of Romans who knew better than any others how to live & how to die, it is reticent, & it reveals a life of 'joy & woe' which stays the rot of time. Who was this Figgy & who this Diana. Mortals who made themselves immortal.

20[73]

This evening the 'Down Your Way' programme came from Chatteris, that bleak out-post of human life in the Fen Country. One of those interviewed was an

---

[23] Llewelyn Powys (1884–1939), writer, younger brother of Theodore Francis Powys and John Cowper Powys, author of *The Meaning of Culture*, reviewed by Oakeshott in 1930: see *SW* iii.58–60. Powys, however, died in Switzerland.

engineer who looked after the pumping station. A simple, true man who understood his engines, who had lived all his life between land & water, who no doubt went fishing on a Saturday, who perhaps had to wait a life-time for an emergency, like 1947, but when it came found that he was a soldier. Why was it so moving that when he was asked to choose a piece of music he chose 'Jesu Joy of Man's desiring'? Almost anything else would have done — '*Aufwiedersehen*,' or 'Wherever you walk,' or even 'You are my sunshine.' Whatever he had said it would be echoing Wyatt — 'I am here in Kent & Christendom' — a miracle of civilization which will not last much longer.

20[74]

If I were asked to choose the triumphant moments which represent the achievements of our civilization it would not be the great & magnificent exhibition of *majestas*, nor perhaps great moments in the history of art or music, but the unobtrusive moments of magnificence in which, not one but many show their education: the tumult of applause which, in defiance of all propriety, followed the five-hour closing speech of Edward Clarke's defence of Mrs Adelaide Bartlett at the Old Bailey in April 1886 & the ovation he received when he was recognized in a London theatre on the eve of that day. Mrs Adelaide was probably guilty of what she was accused — murder.

20[75]

'I'm a psychology major, so I know something about people!'

Dear deluded girl.

20[75]

Why do I find it so moving that it was the 1st Queen's Regiment (the West Surreys) who in far distant Assam at the battle of Jail Hill turned the tide of the Japanese invasion of Asia on 13 May 1944? There must have been Centuries in the Roman army in the 3rd century which fought battles like this. And Roland's horn echoes down the ages. But nothing stays the rot of time.

20[76]

To love the world without being worldly.

20[76]

That facility for starting off again on a new adventure. The *voyageur*.

20[76]

What was between them was like those legends of rings exchanged or coins broken, to be sent as a summons only in some circumstance of finality.

20[77]

In the devastation in which we live the greatest of all the destructions is the self-destruction of women.

20[77]

Until the middle of the nineteenth century British juries blinked the evidence because of the harshness of the law; we are now entering upon a period in which it is difficult (at least in London) to empanel a jury which, if not composed as to one half of criminals, is certainly profoundly in favour of crime, in courts served by barristers concerned with 'social forces' & 'psychological urges' & magistrates who add their quota to the rubbish uttered.

20[78]

The immuring of a delinquent nun was announced in these words:

> Sister, let thy sorrow cease
> Sinful brother, part in peace.

Imagine it.[24]

20[78]

'We must uproot & destroy everything, however sacred it may seem to some, which is a hindrance to the proper development of society towards its proper goal.'

Canon Collins 21 July 1963.

Dear, mad, bemused Canon.

20[79]

Of a book about Amsterdam – 'This chronicles the growth of Amsterdam from an insignificant fishing village to a major tourist centre.'

Oh what a fall is here.

20[80]

The emblem of the human predicament is not exclusion from that Eden-world where every want is satisfied, but the fatality of Babel; not the lack of knowledge but of mutual self-understanding.

20[81]

Life is not a honeymoon, but never to have had a honeymoon is to have missed the sweetness of life. The unfortunate are those for whom one is not enough.

---

[24] Oakeshott's note: 'But see, Maitland, *Canon Law in the Church of England* p. 175.'

20[81]

A scorpion came to the bank of the Dog River & could not cross because the river was in flood. He saw a fish, nibbling placidly among the weeds. 'Please, fish,' said the scorpion, 'take me on your back & carry me across the river.' The fish was unhappy about this. 'If I carry you on my back,' said he, 'you will sting me & I shall die.' But the scorpion had an answer for him. 'If I sting you & you die in the middle of the river, I will be lost too because I cannot swim.' So the fish was reassured. He took the scorpion on his back & began to swim across the flooded river. Half-way over, the scorpion stung him. With his dying breath, the fish asked plaintively, 'Why did you do it? Now we shall both die.' To which the scorpion replied, 'I wish I knew, little friend — but this is Lebanon.'

20[82]

To hear the soft utterances of spring.

20[82]

When will they ever learn, when will they ever learn?

20[83]

A swallow speeds through the air to catch a gnat & to satisfy its hunger; not to verify a principle.

20[84]

Augustinian Christianity is severe & remorseful; it had wit & charm & irony, but it lacked gaiety. It was *il Francesco*, the 'little Frenchman,' who translated it into the language of the Troubadors.

20[84]

Friendship, like everything else human, has to be learned; in children it has no roots.

20[84]

To try, perhaps to try again; but not to grumble.

20[84]

...Since the earth rose out of the sea.

20[85]

In 1968 a 25-year old Punjabi 'farmer' entered England illegally, having paid about £1000 to do so.

Subsequently, he alleges, he paid about £700 'blackmail' to conceal the illegality of his entry.

He stayed 3 years in Birmingham with a 'friend'; what he was doing during this period is not divulged.

In 1971 he came to London and worked for a time as a builder's labourer. In 1974 he was employed as a 'machine operator' earning £50 per week net.

In 1973 he bought a 3 bedroomed house in Southall for £11,000, paying a deposit of £3000 & taking out a mortgage for £8000.

In 1974, by fiat of the Home Secretary (April), he became a legal citizen and disclosed to a journalist the 'misery' of his life as an illegal immigrant.

20[86]

I was eating my chicken pie.

'What are you thinking about,' she asked.

Well, to tell the truth, I was thinking about the village carpenter who took Hölderlin in when he went mad & looked after him all the long years of his later life. The village must have been high in the hills of his beloved Schwabenland. I saw Hölderlin sitting on a bench in front of the cottage in the sun. It was a summer evening & the carpenter, smoking his pipe, came & sat beside him. They did not speak.

Nor did I.

20[86]

Oh to have composed a tune, a polka, a waltz, a song.

20[87]

'To play with the gypsies in the wood.' The pipes of Pan, the magic flute, the enticement of the wild; these can be heard only be those who have been brought up in nurseries or inhabit gardens. Never to have heard them is like never having seen the moon for the first time; but oh do not let them steal your children's hearts away.

20[87]

Das goldene Wiener Herz was destroyed by immigrants.

20[89]

Man, please thy Maker, and be merry,
And give not for this world a cherry[25]

Please put this on my grave.

---

[25]   Oakeshott's note: 'Dunbar.' William Dunbar (c.1460–c.1520), Scottish poet.

20[89]

The passing of time, terrible & yet blessed; to understand this is to understand the human condition.

20[90]

June, I do not know what it may mean to be with you in heaven where, I suppose, we are what we are in terms of our love of God, & so I do not think much about this. But I often think of meeting you in Purgatory. You will be surrounded by your friends, by those you have loved & those who have loved you; and I shall be standing shyly apart. But were I to send a message to you who should say: 'There is one here who has made a fire upon the sea shore & cooked a fish & would have you eat with him,' would you answer: 'Say to him that I will come'? And were it merely for 'old time's sake' you came, I would be almost content — for this is Purgatory, not Heaven. 'Come close to me sweet comrade of the past.' Purgatory, that most human of all inventions, far surpassing 'heaven.'

20[91]

Priscilla told me that when she was a child she really believed in the Greenwood as a place where one might go and be exempt from the troubles & the confusion of the world. The forest of Arden.

20[91]

It is not the wheat which came out of what was then, in 1820, the North West, but the songs. These people were often the victims of crooks, they were credulous, they were deceived; but they did not deceive themselves & they were not Baconians. They retrieved the Wabash from nonentity. How much religion did it take to settle Indiana?

20[92]

Un vivant is a much more significant person than the rather vulgar *bon viveur*.

20[92]

It was a smile debased by no accessory expression of benevolence, or irony, pity, cruelty, or invitation; it expressed nothing but itself, a divine delight in existence.

20[92]

A drummer boy.
The American drummer boy of Castine, Maine. *The Little Locksmith*.[26]

---

[26] K.B. Hathaway, *The Little Locksmith* (New York: Coward-McCann, 1943).

'The Minstrel boy': that is what I was born to be — in those totally pointless Scottish wars; a life devoid of all irrelevancies; a life of self-fulfilment.

20[93]

Lampedusa records that the refugees in Palermo from the earthquake in Messina in 1908 were reported to be 'behaving most indecently' when they were billeted in the Palermo theatres, & his father remarking 'they felt the urge to replace the dead.'[27]

I remember as a boy finding an account of the earthquake in a book in the school library & reading that, after the shock had passed & the town lay in ruins, those who had escaped, even strangers, made love together on the hill side, & I remember thinking: how poetic a way to celebrate an escape from death.

20[93]

The sleepless grudge of unsatisfied curiosity.

20[95]

'This Government, I am proud to say, has sought to fulfil the long-standing obligations of the Labour Movement to the miners, & the whole nation may rejoice that we have done so.'

Michael Foot on the Miner's Wages Settlement, 14 February 1975.[28]

And this is what they called 'politics'!

20[97]

'I weigh my words well when I assert that the men who should know the true history of the bit of chalk which every carpenter carries about in his breeches pocket, though ignorant of all other history, is likely, if he will think his knowledge out to its ultimate results, to have a truer, & therefore a better conception of this wonderful universe & of man's relation to it than the most learned student who is deep-read in the records of humanity & ignorant of those of nature.'

T.H. Huxley, 'On a Piece of Chalk,' 1868. Address to working men in Norwich.[29]

What confusion! Huxley thinks that the 'history' here is 'geology.'

---

[27] Giuseppe Tomasi di Lampedusa (1896–1957), Italian aristocrat and author.

[28] Michael Foot (1913–2010), Labour MP 1945–55, 1960–92, leader of the Labour Party 1980–83.

[29] See T.H. Huxley, 'On a Piece of Chalk,' in *Discourses Biological and Geological* (New York D. Appleton and Company, 1896), pp. 1–36, at p. 4.

20[98]

The once born & the twice born; this is a <u>different</u> contrast.

To be 'born again,' to make the leap — this is not necessary; it is only circumstantial.

We are <u>never without</u> the <u>Or</u>; we are born into a world of the <u>Or</u>; we do not have to <u>get out</u> of the <u>Either</u>, both are abstractions; feeling & thought, action & the conditions of action.

The <u>Either</u> is not 'natural,' it is no less learned than the <u>Or</u> & both are learned together.

20[99]

It is glorious & it is wretched to be a human being. We look at the world & can never see enough of it. Each must manage his wants & his satisfactions for himself as best he may. We are <u>joined</u> only in love (where choice & chance are one, at last), in a conversation, & in observing some conditions of law & morals in whatever we choose to do or say.

Live, but live nobly.

Be ruled by courage.

20[99a]³⁰

A sword from Culloden. That would be something for a man to keep up-stairs or for a girl to bring with her when she married.

20[100]

God died, not in battle or in peace with his dogs around him, but by treachery.

20[101]

According to the Chaldean account of the creation of the world, of man & of his Fall, the consequences of this fall for man were:

That his knowledge was capable of injuring him.

That the human race became disputatious, notable for its hostility.

That they were forced to submit to tyranny.

That his desires were often unsatisfied & when satisfied often disappointing.

That his labour was often frustrated in its purposes.

That he was troubled in mind and body.

20[101]

What constitutes civil freedom is not that our natural desires are unlawful but that our lawful desires are not themselves law-like.

---

30 Oakeshott numbered two consecutive folios 20[99]; to distinguish them the second is referred to here as 20[99]a.

20[101]

There cannot be an <u>obligation</u> to believe something. In other words no <u>belief</u> is authoritative. Belief on 'evidence' is not belief on the 'authority' of evidence (it has none) but on the grounds of evidence.

20[101]

In 'politics' a Jacobite or a Confederate.

20[102]

Later generations, especially after 1945, have expressed astonishment & incredulity at the 'gaiety' of those who went to war & were killed in the so-called 'first' war. Julian & Billy Grenfell, for example, are regarded as sentimental, deceived characters, representative of a sort of decadence. But when I recollect my boyhood & what that war was to us at school, with the almost daily news of an elder boy (who had left a few months before) killed, I know that both the astonishment & the incredulity is misplaced. They were like that, & we who were 15 or 16 were also like that. We did not think of the war as, in any crude sense, a 'religious' war, a 'crusade,' nor were we in love with death; and we floated upon no nonsense about making 'the world safe for democracy.' That 'gaiety' was not a meaningless display of fireworks; it was the dissipation of centuries of religious belief.

20[103]

C.D. Broad seems to have thought the brain was a mechanism for protecting the organism from the confusion of a rush of messages from the universe.

20[103]

'The basic human right to reproduce'!
  Mrs Justice Heilbron, September 1975.

Said in relation to a case concerning an idiot girl of 15 or so whose mother, disturbed by her daughter's escapades with both boys & adults, sought permission of the court to have her castrated.

20[104]

1975. It has taken only thirty years to forget all about the white cliffs of Dover.

20[104]

Poverty — the poverty of desires.
Pauperization — deprivation of desires.

20[104]

Our lives are contests, not with what is without us but with what is within us.

20[105]

There are some people who one does not know how the world can have got on without them & yet they were a very long time coming. We could not have got on without Abraham & appropriately he came early, & we could easily afford to wait for Hegel; but how did all those centuries do without Offenbach?[31]

20[105]

A man incapable of being happily resigned to being a nobody is never likely to be a somebody.

20[105]

A memory: June polishing up her brass Woolworth's 'wedding' ring on our bedroom carpet before going down to dinner in the Inn at Brendon; and how I loved her & admired her at that moment. It seemed as if all the gaiety & all the courage of all the girls in the world was for a moment there in her, triumphing over all the misgivings girls in such situations have ever felt.

20[106]

A world without names — the world upon which an animal opens its eyes. A world in which sight is the least important of the senses.

20[106]

There ought to be a law against eye-witnesses.

20[106]

To notice, to wonder, to marvel, to be astonished, perhaps to be dismayed — *la chasse* — & then what? To understand that one never completely understands.

20[106]

The belief that a night-cap carries in it the dreams of its first owner.

20[107]

'Il est difficile de comprendre combien est grande la ressemblance et la différence qu'il y a entre tous les homes.'[32]

---

31 Possibly Jacques Offenbach (1819–80), French cellist and composer.
32 Oakeshott's note: 'La Rochefoucauld.'

The resemblances are formal & therefore not really 'likenesses' but identities; the differences are individual and governed by education.

20[107]

So-called 'middle-class' morality, middle-class 'values' — to be honest, prudent, provident, punctual, punctilious, self-controlled, responsible, respectable, just, worth, temperate, chaste, decent, modest, square. There is nothing wrong with any or all of this except that by itself it is not a 'morality'; & of course only the very foolish have ever supposed that it was. Its partiality is, first, that it says nothing about motives; & secondly it is (so far as it goes) a morality, not for a middle-class, but for 'middle life.' To be recognizable as a concrete morality it must be filled out by the spontaneous devotion & affection of children (even their delight in wickedness) & by the not less anomalous, even libertine, devotions, affections, generosities & laxities of the old.

And, of course, what is fatal is when this 'morality of middle life' is identified with 'religion.'

20[108]

'Whither thou goest, I will go; & where thou lodgest I will lodge; thy people shall be my people & thy god my god. Where thou diest I will die, & there will I be buried: the Lord do so to me & more also if aught but death part thee & me.'[33]

This was said, not by one who loved to her beloved, but by a widowed daughter-in-law to her mother-in-law: Ruth, the Moabitess, who became the great, great grandmother of David. But the voice is that of a girl speaking to her lover. That mother-in-law must have been a remarkable woman, & so also her dead son.

20[108]

Nothing comes of nothing; but the best comes of very little, & the worst of too much.

20[108]

Asceticism is not denial, it is release from distraction.

20[109]

It was as if the larks were going up for the first time, on a cloudless February morning. Never to have heard it is to have missed something; each year to be reminded of it, even to old age, is to keep one's place among the vivants; but to <u>hear</u> it more than once (or perhaps twice) in a life-time is to hear something else.

'I saw you first.'

---

33   Ruth 1:16.

20[109]

Those terrible words: 'You're young, you'll make it.' It is the 'it' that is so terrible; 'make the grade.' As if life were not a dream.

20[109]

Tobias & the fish. What far-off folk memory is it that reveals to be me the sacredness of the fish upon the Soho fishmonger's slab, and Orpheus in the flute player across the street? And in how many centuries will this be obliterated?

20[110]

The <u>cheerfulness</u> of 'Puritanism' survived in Bunyan; the original cheerfulness of the feeling of being emancipated.

20[110]

Some people take everything for granted; to others everything is wonderful and mysterious. What else is there to do with the mystery of human life but to fall in love with it!

20[111]

To be loved is to be remade — that is why it may be resented.

20[111]

To love may be a summer's day or a winter's night; but it is to wish that, whatever it is, it might never end.

20[111]

Christianity is a stupendous imaginative engagement, a poem whose first languages were Hebrew & Greek & Latin but which has since been written in all the languages of the world. Each generation must rewrite it for itself.

20[112]

That journey on foot of Hölderlin's from Bordeaux to Tübingen after he had heard of the death of Susette Gontard in 1802: begun in grief & ended in madness.

20[113]

Poems may come to be seen as a perpetual conversation between the generations, images of life & death expressed in the languages, common & contested, of a civilization, intelligible for their immediate meaning but more deeply intelligible only by those whose acquaintance with these languages is profound. And the recognition of every great poem as also an extension of these languages.

20[114]

The twentieth century is marked more conspicuously than any other preceding century by the success with which governments have persuaded large numbers of individuals that their value as such is nothing as compared with the overriding requirements of the state or 'society.'

20[115]

'It is better to suffer injustice than to perpetrate it.' This is the heart of a morality.

20[116]

There is a story, appended to the account of St Francis preaching to the Saracens, in which the Sultan, the King of Egypt, 'asked him in secret to entreat God to reveal to him, by some miracle, <u>which is the best religion.</u>'

'Rationalism' did not begin with Descartes.

20[117]

½ the truth, or thereabouts, is that I went to war as a Cherubino.

20[117]

How different it would all be if the Garden of Eden had been told as the story of a boy & a girl. It would, of course, be something more than the story of Daphnis & Chloe, but I could rewrite D&C so as to contain all that there is Genesis.

20[117]

Legitimate are all children got out of doors. May boys.

20[118]

Whispering grass.
    The trees don't need to know.

20[118]

Cranage (Bert), Canadian, killed on the Somme Sept 16, 1916. <u>Always</u> remembered.
    Daily Telegraph, 16 September 1977.

<u>Death</u> comes when there is no-one left who remembers.

20[119]

All proper love songs are sad. Yes, there is room for rollick, but the joy is religious not sensual. My winsome, handsome Johnny.[34] The words may rollick but the music is sad.

Mutabilité.

20[120]

Law is an equalizer: what is lawful is the same for everybody. But morality is not an equalizer: 'It was right for him (or for her).' Anyone who does not understand this is morally blind. It was right for Jane Digby to live as she did;[35] but it would not be right for you or me. The first principle of morality is 'Be yourself' — to be more or less than yourself is 'wrong.' And I think Aristotle would have understood this, although he never quite said it. There is, of course, something else than this, but this should be said because it is often forgotten. But it is not forgotten by the uncorrupted, the humble: they know who they are & they know, & happily admit, that there are others who are not like them.

20[121]

Ponce de Leon discovered Florida while searching for the Fountains of Youth. Juana Maria de Los Dolores de Leon, the 14 year old girl who, with her elder sister, escaped from the ruins of Badajoz & became the wife (then & there) of Lieut. Harry Smith (later Sir Harry Smith) was his lineal descendant.

20[121]

'*La vie tumultueuse est agréable aux grands esprits, mais ceux qui sont mediocre n'y ont aucun plaisir.*'[36]

How various is this *vie tumultueuse*, and to engage in it does not itself constitute a *grand esprit*. Sometimes it is almost a penalty.

20[121]

There is more misery in having what one does not want than in being deprived of what one has set one's heart upon or even in losing what one has enjoyed. Contrary to the common opinion, it takes all the religion we can muster to live with what we have.

---

[34] Anonymous, 'I know where I'm going': 'Feather beds are soft / And painted rooms are bonnie / But I would give them all / For my handsome winsome Johnny.'

[35] Jane Elizabeth Digby (1807–81), adventuress, successively Lady Ellenborough, Baroness von Venningen Üllner, Countess Theotoky, and the Honourable Mrs Digby el Mesreb.

[36] Oakeshott's note: 'Pascal.'

20[122]

'I think in order to be great in any sphere it is necessary to be oneself.'[37]

This is very Stendhalian; one could be more modest: It is necessary to be oneself in order to be <u>anyone</u>.

20[122]

It is the second girl who is interesting — the one who goes along with the couple who have begun to belong to one another, not as a chaperone, but as a kind of 'companion,' 'mediator.' She is more self-possessed & when she has imparted her self-possession she will drop out. She stands, of course, not next to the boy but next to the girl.

20[122]

Benignitas, simplicitas, hilaritas.

20[123]

Liane de Pougy, *Mes cahiers bleus.*[38]

Here is everything save Augustinian passion. How may we distinguish between the once born who achieve perfection in a life of 15 or 20 years & the twice born in whom the *rerum mortalia* are transformed without being denied. So little feeling of guilt: that is the miracle. Her confession before being married in church in 1920 at the age of 41 to an impoverished Romanian prince: 'Father, except for murder & robbery, I have done pretty much everything.' Perhaps she really did keep 'unspotted by the world.'

20[123]

'The most enduring of all human passions: the love of self.' But, oddly enough, the one person one <u>cannot love</u> is oneself. And there is no <u>love</u> in masturbation.

20[124]

'It's all nylon.' Said to me by an elderly man as we walked round a super-market grocery. 'Including even the cheese.'

20[125]

You're lucky if once in your life-time there appears a Carmen who not only sings but looks the part.

---

[37] Oakeshott's note: 'Stendhal (aged 35).'

[38] Liane de Pougy, *Mes cahiers bleus* (Paris: Plon, 1977).

20[125]

'Lewis Mumford had the idea of a culture that takes its cues from Darwin and the idea of organic growth, not from Newton & mechanical movement expressed in mathematical terms.'

But this is a great muddle: a distinction without a difference. Organic growth, metabolism, genes — this is chemistry & no less quantifiable than physics.

20[126]

In a human relationship one may provide light or shade: to do both is a supreme achievement. It is difficult to provide light: it must be unobtrusive if it is not to be destructive. Fortunately, when one is old one can provide only shade.

20[126]

One day, when I was about 12 years old, I was sent out of class to fetch something or other (I forget what) from the Master's Common Room. When I was there I opened a cupboard door: it was the cupboard which belonged to a mathematics master named C.D. Hardingham. Pinned on the inside of the door was a piece of paper on which, carefully inscribed in somewhat Gothic lettering, were the words: Duty, Dignity, Difficulty. In a flash of recognition I knew it said all — all about Hardingham & nearly all about life.

20[127]

In one version of the story, Roland was not killed at Roncevalles but was found alive under a mound of corpses by one who is described as 'a noble Saracen,' who cared for him, set him once more upon his feet, put him upon his horse that he might return to Nonnewerth & to Hildegarde his betrothed. Here and elsewhere (in Ariosto, for example) the relations between Christians & Moslems are represented as 'civil.'[39] There is no profound animosity and nothing like the limitless hatred of orthodox & heretic Christians. This, perhaps, was because they were at 'war' with one another. There is a 'dauntless decency' of the battlefield which owes nothing to Grotius and is unknown in commercial & so-called 'social' relationships.

20[128]

'The dangerous edge of things'; the equilibrium of ambiguities.

---

[39] Ludovico Ariosto (1474–1533), Italian poet, author of *Orlando Furioso* (1516).

20[128]

Forseeing that he must before long retire from the world, he retired from the business of the world & went to live in Dorset with the memories he had gathered, the books he had collected & the trees he had planted.

20[130]

My mother said that I never should
Play with the gypsies in the wood

I remember how disapproving Eleanor (his mother) was when I told Peter that this is just what he should be doing: listening to the pipes of Pan.

20[130]

Petrarch first saw Laura 'in the Cathedral on Good Friday.'

20[130]

Rufus told me that his mother, in exile from the Ukraine in Australia, told him that when he dropped a piece of bread he should kiss it when he picked it up.

20[130]

Politics used to be about loyalties, now it is about the price of bacon.

20[131]

We all have to invent life for ourselves.

20[131]

To live at the end of one's tether.

20[131]

Tithonus was a beautiful young man who was so delighted in being alive that he asked Aurora, goddess of the morning, to make him immortal. She did, but as it had not occurred to him to ask also for perpetual youth, he simply became an old man who could not die.

20[131]

His soul lacked the elasticity of irony.

20[132]

A child is a miracle, but oh how few children there are now.

20[132]

As carefree as a ne'er-do-well.

20[132]

'Science' is the disease of which it purports to be the diagnosis. Karl Kraus would have understood this. It was 'science' which destroyed Vienna in the early years of this century.

20[133]

What one needs to explain in trying to understand a writer is the <u>tensions</u> in his thought.

20[133]

Circumstance: the foreigner who came out of the sea to marry Conrad's Amy Foster.

20[133]

Augustine.
   Only a tragic religion can protect us from the final solution & the apparatchik's paradise. But it will appear to be a religion of despair only when it is circumstantially compelled to resist the pressure for a final solution. What constitutes the character of a human life is that there is no final solution.
   Montaigne; Pascal.

20[134]

Once again.
   Simply as an agent a man is without a law, moral or civil; he is subject only to his own purposes, to the success or otherwise of his actions related solely to his purposes. The only considerations are prudential. Such an agent is, of course, an abstraction. Every human being is also a moral agent — his actions are not unconditional or conditional only upon their consequences. The concrete act is not justifiable in terms of its consequences — & this goes as much for generally beneficial consequences as any others. It is morally justifiable in terms of its subscription to moral considerations — non-instrumental considerations.

20[135]

'Never does a labyrinthine man seek the truth, only his Ariadne.'[40]

The first thing we learn is that we inhabit a labyrinth — the labyrinth of the world. To some (Gnostics) this is intolerable; they wish only to escape. Ariadne

---

[40]   Oakeshott's note: 'Nietzsche, *Beyond Good & Evil*, p. 259.'

they recognize as their Saviour. But, having escaped, they desert her, and they become lost & frustrated wanderers in a wilderness. Some (scientists & technologists) engage themselves to understand the structure of the labyrinth. They measure it, exploit its resources, subdue it to their desires, & devote themselves to making it profitable & to keeping it neat. They do not understand that this is only another sort of escape, and they have forgotten all about Ariadne. But there are others who have learned to accept the mysteries of the labyrinth, its twists and turns, its light & shade, its joys & sorrows with patience, with wonder & without misgiving. From time to time they are visited by a shadowy self-reproach; their unkept promise to return to Ariadne. But they have no thought of escape, and the secret of their serenity lies in the obscure belief that the labyrinth in which they dwell is Ariadne herself.

20[136]

When skies are blue
And hearts are true.

Yes; a kind of easy heaven. But inferior to the heaven of Augustine and the earth of the ballads.

20[137]

For the Cardinal de Retz an intention frustrated, a failure, a defeat are more interesting & more important than a want satisfied or a successful *coup*. The ambivalence of a poet in politics.

20[138]

We were at supper. The garden door was open and I could see the willow, its slender branches gently swaying: Diana's hair lifted in the wind. 'You are so silent; what are you thinking?'; 'I was thinking how fine the willow-tree is this year.'

But I had gone far past that. I was thinking of that moment in the spring of 1537 when Thomas Wyatt and Louis Labé met in Lyons.

But all is turned through my gentilness
Into a strange fashion of forsaking

Tout aussitôt que je commence à prendre
Dans le mol lit le repose désiré[41]

---

41 Louise Labé, '*Tout aussitôt que je commence à prendre.*' The first verse runs: '*Tout aussitôt que je commence à prendre / Dans le mol lit le repos désiré, / Mon triste esprit, hors de moi retiré, / S'en va vers toi incontinent se rendre.*'

20[A]⁴²

Kierkegaard. The 'ethical' does not 'annihilate' the 'aesthetical' but 'transfigures' it.

Aesthetical — pleasure (pain) — 'for the moment.' Individual not 'in control' — determined by the external situation or accident, such as physical beauty.

'Experimental.'

In the power of 'what may or may not be.'

What 'happens,' both within & without himself.

No self-understanding — only knowledge of one's wants & impulses.

Ethical — 'personal' or 'choosing oneself.'

Self-disclosure & self enactment.

(1) A task set; a rule (2) a motive.

Not what you do — but how.

At once 'authoritative' — 'objective' — and 'free,' personal. A personal subscription.

20[B]⁴³

Aristocracy

Virtue		Vice
Graciousness		Uninterest of others: ignorance
Magnanimity	Carelessness	Contempt: indifference
Independence		Ostentatiousness
Compassion		Irresponsibility
Honour		

Bourgeois

Virtue		Vice
Modesty	Punctiliousness	Careerism
Truthfulness	literalness	Touchiness: uncertainty
Industriousness		Miserliness
Thrift		
Incorruptbility		
Studiousness		
Responsibility		
Honesty		

---

⁴² On a loose sheet inserted at 20[98].
⁴³ On a loose sheet inserted at 20[105].

21[01]

The driver of a carriage for hire: 'Where to, sir?'
 The answer: 'Leave it to the horse.'

21[01]

The most fruitless of all actions; to shake the hour-glass.

21[02]

A Parisian taxi-driver's vocabulary of abuse in 1980: '*Hé, va donc, structuraliste!*'

21[03]

A 'May Boy': the child begotten under a hedge. Almost certainly a Sagittarian: gentle, perhaps a little sad, & quietly self-possessed.

21[03]

The legend that St Paul wept at Virgil's tomb in Naples.

21[04]

Charles Sorley, killed at Loos in 1915: 'I regard this war as one between sisters, between Martha & Mary, the efficient & intolerant against the casual and sympathetic. Each side has a virtue for which it is fighting, and each of that virtues' supplementary vice.'

(1) If one speaks in this, Aristotelian, idiom every virtue has its <u>corresponding</u> vice. But is the vice a degeneracy to which one who has the virtue is, in some manner, prone; is the courageous <u>man</u> liable to be foolhardy; or are such virtues and vices logical opposites?

(2) 'for which it is fighting.' If this is a statement about consciousness, then it is certainly false; no man ever fought to maintain or even exhibit a 'virtue.' To fight is to exercise power and its outcome can only be power. 'Rightful power' is only defended.

---

¹   LSE 2/1/21. Soft cover, red with gold border, 21 cm x 14.5 cm, ruled. Autograph, ink. Recto folios numbered 1–31. Title page: 'XXI.' Dated: '1 January 1981.'

21[04]

'Er spricht zu uns' — Wilamowitz in respect of Aristotle on the Aristotelian Polity (constitution).[2] But in what voice does he speak? And to what ears? Every such survival may be made to speak in the voice of 'history'; some such survivals may also be made to speak in the 'practical' mode, delivering advice about what we should do, or purporting to inform us of the probable consequences of doing this or that. Wilamowitz, I suspect, made no such distinction.

21[05]

'Human Rights' transfer familiar & useful conditionals into meaningless absolutes.

Cp. the definition of Papal Infallibility of the first Vatican Council, 1869–70.

Newman perceived the infelicity. A formal definition of Papal infallibility, he said, was provocative, inopportune, and unnecessary; it turned a 'theological opinion' into a 'dogma' — a conditional into an absolute. This opened the door to judicial casuistry; what is *ex cathedra*, and how is one papal pronouncement to be related to another: Intellectual chaos & moral deviousness.

21[05]

Thomas Hardy clearly preferred his women dead.

21[06]

'If a writer has been entrusted with sources of major historical importance out of which to construct a narrative dealing as this does with some very important & highly controversial episodes, he is surely morally obliged to indicate upon what sources he has relied, and his reasons for preferring one version of events to another.'[3]

This attributes to an historian the character of Housman's 'donkey between two bales of hay' — which shall he choose and why? An historical account cannot <u>be</u> a preference for one non-historical account over another.

21[06]

A lie can tell the truth about the speaker.

---

2   Enno Friedrich Wichard Ulrich von Wilamowitz-Moellendorff (1845–1931), German classical philologist.

3   Oakeshott's note: 'Beloff in a review of K. Harris, *Attlee.*' K. Harris, *Attlee* (London: Weidenfeld & Nicolson, 1982).

21[07]

There was so much youthful pride about him, such absence of any calculation of the consequences to himself, that all the madness of the world was right for him. <u>Right</u>?

21[07]

'Instead of a struggle to repress given evils or to achieve given goals, human existence becomes an exploration in which the destination is always being discovered in the course of arriving.'

There may be a break from a 'scent' to a 'view' but there is no 'kill.'

21[07]

Flucht nach Vorn.
Burning one's boats?

21[07]

'But <u>why</u> the sun do shine upon the just & the unjust, that's what the books do not tell me.'[4]

21[08]

'Eternity is in love with the productions of time.'

> But oh, the very reason why
> I clasp them, is because they die.[5]

And it is the love that bestows immortality on the lover & beloved.

21[08]

Uncertainty belongs not only to what is not accomplished but also to what is; every conclusion is a beginning. We little know the things for which we pray.

21[08]

History. 'Break the drowsy spell of narrative: ask yourself questions: set yourself problems.'[6]

But they are questions which may be answered only in an assemblage of contingencies: 'narrative.'

---

4 See Thomas Hardy, *Tess of the D'Urbervilles* (London: Egoist Press, 2012), Ch. XIX, at 119.
5 Oakeshott's note: 'William Cory.'
6 Oakeshott's note: 'J.R. Seeley, *The Expansion of England Two Courses of Lectures* (London: Macmillan and Co., 1883), p. 175.'

21[09]

Christianity

It has often been thought the strength of Christianity lies in its component of 'evidences,' in its 'foundation' in alleged, & 'provable' occurrences and endless trouble has been taken to 'establish' them (often confused with the identification of Christianity as 'the religion of Jesus'). Oh, 'the scriptures'; we could not do without them, but they have been fatally misrepresented.

There are (1) 'Evidences' (from which historical events may be inferred); (2) Myths; (3) Theology. Each is the transformation of the one before: Myth = 'evidences' turned into parables; theology is myth turned into abstract ideas. But all deities reside in the human breast[7] & what is extraordinary is the belief that we must start with 'evidences' and the illusion that we do: that the creation was an occurrence (with speculation about its date), that Adam & Eve were 'historical' characters (& the inference that they had no navels), that 'Christ' was 'born' & represents a 'divine event,' a change in the character of God announced. So-called 'evidences' are 'events' in the history of human imagination, in human self-understanding.

21[11]

Having identified Jesus as the 'son' of God & thus the relation of God to the human race, there was a vast opportunity for exploring the implications of this, including the Virgin Birth. The Second Nun in the *Canterbury Tales* even speaks of her as 'the daughter of thy son.'[8]

21[11]

There is no such thing nowadays (& perhaps there never was) as a virgin word, free from ambiguous multiplicity.

21[13]

'Most reflective Christians are intellectually aware that without the idea of redemption through Christ's death on the cross, the Christian religion would not be Christianity as we know it.'

Perhaps it was unavoidable that sin & salvation should have been made the centre of early Christianity — though this is an exaggeration. But that Redemption as a <u>consequence</u> of the Cross is its central doctrine, unchallenged, is not the case. Great efforts (Augustine, Anselm in early times) were made to supersede it in a doctrine in which the Cross was understood as a <u>symbol</u> of the character of God. It was Jesus who was born and died, not Christ. The Augustinian doctrine

---

7 See W. Blake, 'Proverbs of Hell,' in *The Marriage of Heaven and Hell.*
8 See G. Chaucer, 'The Second Nun's Tale,' in *The Canterbury Tales*, l. 38: 'Thou Maid and Mother, Daughter of Thy Son.'

of the 'love' of God could not be tied to a dated event — 'suffered under Pontius Pilate.' The new era dawned, not with an 'act' of God but with an idea of God.

The notion that God had to perform an 'act' in order to give us an 'idea' is absurd.

21[14]

Christianity

(1) As the worship of Jesus: an 'historical' person.

(2) As the worship of a God into whom the person & attributes of Christ had been incorporated. The 'suffering' God: 'the Cross' not as an event but as the revelation of the character of God.

21[15]

'A statement of probability always refers to the available evidence and cannot be refuted or confirmed by subsequent events.'[9]

A statement of probability always refers to an occurrence understood in terms of its kind.

21[15]

A 'religious' life: not one filled with extraordinary performances, nor necessarily one in which ordinary actions are given extraordinary, symbolic, meanings, but one in which they are performed with the 'grace' which belongs to something done for its own sake or as an expression of love. A life whose coherence & significance lies, not in carefully pursued designs whose successful outcome gives it a touch of 'immortality,' but in which every engagement is an *aventure*, an eternal moment because its character is its 'style.'

21[16]

Comedy is a world whose reality is the creation of human imagination.

21[17]

'An invincible belief in the advent of a loving concord springing like a heavenly flower from the soil of men's earth, soaked in blood, torn by struggles, watered with tears.'[10]

---

[9] Oakeshott's note: 'J.M. Keynes.' Oakeshott may have been reading R. Skidelsky, *John Maynard Keynes: A Biography*, 3 vols. (London: Macmillan, 1983–2000), vol. 1, *Hopes Betrayed 1883–1920*, where this sentence from an unpublished MS by Keynes on probability is quoted at 153.

[10] Conrad, *Under Western Eyes*, p. 372.

No; not quite. There are many such flowers, immortal moments of love hidden in mortal blood & tears. But this, too, is not quite right.

21[17]

'She was wholly lacking in the capacity to behave with what may be called that hypocrisy without which life may scarcely be carried on.'[11]

Some eccentricities we abhor, but they are the price we pay for that absence of uniformity which is the virtue of human life.

21[18-20]

Foucault, *Histoire de la Sexualité*.[12]

In classical discourse, sexual activity was understood as a social practice, while in the language of the Church it was understood as a sign of man's fall, a mark of his sin.

In Christian language, sex for the first time became the secret truth of fallen man, the central sign of his fall & therefore the central preoccupation of his moral life.

With us, now, there is on the one hand a vestigial Christian moral Puritanism, shorn of a theology of salvation which made it credible; & on the other, a hedonism, pop psychology & commercial marketing of sexual fantasy & sexual apparatus.

This is puzzling. This view of the matter cannot, I think, be got out of the Book of Genesis, and it is not how the ancient Hebrews thought. Their 'doctrine' of sex was concerned with monogamy: 'thou shalt not commit adultery.' But Solomon! But, in some respect, it did come to belong to Christianity, or at least hover over what was considered to be 'Christian behaviour.' How did it do so?

Copulation was never detached from progeniture, & progeniture for the Christian was the begetting of immortal souls. But since, according to the earliest Christian belief the 'end of the world' was an event which would occur within 30 to 40 years, there was no point in engaging in worldly affairs, making a fortune, overthrowing a tyranny, or begetting children. This was the meaning of Faith, Hope & Charity. The situation of the human race (fully appreciated only in Christian belief) was that of 'waiting' & being 'ready' (the wise Virgin). The time of waiting was to be relatively short, so it was appropriate that the main

---

[11] Oakeshott's note: 'Mrs Belloc-Lowndes (sister of Hillaire) on Margot Asquith.' Mrs Belloc-Lowndes (sister of Hillaire) on Margot Asquith. Mary Adelaide Elizabeth Rayner Lowndes, née Belloc (1868–1947), English novelist, sister of Hilaire Belloc (1870–1953), Anglo-French Catholic poet, critic, and historian, was a close friend of Margot Asquith (1864–1945), Anglo-Scottish writer, wife of Henry Herbert Asquith (1852–1928), Prime Minister 1908–16. The quotation has not been traced.

[12] M. Foucault, *Histoire de la sexualité*, 3 vols. (Paris: Editions Gallimard, 1976–84).

human relationship should be that of 'charity' — quiet 'goodwill,' 'tolerance' & 'expectation' of an event which the human race could do nothing to bring about.

This view of 'the world' & of human destiny gradually receded; it is seen to be recessive even in St Paul's writings. It has no place in Augustinian Christianity where what is substituted for it is the first fully-worked-out doctrine of Christian 'salvation.' 'Salvation' was God's business. Christians, although they were always to have identifiable enemies, ceased to be a 'sect' & came to compose a civilization which succeeded in accommodating itself to the beliefs & mythologies of the peoples who became 'converted' to it: the Virgin Mary & Diana. This was made easier because the Roman religion was a religion without a theology.

The earlier belief in the imminent 'end of the world,' however, made Christianity vulnerable to corruption by the beliefs which emanated from Mani & his successors, the doctrine of the fundamental <u>evil</u> of the world as it was created, of the war between the forces of 'good' & 'evil' & the doctrines about human relationships, sex etc. etc. which found place in his doctrine. And although these beliefs were recognized as 'heretical,' they have never been successfully excluded from Christianity which has remained vulnerable to this corruption because it never succeeded in divesting itself of a notion of 'salvation' as a future condition to be awaited or promoted.

21[20]

The 'coal cellar.' I once lived, as a child, in a house which had a 'coal cellar.' The Red Lodge, Berkhamsted. It was as significant as our 'governess' & 'the garden shed.'

21[20]

'The chicken was a clear statement of humility.'[13]

Yes, yes: it was the only way we knew of giving 'honour' to those whom we 'honoured' & knew were 'above us' and delighted in being able to recognize them.

21[21]

Aidos. The human ability to distinguish, first, decency from indecency, and then moral good & evil, virtue & vice in human conduct, reflected in the *nemesis* which follows the choice of evil: Shame. Human conduct understood in terms of its motive; vice as self-betrayal. A man 'ashamed' not of what he has done, but of

---

[13] See 'Cambridge Wives,' in *The Incorporated Wife In the Police Oil Companies Armed Services Expatriate Communities Colonial Administrations Oxford and Cambridge Colleges,* ed. H. Callan and S. Ardener, 1984, p. 66.

himself. Moral virtues are emotive dispositions, adverbial qualifications of conduct.

21[21]

O Rus.

21[21]

An idea is a love-child.

21[22]

'The terrible aboriginal calamity.'[14] But Newman, who is usually right, was here unexpectedly astray. It must be understood not as a weakness in the design of the Creation but as a subtility which distinguishes the Creation from a piece of commonplace engineering.

For Augustine (who unfortunately got caught up with the notion of 'salvation' & who erred in some of the eccentric parts of his doctrine of 'salvation') the 'Fall,' 'Original Sin' was not a simple 'calamity,' the outcome of a flaw in the design, but an unavoidable consequence of the character with which God had endowed mankind: imagination, the capability of choosing & doing: self-creation. And when Augustine was asked why God did not endow mankind with unattainable 'perfection,' he replied that God created Man because he was lonely, & that a companion who was himself a God, or a faultless automaton, would be incontestably boring. There was no point in creating the possibility of 'sin' if in fact there were to be no sinners. What (among much else) Augustine meant when he understood the relationship of God to mankind was one of love was that God was interested in something other than perfection. 'Love' is a delight in difference which must be capable of including the acceptance of errancy. Zeus had to suffer the errancy of man & responded with displeasure & anger. Jehova had to suffer the errancy of his Chosen & responded with punishment (which recognized responsibility) and forgiveness. The Christian (Augustinian) God purposely created the uncontrollable and responded (to at least the more endearing antics of his creation) with 'love.' But this is not quite the whole story.

21[23]

Feminine divinities (imagined and invented by men) are not notably feminine: Artemis the unpossessed, Athena pure intellect, Aphrodite passionate delight.

---

[14] J.H. Newman, *Apologia pro vita sua: Being A Reply to a Pamphlet Entitled 'What, Then, Does Dr. Newman Mean?'* (London: Longman, Green, Longman, Roberts, and Green, 1864), p. 379: 'And so I argue about the world; —*if* there be a God, *since* there is a God, the human race is implicated in some terrible aboriginal calamity.'

Yet Troy was sacked for a runaway wife, and Aucussin preferred hell with Nicolette to heaven without her. Follow some Helen for her gift of grief.

21[24]

'The Faith to die in.'

That is what is wrong: life lived for what comes after. 'What comes after' understood as what we have earned here & made the ideal of a consequential moral & religious life. What matters is here & now. Death is the most important event in life, but because of what it ends, <u>not</u> what it may begin. A religion dominated by the notion of 'salvation' is as corrupt (& unchristian) as a morality dominated by the natural or penal consequences of ill-doing.

21[24]

Philosophy: making riddles out of solutions.

21[25]

In the figure of Laura, Petrarch expressed not only the duality often attributed to feminine character, but the ambiguity of human life. She is both Eve & the Virgin Mary. Eve not only deprived Adam of his 'solitude' (indeed, banished it from the world), what sprang from her naïve gullibility was a world of successive incidents (often designed), evanescent responses to circumstances yielding momentary satisfactions — the Laura of 'laurels' to be sought and won in a world which identified immortality with posterity. And the Virgin who represented the restoration of 'solitude' composed not of, at best, satisfactory outcomes, but of *'avantures'* each an imperishable moment; a world redeemed, not by a vision of better things to come but by being itself understood, not in terms of success & failure, but composed of immortal moments.

21[26]

One of Hegel's principle targets in his mature writings is the view of morality as the privileged preserve of individual conviction.

But to deny the <u>sovereignty</u> of the individual 'conscience' is not to identify moral with legal obligations, which clearly are not a matter of individual conviction. Nor does it deny that the recognition of the obligatory considerations which compose a morality is incoherent, the occasion of tension & self-division, & may be morally destructive, where it is not a 'conscientious' (or better, an 'affectionate') recognition. It denies only that the content of moral obligations is to be identified with the manner of their recognition. And somehow there must be room for the recognition that perhaps 'all the madness of the world was right <u>for him</u>.'

There is, then, a distinction between moral & legal conditions (obligation), but they are alike in their noninstrumentality—the absence of a concern with either individual or communal substantive interests or satisfactions.

21[28]

The mistake of supposing that happiness consists in the satisfaction of our desires.

21[28]

How can we stop education from killing the sense of wonder? I was lucky: my schooldays were filled with wonder.

21[29]

I am acquainted with Mr X.
I know Mr X.
I understand Mr X.

21[29]

The business of a teacher is to exercise a formative influence of good example upon his pupils—the only kind of influence which can be executed without impertinence & accepted without indignity.

21[29]

Not 'knowledge' & 'the known,' but 'understanding' & what is 'understood'; this preserves the notion of modality. It also escapes from 'the ruinously inapplicable metaphor of firm foundations,' the architectural imagery etc. which corrupts the notion of 'knowledge.'

21[30]

So-called psychoanalysis is the occupation of rationalists who trace everything in the world to sexual causes—with the exception of their own occupation. Karl Kraus.[15]

21[30]

'A new view of life opened before me. The essence of that view lay in the conviction that the destiny of man is to strive for moral improvement, and that such improvement is at once easy, possible & lasting.'[16]

---

[15] Karl Krauss (1874–1936), Austrian satirist and critic of psychoanalysis.
[16] Oakeshott's note: 'Tolstoy, *Childhood, Boyhood & Youth*, opening of Part III, Youth.' See L. Tolstoy, *Childhood, Boyhood & Youth*, tr. C.J. Hogarth (London: J.M. Dent & Sons, 1912), p. 163.

That is the puzzle. A life devoted wholly & exclusively to being good is impossible. No action or utterance is specifiable in exclusively moral terms.

Faust.

21[A]

De Mandeville's proposition 'Private vices, public virtues' is not a proposition in moral philosophy: it has to do only with substantive consequences of acting. What he is saying is that from the pursuit of private interests (that is self-satisfactions) emerges more general benefits.[17]

21[B][18]

Garden of Eden

'Knowledge' & sin.

The 'virtue' of ignorance. The devil, not God.

An 'all-knowing God' & a 'doomed experiment in human nescience'?

A Creator who created trees & animals — & then saw that his creation could not respond to him?

The condition of response, the self-consciousness of man. All that Adam & Eve lacked before the 'Fall' was self-consciousness — not 'knowledge.'

'Self-knowledge.'

Was God repairing a mistake or did he intend it all along?

---

[17] On the back of an envelope addressed: 'Professor Michael Oakeshott / Victoria Cottage / Acton / Langton Matravers / Nr. Swanage / Dorset.' Stamped: 'LONDON SW / 9.15 PM / 29 APR / 1986.'

[18] On the back of an envelope. Stamped: '20.5.86.'

Index of Names of People and Places

Index of Subjects

Index of Works

Abélard, Pierre, aka Peter Abelard, *Sic et non* 482 and n.

Abercrombie, Lascalles, 'Emblems of Love' 215 n.

Acton, John Emerich, *Historical Essays and Studies* 15 n.

Alighieri, Dante, *Divine Comedy* 43 n., 518

Amiel, Henri-Frédéric, *Journal intime* 209 n., 215 n., 257 n.?

Anonymous, *Chanson de Roland* 517

Anonymous, *Contes des fées* 386 n.

Anslem, St, *Cur deus homo* 482 and n.

Aquinas, St, *Summa contra gentes* 477 n.

—, *Summa theologica* 386 n.

Aristotle, *Metaphysics* 61 n., 123 n.

—, *Nicomachean Ethics* 30–6 and nn., 45–64 and nn., 74 n., 80, 85, 88, 118 n., 353 n., 359 n., 376 n., 470 n.

—, *Poetics* 437 n.

—, *Politics* 53 n., 62 n., 65–88 and nn., 95

Arnold, Matthew, 'The Better Part' 276 n.

—, *Culture and Anarchy* 37 n., 50 n., 87

Arrian, *The Anabasis of Alexander* 96 n., 164 n.

Auden, Wystan Hugh, *New Year Letter* 282 n. 1

Augustine, St, *Confessions* 215 n., 233 n., 259 n., 512 n.

Austen, Jane, *Emma* 164

Babbitt, Irving, *Rousseau and Romanticism* 241 n.

Bacon, Francis, *Novum organum* 25 n.

Bagehot, W., *Estimates of Some Englishmen and Scotchmen* 282 n.

—, 'The Ignorance of Man' 288 n.

Bailey, Cyril, *Epicurus: The Extant Remains* 135 n.

Baker, A.T. (ed.), *Pensées, maximes et réflexions de Pascal, La Rochefoucauld, Vauvenargues* 314 n.

Balfour, Arthur James, *Essays Speculative and Political* 7 n.

—, *Theism and Humanism* 37 n.

Barth, Karl, *The Christian Life* 190 n.?

Barnfield, Richard, 'A Comparison of the Life of Man' 378 n.

Bastiat, Frédéric, *Harmonies économiques* 73 n.

Beatles, The, 'Sgt. Pepper's Lonely Hearts Club Band' 519

Bennett, Arnold, *Hugo* 11 n.

Bentham, Jeremy, *A Fragment on Government* 221

Berdyaev, Nikolai, *The Destiny of Man* 308 n., 312 n.

—, *The Meaning of History* 308 n., 318 n.?, 325 n.?

Bergson, Henri, *Dreams* 4 n.

—, *Evolution créatrice* 4 n.

—, *Introduction to Metaphysics* 7 n.

—, *Le rire* 4 n.

The Bible 7, 14, 26, 42 and n., 59, 108 n., 116 nn., 123 n., 130 n., 132, 138, 147, 152, 159, 188, 216, 217, 251, 257 n., 287, 403, 431–5, 532 n., 547

Biedermann, Alois Emanuel, *Christliche Dogmatik* 129 n.

Black, Hugh, *Edinburgh Sermons Listening to God* 4 n.

Blackie, John Stuart, *On Beauty* 7 n., 9 n.

Blake, William, *The Marriage of Heaven and Hell* 110 n., 545 n.

—, 'The Question Answered' 404 n.

Bligh, Stanley, *The Direction of Desire* 445 n.

Blixen, Karen (aka Isak Dinesen) 'The Dreamers' 437 n.

—, *Shadows On The Grass* 402 n.

Book of Common Prayer 130, 137

Bos, Camille, *Pessimisme, féminisme, moralisme* 452 n.

—, *Psychologie de la croyance* 452 n.

Bosanquet, Bernard, *Aspects of the Social Problem*, 13